Century of Genocide

D0083586

"I have used this book as the basic text in my courses on genocide since its first edition. It is written by the foremost experts on the major genocides of the twentieth century and, in the new edition, the twenty-first. Most importantly, its first-hand accounts by eyewitnesses expose the personal side of genocide, the most depersonalizing crime against humanity. The stories it tells are unforgettable."

—**Dr. Gregory H. Stanton**, President,
International Association of Genocide Scholars

"The third edition of *Century of Genocide* provides valuable comparative perspectives of colonial, political, and ideological mass killing from the Herero and Armenian cases in the early twentieth century to Rwanda and Darfur at the end of the century and into the next. It is compelling both as an overarching general survey that includes first-person testimony, and as a call for effective measures to prevent and deal with the scourge of genocide and crimes against humanity."

—**Richard G. Hovannisian**, Professor of History and Chair in
Modern Armenian History, University of California, Los Angeles

"This is an important, comprehensive, and at times urgent account of modern genocide. The geographical and historical breadth of cases as well as the combining of thoughtful analysis and powerful eyewitness accounts make this book a very valuable contribution for scholars and students alike."

—**Scott Straus**, Associate Professor of Political Science,
University of Wisconsin, Madison

Through powerful first-person accounts, scholarly analysis, and compelling narrative, *Century of Genocide* details the causes and ramifications of the genocides perpetrated in the twentieth century and into the twenty-first. Historical context provides the necessary background on the actors and victims to help us better understand these episodes of atrocious political violence.

The third edition has been carefully updated and features new chapters on the genocides in Darfur, in Guatemala, and against indigenous peoples the world over. The volume concludes with a consideration of the methods of prevention and intervention of future genocides.

Samuel Totten is a professor at the University of Arkansas, Fayetteville, and co-founding editor of *Genocide Studies and Prevention: An International Journal*. He has also been a Fulbright Fellow at the Centre for Conflict Management, National University of Rwanda.

William S. Parsons is Chief of Staff for the United States Holocaust Memorial Museum in Washington, D.C.

Century of Genocide
Critical Essays and Eyewitness Accounts

Third Edition

Edited by Samuel Totten and William S. Parsons

Routledge
Taylor & Francis Group

NEW YORK AND LONDON

First edition published 1997
Second edition published 2004 by RoutledgeFalmer
This edition published 2009
by Routledge
270 Madison Ave, New York, NY 10016

Simultaneously published in the UK
by Routledge
2 Park Square, Milton Park, Abingdon, Oxon OX14 4RN

Routledge is an imprint of the Taylor & Francis Group, an informa business

© 1997 Samuel Totten, William S. Parsons, and Israel W. Charny, except chapter 6: "Holocaust: The Gypsies," © 1994 Sybil Milton, © 2004; 2009 Taylor & Francis

Typeset in Minion by
RefineCatch Limited, Bungay, Suffolk
Printed and bound in the United States of America on acid-free paper by
Sheridan Books, Inc.

All rights reserved. No part of this book may be reprinted or reproduced or utilized in any form or by any electronic, mechanical or other means, now known or hereafter invented, including photocopying and recording, or in any information storage or retrieval system, without permission in writing from the publishers.

Trademark Notice: Product or corporate names may be trademarks or registered trademarks, and are used only for identification and explanation without intent to infringe.

Library of Congress Cataloging in Publication Data
Century of genocide : critical essays and eyewitness accounts / edited by Samuel Totten and William S. Parsons. – 3rd ed.
    p. cm.
    Includes bibliographical references and index.
    ISBN 978–0–415–99084–4 (hbk : alk. paper) – ISBN 978–0–415–99085–1 (pbk : alk. paper) – ISBN 978–0–203–89043–1 (ebook) 1. Genocide–History–20th century. 2. Crimes against humanity–History–20th century. I. Totten, Samuel. II. Parsons, William S.
HV6322.7.C46 2008
909.82–dc22

2008015000

ISBN10: 0–415–99084–X (hbk)
ISBN10: 0–415–99085–8 (pbk)
ISBN10: 0–203–89043–4 (ebk)

ISBN13: 978–0–415–99084–4 (hbk)
ISBN13: 978–0–415–99085–1 (pbk)
ISBN13: 978–0–203–89043–1 (ebk)

Contents

Acknowledgments

Once again, we wish to sincerely thank all of the contributors to this book. All are extremely busy and dedicated scholars, and we greatly appreciate their contributions. At Routledge we wish to thank our acquisitions editor, Michael Kerns, and Felisa Salvago-Keyes.

We also wish to thank George F. McCleary, Jr. and his students (Lauren James, John Michael Jones, Luke Rahjes, Lacey Gray, and Kassandra Shelton) in the Geography Department at the University of Kansas for the research, thought, and hard work they put into the development of the maps that accompany each of the case studies of genocide in this new edition of *Century of Genocide*. Darin Grauberger, Director of Cartographic and GIS Services, University of Kansas, provided the technical processing for the maps. Michael K. Steinberg, The New College and Department of Geography, University of Alabama, Tuscaloosa, and George Lovell, Professor of Geography at Queen's University, Kingston, Ontario and Visiting Professor in Latin American History at Universidad Pablo de Olavide in Seville, Spain, contributed significant information for the map on Guatemala.

As we did in the first edition, we wish to thank Kristy L. Brosius and the late Sybil Milton for their excellent work in translating court testimonies that appear in Chapter 6, "Holocaust: The Genocide of Disabled Peoples." With Rouben Adalian, we offer a heartfelt thanks to Donald E. Miller and Lorna Touryan Miller for granting us permission to publish several of the interviews they conducted with survivors of the Armenian genocide. René Lemarchand and the editors also wish to acknowledge and sincerely thank Liisa Malkki for granting us the right to reproduce the accounts of the Burundi genocide from her doctoral dissertation, *Purity and Exile: Transformation in Historical-National Consciousness among Hutu Refugees in Tanzania*. Appreciation goes to Tanya Barbour for helping us achieve the tight timeline for revising this fourth edition. Finally, we greatly appreciate, too, all of the publishers and organizations that provided us with permission to use excerpts of various eyewitness accounts that previously appeared in their publications.

Permission Acknowledgment

Accounts 1 and 3 in Chapter 14, "The *Anfal* Operations in Iraqi Kurdistan," from *Cruelty and Silence: War, Tyranny, Uprising, and the Arab World* by Kanan Makiya. Copyright © 1993 by Kanan Makiya. Used by permission of W.W. Norton & Company, Inc.

Editors

Samuel Totten is a scholar of genocide studies based at the University of Arkansas, Fayetteville.

One of the founding editors of *Genocide Studies and Prevention (GSP): An International Journal*, he has served thus far as the editor of two special issues, one on Darfur (with Dr. Eric Markusen) and one on Rwanda.

During the summer of 2004, Totten was one of the 24 investigators on the U.S. State Department's Darfur Atrocities Documentation Team. The data collected by the investigators in their interviews of Darfurian refugees housed in refugee camps in Chad along the Chad/Sudan border was used by Secretary of State Colin Powell to make the determination that the Government of Sudan had perpetrated genocide in Darfur.

Among the books Totten has most recently edited and co-edited on genocide are: *Century of Genocide: Critical Essays and Eyewitness Accounts* (New York: Routledge, 2004); *Genocide in Darfur: Investigating Atrocities in the Sudan* (New York: Routledge, 2006); *Genocide at the Millennium* (New Brunswick, NJ: Transaction Publishers 2006); *The Prevention and Intervention of Genocide: An Annotated Bibliography* (New York: Routledge, 2006); *The Prevention and Intervention of Genocide: A Critical Bibliographic Review* (New Brunswick, NJ: Transaction, 2007); and *The Plight and Fate of Females During and Following Genocide: A Critical Bibliographic Review* (New Brunswick, NJ: Transaction Publishers, forthcoming). Most recently, he co-authored, with Dr. Paul Bartrop, the two-volume *Dictionary of Genocide* (Westport, CT: Greenwood Publishers, 2008).

Among the most recent essays and articles on genocide Totten has published are: "The Intervention and Prevention of Genocide: Sisyphean or Doable?," *Journal of Genocide Research*, June 2004, 6(2); "The U.S.

Government Darfur Genocide Investigation," *Journal of Genocide Research*, June 2005, 7(2); and "Investigating Allegations of Genocide in Darfur: The U.S. Atrocities Documentation Team and the UN Commission of Inquiry" (with Eric Markusen) in Joyce Apsel (Ed.) *Darfur: Genocide Before Our Eyes*, New York: Institute for the Study of Genocide, 2005.

William S. Parsons is Chief of Staff of the United States Holocaust Memorial Museum in Washington, DC. Before becoming Chief of Staff, he served as the Museum's Director of Education and was responsible for developing educational programs both in Washington and throughout the nation. For the past thirty-five years, he has been involved in writing, speaking, and creating programs that advance public awareness and knowledge about the Holocaust and genocide and the implications of this history for the world we live in today.

His published works include: *Facing History and Ourselves: Holocaust and Human Behavior* (Margot Strom, co-author, 1982); *The Middle Passage* (contributing writer and editor, 1986); *A World of Difference: Teacher/Student Study Guide* (contributing writer, 1987); *The African Meeting House: A Sourcebook* (Margaret Drew, co-author, 1988); *Everyone's Not Here: Families of the Armenian Genocide, A Study Guide* (1989); and *Century of Genocide: Eyewitness Accounts and Critical Views* (co-editor with Samuel Totten and Israel Charny, 1996).

Parsons holds a BA in History from Cornell College and a MA in Teaching from the University of Wisconsin. In 2002, he received the "Distinguished Achievement Award" from Cornell College for his career work in Holocaust and genocide education.

Contributors

Rouben Paul Adalian is the director of the Armenian National Institute (ANI) and of the Armenian Genocide of America Project in Washington. He is a specialist on the Caucasus and the Middle East, and has taught at a number of universities, including the School of Foreign Service, Georgetown University, and the School of Advanced International Studies, Johns Hopkins University.

In 1993 he completed a project to document the Armenian genocide in the United States National Archives, which resulted in Chadwyck-Healey Inc. publishing the 37,000 pages of American evidence on microfiche. The accompanying 476-page *Guide to the Armenian Genocide in the U.S. Archives 1915–1918* was issued in 1994.

Adalian is the associate editor and resource editor on the Armenian genocide of the award-winning *Encyclopedia of Genocide* (1999) and has contributed to a number of publications, including *Genocide in Our Time* (1992), *Genocide in the Twentieth Century* (1995), *Studies in Comparative Genocide* (1999), *Genocide: Essays Toward Understanding, Early-Warning, and Prevention* (1999), *Actualité du genocide des Arméniens* (1999), *America and the Armenian Genocide* (2003) and *Defining the Horrific Readings on Genocide and Holocaust in the Twentieth Century* (2004).

He is also the author of *From Humanism to Rationalism: Armenian Scholarship in the Nineteenth Century* (1992) and the *Historical Dictionary of Armenia* (2002). Furthermore, Adalian is the compiler and editor of the ANI Web site (http://www.armenian-genocide.org), which holds extensive information on the Armenian genocide. He received his Ph.D. in history from the University of California, Los Angeles.

Jon Bridgman received his Ph.D. from Stanford in 1961 and is a professor of history at the University of Washington, where he teaches classes in modern European history. He is the author of *Revolt of the Hereros* (1981) and *The End of the Holocaust—The Liberation of the Camps* (1990).

Bridget Conley-Zilkic is Project Director for the Committee on Conscience at the United States Holocaust Memorial Museum in Washington, DC. She has worked on the Museum's genocide prevention efforts and has produced, directed or written short films on genocide; conducted teacher training sessions; and curated the Museum's new exhibit on genocide after the Holocaust (due to open in April 2009). In April 2004, she was a member of the official United States delegation to the commemoration ceremonies in Rwanda marking the tenth anniversary of the 1994 genocide. She supervised elections in Bosnia-Herzegovina with the Organization for Security and Cooperation in Europe in 2000. Among her published essays are "'Parler clairement': Tchétchénie : pour défendre autrement les droits humains," (tr. Michel Feher), in *Politique Non Gouvernementale, Vacarme* (no 34, Winter 2006); "Hope Dies Last: On Women Suicide Bombers and Human Rights Abuses in Chechnya," (*Journal of Human Rights*, vol. 3:3, 2004); and "What Barbed Wire Can't Enclose" (*Alphabet City 7: Social Insecurity* (Toronto), Sept. 2000). She received a Ph.D. in Comparative Literature from Binghamton University in 2001, writing about cultural responses to humanitarian interventions in Bosnia and Haiti

Robert Cribb is Senior Fellow in the Research School of Pacific and Asian Studies at the Australian National University in Canberra, Australia. He has written extensively on violence in Indonesia and is the editor of *The Indonesian Killings of 1965–1966: Studies from Java and Bali* (Clayton, Victoria, Australia: Monash University Centre of Southeast Asian Studies, 1990). His most recent book is *Historical Atlas of Indonesia* (London: Curzon, 2000).

James Dunn has degrees in political science and Asian studies from Melbourne University and the Australian National University. Initially, he served as a defense analyst specializing in Asian affairs, then as a diplomat in Western and Eastern Europe, and finally as an Australian Consul to Portuguese Timor. In 1974, he was a member of a two-man fact-finding mission sent to Timor by the Australian government; and in 1975, at the beginning of Indonesian military intervention in East Timor, he led an aid mission. For the ten years prior to his retirement he was senior foreign affairs advisor to the Australian parliament, with a specialization in Soviet affairs, Southeast Asia, and human rights issues. In 2001, Dunn carried out an investigation of crimes against humanity in

East Timor for UNTAET. Dunn is the author of *Timor: A People Betrayed* (Brisbane: Jacaranda-Wiley, 1983).

Hugh Gregory Gallagher died in 2004 and was an independent scholar, was the author of *By Trust Betrayed: Patients, Physicians and the License to Kill in the Third Reich, and FDR's Splendid Deception.* His paper " 'Slapping up Spastics': Euthanasie?" was presented at the first International Conference on the Holocaust sponsored by the United States Holocaust Memorial Museum. Gallagher was a polio quadriplegic and used a wheelchair for 40 years. He resided in Cabin John, Maryland.

Rounaq Jahan is currently affiliated with the Southern Asian Institute at Columbia University as a senior research scholar. She was a professor of political science at Dhaka University, Bangladesh, from 1970–1993. Her publications include *Pakistan: Failure in National Integration* (New York: Columbia University Press, 1972) and *Bangladesh Politics: Problems and Issues* (Dhaka: University Press Ltd., 1980).

Jahan also worked for the United Nations for many years and was the coordinator of the Women's Program at the United Nations Asia-Pacific Development Centre in Kuala Lumpur, Malaysia, from 1982 to 1984. She was also Head of the Rural Women's Employment Program at the International Labour Organization in Geneva, Switzerland, from 1985 to 1989. Jahan received her Ph.D. in political science from Harvard University in 1970 and did post-doctoral research at Columbia, Chicago, and Harvard.

Susanne Jonas teaches Latin American and Latino Studies at the University of California, Santa Cruz. She has been an expert on Central America, particularly Guatemala, for 40 years. In 2000, she published the major in-depth study of the Guatemalan peace process, *Of Centaurs and Doves: Guatemalas Peace Process* (Westview, 2000), which was designated a Choice "Outstanding Academic Book" for 2001; it was also published in Spanish by FLACSO/Guatemala in 2000. Her previous major book on Guatemala was *The Battle for Guatemala: Rebels, Death Squads, and U.S. Power* (Westview, 1991—published in Spanish, by Nueva Sociedad and FLACSO/Guatemala in 1994). She was co-editor of (and major contributor to) the following recent books, since 1998: *Globalization on the Ground: Postbellum Guatemalan Democracy and Development* (2001), *Immigration: A Civil Rights Issue for the Americas* (1999), and *Beyond the Neoliberal Peace: From Conflict Resolution to Social Reconciliation* (1998). Her earlier co-edited books on Guatemala include: *Guatemala: Tyranny on Trial* (1984), and *Guatemala* (1974), published in Spanish in 1976 as *Guatemala: Una Historia Inmediata*. Her authored book, *Guatemala: Plan Piloto para el Continente* was published in 1981. She has written dozens of related journal articles, encyclopedia entries, and book chapters—one major article being "Dangerous Liaisons: The U.S. in Guatemala," in *Foreign Policy*, Summer, 1996—as well as numerous OpEd articles. She is currently working on a co-authored book on Guatemalan migration to the United States.

Robert K. Hitchcock is Professor and Chair of the Department of Anthropology at Michigan State University in East Lansing. His work focuses on human rights, development, and the environment, with particular reference to indigenous peoples, refugees, and small-scale farmers and herders. He has published several papers on genocides of indigenous peoples. He is the author of *Kalahari Communities: Bushmen and the Politics of the Environment in Southern Africa* (1996), and a co-editor of *Hunters and Gatherers in the Modern World: Conflict, Resistance, and Self-Determination* (2000), *Endangered Peoples of Africa and the Middle East: Struggles to Survive and Thrive* (2002), *Indigenous Peoples' Rights in Southern Africa* (2004), and *Updating the San: Myth and Reality of an African People in the 21st Century* (2006) Currently, he is working on a book on the Ju/'hoansi San of Namibia since independence and doing research on dam-related resettlement in Africa.

Ben Kiernan is A. Whitney Griswold Professor of History and director of the Genocide Studies Program at Yale University, and Convenor of the Yale East Timor Project. Kiernan is author of *How Pol Pot Came to Power* (London: Verso Books, 1985), *The Pol Pot Regime: Race, Power and Genocide in Cambodia under the Khmer Rouge, 1975–1999* (New Haven, CT: Yale University Press, 2002), three other works, and a hundred scholarly articles on Southeast Asia and the history of genocide. He is also editor of *Genocide and Democracy in Cambodia: The Khmer Rouge, The United Nations, and the International Community* (New Haven, CT: Yale University Press, 1993).

From 1994 to 1999, Kiernan was founding and managing director of Yale University's Cambodian Genocide Program, which he established with grants from the United States and other governments. He founded Yale's Genocide Studies Program in 1998. Kiernan is a member of the Editorial Boards of *Critical Asian Studies, Human Rights Review*, the *Journal of Human Rights*, and the *Journal of Genocide Research*. Currently, he is writing a global history of genocide since 1500.

Michiel Leezenberg teaches in the Department of Philosophy of the Faculty of Humanities at the University of Amsterdam. He has conducted extensive research on the Anfal operations and subsequent developments in Iraqi Kurdistan, and made several field trips to the region. Among his main publications relevant to the Anfal operations are "Between Assimilation and Deportation: History of the Shabak and the Kakais in Northern Iraq" in B. Kellner-Heinkele and K. Kehl-Bodrogi (Eds.) *Syncretistic Religious Communities in the Near East* (Leiden: Brill, 1997); "De Anfal-operaties in Iraaks Koerdistan: tien jaar straffeloosheid" ("The Anfal Preparations in Iraqi Kurdistan: Ten Years of Impunity") in *Soera,* June 1998; "Politischer Islam bei den Kurden" in *Kurdische Studien,* 2(2001):5–38; and *Genocide and Responsibility: International Reactions to Iraq's Chemical Attack Against Halabja* (in preparation).

René Lemarchand is professor emeritus of political science at the University of Florida (Gainesville). He has written extensively on Rwanda, Burundi, and the Congo. His book, *Rwanda and Burundi* (Praeger, 1970), received the Melville Herskovits Award of the African Studies Association in 1970. He served as Regional Advisor on Governance and Democracy with USAID from 1993 to 1998, first in Abidjan and then in Accra. He has been visiting professor at Smith College, Brown University, the University of Copenhagen, the University of Bordeaux, and Berkeley.

James E. Mace was born in 1952 in Oklahoma, and died in 2004 in Kyiv, Ukraine. He was professor of political science at Kiev-Mohyla Academy National University and a feature writer for *The Day* (a newspaper and Web site in Kiev). Mace was staff director of the U.S. Commission on the Ukraine Famine created by the U.S. Congress. Prior to his work with the Commission on the Ukraine Famine, he had been affiliated with the Russian and European Center at the University of Illinois at Champaign and the Ukrainian Research Institute of Harvard University.

Among his publications are *Communism and the Dilemmas of National Liberation: National Communism in Soviet Ukraine, 1918–1933* (Harvard Series in Ukrainian Studies, Cambridge, MA: Harvard, 1983), "The Man-Made-Famine of 1933 in the Soviet Ukraine: What Happened and Why" in Israel W. Charny (Ed.), *Toward the Understanding and Prevention of Genocide: Proceedings of the International Conference on the Holocaust and Genocide* (Boulder, CO: Westview Press, 1984); "Genocide in the U.S.S.R." in Israel W. Charny (Ed.), *Genocide: A Critical Bibliographic Review, Volume One* (London and New York: Mansell Publishers and Facts on File, 1988); and "The Ukrainian Genocide" in *The Encyclopedia of Genocide* (Santa Barbara, CA: ABC CLIO Publishers, 1999).

Martin Mennecke, who has a LL.M. from the University of Edinburgh, is a doctoral candidate in international law at the University of Kiel, Germany. The focus of his thesis is the most recent evolution of the legal definition of genocide, and it is supported by the Friedrich-Ebert-Stiftung and Herbert-Quandt-Stiftung.

Currently affiliated with the Danish Institute of International Studies, Department for Holocaust and Genocide Studies, he is mainly working on issues of international criminal law. Among his publications are "The International Criminal Tribunal for the Former Yugoslavia and the Crime of Genocide" (with Eric Markusen) in Steven L. B. Jensen (Ed.) *Genocide: Cases, Comparisons and Contemporary Debates*, Copenhagen: The Danish Center for Holocaust and Genocide Studies, 2003.

Sybil Halpern Milton was born in New York City in 1941 and died in Bethesda, Maryland, in 2000. A graduate of Barnard College, she received graduate training at Stanford and Munich. From 1974 to 1984, she served as director of archives of the Leo Baeck Institute in New York; from 1985 to 1997, she was associated with the U.S. Holocaust Memorial Council, and then served as an archival consultant, research curator, and finally senior resident historian with the United States Holocaust Memorial Museum. From 1997 until her death she served as vice president of the Independent Experts Commission: Switzerland—World War II.

In addition, she served as curator or contributor to 11 exhibits and published numerous articles on Nazi Germany and the Holocaust. She was co-author of *Art of the Holocaust* (1981) and author of *In Fitting Memory: The Art and Politics of Holocaust Memorials* (1991). She co-edited the *Simon Wiesenthal Center Annual* (1984–1990) and the 26 volumes of *Archives of the Holocaust* (1990–1995). She also edited or co-edited *The Stroop Report* (1979), *The Holocaust: Ideology, Bureaucracy, and Genocide* (1980), *Genocide: Critical Issues of the Holocaust* (1983), *Innocence and Persecution: The Art of Jewish Children in Nazi Germany, 1936–1941* (1989), *The Story of Karl Stojka: A Childhood in Birkenau* (1992), and a special issue on the Holocaust of the journal *History of Photography* (winter 1999).

Donald L. Niewyk is a professor of modern European history at Southern Methodist University. A specialist in the history of antisemitism, he is the author of six books, including *Fresh Wounds: Early Narratives of Holocaust Survival* (Chapel Hill: University of North Carolina Press, 1998); *The Jews in Weimar Germany* (New Brunswick, NJ: Transaction, 2001); and most recently *The Holocaust: Problems and Perspectives of Interpretation* (Boston: Houghton Mifflin, 2003).

Tara M. Twedt has conducted research on indigenous peoples' rights in Latin America, especially in Chile, where she did an M.A. thesis on the Chilean indigenous law passed in 1993. Her interests range from globalization and its impacts to human rights of indigenous peoples worldwide.

Leslie J. Worley received his Ph.D. from the University of Washington, where he also served as a lecturer in history.

Introduction

SAMUEL TOTTEN AND WILLIAM S. PARSONS

The writing of this book, *Century of Genocide*, began in the early 1990s and resulted in publication in 1995. With each revised edition, new genocides and crimes against humanity have had to be recorded. That is a telling and terrible statement about our contemporary world. Even the title of the book might be reconsidered because the slaughter has now spread into a new century.

"Will the killing ever stop? Will the scourge of genocide ever be eradicated? Will humanity ever be wise enough to prevent the deaths of potential genocidal victims *before* they become yet another set of statistics in the welter of statistics?" We posited those questions in the introduction of the first paperback edition of *Century of Genocide*, which was published in 1997.

We followed the questions up with the following comments and observations: "These and similar thoughts continue to weigh heavily on our minds. . . . How could they not? In the not-too-distant past, daily broadcasts and reams of print journalism issued terrible news about the genocide taking place in Bosnia-Herzegovina; the genocide of some one million Tutsis and moderate Hutus by Rwandan government forces and paramilitary extremists; the Indonesian army-'sponsored' killings in East Timor in the late 1990s; the sporadic and ongoing mass killings in Burundi; the continuing conflict and killing in [southern] Sudan; and the horrific violence and killings that have recently erupted in the Congo. That's not even to mention the hateful epithets and actions of neo-Nazis in Germany, the United States, and elsewhere; the insidious and incremental destruction of indigenous peoples' ways of life across the globe; and the ubiquitous deprivation of various peoples' human rights (which sometimes explodes into genocide)."

1

In the years since we wrote those words, the world has faced yet another genocide: the Government of Sudan's (GOS) and *Janjaweed's* (Arab militia) genocide of the black Africans of Darfur. Over the past four plus years, it is estimated that between 250,000 and over 400,000 people have perished due to the genocidal policies and actions of the GOS and the *Janjaweed*. As we write, the crisis continues; and as the crisis continues unabated so does the mass killing, the mass rape, and the deaths due to what is now being referred to as genocide by attrition.

On January 10, 2008, reports from the Congo indicated that some extremist Hutus were calling for the extermination of the *inyenzi* or Tutsis (*inyenzi* is a Kinyarwanda term which means "cockroaches" and was a term used to denigrate their Tutsi victims during the course of the 1994 genocide).

It is painfully clear that we—humanity and members of the international community—do not yet have "the answer" as to how genocide can be prevented. What humanity is in most need of in this respect is how to cast off addiction to *realpolitik*, the lack of political will to act, and, ultimately, the lack of real care about "others" who face annihilation at the hands of mass murderers. In other words, we, humanity (members all of the international community), have not truly found the humanity that is needed to prevent genocide from reappearing, time and again, like a horrific nightmare.

It is also, to say the least, disconcerting that we live in a world in which certain parties and nations perpetuate the denial of certain genocides that have occurred. Such denial has run the gamut from those who refuse to acknowledge the issue of genocide due to the discomfort the subject causes them to those who distort history for personal or political gain to those who deny and distort out of sheer ignorance or hate. Scholars often arrive at different historical interpretations, but those who purposely distort the historical record and disregard vast amounts of historical documentation know exactly the game they play. As every attorney knows, it is often easier to create doubt and win than it is to prove what actually took place. Indeed, such deniers, minimizers, and obfuscators (Hawk, 1988, p. 151) seem to gain some sort of satisfaction from the fact that they drain the energy and limited resources of legitimate scholars in genocide studies who are compelled to repudiate the distortions in order to keep the historical record intact.

By minimizing or distorting a particular genocide, deniers assault survivors one more time. In fact, one of the key rationales for including accounts by survivors and other eyewitnesses in this book is to send a message that no matter how hard the deniers try to manipulate history, accounts of the genocide will be recorded and remembered.

The essays in this book also reveal the attempts by various governments to cover up genocides or to minimize the destruction of such acts. In essay after essay we read about the efforts of governments to rationalize mass killings; thus, we hear about "security zones," "enemies of the state," and "regrettable losses of life." We also read about the excuses and compromises offered by outside governments as to why they chose not to intervene in order to prevent acts of genocide from being perpetrated.

At times it is difficult not to be disheartened, especially when governments deny and distort the historical record of genocide or do too little or nothing at all when new genocides erupt somewhere across the globe. Indeed, at times it is difficult not to wonder whether all the scholarship, all the words, and all the pledges to "Never Forget" are simply some type of anodyne to ease the pain of the survivors or soothe the conscience of those who deeply care about such tragedies but feel impotent to staunch genocide early on. And at times it is difficult not to wonder whether those of us who hold out hope that genocide can, at a minimum, be halted early on are doing so more out of desperation than any sense of objectivity or reality.

We recognize that these were bleak words and thoughts with which to introduce a book, but we believe that they are apropos. Certain situations demand bluntness and anger, and the continued perpetration of genocide, in our minds, is one of them.

So, why are we taking the time, effort and thought to revise this book yet again? A key reason is to inform, educate, cajole, prod, and encourage people to break out of their mold of silence, to collectively reach out to the victims and the voiceless, and to demand that such atrocities be halted!

Definitional Issues vis-à-vis the Term "Genocide"

Ever since Raphael Lemkin, a Polish Jewish émigré and noted scholar who taught law at Yale and Duke universities, coined the term *genocide* in 1944, there has been an ongoing, and often heated, debate in regard to that which constitutes the most exact and useful definition of "genocide." To form the new term, Lemkin combined the Greek *genos* (race, tribe) and *cide* (killing). He went on to define genocide as:

> ... the coordinated plan of different actions aiming at the destruction of essential foundations of the life of national groups with the aim of annihilating the groups themselves. The objectives of such a plan would be the disintegration of the political and social institutions of culture, language, national feelings,

religion, economic existence, of national groups and the destruction of the personal security, liberty, health, dignity, and even the lives of the individuals belonging to such groups. Genocide is directed against the national group as an entity, and the actions involved are directed against individuals, not in their individual capacity, but as members of the national group. (Lemkin, 1944, p. 79)

As one can readily ascertain, Lemkin's definition is extremely broad.

After lengthy debate over the definition of genocide and ample compromise on how it should be defined by the international community, the United Nations adopted the Genocide Convention on December 9, 1948, and in doing so defined genocide in the following manner:

In the present Convention, genocide means any of the following acts committed with the intent to destroy, in whole or in part, a national, ethnical, racial, or religious group, as such:

a. Killing members of the group
b. Causing serious bodily or mental harm to members of the group
c. Deliberately inflicting on the group conditions of life calculated to bring about its physical destruction in whole or in part
d. Imposing measures intended to prevent births within the group
e. Forcibly transferring children of the group to another group

This definition is, at one and the same time, extremely broad and extremely narrow. As a result, it is not surprising that over the years many scholars have proposed alternative definitions of genocide (Chalk and Jonassohn, 1990, p. 23; Charny, 1988a, p. 4; Drost, 1975; Fein, 1990, pp. 23–25; Horowitz, 1980). To this day, though, no single definition has been generally accepted as definitive. This constitutes a serious problem, especially as it relates to the intervention and prevention of genocide—not to mention the prosecution of cases that involve genocidal-like actions. It also complicates the work of scholars as they undertake the study of the preconditions, processes, and ramifications of genocide.[1]

It should be noted that we, along with many other scholars (Charny, 1988a; Charny, 1988b; Drost, 1975; Kuper, 1981; Kuper, 1985; Whitaker, 1985; Totten, 2002), believe that both political and social groups should be included in any definition of genocide. In light of that, we have purposely chosen to include certain cases of mass destruction of political and social groups in this book.

Focus of the Book

Century of Genocide is comprised of critical essays by some of the most noted scholars in the field of genocide studies about various genocidal acts committed during the course of the 20th and 21st centuries. Each essay on a particular genocide is accompanied by oral testimony about the genocide. Many of the essays have been revised and updated. That is true of the chapters on the Iraqi gassing of the Iraqi Kurds, the 1994 Rwandan genocide, genocide in the former Yugoslavia, and the chapter on the prevention and intervention of genocide. Several were not revised due to the deaths of our colleagues who contributed chapters to the original volume back in 1995. This was true of the chapters by Sybil Milton, James Mace, and Hugh Gallagher. Due to the death of our friend and colleague Eric Markusen, his good friend and long-time colleague and co-author, Martin Mennecke, revised their chapter on his own.

Two genocides not previously addressed in *Century of Genocide* are included herein: the genocide of the Mayans in Guatemala by Suzanne Jonas and the genocide of the black Africans in Darfur by Samuel Totten. Additionally, a chapter that appeared in the first volume but not the second, one that addresses the plight and fate of indigenous peoples across the globe, reappears in this third edition. It, too, has been radically revised by its original authors, Robert K. Hitchcock and Tara M. Twedt.

The historical cases addressed in this revised edition are as follows: genocide of the Hereros; the Armenian genocide; the Soviet man-made famine in Ukraine; the Nazi genocide of Jews, Gypsies, and disabled peoples; the Indonesian massacre of suspected "Communists"; the genocide in East Timor; the Bangladesh genocide; the genocide of the Hutu in Burundi; the Cambodian genocide; the genocide of the Mayans in Guatemala; the Iraqi genocide of the Kurds in the late 1980s; the ongoing genocide of indigenous peoples across the globe; the 1994 Rwandan genocide; the genocide perpetrated in the former Yugoslavia in the 1990s; and the ongoing genocide in Darfur, Sudan.

The cases presented in this book were chosen because the editors believe that each one constitutes an act of genocide or, at the very least, constitutes an action that involved a genocidal process. Another factor that was taken into consideration was whether eyewitness accounts were available. If no such documentation was available, then a genocide was not included herein.

In order to assure some semblance of continuity, each author was asked to address a series of questions posited by the editors: Who committed the genocide? How was the genocide committed? Why was the genocide committed? Who were the victims? Who was involved (e.g., state, societal institutions, various peoples: ethnic groups, individuals with certain job roles/professions, bystanders, etc.)? What were the outstanding historical forces and trends at work that led to the genocide? What was the long-range impact of the genocide on the victim group? What have been the responses of individuals, groups, and nations to this particular genocide? Is there agreement or disagreement among "legitimate scholars" as to the interpretation of this particular genocide (e.g., preconditions, implementation, ramifications)? Do people care about this genocide today? If so, how is that concern manifested? And what does a study of this genocide contribute to the field of genocide studies?

Since the intent of this book is to highlight a range of genocides, readers need to keep in mind that the essays provide only a basic overview, detailed though they are, of the various historical events.

Each of the contributing authors was also asked to select one to four of the most informative eyewitness accounts that they could locate in regard to the genocide that they discussed in their essay. A couple of the authors were hard-pressed to locate much at all in the way of eyewitness accounts. This is an acute problem, and one that will be discussed in more detail elsewhere in this Introduction.

Value and Limitation of Eyewitness Accounts

Time and again, scholars have noted the unique contribution such eyewitness accounts make in regard to providing a more thorough understanding of the genocidal process. In speaking about eyewitness accounts of the Armenian genocide, Richard Hovannisian (1973), professor of history and director of the Near Eastern Center at the University of California at Los Angeles, asserted: "Eyewitness accounts of decisive events may be as valuable as official dispatches and reports. It is in such versions especially that the human element becomes manifest, affording insights not to be found in documents" (p. xxiii).

Totten (1991b) commented: "First-person accounts by victims and others are capable of breaking through the numbing mass of numbers in that they provide the thoughts, the passions and the voices of those who experienced and/or witnessed the terrible calamity now referred to as genocide. And while first-person accounts serve many purposes among the most significant is the fact that authentic accounts constitute valuable testimony as to what it means to be caught up in the maelstrom of hatred and savagery that is genocide" (p. xi).

Oral accounts also remind scholars, educators, and students who record or study statistics, examine documents, and argue over definitions of genocide and interpretations of genocidal actions that the victims are human beings just as they and their family members are—that is, innocent men, women, and children.

Although eyewitness accounts are a valuable means of documenting historical events, their validity as a primary source is only as good as the procedures by which they are collected as well as the accuracy of the witnesses whose accounts are documented. The same research standards used to develop historical works need to be applied to gathering, recording, authenticating, and interpreting eyewitness accounts.

Dearth of Oral Testimony

Just as the documentation and scholarship is much richer for certain genocides and genocidal processes than others, the same is true of the availability of eyewitness accounts of certain genocidal situations.

There are numerous reasons as to why there is a dearth of first-person accounts of various genocidal acts, but among the main ones are the following: The survivors may not have been literate, and thus did not have the means to develop a written record; in the aftermath of the genocide the survivors may have had to struggle simply to survive, thus documenting their tragedy was not foremost on their minds; the survivors may not have had the financial means to take the time to record and collect testimony; the survivors may not have had a constituency that was interested in their plight, and thus no one collected or supported documentation of their tragedy; the survivors may have been (or continue to be) leery of people who question them about their plight; and some survivors may have continued to live under the very regime that perpetrated the genocide, which, in turn, prevented (through censorship, coercion, or threats of violence) the survivors or others from documenting the atrocities (Totten, 1991b, pp. xliii–liii).

In the introductions to the oral testimony that accompany their essays herein, a number of contributing authors address the dearth of first-person accounts. For example, in his introduction to the eyewitness accounts of the Burundi genocide, René Lemarchand notes that "oral witness accounts of the events surrounding the 1972 genocide are extremely scarce, in part because of the restrictions placed by the Burundi authorities on unaccompanied travel throughout the countryside—especially when the aim is to interview survivors of the genocide—and in part because of the logistical, administrative, and political difficulties involved in gaining access to refugee camps in neighboring states."

Speaking about the dearth of eyewitness accounts of the Indonesian genocide of suspected "Communists," Robert Cribb reports that:

> ... the Indonesian killings have produced remarkably few direct testimonies by survivors or participants. . . . [In fact,] few records of any kind were made or kept of the killings as they took place. The few foreign journalists who were in the country found access to the countryside very difficult and were in any case kept busy reporting the complex political changes taking place in national politics. . . . Indonesians on the whole have remained reluctant to speak about the killings, except in very general terms. This reluctance probably stems both from a sense of shame at the magnitude of the massacres and an unwillingness to discuss what is still a sensitive topic in a country dominated by the military who presided over the killings in the first place.

Despite the aforementioned impediments and difficulties that scholars, activists, and others face in regard to collecting eyewitness accounts of certain genocidal acts, it is still disturbing that there has not been a concerted and collective effort by both the scholarly and activist communities to collect as many accounts as possible of the least-documented genocides in this century. While not wishing to appear cynical, it seems that by not assisting those who have largely remained voiceless, we (the scholars and the activists) have contributed to, rather than ameliorated, the problem. Instead of locating the survivors and other witnesses in order to "return" the voices to the voiceless, we have remained on the sidelines.[2] Certainly a place to begin the collection of such testimony would be many of the refugee camps located across the globe. Other places are those communities and enclaves in various parts of the globe where relatively large numbers of survivors of the same genocide now reside and where censorship and political constraints do not pose a problem to the researchers or the witnesses.

In regard to those genocidal acts where survivors and witnesses to the genocide are still alive, it is incumbent upon scholars and activists to collect as many accounts as possible. Not to do so leaves the historical record bereft of what could prove to be invaluable information. It also constitutes a further injustice to the victims.

Scholarly Activity: The Critical Need for an Intensified Study of Genocide, its Preconditions, and Methods of Prevention and Intervention

The amount and quality of scholarly study of different genocidal acts has varied greatly over the years. While the Holocaust is certainly the most heavily documented and studied genocide, other genocidal events suffer from a dearth of scholarly examination. This must be addressed.

There is also a great need to continue the scholarly work that has been undertaken of late to understand the processes that lead up to and eventuate in acts of genocide.

Certain scholars and activists seem to have come to the conclusion that if there is ever going to be any hope at all in regard to preventing genocide then they (and not governments) are going to have to be the catalyst behind such hope. Numerous times throughout this century no government (either individually or collectively) has taken it upon itself to address this issue or to be proactive in this regard. (In regard to the United States' actions and inaction, see Samantha Power's "*A Problem from Hell*": *America and the Age of Genocide*, New York: Basic Books, 2002.)

Although Leo Kuper (1985), the late genocide scholar, made the following comments about the role of the United Nations some two decades ago, his assessment remains relevant today: "I assume that realistically, only a small contribution can be expected from the United Nations, at any rate in the immediate future" (p. 21). Later in the book, he asserts: "The performance of the United Nations in response to genocide is as negative as its performance on charges of political mass murder. There are the same evasions of responsibility and protection of offending governments and the same overriding concern for state inter-ests and preoccupation with ideological and regional alliances" (p. 160). Sadly, the genocides perpetrated in Iraq in 1988, Rwanda in 1994, Yugoslavia in the 1990s and Darfur, Sudan, in early 2005, bear out his comments.

We believe that a concerted effort needs to be made by as many scholars, activists, and nongovernmental bodies as possible to continue to study all aspects of genocide and human rights violations with an eye toward developing, as soon as possible, a highly effective genocide early warning system—and then, finding a way to prod the United Nations and independent nations to summon the political will to act on such a system's findings.

Individuals, NGOs, and the International Community: The Need for a Well-Organized, Collective, and Concerted Effort to Intervene or Prevent Genocide

Individually, a person can only do so much to protest genocidal actions or to work on behalf of oppressed individuals. Collectively, people have a much better chance of effecting positive change. Today there are literally thousands of nongovernmental organizations working on various issues vis-à-vis the protection of international human rights. A small number of these organizations are working, in one way or another, on the issue of genocide. Many of them face a constant struggle to continue to remain in existence; this is due, in large part, to the limited resources they have at their disposal. As a result of this situation, both the focus of their efforts as well as their influence is limited. Certainly a key way for these organizations to gain more clout is to band together in order to complement and supplement one another's strengths as well as to act as a single body and to speak in one voice when addressing issues that they hold in common (Totten, 1994).

To be more effective, those working on the issue of genocide need to begin to initiate campaigns against genocide with an eye towards influencing international public opinion as well as the decisions and actions of governmental organizations. They also need to establish themselves as a main source of documentation for investigating the perpetration of genocide. As it now stands, most individuals and organizations dealing with the issue of genocide are putting more time into working on the scholarly examination of genocide (including issues of intervention and prevention) than the actual prevention of or intervention in genocide. There are, though, several major exceptions to this rule, and among the most notable are the Germany-based *Gesellschaft fur Bedrohte Volker* (Society for Threatened Peoples); the London-based International Alert (IA) Standing International Forum on Ethnic Conflict, Genocide and Human Rights; the Denmark-based International Work Group for Indigenous Affairs (IWGIA); STAND: A Student Anti-Genocide Coalition; and the United States Holocaust Memorial Museum's Committee on Conscience.

Educating about Genocide

In his hard-hitting and perspicacious report, *Revised and Updated Report on the Question of Prevention and Punishment of the Crime of Genocide*, Ben Whitaker's arguments still hold true today:

> The results of research [on the causes of genocide] could help form one part of a wide educational programme throughout the world against such aberrations (e.g., genocide), starting at an early age in schools. Without a strong basis of international public support, even the most perfectly redrafted [U.N.] Convention [on Genocide] will be of little value. Conventions and good governments can give a lead, but the mobilization of public awareness and vigilance is essential to guard against any recurrence of genocide and other crimes against humanity and human rights. . . .

As a further safeguard, public awareness should be developed internationally to reinforce the individual's responsibility, based on the knowledge that it is illegal to obey a superior order or law that violates human rights. (1985, p. 42)

We agree with Whitaker that it is crucial for educational institutions across the globe to teach their students about the causes and ramifications of genocide as well as the fact that it is each person's responsibility to act in a moral manner when human rights infractions (including genocide) rear their ugly face. As for the goal of Holocaust and genocide education, Israel Charny (1993) makes the perceptive point that the goal "must be to make awareness of Holocaust and genocide part of human culture, so that more and more people are helped to grow out of killing and from being accomplices to killers, or from being bystanders who allow the torture and killing of others" (p. 3).

The sort of study that we advocate is one that is immersed in both the cognitive and the affective domains (values and feelings). More specifically, it is one that (1) engages the students in a study of accurate and in-depth theories, research, and facts; (2) contextualizes the history; (3) avoids simple answers to complex history; and (4) addresses issues of personal and societal responsibility both from a historical as well as a contemporary perspective. (For a more in-depth discussion of such concerns, see Totten's *Teaching About Genocide: Issues, Approaches and Resources*, Greenwich, CT: Information Age Publishing, 2004.)

Indeed, an all-out educational effort by scholars, activist organizations, and educators is needed. Working together, these three groups could produce accurate and engaging curricular materials on various facets of genocide and reach students in a way that has not been attempted thus far. While such organizations could approach educational endeavors in a host of ways, we think the following avenues would prove to be a good starting point: (1) develop engaging and highly readable resource books on genocide; (2) develop accurate, informative, and engaging films and videos on various aspects of genocide; (3) develop state-of-the-art computer software on various aspects of genocide; (4) develop teacher manuals and curriculum guides that help integrate the study of genocide into existing courses such as social studies, history, geography, economics, anthropology, humanities, government studies, contemporary issues, English, and art; (5) establish international computer conferences on genocide specifically for secondary and university students (such conferences could lead to a global network of people engaged in thought-provoking discussions about genocide, its causes and ramifications, and the ways individuals and groups are working to intervene in current crises to prevent future genocides); (6) collect video testimonies of survivors and eyewitness accounts, and edit the collection for use in secondary, college, and university classrooms; and (7) conduct research into the efficacy of current efforts to teach about genocide.

Conclusion

The scholars who have contributed essays to this volume are doing vitally significant and, in many cases, groundbreaking work in regard to assisting humanity to gain a clearer understanding as to how, why, and when genocide is perpetrated. They, and others like them, are to be commended. At the same time, what is still needed is the development of a critical mass of humanity across the globe to work for the intervention and prevention of genocide. To develop such a critical mass, individuals, communities, and states need to undertake an effort to educate themselves and their young about genocide; speak out against injustices anywhere against anybody; remain vigilant; and finally, encourage and prod one's family, friends, community, and nation to be vigilant.

In that vein, we agree with Charny (1988a) when he argues that:

> There needs to be a growing consensus on the part of human beings and organized society that penetrates the very basis of human culture that mass killing is unacceptable to civilized peoples, otherwise the prevailing momentum of historical experience will continue to confirm for generation after generation that genocide is a phenomenon of nature, like other disasters, and this view of the inevitability of genocide as an almost natural event will continue to justify it in the sense of convincing people that nothing can be done (p. 23).

Further, as Totten (1991a) has written:

> . . . it is easy to call for the prevention of genocide. In fact, far too often in [books] of this sort, as well as at commemorative ceremonies for the victims and survivors, well-intentioned people almost perfunctorily recall Santayana's admonition, "Those who do not remember the past are condemned to repeat it." Through its repeated use, this finely wrought and powerful notion has become not much more than a cliché. The past must be remembered, yes; but humanity must go beyond merely remembering a particular genocidal act. Inherent in authentic remembrance is vigilance and action. More often than not, remembrance has been bereft of such crucial components. As Elie Wiesel has eloquently and powerfully stated: "Memory can be a

graveyard, but it also can be the true kingdom of man." The choice is before humanity (pp. 334–335).

Each generation has its great accomplishments, and each generation expresses a desire to shape a more humane world, and yet, we still seem to be in the Stone Age when it comes to mass killings and atrocities. It seems as though human beings, organizations and governments are incapable of preventing genocide once and for all, and it is clear that the perpetrators of mass killing learn from one another. That said, there are thousands upon thousands of individuals throughout the world who are pushing back on the perpetrators of mass atrocities, and this book is one small effort in that direction. The ultimate question is whether or not those of us who push back have greater determination and clout than the perpetrators.

Notes

1. What has been delineated here in regard to the definition of genocide is, quite obviously, a synopsis of a complex issue. For more detailed discussions, see the following: Chalk and Jonassohn, 1990, pp. 8–27; Charny, 1988a, pp. 20–38; Charny, 1988b, pp. 1–19; Dadrian, 1975; Drost, 1975; Fein, 1990; Kuper, 1981, pp. 19–39; Kuper, 1985, pp. 8–22; Whitaker, 1985, and Schabas, 2000.

2. We, of course, commend the efforts of many of the contributors to this volume in regard to their Herculean efforts to collect eyewitness accounts under extremely difficult conditions.

References

Chalk, Frank, and Jonassohn, Kurt (1990). *The History and Sociology of Genocide: Analyses and Case Studies.* New Haven, CT: Yale University Press.

Charny, Israel W. (1988a). "Intervention and Prevention of Genocide," pp. 20–38. In Israel W. Charny (Ed.) *Genocide: A Critical Bibliographic Review.* New York: Facts on File.

Charny, Israel W. (1988b). "The Study of Genocide," pp. 1–19. In Israel W. Charny (Ed.) *Genocide: A Critical Bibliographic Review.* New York: Facts on File.

Charny, Israel W. (1993). "Editorial Comment." *Internet on the Holocaust and Genocide,* April, 43, p. 3.

Dadrian, Vahakn (Fall 1975). "A Typology of Genocide." *International Review of Modern Sociology,* 5, 201–12.

Drost, Pieter (1975). *The Crime of State* (Vol. 2). Leyden: A.W. Sythoff.

Fein, Helen (1990). "Genocide: A Sociological Perspective." *Current Sociology,* 38(1):1–126.

Hawk, David (1988). "The Cambodian Genocide," pp. 137–54. In Israel W. Charny (Ed.) *Genocide: A Critical Bibliographic Review.* New York: Facts on File.

Horowitz, Irving Louis (1980). *Taking Lives: Genocide and State Power.* New Brunswick, NJ: Transaction Publishers.

Hovannisian, Richard (1973). "Introduction," pp. xix–xxv. In Stanley E. Kerr's *The Lions of Marash: Personal Experiences With Near East Relief, 1919–1922.* Albany: State University of New York Press.

Kuper, Leo (1981). *Genocide: Its Political Use in the Twentieth Century.* New Haven, CT: Yale University Press.

Kuper, Leo (1985). *The Prevention of Genocide.* New Haven, CT: Yale University Press.

Lemkin, Raphael (1944). *Axis Rule in Occupied Europe: Laws of Occupation, Analysis of Government, and Proposals for Redress.* Washington: Carnegie Foundation for International Peace. [Reprint, New York: Howard Fertig, 1973.]

Schabas, William A. (2000). *Genocide in International Law.* New York: Cambridge University Press.

Totten, Samuel (1991a). "First-Person Accounts of Genocidal Acts," pp. 321–62. In Israel W. Charny (Ed.) *Genocide: A Critical Bibliographic Review. Volume 2.* London and New York: Mansell Publishers and Facts on File, respectively.

Totten, Samuel (1991b). *First-Person Accounts of Genocidal Acts Committed in the Twentieth Century: An Annotated Bibliography.* Westport, CT: Greenwood Press.

Totten, Samuel (1994). "Non-Governmental Organizations Working on the Issue of Genocide," pp. 325–57. In Israel W. Charny (Ed.) *The Widening Circle of Genocide—Genocide: A Critical Bibliographic Review, Volume 3.* New Brunswick, NJ: Transaction Publishers.

Totten, Samuel (2002). "A Matter of Conscience," pp. 545–80. In Samuel Totten and Steven Jacobs (Eds.) *Pioneers of Genocide Studies.* New Brunswick, NJ: Transaction Publishers.

Whitaker, Ben (1985). *Revised and Updated Report on the Question of the Prevention and Punishment of the Crime of Genocide.* pp. 62 (E/CN.4/Sub.2/1985/6, 2 July 1985).

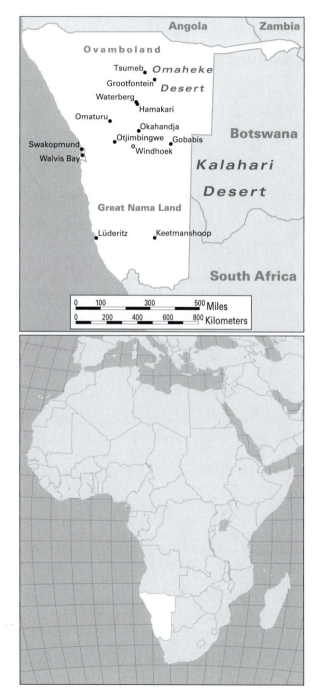

South West Africa

CHAPTER 1

Genocide of the Hereros

JON BRIDGMAN AND LESLIE J. WORLEY

In January 1904, a revolt broke out in German South West Africa. The Hereros, who inhabited most of the best grazing land in the colony, rose against the Germans. Two years later, when the German army finally succeeded in stamping out the last embers of the revolt, the Hereros all but ceased to exist as a cultural entity. Of the original 80,000 Hereros, only 20,000 remained alive and the survivors were so shaken by the catastrophe that they lapsed into a terrible lethargy that lasted for decades.[1]

On the face of it, the destruction of the Hereros might appear a paradigm of genocide, but there are some complications. By definition, genocide usually refers to the deliberate policy of a government as opposed to a random massacre by a local commander. To a large extent, the destruction of the Hereros was not the deliberate policy of the German government in Berlin, but rather the decision of the local commander.

This is not to say that the German actions during the revolt were not morally repulsive, but whether they should be subsumed under the rubric of "genocide" is another matter. When the Nazi regime and its collaborators set out to annihilate the Jews of Europe, the whole administrative structure of the government was pressed into service to carry out this diabolical policy, and the few voices of protest that were heard were in vain. When the Germans began the annihilation of the Hereros, loud and insistent protests were raised in Germany, and many agencies of the German government refused to be involved in what they considered an immoral act.

These protests were not totally in vain. Eventually, the German forces in South West Africa were forced to halt the overt slaughter of the Hereros before the entire tribe had perished. And yet, this was genocide because it was an attempt by representatives of the German government to destroy a whole people with the knowledge and the tacit approval of the Kaiser and the General Staff, the two most important elements of the government.

The Victims

The Hereros were part of the Bantu tribal peoples, and related to the Ovambo, a tribe so fierce and warlike that the Germans for the most part left it alone. Early European travellers among the Hereros were impressed by their physical, handsome appearance. Charles Andersson (1856), a Swedish explorer, wrote, "The Damara [the Hottentot name for the Hereros], speaking generally, are an exceeding fine race of men ... . Indeed, it is by no means unusual to meet individuals six feet and some inches in height, and symmetrically proportioned withal. Their features are, besides, good and regular; and many might serve as models of the human figure" (p. 49). Andersson was less impressed with the personal hygiene of the Hereros. "Both sexes are exceedingly filthy in their habits. Dirt often accumulates to such a degree on their persons, as to make the colour of their skin totally indistinguishable; while to complete the disguise, they smear themselves with a profusion of red ochre and grease. Hence the exhalation hovering about them is disgusting" (Andersson, 1856, p. 50).

Traditionally, the social and political organization of the Hereros was fairly complex and centered around paternal and maternal groupings. The nation was divided into almost 20 different *oruzo* or paternal groups. Each had a chief (who generally acquired his position through inheritance), had a herd of sacred cattle (which was inalienable), and lived in a *werft* or village of mud and dung huts. If a *werft* became too large, the chief usually permitted the founding of a new and separate village, but this had to remain dependent on and subordinate to the *oruzo* chief. Parallel to the *oruzo* groups were the *eanda* groups, which were maternal. The cattle of these were used to pay debts and at times loaned to poor members of the group. *Eanda* members were generally not allowed to live in the same *oruzo*. Thus the *eanda* organization formed a network that bound the Herero people as a whole together. All land was held to be common property of the tribe and could not be alienated except for temporary purposes.

By 1903, this traditional organization had deteriorated and altered somewhat, in large part due to the increased presence and influence of the Germans and other Europeans. As the possibility of selling cattle for cash expanded, some Hereros became cattle ranchers. This caused social distinctions to appear between the poor "field Hereros," who owned few or no cattle and were obliged to work, and the richer Hereros, mainly chiefs, who had acquired large herds by means fair and foul. The Herero nation was divided into nine tribes. The largest of these was centered on Okahandja and was estimated to have some 23,000 members living in about 150 villages. Other large tribes existed near Omaruru, Otijimb-ingwe, and Waterberg, while the five tribes of eastern Hereroland were all fairly small. The total Herero population was estimated to be roughly 80,000 men, women, and children.[2]

While each tribe had a chief who was its nominal leader, in fact even the richest chief was no more than a *primus inter pares*, since all the cattleowners in the tribe shared in the decision-making process. Samuel Maherero held the position of Paramount Chief, a fairly new office, because he was chief of the tribe located in the Okahandja area, the largest single grouping of Hereros, and was supported by the German colonial authorities and the Rhenish Missionaries, since he was a Christian. In actual practice, intertribal authority was almost nonexistent, as each chief ruled his own tribe, and the agreement of all the chiefs was needed for common action.

Even in 1903, the Hereros sought to preserve their traditional way of life. They were a pastoral people whose entire way of life centered on their cattle. The Herero language, while limited in its vocabulary for most areas, contained over a thousand words for the colors and markings of cattle. Herero myths extolled the fact that the creator gave them the cow and the bull, while the rest of mankind suffered with lesser gifts. So much did the Hereros love their animals that they rarely slaughtered them. The basis of their diet was sour milk mixed with blood drawn from the cattle and the wild fruits and berries that they found in the bush. The Hereros were content to live in peace as long as their cattle were safe and well-pastured; but when their cattle were threatened, the peaceful Hereros became formidable warriors.[3]

The Perpetrators

In the early 1880s, German influence in South West Africa was stronger than that of any other European power, but for all that it was still minuscule. Furthermore, the government in Berlin, under Chancellor Bismarck, had no interest in imperial expansion. Bismarck modified his position somewhat in 1882 when he gave Adolf Lüderitz, a German trader, a guarantee of imperial protection for such lands as he might acquire in Africa, providing Lüderitz acquired a harbor and "clear title." Subsequently, Lüderitz purchased several large parcels of land and the harbor of Angra Pequena in South West Africa from the Orlam tribe, and he asked the German government for official recognition and protection. After a two-year period of inquiries to Whitehall and the Cape government concerning the British position on South West Africa, which resulted in no clear statement or policy, Bismarck in April 1884 had all parties notified that Lüderitz and his property were under the protection of the Reich.

In April 1885, Dr. Goering, the father of Hermann Goering, the future *Reichsfeldmarschall* of the Third Reich, arrived in South West Africa as Imperial Commissioner. Goering's main task was to extend German control and influence beyond Lüderitz's holdings by persuading the various tribal chiefs to sign treaties of protection. Kamaherero, the Herero chief, signed such a treaty on October 21, 1885. Within four years, the Herero leader repudiated this treaty. Kamaherero felt the treaty was utterly useless since it provided him with neither men, money, nor arms and equipment to protect the Herero cattle and to fight the Orlam, a neighboring tribe with whom the Herero had cattle wars.

To add insult to injury, Kamaherero told Goering that he was giving Robert Lewis, an English adventurer, power of attorney to exercise control and authority over the territory. The threat of English intervention along with the collapse of the *Deutsche Kolonialgesellschaft für Südwestafrika* forced Bismarck to dispatch Captain Curt von François with a small detachment of soldiers to South West Africa. For better or worse, South West Africa now became a German colony and the direct responsibility of the German government. The people of this colony were to obey the Germans not because they had agreed to, but because the Germans had the force to coerce them.

Why the Genocide Was Committed

In the autumn of 1903, the German administrators and officials in South West Africa were quietly confident that the colony was advancing in an orderly way along the path that led to "civilization."[4] Since the last native uprising in 1896, law and order had, for the most part, prevailed. Year after year the governor, Major Theodor Leutwein, had travelled throughout the colony visiting the chiefs and dispensing justice. In the summer of 1903 he had demanded that the old Herero chief Tjetjo and his tribe turn in all their weapons. Backed by the support of the principal Herero chief, Maherero, who had been a long-time enemy of Tjetjo, Leutwein was able to enforce compliance without recourse to arms (Schwabe, 1904, p. 67). The whole incident seemed to prove to Leutwein that the Hereros had lost the will to resist the white man. Therefore, in the autumn of 1903, he withdrew over half of the troops stationed in Hereroland for duty in the extreme south of the colony.

Yet beneath the tranquil surface there was growing bitterness among the Hereros, and indeed most of the other tribes as well, at the treatment they received at the hands of the German settlers and traders. On the eve of the rebellion, a Herero told a German officer that "if the Herero is angry and storms at you there is nothing to fear, but when he laughs and is friendly be on your guard ... . Sir, they are so crafty that [even] if you understand their speech and sit with them at the fire, they can be deciding your death whilst you think they are talking about flowers" (Wellington, 1967, p. 67). And so it was in the last days of 1903; the Germans deluded themselves into thinking their subjects were quiescent when in reality they were planning an uprising that would shake the German rule to its foundations.

By 1904, the Hereros had so many reasons for rebelling that it might be more profitable to ask why they had not acted sooner, rather than why they revolted when they did. First, every Herero was alarmed at the progressive loss of land. Up to 1900, only a minor portion of the Herero hereditary lands had been alienated, but with the completion of the railroad from the coast to the capital of the colony, Windhoek, the pace of alienation accelerated rapidly, so that by the end of 1903, 3.5 million hectares out of a total of 13 million had been lost, and the day when the Hereros would not have enough land to continue their traditional way of life was fast approaching. The loss of land, frightening as it was to any Herero who looked only a few years into the future, did not yet in 1903 affect the daily life of the Hereros.

The problem of debt was another matter. For many years, Hereros had fallen into the habit of borrowing money from the white traders at usurious rates of interest. Leutwein had long been concerned about this practice, which he considered not only immoral, but also politically explosive; however, all his attempts to find a solution had been frustrated by the powerful colonial interests, which grew rich on the profits. Finally, on July 23, 1903, Leutwein grasped the nettle and issued an ordinance that provided that all outstanding debts not collected within a year would be null and void.[5] The ordinance went into effect on November 1, 1903. This law, whose sole purpose was to wipe the slate clean after a reasonable period of time and then discourage further abuse of the credit system, had — in the short run — the opposite effect.

The German traders, knowing that if they did not collect all outstanding debts within a year they would lose them forever, not unnaturally began recalling their loans as quickly as possible. To facilitate the collection process, government officials, and on some occasions even soldiers, were pressed into service to aid traders. In some cases, traders turned over lists of their debtors to local officials; in others, the traders themselves expropriated as many cattle as they thought necessary to cover claims — and, as one trader remarked, a few extra to cover any future claims.[6]

Moderate German newspapers were almost unanimous in citing the credit ordinance as the principal reason for the uprising. On January 25,

1904, the *Kölnische Zeitung* editorialized: "The credit ordinance … is one of the direct causes of dissatisfaction among the Hereros. The dubious past of the traders in Europe is quite often the reason for their being down there in the first place" (Bridgman, 1981, p. 60).

The Outstanding Historical Forces and Trends at Work that Led to the Genocide

The naked economic exploitation of the natives was a major reason for the rebellion, but a purely economic explanation is too simple. Racial tension, also a major factor, was real and very intense by 1903. Every year saw more and more white settlers coming into the colony "as conquerors, in a land which had not been conquered," as Leutwein put it.[7] Typically these new settlers were ne'er-do-wells, and not a few of them were criminally inclined younger sons of the aristocracy, packed off to "darkest" Africa to prevent them from disgracing the family name at home. The old colonial hands like Leutwein had a real respect for Africans as men, because they knew them as soldiers and because they had fought against them. The newer arrivals saw the black African as nothing but a potential source of cheap labor at best, and some even raised the question whether the colony would not be better off if the black population were completely eliminated.

Indeed, when the rebellion broke out, a number of settlers voiced the opinion that the uprising was a positive advantage because it gave the Germans a chance to annihilate the natives. This prompted one missionary to exclaim in horror: "The Germans are consumed with inexpiable hatred and a terrible thirst for revenge, one might even say they are thirsting for the blood of the Hereros. All you hear these days is words like 'make a clean sweep, hang them, shoot them to the last man, give no quarter.' I shudder to think of what may happen in the months ahead. The Germans will doubtless exact a grim vengeance" (Imperial Colonial Office, File No. 2114, pp. 80–82).[8]

The consciousness of being white, which had no doubt played a major role in German actions from the very beginning, became a dominate factor for many colonists. White settlers normally referred to black Africans as "baboons" and treated them accordingly. As one missionary reported: "The real cause of the bitterness among the Hereros toward the Germans is without question the fact that the average German looks down upon the natives as being about on the same level as the higher primates ('baboon' being their favorite term for the natives) and treats them like animals. The settler holds that the native has a right to exist only in so far as he is useful to the white man. It follows that the whites value their horses and even their oxen more than they value the natives"

(Drechsler, 1980, p. 133, no. 6). Among other things, this attitude manifested itself in the mistreatment of native women. In 1903, there were about 4000 white males in South West Africa and only 700 white women. The inevitable result of this imbalance was what the Germans referred to as *"Verkafferung"* or *"Schmutzwirtschaft."* From the perspective of the natives, *"Verkafferung"* meant that the German men took their woman, peacefully if possible, but otherwise by force.

This contempt for the black African was held to be the reason for many acts of violence that whites perpetrated on the Hereros. Indeed, settlers were wont to explain such behavior in quasi-medical terms, inventing a disease called "tropical frenzy," which was said to overtake white men in the tropics. A German doctor writing in 1902, however, rejected such an explanation: "I have never found anywhere any evidence of the disease which in the accounts of murders in the daily newspapers from the colonies plays such a role, that is 'tropical frenzy'.... There are a relatively large number of men of a passionate temperament among the Europeans in the colonies because the average man of mild temperament would rather remain in his homeland. For a man of weak character there are, out under the palms, opportunities greater than in Europe to avoid the moral imperatives" (Drechsler, 1980, p. 133, no. 8). This contemptuous attitude was not confined to settlers. The Kaiser and his Chief of Staff, Count von Schlieffen, displayed attitudes hardly different from those of the average settler in South West Africa; the Kaiser was known to have said that Christian precepts were not applicable to heathens and savages (von Bülow, 1930–1931, 1:24). And when Matthias Erzberger, speaking in the *Reichstag*, pointed out that the black men had immortal souls just as the Germans did, he was hooted down by the whole right side of the house (Epstein, 1959, p. 637).

Such, then, was the temper of the whites and blacks in Hereroland on the eve of the rebellion. The Hereros, or at least a large portion of them, had decided that German rule meant not only personal humiliation and economic ruin, but the end of their traditional way of life. Given this conviction, they saw little reason to wait and see if conditions would improve. By 1903, the tinder was ready and only a spark was needed to set Hereroland aflame. That spark was provided in an unexpected way and from an unexpected quarter. Almost 500 miles to the south of Windhoek lived a Hottentot tribe called the Bondelzwarts. (See *Kriegsgeschichtliche Abteilung, Grosser Generalstab*, 1906–1907 for a detailed account.) Their land, which lay between the Karras Hills and the Orange River, was bleak and arid. Just how many Bondelzwarts there were was not known; the Germans, however, estimated that the tribe could muster somewhere between 300 and 700 warriors. A total of 161 white men lived in the area; included in this number were the military force, which consisted of one officer, three noncommissioned officers, twelve men, and two civilian policemen. Since 1890, the Bondelzwarts had lived in peace with the Germans.

Then, in 1903, the local German authorities ordered the Bondelzwarts to register their guns. This demand, which the Bondelzwarts correctly interpreted as a prelude to total disarmament, was rejected by their chief, Willem Christian. To enforce compliance, the district chief, accompanied by five men, rode into Christian's encampment. A fire-fight ensued in which three Germans were killed and a fourth wounded. Four days later (October 29, 1903) Leutwein in Windhoek received news of the affair. He at once dispatched two companies of regulars to restore order in the south. After a month of desultory fighting, the situation had not improved, but had actually deteriorated. The Bondelzwarts were by then cooperating with small bands of robbers who infested the Karras Hills and Leutwein himself went to the south to take personal command, leaving almost no troops in the north.

The Hereros sensed at once that they had an opportunity that might not come again. However, the absence of the soldiers and Leutwein was also a danger to them. No sooner was the restraining hand of Leutwein removed than the settlers began pushing the natives, hoping to drive them to some desperate act that would permit a final solution of the "black problem." The Hereros trusted Leutwein (whom they called "Majora," with a mixture of deference and affection), but to the whites he was a traitor to his race. One German asserted, "Leniency toward blacks is cruelty toward whites."[9] And the German Colonial League produced a pamphlet that demanded that "the policy pursued so far towards the natives be changed in favor of our race" (Imperial Colonial Office, 1904, File No. 2111, p. 26). Shortly after his departure, rumors were abroad in the land that the Germans had suffered a major military defeat in the south. Some said that Leutwein and 75 men had been killed; according to another version, Leutwein had been driven across the frontier and interned by the British. In a letter to Leutwein, Maherero described the situation in Hereroland at the time:

> And now in those days the white people said to us that you [Leutwein] who were at peace with us and loved us, were gone, and they said to us: The governor who loved you has gone to fight a difficult war; he is dead and because he is dead you [Hereros] must die also. They went so far as to kill two men of Chief Tjetjo's tribe. Even Lieutenant N began to kill my people in jail. Ten died and it was said they died of sickness, but they died at the hands of the labor overseer and by the lash. Eventually Lieutenant N began to treat me so badly and to look for a reason for killing me, so he said:

the people of Kambasembi and Uanja are making war. Then he called me to question me, I answered truthfully "No," but he did not believe me. I did not go; I saw his intentions and so I fled … . Because of these things I became angry and said, "Now I must kill the white people even if I die." (Leutwein, 1908, p. 512)

During the last days of 1903 and the first of 1904, the Hereros made their final plans for a concerted attack that, they hoped, would undermine the sources of German power in their land. Their greatest single advantage was the element of surprise, and they exploited it to the utmost. Leutwein knew Maherero very well and was absolutely convinced that the old chief was far too fond of the good life, particularly of alcohol and women, to take up arms against his friends and patrons the Germans who, after all, supplied him with the wherewithal to sustain his pleasures. Leutwein said of Maherero that he was "a large man, imposing and of proud mien, a man not without spirit and understanding"; but he added that Maherero was "lacking in character" and sacrificed the duties of his office as Paramount Chief to pleasure. Leutwein was convinced that without Maherero's name and authority, no common action on the part of the Hereros was possible.

The ultimate objective of the revolt was, of course, to drive the Germans out of Hereroland. This goal was to be achieved by undermining the German power structure from two different angles. First, an attack was to be made on German outposts and garrisons as well as on the transportation and communication systems, with the objective of crippling German military power so that the German government would lose the ability to protect the colony. Second, an all-out attack was to be made on German farmers. They offered a tempting target, controlling as they did hundreds of thousands of acres of land and having 42,000 cattle, 3,000 horses, and 210,000 sheep and goats. The farms all tended to be very large and isolated, and were thus hardly defensible. In all, there were only 267 farms in the northern part of the colony. The Hereros reasoned that since the colonial government existed largely for the sake of those farms, if the settlers became discouraged and left the land, then the rest of the Germans would also pack up and leave.

While male Germans, both military personnel and farmers, were targets of the Hereros, Maherero feared that a general attack on defenseless civilians might easily lead to an orgy of wanton killing, and this he wanted to avoid at all costs. Therefore, on the eve of the revolt, he issued a strikingly unequivocal manifesto in which he declared: "I am the principal chief of the Hereros. I have proclaimed the law and the just word, and I mean for all my people. They should not lay hands on any of the following: Englishmen, Basters, Berg Damaras, Namas, and Boers. On none of these shall hands be laid. I have pledged my honor that this thing shall not take place. Nor shall missionaries be harmed. Enough!" (Great Britain, 1918, p. 57).[10]

While the Germans found this unexpected streak of humanity hard to understand, from Maherero's point of view there were several good reasons for this manifesto. Militarily, the Herero chief wanted to reduce the number of his enemies and obtain, if possible, allies in the struggle against the Germans. The Basters, the Berg Damaras, and the Namas were all traditional enemies of the Hereros. However, if the latter refrained from attacking these other tribes, they probably would not join the Germans and might be persuaded to cooperate with the Herero against the common oppressor.[11] This same logic held true for the British and the Boers; by not attacking them, Maherero held open the possibility of British assistance in the event the rebellion sparked a colonial war (Drechsler, 1980, p. 144).

Politically, Maherero also needed an ally or allies, someone to plead the Herero cause, particularly in Germany. The most obvious choice was the Rhenish Missionary Society. The missionaries in the past had supported Maherero, and he owed his position as Paramount Chief to their influence. There was no reason to believe that if the missionaries were left unhurt and unmolested in this rebellion that the Rhenish Missionary Society would not use its influence in Germany and argue for justice and the just cause of the Herero.[12] And finally, Maherero seems to have had a sense of destiny. From the missionaries and colonial officials, he had been taught that he was a "barbarian" and that they were "civilized." One of the most commonly cited proofs of the barbarism of the natives was their manner of making war — with indiscriminate slaughters of prisoners, massacres of women and children, torture, cruelty, and unrestrained sadism.[13] Maherero seemed to realize that he and his people at this moment in history had to surpass the standards of civilization as defined by their enemy.

On January 12, 1904, the Hereros launched their first attacks. During the next ten days almost every farm, village, and fort in Hereroland was attacked or, at least, threatened by marauding bands. The majority of the German farms were destroyed during those hectic days. By January 20, in the Windhoek area, alone, civilian casualties had reached thirteen: six farmers, one farm hand, two surveyors, two merchants, one policeman, and a 14-year-old boy. No women or children had been killed. Of those farmers who survived, all fled to Windhoek; in most cases, they had lost everything: their livestock had been stolen, their possessions looted, and their buildings burned. In addition, all the major fortified places in Hereroland were loosely besieged, though no fortified place had fallen.

Leutwein called the first days of the uprising "nerve-shattering," but despite the initial success of the Hereros, by late spring of 1904 German troops were pouring into the colony, and the defeat of the Hereros was only a matter of time. In August, the day of reckoning arrived when the main Herero forces were surrounded and crushed at the Battle of Waterberg.

How the Genocide Was Committed and Those Who Were Involved

General Lothar von Trotha, the newly arrived commander of German forces in South West Africa, had one aim: to utterly destroy the Hereros. With this in mind, he deployed his strongest units on three sides of Waterberg, while placing a weak force on the southeast. Thus, the Hereros could either stay trapped in a killing zone or fight their way out to the southeast and into the vast wastes of the Omaheke Desert. In fact, von Trotha was following the results of a study prepared by the German General Staff: "If, however, the Hereros were to break through, such an outcome of the battle could only be even more desirable in the eyes of the German Command because the enemy would seal his own fate, being doomed to die of thirst in the arid sandveld" (*Grosser* Generalstab, 1906–1907, 1:132). After two days of fierce fighting, Maherero and the other Herero chiefs were forced to recognize the uselessness of facing the superior firepower of the German forces, equipped with 30 pieces of artillery and 12 machine guns. The Herero broke through the German lines in the southeast and fled toward the desert.

Von Trotha pursued and kept constant pressure on the fleeing tribe, driving it southeast. When groups of Hereros broke off from the main body and tried to flee north or south, in either case away from the line-of-march and the desert, German units made sweeping, flanking movements to force the natives back into the main body and toward the sandveld. As this march continued, exhausted Hereros lagged behind and fell to the ground unable to move. The pursuing Germans, acting on orders, took no prisoners, but instead killed men, women, and children indiscriminately. Jan Cloete from Omaruru, who acted as a guide/scout for the Germans, later testified: "I was present when the Hereros were defeated in the battle at Hamakiri in the vicinity of Waterberg. After the battle all men, women, and children who fell into German hands, wounded or otherwise, were mercilessly put to death. Then the Germans set off in pursuit of the rest, and all those found by the wayside and in the sandveld were shot down or bayoneted to death. The mass of the Herero men were unarmed and thus unable to offer resistance. They were just trying to get away with their cattle" (Great Britain, 1918, p. 64).

By the end of August, the Hereros had been forced into the Omaheke. Now the tactics changed from direct contact and conflict with the natives to the elimination of their water. Von Trotha had German units patrol the water holes and drive away or kill any natives attempting to obtain water.

The German commander defended his orders as necessary in the *Berliner Neueste Nachrichten* on February 3, 1909: "My force was on the verge of disaster. If I had made the small water holes accessible to the womenfolk, I would have run the risk of an African catastrophe comparable to the Battle of Beresonia" (Drechsler, 1980, p. 158). At some point, the Germans poisoned these water holes; now, the choice for the Hereros was to die from poison or to die from thirst.[14] German patrols subsequently found hand-dug holes 40 feet deep, grim evidence of the Hereros' futile attempts to find water in the Omaheke Desert.

To prevent the Hereros from returning to German South West Africa, von Trotha sealed off the western rim of the desert with a series of forts and fortified positions stretching for several hundred miles. On September 28, 1904, a small band of Hereros tried to break through the German lines; they were repulsed almost without a fight. "All contacts with the enemy since the Battle of Waterberg have demonstrated (that) strength of will, unity of command, and the last remnants of resistance have been lost," wrote von Trotha (*Grosser Generalstab*, 1906–1907, 1:206). The trails through the desert were littered with hundreds of carcasses. Prisoners reported that people were weary of the war and willing to surrender. They also stated that Maherero and several other leaders had crossed the desert and found refuge in British territory.

On October 2, 1904, von Trotha promulgated his infamous *Schrecklichkeit* (Atrocity or Extermination) order in an attempt to stamp out the last embers of the revolt before the end of the year. The order read as follows (Drechsler, 1980, p. 156):

Osombo-Windimbe October 2, 1904

I, the great general of the German troops, send this letter to the Herero people. Hereros are no longer German subjects. They have murdered, stolen, they have cut off the noses, ears, and other bodily parts of wounded soldiers and now, because of cowardice, they will fight no more. I say to the people: anyone who delivers one of the Herero captains to my station as a prisoner will receive 1000 marks. He who brings in Samuel Maherero will receive 5000 marks. All the Hereros must leave the land. If the people do not do this, then I will force them to do it with the great guns. Any Herero found within the German borders with or without a gun, with or without cattle, will be shot. I shall no longer receive any women or children. I will drive them back to their people or I will shoot them. This is my decision for the Herero people.

Signed: The Great General of the Mighty Kaiser,

von Trotha

This order is to be read to the troops at quarters with the additional statement that even if a trooper captures a captain of the Hereros he will receive the reward, and the shooting of women and children is to be understood to mean that one can shoot over them to force them to run faster. I definitely mean that this order will be carried out and that no male prisoners will be taken, but it should not degenerate into killing women and children. This will be accomplished if one shoots over their heads a couple of times. The soldiers will remain conscious of the good reputation of German soldiers.

The General Command

Signed: Lieutenant-General von Trotha

Two days later von Trotha explained his order to General von Schlieffen, Chief of the General Staff:

There is only one question to me: how to end the war? The ideas of the governor and the other old African hands and my ideas are diametrically opposed. For a long time they have wanted to negotiate and have insisted that the Hereros are a necessary raw material for the future of the land. I totally oppose this view. I believe that the nation as such must be annihilated or if this is not possible from a military standpoint then they must be driven from the land. It is possible by occupying the water holes from Grootfontein to Gobabis and by vigorous patrol activity to stop those trying to move to the west and gradually wipe them out … . My knowledge of many central African peoples, Bantu and others, convinces me that the Negro will never submit to a treaty but only to naked force. Yesterday before my departure I ordered the execution of those prisoners captured and condemned in the last few days and I have also driven all the women and children back to the desert to carry the news of my proclamation … . The receiving of women and children is a definite danger for our troops, to take care of them is an impossibility … . This uprising is and remains the beginning of a racial war (Drechsler, 1980, p. 161).

The immediate impact of von Trotha's decision to annihilate the Hereros was unfavorable. Leutwein cabled the Foreign Office: "According to reliable reports the Hereros have asked for terms. Up to now the question of negotiation has been decided without consulting me. Therefore I ask for clarification: How far does my authority extend?" (Drechsler, 1980, pp. 161f). When the Foreign Office answered that von Trotha alone had authority to deal with the natives, Leutwein asked to be relieved of his duties (Drechsler, 1980, p. 162). Nor was Leutwein the only German disturbed by von Trotha's *modus operandi*. The highest civilian in the colony after the dismissal of Leutwein, Regierungsrat Tecklenburg, said that, in his opinion, German prestige with the natives was "lost beyond recall" by von Trotha's actions (Bridgman, 1981, p. 129). Also from the colony, the self-interested voices of the Rhenish Missionary Society and some of the settlers complained; the former feared that if the slaughter continued, the discontinuation of all missionary work was only a matter of time, and the latter feared the complete loss of the native labor needed on the farms. In Berlin, dissent was heard in the *Reichstag* where liberal Social Democrats criticized the von Trotha policy (Drechsler, 1980, p. 151; Swan, 1991, p. 51). Even the government in Berlin was alarmed by the bad press that the military action in South West Africa was receiving. On November 23, 1904, von Schlieffen informed the Chancellor, Bernard von Bülow, of the Army's position:

> According to all appearances our troops will be forced to stop the enemy from returning to the west by a system of extended posts and will have to carry on a war of attrition with all its horrors such as typhus, malaria, and heart attacks … . It is conceivable that in such circumstances the call for a quick peace will be raised. With rebels, however, a peace can only be concluded on the basis of unconditional surrender. Up to now neither the whole Herero nation nor even part of it is amenable to such conditions. Prisoners whom Major von Estorff had captured were released after good treatment in order to win their fellow countrymen over to the idea of accepting German protection, but they have not been seen since. If the Hereros will not come in freely then they must be forced and encouraged to give up. To enter into negotiations with the Herero captains for this purpose is out of the question. They have forfeited their lives and in order to create acceptable conditions in the protectorate, they must be removed from office. If General von Trotha has put a price on the heads of the captains, then he adopted the customary way of getting rid of them. The sums which he offered are, however, clearly too low and must be expressed not in terms of money but rather in terms of head of cattle. When the influence of the captains is broken, then one can hope for the surrender of Hereros in meaningful numbers.

The measures which von Trotha has taken … are prejudicial to such an outcome. One can agree with his plan of annihilating the whole people or driving them from the land. The possibility of whites living peacefully together with blacks after what has happened is very slight unless at first the blacks are reduced to forced labor, that is, a sort of slavery. An enflamed racial war can be ended only through the annihilation or complete subjugation of one of the parties. The latter course is, however, not feasible considering the present estimate of the length of the struggle. The intention of General von Trotha can therefore be approved. The only problem is that he does not have the power to carry it out. He must remain on the western edge of the Omaheke and cannot force the Hereros to leave it. If they should voluntarily leave the land we would not have gained much. They would present a constant threat in Bechuanaland in the event that the Cape government would not or could not render them harmless.

There is therefore scarcely any other alternative but to try to persuade the Hereros to give up. That is made more difficult by the proclamation of General von Trotha which states that any Herero who tries to give up will be shot. If a new proclamation is issued which states that any Herero who gives up will be spared, they will scarcely trust this statement. Yet it must be tried. I believe therefore that it must be proposed to General von Trotha that (1) a higher price be put on the heads of the captains and the leaders; (2) by means of a new proclamation or in some other suitable way we spare the lives of those Hereros who give themselves up (Drechsler, 1980, pp. 162f).

Put another way, von Schlieffen did not suggest that he was offended by von Trotha's way of making war, but he was convinced that it would not be successful. On the strength of this letter, von Bülow asked the Kaiser to lift the *Schrecklichkeit* order. He gave four reasons for doing so: (1) A policy of total annihilation was un-Christian; (2) it was not feasible; (3) it was economically senseless; and (4) such a way of making war would give the Germans a bad reputation among civilized people. The Kaiser, even when pressured by his Chancellor and Chief of the General Staff, was reluctant to command von Trotha to lift the order. For over three weeks he delayed, despite pressure from von Bülow, until finally in late December he gave in. Von Trotha was equally reluctant, and when he finally bowed to the inevitable, he did it with as bad grace as possible. Those Hereros who surrendered would not be shot, that much he conceded, but they were to be chained, used for forced labor, and branded with the letters GH (*gefangene Herero*); any who refused to reveal the whereabouts of weapons caches were to be shot out of hand.

When the new policy went into effect in the beginning of 1905, the Herero revolt, or what was left of it, quickly flickered out. The surviving Hereros either voluntarily presented themselves at collecting stations or were driven there by German patrols. This once proud tribe that had numbered about 80,000 people had apparently suffered 20,000 to 30,000 dead in the period from the start of the rebellion to the conclusion of the Battle of Waterberg, most of these no doubt the result of the one major confrontation. While there is no way of knowing how many Hereros were killed outright, since the Germans did not do a body count, in modern combat, combat employing the machine gun and artillery, there are usually three or four wounded for every individual killed in action. With this in mind, the Hereros had 5000 to 6000 killed in action, while the remainder of the casualties had initially been wounded and fell victim to von Trotha's no-prisoner policy. These numbers included men, women, and children because the entire tribe, or most of it, was in a single locale at the time. Between 50,000 and 60,000 Hereros survived the Battle of Waterberg and went to the Omaheke. Of these, about 1000 reached British territory; rather less than 1000 found refuge in Ovamboland; and perhaps the same number escaped to Namaland. An undetermined number filtered back through the German lines to their old homeland, where they scratched out a living stealing cattle.

In September 1905, a sweep was made through Hereroland that netted 260 prisoners and 86 guns. During this operation, about 1000 Hereros were killed. After September, there could hardly have been more than a few dozen free Hereros in all of Hereroland. In the German prison labor camps there were 10,632 women and children, and 4,137 men (Imperial Colonial Office, 1904, File No. 2119, p. 44; Drechsler, 1980, p. 208; and Bridgman, 1981, p. 131). Subsequently, in the next year, 7682 of the imprisoned natives died as a result of forced labor and harsh treatment (Imperial Colonial Office, 1904, File, No. 2140, p. 161; Drechsler, 1980, p. 213; and Swan, 1991, p. 53). It should be noted that this number includes some natives from other tribes, but the vast majority were Hereros. In 1911, the official census taken by colonial officials showed that there were a mere 15,130 Hereros in South West Africa. Thus, out of the original 80,000 people, the Herero population had been reduced by 81 percent (Great Britain, 1916, p. 35; and Drechsler, 1980, p. 214). Truly a genocide had taken place.

The Long-Range Impact of the Genocide on the Victim Group

"The death-rattle of the dying and the shrieks of the mad ... they echo in the sublime stillness of infinity!" (*Grosser Generalstab*, 1906–1907, 1:214)

So one German soldier described the end of the Hereros. The German official historians were blunter: "The Hereros ceased to exist as a tribe" (*Grosser Generalstab*, 1906–1907, 1:214). In fact, the German official historians recorded the truth. The Herero tribe ceased to exist as a functioning social, political, and cultural entity. Further, the German colonial authorities took definite steps to insure that the tribe would not be a phoenix and rise again from the ashes of war and genocide.

In August 1906, the labor camps were closed and the surviving Hereros were divided up into small groups and shipped off to work on the farms and ranches of the German settlers. This move, in part, was motivated out of fear that the concentration of large numbers of Hereros in camps might possibly lead to a reorganization of the tribe and another uprising (Drechsler, 1980, p. 208). With small groups of Herero dispersed on hundreds of ranches and farms spread over thousands of square miles, there was little chance of a tribal reorganization, let alone a renewed rebellion.

To insure that the traditional Herero lifestyle ceased, Hereroland was confiscated by the Germans. Hans Tecklenberg, deputy governor of South West Africa, outlined the Colonial Administration's policy in a report: "The tribal property of the tribes fully or partly involved in the rebellion will be subject to confiscation. Whether they have carried out, or aided and abetted, warlike acts will make no difference. It would be a sign of weakness, for which we would have to pay dearly, if we allowed the present opportunity of declaring all native lands to be Crown territory to slip by … . With the confiscation of their land, the natives will be deprived of the possibility of raising cattle. All objections notwithstanding, they must not, as a matter of principle, be allowed to own cattle because they cannot be conceded the grazing land required for this purpose" (Imperial Colonial Office, 19XX, File No. 1220, pp. 28–35).[15]

This policy was formalized on August 18, 1907, with the issuance of three orders. First, no native could own land or cattle. Second, all males over 17 had to carry passes. And third, any native unable to prove the source of his or her livelihood was subject to prosecution for "vagrancy" (Bridgman, 1981, p. 165; and Drechsler, 1980, p. 231).

Now the remnants of the Herero people were reduced to a permanent class of forced labor for German masters. Natives whose work was deemed unsatisfactory by their masters were turned over to the local authorities for punishment, which usually took the form of floggings. During 1911, 1655 cases of official floggings of natives were recorded. Yet, without a doubt, this number is nowhere near the actual number of floggings that occurred in South West Africa in that year since most white masters administered their own punishments. A farmer named Kramer, for instance, was charged with abusing seven women and one man. It was revealed that he flogged the man all afternoon, and one woman all evening. Two pregnant women had been so brutally whipped on two successive days that they miscarried, and two others had died from their punishments. Virtually all of Kramer's native laborers were found to have festered, whip-inflicted wounds. For his crimes, Kramer was sentenced to 21 months in prison, but on appeal his sentence was reduced to 3 months in prison and a fine of 2700 marks (Bridgman, 1981, p. 165ff; and Drechsler, 1980, p. 235).

Although the Germans lost South West Africa to a British invasion in 1915, the plight of the Hereros remained the same. They soon learned that while the colonial imperialists would wage war on one another, in the end the Europeans would come to terms in order to continue the oppression of the native labor force. Even the end of British colonial rule did not end the struggle for existence of the Herero. Only the administrative officials changed. Just as British officials had taken over from the Germans, South African officials replaced the British. But the Germans still ran the farms and the ranches, and life for the native laborer changed not at all. Now that South West Africa has become the independent nation of Namibia, only time will tell the fate of the descendants of the Herero.

The Response of Individuals, Groups, and Nations to this Particular Genocide

In fact, the decimation of the Hereros was largely ignored by most of Europe and the world. For some, particularly the imperialistic segments of German society and government, including the Colonial Office, complacency was a form of expediency. The colonial officials saw in the elimination of the natives the quickest and most efficient solution to the problem of ruling South West Africa. Without the natives the land could be settled by Germans and ruled as a German territory. It seemed to them a sensible solution for a knotty problem. When two minor officials in the Colonial Office brought forward to their superiors evidence of widespread misconduct by German officials in South West Africa, the reports were quickly filed and no action taken, except to force the retirement of the two officials on the grounds of "mental incapacity." Ultimately this information was leaked to a member of the *Reichstag*, who presented it to Chancellor von Bülow. The Chancellor's only concern was that confidentiality and secrecy had been violated (Epstein, 1959, p. 647ff).

For two years, from 1904 to 1906, the anticolonial parties — the Socialists, the Center, and the Radicals — in the Reichstag, time and again, protested the misconduct in South West Africa, among other things, by voting down budgetary requests. Then in December 1906 von Bülow dissolved the house and went to the German people asking for a mandate to carry on colonial affairs. In the only election in European history fought exclusively on imperial and colonial issues, the anticolonial coalition suffered a severe setback. The German voters gave those parties and politicians favoring colonial expansion a massive mandate. Von Bülow took a record of inhumane cruelty and military failure to the people, and the people chose imperialism by a great majority.[16]

For Europeans as a whole, the revolt of the Hereros, and its subsequent consequences, was an all-too-familiar occurrence for all colonial powers, and thus easy to ignore or rationalize. While by European standards the behavior of the Germans in South West Africa could be described as at best harsh and at worst sadistic, the Germans were not the only Europeans, let alone the only colonial power, to use their subject peoples cruelly. The French — in Madagascar, in Equatorial Africa, and in Indochina — had suppressed uprisings with methods not much different than the Germans. The Belgians in the Congo, the Americans in the Philippines, the Dutch in the East Indies, and the Japanese in Korea had all used the machine gun, the whip, and forced labor to bring their subjects to heel. Even the British could be ruthless when they thought it served their interests.

The general European attitude can find no more eloquent expression than in "The Report of the Commissioners into the Administration of the Congo State." King Leopold appointed this commission in 1904, after intense international pressure, to investigate the allegations that Belgians had employed means repugnant to civilized men in order to control the Congo Free State. After cataloguing repeated instances of shocking treatment of the native population, the commissioners concluded that although such behavior was not exemplary, it was absolutely necessary to rule inferior races and bring them along the road to civilization. "In a word, it is by this basis alone that the Congo can enter into the pathway of modern civilization and the population be reclaimed from its natural state of barbarism" (Bridgman, 1981, p. 167).

After South West Africa was occupied by British forces in 1915, an attempt was made to document the German atrocities against the natives. Two officers were assigned the task of investigating and drawing up a report detailing the treatment of the South West Africans by German colonial authorities. This report was submitted in 1918 and provided an explicit, unbiased account of the German domination of the region and its consequences. While this could have brought the Herero genocide out of the shadows and into the light for all to see, the apparent purpose of the report was not humanitarian but political, namely to document the incompetence of the Germans as colonial administrators and thus rule out a possible return of South West Africa to Germany after World War I. In fact, the League of Nations mandated South West Africa to the Union of South Africa. This move placed British–South African officials and German farmers on the same side, one desiring a peaceful and prosperous region. At a session of the South West African Legislative Assembly on July 19, 1926, a resolution was adopted that (1) labeled the report an "instrument of war" and said it was time for all such instruments to be set aside; (2) asked for the removal of the report from the official files of the Government of the Union and the British government; and (3) requested the removal and destruction of all copies of the report found in public libraries and official bookstores (Drechsler, 1980, p. 10). This relegated the most damning record of the German genocide of the Hereros to virtual oblivion, instead of placing it before the world as a possible warning of things to come.

Scholars' Interpretations of this Particular Genocide

It is possible that the general public and the world might become more conscious of and knowledgeable about the genocide of the Hereros if scholars were more united in their evaluations and interpretations of German conduct in South West Africa. This is unlikely to occur, and thus for the present, at least, two distinct schools of thought exist and oppose one another.

The first, or what can be called the "genocide school," believes that the German authorities committed genocide in South West Africa. Obviously, this chapter supports this belief. Two of the leading scholars of this school are Horst Drechsler and Jon Bridgman. Drechsler's *Südwestafrika unter deutschen Kolonialherrschaft,* which appeared in 1966, is the most complete and carefully documented work to date dealing with the German colonial activity and the natives of South West Africa. Bridgman's *The Revolt of the Hereros,* published in 1981, is the first work in English to detail the struggle of the Hereros and their destruction. Jon Swan (1991) added his voice and pen to the "genocide school" with an article entitled "The Final Solution in South West Africa."

On the other side, the "non-genocide school," the opposing view is set forth mostly by West German ethnologists. Katesa Schlosser (1955) recounts her visit to a Herero settlement in Bechuanaland and plays down the consequences of the Herero Revolt.[17] The logic of her argument is that since 5000 Hereros were in Bechuanaland in 1936, the number of Hereros who escaped the Germans and successfully crossed the desert must have been greater than previously thought. Thus, the number of dead was less than 60,000, and genocide did not occur.

In 1985, Karla Poewe took up the non-genocide cause. In *The Namibian Herero — A History of their Psychosocial Disintegration and Survival,* Poewe (1985), who also questions the accuracy of the numbers regarding the Herero dead, explains von Trotha's "extermination order" as attempted psychological warfare. "The intent was to keep small guerilla bands away from the German troops. The former shot upon the latter unexpectedly and cruelly mutilated dead German soldiers" (Poewe, 1985, p. 65). She also denies that von Trotha's order really called for extermination. "The use of the word '*vernichten*' which unknowledgeable people translate as 'extermination,' in fact, meant, in the usage of the time, breaking the military, national, or economic resistance" (Poewe, 1985, p. 60). Thus, according to Poewe, no genocide was intended.

With two such schools of thought in existence, the stage is set for the debate to continue for some time to come.

What this Genocide Can Teach Us in Regard to Our Effort to Protect Others from Such a Tragedy

Yet, the study of and discussion about the genocide of the Hereros must continue for the valuable lesson, or lessons, it offers concerning genocide in general. Genocide is not a random, unconscious, or unplanned act. Genocide is always initiated and committed by deliberate, calculating, and thinking men. While a few of these may be irrational or insane, the majority are not. The majority are generally followers who see nothing wrong in their actions. The rational participants in genocide have, unfortunately, developed an irrational attitude or mindset that allows them to kill thousands, or even millions, without remorse. Often these attitudes are culturally or nationally inspired and concern the superiority of one group and the inferiority of the other. Such attitudes and their development can be identified by the study of the Herero genocide, and in fact all genocides, and serve as a lesson or warning for future generations. With such lessons from the past, hopefully future generations will be able to identify possible targeted groups and prevent new genocides.

The overriding lesson from the genocide of the Hereros is that dehumanization or degradation of a people or peoples can lead to atrocities and genocide. It is easy to kill "subhumans" or "nonhumans." Too many German settlers and officials of South West Africa thought of the natives as "baboons." Baboons were not human and therefore did not have the same feelings and emotions, let alone rights, as humans. Baboons were wild animals. This labeling not only dehumanized the labelled but desensitized the labelers. There was no moral or ethical penalty to be considered in the treatment of baboons or wild animals, particularly when those wild animals bared their fangs and demonstrated their basic bestial nature. In fact, it was only prudent to destroy all such animals in the vicinity in order to protect peaceful, civilized white people from future attacks. Thus, the Herero were exterminated.

Eyewitness Accounts: Genocide of the Hereros

First-hand accounts of the events in South West Africa during the native uprisings are fairly numerous but vary dramatically in style, factuality, and perspective. Generally, these fall into three categories.

The first of these are the memoirs and journals of a popular nature. As one would expect, these were almost exclusively written by German soldiers and officials who served in the colony. Obviously, these were written from the perspective of the victors and treat favorably the Imperial colonial policy and the conduct of the war.

The second source, also German, is the files of the Imperial Colonial Office. Until 1955 these records were unavailable to scholars and other interested parties. In the Kaiser's day, these documents were held in strict confidentiality. During the Weimar Republic and the Third Reich, the Imperial Colonial Office files were suppressed for fear they might damage Germany's image and interests. And after World War II, all German government records were seized by the Allies, with those of the Imperial Colonial Office falling into Soviet hands.

These files were returned in 1955 and placed in the *Deutschen Zentralarchiv Potsdam*. While East Germany gradually allowed more and more access to these files, restrictions continued to apply until the fall of East Germany. Thus even today only a very small portion of the Imperial Colonial Office files have been published, and a trip to the archives is often necessary. Interestingly, such a trip usually reveals that the German colonists and authorities, knowing that their reports were not intended for publication, submitted fairly accurate and straightforward accounts of the conditions in the colony.

The only account from the native viewpoint and in English, and the one used in this Eyewitness Accounts section, is *The Report on the Natives of South West Africa and their Treatment by Germany,* which can be found in *The Sessional Papers of the House of Lords* (Vol. 13, 1918). Although the report in its narrative is anti-German, and at times quite dramatic and defamatory — von Trotha is called "no more worthy son of Attila," which of course is a reference to the great leader of the Huns, their barbaric warfare, and the derogatory name applied to the Germans during World War I — it does contain an extensive body of testimony from survivors of and witnesses to the Herero Revolt and the genocidal nature of the warfare.

What follows are a number of excerpts from the *Report* (using the headings found in it):

The Outbreak of the Herero Rising and the Humanity of the Herero

Under-Chief Daniel Kariko, who is noted as a bitter life-long enemy of the Germans, stated:

We decided that we should wage war in a humane manner and would kill only the German men who were soldiers, or who would become soldiers. We met at secret councils and there our chiefs decided that we should spare the lives of all German women and children. The missionaries, too, were to be spared, and they, their wives and families and possessions were to be protected by our people from all harm. We also decided to protect all British and Dutch farmers and settlers and their wives and children and property as they had always been good to us. Only German males were regarded as our enemies, and then not young boys who could not fight — these also we spared: We gave the Germans and all others notice that we had declared war (p. 57).

An unidentified Dutch housewife, who was alone at the time the rebellion started, reported on a visit by Michael Tysesita in which he said:

I have come to assure you that you and your children will be quite safe in your own home. You are under my protection. Do not go into the German fort. The Germans are foolish to take their women and children there, as they may be killed by our bullets, and we are not making war on women and children. Keep calm and stay indoors when there is fighting, I assure you my people will do you no harm. [In reply to a question about her husband, Tysesita responded:] We are not barbarians. Your husband is our friend; he is not a German. I have already sent a special messenger to him, to tell him he is under my protection as long as he remains quietly on his farm. His cattle and sheep are safe also. In order not to inconvenience your husband, I have specially ordered my people who are working for him to remain there and do their work loyally until I send further instructions (p. 57).

Barmenias Zerua, son of Chief Zacharias Zerus of Otjimbingwe, testified on the conditions of armament:

He [our chief] knew that if we rose we would be crushed in battle, as our people were nearly all unarmed and without ammunition. We were driven to desperation by the cruelty and injustice of the

Germans, and our chiefs and people felt that death would be less terrible than the conditions under which we lived (p. 58).

Preliminary Steps and Treachery of the Germans

Gottlob Kamatoto, a servant to one of the German officers, stated:

> I accompanied the troops to Ombakaha above Gobabis and near Epikiro in the Sandveld. At a farm called Otjihaenena the Germans sent out messages to the Hereros that the war was now over and they were to come in and make peace. As a result of this message seven Herero leaders came into the German camp to discuss peace terms. As soon as they came in they were asked where Samuel Maherero the chief was. They said he had gone towards the desert on his way to British Bechuanaland. That evening at sunset the seven peace envoys were caught and tied with ropes. They were led aside and shot. Before being shot they protested bitterly; but seeing that they were doomed they accepted their fate (p. 59).

Gerard Kamaheke, a former leader of the Hereros in the uprising and at the time he testified a Headman at Windhoek, recalled:

> The Chiefs Saul, Joel, and I with a number of our followers were camped in the veld at Ombuyonungondo, about 30 km. from Ombakaha. This was in September. A messenger, a German soldier, came to our camp on horseback. He said he had come from the German commander at Ombakaha, who had sent him to tell us to come to Ombakaha and make peace. Joel then sent the schoolmaster Traugott Tjongarero personally to Ombakaha to confirm the truth of the soldier's message and to inquire if peace were intended, whether the Herero leaders would be given safe conduct and protection if they went to Ombakaha. Traugott came back a few days later and said he had seen the German commander, who confirmed the message brought by the soldier. Traugott said that the German commander had invited us all to come in and make peace; that our lives would all be spared; that we would be allowed to retain our cattle and other possessions; and that we would be allowed to go to Okahandja to live. I fell in with the wishes of the majority and we left for Ombakaha in the evening, and arrived at the German camp at noon the next day. With me were the Chiefs Saul and Joel, and the Under-Chiefs Traugott, Elephas, Albanus, Johannes Munqunda, Elephas Munpurua, and two others whose

names I now forget. We had with us 70 Herero soldiers. The wives and children we had left at our camp. On arrival at Ombakaha the 70 men who were under my command were halted near the German camp under some trees, as the sun was hot and we were very tired. Joel and the other leaders went on to the German commander's quarters about 100 yards away; they left their arms with us. The Germans then came to me and said we were to hand over our arms. I said, "I cannot do so until I know that Joel and the other leaders who are now in the camp have made peace." I sat there waiting, when suddenly the Germans opened fire on us. We were nearly surrounded, and my people tried to make their escape. I tried to fight my way through, but was shot in the right shoulder and fell to the ground [I show the wound], and I lay quite still and pretended to be dead. I was covered with blood. The German soldiers came along bayoneting the wounded; and as I did not move they thought I was dead already and left me. The Chiefs Saul and Joel and all other Headmen were killed. I got up in the night and fled back to our camp, where I found our women and children still safe and also some survivors of my 70 men. We then fled further towards the Sandveld and scattered in all directions (pp. 59f).

How the Hereros Were Exterminated

Daniel Kariko, Under-Chief of Omaruru, recalled:

The result of the war is known to everyone. Our people, men, women, and children were shot like dogs and wild animals. Our people have disappeared now. I see only a few left; their cattle and sheep are gone too, and all our land is owned by the Germans ... . After the fight at Waterberg we asked for peace; but von Trotha said there would only be peace when we were all dead, as he intended to exterminate us. I fled to the desert with a few remnants of my stock and managed more dead than alive to get away far north. I turned to the west and placed myself under the protection of the Ovambo Chief Uejulu, who knew that I was a big man among the Hereros ... . In 1915 they told me that the British were in Hereroland, and I hurried down to meet them ... . I was allowed to return to Hereroland after 10 years of exile (p. 63).

Hosea Mungunda, Headman of the Hereros at Windhoek, stated:

We were crushed and well-nigh exterminated by the Germans in the rising. With the exception of Samuel Maherero, Mutati, Traugott, Tjetjoo, Hosea, and Kaijata [who fled to British territory] all our big chiefs and leaders died or were killed in the rising, and also the great majority of our people. All our cattle were lost and all other possessions such as wagons and sheep. At first the Germans took prisoners, but when General von Trotha took command no prisoners were taken. General von Trotha said, "No one is to live; men, women, and children must all die." We can't say how many were killed (p. 63).

Samuel Kariko, son of Daniel Kariko and former secretary to the Omaruru Chief, testified:

A new general named von Trotha came, and he ordered that all Hereros were to be exterminated, regardless of age or sex. It was then that the wholesale slaughter of our people began. That was towards the end of 1904. Our people had already been defeated in battle, and we had no more ammunition ... . We saw we were beaten and asked for peace, but the German General refused peace and said all should die. We then fled towards the Sandveld of the Kalahari Desert. Those of our people who escaped the bullets and bayonets died miserably of hunger and thirst in the desert. A few thousand managed to turn back and sneak through the German lines to where there were water and roots and berries to live on (p. 63).

Manuel Timbu, a Cape Bastard and Court Interpreter in native languages at Omaruru, described his experiences with the Germans:

I was sent to Okahandja and appointed groom to the German commander, General von Trotha. I had to look after his horses and to do odd jobs at his headquarters. We followed the retreating Hereros from Okahandja to Waterberg, and from there to the borders of the Kalahari Desert. When leaving Okahandja, General von Trotha issued orders to his troops that no quarter was to be given to the enemy. No prisoners were to be taken, but all, regardless of age or sex, were to be killed. General von Trotha said, "We must exterminate them, so that we won't be bothered with rebellions in the future." As a result of this order the soldiers shot all natives we came across. It did not matter who they were. Some were peaceful people who had not gone into rebellion; others, such as old men and old women, had never left their homes; yet they were all shot. I often saw this done. Once while on the march near Hamakari beyond Waterberg, we came to some water holes. It was winter time and very cold. We came on two very old Herero women. They had made a small fire and were warming themselves. They had dropped back from the main body of Hereros owing to exhaustion. Von Trotha and his staff were present. A German soldier dismounted, walked up to the old women, and shot them both as they lay there. Riding along we got to a *vlei*, where we camped. While we were there a Herero woman came walking up to us from the bush. I was the Herero interpreter. I was told to take the woman to the General to see if she could give information as to the whereabouts of the enemy. I took her to General von Trotha; she was quite a young woman and looked tired and hungry. Von Trotha asked her several questions, but she did not seem inclined to give information. She said her people had all gone toward the east, but as she was a weak woman she could not keep up with them. Von Trotha then ordered that she should be taken aside and bayoneted. I took the woman away and a soldier came up with his bayonet in his hand. He offered it to me and said I had better stab the woman. I said I would never dream of doing such a thing and asked why the poor woman could not be allowed to live. The soldier laughed, and said, "If you won't do it, I will show you what a German soldier can do." He took the woman aside a few paces and drove the bayonet through her body. He then withdrew the bayonet and brought it all dripping with blood and poked it under my nose in a jeering way, saying, "You see, I have done it." Officers and soldiers were standing around looking on, but no one interfered to save the woman. Her body was not buried, but, like all others they killed, simply allowed to lie and rot and be eaten by wild animals.

A little further ahead we came to a place where the Hereros had abandoned some goats which were too weak to go further. There was no water to be had for miles around. There we found a young Herero, a boy of about 10 years of age. He apparently lost his people. As we passed he called out to us that he was hungry and thirsty. I would have given him something, but was forbidden to do so. The Germans discussed the advisability of killing him, and someone said that he would die of thirst in a day or so and it was not worth while bothering, so they passed on and left him there. On our return journey we again halted at Hamakari. There, near a hut, we saw an old Herero woman of about 50 or 60 years digging in the ground for wild onions. Von Trotha and his staff were present. A soldier named Konig jumped off his horse and shot the woman through the forehead at point-blank range. Before he shot her, he said, "I am going to kill you." She simply looked up and said, "I thank you." That night we slept at Hamakari. The next day we moved off again and came across another woman of about 30. She was also busy digging wild onions and took no notice of us. A soldier named Schilling walked up behind her and shot her through the back. I was an eyewitness of everything I related. In addition I saw the bleeding bodies of hundreds of men, women, and children, old and young, lying along the road as we passed. They had all been killed by our advanced guards. I was for nearly two years with the German troops and always with General von Trotha. I know of no instance in which prisoners were spared (pp. 63f).

Jan Cloete, a Bastard, of Omaruru, stated:

I was in Omaruru in 1904. I was commandeered by the Germans to act as a guide for them to the Waterberg district, as I knew the country well. I was with the 4th Field Company under Hauptmann Richardt. The commander of the troops was General von Trotha. I was present at Hamakari, near Waterberg, when the Hereros were defeated in battle. After the battle, all men, women, and children, wounded and unwounded, who fell into the hands of the Germans were killed without mercy. The Germans then pursued the others, and all stragglers on the roadside and in the veld were shot down and bayoneted. The great majority of the Herero men were unarmed and could make no fight. They were merely trying to get away with their cattle. Some distance beyond Hamakari we camped at a water hole. While there, a German soldier found a little Herero baby boy about nine months old lying in the bush. The child was crying. He brought it into the camp where I was. The soldiers formed a ring and started throwing the child to one another and catching it as if it were a ball. The child was terrified and hurt and was crying very much. After a time they got tired of this and one of the soldiers fixed his bayonet on his rifle and said he would catch the boy. The child was tossed into the air towards him and as it fell he caught it and transfixed the body with the bayonet. The child died in a few minutes and the incident was greeted with roars of laughter by the Germans, who seemed to think it was a great joke. I felt quite ill and turned away in disgust because, although I knew they had orders to kill all, I thought they would have pity on the child. I decided to go no further, as the horrible things I saw upset me, so I pretended that I was ill, and as the Captain got ill too and had to return, I was ordered to go back with him as guide. After I got home I flatly refused to go out with the soldiers again (pp. 64f).

Johannes Kruger, appointed by Leutwein as "Chief" of the Bushmen and Berg Damaras of the Gootfontein area, and a Bastard of Ghaub, testified:

I went with the German troops right through the Herero rebellion. The Afrikaner Hottentots of my *werft* were with me. We refused to kill Herero women and children, but the Germans spared none. They killed thousands and thousands. I saw this bloody work for days and days and every day. Often, and especially at Waterberg, the young Herero women and girls were violated by the German soldiers before being killed. Two of my Hottentots, Jan Wint and David Swartbooi (who is now dead), were invited by the German soldiers to join them in violating Herero girls. The two Hottentots refused to do so (p. 65).

Jan Kubas, a Griqua living at Gootfontein, stated:

I went with the German troops to Hamakari and beyond ... . The Germans took no prisoners. They killed thousands and thousands of women and children along the roadsides. They bayoneted them and hit them to death with the butt ends of their guns. Words cannot be found to relate what happened; it was too terrible. They were lying exhausted and harmless along the roads, and as the soldiers passed they simply slaughtered them in cold blood. Mothers holding babies at their breasts, little boys and little girls; old people too old to fight and old grandmothers, none received mercy; they were killed, all of them, and left to lie and rot on the veld for the vultures and wild animals to eat. They slaughtered until there were no more Hereros left to kill. I saw this every day; I was with them. A few Hereros managed to escape in the bush and wandered about, living on roots and wild fruits. Von Trotha was the German General in charge (p. 65).

Hendrik Campbell, War Commandant of the Bastard tribe of Rehoboth and Commander of the Bastard Contingent called out by the Germans to help them, testified:

At Katjura we had a fight with the Hereros, and drove them from their position. After the fight was over, we discovered eight or nine sick Herero women who had been left behind. Some of them were blind. Water and food had been left with them. The German soldiers burnt them alive in the hut in which the were living. The Bastard soldiers intervened and tried to prevent this, but when they failed, Hendrik van Wyk reported the matter to me. I immediately went to the German commander and complained. He said to me "that does not matter, they might have infected us with some disease." ... Afterward at Otjimbende we [the Bastards] captured 70 Hereros. I handed them over to Ober-Leutenants Volkmann and Zelow. I then went on patrol, and returned two days later, to find the Hereros lying dead in a *kraal*. My men reported to me that they had all been shot and bayoneted by German soldiers. Shortly afterwards, General von Trotha and his staff, accompanied by two missionaries, visited the camp. He said to me, "You look dissatisfied. Do you already wish to go home?"

"No," I replied, "the German government has an agreement with us and I want to have no misunderstandings on the part of the Bastard government, otherwise the same may happen to us weak people as has happened to those lying in the kraal yonder."

Lieut. Zelow gave answer: "The Hereros also do so." I said, "But, Lieutenant, as a civilized people you should give us a better example." To this von Trotha remarked, "The entire Herero people must be exterminated." (p. 65)

Daniel Esma, a European who lived at Omaruru and drove transport wagons for the Germans, stated:

I was present at the fight at Gross Barmen, near Okahandja, in 1904. After the fight the soldiers (marines from the warship *Habicht*) were searching the bush. I went with them out of curiosity. We came across a wounded Herero lying in the shade of a tree. He was a very tall, powerful man and looked like one of their headmen. He had his Bible next to his head and his hat over his face. I walked up to him and saw that he was wounded high up in the left hip. I took the hat off his face and asked him if he felt bad. He replied to me in Herero, "Yes, I feel I am going to die." The German marines, whose bayonets were fixed, were looking on. One of them said to me, "What does he reply?" I told him. "Well," remarked the soldier, "if he is keen on dying he had better have this also." With that he stooped down and drove his bayonet into the body of the prostrate Herero, ripping up his stomach and chest and exposing the intestines. I was so horrified that I returned to my wagons at once.

In August 1904, I was taking a convoy of provisions to the troops at the front line. At a place called Ouparakane, in the Waterberg district, we were outspanned for breakfast when two Hereros, a man and his wife, came walking up to us out of the bush. Under-Officer Wolff and a few German soldiers were escort to the wagons and were with me. The Herero man was a cripple, and walked with difficulty, leaning on a stick and on his wife's arm. He had a bullet wound through the leg. They came to my wagon, and I spoke to them in Herero. The man said he had decided to return to Omaruru and surrender to the authorities, as he could not possibly keep up with his people who were retreating to the desert, and that his wife had decided to accompany him. He was quite unarmed and famished. I gave them some food and coffee and they sat there for over an hour telling me of their hardships and privations. The German soldiers looked on, but did not interfere. I then gave the two natives a little food for their journey. They thanked me and then started to walk along the road slowly to Omaruru. When they had gone about 60 yards away from us I saw Wolff, the Under-Officer, and a soldier taking aim at them. I called out, but it was too late. They shot both of them. I said to Wolff, "How on earth did you have the heart to do such a thing? It is nothing but cruel murder." He merely laughed, and said, "Oh! These swine must all be killed; we are not going to spare a single one."

I spent a great part of my time during the rebellion at Okahandja, loading stores at the depot. There the hanging of natives was a common occurrence. A German officer had the right to order a native to be hanged. No trial or court was necessary. Many were hanged merely on suspicion. One day alone I saw seven Hereros hanged in a row, and on other days twos and threes. The Germans did not worry about rope. They used ordinary fencing wire, and the unfortunate native was hoisted up by the neck and allowed to die of slow strangulation. This was all done in public, and the bodies were allowed to hang a day or so as an example to the other natives. Natives who were placed in gaol at the time never came out alive. Many died of sheer starvation and brutal treatment … . The Hereros were far more humane in the field than the Germans. They were once a fine race. Now we have only a miserable remnant left (p. 66).

Johann Noothout, a Hollander and naturalized British subject, testified:

I left Cape Town during the year 1906, and signed on with the Protectorate troops in South West Africa. I arrived at Luderitzbucht, and after staying there a few minutes I perceived nearly 500 native women lying on the beach, all bearing indications of being slowly starved to death. Every morning and towards evening four women carried a stretcher containing about four or five corpses, and they had also to dig the graves and bury them. I then started to trek to Kubub and Aus, and on the road I discovered bodies of native women lying between stones and devoured by birds of prey. Some bore signs of having been beaten to death … . If a prisoner were found outside the Herero prisoners' camp, he would be brought before the Lieutenant and flogged with a *sjambok*. Fifty lashes were generally imposed. The manner in which the flogging was carried out was the most cruel imaginable … pieces of flesh would fly from the victim's body into the air … .

My observations during my stay in the country [in the German time] gave me the opinion that the Germans are absolutely unfit to colonise, as their atrocious crimes and cold-blooded murders were committed with one object — to extinguish the native race (p. 100).

Hendrick Fraser swore under oath:

When I got to Swakopmund I saw very many Herero prisoners of war who had been captured in the rebellion which was still going on in the country. [Note — these were prisoners captured before von Trotha's arrival.] There must have been about 600 men, women, and children prisoners. They were in an enclosure on the beach, fenced in with barbed wire. The women were made to do hard labor just like the men. The sand is very deep and heavy there. The women had to load carts and trolleys, and also to draw Scotch-cart loads of goods to Nonidas (9–10 km. away) where there was a depot. The women were put in spans of eight to each Scotch-cart and were made to pull like draught animals. Many were half-starved and weak, and died of sheer exhaustion. Those who did not work well were brutally flogged with sjamboks. I even saw women knocked down with pick handles. The German soldiers did this. I personally saw six women [Herero girls] murdered by German soldiers. They were ripped open with bayonets. I saw the bodies. I was there six months, and the Hereros died daily in large numbers as a result of exhaustion, ill-treatment and exposure. They were poorly fed, and often begged me and other Cape boys for a little food ... . The soldiers used the young Herero girls to satisfy their passions. Prisoners continued to come in while I was there; but I don't think half of them survived the treatment they received.

After six months at Swakopmund I was sent to Karibib towards the end of September 1904. [Note — Von Trotha's extermination order was issued about August 1904.] There I also saw an enclosure with Hereros waiting for transport to Swakopmund. Many were dying of starvation and exhaustion. They were all thin and worn out. They were not made to work so hard at Karibib, and appeared to be less harshly treated (p. 100).

Samuel Kariko, Herero schoolmaster and son of Under-Chief Daniel Kariko, stated:

When von Trotha left, we were advised of a circular which the new Governor, von Lindequist, had issued in which he promised to spare the lives of our people if we came in from the bush and mountains where we lived liked hunted game. We then began to come in. I went to Okambahe, near my old home, and surrendered. We then had no cattle left, and more than three quarters of our people had perished, far more. There were only a few thousands of us left, and we were walking skeletons, with no flesh, only skin and bones. They collected us in groups and made us work for the little food we got. I was sent down with others to an island far in the south, at Luderitzbucht. There on that island were thousands of Herero and Hottentot prisoners. We had to live there. Men, women and children were all huddled together. We had no proper clothing, no blankets, and the night air on the sea was bitterly cold. The wet sea fogs drenched us and made our teeth chatter. The people died there like flies that had been poisoned. The great majority died there. The little children and the old people died first, and then the women and the weaker men. No day passed without many deaths. We begged and prayed and appealed for leave to go back to our country, which is warmer, but the Germans refused. Those men who were fit had to work during the day in the harbour and railway depots. The younger women were selected by the soldiers and taken to their camps as concubines.

Soon the great majority of the prisoners had died and then the Germans began to treat us better. A Captain von Zulow took charge, and he was more humane than the others. After being there over a year, those of us who had survived were allowed to return home.

After all was over, the survivors of our race were merely slaves (p. 101).

Hosea Mungunda, Herero-Headman at Windhoek, stated:

Those who were left after the rebellion were put into compounds and made to work for their food only. They were sent to farms, and also to the railways and elsewhere. Many were sent to Luderitzbucht and Swakopmund. Many died in captivity; and many were hanged and flogged nearly to death and died as the result of ill-treatment. Many were mere skeletons when they came in and surrendered, and they could not stand bad food and ill-treatment.

The young girls were selected and taken as concubines for the soldiers; but even the married women were assaulted and interfered with. . . . It was one continuous ill-treatment. . . . When the railways were completed and the harbour works, we were sent out to towns and to farms to work. We were distributed and allocated to farmers, whether we liked them or not (p. 101).

Traugott Tjienda, Headman of the Hereros of Tsumeb, who also surrendered under von Lindequist's amnesty order, testified:

I was made to work on the Otavi line which was being built. We were not paid for our work, we were regarded as prisoners. I worked for two years without pay ... . As our people came in from the bush they were made to work at once, they were merely skin and bones, they were so thin that one could see through their bones — they looked like broomsticks. Bad as they were, they were made to work; and whether they worked or were lazy they were repeatedly *sjambokked* by the German overseers. The soldiers guarded us at night in a big compound made of thorn bushes. I was a kind of foreman over the labourers. I had 528 people, all Hereros, in my work party. Of these 148 died while working on the line. The Herero women were compounded with the men. They were made to do manual labour as well. They did not carry the heavy rails, but they had to load and unload wagons and trucks and to work with picks and shovels. The totals above given include women and children ... . When our women were prisoners on the railway work they were compelled to cohabit with soldiers and white railway labourers. The fact that a woman was married was no protection. Young girls were raped and very badly used. They were taken out of the compounds into the bush and there assaulted. I don't think any of them escaped this, except the older ones (pp. 101f).

Edward Lionel Pinches, an English resident of Keetmanshoop, confirmed the native reports:

At the time I entered the country then known as German South West Africa in the year 1896 the Hottentots and Damaras were divided into tribes and were living under the jurisdiction of their Chiefs. The natives were prosperous and the country was fairly well populated. Any estimation of the actual native population would be extremely difficult to give. At this time I was continuously travelling about the country, and I got a fairly accurate idea of the number of natives of the different tribes I came in contact with. On the outbreak of the Hottentot war the natives were about the same in number as when I entered the country, but on the conclusion of that war in my estimation the total native population was not more than one fifth of its former number. The war was to all intents and purposes a war of extinction of the native races, and has been admitted to be so by Germans of high standing. This tremendous reduction of population was by no means owing to actual losses through the war, but is directly due to the treatment received by the natives during captivity. I have myself been several times in Luderitzbucht, where large numbers of Damaras were kept in confinement, and have seen them being buried by their fellows, who were little better than dead themselves, at the rate of 12 to 15 per diem. Judging by the appearance of these natives, they were dying from sheer starvation (p. 102).

Leslie Cruikshank Bartlet, an Englishman residing in South West Africa, reported:

I came to German South West Africa with the first transport during the Hottentot war in 1905. The prisoners, Hereros and Hottentots, mostly women, and all in a terribly emaciated condition, were imprisoned on an island adjoining Luderitzbucht. The mortality amongst the prisoners was excessive, funerals taking place at the rate of 10 to 15 daily. Many are said to have attempted escape by swimming, and I have seen corpses of women prisoners washed up on the beach between Luderitzbucht and the cemetery. One corpse, I remember, was that of a young woman with practically fleshless limbs whose breasts had been eaten by jackals. This I reported at the German Police Station, but on passing the same way three or four days later the body was still where I saw it first. The German soldiery spoke freely of atrocities committed by Hereros and Hottentots during the war, and seemed to take a pride in wrecking vengeance on those unfortunate women. When the railway from Luderitzbucht to Keetmanshoop was started, gangs of prisoners, mostly women scarcely able to walk from weakness and starvation, were employed as labourers. They were brutally treated. I personally saw a gang of these prisoners, all women, carrying a heavy double line of rails with iron sleepers attached on their shoulders, and unable to bear the weight they fell. One woman fell under the rails which broke her leg and held it fast. The *Schachtmeister* [ganger], without causing the rail to be lifted, dragged the woman from under and threw her on one side, where she died untended. The general treatment was cruel, and many instances were told to me, but that which I have stated, I personally saw (p. 102).

Notes

1. For a more detailed consideration of the Hereros' genocide see Jon Bridgman's *Revolt of the Hereros* (1981) or Horst Drechsler's *"Let Us Die Fighting"* (1980); Drechsler's work was originally published as *Südwestafrika unter deutschen Kolonialherrschaft* (Berlin: Academie-Verlag, 1966).
2. See Drechsler (1980, p. 55, no. 8) for a discussion of the various population estimates, which in fact went as high as more than 100,000.
3. See Bridgman (1981, Chapter 1) for a fuller discussion of the tribal peoples of South West Africa at this time.
4. See Helmut Bley's *Kolonialherrschaft und Sozialstruktur in Deutsche-Südwestafrika* (1968, pp. 160ff) for a more detailed analysis.
5. Theodor Leutwein (1908, p. 559) said that the government had not issued the ordinance out of any love of the natives, but rather to preserve the life and possessions of those whites who were living among the natives.
6. See Wellington (1967, pp. 198f) and Drechsler (1980, pp. 118f); the Hereros named each year according to the most significant event that occurred during its course, and the year 1903 was named "*ojovuronde juviuego*," which meant the year of traders and fraud.
7. For the most perceptive analysis of Leutwein's attitude, see Bley, 1968.
8. This passage was contained in a message from Missionary Elger to the Rhenish Missionary Society; see also Drechsler (1980, p. 145) and Jon Swan's "The Final Solution in South West Africa" (1991).
9. Bridgman (1981, p. 65) notes that Paul Rohrbach, the colonial propagandist, is generally credited with this expression.
10. Sub-Chief Daniel Kariko testified later that the war was aimed exclusively at German men.

11. Maherero actually sent messages to several tribes seeking alliances against the Germans; cf. Imperial Colonial Office Files (1904, pp. 21f, 23), Leutwein (1908, p. 468), and Drechsler (1980, p. 143).
12. Maherero's judgment here was correct, the Rhenish Missionary Society or at least some of its members did plead the native cause in the German press; cf. Drechsler (1980, p. 140).
13. Wellington (1967, p. 148) reports on the Herero treatment of a Hottentot prisoner that apparently was typical: First the Hereros cut off his ears, then his nose and lips, and finally they slit his throat.
14. Swan (1991, p. 51); Great Britain (1916, pp. 74–80) shows the German army poisoned wells in South West Africa to hinder the British invasion in 1915, and implies that this had been done in earlier wars.
15. Also see Drechsler (1980, pp. 214ff).
16. See George Crothers (1941) for a detailed account of this unusual election.
17. This article can be found in Schlosser (1955).

References

Andersson, Charles (1856). *Lake Ngami or Exploration and Discovery During Four Years Wanderings in the Wilds of South-Western Africa*. New York: Harper & Brothers.
Bley, Helmut (1968). *Kolonialherrschaft und Sozialstruktur in Deutsch Südwestafrika 1894–1914*. Hamburg: Leibniz-Verlag.
Bridgman, Jon (1981). *The Revolt of the Hereros*. Berkeley: University of California Press.
Bülow, Bernhard von (1930–1931). *Denkwürdigkeiten*. Four volumes. Berlin: Ullstein.
Crothers, George (1941). *The German Elections of 1907*. P. S. King & Son, Ltd.
Drechsler, Horst (1980). *"Let Us Die Fighting."* London: Zed Press. Translated by Bernd Zöllner. Originally published (1966) under the title *Südwestafrika unter deutsche Kolonialherrschaft*. Berlin: Akademie-Verlag.
Epstein, Klaus (1959). "Erzberger and the German Colonial Scandals, 1905–1910." *English Historical Review*, 74(293):637–663.
Great Britain (1916). "German Atrocities, and Breaches of the Rules of War, in Africa," in *The Sessional Papers of the House of Lords*. Vols. 5 and 6. London: H.M. Stationery Office.
Great Britain (1918). "Report on the Natives of South West Africa and their Treatment by Germany," in *The Sessional Papers of the House of Lords*. Vol. 13. London: H.M. Stationery Office.
Imperial Colonial Office Files (1904). Nos. 2111, 2114, 2119, 2140. Archival records.
Kriegsgeschichtliche Abteilung, Grosser Generalstab, Armée Prussia (1906–1907). *Die Kampfe der deutschen Truppen in Südwestafrika*. Two volumes. Berlin: E. S. Mittler.
Leutwein, Theodor (1908). *Elf Jahre Gouverneur in Deutsch-Südwestafrika*. Berlin: E. S. Mittler.
Poewe, Karla (1985). *The Namibian Herero — A History of their Psychosocial Disintegration and Survival*. Lewiston, New York: The Edwin Mellen Press.
Schlosser, Katesa (1955). "Der Herero im Britisch-Betschuana-Protektorat und ein Besuch in einer ihrer Siedlunger: Newe-le-tau." *Zeitschrift für Ethnologie*, 80(2):200–218.
Schwabe, Kurd (1904). *Mit Schwert und Pflug in Deutsch-Südwestafrika*. Berlin: E. S. Mittler.
Swan, Jon (1991). "The Final Solution in South West Africa." *MHQ: The Quarterly Journal of Military History*, 3(3):36–55.
Wellington, John H (1967). *South West Africa and Its Human Issues*. Oxford: Oxford University Press.

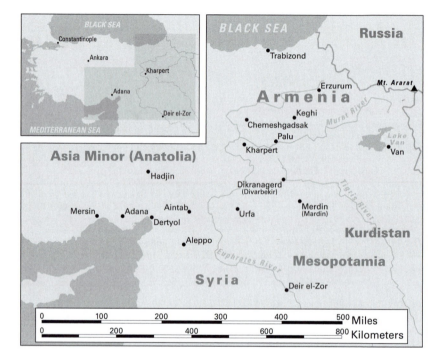

Armenia

CHAPTER 2

The Armenian Genocide

ROUBEN PAUL ADALIAN

Between the years 1915 and 1923 the Armenian population of Anatolia and historic West Armenia was eliminated. The Armenians had lived in the area for some 3000 years. Since the 11th century, when Turkish tribal armies prevailed over the Christian forces that were resisting their incursions, the Armenians had lived as subjects of various Turkish dynasties. The last and longest-lived of these dynasties were the Ottomans, who created a vast empire stretching from Eastern Europe to Western Asia and North Africa. To govern this immense country, the Ottomans imposed a strictly hierarchical social system that subordinated non-Muslims as second-class subjects deprived of basic rights. In its waning days, with the empire in decline and territorially confined to the Middle East, the Ottoman leaders decided that the only way to save the Turkish state was to reduce the Christian populations. Beginning in April 1915, the Armenians of Anatolia were deported to Syria and the Armenian population of West Armenia was driven to Mesopotamia. Described euphemistically as a resettlement policy by the perpetrators, the deportations, in fact, constituted and resulted in genocide. In the end, after eight years of warfare and turmoil in the region, the Armenians had disappeared from their homeland.

Who Committed the Genocide?

In 1915 the Ottoman Empire was governed by a dictatorial triumvirate. Enver was Minister of War. Talaat was Minister of the Interior. Jemal was Minister of the Navy and military governor of Syria. All were members of the Committee of Union and Progress (CUP), called Unionists for short. They were known in the West as the Young Turks. They had started out as members of a clandestine political organization that staged a revolution in 1908, replaced the ruler of the country in 1909, and finally seized power by a coup in 1913 (Ramsaur, 1957; Zürcher, 1998; Charny, 1999).

When World War I started, the CUP exercised near total control in the government. Party functionaries had been appointed to posts all across the empire. Unionist cells had been organized in every major town and city. Unionist officers commanded virtually all of the Ottoman army. The cabinet was entirely beholden to the CUP. Key decisions were made by the triumvirs in consultation with their party ideologues and in conformity with overt and covert party objectives. As heads of government and leaders of the CUP, Enver, Talaat, and Jemal had at their disposal immense resources of power and an arsenal of formal and informal instruments of coercion (Libaridian, 1985, pp. 37–49).

Organized in reaction to the autocratic regime of the sultan Abdul-Hamid II (1876–1909), the Young Turks originally advocated a platform of constitutionalism, egalitarianism, and liberalism. They attributed the weakness of the Ottoman Empire to its retrograde system of government. They hoped to reform the state along the progressive and modernizing course of the Western European countries. However, after the revolution, they were surprised by the strength of conservative and reactionary forces in Ottoman society and were just as quickly disillusioned by the aggressive posture of the European powers, which vied with one another for influence in the Ottoman Empire. Their realization that the problems of the Ottoman Empire were systemic and endemic became the source of their own retrenchment and growing intransigence. Also, suspicious of British, French, and Russian colonialist designs, defeated in war by the Italians, and challenged militarily by neighboring Greece, Serbia, and Bulgaria (countries that were formerly subject states of the empire), the Young Turks increasingly looked toward Germany as an ally and as the model nation-state to emulate. By 1913, the advocates of liberalism had lost out to radicals in the party who promoted a program of forcible Turkification.

By the time the first shots of the war were fired in August 1914, the CUP had become a dictatorial, xenophobic, intolerant clique intent on pursuing a policy of racial exclusivity. Emboldened by their alliance with Imperial Germany, the CUP also prepared to embark on a parallel course of militarism. German war materiel poured into the country, and Turkish officers trained at military schools in Germany. German army and navy officers drilled the Ottoman forces, drew their battle plans, built fortifications, and, when war erupted, stayed on as advisors whose influence often exceeded that of the local commanders (Sachar, 1969, pp. 5–31; Trumpener, 1968, pp. 62–107; Dinkel, 1991, pp. 77–133).

Because of the preponderance of the Germans in Ottoman military affairs, the lurking question of the degree of their involvement in either advising or permitting the deportation of the Armenians has been asked many times (Dadrian, 1996). Ultimate responsibility for the Armenian genocide, however, rests with those who considered and took the decision to deport and massacre the Armenian population of the Ottoman Empire. It also rests with those who implemented the policy of the central government and, finally, with those who personally carried out the acts that extinguished Armenian society in its birthplace. In this equation, the largest share of responsibility falls on the members of the Committee of Union and Progress. At every level of the operation against the Armenians, party functionaries relayed, received, and enforced the orders of the government. The state's responsibility to protect its citizens was disregarded by the CUP. The Ministries of the Interior and of War were charged with the task of expelling the Armenians from their homes and driving them into the Syrian desert (Dadrian, 1986). The army detailed soldiers and officers to oversee the deportation process (Great Britain, 1916, pp. 637–53; Ternon, 1981, pp. 22–39). Killing units were organized to slaughter the Armenians (Dadrian, 1989, pp. 274–77). By withholding from them the protection of the state and by exposing them to all the vagaries of nature, the Young Turk government also disposed of large numbers of Armenians through starvation (Ternon, 1981, pp. 249–60). In the absence of even minimal sanitation, let alone health care, epidemics broke out in the concentration camps and contributed to the death toll.

How Was the Genocide Committed?

The genocide of the Armenians involved a three-part plan conceived with secrecy and deliberation and implemented with organization and efficiency. The plan consisted of deportation, execution, and starvation. Each part of the plan had its specific purpose.

The most thoroughly implemented part of the plan was the deportation of the Armenian population. The Armenians in historic Armenia in the east, in Anatolia to the west, and even in European Turkey were all driven from their homes. Beginning in April 1915 and continuing through the summer and fall, the vast majority of the Armenians in the Ottoman Empire were deported. Upon the orders of the Ottoman government, often with only three days' notice, village after village and town after town was emptied of its Armenian inhabitants.

Many were moved by train (Bryce, 1916, pp. 407–63). Some relied on horse-drawn wagons. A few farmers took their mules and were able to carry some belongings part of the way. Most Armenians walked. As more and more people were displaced, long convoys of deportees, comprised mostly of women and children, formed along the roads of Anatolia and Armenia, all headed in one direction, south to the Syrian desert. Many never made it that far. Only a quarter of all deportees survived the hundreds of miles and weeks of walking. Exhaustion, exposure, and fright took a heavy toll especially on the old and the young (Hairapetian, 1984, pp. 41–145).

The Ottoman government had made no provisions for the feeding and the housing of the hundreds of thousands of Armenian deportees on the road (Bryce, 1916, pp. 545–69). Indeed, local authorities went to great length to make travel an ordeal from which there was little chance of survival (Davis, 1989, pp. 69–70). At every turn, Armenians were robbed of their possessions, had their loved ones held at ransom, and even had their clothing taken off their backs. In some areas, Kurdish horsemen given to marauding and kidnapping were let loose upon the helpless caravans of deportees (Hairapetian, 1984, p. 96; Kloian, 1985, p. 8). Apart from the sheer bedlam of their raids and the killing that accompanied it, they carried away the goods they snatched and frequently seized Armenian children and women.

The deportations were not intended to be an orderly relocation process (Walker, 1980, pp. 227–30). They were meant to drive the Armenians into the open and expose them to every conceivable abuse (Hovannisian, 1967, pp. 50–51) At remote sites along the routes traversed by the convoys of deportees, the killing units slaughtered the Armenians with sword and bayonet (Dadrian, 1989, p. 272; Walker, 1980, p. 213). In a random frenzy of butchering, they cut down persons of all ages and of both genders. These periodic attacks upon the unarmed and starving Armenians continued until they reached the Syrian desert.

To minimize resistance to the deportations, the Ottoman government had taken precautionary measures. The most lethal of these measures consisted of the execution of the able-bodied men in the Armenian population. The first group in Armenian society targeted for collective execution were the men conscripted into the Turkish armies. Upon the instruction of the War Ministry, these men were disarmed, forced into labor battalions, and either worked to death or outright murdered (Morgenthau, 1918, p. 302; Kuper, 1986, pp. 46–7; Sachar, 1969, p. 98).

Subsequently, the older males who had stayed behind to till the fields and run the stores were summoned by the government and ordered to prepare themselves for removal from their places of habitation. Virtually all the men turned themselves over without an inkling that their government contemplated their murder. They were immediately imprisoned, many were tortured, and all of them were taken away, sometimes in chains, and felled in mass executions (Bryce, 1916, pp. 640–41).

To assure the complete subservience of the Armenian people to the government's deportation edicts and to eliminate the possibility of protestation, prominent leaders were specially selected for swift excision from their communities (Davis, 1989, p. 51). Although the wholesale measures against the Armenians were already in the process of implementation by late April, the symbolic beginning of the Armenian genocide is dated the evening of April 24, 1915. That night, the most gifted men of letters, the most notable jurists, the most respected educators, and many others, including high-ranking clergy, were summarily arrested in Constantinople, the capital of the Ottoman Empire, sent to the interior, and many were never heard from again (Ternon, 1981, pp. 216–19).

The Armenians were brought to the Syrian desert for their final expiration (Walker, 1980, pp. 227–30). Tens of thousands died from exposure to the scorching heat of the summer days and the cold of the night in the open. Men and women dying of thirst were shot for approaching the Euphrates River. Women were stripped naked, abused, and murdered. Others despairing of their fate threw themselves into the river and drowned. Mothers gave their children away to Arab Bedouins to spare them from certain death. The killing units completed their task at a place called Deir el-Zor. In this final carnage, children were smashed against rocks, women were torn apart with swords, men were mutilated, others were thrown into flames alive. Every cruelty was inflicted on the remnants of the Armenian people.

Why Was the Genocide Committed?

The Armenian genocide was committed to solve the "Armenian Question" in the Ottoman Empire. There were, at the very least, five basic reasons for the emergence of this so-called question. The first had to do with the decline of the Ottoman Empire and the internal demographic and economic pressures created upon the non-Muslim minority communities that began to experience ever-increasing and violent competition for the land and resources they historically controlled. The government's failure to guarantee security of life and property led the Armenians to seek internal reforms that would improve their living conditions. These demands only invited resistance and intransigence from the government, which convinced many Armenians that the Ottoman regime was not interested in providing them the protection they needed and the civil rights they desired (Nalbandian, 1963, pp. 67–89).

Second, Great Power diplomacy that offered the hope of redressing the injustices and inequities of the Ottoman system proved inadequate to the task. The greater interest in maintaining the balance of power in Europe only resulted in half-hearted measures at humanitarian intervention in response to crises and atrocities. As the Armenians turned to the European powers in order to invite attention to their plight, the Ottomans only grew more suspicious of the intentions of the Armenians. Thus, the appeal of the Armenians to the Christian countries of Europe was viewed as seditious by the Ottomans. On earlier occasions European powers had exploited the tensions in Ottoman society to intervene on behalf of Christian populations. With the passage of time, the Ottomans became more resolved to prevent the recurrence of such intervention by quickly and violently suppressing expressions of social and political discontent (Dadrian, 1989, pp. 242–55; Dadrian, 1995, 61–97).

Third, the military weakness of the Ottoman Empire left it exposed to external threats and therefore made it prone to resorting to brutality as a method of containing domestic dissent, especially with disaffected non-Muslim minorities. In fact, a cycle of escalating violence against the Armenians had set in by the late 1800s (Dadrian, 1989, pp. 232–42).

Fourth, the reform measures introduced in the 19th century to modernize the Turkish state had initially encouraged increased expectations among Armenians that better government and even representation were imminent possibilities. The periodic massacre of large numbers of Armenians, however, undermined the confidence of the community in its government and in the prevailing international order. This disaffection became the source of a growing Armenian national consciousness and resulted in the formation of political organizations seeking emancipation from lawlessness and discrimination.

Last, the rapid modernization experienced by the Armenians, who were more open to European concepts of progress through education than the rest of the population, only registered resentment among the Muslims of the Ottoman Empire who saw the interests of Armenians more in alignment with countries they regarded as infidels than with the state ruling over them.

By the early 20th century, the Ottomans had been forced out of southeastern Europe. Having relinquished the mostly Christian and Slavic regions of the Balkans whence the early Ottomans had created their empire, the Young Turks sought to restore the empire on new foundations. They found their justification in the concepts of Turkism and Pan-Turanism. Turkism altered Ottoman self-perceptions from a religious to a national identity by emphasizing the ethnicity of the Turks of Anatolia to the exclusion of other populations and promoted the idea that the region should be the exclusive domain of the Turkish nation. Pan-Turanism advanced the idea of conquering lands stretching into Central Asia inhabited by other Turkic-speaking peoples. Many of these Turkic peoples were living under Russian rule, and the Young Turks believed that the advancing Ottoman armies would be received as liberators (Walker, 1980, pp. 189–91). The Pan-Turanian goal was to unify all the Turkic peoples into a single empire led by the Ottoman Turks (Parla, 1985).

In this formulation, the Armenians presented an ethno-religious anomaly. They were an indigenous Christian people of the Middle East who, despite more than 14 centuries of Muslim domination, had avoided Islamification. When the CUP began to implement its policy of Turkification, the Armenians resisted the CUP plans. For example, the Armenians had worked hard to build up the infrastructure of their communities, including an extensive network of elementary and secondary schools. Through education, they hoped to preserve their culture and identity and to obtain participation in the government. The new emphasis on Turkism and the heightened suspicion of the subject nationalities was warning enough for the Armenians to redouble their effort to gain a say in at least the governance of regions with a heavy Armenian concentration (Libaridian, 1987, pp. 219–23).

In the increasing tension between the assimilationist policies of the Young Turk government and Armenian hopes for administrative reforms and aspirations for a measure of local self-government, the coincidence of resistance to Unionist policies and the beginning of World War I proved fatal for the Armenians. As the German forces were prevailing against Russia in Europe, a second front in Asia seemed to guarantee success for the Ottomans. Confident of their strength and witness to the early military victories of the German army, the Young Turks chose to enter the war. They believed that the great conflict among the imperial powers of Europe offered the Ottoman Empire an opportunity to regain a position of dominance in the region.

The war placed the Armenians in an extremely precarious situation. Tragically for them, their difficulties with the Young Turk regime were compounded by the fact that this second front against Russia would be fought in the very lands of historic Armenia where the bulk of the Armenian population lived. Straddled on both sides of the Russian–Turkish border, their homeland was turned into a battlefield. Long chafing from the exploitation of Muslim overlords, the Armenians had welcomed the Russians into Transcaucasia. After nearly a century of relative peace and prosperous existence under Russian administration, the prospect of falling under the rule of the Ottomans was unthinkable for the Armenians living in Russia. While thousands of Armenian conscripts were serving on the Russian front in the war against Germany, many others volunteered to fight the Ottomans.

The fate of the Armenians was sealed in early 1915 with the defeat of the Ottoman offensive into Russian territory. The Russians not only stopped the Ottoman advance but slowly moved into Ottoman territory. The failure of the campaign was principally the fault of Enver, the Minister of War, who had taken personal command of the eastern front and chosen to fight a major battle in the dead of winter in rugged and snowbound terrain. With his ambitions dashed, this would-be conqueror and self-styled liberator exacted vengeance from the Armenian population.

Instead of accepting responsibility for their ill-conceived invasion plans and the consequential defeat of their armies, the Young Turks placed the blame on the Armenians by accusing them of collaboration with the enemy (Morgenthau, 1918, pp. 293–300). Charging the entire Armenian population with treason and sedition, they decided to kill the innocent for the actions of those who had chosen to put a stop to their planned conquests. That was the reason, at least, given by the Minister of the Interior when asked about the CUP policy of deporting the Armenians (Morgenthau, 1918, p. 327; Trumpener, 1968, pp. 207–10).

The war, in effect, provided the opportunity to implement the Turkification of the Ottoman Empire by methods that exceeded legislation, intimidation, and expropriation. Under the cover of war, with no obligation to uphold international agreements, and in an atmosphere of heightened tensions, the Unionists found their justification and opportunity to resort to extreme measures. The Turkish state now could be created internally. With the Armenians eradicated, one less racial grouping would be living on Ottoman territory. One less disenchanted group would have to be tolerated. The problems with the Armenians would be automatically resolved by eliminating the Armenians. In a country of 20 million people, the Armenians constituted only about 10 percent of the population. It was easily within the reach of the Ottoman government to displace and kill that many people.

For all the historical, political, and military reasons that may be cited to explain the Young Turk policy of destroying the Armenians, it must be understood that ultimately the decision to commit genocide was taken consciously. Genocide is not explained by circumstance. Mass murder is an act deliberately conceived. Decision-makers can always exercise other options in dealing with serious conflicts. The real cause of genocide lies in the self-licensing of those in charge of government with irresponsibility toward human life and amorality in the conception of their social policies. Genocide is the fulfillment of absolute tyranny. In the new social order conceived by the Young Turks, there was no room for the Armenians. They had become that excess population of which tyrants are prone to dispose.

Who Were the Victims?

The Armenians were an ancient people who from the first millennium B.C. lived in a mountainous plateau in Asia Minor, a country to which they gave their name. This was their homeland. The area was absorbed as the eastern provinces of the Ottoman Empire in the 16th century. Two thousand years earlier the Armenians had formed one of the more durable states in the region. A series of monarchical dynasties and princely families had been at the head of the Armenian nation. Early in the fourth century, the king of Armenia accepted Christianity, making his country the first to formally recognize the new faith. Armenians developed their own culture and spoke a unique language. A distinct alphabet, a native poetry, original folk music, an authentic architectural style, and centuries-old traditions characterized their separate civilization (Lang, 1970; Lang, 1981; Bournoutian, 2002; Adalian, 2002).

The remoteness of Armenia from the centers of urban life in the ancient world kept the Armenians on the periphery of the empires of antiquity. Their distinctiveness was reinforced by the mountainous country and the harsh and long winters, which discouraged new settlers. Their own armies fought off many invaders; but through the course of the centuries, Armenia proved too small a country to withstand the continued menace of outside aggression. The strength of its armies was sapped. Its leaders were defeated in battle, and its kings were exiled and never returned. Increasingly exposed to invasions, the Armenians finally succumbed to the occupying forces of a new people that emerged from the east.

Persians, Greeks, Romans, Arabs, Byzantines, and Mongols each in turn lorded over the Armenians; however, only the Turks made permanent settlements in Armenia. The seeds of a mortal conflict were planted as the Turks grew in number and periodically displaced the Armenians. Beginning from the 11th century, towns, cities, and sometimes entire districts of Armenia were abandoned by the Armenians as they fled from the exactions of their new rulers. Unlike all the other conquerors of Armenia, the Turks never left. In time, Armenia became Turkey. The genocide of 1915 brought to a brutal culmination a thousand-year struggle of the Armenian people to hold on to their homeland and of the Turks to take it away from them.

The Ottoman Turks, who built an empire around the city of Constantinople after conquering it in 1453, and who eventually seized the areas of historic Armenia, developed a hierarchically organized society. Non-Muslims were relegated to second-class status and were subjected to discriminatory laws. The constant pressure on the Armenian population resulted in the further dispersion of the Armenians. Yet, despite the difficulties they endured and the disadvantages they faced, Armenian communities throughout the cities of the Ottoman Empire attained a tolerable living standard. By the 19th century a prosperous middle class emerged that became the envy of the Turkish population and a source of distrust for the Ottoman government (Barsoumian, 1982, pp. 171–84).

As the Armenians recovered their national confidence, they increased their demands for reforms in Armenia, where conditions continued to deteriorate. The government, however, was opposed to the idea of introducing measures and policies that would have enhanced the progress of an industrious minority that already managed a sizable portion of Ottoman commerce and industry. This reluctance only contributed to the alienation of the Armenians from the Ottoman regime. The more the Armenians complained, objected, and dissented, the more the Ottoman government grew annoyed, resistant, and impatient. By refusing to introduce significant reform in its autocratic form of government and to restrain the arbitariness of local administration, the Ottoman rulers placed the Armenian and the Turkish peoples on a collision course (Astourian, 1992, 1998).

Who Was Involved in the Genocide?

The Armenian genocide was organized in secret but carried out in the open (Dadrian, 1989, p. 299; 1991, p. 558). The public proclamations ordering the removal and departure of the Armenians from their homes alerted all of Ottoman society that its government had chosen a course of action specifically targeting this one minority for unusual treatment. At no time throughout its existence had the Ottoman state taken such a step against an entire population. The manner in which the deportations were carried out notified the rest of society that the measures were intended to yield a permanent outcome.

A policy directed against a select population requires the agencies of government to organize, command, implement, and complete the separation and isolation of the group from the rest of society. When the measures affect a population spread across a vast stretch of territory, it cannot be a matter of accident, or coincidence, that persons of the same ethnic background become the object of mistreatment.

Although the decision to proceed with genocide was taken by the CUP, the entire Ottoman state became implicated in its implementation. First, cabinet decisions were taken to deport and massacre the Armenians (Dadrian, 1989, pp. 265–67). Disguised as a relocation policy, their purpose was understood by all concerned. Second, the Ottoman parliament avowedly enacted legislation legalizing the decisions of the cabinet (Dadrian, 1989, pp. 267–74). Third, the Ministry of the Interior was delegated the responsibility of overseeing the displacement, deportation, and relocation process. This Ministry, in turn, instructed local authorities on procedure, the timing of deportation, and the routing of the convoys of exiles (Dadrian, 1986, pp. 326–28). The Ministry of War was charged with the disarming of the Armenian population, the posting of officers and soldiers to herd the deportees into the desert, and the execution of the Armenian conscripts. The agencies in charge of transport also were inducted into service. To expedite the transfer of the Armenians of western Anatolia, the deportees were loaded on cattle cars and shipped en masse to points east by train. The telegraph service encoded and decoded the orders of the ministers and governors. The governors of the provinces relayed the orders to the district governors, who in turn entrusted the local authorities, courts, and constabularies to proceed with instructions. The chain of command that put the Armenian genocide into motion joined every link in the administration of the Ottoman state.

Orders, however, were not obeyed uniformly. A few governors downright refused to deport the Armenians in their districts (Dadrian, 1986, pp. 326–27). Aware that some government personnel might be reluctant to sign the death warrant of the Armenian people, the CUP had made provisions to enforce its will on the entire corps of Ottoman officials. Young Turk Party members were entrusted by the central leaders with extraordinary power in situations requiring the disciplining of local authority. Disobedient governors were removed from their posts, and CUP partisans with a more reliable record were assigned to carry out the state's policies in these districts. Frequently, the most notorious among the latter happened to be army officers who were also ideological adherents of the CUP, a combination that gave them complete license to satisfy — at the expense of the Armenians — their every whim and that of the men under their command (Dadrian, 1986, pp. 311–59).

To implement the various aspects of its policy, the CUP cabinet had to go so far as to establish new agencies. One of these was a secret extra-legal body called the Special Organization. Its mission was organized mass murder (Dadrian, 1989, pp. 274–77). It was mainly composed of convicted criminals released from prisons, who were divided into units stationed at critical sites along the deportation routes and near the concentration camps in Syria. Their assignment consisted solely of reducing the number of the Armenians by carrying out massacres. Sparing bullets, which were needed for the war effort, the slaughter of the Armenians frequently was carried out with medieval weaponry: scimitars and daggers. The physical proximity with which the butchering went on left a terrifying image of the Turk among those who happened to survive an attack by squads of the Special Organization.

Additionally, the government set up a Commission on Immigrants, whose stated purpose was to facilitate "the resettlement" process. In fact, the commission served as an on-site committee to report on the progress of the destruction of the Armenians as they were further and further removed from the inhabitable regions of Anatolia and Syria. As for the Commission on Abandoned Goods, which impounded, logged, and auctioned off Armenian possessions, this was the government's method of disposing the immovable property of the Armenians by means that rewarded its supporters. Generally, the local CUP officials pocketed the profit. It is not known what sums might have been transferred to party coffers (Baghdjian, 1987, pp. 64–87).

The CUP orchestrated a much wider system of rewards in order to obtain the consent of the Turkish population (Baghdjian, 1987, pp. 121–71). By implicating large numbers of people in the illegal methods of acquisition, the Young Turk government purchased the silence and cooperation of the populace. Many enriched themselves by misappropriating the forcibly abandoned properties of the Armenians. There was easy gain in plunder.

The same impulse motivated the Special Organization and the Kurdish tribesmen, who were given license to raid the convoys of deportees. In their case, the booty included human beings as well. It was a form of enslavement limited to younger boys and girls, who, separated from their kinsmen, would be converted to Islam and either Kurdified or Turkified in language and custom. Lastly, the public auction of Armenian girls revived a form of human bondage that was, for the most part, erased elsewhere in the world. The auctioneer made money. The purchaser had a slave servant and a harem woman added to his household. This kind of brutalization scarred countless Armenian women. Many, incapable of bearing the shame of giving birth out of wedlock to children conceived from rape and abuse by their Kurdish and Turkish owners, chose to forgo Armenian society after the war and remained with their Muslim families. Some were rescued and a few escaped, some taking their children with them, while others, fearing reprisal, abandoned them. Some Armenian women taken into harems against their will were often tattooed on their arms, chest, or face, as signs of their being owned and as a way to discourage escape (Sanasarian, 1989, pp. 449–61).

The gender, age, occupational, and regional differences in the treatment of the Armenians reflected the varying operative value systems prevailing in Ottoman society. The Young Turk ideologues in Constantinople conceived and implemented genocide, a total destruction of Armenian society. Military officers and soldiers regarded the policy as a security measure. Others in Ottoman society saw it a convenient way of ridding themselves of effective economic competitors, not to mention creditors. Others justified the slaughter of the Armenians as religious duty called upon by the concept of *jihad*, or warfare against infidels or nonbelievers in Islam. All essentially aimed at eliminating the Armenian male population. Traditional society in the Middle East still looked upon women and children as chattel, persons lacking political personality and of transmutable ethnic identity. The cultural values of children and of females could be erased or reprogrammed. Genetic continuity was a male proposition. For many, but not the CUP, the annihilation of Armenian males would have been sufficient to block or impede the perpetuation of the Armenian people (Davis, 1989, pp. 54–63).

What Were the Outstanding Historical Forces and Trends at Work that Led to the Genocide?

The Armenian genocide was the result of the intensifying differences between two societies inhabiting the territories of a single state. One society was dominant, the other subordinate; one Muslim, the other Christian; one in the majority, the other in the minority. At its source, the conflict stemmed from two divergent views of the world. The Turks had established their state as a world empire. They had always ruled over lands and peoples they conquered. The receding of their empire from its far-flung provinces challenged their image of themselves. Virtually undefeated in war before 1700, in the 18th and 19th centuries the Ottomans lost battle after battle as their once-mighty armies were no longer a match for the modern tactics and weaponry of the armies of the European states. New empires taking form on the European continent began to carve away Ottoman territory. France, England, Austria, and Russia, each in turn, imposed its demands on the weakening Turkish state. By the second half of the 19th century, however, these European powers, soon joined by a Germany unified by Prussian arms, balanced out each other in their competition for global influence.

A new type of challenge arose to force the Ottomans into retreating further. Whereas the Ottomans were in part successful in checking the territorial aggrandizement of their neighbors by relying on the balance-of-power system, the rise of nationalist movements among the subject peoples of the empire posed a different predicament. As imperial states are wont to do, the Ottomans resorted to brutal methods of suppressing national liberation and other separatist movements. The response of the Ottomans to the uprisings in Greece, Serbia, Bulgaria, and elsewhere was mass action against the affected population. These tactics only invited European intervention, and the settlement often resulted in the formation of a small autonomous state from a former Ottoman province as a way of providing a national territory to the subject people.

Unlike the Greeks, Serbians, or Bulgarians, the case of the Armenians was more complicated. They had long been ruled by the Turks, and by the early 20th century they were widely dispersed. In historic Armenia, the Armenians formed a majority of the population only in certain districts. This was due to the fact that a substantial Kurdish and Turkish population lived in these lands. When the Armenians also began to aspire for a national home, the Ottomans regarded it a far more serious threat than earlier and similar nationalist movements, for they had come to regard historic Armenia as part of their permanent patrimony.

The fracturing of the status of the Armenians in the Ottoman Empire has a complicated diplomatic history to it. The Russo–Turkish War of 1877–1878 was concluded with the signing of the Treaty of San Stefano, which ceded the Russians considerable Ottoman territory. The European powers vehemently opposed the sudden expansion of Russian influence in the Balkans and the Middle East, and compelled the Russian monarch to agree to terms more favorable to the Ottomans in the Treaty of Berlin. All the European powers became signatories to this treaty. One of the terms in the Treaty of Berlin promised reforms in the so-called Armenian provinces of the Ottoman Empire. Armenians saw hope in this treaty. They thought an international covenant would have greater force in compelling the Ottomans to consider reorganizing the ramshackle administration of their remote provinces. When the European powers failed to persist in requiring the Ottoman sultan to abide by the terms of the treaty, the Armenians faced a rude awakening. Not only were they disappointed with a government that did not keep its promises, but they also realized that the powers had little interest in devoting time to the problems of the Armenians (Hovanissian, 1986c, pp. 19–41).

The fundamental issue separating Armenians and Ottomans was their diametrically opposed definitions of equality. Empires are inherently unequal systems. They divide the people into the rulers and the ruled. The Islamic empires, including the Ottoman state, compounded this system of inequality because the legal and judicial precepts of Islam also subordinated non-Muslim subjects to second-class status. Not only was the Ottoman system unequal, Ottoman society was unaccustomed to a concept of equality among men irrespective of their racial or religious background.

Although laws were issued accepting the principle of equality among the various confessional groups in the Ottoman Empire, the Muslim populace remained unconvinced that they should accept these secular ideas. Instead of leading to a new adjustment in Ottoman society, these laws became the source of consternation among Muslims, who believed these notions upset the established social order. The hierarchy of faiths had never been reconsidered in an Islamic society since the religion was founded in the seventh century. On the contrary, to the Muslims, the combination of European states sponsoring reforms on behalf of Christian minorities and these peoples, in turn, aspiring for equal treatment under the law, appeared to be a bid by the subject Christians for power over the Muslims (Dadrian, 1999, pp. 5–26).

Islamic law disenfranchised Christians and Jews. Their testimony was inadmissible in court, thus frequently denying them fair treatment by the justice system. Christians and Jews were also required to pay additional levies, such as a poll tax. For a peasantry eking out a living on the farm, the extra taxes often became an obligation that could not be met in a difficult year. The end result was commonly foreclosure and eviction. Disallowed from bearing arms, non-Muslims had no means for self-defense. They could protect neither their persons and families nor their properties. In certain places, dress codes restricting types of fabric used by the Christians helped differentiate them from the population at large, exposing them to further intimidation. At times a language restriction meant speaking a language other than Turkish at the risk of having one's tongue cut out. As a result, in many areas of the Ottoman Empire Armenians had lost the use of their native language (Ye'or, 1985, pp. 51–77).

These disabilities would have been impairing under normal circumstances. In areas closer to the capital, competent governors oversaw the administration of the provinces, and Armenians flocked to these safer parts of the empire. In the remoter provinces, such as the areas of historic Armenia, the hardships faced by the ordinary people were insurmountable. Avaricious officials exacted legal and illegal taxes. The justice system was hopelessly rigged. The maintenance of law and order was entrusted to men who only saw in their positions the opportunity for reckless exploitation. Extortion and bribery were the custom. In the countryside, the army demanded quartering in the houses of the Armenian peasants, which made their families hostages in their own homes. Unable to defend themselves, these people were also at the mercy of tribesmen, who descended upon their villages and carried off goods, flocks, and women. With no recourse left, Armenians were being driven to desperation.

The disappointment over the failure of the European powers to intervene effectively, combined with the dismay over the delays of the Ottoman government, continued to fuel the crisis in the Armenian provinces. Some Armenians decided to take matters into their own hands. In certain parts of Armenia, during the 1880s and 1890s, individuals began arming themselves and forming bands that, for instance, resisted Kurdish incursions on Armenian villages. Others joined political organizations advocating revolutionary changes at all levels of society. They demanded equal treatment, an adequate justice system, fair taxation, and the appointment of officials prepared to act responsibly (Nalbandian, 1963, pp. 167–68).

The Ottoman authorities refused to consider the demands. In response to the rise of nationalist sentiment among the subject peoples, and other internal and external security concerns, the Ottoman sultans had been striving to centralize power in their hands and had been creating a modernized bureaucracy that would help expand the authority of the government in all areas of Ottoman society. Among the measures introduced by the sultan Abdul-Hamid was a secret police and irregular cavalry regiments, called in his honor the Hamidiye corps, to act both as border guards and local *gendarmerie*. They became his instrument for suppression. In 1894, at a time of increasing tension between the Armenian population and the Ottoman government, which also coincided with increased political activism by Armenians and inadequate efforts at intervention by some of the European powers, the sultan unleashed his forces. Over the next three years, a series of massacres were staged throughout Armenia. Anywhere between 100,000 and 300,000 persons were killed, others were wounded, robbed, thrown out of their homes, or kidnapped. Many also fled the country (Bliss, 1982, pp. 368–501; Greene, 1896, pp. 185–242; Walker, 1980, pp. 156–73).

The Armenian massacres of 1894–1896 made headline news around the world. They engendered international awareness of the plight of the Armenians, and their horrendous treatment by the sultan's regiments resulted in condemnation of the Ottoman system (Nassibian, 1984, pp. 33–57). The European powers were compelled by public clamor in their own countries to urge the sultan to show restraint. The massacres were halted, but nothing was done to punish the perpetrators or to remedy the damage.

This cycle of violence against the Armenian population repeated itself in 1909 in the province of Adana, a region along the Mediterranean coast densely settled by Armenians, where again the Armenian neighborhoods were raided and burned. The estimate of the number of victims runs between 10,000 and 30,000 (Walker, 1980, pp. 182–88). The Adana massacre coincided with an event known as the Hamidian counter-revolution. The Young Turks had achieved political prominence by staging a military revolution in 1908. They had compelled the sultan, Abdul-Hamid, to restore the Ottoman Constitution, which he himself had issued in 1876 and soon after suspended. The sultan was suspected of having plotted to recover his autocratic powers by dislodging the Young Turks from Constantinople. In the ensuing climate of tension and suspicion the Adana massacre erupted.

The Young Turks blamed the Hamidian supporters of igniting strife in order to embarrass the progressive forces in Ottoman society, but the Young Turks themselves were also implicated in the atrocities. It augured badly for the Armenians. The Adana massacre demonstrated that even in a power struggle within Turkish society, the Armenians could be scapegoated by the disaffected and made the object of violence. In this context, Enver's embarrassment at his defeat in early 1915 and the government's casting of blame on the Armenians had a precedent. In this chain of events, the genocide of 1915 was the final, and mortal, blow dealt the Armenians by their Ottoman masters (Libaridian, 1987, pp. 203–35).

What Was the Long-Range Impact of the Genocide on the Victim Group?

The Armenians in the Ottoman Empire never achieved equality and were never guaranteed security of life and property. They entered the Ottoman Empire as a subject people and left it as a murdered or exiled population. It is estimated that the Armenian genocide resulted in the death of over one and a half million people. Beyond the demographic demise of the Armenians in the larger part of historic Armenia, the Armenian genocide brought to a conclusion the transfer of the Armenian homeland to the Turkish people. The Young Turks had planned not only to deprive the Armenians of life and property, but also conspired to deny to the Armenians the possibility of ever recovering their dignity and liberty in their own country.

Whole communities and towns were wiped off the map. The massive loss in population threatened the very existence of the Armenian people. Hardly a family was left intact. The survivors consisted mostly of orphans, widows, and widowers. The Armenian nation was saved only through the direct delivery of American relief aid to the "starving Armenians." Millions of dollars were collected in the United States to feed and house the destitute Armenians, both in the Middle East and in Russia, where tens of thousands took refuge. Hundreds of thousands eventually received some sort of aid, be it food, clothing, shelter, employment, resettlement, or emigration to the United States and elsewhere.

The tremendous difficulty faced by the Armenians in recovering from the devastating impact of the genocide had much to do with the fact that they, as a collectivity, had been robbed of all their wealth. They were forced to abandon their fixed assets. They received neither compensation nor reparations. As deportees, Armenians were unable to carry with them anything beside some clothing or bedding. All their businesses were lost. All their farms were left untended. Schools, churches, hospitals, orphanages, monasteries, graveyards, and other communal holdings became Turkish state property. The genocide left the Armenians penniless.

Those who survived and returned to reclaim their homes and properties after the end of World War I were driven out again by the Nationalist Turks who had risen to power in Turkey (Kerr, 1973, pp. 214–54). For the Armenians, the only choice was reconciliation with their status as exiles and resettlement wherever they could find a means of earning a living. With the inability to recongregate as a people in their homeland, the Armenians dispersed to the four corners of the world (Adalian, 1989, pp. 81–114; Adalian, 2002).

Lastly, the genocide shattered the historic bond of the Armenian people with their homeland. The record of their millennial existence in that country turned to dust. Libraries, archives, registries, the entire recorded memory of the Armenians as accumulated in their country was lost for all time (Adalian, 1999a).

What Were the Responses to this Particular Genocide?

At the time, the horror story of the Armenian genocide shocked the world. The Allies threatened to hold the Young Turks responsible for the massacres (Dadrian, 1989, p. 262), but the warning had no effect. The Allies were preoccupied with the war in Europe and did not commit resources to deliver the Armenians from their fate. Locally, however, humanitarian intervention by individual Turks, Kurds, and Arabs saved many lives (Hovannisian, 1992, pp. 173–207). While some Turks robbed their Armenian neighbors, others helped by hiding them in safe dwellings. While some Kurds willingly participated in the massacres, others guided groups of Armenians through the mountain passes to refuge in Russian territory. And while some Arabs only saw the Armenians as hopeless victims, others shared their food.

Among the first people to see the deplorable condition of the mass of the Armenians were the American missionaries and diplomats stationed in Turkey. Their appeals to their government, the religious institutions in the United States, and the general public were the earliest of the active responses to the predicament of genocide. They strove to deliver aid even during the war (Sachar, 1969, p. 343; Winter, 2003).

After the war, the European nations were little disposed to help the Armenians, as they themselves were trying to recover from their losses. Nevertheless, Britain and France, which had occupied Ottoman territory in the Middle East, were strongly positioned to influence the political outcome in the region, but neither chose to do so on behalf of the Armenians. Their interest in retaining control of these lands also conflicted with the wider goals of Woodrow Wilson in establishing a stable world order. The American president's laudable policies were welcomed by the peoples of Europe and Asia, such as the Poles, Czechs, Arabs, and Indians, who saw in his principles for international reconciliation the possibility of attaining their national independence. He too, however, was unable to deliver more than words. The United States Congress was disinclined to involve America in foreign lands. Consequently, many territorial issues were solved through the pure exercise of might. Diplomacy had little chance of extending help to the Armenian refugees.

For the Turks, the failure of diplomacy provided an opportunity to regroup under new leadership and to begin their own national effort at building a new state upon the ruins of the Ottoman Empire. With Mustafa Kemal at their head, the Nationalist Turks forged a new government and secured the boundaries of modern-day Turkey. Their policy of national consolidation excluded despised minorities (Dadrian, 1989, pp. 327–33). The Armenians, the weakest element, headed the list. By 1923, when the

Republic of Turkey was formally recognized as a sovereign state, the Armenians remaining in the territories of that state, with the exception of those in Constantinople, had been driven out. For many survivors of the deportations who had returned to their former homes, this was their second expulsion (Kinross, 1964, p. 235).

Before the Turkish borders were finally sealed and the Armenians conclusively denied the right to their former homes, the absence of moral resolve in Turkish governmental circles to confront the consequences of the Armenian genocide was made abundantly clear. The postwar government proved reluctant to put on trial the Young Turk officials suspected of organizing the massacres. Only upon the insistence of the Allies were a series of trials initiated. Some dramatic evidence was given in testimony, and verdicts were handed down explicitly charging those found guilty of pursuing a course of action resulting in the destruction of the Armenian population. Even so, popular sentiment in Turkish society did not support the punishment of the guilty, and the government chose to forgo the sentences of the court. The triumvirs —Enver, Talaat, and Jemal — were condemned to death, but their trials were held in absentia since they had fled the country and their extradition was not a matter of priority (Dadrian, 1989, pp. 221–334).

Under these circumstances, no legal recourse to justice remained open. A clandestine Armenian group called Nemesis decided to mete out punishment to the accused individuals. The principal figures in the Young Turk Party, such as Talaat and Jemal, who conceived and implemented the genocide, were assassinated. All of them had fled Turkey, since their enemies included more than just Armenians. They also had much to account to the Turkish people for having taken them into a war which they lost so disastrously. Although the acts of retribution against Talaat and some of the others had a profound emotional effect on the Armenians, politically they were insignificant. The Armenians were never compensated for their losses (Derogy, 1990; Power, 2002, pp. 1–16).

Is There Agreement or Disagreement Among Legitimate Scholars as to the Interpretation of this Particular Genocide (e.g., Preconditions, Implementation, and Ramifications)?

Two schools of thought have emerged over the years. Scholars who study the Armenian genocide look at the phenomenon as either an exceptionally catastrophic occurrence coincident to a global conflict such as World War I (Fein, 1979, pp. 10–18; Horowitz, 1982, pp. 46–51), or the final chapter in the peculiar fate of the Armenians as a people who lost their independence many centuries earlier (Kuper, 1981, pp. 101–19; Walker, 1980, pp. 169, 236–37).

All agree that the preconditions to the genocide were highly consistent with other examples where a dominant group targets a minority. They also agree on the structural inequalities of Ottoman society and how it disadvantaged the Armenians. They differ on their interpretation of the causes and consequences of Armenian nationalism. Some think that the appearance of political organization among the Armenians can be regarded as the critical breaking point. Others see these developments as inevitable and entirely consistent with global trends and not particular to the Armenians. Two questions are often debated: whether the massacres during the reign of Abdul-Hamid were sufficiently precedental to be regarded as the beginning of the Armenian catastrophe, or whether the Young Turks aggravated conditions in ways that exceeded the designs of Abdul-Hamid (Kuper, 1981, pp. 101–19; Horowitz, 1982, pp. 46–51).

In the implementation of the genocide, one thing is clear. The earlier massacres were episodic and affected select communities. The genocide was systematic, comprehensive, and directed practically against everyone. The sultan's policy did not aim for the extermination of the Armenians; rather, it was brutal punishment for aspiring to gain charge of their political destiny. As many scholars have pointed out, at one time the Ottoman system extended a considerable measure of security to its minorities. Although for the most part they were excluded from government and at a disadvantage in holding large-scale property, Christians and Jews were allowed to practice their faiths and distinguish themselves in commerce and finance. Therefore, it was not in the interest of the sultan to dismantle his imperial inheritance. His objective remained the continuance of his autocratic power and his rule over the lands bequeathed him by his conquering forebears.

Those studying the Young Turks have pointed out that the CUP organized its committees and conducted its activities outside this system. They were opponents of imperial autocracy. Their own political radicalism also meant that they were predisposed to think in exclusionary terms. Some of these scholars contend that the Young Turk period can be seen as a transitional phase in Turkish society where the pluralistic construct of the multiethnic and multiconfessional Ottoman system was violently smashed and the ground was prepared for the emergence of a state based on ethnic singularism (Ahmad, 1982, pp. 418–25; Staub, 1989, pp. 173–87; Melson, 1986, pp. 61–84).

Perhaps the issue debated most frequently revolves around the matter of postgenocide responsibility. There is a wide divergence of opinion on the question whether modern Turkey is liable to the Armenians for their losses, or whether it is absolved of such liability because the crime was committed under the jurisdiction of prior state authorities (Libaridian, 1985, pp. 211–27). The Turkish government dismisses all such claims since it denies that the policies implemented in 1915 constitute genocide. Some in the academic and legal community are supportive of the Turkish position (Gürün, 1985). On the other hand, that stance raises a more complex problem. Who exactly should be held responsible for genocide: the government, the state, society? If governments put the blame on prior regimes, all they have done is merely certify the former policy by disregarding the consequences of genocide. The reluctance by a successor state to shoulder responsibility is only another form of reaping the benefits of mass murder.

Do People Care about this Genocide Today? If So, How Is that Concern Manifested? If Not, Why Not?

For a period of about 50 years, the world fell into an apathetic silence over the Armenian genocide. Its results had been so grievous for the Armenians and the failure of the international community to redress the consequent problems was so thoroughgoing that the world chose to ignore the legacy of the Armenian genocide. With the consolidation of Communist rule in Russia and of Nationalist rule in Turkey, the chapter on the Armenians was considered closed. People wanted to forget about the Great War and its misery. As for the Armenians, they were too few, too widely dispersed, and too preoccupied with their own survival to know how to respond.

The concern over the fate of the Armenians manifested mostly in literature, as various authors wrote about the massacres and memorialized the rare instances of resistance (Lepsius, 1987; Gibbons, 1916; Werfel, 1934). After a life of struggle, upon reaching retirement age, Armenians also began to write down their memoirs. Slowly a small corpus of literature emerged, documenting in personal accounts the genocide and its consequences for individuals, their families, and communities (Hovannisian, 1987; Totten, 1991). This body of work began to serve as evidence for the study of the Armenian genocide. In the 1960s, as government archives holding vast collections of diplomatic correspondence on the deportations and massacres were opened, a significant amount of contemporaneous documentation also became available (Hovannisian, 1987; Beylerian, 1983; Ohandjanian, 1988; Adalian, 1991–1993; Dadrian, 1994). This further encouraged research in the subject. Interest in the Armenian genocide has since been growing as more researchers, writers, and educators examine the evidence and attempt to understand what happened in 1915 (Adalian, 1999b).

Commensurate to this interest, however, has been a phenomenon growing at an even faster pace. This is the denial of the Armenian genocide. For many Turks the reminder of the Ottoman past is offensive. The Turkish government's stated policy has been a complete denial

(Foreign Policy Institute, 1982). The denial ranges beyond the question of political responsibility. This type of denial questions the very historical fact of the occurrence of genocide, and even of atrocities. A whole body of revisionist historiography has been generated to explain, to excuse, or to dismiss the Armenian genocide (Hovannisian, 1986a, pp. 111–33; Dobkin, 1986, pp. 97–109; Adalian, 1992, pp. 85–105).

Some authors have gone so far as to place the blame for the genocide on the Armenians themselves, describing the deportations and massacres as self-inflicted, since, they say, the deportations were only counter-measures taken by the Ottoman government against a disobedient and disloyal population (Uras, 1988, pp. 855–86; Gürün, 1985). Such arguments do not convince serious scholars (Guroian, 1986, pp. 135–52; Smith, 1989, pp. 1–38). Others, regrettably, are more prone to listening to revisionist argumentation (Shaw and Shaw, 1977, pp. 314–17; McCarthy, 1983, pp. 47–81, 117–30). These kinds of debates fail to address, however, the central questions about the Young Turk policy toward the Armenian population. Was every Armenian, young and old, man and woman, disloyal? How does one explain the deportation of Armenians from places that were nowhere near the war zones, if removing them from high-risk areas was the purpose of the policy? And always, one must ask about the treatment of children. What chance did they stand of surviving deportation, starvation, and dehydration in the desert?

What Does this Genocide Teach Us if We Wish to Protect Others from Such Horrors?

Although, ultimately, it is the exercise of political power in the absence of moral restraint that explains the occurrence of genocide, the demographic status of a people is demonstrated by the Armenian genocide to be a significant factor in the perpetration of genocide. A dispersed people jurid-ically designated by a state as a minority, both in the numerical and politi-cal sense of the word, is extremely vulnerable to abusive policy. It lacks the capacity for any coordinated action to respond to, or resist, genocidal mea-sures. It is evident that a government inclined to engage in the extermina-tion of a minority can only be restrained by pressures and sanctions imposed by greater powers.

Geography was no less a contributing factor in exposing the Armenians to genocide. A people inhabiting a remote part of the world is all the more at the mercy of a brutal government, especially if it is questioning the policies of the state. Since exposure is the principal foil of crime, the more hidden from view a people lives, the more likely it is to be repressed. Of all the places where the Armenians in the Ottoman Empire might have hampered the war effort, if indeed they were a seditious population, the most likely spot would have been the capital city. Yet the government spared most of the Armenians in Constantinople because many foreigners lived there, and they would have been alarmed to witness mass deportations. That signal exception underscores the importance and the high likelihood of successfully monitoring the living conditions of an endangered population.

That exception also points to another lesson, which is specially pronounced in the Armenian case. Since many foreign communities had a presence in Constantinople, getting the word out to the rest of the world would not have been difficult with such corroboration. Thereby the Armenians in this one city remained in a protected enclave. This principle applies no less to the international status extended an entire people, as the European powers once did for the Armenians. Their interest in the Armenians acted as a partial restraint on the Ottoman government. The sudden alteration of the international order as a result of global conflict left the Armenians wholly exposed. Whatever the level of international protection extended to an endangered minority, the withdrawal of those guarantees, tenuous as they might be, only acts as an inducement for genocide. Denying opportunity to a criminal regime is critical for the prevention of genocide.

The experience of the Armenian people in the period after the genocide teaches another important lesson. Unless the consequences of genocide are addressed in the immediate aftermath of the event, the element of time very soon puts survivors at a serious disadvantage. Without the attention of the international community, without the intervention of major states seeking to stabilize the affected region, without the swift apprehension of the guilty, and without the full exposure of the evidence, the victims stand no chance of recovering from their losses. In the absence of a response and of universal condemnation, a genocide becomes "legitimized." Following the war, the Ottoman government never gave a full accounting of what happened to the Armenians, and the successor state of Turkey chose to bury the matter entirely (Adalian, 1991, pp. 99–104).

Though all too frequently unwilling to take concerted action to save populations clearly in danger of annihilation, whether through monitoring and reporting systems, the activation of legal and economic sanctions, or political or military intervention, the international community is far better equipped to respond to genocidal crises than ever before. When the Armenian genocide occurred there was no alarm and there was no rescue. Without alarm there can be no rescue, and that is the least that the Armenian experience teaches.

Eyewitness Accounts: The Armenian Genocide

Eyewitness and survivor accounts of the Armenian genocide were audiotaped and videotaped more than a half century after the events. That means the recorded testimony was provided by persons in their 70s and 80s who were reflecting upon a life that took a sudden turn when they were still children or very young adults. Hence, the problem of the great length of time that passed since the events of 1915 and the fact that those events were seen through the eyes of children who were looking at the world from their very narrow frames of reference needs to be kept in mind when dealing with testimony of this type. Certainly children have the greatest difficulty gauging an accurate measure of time. Therefore, the episodes from their personal narratives occur at approximated intervals. Their memory, for instance, preserves the first names of numerous acquaintances, but last names are less frequently known.

A contrast to these limitations is the accuracy, with virtually all survivors, in their depiction of the geography and the topography that was the setting of their life's most tragic period. Because they were deported, knowledge of where they originated and the places they saw and stopped along the way and the spots they reached at the end of their journeys became vital information not only for their physical and emotional survival, but also for their ability to reconnect with other survivors of the communities from which they were separated. Most interesting, however, and useful for the documentary record it turns out, was their very limited sense of the world around them. Whereas adults would have attempted to understand the events they witnessed in terms of their community and society, children describe their experiences strictly from within the confines of their immediate family and circle of friends. As such, therefore, they preserve a sense of greater pathos undiluted by either fatalism or drama. Most seem to have retained their horror of genocide through their inability to offer any larger suggestion than their very incomprehension at what happened and why.

Helen Tatarian's account is an exceptionally rare one because it describes a massacre of Armenians that happened in 1909. When these records were created, very few survivors were old enough to have lived through occurrences of massacres earlier than 1915. The details of her account are also a valuable contrast to the pattern of the 1915 genocide. The Adana massacre is characterized by random mob action occurring within the perimeter of the city. Government forces are described as a party that simply stayed out of the way and, in this case, provided safe conduct where foreigners, specifically Americans, were concerned. More importantly, she verifies the significance of the protection provided by the missionary, and other third-party, presence. During the genocide none of these factors came into play. The missionaries were unable to protect their parishioners. The government was an active participant in the dislocation and the execution of the Armenian population. Lastly, with the exception of some towns in the farthest eastern reaches of Anatolia, little killing occurred within the towns. The other survivors all testify to a consistent pattern of separation, deportation, and subsequent mass executions in places away from urban centers during the period of the genocide.

Sarkis Agojian records the treatment of the adult male population that was never deported. He testifies that they were arrested, tortured, and murdered very early in the process. The deportations, as he recalls, occurred after the segment of the Armenian population capable of resistance was eliminated. Lastly, his memory preserves, with a powerful poignancy, the trauma of Armenian children who were spared deportation and starvation by adoption into Turkish families. The deafening silence at his last glimpse of his mother and the shattering news of her death capture the maddening grief that seized their young lives, and which marked them for all their years.

Takouhi Levonian gives an eyewitness account of an actual episode of wholesale slaughter. Her description of the physical cruelties inflicted upon the Armenian population is especially riveting. Her description of the kinds of privations endured is no less powerful. Her testimony incontrovertibly underscores the extreme vulnerability of the Armenian young female population. It would appear that the treatment they received was most abusive. The horrific sadism practiced by the perpetrators of the Armenian genocide is hereto testified in this single account.

Yevnig Adrouni's story redeems humanity through a personal narrative of survival and rescue. Too young to be mistreated sexually, her exploits are testament to the spirit of an alert child who would not submit to degradation. Spared physical torment, she committed herself to escaping her fate. Clutching onto the last shreds of her Armenian identity, she proves to herself and her rescuers that determination and defiance can, sometimes, defeat evil. As she so vividly recounts, from the survival of a single human being springs forth the new hope of larger victories.

Helen Tatarian, native of Dertyol, born c. 1893. Audiotaped on April 17, 1977, Los Angeles, California by Rouben Adalian. (Dertyol was a town inhabited mostly by Armenians. It is located on the Mediterranean coast in the region of Adana. Adana is also the name of the largest town in the area.)

There was a massacre in 1909. I was in school at Adana. Miss Webb and Miss Mary, two American sisters, ran the school. Miss Webb was the older, Miss Mary the younger.

In 1909, right in the month of April, we suddenly heard guns being fired and saw flames rising. The houses of the Armenians were set on fire.

There was a French school right next to ours. They burned it down completely.

At first the Turks killed quite a lot of people, then they stopped for a while. Eight days later they started firing their guns again. Reverend Sisak Manoogian came running. "Do not be afraid children, a hog had gone wild," he said, "and they are shooting it." But it was a lie, nor had a hog gone wild. The Turks had gone wild. They were about to start again.

The son-in-law of our American missionary, Mr. Chambers, had climbed on the roof. He had climbed on the roof of our laundry room to look at what was going on in the city. They shot the man.

There was a window, a small window up high. We used to look from there to see that behind the school building there were people lying dead. The Turks were shooting the Armenians. This was a massacre specifically aimed at the Armenians.

During the fire those who managed to hide remained in hiding, those who did not hide were cut down. Just like Surpik grandmother, the poor woman who was going to her brother-in-law's house. Surpik grandmother was shot in the arm, great grandmother Surpik. Later they had shot dead her husband and son. This woman owned fields. She was a rich woman. She used to travel on horseback. But it so happened that she was going in the direction of her relatives, her brother-in-law's house. Fortunately she was not killed.

We could not go out and we remained in hiding in the school building. We heard the sounds of guns, and from the sounds alone we were afraid. We were children. We cried, but we had no communication with anyone outside. Across from our building there lived an American, Miss Farris. The Turks burned her building so that our school would catch on fire and the children would have to run outside and thus they could kidnap the girls. The American missionary immediately notified the government. Soldiers came from the government and while putting out the fire a soldier fell and was burned inside.

Later we opened a hole in the wall. The missionaries did this. They opened a hole big enough to go through it in order to cross from our end of the block to the other end, to Mr. Chambers' house, the missionary's house. All the girls were there, 250, 300 girls. We piled up in the man's house. The Turks were going to burn this house also. The man held out a surrender flag. They had poured gas and threatened to burn us in that house. We asked him: "Reverend, if the Turks forced you, would you hand us over to them?" "If they press me hard. If they insist," said the man. What could he do? Or else they would kill him too. Later we remained there for a night. There, we cried. The girls began such a weeping. The following morning, the government soldiers took us to the train station. By train we went to Mersin.

There was no fighting [in Adana between Armenians and Turks]. The Turks knew anyway which was the house of an Armenian. They went in and cut him down and shot the people inside and they took whatever was in the house. They robbed the houses and set them on fire. They entered them since it was the property of the Armenians. They also burned the churches, but I believe a considerable crowd had gathered in a French church. They did nothing there at that time. There were those who took refuge with our American missionaries also, but it was a little difficult to cross the street. If the Turks saw you, they were ready to shoot.

Sarkis Agojian, native of Chemeshgadsak, born 1906. Audiotaped on May 25, 1983, in Pasadena, California, by Donald and Lorna Miller (Chemeshgadsak was a town inhabited by Armenians in the region of Kharpert in the western portion of historic Armenia.)

We were in school having physical education. We had lined up when the wife of our coach, Mr. Boghos, came and told her husband that the Turks had just arrested the principal, Pastor Arshag. You see, they first took the educated, the intellectuals. They took these people to a home which they had converted into a prison and tortured them in order to get them to talk. The mailman, who was Armenian, was also arrested and tortured. They pulled out his fingernails saying that while he was carrying mail he also was transporting secret letters; mail was carried in those days on horseback in large leather bags fastened to either side of the horse. He was Sarkis Mendishian. So upon the news that Pastor Arshag was arrested, they dismissed us from school and asked all of us to go home.

We went home. My father was not there. My uncle had run away. They had put a dress on my uncle's son, even though he was not young, to disguise him. My father's uncle was also in prison, for, after taking the younger educated men, they also took the elderly. I was young so they used to send me to take food to him. I did this a few times. I would go in and sit with him. One day when I was taking his food, I met a lot of police who were saying that on that day we could not deliver food — that all the prisoners were going to leave. I saw them in twos, all chained together. I could not take the food, so I returned and gave the news. I told them that they were chained and they were coming this way and would pass by our house, there being no other way to leave town toward Kharpert.

By now, all the families had heard, so they were all in the streets to see their loved ones. I got on top of the roof and was yelling "uncle." There was a doctor in this procession, and when his wife saw him, she ran out to greet him, but with the butt of the rifle the police pushed her away — even though he was an elderly man. So the men marched on, leaving all the women and families crying and grieving. There was a place outside of town about 20 minutes with trees and water. There they took their names to see if anyone was missing. Then they marched them to the edge of the Euphrates and killed them. Apparently my great uncle had some red gold with him; he gave it to the police who took it and then killed him.

Now that all the men were gone, deportation orders were issued for women and children. Our town was deported in two different groups, 15 days apart. I wish we were in the first group because they made it all the way to Aleppo. When we were to leave our home, we left our bedding and other things with the landlord so that if we returned we would get it back. Also, we threw our rugs to the people at the public bath next door so that they would keep them for us. We said that we would get them when we returned. We are still to return!

Because we could afford it, we had rented a cart to carry some of our things. It was five hours from our town to the Euphrates River. On the way we had to pass on a bridge. We were told that one of our neighbor's boys had been killed and thrown over there. In fact, I heard some Turk boys saying to each other that there was a gold piece in the pocket of our neighbor's son. We could see the injured who had been shot but were not yet dead.

The first village that we reached was one in which our landlord lived. We saw that the fruit was getting ripe. My brother, sister, uncle's son and daughter took some money to our landlord to see if he would save their lives, and they remained with him. I stayed with my mother, my uncle's wife, and her five-year-old grandchild. We left the village of Bederatil and went to the next town, Leloushaghen, which took us a day to reach. There was a Turk man who was taking Armenian boys away, and I said that I would go with him.

That night, I and two other boys slept at this Turkish agha's house. In the morning my mother brought a bundle of clothes for me and left it with a Turkish woman whose husband had worked in my father's bakery and who had lived with this agha for years. I was there when she came to the house to leave my clothes. I was sitting there and I saw her, but it was as though I was in a trance; we never talked and she never kissed me. I don't know if it was because she could not bear it from sadness. I never saw again any of those clothes or anything that my mother might have left in them for me.

The deportation caravan now went on without me; they still had two hours to make it to the Euphrates River. When they got there, they were all killed. The way we heard this was that some of the police brought to the agha a pretty young girl and her brother that this Turk wanted. These police told the agha that in a matter of a few minutes they wiped them all out. But this young Armenian girl told us that she saw the *gendarmes* force the deportees to take off their clothes and then shove them off a cliff into the Euphrates River far below. According to this girl, when it came time for my mother, she took gold from her bundle, threw it in the river, grabbed my four-year-old brother, and jumped down with the child in her arms. When I heard this, all of a sudden I began to weep. It's the feelings you know. I was about nine years old. As soon as this girl finished telling her story, the agha's son tried to distract me and those listening by calling me a *gavour* [infidel], making fun of the cross. I covered my head with the blanket and cried and cried.

Takouhi Levonian, native of Keghi, born 1900. Audiotaped on April 8, 1981, in Los Angeles, California (Keghi was another Armenian town in the region of Kharpert.)

When the war began, I could see and sense the men of our town gathering in groups. They were talking and looking very sad. The women used to sigh. The schools shut down and their grounds, as well as the churches, became filled with soldiers. That's how winter passed. In April, there was talk that they were going to move us out. I was 15 years old then ... .

Between April 29 and 30 [of 1915], word came that they were going to transfer us to Kharpert. On May first, that news was confirmed and until the fourth [of May] every household began preparations by making *kete* [Armenian bread], preparing chickens, other meats, and so on. My father told my mother not to bother with any of these preparations. He said to just take our bedding on the mules and not to bother burying anything, like so many others had done who thought that they would return to them. He said that if we ever returned, he would be glad to come back to four walls. He was farsighted.

At the onset of the war he imported large amounts of oil, sugar, matches, and all the things that had to be imported. When we left [on the deportation], we distributed all this to our neighbors. They arrested only a few people from our town. The rest they left unharmed. They did not do anything to my father because he was respected by all, since he was so fair with every one — regardless of nationality. He did good equally to all.

We were the first caravan to leave with much tears and anguish since it meant separation for so many. They assigned a few soldiers to us and thus we began. We used to travel by day, and in the evenings we stopped to eat and rest. In five to six days we reached Palu. There, while we were washing up, I will never, never forget, they took my father away, along with all the men down to 12 years of age. The next day our camp was filled with the Turks and Kurds of Palu, looting, dragging away whatever they could, both possessions and young women. They knocked the mules down to kill them. I was grabbing onto my six-year-old brother; my sister was holding her baby, and my two young sisters were grabbing her skirt; my mother was holding the basket of bread. There was so much confusion, and the noise of bullets shooting by us. Some people were getting shot, and the rest of us were running in the field, not knowing where to go … .

Then I saw with my own eyes the Turks beating a fellow name Sahag, who had hid under his wife's dress. They were beating him with hammers, axes right in front of me and his wife. He yelled to her to run away, that we are all going to die a "donkey death." And then I saw the husband of my aunt, who was too old to have been taken previously, and he was being beaten in the head with an ax. They then threw him in the river. It finally calmed down. The Turks left some dead, took some with them, and the rest of us found each other.

At this time it was announced that anyone who would become a Turk could remain here. Otherwise, we must continue on. Many stayed. So we took off again. [We felt] much loss, that was not material loss only, but human loss. We were in tears and anguish as we left.

From Palu to Dikranagerd they tormented us a great deal. We suffered a lot. There was no water or food. Whatever my mom had in her bag, she gave us a little at a time. We walked the whole day, 10 to 15 days. No shoes remained on our feet. We finally reached Dikranagerd. There, by the water, we washed, and whatever little dry bread we had we wetted it and ate it.

Word came that the *vali* [governor] wanted from the Armenians a very pretty 12-year-old girl … . So by night, they came with their lamps looking for such a girl. They found one, dragged her from the mother, saying to the weeping mother that they will return her. Later, they returned the child, in horrible condition, almost dead, and left her at her mother's knees.

The mother was weeping so badly, and, of course, the child could not make it and died. The women could not comfort her. Finally, several of the women tried to dig a hole, and with the help of one of the *gendarme's* guns, they buried the girl and covered her. Dikranagerd had a large wall around it, so my mother and a few other women wrote on it, "Shushan buried here."

We remained under the walls [where Shushan was buried] for two to three days. Then they made us leave again. This time they assigned to us an elderly *gendarme*. He had tied to his horse a large container of water and the whole way he kept giving it to children and never himself rode the horse, but allowed old women to take turns on it. We went to Mardin. He also always took us near the villages so we could buy some food, and he would not allow the villagers to sell food at expensive prices. A lot of people either died on the way or stayed behind, because they could not keep up. So by the time we reached Mardin we were a lot less in number, although still a lot. They deposited us in a large field. There they gave us food … . At this point my mother was not with us.

A Kurd women came and told my sister that two horsemen were going to kidnap me. She panicked and started looking for my mom, but she was not around. So she thought of giving the baby, who was in her arms, to the Kurd woman, so that she would help me. So she disguised me, but when we turned around, the woman was gone with the baby.

Turks used to pay high prices for babies, probably the woman sold him. My poor sister, Zarouhi, went crazy. I, too, was going crazy, feeling that I was the cause. I cried and cried. We remained in Mardin for five days and never found the baby. My poor sister was lactating, and her milk was full but there was no baby to nurse ... .

It came time to leave, and we had to leave the baby behind with uncontrollable tears. The journey was dreadful. With no shoes on our feet, it was so painful to walk on the paths they took us on. We used to wrap cloth on them to ease the pain, but it didn't really help much. There was no water. In fact, at one stretch, for three full days, we had no water at all. The children would cry: "Water, water, water." One of the children died.

Then toward morning one day, my sister and another woman crawled out of camp to a far place and brought some water in a tin can. Finally, they dumped us next to a small river. There my mother took me to the river to wash my face which was always covered up, except for my eyes. But one of the *gendarmes*, having spotted my eyes, showed up and grabbed me. My mother fainted, and, acting bravely, I shook his hand loose and ran, mingling among the people. I could hear the women yelling to my mother to wake up, that I got away. As the caravan moved again, I kept watching that man, always trying to stay behind him ... .

Yevnig Adrouni, native of Hoghe, born c. 1905. Audiotaped on August 13, 1978, by Rouben Adalian. (Hoghe was an Armenian village in the Kharpert region.)

My uncle, my cousin, the government took them away. Later they gathered the noteworthy people, including my father. They took him to prison, to Kharpert. After this they began to gather the men and to take them to the place called Keghvank. That place was a slaughterhouse. I remember my uncle's wife and others used to go there. My father was still in prison at this time. They used to go there and find that their men were missing. They [the Turks] had taken them and killed them with axes even then.

During the time when my father was in prison, there occurred the thing called *Emeliet Tabure*. They recalled all the Armenian soldiers. They set them to work at road construction. In this way they gathered all of them, including the Armenian soldiers, and filled them in the prisons. Later, when my father was still in prison, they set fire to the prison so that the Armenians would be killed. Already they were torturing them every day.

When he escaped from prison, a Kurd saw my father. He was an acquaintance. My father fled with the Kurd to our village. But his nails were pulled out and his body was black and blue. They had tortured my father continuously. He lived but a few days. He died.

This is in 1915. My mother was deported first. A Turk was going to keep us, but he proposed that we Turkify. My mother did not accept. Therefore, since I was young, they thought that if my mother was not with me, they might be able to convince me to Turkify. My mother was deported three months before the rest of us. This happened in spring. As for me, they would say: "Would the daughter of a tough infidel become a Muslim?"

They deported me also, thirsty and hungry, all the way to Deir el Zor. They did not even allow us to drink water. Along the way they took us by very narrow roads. Many of the old people who were hungry and thirsty could not walk. They used to strike them with stones and roll them down the slope. Pregnant women, I have seen with my own eyes ... I cried a lot. Whenever I go to church, the whole thing is in front of my eyes, the scene, the deportation. They tore open the bellies of pregnant women so that the child was born. It fell free. They used to do that. I have seen such things.

There were some men. They killed them at that time. All of us, hungry, thirsty, we walked all the way to Deir el Zor. They came, Kurds, Arabs, and carried us away from the caravan. When a piece of bread fell in my hands for the first time, I chewed it but could not swallow it because I was starved.

Along the way they did not allow us to drink water. The river was there. It flowed. They did not let us go and drink. A girl, she was 13, 14 perhaps ... we suddenly saw that the caravan was stopped there in the field. That girl came, her face scratched, bloodied, all her clothes torn. Her mother had sent her secretly in order to fetch water. There were Kurdish boys ... all the things they have done to the poor girl. The Turkish guards caught her mother. They asked: "Who is her mother? Let her come forward." The caravan was seated. A woman moved her lips. The guards said: "This is her mother." The child was in her lap. They seized the woman and in front of our eyes, they shot her [daughter] dead, saying: "Because you did not have the right. We had forbidden you to send anyone to the river."

They used to take the little ones and carry them away. The Kurds carried me away as well. For eight years I remained lost among the Kurds, the Turks, and the Arabs. I was among the Kurds. I forgot much of the Armenian language, but I did not forget the Lord's Prayer. Later they used to have me tend sheep. They gave me a dog with the name of Khutto. I used to write in the dirt with my finger my name, my last name, and the name of my birthplace. I used to write the alphabet in the dirt and in this way I did not forget the Armenian letters. I did not forget the Lord's Prayer and I did not forget where I was from.

First I was with an Assyrian. They took me to Merdin. Later I was placed with Muslims to be brought up as their child, but I became ill. They returned me to the Assyrians. The Assyrians helped us a great deal. From the church, the sister of the patriarch of the Assyrians took me to her house. They were poor as well. The Assyrians used to go to the road in order to break stones and make a living, and I went along with them. We used to go there to break stones. When that finished, it seems the war was ended, I said I am going to Aleppo. Instead of going to Aleppo, Kurdish tribesmen carried me away. They took me to their villages as a servant. I knew that I had relatives in Aleppo but how would I find them, how would I get there? I was among Kurds.

They took me to the place called Tersellor. Tersellor was a village of Kurds in the environs of Aleppo at the place called Musulme. I remained there tending sheep, but I had made up my mind that I would go to Aleppo. I did not know any other Armenians. There were no Armenians. There was nobody, but I thought to myself that my cousin might be there. By night I escaped. I went down the road. I hid from the Kurds. I saw a traveler on horseback with young ones around him. They saw me.

Now the languages, Arabic, Kurdish, I spoke fluently already. They asked me: "Where are you going?" I said: "I am going to Aleppo." They looked at each other's faces. They said: "We are going to Aleppo. We will take you along." They took me with them. They were from Aleppo, but Muslims. They have villages. In the summer they go to their villages. In the winter they return to Aleppo. They took me with them, but they did not let me out of their house in Aleppo. Next door to the house I was staying in there was an Armenian girl. She was younger than I. She remembered only her name, Mary. She brought news from the outside. She is also Armenian and I am Armenian, but I acted as if I was a Kurd since I had presented myself as a Kurd to the others. I was afraid to tell the truth to that Armenian girl. She was younger than I.

One day she had fallen down the stairs and broken her foot. They took her to the hospital. At the hospital they told her: "You are Armenian." "No, my name is Fatma," she had said.

I saw that she had come back. When we were taking out the garbage, I asked her: "Where were you?" She related what had taken place. "I was at the hospital." She said that they told her: "You are Armenian." She said: "At first I denied it." After talking for a while she conceded. "Yes, I only remember that we were under a tent. My father, my mother, all, they killed and they took me. Only that much I remember." They [the hospital personnel] said: "Do not go [back to the house]. Now there are Armenians. We have an Armenia." This is at the end of 1922. After I was freed I discovered what the date was. She said [to the hospital personnel]: "No. I go back because they spent ten red gold pieces for my foot."

Look, God sent her for me. I believe that God sent her for me. "But I will escape," she said. "I will escape." I said: "Alright, we will escape together." We had a shoemaker who was Armenian. We did not know that he was Armenian. He was from Aintab. Now I regret very much that I did not take down his name. Eventually, through his assistance, we managed to escape.

I told the girl: "Tell that boy from Aintab that there is another Armenian girl." He asked her: "Does she use a veil?" At that time I had been given a small veil since I was with a Muslim. He made me work as a servant. She said: "Yes." "Do not believe that she is Armenian," he said. The girl came and told me this. I said: "Tell him I know the Lord's Prayer." She went and told him. He said: "Anyone from another race can learn that by heart just as they learn languages." It so happened that Armenian men had attempted to rescue girls from the houses of other Arabs only to discover that they were not Armenians. I said: "Tell him that I know how to read Armenian." He said: "If she knows how to read Armenian, let her write." I wrote my name, my last name, where I was from, but I wrote in Turkish with Armenian letters. When she gave him the letter, he told her: "We will not rescue you until she is ready too. Now we believe that this girl is Armenian." If I had not known how to read and write Armenian I would not be here today. The Armenian letters saved me. This letter was handed to Nishan Der-Bedrosian, a man from Kharpert. It came into his hands and he wrote me a letter which reached me through that girl. "Try in every way to escape ... ."

The shop of the shoemaker was close to where we lived. The first day I found that he had locked the door to the shop and left. I went the following day. He said: "You know I cannot keep the store open after a certain hour. It is against the law." Then I found the means to escape. When I was escaping, they realized that I was escaping so they locked the door with two keys. But finally I found the way. I escaped by night. A man was standing in the dark and the shoemaker had not closed his shop. They took me and we left. It was a feast day. It was Christmas day. Apparently it was December or January, perhaps the beginning of 1923. I was free.

So this is my story. But the things which the Turks did, the massacres, I never forget. In front of our eyes ... Haygaz ... on his mother's knees, they butchered him. These sort of things I have seen. And I always cry. I cannot forget.

References

Adalian, Rouben P. (1989). "The Historical Evolution of the Armenian Diasporas." *Journal of Modern Hellenism*, 6:81–114.

Adalian, Rouben P. (1991). "The Armenian Genocide: Context and Legacy." Special Issue on Teaching about Genocide edited by William S. Parsons and Samuel Totten of *Social Education*, 55(2):99–104.

Adalian, Rouben P. (Ed.) (1991–1993). *The Armenian Genocide in the U.S. Archives 1915–1918*. Alexandria, VA, and Cambridge, UK: Chadwyck-Healey, Inc.

Adalian, Rouben P. (1992). "The Armenian Genocide: Revisionism and Denial," pp. 85–105. In Michael N. Dobkowski and Isidor Wallimann (Eds.) *Genocide In Our Time: An Annotated Bibliography with Analytical Introductions*. Ann Arbor, MI: The Pierian Press.

Adalian, Rouben P. (1999a). "A Conceptual Method for Examining the Consequences of the Armenian Genocide," pp. 47–59. In Levon Chorbajian and George Shirinian (Eds.) *Studies in Comparative Genocide*. New York: St. Martin's Press, Inc.

Adalian, Rouben P. (1999b) "Evidence, Source, and Authority: Documenting the Armenian Genocide Against the Background of Denial," pp. 67–77. In Roger W. Smith (Ed.) *Genocide: Essays Toward Understanding, Early-Warning, and Prevention*. Williamsburg, VA: Association of Genocide Scholars.

Adalian, Rouben P. (2002). *Historical Dictionary of Armenia*. Lanham, MD: Scarecrow Press, Inc.

Adalian, Rouben P. (2003). "American Diplomatic Correspondence in the Age of Mass Murder: Documents of the Armenian Genocide in the U.S. Archives," pp. 146–184. In Jay Winter (Ed.) *America and the Armenian Genocide of 1915*. Cambridge, UK: Cambridge University Press.

Ahmed, Feroz (1982). "Unionist Relations with the Greek, Armenian, and Jewish Communities of the Ottoman Empire, 1908–1914," pp. 387–434. In Benjamin Braude and Bernard Lewis (Eds.) *Christians and Jews in the Ottoman Empire, Volume I, The Central Lands*. New York: Holmes & Meier Publishers Inc.

Astourian, Stephan H. (1992). "Genocidal Process: Reflections on the Armeno-Turkish Polarization," pp. 53–79. In Richard G. Hovannisian (Ed.) *The Armenian Genocide: History, Politics, Ethics*. New York: St. Martin's Press.

Astourian, Stephan H. (1998). "Modern Turkish Identity and the Armenian Genocide," pp. 23–49. In Richard G. Hovannisian (Ed.) *Remembrance and Denial: The Case of the Armenian Genocide*. Detroit, MI: Wayne State University Press.

Baghdjian, Kevork K. (1987). *La Confiscation, par le Gouvernement Turc, des Biens Arméniens ... Dits "Abandonnés."* Montreal: Payette & Simms Inc.

Barsoumian, Hagop (1982). "The Dual Role of the Amira Class within the Ottoman Government and the Armenian Millet (1750–1850)," pp. 171–184. In Benjamin Braude and Bernard Lewis (Eds.) *Christians and Jews in the Ottoman Empire, Volume I, The Central Lands*. New York: Holmes & Meier Publishers Inc.

Beylerian, Arthur (1983). *Les Grande Puissances l'Empire Ottoman et les Arméniens dans les Archives Francaises (1914–1918): Recueil de documents*. Paris: Publications de la Sorbonne.

Bliss, Edwin M. (1982). *Turkey and the Armenian Atrocities*. Fresno, CA: Meshag Publishers. [Originally published in 1896.]

Bournoutian, George A. (2002). *A Concise History of the Armenian People*. Costa Mesa, CA: Mazda Publishers.

Braude, Benjamin, and Lewis, Bernard (Eds.) (1982). *Christians and Jews in the Ottoman Empire, Volume 1, The Central Lands*. New York: Holmes & Meier Publishers Inc.

Charny, Israel W. (1999). *Encyclopedia of Genocide*. Santa Barbara: ABC CLIO. (See multiple entries on the Armenian genocide.)

Dadrian, Vahakn N. (1986). "The Naim-Andonian Documents on the World War I Destruction of Ottoman Armenians: The Anatomy of a Genocide." *International Journal of Middle East Studies*, 18(3):311–360.

Dadrian, Vahakn N. (1989). "Genocide as a Problem of National and International Law: The World War I Armenian Case and its Contemporary Legal Ramifications." *Yale Journal of International Law*, 14(2):221–334.

Dadrian, Vahakn N. (1991). "The Documentation of the World War I Armenian Massacres in the Proceedings of the Turkish Military Tribunal." *International Journal of Middle East Studies*, 23(4): 549–576.

Dadrian, Vahakn N. (1994). "Documentation of the Armenian Genocide in German and Austrian Source," pp. 77–125. In Israel W. Charny (Ed.), *The Widening Circle of Genocide: A Critical Bibliographic Review*. New Brunswick, NJ: Transaction Publishers.

Dadrian, Vahakn N. (1995). *The History of the Armenian Genocide: Ethnic Conflict from the Balkans to Anatolia to the Caucasus*. Providence, RI: Berghahn Books.

Dadrian, Vahakn N. (1996). *German Responsibility in the Armenian Genocide: A Review of the Historical Evidence of German Complicity*. Cambridge, MA: Blue Crane Books.

Dadrian, Vahakn N. (1999). *Warrant for Genocide: Key Elements of Turko-Armenian Conflict*. New Brunswick, NJ: Transaction Publishers.

Davis, Leslie A. (1989). *The Slaughterhouse Province: An American Diplomat's Report on the Armenian Genocide, 1915–1917*. New Rochelle, NY: Aristide D. Caratzas, Publisher.

Derogy, Jacques (1990). *Resistance and Revenge: The Armenian Assassination of the Turkish Leaders Responsible for the 1915 Massacres and Deportations*. New Brunswick, NJ: Transaction Publishers.

Dinkel, Christoph (1991). "German Officers and the Armenian Genocide," *Armenian Review,* 44(1):77–133.

Dobkin, Marjorie Housepian (1986). "What Genocide? What Holocaust? News from Turkey, 1915–1923: A Case Study," pp. 97–109. In Richard Hovannisian (Ed.) *The Armenian Genocide in Perspective*. New Brunswick, NJ: Transaction Books.

Fein, Helen (1979). *Accounting for Genocide: National Responses and Jewish Victimization during the Holocaust*. New York: The Free Press.

Foreign Policy Institute (1982). *The Armenian Issue in Nine Questions and Answers*. Ankara: FPI.

Gibbons, Herbert Adams (1916). *The Blackest Page of Modern History. Events in Armenia in 1915. The Facts and the Responsibilities*. New York and London: G.P. Putnam's Sons.

Great Britain, Parliament (1916). *The Treatment of the Armenians in the Ottoman Empire: Documents Presented to Viscount Grey of Fallodon, Secretary of State for Foreign Affairs*. Preface by Viscount Bryce. London: Sir Joseph Causton & Sons.

Greene, Frederick Davis (1896). *Armenian Massacres and Turkish Tyranny*. Philadelphia and Chicago: International Publishing Co.

Guroian, Vigen (1986). "Collective Responsibility and Official Excuse Making: The Case of the Turkish Genocide of the Armenians," pp. 135–52. In Richard Hovannisian (Ed.) *The Armenian Genocide in Perspective*. New Brunswick, NJ: Transaction Books.

Gürün, Kâmuran (1985). *The Armenian File: The Myth of Innocence Exposed*. London and Nicosia, Istanbul: K. Rustem & Bros. and Weidenfeld and Nicolson Ltd.

Hairapetian, Armen (1984). "'Race Problems' and the Armenian Genocide: The State Department File," and "Documents: The State Department File." *Armenian Review*, 37(1):41–145.

Horowitz, Irving Louis (1982). *Taking Lives: Genocide and State Power*. New Brunswick, NJ: Transaction Books.

Hovannisian, Richard G. (1967). *Armenia on the Road to Independence 1918*. Berkeley: University of California Press.

Hovannisian, Richard G. (1986a). "The Armenian Genocide and Patterns of Denial," pp. 111–33. In Richard G. Hovannisian (Ed.) *The Armenian Genocide in Perspective*. New Brunswick, NJ: Transaction Books.

Hovannisian, Richard G. (Ed.) (1986b). *The Armenian Genocide in Perspective*. New Brunswick, NJ: Transaction Books.

Hovannisian, Richard G. (1986c). "The Historical Dimensions of the Armenian Question, 1878–1923," pp. 19–41. In Richard G. Hovannisian (Ed.) *The Armenian Genocide in Perspective*. New Brunswick, NJ: Transaction Books.

Hovannisian, Richard G. (1987). *The Armenian Holocaust: A Bibliography Relating to the Deportations, Massacres, and Dispersion of the Armenian People, 1915–1923*. Cambridge, MA: National Association for Armenian Studies and Research.

Hovannisian, Richard G. (1992). "Intervention and Shades of Altruism During the Armenian Genocide," pp. 173–207. In Richard G. Hovannisian (Ed.) *The Armenian Genocide: History, Politics, Ethics*. New York: St. Martin's Press.

Kerr, Stanley E. (1973). *The Lions of Marash: Personal Experiences with American Near East Relief, 1919–1922*. Albany: State University of New York Press.

Kinross, Lord (1964). *Ataturk: The Birth of a Nation*. London: Weidenfeld and Nicolson.

Kloian, Richard D. (1985). *The Armenian Genocide: News Accounts from the American Press: 1915–1922*. Berkeley, CA: Anto Printing.

Kuper, Leo (1981). *Genocide: Its Political Use in the Twentieth Century*. New Haven, CT: Yale University Press.

Kuper, Leo (1986). "The Turkish Genocide of Armenians, 1915–1917," pp. 43–59. In Richard G. Hovannisian (Ed.) *The Armenian Genocide in Perspective*. New Brunswick, NJ: Transaction Books.

Lang, David Marshall (1970). *Armenia: Cradle of Civilization*. London: George Allen & Unwin.

Lang, David Marshal (1981). *The Armenians: A People in Exile*. London: George Allen & Unwin.

Lepsius, Johannes (1987). *Rapport Secret sur les Massacres d'Arménie (1915–1916)*. Paris: Edition Payot.

Libaridian, Gerard (1985). "The Ideology of the Young Turk Movement," pp. 37–49. In Gerard Libaridian (Ed.) *A Crime of Silence, The Armenian Genocide: Permanent Peoples' Tribunal*. London: Zed Books.

Libaridian, Gerard (1987). "The Ultimate Repression: The Genocide of the Armenians, 1915–1917," pp. 203–35. In Isidor Wallimann and Michael N. Dobkowski (Eds.) *Genocide and the Modern Age: Etiology and Case Studies of Mass Death*. Westport, CT: Greenwood Press.

McCarthy, Justin (1983). *Muslims and Minorities: The Population of Ottoman Anatolia and the End of the Empire*. New York: New York University Press.

Melson, Robert (1986). "Provocation or Nationalism: A Critical Inquiry into the Armenian Genocide of 1915," pp. 61–84. In Richard G. Hovannisian (Ed.) *The Armenian Genocide in Perspective*. New Brunswick, NJ: Transaction Books.

Miller, Donald E., and Miller, Lorna Touryan (1993). *Survivors: An Oral History of the Armenian Genocide*. Berkeley: University of California Press.

Morgenthau, Henry (1918). *Ambassador Morgenthau's Story*. Garden City, New York: Doubleday, Page and Co. [Reprinted in 2003 by Wayne State University Press, Detroit, MI.]

Nalbandian, Louise (1963). *The Armenian Revolutionary Movement*. Berkeley: University of California Press.

Nassibian, Akaby (1984). *Britain and the Armenian Question 1915–1923*. New York: St. Martin's Press.

Ohandjanian, Artem (Ed.) (1988). *The Armenian Genocide, Volume 2 Documentation*. Munich: Institute fur Armenische Fragen.

Parla, Taha (1985). *The Social and Political Thought of Ziya Gökalp 1876–1924*. Leiden: E.J. Brill.

Power, Samantha (2002). *"A Problem From Hell": America and the Age of Genocide*. New York: Basic Books.

Ramsaur, Jr., Ernest Edmondson (1957). *The Young Turks: Prelude to the Revolution of 1908*. New York: Russell & Russell.

Sachar, Howard M. (1969). *The Emergence of the Middle East 1914–1924*. New York: Alfred A. Knopf.

Sanasarian, Eliz (1989). "Gender Distinction in the Genocide Process: A Preliminary Study of the Armenian Case." *Holocaust and Genocide Studies*, 4(4):449–61.

Shaw, Stanford J., and Shaw, Ezel Kural (1977). *History of the Ottoman Empire and Modern Turkey. Volume 2*. New York: Cambridge University Press.

Smith, Roger (1989) "Genocide and Denial: The Armenian Case and Its Implications." *Armenian Review*, 42(1):1–38.

Staub, Ervin (1989). *The Roots of Evil: The Origins of Genocide and Other Group Violence*. New York: Cambridge University Press.

Ternon, Yves (1981). *The Armenians: History of a Genocide*. Delmar, NY: Caravan Books.

Totten, Samuel (1991). "The Ottoman Genocide of the Armenians," pp. 7–43. In Samuel Totten (Ed.) *First-Person Accounts of Genocidal Acts Committed in the Twentieth Century: An Annotated Bibliography*. Westport, CT: Greenwood Press.

Toynbee, Arnold J. (Ed.) (1916). *The Treatment of Armenians in the Ottoman Empire, 1915–1916*. London: Sir Joseph Causton and Sons, Limited. [Preface by Viscount Bryce.] [Reprinted in Beirut, Lebanon, by G. Doniguian & Sons, 1979.]

Trumpener, Ulrich (1968). *Germany and the Ottoman Empire 1914–1918*. New Jersey: Princeton University Press. [Reprinted in 1989 by Caravan Books in Delmar, NY.]

Uras, Esat (1988). *The Armenians in History and the Armenian Question*. Istanbul: Foundation for the Establishment and Promotion of Centers for Historical Research and Documentation, and Istanbul Research Center.

Walker, Christopher J. (1980). *Armenia: The Survival of a Nation*. New York: St. Martin's Press.

Werfel, Franz. (1934). *The Forty Days of Musa Dagh*. New York: The Modern Library.

Winter, Jay (2003). *America and the Armenian Genocide of 1915*. Cambridge: Cambridge University Press.

Ye'or, Bat (Y. Masriya) (1985). *The Dhimmi: Jews and Christians Under Islam*. Teaneck, NJ: Fairleigh Dickenson University Press.

Zürcher, Erik J. (1998) *Turkey A Modern History*. London and New York: I.B. Tauris & Co Ltd.

Ukraine

CHAPTER 3

Soviet Man-Made Famine in Ukraine

JAMES E. MACE

It is now generally accepted that in 1932–1933 several million peasants — most of them Ukrainians living in Ukraine and the traditionally Cossack territories of the North Caucasus (now the Krasnodar, Stavropol, and Rostov on the Don regions of the Russian Federation) — starved to death because the government of the Soviet Union seized with unprecedented force and thoroughness the 1932 crop and foodstuffs from the agricultural population (Mace, 1984; Conquest, 1986). After over half a century of denial, in January 1990 the Communist Party of Ukraine adopted a special resolution admitting that the Ukrainian Famine had indeed occurred, cost millions of lives, had been artificially brought about by official actions, and that Stalin and his associates bore criminal responsibility for those actions (*Holod*, 1990, pp. 3–4).

The Ukrainian Famine corresponded in time with a reversal of official policies that had hitherto permitted significant self-expression of the USSR's non-Russian nations. During and after the Famine, non-Russian national self-assertion was labeled bourgeois nationalism and suppressed. The elites who had been associated with these policies were eliminated (Mace, 1983, pp. 264–301). The authorities of the period denied that a famine was taking place at the time, sought to discredit reports on the factual situation, insofar as possible prevented the starving from traveling to areas where food was available, and refused all offers of aid to the starving (Conquest, 1986; U.S. Commission on the Ukraine Famine, 1988: vi–xxv). They were assisted in this policy of denial by certain Western journalists, most notably Walter Duranty of *The New York Times* (Taylor, 1990, pp. 210–23).

In order to understand the Ukrainian Famine, a brief excursion into the period that preceded it is necessary. Despite their numerical strength as the second-largest of the Slavic-speaking nations, Ukrainians may be classed with what Czech scholar Miroslav Hroch (1985) designated the "small nations" of Europe. Such nations "were in subjection for such a long period that the relation of subjection took on a structural character;" that is, the majority of the ruling class belonged to the ruling nation, while the subjugated nation possessed an incomplete social structure partially or entirely lacking its own ruling class (Hroch, 1985, p. 9). The Ukrainians were basically a nation of peasants, their national movement being led by a numerically small intelligentsia. As in other areas occupied by subject nations in Imperial Russia and early Soviet history, the local nobility, bourgeoisie, and urban population in Ukraine were overwhelmingly Russian or Russian-speaking (Liber, 1990, pp. 12–15).

In the 19th century, Ukrainians underwent a national revival similar to that of Czechs and other "small nations"; that is, romantic scholarly excursions into the local language and history, along with the creation of a vernacular literature, brought a spreading sense of local patriotism and national identity that in turn gave way to political aspirations and, ultimately, territorial home rule. Yet, when in 1925 Stalin wrote, "The national question is, *according to its essence,* a question of the peasantry" (Stalin, 1946–1951, Volume 7, p. 72), this held true for almost all the non-Russian peoples of the Soviet Union and certainly for Ukrainians.

The social development of Ukrainians in the Russian Empire had been retarded by extraordinarily repressive policies. In 1863, the Imperial Russian government responded to what it perceived as a nascent threat of "Ukrainian separatism" by banning education and publications (except for folk songs and historical documents) in the Ukrainian language, declaring it to be a substandard variant of Russian. This ban was broadened in 1876 to eliminate the modest exemptions in the earlier measure and remained in effect until 1905 (Savchenko, 1930). After 1905, a Ukrainian language press enjoyed a brief flowering in central Ukraine, but creeping reimposition of the old prohibitions all but eliminated it within a few years. Because repressive tsarist policies had stunted the growth of social differentiation within Ukrainian society, Ukrainian activists could expect to gain mass support only among the peasantry. Consequently, when Ukrainian political parties evolved in Imperial Russia at the turn of the century, they assumed a revolutionary socialist character, and the form in which Ukrainian political aspirations gained majority support during the Russian Revolution of 1917 was through the agrarian socialism of the Ukrainian Party of Socialist Revolutionaries (Hermaize, 1926; Khrystiuk, 1921–22, Volume 1, p. 35).

After the collapse of the Russian imperial authority in 1917, the national movements that attempted to establish local governments throughout the former empire's non-Russian periphery, including the Ukrainian movement, drew most of their mass support from the village, while in the cities various groups competed more or less as they did in Russia proper.

The group that seized power in the center, Lenin's Bolsheviks, mistrusted the peasants as petty property owners and relied on forced requisitions of agricultural produce in order to keep the urban population fed. Thus, the national struggle between Russians ("Red" or "White") and the subject peoples was at the same time a social struggle of the countryside versus the town, where even the working class was drawn from the oppressor nation or had assimilated its culture. As Ukrainian Communist spokesmen recognized as early as 1920, the Russian-speaking worker, who provided the main source of support for Soviet rule in Ukraine, sneered at the Ukrainian village and wanted nothing to do with it (Mace, 1983, pp. 68–69). During the wars that followed the Russian Revolution of 1917, a Soviet regime had been imposed on Ukraine by Russia against the will of most of Ukraine's inhabitants, an absolute majority of whom had voted in free elections for groups that supported Ukrainian self-rule (Borys, 1980, p. 170, table).

In order to overcome rural resistance to the Soviet order, in 1921 Lenin proclaimed the New Economic Policy (NEP), which ended forced procurements and allowed a private market in which agricultural producers could sell what they had produced. In 1923, in order to overcome the continued national resistance of the non-Russian countryside, Lenin proclaimed a policy of indigenization (*korenizatsiia*), which attempted to give non-Russian Soviet regimes a veneer of national legitimacy by promoting the spread of the local language and culture in the cities, recruiting local people into the regime, ordering Russian officials to learn the local language, and fostering a broad range of cultural activities (Mace, 1983, pp. 87–95; Liber, 1990, pp. 33–46).

The Ukrainian Famine of 1932–1933 occurred within the context of the so-called "Stalinist Revolution from Above," a violent experiment in social transformation in which state-orchestrated paranoia about internal and external enemies was used to blame shortcomings on the machinations of class enemies. Like Nazism, Stalinism attempted to explain the world as a struggle between different categories of people, some of whom were considered inherently deleterious and whose elimination was an essential prerequisite toward the attainment of a new and better state of affairs. As a degenerated offshoot of Marxism, Stalinism attempted to explain the world by using class categories, rather than the racial ones employed by the Nazis. But what Hitler and Stalin had in common was a dualistic view of human society as composed of two implacably hostile forces: the "good" force destined for victory (Aryans for Hitler and the proletariat for Stalin), which could only liberate itself and achieve its destiny by destroying utterly the forces of evil (for Hitler, Jews and Gypsies, which he considered racially polluting elements, and for Stalin, representatives of "exploiter classes").

A major difference between Stalinism and racism (like Nazism) is that racism at least knows how to define what it hates: people who look or speak differently or have different ancestors. Class warfare, however, is a sociological concept. Sociological categories are much easier to manipulate than racial ones, especially when applied in and by a state that claims, as did Stalin's, a monopoly on truth and science thanks to its "correct" understanding and application of a theory based on claims of holistic scientism; that is, claims that it explains everything with the certainty of (pseudo) scientific laws. By redefining and manipulating such notions as class enemies and enemies of the people, and objectively serving the interests of such dark forces, Stalin was able to declare practically any group or individual worthy of destruction. This enabled Stalin to reduce Marxism, one of the great (if flawed) intellectual systems of the 19th century, to the level of a sanctioning ideology for perhaps the paradigmatic example of what Leo Kuper (1990) has called the genocide state.

Marxism views history as class struggle. It holds that modern capitalism is defined by the struggle between proletarians and capitalists, the former being destined to triumph over the latter and thereby create a new socialist stage of human history in which the economic exploitation of one person by another will be abolished. Independent small-holding peasants are viewed as peripheral in this struggle, a petty capitalist holdover of an earlier era. Leninists saw an inevitable process of class differentiation among peasants into three strata: the relatively wealthier *kulaks* (Ukrainian *kurkuls*) or village exploiters, the middle peasants or subsistence farmers who did not hire labor or depend on outside employment to get by, and the poor peasants, who could only make ends meet by working for others and thus were at least partially a rural proletarian. The middle and poor peasants were often lumped together as the *toiling peasantry* in order to mark them off from the kulaks. However, such a division of the peasantry into such categories was arbitrary, and just who was a kulak was never defined with any precision (Lewin, 1985, pp. 121–41).

As for the national question, most varieties of Marxism reject nationalism as a species of false consciousness that reflects the interests of an exploitative bourgeois class by convincing the exploited that they owe loyalty to their capitalist-ruled nation rather than to the international working class. Orthodox Marxists believe that only internationalism can serve the interests of the working class. There have been many conflicting policy prescriptions advocated by Marxists designed to overcome nationalistic prejudices and achieve the internationalist unity of the toiling classes.

Just as nationalism can have a variety of meanings, so can internationalism. In the pre-Stalinist period, the Soviet authorities found what they considered the "correct" internationalist approach to building socialism by attempting to combat the imperial pretensions of Russians (the dominant group) and by assisting the formerly subject peoples of the Russian Empire to overcome the legacy of colonial domination by rebuilding their various national cultures and societies — under the Party's guidance, of course. This ideological prescription actually reflected political necessity: Before the adoption of such a policy, non-Russian peasant dissatisfaction had threatened political stability in wide areas of the new Soviet Union. But there were certainly other Marxist views of internationalism. For example, Rosa Luxemburg advocated a view often criticized as "national nihilism" when she argued that national self-determination was a chimera: It was utopian so long as capitalist exploitation survived and would be rendered irrelevant once socialism had brought about the final end of all forms of exploitation (Luxemburg, 1986, pp. 308–14).

Once an ideology comes to power, theory becomes the stuff of practical politics, influencing and being influenced by considerations of power. *Ukrainization,* the Ukrainian version of indigenization, went further than elsewhere in the Soviet Union because roughly 30 million Ukrainians were several times more numerous than any other single national group. On the eve of the Famine they constituted about two-fifths of all non-Russian inhabitants of the USSR. The policies of indigenization, designed to placate the national aspirations of the non-Russian overwhelmingly peasant nations, went hand-in-hand with the limited free market policies of the New Economic Policy, which were designed to satisfy the economic aspirations of both Russian and non-Russian peasants.

With indigenization having legitimized national priorities among non-Russian Communists and the high politics in Moscow centering on a protracted struggle for power, throughout the 1920s national Communists in the constituent republics of the USSR accumulated a large measure of autonomy from central dictates. When, at the end of the decade, Joseph Stalin emerged victorious in the succession struggle, he abruptly changed course by announcing the crash collectivization of agriculture on the basis of the liquidation (that is, destruction) of the *kulaks* as a class.

Collectivization meant forcing millions of small farmers into large collective farms, which many peasants saw — not without reason — as a reinstitution of serfdom, the only difference being that the state was now taking the place of the nobleman who owned the peasants' grandparents. Forcing the majority of the population to restructure their lives in a way they did not wish to meant provoking a degree of hostility, which rendered concessions that had been designed to placate the non-Russian peasants on national grounds politically irrelevant.

The changed political situation enabled Stalin to pursue four objectives toward the non-Russians. Donald Treadgold (1964) rightly has summarized them as follows: (1) the elimination of centrifugal pressures by stifling local nationalism; (2) subversion of neighboring states by having members of a given Soviet nationality conduct propaganda among their co-nationals in neighboring areas; (3) "economic and social transformation designed to destroy native society and substitute a social system susceptible of control by Moscow"; and (4) the economic exploitation of non-Russian areas (pp. 297–98).

Transforming society by force far exceeded the capacity of any traditional authoritarian state. It required the mobilization and motivation of mass constituencies who could be called upon to do the regime's will. Starting with a phony war scare in 1927 and followed by show trials designed to point out various social groups (managers and engineers held over from the old regime, academicians, people who had been associated with national or religious movements, etc.) as nests of plotters in the pay of world capitalism, a massive propaganda campaign was carried out designed to convince people that the Soviet Union was under siege by the hostile capitalist world that encircled it. Soviet society had to catch up with the capitalist West or be crushed. The crash collectivization of agriculture was portrayed as essential in order to do this.

In order to expropriate kulaks, enforce collectivization, and take possession of agricultural produce, the authorities mobilized anyone they could. As a self-proclaimed workers' state, it was logical that the regime would turn first to the workers and trade unions for personnel to impose its will. The entire network of officially sanctioned social organizations was mobilized. The resistance they faced was interpreted in class terms as kulak terrorism, for who but a kulak or his agent could oppose the socialist transformation of the countryside? Ultimately, any problem was blamed on "kulaks" or their "agents," and repressive policies were justified by the need to combat an enemy presence that was ever more broadly defined. The village itself became an object of official mistrust as tens of thousands of factory workers were issued revolvers and sent into villages with the power to completely reorganize life as well as to circumvent or abolish village-level governmental bodies. Workers were sent from factories, and sometimes a factory would be named "patron" of a given number of villages; that is, the factory would be assigned villages in which to enforce collectivization and seize food.

Local "activists," that is, individuals whose positions gave them an active role in officially sanctioned social and political life, would also be given these responsibilities. Special peasant "tow" (*buksyr*) brigades were organized and given the task of "taking the kulaks in tow," which meant ejecting those selected by the local authorities from their houses or searching for and expropriating concealed foodstuffs. The members of these brigades did not always volunteer; sometimes county or district authorities would simply call up the able-bodied men in one village to act as a tow brigade in a neighboring village. A schoolteacher, for example, had no choice but to take part in the work of the local activists. At the height of the Famine, when most peasants were physically incapable of work, lines in front of city stores were raided from time to time, and the unfortunates rounded up were sent to weed sugar beets (U.S. Commission on the Ukraine Famine, 1988, pp. 448–49).

The essence of the collective farm system was official control over agricultural production and distribution. The state's "procurement" of agricultural produce was carried out by force such that procurements (purchases) really became forced requisitions. Since, however, the collective farm was, in theory, a private cooperative, not a state enterprise, the authorities assumed no responsibility for the welfare of the collective farmers. Whatever the state required came from the "first proceeds" of the harvest; that is, the state took its quota first. If there was anything left, it went first to what was needed to run the farm, such as seed reserves, and what was left over was then shared among the collective farmers according to the labor days (*trudodni*) they had earned (Jasny, 1949, pp. 64–85).

These "labor days" were not actual days worked. Rather, they were allocated according to a complex formula designed to calculate the different values of different kinds of labor by converting all types of labor on the farm into the Marxist concept of simple labor time. Skilled workers, like a tractor driver, might earn two labor days for each day worked, while a simple farmer without any particular skill might have to work two days in order to earn one labor day. This, however, was of no consequence if there was nothing left; in that case, of course, the labor days of the collective farmers were worthless.

At the time of the Famine, roughly 20 percent of the Ukrainian peasantry was still outside the collective farms. They had their own household quotas, which were imposed by local authorities. If they could not meet a given quota, they were fined, and their farms searched with the aid of metal prods.

Collectivization led to a crisis in agricultural production that the regime met sometimes with force and sometimes with promises to overcome "errors" or "excesses" or "deviations" from the Party's "Leninist general line." Such shortcomings were always blamed on subordinate officials, never on the policies of the Communist Party and Soviet state, which were held to be infallible. The first agricultural procurement campaign after crash collectivization, that of 1930, was met, thanks to a fortunate harvest. The following year, the quota was not met in spite of considerable force that succeeded only in creating pockets of starvation. In the first half of 1932, the regime announced that there had been a crop failure in parts of the Volga Basin and Asiatic Russia and sent aid there from other regions. In May, agricultural quotas for the coming crop were lowered to about the level of what had been obtained from the 1931 crop. Various officials were denounced for having used excessive force in seizing agricultural produce and promises were made that such "distortions" of the official policy would not be tolerated in the future. Some local officials who had been particularly harsh toward peasants in their charge were publicly tried and punished. For a few weeks, even Ukraine received limited food aid.

Then, in the summer of 1932, with Ukraine on the verge of mass starvation, Stalin abruptly changed course. At a Ukrainian Communist Party conference in July, amid reports that the situation in the Ukrainian countryside was growing desperate, Stalin's top assistants — Prime Minister Viacheslav Molotov and Agriculture Minister Lazar Kaganovich — announced that Ukraine's quotas for bread grain deliveries would stand at the level announced the previous May. But once the harvest was in, there simply wasn't enough grain to meet the quota. The Ukrainian authorities appealed to Moscow for an end to the grain seizures, but to no avail. Throughout the fall of 1932, Stalin sent various high officials to Ukraine to supervise the local Communists. In November, bread that had been "advanced" to the collective farmers at harvest time was declared to have been illegally distributed and was therefore seized. In order to make up for shortfalls elsewhere, those farms that met their quotas were subjected to supplementary quotas of foodstuffs that had to be delivered to the state. Local officials were ordered to determine how much bread there was in every collective farm and to put it toward the quota.

On December 14, Stalin's intimate involvement in the Ukrainian Famine became clear when he called the top leaders of Ukraine, the North Caucasus, and the Western (Smolensk) District to Moscow. The meeting produced a secret decree signed by Stalin as head of the Party and Molotov as head of government. While the leader of the Western District was let off with a simple admonition to meet its quotas, the Ukrainian and North Caucasus representatives were blasted for having failed to root out Ukrainian nationalism:

As a result of the extremely weak efforts and lack of revolutionary vigilance of a number of local Party organizations in Ukraine and the North Caucasus, in a substantial portion of these organizations counterrevolutionary elements — kulaks, former officers, Petliurists, adherents of the Kuban Rada, and so forth — have been able to worm their way into the collective farms as chairmen or as influential members of their administration, bookkeepers, store managers, threshing brigade leaders, and so forth, were able to worm their way into village councils, agricultural offices, cooperatives, and attempted to direct the work of these organizations against the interests of the proletarian state and the Party's policy, attempted to organize a counterrevolutionary movement, to sabotage the grain procurements, and to sabotage the sowing, the All-Union Communist Party Central Committee and Council of Peoples Commissars of the USSR direct the Communist Party and government leadership of Ukraine and the North Caucasus to resolutely root out the counterrevolutionary elements by means of their arrest, long sentences of confinement in concentration camps, and not excluding application of the highest measure of legality (that is, execution) in the most criminal cases (*Postanova*, 1991, p. 78).

The decree went on to name officials on the local level who had failed to make their quotas, mentioning the officials by name and detailing which of them were to be given prison sentences and which of them were to be shot. In addition, Ukrainian officials were condemned for their "mechanistic" (that is, overzealous) implementation of Ukrainization, while Ukrainization was ordered halted in the North Caucasus (*Postanova*, 1991).

A week later, Stalin's representatives in Ukraine ordered *the seizure of even the seed that had been put aside for spring planting.* In January 1933, Stalin took direct control of the Ukrainian Communist Party apparatus. His appointees, accompanied by tens of thousands of subordinates, initiated a campaign that led to the destruction of nationally self-assertive Ukrainian elites, the end of the Ukrainization policy and virtually all Ukrainian cultural self-expression, and the gradual return to the exclusive use of the Russian language in Ukraine's cities and educational institutions (U.S. Commission on the Ukraine Famine, 1988: xi–xvii; *Holod*, 1990, pp. 148–235).

The food seized, people began to starve. Millions died either from starvation — an agonizingly slow process in which the body literally consumes itself until the muscles of the chest can no longer lift the rib cage to inflate the lungs and the victim suffocates — or, more commonly, from diseases that in such a weakened condition the body can no longer fend off. But to report deaths from starvation or from diseases like typhus, which are associated with famine, was considered anti-Soviet. Physicians used euphemisms like vitamin or protein deficiency (which does usually accompany caloric deficiency), heart failure (because the heart stops), diarrhea (from eating plants the body cannot digest), or "exhaustion of the organism" (Gannt, 1937, pp. 147–162).

Estimates of the number of victims in Ukraine range from 3 to 8 million. According to the long-suppressed 1937 census, released only in 1991, in 1937 Ukraine had a million fewer inhabitants than in 1926, 3 million fewer than official estimates of the early 1930s, which were probably not far off the mark (*Vsesoiuznaia,* 1991, p. 28, table). Using these and other long-suppressed figures, demographers in the former Soviet Union have calculated that, while the population of the USSR increased from 148.7 million in 1927 to 162.5 million in 1937, during the year 1933 the population decreased by 5.9 million. Their figures further suggest that the number of victims of famine in 1933 was between 7.2 and 8.1 million (summarized in Ellman, 1991, pp. 375–79). Given that all but 1 or 2 million of these victims perished in Ukraine, the number of victims of the Ukrainian Famine would be in the range of 5 to 7 million.

As living conditions worsened, the authorities expanded the system of hard currency stores, the *torgsin.* The name was an abbreviation for the Russian phrase, *torgovlia s inostrantsami* (trade with foreigners), because only foreigners had the right to possess precious metals and convertible currency. In exchange for food, these stores helped extract the last valuables remaining in the countryside. Often a small piece of jewelry, a gold tooth, or a concealed silver or gold coin meant the difference between life and death.

The famine had a major long-range impact on Ukrainians. The adoption in 1932–1933 of an internal passport system from which peasants were excluded meant that the agricultural population could not leave the countryside without official permission. This meant attaching the peasantry to the land in a way not entirely different from traditional serfdom. The psychological traumatization inevitable in any situation of mass mortality was undoubtedly compounded by a policy of official denial extending to the most remote village. At the height of the Famine, Stalin adopted the slogan: "Life has become better; life has become more fun," and even the starving had to repeat it. To speak openly of everyday reality meant running the risk of punishment for propagating anti-Soviet propaganda.

Children were encouraged to inform on their parents, and Pavlik Morozov, a boy who had informed on his parents and was killed by villagers after the parents' subsequent arrest, was held up as a model for

Soviet young people. As a result, parents became afraid to talk openly in front of their own children. While Stalin's rapid industrialization brought millions of Ukrainian peasants to Ukraine's cities, mines, and factories, the abandonment of policies promoting the use of the Ukrainian language there often meant the rapid linguistic and cultural Russification of these new workers and city-dwellers.

As a result of the Famine and accompanying destruction of national elites, the Ukrainian nation was literally crushed. Their leadership (including the natural village leadership, the more prosperous and industrious peasants) was destroyed. Their language and culture, which had made significant inroads in the cities in the 1920s, was largely pushed back to the countryside whence it came. And in the countryside, about one out of every five people had perished. As a result, the development of Ukrainians as a nation was violently and traumatically set back.

The Ukrainians might never have recovered as a nation had it not been for Stalin's 1939 pact with Hitler, by which the Soviet Union annexed Western Ukraine as its share of the dismembered Polish Republic. Western Ukraine contained areas that had never been under Russian rule and were consequently the most developed and nationally conscious regions of Ukraine. The joining of Western Ukraine to the devastated central and eastern Ukrainian territories largely undermined Stalin's deconstruction of the Ukrainian nation in the 1930s, paving the way for Ukrainian independence in the 1990s.

Drawing lessons from history is always a risky business, but surely one of the principle lessons of the Ukrainian Famine has to do with the dangers of pseudo-scientific totalitarian ideologies. Such ideologies, which often claim scientific validity, explain problems within a given society by blaming them on the presence of permanent enemies that by virtue of their very existence prevent the bulk of society from achieving its destiny, living the good life, or otherwise solving its problems. Such enemies may be racial, national, political, or social, but however defined, such ideologies may easily be used as warrants for mass murder and genocide. The monopolies or near-monopolies of propaganda, reward, and coercion that totalitarian societies possess in turn make it possible for totalitarian regimes to attract sufficient mass participation to carry out such designs.

Moreover, as George Orwell demonstrated over a half a century ago in 1984, the totalitarian monopoly of official expression allowed the Stalin regime to define and redefine concepts in order to radically change their meaning. Thus, in the Ukrainian case, class categories were manipulated in order to redefine national issues as class ones. Thus, the Ukrainian Famine further shows that the Fascist Right has no monopoly on genocide. Even ideologies espousing internationalism and social justice can be manipulated so as to target ethnic groups by redefining their terms to mean whatever might seem expedient at a given moment.

The refusal of even the moderate Left to perceive the full horror of Stalinism also carries lessons about the selective perception of evil. While it is understandable that one is more charitable to actions taken by regimes that profess adherence to "one's own" side of the political spectrum, civilized adherents of both the Left and the Right should realize that the most important issue of political life is not between continuity and change but between those who uphold such universal human values as the right of living people to remain among the living and those who do not recognize such a right for members of a given out-group. For those who profess humane values, the willingness to countenance the death of millions for their goals ceases to have anything in common with political progress: it is simply mass murder on an unspeakable scale.

Eyewitness Accounts: Soviet Man-Made Famine in Ukraine

Account 1

S. Lozovy, "What Happened in Hadyach County," pp. 246–55. In S. Pidhainy, et al. (Eds.) *The Black Deeds of the Kremlin: A White Book.* Toronto and Detroit, 1953–1955. *The Black Deeds* is the classic collection of eyewitness accounts of the Famine, compiled by the Democratic Association of Ukrainians Who had Been Repressed By the Soviets (DOBRUS), which was associated with the Ukrainian Revolutionary Democratic Party, a socialist group formed after World War II by Ukrainians who had emigrated from Central and Eastern Ukraine.

Having received from comrade Kolotov, boss of the county seat, instructions to establish a commune, the chairman of the village soviet, Tereshko Myshchachenko, took great pains to carry them out. He gave them wide publicity and, as a further incentive, put his name first on the list of commune farmers. Another reason was comrade Gapon from the city of Orel who certainly would have been made chairman if Tereshko had failed in his "duties."

This was in 1930. The village of Kharkivtsi then numbered 780 individual farmers. Out of this number, only four followed his lead and joined the commune. It was easy for them to do so because they had never had places of their own, or else had sold their houses shortly before the instructions were received.

But this venture was stillborn. Even these four, having tasted commune life for one season, turned against it and began to think of leaving it.

The authorities, aware of the fact that people were reluctant to join a commune, changed their tune and began to encourage the idea of a collective farm. With this object in view, there appeared Demen Karasyuk from the city of Tambov. He spoke a Russian-Ukrainian jargon, while his family spoke only Russian. Karasyuk appropriated the house of *seredniak* [middle peasant] Brychko and sent him to Siberia, where the poor fellow was worked to death six months later. Thus began collectivization and the liquidation of *kurkuls* [*kulaks*] as a class.

Rallies were held in the center of the village each day, at which Communists from the county seat agitated for collectives. But people did not want to join them and said so, arguing that the government had divided the land against them. And every day GPU agents arrested two or three men.

The village soviet, seeing that people did not want to attend these rallies, hired a boy of 12 to go around with a list and ask people to sign promises that they would attend the gathering. The measure was not successful because men would hide, and their wives would sign their own names arguing that the law gave both sexes equal rights. They also caused a lot of confusion at the rallies by making a terrible noise. The GPU stopped this by sentencing Maria Treba to one year in jail.

The Communists changed their tactics. The farmers were called out individually. Under threat of reprisals they were asked to sign papers agreeing to have their property nationalized.

The farmers began to sell their livestock and horses. Their unwillingness to join the collective was stimulated by the fact that people from the neighboring counties of Komyshany and Myrhorod, from villages already collectivized a year ago, came to the village begging for bread. This was an indication as to what they could expect from a collective farm and "Communist Socialism."

The taxes had to be paid in kind and those who paid them received additional demands, sometimes even greater than the first time, to pay with their products, especially grain.

Seeing no end to this the people began to hide their grain and potatoes if they had any left. A new arrival from the Hadyach Center, comrade Shukhman, who was commissioned to collect grain in three or four counties, gave orders to form *buksyr* [tow] brigades who had authority to manhandle every farmer until he gave all his grain to the state. These brigades were supplied with special tools made in advance in some factory to facilitate the "grain hunt." These were steel rods about 5/8 inch in diameter, three to ten feet long, with one end sharpened to a point and the other equipped with an oval-shaped handle. Some had a kind of drill on the end instead of a point. The *buksyrs* would attack piles of straw, first of all sticking their rods into it to see if sacks of grain were hidden in it. The other tool was used to drill in the gardens and other likely places. The grain when found was, of course, confiscated and the owner was forbidden to remain in Ukraine and was sent to Russia [Solovky, Siberia, etc.]. The collective farmers did not hide the grain they received for their labor days [*trudodni*] because there was very little of it.

In October 1932, comrades Shukhman and Kolotov organized a "Red Column." Commandeering about 60 farm wagons, they filled them with toughs and sent them to the villages. Coming to a village, the toughs would scatter, go to the houses of the collective farmers and ask how much grain each had, pretending this was only for registration purposes. When the information was in hand, teams would come up to each house and the grain would be taken away. When all the farmers had been robbed of their grain, the wagons would be decorated with banners and slogans which proclaimed that the farmers had voluntarily, and in an organized manner, given their grain to the state.

This Red Column passed through villages to be observed, but it was always under GPU protection. When guards were absent, the columns would run into the woods or be robbed by former prisoners who escaped. Such columns took their toll from all the neighboring villages.

It should be observed here that the Communists robbed people not only of grain but also of potatoes and any other thing that could be eaten. In some cases, farmers were ordered to thresh the straw when the records showed a yield to have been poor. Combatting the Communist menace, farmers would leave some grain in the straw by breaking the teeth in the cylinder of the threshing machine. Sometimes they succeeded in concealing up to 30 percent of grain which remained unthreshed in the straw. They hoped to thresh out this grain later, and thus save themselves and their families. But cases where farmers, in desperation, burned the straw together with their sheds were common.

Searches and arrests led people to despair. The indignation reached its culminating point on November 21, 1932, when great unrest in the village made the village soviet and all the *buksyrs* flee to the country seat for protection. The collective flew to pieces in half an hour. It was exclusively the work of women. They took their horses and cattle home, and the next day went to the approximate location of their former fields because all the field boundaries were destroyed.

The Communists were prompt in checking the incipient rebellion. They arrived in force in GPU cars the next night, arrested five persons and ordered that all collective farm property be returned. This order was carried out.

A stranger was now the chairman of the village soviet. Nobody knew where he came from, though he had a Ukrainian name, Boyko. He began to continue the work of his worthy predecessor, paying special attention to the Ukrainian movement for independence. "This is the work of our arch-enemy, Petlyura," he said. Then he tried to find out who had served in Petlyura's army.

Alarmed by the prospect of inevitable doom which was approaching, the people carried off one night all the grain from the collective farm stores, covering their tracks with pepper to protect themselves from detection by GPU hunting dogs. Some went to the forest to gather acorns, but this practice was soon stopped by Boyko, who declared the woods to be state property. It was forbidden to go there.

It was impossible to grind grain in the mill because the government grain quotas were not fulfilled. The farmers constructed hand mills and stampers. Boyko issued an order for the immediate arrest of the man who had built these machines, O. Khrynenko, but he was warned in time and ran away to the Donbas [industrial region of the Donets River Basin]. His wife was thrown out of the house, and it was locked by the GPU. Then she was tortured to reveal the whereabouts of her husband and where he had hidden some gold coins. She gave them 230 rubles in gold but did not know where her husband was and died in their hands.

The former chairman of the village soviet, Myshchachenko, sold his house to buy liquor. Then he took a house from Petro Yarosh and, with the assistance of Boyko, managed to have the Yarosh family exiled to the region of Sverdlovsk where all eight family members died from hard labor and ill treatment. Another case was that of F. Shobar, who did the same thing with the brothers Mykola and Stepan Nedvyha. One of them escaped and the other perished in Siberia, together with his family of ten.

A week or so later, the GPU arrested the following families: Borobavko — 5 persons, V. Brychko — 7 persons, Ostap Ilchenko — 5 persons, Nykyfor and Zakhar Koronivsky — 3 persons, O. Perepadya — 4 persons, K. Riznyk — 7 persons, Shyka — 4 persons, Taras Elesey — 6 persons, Vasyukno — 4 persons, and others. All of them received life terms with hard labor and were sent 280 miles north of Sverdlovsk. In 1942, 5 of them returned and said that all the others had died from hard labor and scurvy. They were lucky to get forged papers and escaped to Donbas, where they worked in the mines. [During their terms] they had not stayed long in any one place, because as soon as they cleared a patch in the forest and built barracks and other buildings, they were sent to another place in the wilderness 18 to 24 miles away where the same thing was repeated. The direction was always further north. Their address was Sverdlovsk 5, Letter G.

"There are no *kurkuls* now and presumably no Petlyura partisans, and we can build up our collective farm in peace," said Boyko. "But you should keep in mind that there are many *sub-kurkuls* whom we have to watch and, if they are going to harm our Soviet government, we will send them after the others." He again held meetings urging people to join the collective farm. The government took away grain and meat for taxes. There were no cows or sheep in the village.

In the evening of November 2, an unknown group of farmers attacked a *buksyr* brigade. Makar Verba was killed, and three men ran away. The next day the GPU confiscated all the shotguns in the village. The attackers were not caught. Boyko then threatened that the Soviet Red Army would come and wipe out all the farmers.

The people were terrified. It was hard to find a farmer who had not served a jail term. Practically all joined the collective farm now; only 12 swore that they would not do it and did not until 1941. But these were all women and children whose husbands were in exile in Siberia.

After the fall of 1932, it became customary to go around and beg for bread or food from neighbors. These beggars were usually children and old people.

A new *buksyr* brigade appeared in the village, more cruel than the first one.

In the spring of 1933 one-third of the people in the village were starving. The others had a little food and ate once a day to keep from swelling. To save themselves and their families from starvation, men began to offer their properties for sale or in exchange for food. Some went to Kharkiv, Kiev, or Poltava [major cities of Ukraine] to buy a little food and came back disappointed. Those cities were no better than Hadyach. Then they went to Moscow, Stalingrad, Voronezh, and Orel [cities in Russia] where food could be obtained. But the GPU soon found this out and the people were searched on the trains, food confiscated, and they themselves were charged with speculation. Then an order was issued that no farmer would be allowed to travel by train without a permit from the county soviet executive.

In March 1933 all the people from the collective farm went to the authorities, asking for bread. They were not even allowed to enter the courtyard.

On March 28, 1933, we were shocked by the news that Myron Yemets and his wife, Maria, had become cannibals. Having cut off their children's heads, they salted them away for meat. The neighbors smelled meat frying in the smoke coming from their chimney and, noticing the absence of children, went into the house. When they asked about the children, the parents began to weep and told the whole story. The perpetrators of this act said that they would have children again. Otherwise, they would die in great pain and that would be the end of the family.

Chairman Boyko arrested them himself, and about six hours later the GPU began to question them. "Who has so cunningly persuaded you to do this, *kurkuls*, near-*kurkuls*, or Petlyura henchmen? You know that this is the work of our enemies to cast dishonor upon our country, the Soviet

Union, the most advanced country in the world. You have to tell us who did it!" Hoping to save themselves in this way, the accused pointed to Pavlo Lytvynenko, who was supposed to have said: "If you have nothing to eat, butcher the children and eat them!" Lytvynenko was arrested and shot as an example to the others. Myron and Maria were sentenced to ten years in prison. However, they were shot about three months later because even the Soviet government was ashamed to let them live.

At the end of March or the beginning of April, a big department store was opened in Hadyach on Poltavska Street, by the park, across the street from Lenin's monument. It was called *Torgsin*. Stocked very well, even with goods from abroad, it had one fault, that of selling [goods] only for platinum, gold, silver, or precious stones. The prices were: For 10 gold rubles one could buy there 17 pounds of bread, 22 pounds of buckwheat cereal, 6 2/3 pounds of millet, and 10 herrings.

As soon as people learned about this, all who had any gold or silver flocked to the city. There was a line eight abreast and 1/3 mile long in front of the store. There were always 50–70 people who could not get in before the store closed for the day. They spent their nights on the sidewalk disregarding cold, storm, or rain. Thefts were very common, but most died from hunger or stomach cramps after eating too much and too greedily the food they bought. The corpses were removed every morning by a GPU truck.

I also stood in line with my mother. There I saw with my own eyes ten dead bodies thrown on the truck like so many logs and, in addition, three men that were still alive. The dead were hauled to Hlyboky Yar [Deep Ravine] and dumped there.

None of the clerks in this store were Ukrainians and the store belonged to the state.

A month later, in April, this store was broken into and robbed. Half an hour before the opening an alarm was sounded that the store had been robbed at daybreak. The militia with dogs began to search the people waiting in line. All who were a little stronger, had little or no swelling and, perhaps, some gold, were arrested and taken to the building of the country executive committee which was quite close and had a large basement. The prisoners were searched and the gold coins or any other valuables they might have had were confiscated. Other GPU agents without dogs did the same.

One woman, Maria Bovt, had a gold "ship" which had been awarded her husband during the Russo–Japanese War for his bravery in saving a Russian ship. She was also arrested during this investigation and was sent to work at construction projects in Komsomolsk on the Amur River near the Pacific Ocean. All trace of her vanished. The ship must have been taken to swell the Russian treasury or went into the pocket of some GPU agent.

Two weeks later, it was discovered that the real culprits had been the clerks in collusion with the militia. They were not punished because they had false documents prepared in advance, and they escaped arrest. This explanation was given out by comrades Shukhman and Kolotov.

The department store had its good and bad sides. The Russians robbed the people of practically all the gold they had. On the other hand, it saved many people's lives because 6 to 11 pounds of grain often saved one from starving to death. Those who had no gold for food died like flies or went to the cemeteries in search of corpses.

The most critical point was reached just before harvest. More and more people starved to death each day. Everything was eaten that could be swallowed: dogs, cats, frogs, mice, birds, grass, but mostly thistles, which were delicious if the plants were about 15 inches high and cleaned of spines. Many people went to graze and often died in the "grazing fields."

When rye ears began to fill out and were at least half full, the danger of death from starvation receded. The people cut ears of grain in the fields, dried them and, rubbing them down, they ate the precious green grains.

The Communists now began to combat "the grain barber menace," that is, people who cut off ears of grain with scissors. Mounted guards on watchtowers protected the grain from the "barbers." One of these watchmen, Fanasiy Hursky, killed a fellow who dared to "steal government property." But sometimes the "barbers" struck back. Some of them sawed through the props under the tower of Ivan Palchenkov when he was asleep. When the wind blew, the tower toppled down, and Ivan was killed.

In the spring of 1933, 138 people died in the village of Kharkivtsi. In comparison with some places this was very good. A great many people died from diseases caused by hunger, especially dysentery. There was only one child born at that time in the whole administrative unit to which Kharkivtsi belonged.

The 1940–1941 school year saw no beginners at all, while previously there had been about 25 each year. The new school principal, a Communist, saw the implication, and to save face made a first grade out of children a year younger if they were a little better developed than others. The same thing happened in neighboring villages.

The orphans who survived the Famine were taken to a children's home in the village. They were well cared for and most of them grew up properly and reached maturity in the years 1939–1941. The boys raised in these homes when inducted into the army in 1941 were the first to desert with arms and go back to avenge themselves on the Communists in their home villages, who deserved punishment.

Account 2

Case History SW34 (U.S. Commission on the Ukraine Famine, 1988, pp. 385–93). The interview was conducted as an oral life history in 1987 by Sue Ellen Webber and translated by Darian Diachok under the auspices of the U.S. Commission on the Ukraine Famine.

Q: Please state your year of birth.
A: 1922.

Q: Where were you born?
A: In Stavyshche, in Kiev Province.

Q: In which district?
A: The Stavyshche District.

Q: Where did you live during the 1920s and the 1930s?
A: In Stavyshche.

Q: What was your parents' profession?
A: My father worked in a bank, and my mother worked as a saleslady in a store.

Q: I see. So they weren't peasants, is that correct?
A: No, they weren't.

Q: And you had said you were born in …
A: 1922.

Q: Do you remember anything from the NEP period?
A: Well, I might have been, oh, about seven or eight years old at the time. People lived well then. But this was only for a few years. Then people were milked dry. Every single drop was wrung out of them.

Q: What can you recall about collectivization?
A: I only remember that they took away horses, farming implements, tools. Everything was taken from people against their will. And then they shoved you into a collective farm.

Q: And what social category were you given, given the fact that your family wasn't a peasant family, how were you designated?
A: Well, I come from the peasant class, but I'm not a peasant. It was a painful experience looking at all that was going on, seeing how the people were being uprooted and scattered about, how the dying were being brought in. At the time I lived close to the hospital. People were being driven in from villages near and far, as well as from Stavyshche, my native village. People were even bringing in their own children, who were already

swollen. They would come to spend the night. And they would spend the night, and then they would be ...

Close by, there was a park belonging to the hospital. It was quite a large park. There were yellow acacias planted in the center of the park and fenced off. Well, this is right where the cemetery was. Enormous open pits were dug and the doctors carried on stretchers the bodies of those who had died and tossed them into the pits. The process would be repeated each day until the open pit was filled and covered over with dirt shoveled over it. I know the earth over the pits has settled quite a bit since that time. But today you can still locate the exact burial spot, right by the cemetery. This was the hospital morgue where they took patients who had died. Later, they didn't bother with the morgue anymore, but took the corpses straight to the open pits on stretchers. Often nurses carried as many as ten children on stretchers and tossed them into the pit.

Q: When did people begin to die?

A: The precise time? When spring came. People were wandering about the gardens and hoping to come upon something left behind in the gardens; they would dig and dig, and examine every clump of earth. If they came upon a smelly old potato, they would clean it and take the starchy residue. They would also dry and grind acacia blossoms. Linden leaves would also be dried and made into ersatz pancakes. People dug up all sorts of roots. It was terrible, absolutely terrible. People scattered all over; they wandered here and there. Sometimes, they'd spot some small creature in the water, like a turtle and eat it as food. It was terrible. People were reduced to this state. I was right there. Some of the starving were in such a bad way that they had begun to stink already. Their feet would swell up; their wounds would open and fester. It was terrible. You would see them walking about, just walking and walking, and one would drop, and then another, and so on it went.

Q: How many were there in your family?

A: Well, there were four children, my mother, father, and grandmother, who was already quite old.

Q: And how did you survive?

A: How I survived? I'll tell you. We always had a supply of pickled cabbage, which we would prepare for the winter, as well as a supply of onions and potatoes. And that's all we had. This was the common practice. In villages, there were various ways to prepare provisions. Some people had had all their provisions, all their potato crop, seized, and they themselves had been thrown out of their houses. That's all that I remember, because I was still small then. It all began in 1929, and at that time I was only seven years old. And I can recall how they would deport people, people who never returned. And where they exiled these people, I can't say. Everything that they had was destroyed.

Q: Was there a church in your village?

A: We had three churches, in fact. One of them was called the Rozkishna Church. It belonged to a rather large town of over 10,000 inhabitants. The town was located on the other side of a dam and could be reached by taking the bridge. But for some reason Rozkishna Church was on our side. I recall going past it in 1931 when the cross was being taken down. But I was not an actual witness to the dismantling of the bells. Apparently, they needed the metal to make weapons. During the dismantling, a band of the women assembled at the church to protest what was going on. The militia was called; the women were roughed up, hit over the head. The next day, activists arrived at night and quietly cut down the bells.

The church was converted into a grain storage building. They would bring grain from Zhazhkiv, 18 miles away from our village, which was once part of Kiev Region, but which is now part of Cherkasy Region. And that's one of the places from where they were trucking the grain out. They had an enormous grain elevator there, and day and night they transported the grain from there, grain collected from the collective farms. Day and night!

This was all done at the MTS, the Machine-Tractor Station. And everywhere there were placards with the inscriptions, "MORE GRAIN!," and other similar exhortations. More grain for the government. They literally pumped the grain out of the countryside, and all for the use of the government. In the spring the Party sent in Komsomol members, who walked about the villages with pikes to which small scoops were attached. The Komsomol members searched literally everywhere to find hidden grain. They looked especially in places like hay piles in barns. They dug everywhere. And if they happened to find some grain that someone had hidden away, well, that was pretty much the end of him. He would never see the light of day again. That's how it was.

Q: And who exactly were these Komsomol members? Whose children were they?

A: The Komsomol members? Well, there were some Ukrainians among them, that's true. But the vast majority were sent from Moscow. At one point, the so-called 10,000-ers had been sent; there were supposed to have been 10,000 of them sent. Later, the government realized that this number was not enough, so it brought in the so-called 25,000-ers. And it was these groups that confiscated the grain all over the countryside. And if you happened to be a member of the Komsomol, you were forced to do these things, too. But the possibility was always open to you, that if you did find hidden grain, you could fail to report it, or you pretended you hadn't seen anything.

Q: Did the Committees of Non-Wealthy Peasants exist at this time?

A: Non-Wealthy Peasants? Yes, there were such committees; in fact, pretty much all over the countryside but they were quickly suppressed. Even though I was quite young, I remember that during the SVU [in 1930], they were branded as "enemies of the people." I myself was also considered "an enemy of the people." They took away my father in 1937.

Q: Why was he taken away?

A: Why? Well, he had been branded an "enemy of the people," and they took him away in 1937. And they also took away one of my father's brothers, and another brother, as well. And to this day, we don't know what happened to them. And when my mother went to inquire as to my father's whereabouts at the militia, they told her that he had been sentenced to ten years without the right of correspondence. It was common knowledge that this meant he had been shot. Most likely, his body is somewhere in Vinnytsia. So, the four of us were left. Yurii was the youngest, just six months old at the time. And that was how my mother was left to fend for herself. Many of the other women were sent off to Kazakhstan. It was common practice for wives of the men that had been sentenced to be sent for five years to Kazakhstan to pick cotton, or to perform similar tasks. Five years! My own Godmother was sent there and actually returned. But this was during the war. After the war, my mother came here for a visit, and told us that it became standard practice to tell the wives whose husbands had been sentenced without the right of correspondence: "Your husband was killed in 1945." This was the standard line they gave everyone during the Khrushchev era.

Q: Do you recall how many people died of hunger during the Famine? What was the percentage?

A: In our village, you mean?

Q: Yes. Would you say it was about a half of the villagers?

A: Well, there was a village not far away from us called Krasenivka, which had a population of about 10,000. It was a rather large village. They had to put up a black flag at one end of the village, and another one at the other end which indicated that absolutely no one had survived, not even a dog, or cat. The houses were all overgrown with goosefoot and other weeds. And our village? Well, what can I tell you? About ten percent of our village died of hunger. It was terrifying. Utterly terrifying.

Q: Were you yourself repressed during collectivization?

A: Well, in the beginning, you know, we had our own house, which later became my uncle's house. They evicted us and told us that they needed our house as part of the new collective farm, and they made an office out of my uncle's house. And they also confiscated 90 percent of everything we had. They took the land together with the house and all our belongings. We had had this garden there — and we lost all of this.

Q: And they didn't tell you anything?

A: At that point, they took whatever they wanted to, since technically these things were no longer ours. They would walk all over our fields, probing the latter with the sharp pikes. The pike was jammed into the ground and pulled up. If any grains of wheat were picked up, the conclusion was that grain was being hidden from the state. The men with the pikes were everywhere.

Q: Were you going to school at the time? And if so, was it a Ukrainian school?

A: Yes, it was. In our school, whenever any of the children mentioned the Famine, they were corrected by the teachers. They were told that there was no Famine, simply a year of difficulties. They confiscated all that we had and designated the year as one of difficulties!

Not far from us was a cemetery. There were many beautifully made crosses and memorials there. This was during the Famine. Every night there were two or three graves dug up. Wealthy people had been buried there, and, naturally, there were valuables in the caskets — a ring perhaps, a watch, or earring. The robbers were caught: a man by the name of Abramovich and his son. The father had forced the son into it. Well, they had been trying to break into a tomb — the rich people had all been buried in tombs. The valuables buried with them were just waiting to be taken. Nothing was done to prevent theft. The entire site was ruined and everything of value was taken.

Well, when someone like a priest was buried, a gold cross was often placed in his casket. During the Famine hundreds of graves were unearthed ....

During the Famine they used to give us tea and a small piece of bread at school. The tea was made in the following fashion. It was simply overcooked sugar and some coloring. And that was our tea. A lot of children did not go to school; they were no longer able to, because they had already reached the stage where their bodies had swelled. A large number of children died.

A few of the villagers had planted potatoes in the spring, but they had to do the plowing with shovels, because by this time, all the horses had died and no implements were left. They dug the earth with shovels and planted the potatoes. But the problem was that anyone could easily figure out where it was that you planted the potatoes, and the next day, usually at night, someone would come and dig up what you had planted. The field would again be barren. That's what went on. So, as a result, people would try to cover their tracks by raking over the newly sowed ground. We used to plant small potato cuttings which were little more than peels. Well, we planted these in our garden, and the potatoes grew beautifully. Something so simple, it could only have come from God. It was just a potato peel with some eyes on it. We planted the peels and got perfectly good potatoes that way. That's how we did it.

The greatest number of deaths from starvation actually occurred when the wheat-ears had matured. People began to steal the wheat-ears. They were starving, you understand, and all at once the wheat-ears were available. And when the people began eating great quantities of wheat-ears, they died even more rapidly, because their intestines would rupture. That's when the greatest number of corpses began appearing.

Q: And what did they do with the corpses?

A: What indeed! Well, they went looking for them; they collected the corpses and dumped them into pits. And if the authorities happened to come across someone who was somehow managing to stay relatively healthy, well, they gave him the job of watching over the pit that they had dug out to make sure that it wasn't used by anyone else.

Q: Are you aware of any cases of cannibalism?

A: I heard of instances, but had never witnessed anything personally. But everyone talked about it. We had our own newspaper, *The Red Collectivist*. The newspaper mentioned that someone had been apprehended in connection with the discovery of barrels of salted meat. I can't recall the entire episode. Rumors were circulating involving the activists. There were Ukrainians among them, and there may have been others as well. They were the real activists, you know. They were involved in dekulakization, and they used to go drinking in the gardens. In fact, they didn't do much of anything else, except when it came time to dekulakize someone, they'd come and confiscate everything, throwing the children out, like unwanted puppies, into the courtyard. And this was in the dead of winter. The head of the household would go to the village soviet and request help for his seven children, and the activists would tell him something like, "Get out of here, and take those little mongrels with you!" That's how it was. And no one would help these people out. And so they would just die ....

Q: Who was the head of the village soviet at the time?

A: The head of the village soviet? A man by the name of Makharynsky. I've forgotten his first name. And later they took him away as well. I don't know what the cause of that was.

Q: And what sort of man was he? Can you describe him?
A: What kind of man? Well, he did whatever they ordered him to do.

Q: I see, a bureaucrat.
A: Whatever the bureaucracy told him to do, he'd do. You know, he himself didn't actually participate in the dirty work of dekulakization; and whenever they told him to pump the grain out of a particular village, he would send in the activists, the so-called 10,000-ers, and later the 25,000-ers sent by Moscow. And these were all foreigners, outsiders.

The Famine existed only in Ukraine. There were a lot of people, a lot of people who wanted to go to Russia. People figured they could go there with the shirt on their backs and sell it for bread. On their way back everything they were carrying would be confiscated. And they would be arrested and sentenced. I myself know of several people who went there. You see, Russia was some distance away from us. The people who lived closer did try to go, but the ones who made it never returned with anything. Everything they managed to get was confiscated. By this time, the passport system had already been introduced. According to this system, you would be arrested and in great difficulties if you happened to be somewhere for nine days without reporting. So, whatever you did, you would invariably find yourself in hot water.

Q: Did you leave the village during the Famine?
A: My father was still around. I remember once we bought some coffee. The so-called coffee had actually been made out of barley. It was just over-roasted barley. Well, since there was nothing to eat, we were told to mix some of this and some of that into this coffee. This mixture was awfully bitter! Yecch!

Q: Do you remember how the Famine came to an end?
A: How the Famine ended? Well, they began to provide a little something for the people; people began to go to the collective farms for soup. But as far as to how the Famine actually ended? Well, it happened gradually, in stages. How can I explain? Well, the thing is that it never really completely ended. That's the way it is over there. People were no longer dying en masse, but in a sense the Famine still continued. In fact, it recurred in 1947. Once again there was a great Famine in Ukraine. My mother recounted how there was a great migration to the cities. Life was a bit better in the cities. But even in the cities, people were dying of hunger ....

Q: What sort of people joined the Party in your village?

A: There were very few Party members in our village.

Q: Well, what sort of people were the Party members?

A: What sort? There was a man by the name of Pokotylo who shot himself during the Famine. I believe he was in the District Party Committee, but I don't know what his rank was. I just know that he was a Communist and that he shot himself. There was another by the name of Nahornyi who also shot himself. This all happened during the Famine. These Communists committed suicide during the Famine, as did Mykola Khvyliovy, the writer, and Skrypnyk. Others committed suicide, too, because they saw what was actually going on. At one time they had embraced Lenin's slogans that Ukraine would be allowed to separate from the Soviet Union if it chose to. They believed the slogans, or at least I suppose they did. But later, when they understood the truth, they shot themselves. They had to. And that's how it was with our Party members.

And then came the Party purges. They were directed from Moscow. Party purges. And these were public spectacles. There was a building in our village that served as a club. And this is where the proclamations were made. When the Party purge began, they zeroed in on this fellow named Hrynchenko. They started in on him, tagging him with all sorts of accusations — that he had pumped out insufficient quantities of grain, that there was too little of this and too little of that. Although there was already nothing at all left to pump out, and they were still accusing him of falling short. "Too little!" they shouted at him.

By 1934 they were already giving out 250 grams for one labor day. This is about half a pound of bread a day. But you really had to work to earn this ration. This was a very difficult life, but people began to manage. They planted potatoes and different varieties of pumpkins, beets, and other staples. But during the Famine, a group of Soviet ruffians would come through the villages and would even pull out whatever people happened to be baking in the oven. In the markets, they would even confiscate and destroy such items as beans in jars. It was terrible. Well, this is what I myself know and saw.

Q: How did people rebuild their lives after the Famine?

A: Slowly. Before collectivization, there were still large barns around the countryside, but all these were burned as firewood. Whoever had fences for keeping in domestic livestock, these were burned also because people didn't have anything to keep themselves warm. The only housing that was left were so-called "houses on chicken legs." Reconstruction was simply awful. It was repulsive just to look at these buildings. It's probably the same way today. They say that there have been some changes, some minor changes made, that some sidewalks have been added, that electrical lines have been added, and that sort of thing ....

Q: Did people ever talk about the Famine after it was over?

A: They talked about it constantly. If I knew you well, then I would feel free to talk about it; but if I didn't know you well, I wouldn't feel comfortable talking. I would be afraid of your denouncing me to the NKVD. There were so-called Judases who were capable of turning you in. Whatever you would say, they would immediately report it, and you would be in for some real trouble.

Q: You were only 11 years old during the Famine?

A: Yes.

Q: But did you hear the adults talking about the political affairs of the day? Did you know at the time who Skrypnyk was? Kaganovich? What was being said about these political figures?

A: We all knew! Kaganovich, Molotov. Except that at that time no one could speak openly about these matters. We couldn't speak openly. Let me tell you about this little song that we had from that period. I can still remember this song from my school days.

During the Famine, they sent this fellow, Postyshev, as secretary to Ukraine. And then there was this other fellow, Kossior, who was Polish. He was in the Politburo. So you can see for yourself what lovely songs we had to sing as we starved.

> Hey, our harvest knows no limits or measures.
> It grows, ripens, and even spills over onto the earth,
> Boundless over the fields; while the patrolling pioneers
> Come out to guard the ripening wheat-ears of grain.

And now here's the refrain:

> We've hardened our song in the kiln's fires
> And carry it aloft like a banner, offering it to you;
> And in this way, Comrade Postyshev, we are submitting
> Our report of the work we've done.

I remember the song as if it were yesterday. We had a very beautiful park in our village, with a stream flowing by. A gorgeous park. And in all the parks, there were loudspeakers placed, as part of this radio network, which was itself linked to the post office. And in these parks, you could always hear songs in Russian being sung, one song in particular:

Swiftly as birds, one after another,
Fly over our Soviet homeland
The joyous refrains of town and country:
Our burdens have lightened
Our lives have gladdened.

They broadcast this song while people were dying in the Famine. "Our lives have gladdened." I can recall this song from my school years, when they were teaching the children to sing *The Patrolling Pioneer*. What kind of a country is this in which they keep bread from the people for the sake of a "better life"? They themselves sang, "The joyous refrains of town and country." And this song would play every day, ten times a day, and as you listened to the song, everywhere all around you people are screaming, and starving to death, while the song played on: "Our burdens have lightened."

Q: And what were you thinking?
A: What could I think?! All I could think of was where could I get some food. I didn't think anything. They let the Ukrainians have it because they had wanted to separate from Russia. That's what I think. The Ukrainian nation is still paying for that even up to this very day.

Q: Would you like to add anything to what you've said?
A: What is there that I could add? As long as you have Communism there, you will have this endless agony there. They can always institute another policy similar to NEP; they can always try something like that again. From what I hear, they want to give the people a greater share, a greater share of land as well — the primary reason being that the private plots of land yield more crops per acre than the collective farms. But people aren't going to fall for this. First of all, they don't have the implements with which to farm private land; and, secondly, let's say, if a man does work his field, and he seeds it and plants something — potatoes, for example — then they'll tell him to pay his taxes. And regardless whether or not something grows or doesn't grow in your garden, you have to come up with the payment. People don't want this system and aren't going to be taken in by it. And as long as this system continues to exist over there, then that's how it will be over there.

Q: Thank you very much indeed for this most interesting testimony.
A: I was quite young, but I saw a great deal. In fact, I can recall the events of those times better than I can recall what I did yesterday.

Q: Oh, yes.
A: It was all so horrible.

Account 3

Vasyl' Pakharenko, "Holodnyi 33-yi," *Molod'* Cherkashchyny, July 18–24, 1988; translated by Vera Kaczmarskyj, *Soviet Ukrainian Affairs*, autumn 1988, pp. 14–15. The author is a schoolteacher in the city of Cherkassy, a regional capital in Ukraine.

Recently I was leafing through a thick notebook filled with eyewitness accounts. I had jotted them down at various times and different villages. They are simple narratives (I tried to record them verbatim). A surrealistic tragedy unfolds behind these words ....

Here is Iaryna Larionivna Tiutiunyk's account of the death of her neighbor's 6-year-old son, Myt'io. [Iaryna was born in 1905 in the village of Subotiv in the Chyhyrin region]: "He was on his way to the kindergarten one morning, where the collective farm was distributing a serving of millet meal the size of a matchbox. And he dropped by, begging — Auntie, give me a piece of bread. I am so hungry. I didn't give him any because I was mad at him for eating the greens I had planted in the garden. To the day I die I will not forgive myself for begrudging the child a piece of bread. In the evening, on our way home from work, we found him sitting right in the middle of the footpath — dead. He was probably returning from the kindergarten, had got tired, sat down, and died."

Antonina Oleksandrivna Polishchuk [born in 1925]. She lived in the village of Buzhanka in the Lysians'kyi raion: "In 1933, our mother pretended to sew some dolls for children, filling them with grain, so that they would not take away all the grain from us. But they found the grain even there and seized it. They took our ox away ... and killed it, taking the meat for themselves ....

"Our father died from hunger, as did my 14-year-old brother, Vasia, and my twin sisters, Katia and Dunia [born in 1927]. We ate only weeds and drank water. The corpses were carted out to the cemeteries on big carts. They pushed 300 bodies into one hole ...."

Tetiana Iakivna Vdovychenko [born in 1911] lived in the same village: "It happened that they took people who were still alive and would throw them into the common graves. This happened with Khotyna Revenko. When they came to her house, she was still alive. They started dragging her to the cart by her feet. 'Where are you pulling me to? Give me a beet. I am hungry, I still want to live.' She was young, not yet 30.

"'You think we are going to come back for you tomorrow?' growled the men in response, pulling her onto the cart by her feet. They brought her to the gravesite and threw her inside. She did not fall on her back, but propped up in a sitting position, her back against the side. They poked at her head and she finally fell back."

"Motria Vdovychenko was also taken to the gravesite and buried alive with her two children [who were also still living]. Such incidents were frequent."

Denys Mykytovych Lebid' [born in 1914] from Iablunivka in Lysians'kyi raion: "I was transported to the gravesite and thrown into the common grave, but they did not cover it up that day. My friend Iaremii Stavenko was passing by and pulled me out."

Stepanida Hryhorivna [born in 1905] from the village of Zhab'ianka in the region by the same name: "In 1933, my neighbor lured my daughter to her house, killed her with a knife and ate her. My daughter was all of 6 years old at the time. When the beast was seized and taken to the *raion* [to be imprisoned], she kept taking out slices of meat and eating them, saying 'Umm, how tasty. Had I known, I would have killed her earlier.' The police could not tolerate this any longer and shot her right there on the road ...."

Account 4

Oleksandr Mishchenko, *Bezkrovna viina* (Kiev, 1991), pp. 48–49. The author, a member of the Union of Writers of Ukraine, collected 42 accounts in the Poltava region in 1990. The following account is that of Petro Ivanovych Bilous, born 1909 in the village of Andriiky, which was formed from four farmsteads (*khutirs*), including the Andreiko farmstead, in Poltava region.

In 1932–1933 the people were terrified. They no longer slept nights but sat in their houses and waited for the brigades to come for bread. In order to survive, some tried to hide some produce somewhere. For example, at Laryvon Andreiko's house the brigade leader found some buried potatoes and beneath them a few poods of wheat. Then they crawled in the attic where there were flowerpots, cast-iron pots, and jars. And in every jar and pot there were beans, dried apples, ground millet, or crab-apples, all covered with charcoal to hide it. They found it all the same. They took it down from the attic and poured it all in one sack. They found a little cask of cheese. They ate his sauerkraut and I ate some, too, because I was hungry. Old man Laryvon was left with nothing. He survived somehow, but his wife died.

In our family, both mother and father perished. Mother died when the rye was already being harvested. She went to look at how they were pouring it. Even though the rye was ripe, they wouldn't allow anyone to cut an ear. Even in their own garden. My brother was already married then. He went to live with his wife's family at Marfyna Andreiko's house. They had a cow, and he survived there. Another brother went around to the small farming communities (*khutirs*) and begged. And I was already near death, so swollen that I couldn't get out of bed, but someone remembered about my army requalification. And I was taken to the hospital. I stayed there a month and got better. I returned home. The house stood empty. All there was were the four walls. I didn't think about that then. All I thought about was going somewhere in order to earn a piece of bread and not die. But in the village there was no place to go. The dead lay in the shadows, in kitchen gardens under a tree; the people wandered sluggishly, apathetically, dazed, and no one even buried the dead.

Over there across the gully lived Kateryna Andreiko. She lost four daughters, and she also gave up her spirit to God, but her two sons, luckily, survived. One was already married, and his younger brother stayed with him. Andrii Vasyl'ovych Andreiko lost two boys and five daughters. The daughters were little, school-age. Andrii Vasyl'ovych from time to time served as chairman of the collective farm, and then they dismissed him, and then he died. His wife, too. Not only did our own people die but even outsiders who had been sent in. There was starvation in every house. At my wife's, thanks to the fact that her father had a cow, nobody died. But everybody was swollen: her mother, father, and brother. She was given a little bread in the collective farm — she didn't eat it herself but brought it home. And that's how she saved her immediate family. At Odarka Andreiko's house, not far from here, the father died, two brothers, and the sisters Mariika, Nastia, and Mylia. Odarka was already married then. She buried them in a pit. She worked on the burial detachment. Nobody made her. She came home and buried them herself. She buried Mariika, she buried Nastia, she buried her father. Before he died, her father asked for a piece of bread: "Give me some, my child, if only some crumbs, because I'm dying." She didn't have any to give him. There just wasn't any bread at all.

References

Borys, Jurij (1980). The Sovietization of Ukraine 1917–1923: The Communist Doctrine and Practice of National Self-Determination. Edmonton: Canadian Institute of Ukrainian Studies.

Conquest, Robert (1986). *The Harvest of Sorrow: Soviet Collectivization and the Terror-Famine.* New York and Oxford: Oxford University Press.

Ellman, Michael (1991). "A Note on the Number of 1933 Famine Victims," *Soviet Studies,* XLIII(2):375–379.

Gannt, William Horsley (1937). *Russian Medicine.* New York: Harper & Brothers.

Hermaize, Osyp (1926). *Narysy z istoriï revoliutsiinoho rukhu na Ukraïni (Sketches from the History of the Revolutionary Movement in Ukraine).* Kharkiv: Knyhospilka.

Holod *1932–1933 rokiv na Ukraïni: Ochyma istorykiv, movoiu dokumentiv (The Famine of 1932–1933 in Ukraine: In the Eyes of Historians and in the Language of the Documents)* (1990). Kiev: Vydavnytstvo politychnoï literatury.

Hroch, Myroslav (1985). *Social Conditions of National Revival in Europe. A Comparative Analysis of the Social Composition of Patriotic Groups among the Smaller European Nations.* Cambridge, London, New York: Cambridge University Press.

Jasny, Naum (1949). *The Socialized Agriculture of the USSR: Plans and Performance.* Stanford: Stanford University Press.

Khrystiuk, Pavlo (1921–1922). *Zamitky i materiialy do istoriï ukraïns'koï revoliutsiï, 1917–1920* *(Notes and Materials on the History of the Ukrainian Revolution, 1917–1920)*. Prague: Ukraïns'kyi sociologychnyi instytut. Four volumes.

Kuper, Leo (1990). "The Genocidal State: An Overview," pp. 19–52. In Pierre L. van den Berghe (Ed.) *State Violence and Ethnicity.* Niwot, CO: University of Colorado Press.

Lewin, Moshe (1985). *The Making of the Soviet System: Essays in the Social History of Interwar Russia.* New York: Pantheon.

Liber, George O. (1990). *Soviet Nationality Policy, Urban Growth and Identity Change in the Ukrainian SSR, 1923–1934.* New York: Cambridge University Press.

Luxemburg, Rosa (1976). *The National Question: Selected Writings.* Ann Arbor, MI: Books on Demand.

Mace, James E. (1983). *Communism and the Dilemmas of National Liberation: National Communism in Soviet Ukraine, 1918–1933.* Cambridge, MA: Harvard University Press.

Mace, James E. (1984). "The Man-Made Famine of 1933 in the Soviet Ukraine: What Happened and Why," pp. 67–83. In Israel W. Charny (Ed.) *Toward the Understanding and Prevention of Genocide.* Boulder, CO: Westview Press.

Mishchenko, Oleksandr (1991). *Bezkrovna viina.* Kiev: Vydanvnytstvo politychnoi literatury.

"Postanova TsK VKP(b) ta RNK SRSR pro khlibozahotivli na Ukraïny, Pivnichnomu Kavkazi ta Zakhidnii oblasti" (Decision of the All-Union Communist Party Central Committee and USSR Council of Peoples Commissars on Grain Procurements in Ukraine, the North Caucasus, and Western District) (1991). Zoloti vorota: Al'manakh, No. 1:78–79.

Savchenko, Fedir (1930). *Zaborone ukraïnstvo 1876 r. (The Suppression of Ukrainian Activities in 1876).* Kharkiv and Kiev: Derzhavne vydavnytstvo Ukraïny.

Stalin, I. V. (1946–1951). *Sochineniia (Works).* Moscow: Gospolitizdat. 14 volumes.

Taylor, S. J. (1990). *Stalin's Apologist: Walter Duranty, The New York Times's Man in Moscow.* New York: Oxford University Press.

Treadgold, Donald (1964). *Twentieth Century Russia.* 2nd ed. Chicago: Rand McNally.

U.S. Commission on the Ukraine Famine (1988). Report to Congress. Washington: U.S. Government Printing Office.

Vsesoiuznaia perepis' naseleniia 1937 g.: Kratkie itogi (All-Union Population Census of 1937: Summary). (1991). Moscow: Institut istorii SSSR.

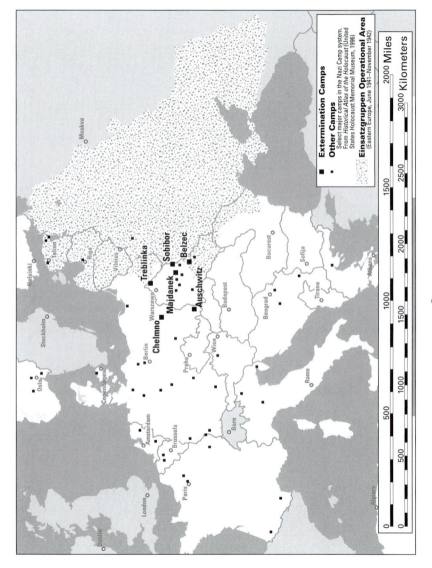

Extermination Camps

■

Other Camps

■ Select major camps in the Nazi Camp system.
From *Historical Atlas of the Holocaust* (United
States Holocaust Memorial Museum, 1996)

Einsatzgruppen Operational Area
(Eastern Europe, June 1941–November 1942)

Treblinka
Sobibor
Belzec
Chelmno
Majdanek
Auschwitz

Moskva

Helsinki
Tallinn
Riga
Vilnius
Warszawa
Berlin
Praha
Wien
Budapest
Beograd
Bucurest
Sofija
Tirane
Athen
Rome
Bern
Paris
Brussels
Amsterdam
London
Dublin
Oslo
Stockholm
Copenhagen
Algiers

Germany

0   500   1000   1500   2000   Miles
0   500   1000   1500   2000   2500   3000   Kilometers

CHAPTER **4**

Holocaust: The Genocide of the Jews

DONALD L. NIEWYK

The Nazi slaughter of the Jews during World War II gave the world the idea of genocide. The Nazis themselves did not use the term, nor was this the first such mass murder. But the systematic extermination of between 5 and 6 million Jews through shootings, gassings, and forced labor was a catastrophe on a massive scale. It was, moreover, closely related to broader Nazi racial policies that led to the murder of very large numbers of Gypsies, Russian and Polish prisoners of war, East European slave laborers, and Germans who were physically disabled or mentally retarded.

Perpetrators

Following Hitler's seizure of power in Germany in 1933, the Nazi state pursued policies designed to isolate and pauperize the 600,000 German Jews. The goal, more or less openly acknowledged, was to make the Jews despair of their future in Germany and emigrate, which many of them did. Violent attacks on Jews were uncommon, and Jews were sent to concentration camps only if they had been prominent in anti-Nazi parties. The exception to these rules was the "Crystal Night" (*Kristallnacht*) pogrom of November 9–10, 1938, when Nazi thugs physically attacked thousands of Jews and sent them to concentration camps. The latter were released only after promising to leave Germany. These actions were clearly the work of virulent anti-Semites in the Nazi Party, supported by government officials who found pogroms useful in advancing economic objectives. Most ordinary Germans ignored these atrocities out of indifference to the Jews or a sense of powerlessness to help them.

These policies aimed at forcing Jewish emigration held for more than a year after World War II began. While many Jews in the part of Poland conquered by Germany in 1939 were mistreated, the Nazi bureaucracy made plans to expel them and all other Jews in German hands farther to the east or else to the Indian Ocean island of Madagascar. Only when Hitler invaded the Soviet Union in 1941 did emigration give way to extermination. Believing that the German people would not understand such a ghastly policy, the Nazis carried out the genocide of the Jews in secrecy and under cover of war. Accordingly, responsibility for mass murder was placed in the hands of the SS (*Schutzstaffel*), Hitler's special guard of policemen and soldiers that had grown into the central agency of terror in Nazi-dominated Europe. Some of its officers were convinced anti-Semites who accepted the view that the Jews were Germany's most dangerous enemies. All of them were convinced Nazis who were sworn to obey orders without question.

Genocide was too vast a process for the SS alone. The German army cooperated in the roundup of victims. Volunteers from the conquered Eastern countries served as auxiliary police and as guards in the camps out of sympathy with the Nazis or the desire to escape some worse fate at German hands. Occasionally local mobs in Poland, the Baltic states, and the Ukraine massacred their Jewish neighbors, with German encouragement. However, unlike the Germans, none of these other groups were dedicated to the systematic slaughter of every single Jew in Europe. The point is, the Holocaust was masterminded and implemented by Hitler's elite guard, the SS.

Genocide: Policies and Procedures

As SS leaders prepared to participate in Hitler's invasion of the Soviet Union in June 1941, they created four mobile killing squads called *Einsatzgruppen* for the purpose of liquidating Jews, Polish and Soviet intellectuals, and Communist Party officials. The 3000 members of these four squads shot and buried in mass graves between 1 and 2 million Jews during the course of the war on the Eastern Front, but their methods were considered slow and inefficient — particularly if all 11 million European Jews were to die. Hence, Hermann Goering placed the formulation of what was to become the Nazis' "Final Solution to the Jewish problem" in the hands of Reinhard Heydrich, the most powerful SS leader after Heinrich Himmler. Heydrich's plan was submitted at a conference of top Nazi officials held in the Berlin suburb of Wannsee in January 1942. It called for concentrating all the Jews under German control in Eastern European ghettos and labor camps, where those capable of doing slave labor for the

Third Reich would be worked to death. Those who could not work or who were not needed would be sent to special camps for immediate extermination.

Existence for the Jews in ghettos and their nearby forced labor camps almost defies description. Overcrowded, overworked, and underfed, they could hope only that producing for the Nazi war machine would buy enough time to save at least a remnant of the Jewish people. That hope, combined with the Nazi policy of holding all the Jews of the ghetto collectively responsible for any attempt at opposition or escape, kept Jewish resistance to a minimum. In 1944, the SS shut down the last of the ghettos and sent their piteous remnants to camps in Germany or else to the extermination centers.

The six extermination centers, all of them situated on what had been Polish territory, ended the lives of 3 million Jews. Four of them — Chelmno, Belzec, Sobibor, and Treblinka — were strictly killing centers, where victims were gassed immediately following their arrival. The Nazis already possessed the technical expertise, having employed poison gas to kill more than 70,000 incurably ill Germans in a "euthanasia" program between 1939 and 1941 (see chapter 6). The remaining two extermination centers — Auschwitz and Majdanek — were both killing and slave labor camps. In them, the able-bodied were selected for work in various military industries; the rest were consigned to the gas chambers or firing squads. To be selected for work often meant only a brief reprieve, since conditions were atrocious. As the SS saw it, the victims were to die eventually anyway, and there was no reason to spare them when a steady stream of replacements kept arriving. Hence tens of thousands were literally worked to death. Others were subjected to grotesque and painful medical experiments. Survival depended on almost superhuman determination to live and often on the good fortune of securing jobs in camp kitchens, offices, or medical wards.

Auschwitz was the last of the extermination centers to be shut down as Soviet forces overran Poland late in 1944. The SS drove the survivors of the various camps to Germany, where they were dumped in already overcrowded concentration camps and their outlying slave labor centers. Deprived of even the most elementary needs in the last days of the war, thousands died of malnutrition, tuberculosis, typhus, and other diseases. The liberating Allied armies found the camps littered with unburied corpses, and many of those still alive were too far gone to be saved. Of the approximately 200,000 Jews who survived, the majority attempted to return to their former homes, while the remainder entered European displaced persons' camps and applied for permission to enter Palestine, the United States, or some other place of permanent refuge.

Why the Jews?

Answering the question "Why the Jews?" requires an understanding of Adolf Hitler, the undeniable author of the Holocaust. His anti-Semitism dates from his youth in Austria before World War I, where Jew-baiting was advanced by the politicians he admired and the tabloids he read. If the psychohistorians are to be believed, it may have been more deeply rooted in some early personal trauma (Binion, 1976; Waite, 1977).

Whatever its sources, Hitler's Judeophobia comprised all the well-established and virtually universal stereotypes: Jews were corrupt and predatory materialists, devoid of patriotism and feelings for others, and they advocated subversive ideas such as liberalism, Marxism, and cultural modernism. Hitler adopted this hackneyed litany in its most extreme, social Darwinian form that interpreted history as a struggle between superior and inferior races. By the time he began his political career in postwar Munich, he was a convinced anti-Semite.

Doubtless, Hitler's anti-Semitism, and that of many of his followers, was intensified by the Bolshevik revolution in Russia, Germany's defeat in World War I, and the abortive Spartacus Revolt by German Communists in 1919. Then Hitler and his fledgling Nazi Party began associating the Jews with the alleged "stab in the back" of the German army, the liberal Weimar Republic established in Germany after the defeat, and the Communist menace. Anti-Semitism was always one of his central teachings. Occasionally Hitler called for the emigration or deportation of the Jews, but more often he blamed problems on a Jewish world conspiracy without specifying a cure beyond inviting Germans to support his movement. Moreover, the Nazi Party tended to use anti-Jewish propaganda opportunistically, playing it up or down depending on the responses it received. Hence no one could know exactly what Hitler and his party planned to do with the Jews, and it cannot be said that the large minority of Germans who came to support him after 1930 deliberately endorsed violent anti-Semitism. Today it is far clearer than it was at the time that genocide was implicit in Hitler's ideology.

That genocidal impulse became explicit as part of the events surrounding Operation Barbarossa, the attack on the USSR in 1941. No one knows exactly when or why the Germans decided to kill all the European Jews (and not just those targeted by the *Einsatzgruppen*). Fragmentary evidence suggests that the euphoric atmosphere surrounding Germany's initial victories on the Eastern Front may have convinced Hitler that the creation of his Aryan utopia was imminent. The dictator's increasingly barbaric campaign against the Soviet Union also sharpened his hatred for what he called "Judeo-Bolshevism" at the same time as it foreclosed opportunities to resettle the Jews. By 1942, Nazi genocide was being aimed at all of European Jewry.

The Victims

Although the Third Reich targeted all the Jews in Nazi-dominated Europe, their fate varied with local conditions. Jews were most vulnerable where German officials managed affairs directly (and did so from the beginning of the Holocaust); where the Jewish communities were large and unassimilated; and where indigenous anti-Semitism encouraged some degree of cooperation with the murderers.

All three of these elements combined to decimate the Jews of Poland, the western USSR, and the Baltic states. There Nazi rule was most openly brutal. First under the guns of the Einsatzgruppen and then in ghettos and labor and extermination camps, Jews from these areas died in numbers amounting to three quarters of the total Holocaust casualties. Very few survived. Direct German control over Serbia, the Protectorate of Bohemia and Moravia, and part of Greece meant that their Jews were deported to Poland and subjected to similar atrocities. Such was also the fate of the remaining German and Austrian Jewish communities. Only small numbers of German Jews who were of mixed race, living in mixed marriages, highly decorated war veterans, or prominent persons were spared. Hungary came under direct German rule only in March 1944, following which the SS, aided by Hungarian officials, swallowed up more than half of the large Jewish population. Doubtless the losses in Hungary would have been even greater had the Nazis taken control earlier.

Unlike Hungary, Germany's other Eastern European allies — Romania, Bulgaria, Slovakia, and Croatia — retained some measure of independence to the end of the war. Slovakia and Croatia, both satellites created by Nazi Germany, willingly established their own forced labor camps for some of the Jews and sent the rest to the extermination centers. Romania and Bulgaria, however, refused to comply with some Nazi demands. Neither was a German creation, and both were fiercely protective of their national rights. Bulgaria confiscated the property of many native-born Jews and forced some of them into slave labor, but it would not hand them over to the Germans. It did, however, deport Jews from lands newly acquired from Greece and Yugoslavia. In Romania, where (unlike Bulgaria) there was considerable anti-Semitism, tens of thousands of Jews in the newly reconquered provinces of Bessarabia and Northern Bukovina were murdered in pogroms or else deported across the Dniester River to be murdered by the Einsatzgruppen or at Auschwitz. And yet, the majority of Bulgarian and Romanian Jews survived the Holocaust.

The Jews of Western Europe, remote from the killing fields and the intense anti-Semitism of Eastern Europe, lost about 40 percent of their numbers to the Nazis. The SS gave priority to exterminating the Jews of the east, and the war ended before it could finish its work in the west. There, too, the pace of extermination varied with local conditions. In

Holland, which had been placed under direct German rule, three quarters of the Jews perished because they were numerous, heavily concentrated in one place (Amsterdam), and led by passive community officials; they also had little opportunity to escape or hide in their heavily populated country. French Jews, too, perished as a result of the Vichy regime's collaboration with the Nazis. And yet, only about 20 percent of them died in the Holocaust because they seized opportunities to hide in remote villages or to flee to neutral Spain and Switzerland.

At the opposite extreme, almost all members of the very small Danish Jewish community were transported the short distance by boat to Sweden by Danes who had no sympathy with anti-Semitism. The Italians, too, although German allies, were not racists. Only after Mussolini's fall and the German takeover of the country were about 16 percent of the Italian Jews sent to their deaths, and the retreating Nazis had to do the job themselves. Hence, in certain circumstances resistance to the occupiers by local officials and private individuals saved lives. The fate of the different Jewish communities was determined by various concatenations of local attitudes, opportunities for flight or concealment, the size and location of the Jewish populations, and the nature of Nazi rule in the several countries (Fein, 1979).

Participants and Bystanders

Direct participation in the Holocaust by SS officials, Einsatzgruppen personnel, and camp guards was required in relatively small numbers. Indirect involvement by police, civil servants, private businessmen who profited from slave labor, and the like was considerably broader. Moreover, news of the exterminations rapidly leaked out of Eastern Europe in 1942, enmeshing much of the world in the catastrophe.

German police and government bureaucrats who defined, identified, assembled, and deported the Jews to the east were not always fanatical Nazis or anti-Semites. Many were careerists and efficient professionals, dedicated to following instructions and improvising solutions to problems in the spirit of their superiors. Amorality was encouraged by specialization; each department and individual was accountable for only one small segment of the program, diffusing personal responsibility. Ordinary Germans who had nothing to do with the Holocaust might hear rumors of crimes against the Jews in Eastern Europe, but they were preoccupied with staying alive and making ends meet in an increasingly disastrous wartime situation. The Jews quite literally were out of sight and out of mind.

In occupied Western Europe, the Nazis were stretched thin and depended heavily on local authorities to deliver the Jews for deportation. Especially in France and Holland, such assistance was widespread, encouraged by careerism and fear of reprisals. Small minorities in all the

Western European countries risked their lives to hide Jews or help them escape to neutral havens. Tens of thousands were saved as a result. Equally small minorities of Nazi sympathizers turned Jews and their helpers in to the authorities. The vast majority, however, were as apathetic and self-absorbed as most Germans.

Neutral countries such as Switzerland, Sweden, Spain, and Turkey accepted limited numbers of refugees, but none wanted to antagonize Hitler while his armies seemed invincible. Once the tide turned against him, however, they became more willing to aid the Jews. The Vatican also held to its traditional neutrality. Pope Pius XII kept silent about the Holocaust, evidently fearing German reprisals and hoping to enhance his role as a mediator. Individual Catholic clerics and laymen, however, did intervene on behalf of the Jews, notably in France, Hungary, and Slovakia.

The nations allied against Hitler reacted to the genocide of the Jews in diverse ways. The Soviet Union gave refuge to large numbers of Eastern European Jews who had fled before the *Wehrmacht*, but it acknowledged no special Nazi program to kill the Jews. In contrast, Great Britain and the United States warned the Germans and their allies that they would be called to account for their acts of genocide. A key question is: Could more have been done? It has been charged that Jewish lives could have been saved if President Roosevelt had not waited until 1944 to establish the War Refugee Board; if Germany and its satellites had been pressed to release their Jews; if the Allied air forces had bombed Auschwitz and its rail approaches in 1944; and if negotiations with the Nazis to ransom the Jews had been pursued. That the measures were not taken may be explained by indifference or even covert anti-Semitism among Allied leaders.

Or it may be argued that the Allies' single-minded preoccupation with the military side of the war was responsible. As they saw it, the best way to help all the victims of fascism was to press for the quickest possible victory. Nor will everyone agree that such measures would have altered the outcome in any significant way. No one should underestimate Nazi determination to exterminate the Jews, regardless of disruptions of the killing centers and promises held out in negotiations.

The Burden of History

A number of historical trends combined to make the Holocaust possible: anti-Semitism, racism, social Darwinism, extreme nationalism, totalitarianism, industrialism, and the nature of modern war. The absence of any one of these trends would have made the genocide of the Jews unlikely.

Anti-Semitism has a long history in most of Europe, not just in Germany. Traditional anti-Semitism arose out of Christian rejection of the Jews as deicides and deliberate misbelievers. Once it had generated pogroms, but in modern times it inspired contempt for the Jews by providing an explanation for their alleged materialism. Having rejected the saving grace of Jesus, so the argument went, they had lost their ethical standards in the pursuit of physical wealth and materialistic philosophies. Religiously based Judeophobia partially merged with newer criticisms of the Jews' role in the modern economy. Having been emancipated from special laws and restrictions only in the 19th century, the Jews were still concentrated in a few highly visible economic sectors such as banking, publishing, and the metal and clothing trades. This made them convenient targets for the victims of industrialization, some of whom blamed the Jews for economic depressions, bankruptcies, and unemployment. At the same time, the Jews' support for liberal political movements that had advocated Jewish emancipation generated anti-Semitism among conservative foes of individualism and representative government. The prominence of Jewish intellectuals such as Karl Marx and Leon Trotsky in the European socialist movements sparked criticisms of Jews for sacrificing patriotism to internationalism.

Although anti-Semitism was widespread before World War I, it was not a central issue. Most Judeophobes advocated solving the "Jewish problem" through assimilation or the restoration of special laws for the Jews, not through violent action. Only in backward Russia were there pogroms against the Jews. Racism, which implied that Jews were incapable of changing their ways, and social Darwinism, some forms of which predicted inevitable struggle between nations and races, gained adherents before 1914. But even their most radical exponents limited themselves to advocating Jewish emigration, and they were marginal figures without much influence.

World War I changed that. Anti-Semitism became entwined in the outraged nationalism of defeated Germany and in the quest for national identity in new states like Poland and Hungary and would-be states like the Ukraine and Croatia. Demagogues — such as Adolf Hitler in Germany — associated the Jews with economic hard times and the foreign oppressors. The growth of threatening Communist movements, some of them led by Jews, added grist to the anti-Jewish mill. Hitler, who had become a racial anti-Semite and social Darwinist as a young man in Vienna before 1914, advocated total solutions to Germany's staggering economic and political problems. Once in power, his totalitarian Third Reich enforced the "leadership principle" of absolute obedience to authority. Like Lenin, Hitler had learned totalitarianism from total war between 1914 and 1918. Then the belligerents had employed political centralization, economic regimentation, and thought-control to mobilize all national resources in a terrible war of attrition. The Third Reich would use them to destroy domestic rivals, to mobilize the German economy for aggressive war, and ultimately to exterminate the Jews.

All of these historical trends came together in 1941 with Hitler's war against the Soviet Union. Having identified the Jews with Communism, the dictator's crusade against "Judeo-Bolshevism" provided both cover and justification for genocide. In Hitler's name, highly specialized bureaucrats used the latest industrial technology to make war on the Jews as part of the larger national struggle for survival. The techniques of mass slaughter developed in the First World War were brought to new levels of perfection, only this time poison gas would be reserved for noncombatants.

Post-Holocaust Victim Responses

Studies of Holocaust survivors have shown that virtually all suffered to some degree from a "survivor syndrome" that included acute anxiety, cognitive and memory disorders, depression, withdrawal, and hypochondria. Some became clinical cases, but most learned to live with their trauma and rebuild old lives or start new ones (Berger, 1988).

Nazi genocide decimated the once-thriving Jewish communities of Eastern Europe. Hundreds of thousands of Holocaust survivors, fearing Communism and renewed outbreaks of anti-Semitism, would not or could not return to their former homes. Stranded in displaced persons' camps in Germany and Austria, virtually all expected to emigrate to Palestine or the United States. The U.S. government, however, limited the entry of refugees and placed heavy pressure on Great Britain to admit large numbers of Jews to Palestine. When Britain chose instead to honor its promises to the Arab majority limiting Jewish immigration, guerrilla uprisings by militant Zionists and international pressure forced Britain to withdraw from the area. The Jewish state that emerged from the partition of Palestine by the United Nations might eventually have come into being anyway, but the creation of Israel in 1948 was greatly facilitated by the need to find a home for large numbers of Holocaust survivors and by the widespread sympathy for Zionism engendered by Hitler's murderous actions.

The genocide of the Jews also had a major impact on Jewish religious thought. For Judaism, God's covenant with the ancient Israelites bound Him and the Jewish people to the end of time. History was viewed as the expression of God's will, working out a divine plan in which the Jews occupied a special place. Judaism conceived of God as merciful, loving, and omnipotent. How, then, could the dehumanization and mass murder of God's people be explained?

For some Jewish scholars this question could not be confronted without challenging traditional Judaism. After Auschwitz, they reasoned, faith in the redeeming God of the covenant, an omnipotent and merciful deity, was no longer possible. Nor did they find it credible any longer to regard the Jews as His chosen people. Just where this reappraisal was leading remained unclear, and other Jewish theologians rushed to the defense of continuity with covenantal Judaism. One such response was to reaffirm orthodoxy by placing the Holocaust within the tradition that heard God's commanding voice in catastrophes such as the destruction of the First and Second Temples. Judaism endured then, and Jews must not hand Hitler a posthumous victory by losing faith as a result of his policies.

A second approach embraced the traditional covenant by distinguishing between God's work and man's. God, for reasons that would become evident at the end of time, voluntarily placed restraints on Himself in order to make history possible. Hence the genocide of the Jews was man's responsibility, not God's. A third line of thought accepted that the covenant had been shattered in the Holocaust but held out the possibility of renewing it by returning to the quest for redemption and redefining tradition by living authentically religious lives (Roth and Berenbaum, 1989, pp. 259–370). In all these viewpoints, the impact of genocide on Judaism and on the Jews' sense of their place in the world was unmistakable.

Other Post-Holocaust Responses

Among Christian thinkers, the Holocaust induced a profound reappraisal of the traditional view of the Jews as living examples of what happens to those who reject Jesus. It is unlikely that those who advanced this view ever intended it to culminate in violence against the Jews, nor would it have done so by itself. And yet, there was no explaining away the contributions made by Christian anti-Semitism to the climate of opinion that made the genocide of the Jews possible in the European heartland of ostensibly Christian Western civilization.

Protestant theologians demanded a critical reappraisal of traditional Christian teachings of contempt for Judaism. They called for a reinterpretation of church Christology and eschatology to affirm the authenticity of the religion of the Jews and Christianity's vital roots in Judaism. The Catholic Church repudiated Judeophobia during the reforming pontificate of John XXIII. One of the key documents that emerged from the Second Vatican Council in 1965 recognized the common patrimony of Christianity and Judaism and denounced "hatred, persecutions, and displays of anti-Semitism, directed at Jews at any time and by anyone." In 1998, the Vatican Commission for Religious Relations with the Jews issued the document "We Remember: A Reflection on the Shoah," apologizing for the Catholic Church's failures during the Holocaust. It aroused controversy, however, because it did not link traditional Christian teachings about the Jews to Nazi genocide. German church scholars of both denominations confronted the lamentable failure of German Christians to stand up for the Jews under Hitler.

Germans as a whole, however, were slow to absorb the implications of the genocide of the Jews. Although a few called it an Allied fabrication, most repressed it and the whole memory of the now-discredited regime that had brought about their downfall. Although the new West German government in 1952 agreed to pay reparations to Jewish survivors, the West German courts were reluctant to pick up prosecutions of war criminals where the Allied jurists left off in 1949.

German consciousness of the Holocaust arose principally during the 1960s when a new generation began asking uncomfortable questions, primed by the sensational 1961 trial of SS Lieutenant Colonel Adolf Eichmann in Jerusalem. Since that time, critical examinations of the Holocaust and the regime that brought it about have entered the media and the school and university curricula. Perhaps the most concrete expression of Germany's reaction to the human rights abuses of the Nazis was its liberal postwar asylum law that up until 1993 made Germany a haven for political refugees from many lands.

The Eichmann trial also caused the Holocaust to have a delayed impact on American Jewry. Before then, little attention was paid to survivors and GI liberators of the concentration camps. The effects of the trial were intensified by the Six-Day War of 1967, which strengthened the Jews' sense of solidarity with Israel and encouraged them to encounter the agony of their coreligionists under Hitler as a means of intensifying their Jewish identity. For some American Jews that suffering imposed a special obligation to become involved in all forms of civil rights movements.

Elsewhere, the genocide of European Jewry had a much smaller impact. Austrians, who had welcomed Hitler in 1938 and perpetrated anti-Semitic outrages, hid behind the cloak of having been passive objects of Nazi aggression. Eastern Europeans, and especially Poles, saw themselves as victims of Nazism on the same level as the Jews. Until recently that view was reinforced by the refusal of Communist governments to acknowledge that the Jews had been singled out for annihilation by the Nazis.

Debates about the Holocaust

How and when did the decision to exterminate the Jews come about? For a group of historians referred to as "intentionalists," Hitler probably planned the extermination all along and certainly gave the order no later than early 1941, when the attack on the Soviet Union was being prepared. Opposing this interpretation is the "functionalist" view that the Nazi leadership replaced resettlement schemes with genocide only after the June 1941 attack on the Soviet Union. Some functionalists explain it as a result of euphoria over early victories in the summer. Others stress Hitler's frustration over stiffening Soviet resistance and the entry of the United States into the war later in the year. Most functionalists refer to a "decision-making process" that involved two or more increasingly radical orders made over several months. Although some functionalists believe that the central decisions were made by Hitler and other top Nazi leaders, others stress initiatives by local and regional officials facing hopelessly over-crowded ghettos and believing (correctly) that Hitler would not disapprove of mass murder. Since documents have been lost and orders were often given orally (and not in writing), the evidence is incomplete. Hence these debates promise to go on indefinitely (Browning, 2000, pp. 1–57).

Some Holocaust scholars have faulted the Jews for failing to offer armed resistance to the Germans or cooperating with them to some degree (Hilberg, 1985, pp. 1030–44). Other scholars have disputed this reasoning, stressing instead the Jews' almost total vulnerability to their tormentors and demanding a broader definition of resistance that embraces all efforts to keep Jews alive. These include measures to make Jews economically useful to the Germans, to smuggle food into the ghettos and Jews out of Nazi-dominated territory, and to provide the victims with morale-building cultural and social support (Bauer, 1979, pp. 26–40).

What motivated the perpetrators? A popular interpretation contends that the killers were "willing executioners" because their German culture had been deeply anti-Semitic long before Hitler came to power. (Goldhagen, 1996) Another stresses the immediate impact of Nazi indoctrination and ideology on the perpetrators (Bartov, 2003). A third viewpoint holds that the killers were mostly "ordinary men" who yielded to peer pressure and deferred to authority (Browning, 1992).

Controversy also surrounds the role of Holocaust bystanders, both those in German-controlled areas and those abroad. Some scholars have criticized the Poles in particular for failing to aid the Jews and even for actively betraying their Jewish neighbors (Gutman and Krakowski, 1986). The contrary view holds that the Poles were themselves so direly persecuted by the Germans that they had few opportunities to assist the Jews (Lukas, 1986). The United States and its allies have been condemned for doing little to rescue the Jews (Wyman, 1984). Opposing this is the view that, given German determination to kill all the Jews, there was nothing more that outsiders could have done except defeat Germany as quickly as possible (Rubinstein, 1997).

People's Perspective of the Holocaust Today

The Holocaust is perhaps the one genocide of which every educated person has heard. Especially in Israel and the United States, its memory is kept alive by schools, the mass media, and the observance of national days of remembrance. A network of Holocaust memorial centers educates the public at large, although they often come under pressure from groups that would vulgarize the genocide of the Jews by placing it at the service of their political agendas.

In the not-too-distant past, German consciousness of this genocide helped spark what has come to be called the "historians' debate." Conservative German historians suggested that their countrymen are much too mindful of past Nazi crimes. It is time, they said, to regard the Holocaust as one of many genocidal acts around the world and pay closer attention to more positive episodes in German history. These conservative scholars were strongly attacked by scholars who stressed the uniqueness of the Holocaust and the need for Germans to confront their heavy historical responsibility for it. It remains to be seen whether and how Germans' continuing preoccupation with the reunification of West and East Germany will affect their receptivity to neoconservative revisionism.

Austrians were shaken out of their historical amnesia in the 1980s by a scandal over their president, Kurt Waldheim. Although he was no war criminal, Waldheim clumsily attempted to cover up his youthful service in Hitler's armed forces; once revealed, it called attention to Austria's role in the atrocities of the Third Reich. Similarly, the 1987 trial in France of Klaus Barbie, the Gestapo "butcher of Lyon" who excelled in deporting the French to Auschwitz, raised uncomfortable questions about French complicity in Nazi crimes against the Jews. In Eastern Europe, however, the post-Communist revival of nationalism seems ill-suited to any similar reconsideration of the Holocaust.

Lessons of the Genocide of the Jews

German history dramatizes the insidious nature of racial prejudice. Many Germans were prejudiced in varying degrees, but only a minority wanted or expected actual violence against the Jews. Although the Nazis were deliberately vague about the practical implications of their anti-Semitism, they were sufficiently bold in their propaganda against the Jews that anyone supporting Hitler had at least to condone his Judeophobia. Moderate anti-Semitism made that possible and helped deliver the German nation into the hands of one of history's most malicious leaders. The Holocaust demonstrates that there is no safe level of racism. On the contrary, it teaches that any agenda that places economic and political concerns above human rights has the potential to result in disaster.

Once the genocide of the Jews began, there was little that outsiders could do to rescue them. Earlier, however, many of the victims might have been saved had other countries opened their doors to Jewish refugees. The time to aid the targets of racial bigotry is before their situation becomes untenable.

Those who were called upon to carry out the extermination process found that the modern state has effective ways of securing obedience and cooperation. Although the threat of coercion and reprisal was always present, compliance was more commonly assured by assigning each person only a single, highly specialized function, often not particularly significant in itself. Overall responsibility rested with someone else, and ultimately with Hitler. Unable or unwilling to answer for anything but their little spheres, well-educated and cultured individuals effectively placed themselves at the service of barbarism. Their participation made possible the bureaucratic organization of modern technology for mass extermination, this genocide's most characteristic feature. It challenges us all to develop sufficient moral sensitivity to take responsibility as individuals for all our fellow human beings.

Eyewitness Accounts: Holocaust — The Jews

Although the Germans kept careful records of their genocide of the Jews, not all of those records survived the downfall of the Third Reich, and in any event they could never view events from the standpoint of the victims. Hence, oral histories of the Holocaust are indispensable sources. Fortunately, interviews of survivors and witnesses have been conducted in many countries. These interviews cover a wide range of topics, including Jewish life before the Holocaust, Nazi policies toward the Jews in many countries, ghettoization, slave labor, resistance, successful and unsuccessful attempts at escape, liberation, and efforts to start over. Naturally, Jewish survivors living in North America, Western Europe, and Israel are most heavily represented.

Among the first scholars to interview Holocaust survivors was the American psychologist David P. Boder (1949). During the summer of 1946, he wire-recorded interviews with 70 displaced persons, many of them Jews, at camps in France, Italy, Germany, and Switzerland. Eight of the interviews were translated and published in book form under the title *I Did Not Interview the Dead*. The interview that follows was conducted by Boder, but was not included in that volume.

The Holocaust can never be encapsulated in a single person's recollections. However, this interview with Nechama Epstein reveals a remarkable breadth of experiences, including survival in ghettos, slave labor camps, and extermination centers. Made soon after World War II ended, it has the advantages of freshness and immediacy. Epstein begins her story in 1941 when the 18-year-old native of Warsaw and her family were herded into the city's ghetto together with 350,000 other Jews. [Note: This interview is housed in the David Boder Collection at the Simon Wiesenthal Center in Los Angeles. Acquisition # 81-992, spools 95, 96, pp. 104A/2593-2668.]

Epstein: When the ghettos began, among us began a great fight of hunger …. We began selling everything, the jewelry …. We finished at the last at the featherbed ….

Q: Who bought it?

A: People who were smuggling. They had. They were earning. Christians bought it …. And then we could already see that it was very bad. We had nothing to sell any more. Eight people were living on a kilo [2.2 lbs.] of beets a day …. With water. And every day, day by day, there remained less strength. We did not have any more strength to walk. My brother's 4-year-old child did not have anything to eat. He was begging for a small baked potato. There was none to give him …. And thus it lasted a year's time. Until … the first burned offering in my home was my father who, talking and walking, said he is fading from hunger, and died. My father was 60 years old …. When my father died, there began among us a still greater hunger. A kilo of bread cost 20 zlotys …. Every day there were other dead, small children, bigger children, older people. All died of a hunger death.

Q: What was done with the dead?

A: The dead were taken … if one fell on the street … he was covered. A stone was put on top, and thus he lay until …. There was not enough time to collect the dead …. And then people drove around with small carts. There were no funeral coaches any more, nothing. People drove around with small carts, collected the dead, loaded them up, took them to the cemetery, and buried them — women, men, children, everybody in one grave …. And we … It had broken out, the first deportation that was in the year 1942 …. I do not remember the exact month. In the beginning of winter [Note: *sic.* Between September 5 and 12, 1942] There came down a whole … a few thousand Germans had come down, with weapons, with machine guns, with cannons, and they … made a blockade. They surrounded from one end of the street to the other …. They began to chase the people out of the houses …. It was terrible. Many ran into the gates. They [the Germans] saw small children. They grabbed them by the legs and knocked them against the walls …. The mothers saw what is being done to their children. They threw themselves out of windows …. They [the Germans] went into a hospital, a Jewish hospital …. And they began taking out all the sick that were there ….

Q: Did you see it yourself?

A: Yes …. I was being led to the rail terminal …. The sick began jumping out the windows. So they [the Germans] ran on the roofs with machine guns and shot down at the sick. And all were shot. And we were led away to the rail terminal. There I was the whole night. That night was a terrible one ....

Q: What sort of a building was it [the rail terminal]? ...

A: A school was there at one time .... Then a depot was made there, and the Jews of the ghetto were all concentrated there. They were led in there, and there they were a night, two nights. They led a railroad siding to the street, and in trains [Jews were] transported to Treblinka .... At night Germans came in, threw hand grenades. At the people .... There were loud screams. We had no place to go out. One lay on top of the other; we had to ... eh ... relieve ourselves on the spot .... It was a frightful experience to live through that night .... In the morning they began to chase us out. "Alle aus!" ... And they began to arrange in rows of five mothers with children, men, everybody together. And whoever could not ... walk straight, he was immediately shot on the spot .... We got into the railroad cars. Two hundred persons were packed into one railroad car. Riding in these wagons everyone saw death before the eyes at any instance. We lay one of top of the other. One pinched pieces from another. We were tearing pieces.

Q: Why?

A: Because everybody wanted to save oneself. Everybody wanted to catch air. One lay suffocating on top of another .... We could do nothing to help ourselves. And then real death began .... After we had traveled for four hours, it became terribly hot. But so fast did the train travel that there was nothing .... We began thinking, the youths, what should we do. The mothers were telling their children they should save themselves, they should jump. Maybe in spite of all they will remain alive.

Q: Were the doors open?
A: Closed, everything! There was a small window with bars.

Q: Then how could one jump?
A: Many had along with them files, knives, hammers .... There had begun a great thirst. It became terribly hot. Everybody undressed .... There were small children who began to cry terribly. "Water!" ... So we started banging on the doors. The Germans should give water .... We were screaming. So they began to shoot inside, from all four sides.

Q: On the stations?
A: Not on the sta-... while traveling. They were sitting on the roofs .... where one steps down, on the steps, Germans were sitting .... And they began to shoot inside. When they began to shoot inside, very many people were killed. I was sitting and looking how one gets hit by a bullet, another one gets hit by a bullet. I, too, expected to get hit in a moment .... And I

saved myself by hiding under the dead. I lay down underneath the dead. The dead lay on top of me. The blood of the killed was flowing over me …. There lay a little girl of four years. She was calling to me, "Give me a little bit of water. Save me." And I could do nothing. Mothers were giving the children urine to drink ….

Q: Is it really true?

A: I saw it! I did it myself, but I could not drink it. I could not stand it any more. The lips were burned from thirst …. I thought this is it, I am going to die …. So I saw that the mother is doing it, and the child said, "Mama, but it is bitter. I cannot drink it." … So she said, "Drink, drink." And the child did not drink it, because it was bitter. And I myself imitated it, but I was not able to drink it, and I did not drink it. But what then? There were girders inside the railroad cars …. From the heat, perspiration was pouring from the girders. This we … one lifted the other one up. It was high up, and we licked the moisture off the girders …. It was very stifling. There was that little window, a tiny one, so we wanted to open it. Every time we opened it, they would shoot in …. And when we wanted to open it, not minding that they were shooting, we did. There were small children, and they were all suffocating …. We could not stand it any more.

Q: And then?

A: And thus I rode all night. Early in the morning — it was about 2 in the morning, maybe 3, just before dawn — my mother began crying very much … . She begged us to save ourselves. The boys took a saw and cut a hole — it [the door] was locked with a chain from the other side…. And we took the bars off the windows…. And we started to jump. No. What does "to jump" mean? One pushed out the other one ….

Q: Aha. Did the Germans let them?

A: They did not let them. They immediately started shooting on the spot. When I jumped out I fell into a ditch …. And I remained lying completely unconscious. And the railroad car … the train passed …. I came to. It was at night, around three in the morning, so I ….

Q: And your mother herself did not jump.

A: No. The mother could not. With the small child she could not jump. And a woman of 60, she could not jump ….

Q: And then? …

A: I came to. I got back my thoughts, so I went to look for my brother …. In the meantime there arrived some sort of a Polish militia man … and told me that I should quickly run away from here, because the Gestapo is all around here. I will be shot here. I should run away. He told me that I had jumped near Radzin and Lukow .... So he told me to go to the Miedzyrzec ghetto. There is a ghetto with Jews .... I began to walk on foot toward Miedzyrzec .... When I jumped out I met a little girl. She had also jumped. She had her entire leg completely torn open. While jumping she had caught on a piece of iron, and she tore open her leg .... And the two of us started to walk. Yes, after getting up I went to look for my brother. I had gone about ten feet. He lay shot. He had a bullet here in the heart .... I could not move away from him, but that Christian [the militia man] said that I should go away quickly. The struggle for life was stronger than anything. I left my brother on the road. I do not know what happened to his bones. And I went on. I had walked with that little girl for about three hours. Dark it was. Through woods, through fields we crawled, crawled, crawled ....

Q: That little girl was a stranger?

A: A strange little girl. I don't know at all that little girl .... She was about 14 years old .... And the little girl with the bleeding leg ... for terror she did not feel the pain .... After having walked thus for perhaps ten kilometers, the two of us remained sitting where the road leads into a forest. And we could not walk any more. The child said that she cannot walk any more. The leg hurts her. We don't know what will be. In the meantime I had heard gentiles saying that Germans prowl on this road looking for Jews. And I saw it is bad. With the child I cannot walk. So I took the child. I did not know what to do. I carried her perhaps ... perhaps, who knows, a kilometer or two. I myself did not have any strength. I was barefoot. My shoes had remained in the railroad car, because I had undressed. I did not have the time to put anything on. I was completely naked and barefoot. And that child remained in the field. And I went away. I could not help any more at all. The child had fallen, and I could not do anything to help any more. I went away. [A pause]

Q: Go on.

A: I had walked thus for about 20 kilometers. I do not know myself how many kilometers I had covered. I came to the Miedzyrzec ghetto .... I went in. It was a day after a large deportation. So I went in .... Entering the ghetto, it became faint before my eyes. It was at night. I did not have anywhere to go. When arriving there, I regretted very much that I had jumped off the train, because at every step, wherever I went, shot people were lying. Broken windows, all stores looted. Terrible things happened there .... In that ghetto I lived eight months.

Q: Did you ... ?

A: ... in deathly fear.

Q: ... register with the ... ?

A: There was a Jewish Community Council. I registered with the Jewish Community Council, and I [just sat there and waited]. It was not worth it. Every four weeks there were new deportations. From the small towns all around and around Jews were brought in there. And there was a sort of an assembly depot for Jews. And from there all the Jews were being sent to Treblinka. There I lived through three terrible deportations. During the first deportation I hid in an open attic and lay there for four weeks. I lived just on raw beets .... I did not have anything to drink. The first snow fell then, so I made a hole in the roof and pulled in the hand a little snow. And this I licked. And this I lived on.

Q: Were you there alone?

A: No. We were about ... there were about 20 people there. There was a father with a mother with child. There were some others .... We had nothing to eat. Thus we lived four weeks. We found raw peas which we ate. I had pared the beets, and afterwards I gathered the rinds of the beets, because I had nothing more to eat. And thus I nourished myself for four weeks, till there was a deportation. It lasted four weeks, that deportation. After the deportation we came down from the attic. At that time a lot of Jews had also been shot. Coming down from the attic, it was a terrible thing to see. We had to ... we were taken to work removing the dead.

Q: Who were the SS? Germans and who else? ...

A: There were a few Ukrainians, too, but not many .... All the streets were splashed with blood. In every ditch Jewish blood had been poured. We went down. We had nothing to eat. We started looking for something to eat so we ...

Q: Was there no council, no Community Council?

A: At the time the chairman had been taken away. The chairman had been shot. He was taken out first. He was the first .... A very fine man. He was taken out the first — with the wife, with the child. They were told to turn around, and they were shot. There were Jewish police, too .... Jewish policemen. So they [the Jews of the ghetto] were shot little by little. During each deportation ten, twenty were taken and also transported into the railroad cars. And they were shot, sent away. Those who escaped were shot .... So there was nobody to turn to. Everybody was afraid to go out. Many were lying [in hiding] there still a few weeks after the deportation. They did not know that it is already safe .... When we came down it was sort of peaceful for about two months. For two months time we lived on that which the Jewish Council gave to those who were strangers [from other towns and waiting for deportation] .... They gave them every day a kilo of potatoes and a piece of bread. The food was not important, because it was

... every day we lived in great fear. People walking in the streets were shot at.

Q: Did you have relatives there? Did you know anyone?

A: Nobody. I was all alone .... Mine had all gone away. I had remained all alone. I had to support myself. By how did I support myself? I carried water.

Q: For whom?

A: For the Jews who lived there I carried water. And for that I received a few pennies. And that is how I supported myself .... In brief, it dragged on till winter, till the Birth of Christ.

Q: That is when? Christmas?

A: Yes. Then there was a frightful night to live through. There came down drunken Gestapo from Radzin .... And in the middle of the night we were asleep in a room. There were perhaps, who knows, 30 people altogether in that house where we were .... And they entered. I was sleeping there with two little girls. These children had also escaped from the Radzin ghetto. Two girls, little ones. One was about eight years old, and one about six years. I was sleeping with them in the room. There were other girls. In our room there were about 15 persons. In the middle of the night we hear ... shooting. We lay in great deathly fear. And they were knocking on our door. And I did not know why they could not enter through the door. In the morning I got up. I opened the door. A shot person fell into ... my room, into the house where we were lying. When we came in [into the other rooms] there lay shot all who were living in those rooms. Two children with a father who were sleeping in bed, everything was shot. A man lay with his stomach completely torn open, his guts outside on the ground. And later Jewish police came in. The Germans had left, and we had to clean up the blood and all that .... During the second deportation I was not able to hide any more. I was led away to a synagogue. There was a large synagogue. There, all the Jews were assembled. In the synagogue it was terrible. They simply came in — if they heard a cry, they shot in. They threw grenades. They beat. They struck. They did not give anything to drink. We had to relieve ourselves on the same place were we slept. I was there a whole night. I saw it was bad. I did not want to go to death. I went on fighting against it. I went over to a window. It was on the first floor. We took two towels, I and another girl. We lowered the towels from the windows, and we crawled down and escaped down into a cellar, and there we again lived through the second deportation .... Again we lived [there] a few months. During the last deportation I was not able to hide any more. I was led away into a transport. It was a beautiful summer day .... It was May Day .... We were loaded on railroad cars. We were led through the streets exactly like we had been driven to Treblinka. They shot at those who did not walk in line. Many people fell, children. [We were] running fast. I myself received from a German ... a [rubber] hose over the head. I got a large bump. I did not pay attention to the pain, but I ran fast ....

Q: What then?

A: We were put into the railroad cars. It was the same as to Treblinka, shooting. We had nothing to drink. We drove a day and a night. We were taken down to Majdanek. Many were saying that we were being taken to Treblinka, but the direction was toward Majdanek. We were taken off at the Majdanek camp. We were all lined up. There were many who were shot. They were taken down, those who were still alive. They were taken down on the square, and they were immediately shot to death. The mothers were put separately, the children separately, the men separately, the women separately .... Everything was separated. The women, the young women, were taken to the Majdanek camp. The men were taken to another camp. The children and the mothers were led to the crematory. All were burned .... We never laid eyes on them again .... I was in Majdanek two months. I lived through many terrible things. We had nothing to eat. We were so starved. At first we did not know yet what such a thing as a camp means. In the morning, at 6 in the morning, came in a German, an SS woman, and started to chase us with a large strap, beating everybody. We were lying on the beds, grieved, with great worries, thinking where the mothers were, where the fathers and the children were. We were crying. Then came in a German woman at 6 in the morning with a large strap and beat us over the head to go out to the inspection. At inspection it could happen that we would stand four, five hours.

Q: Why so long?

A: People were being kept so long because everybody did not know yet what ... what this was all about. Many children of about 16 years hid in the attic. They were afraid to come out. They thought they were going to be shot .... And for that, that they had hidden, we stood five hours as a punishment. Later nobody hid any more. They said whoever will hide himself will be shot. And so I was in Majdanek two months.

Q: Did you work there?

A: Yes. We were sent to do garden work. We were sent to carry the shit which .... There were no toilets there, so we carried it in buckets. We were not given anything to eat. They were hitting us over the legs. They were beating us over the heads. The food consisted of 200 grams [7 ounces] of bread a day, and a little soup of water with [leaves of] nettles. This was the food. And I was there two month's time. The hunger there was so great that when a caldron of food was brought, we could not wait for it to be distributed, but we threw ourselves on the food, and that food would spill on the ground, and, with the mud, we ate it. After having been there two months ... they began to select the healthy, healthy children who are able to work .... They tested the heart. Whoever had the smallest blemish on the body did not come out [any more] from there. Only 600 women were picked out, and I was among them. This was in... July .... I was taken away to Auschwitz. The conditions were then already a little better. Fewer were being packed into a railroad car. They were putting in already 60 to a wagon .... Arriving at Auschwitz, we were led into a large hall before taking us to be bathed. All the women had their hair cut off ....

Q: That was the first time you had that done?
A: For the first time ... just in Auschwitz .... So I had my hair shorn off, and they tattooed numbers on us.... We had very great anguish, because we had our hair cut off. How can a woman live without hair? They took us and dressed us in long pants ...

Q: Who cut off your hair?
A: Our hair was cut off by women who were working there.

Q: Yes. What then? They cut it from the whole body?
A: Completely. On the body, here [she points], everywhere, everywhere, everything .... And we were dressed in trousers and blouses. We were terribly hungry ....

Q: What did you do there? ...
A: We went to work in a detail which was call the death detail. Why? This I will tell, too .... We went to work, the 600 women from Majdanek. It took a month, and there remained no more than 450. We died out of hunger .... We worked carrying stones on barrows, large stones. To eat they did not give us. We were beaten terribly. There were German women who were also prisoners [i.e., prisoner foremen]. They were imprisoned for prostitution .... They [the prostitutes] used to beat us terribly. They said that every day they must kill three, four Jews. And food they did not give us .... We carried stones on ... barrows. We carried sand, stones. We were building a highway — women! The work was very hard. We got heavily beaten with rubber hoses over the legs from those German women overseers, those who also were imprisoned, prisoners .... Thus I labored for three months, until I became sick. I had gotten malaria .... I went around for two weeks with a 41-degree fever [about 105 degrees F]. I was afraid to go to the sick-ward. There was such a sick-ward .... I was afraid to go, because it was said that if one goes there one does not come back any more, one is taken away to the crematory .... I saw that I cannot stand it any more. The legs were buckling under me. Each day I got more and

more beaten, because I did not work. I could not eat any more .... I would accumulate bread from one day to the next. I could not eat it any more. I gave it away to other girls .... I decided to go away to the sick-ward .... There were no medicines. I lay around for about four weeks without medicine .... There was a doctor, also a prisoner, a Jewess .... She was not able to help at all. She had no medicaments. None were given to her. And in this way I pulled through the crisis ....

Q: And then?

A: I lay around in such a way for four weeks. I did not have anything to drink .... I pleaded for a drink of water. They did not want to give it to me, because the water there was contaminated. It was rusty from the pipes. If one drank that water one became still more sick. I passed the crisis, and during that time there were three such ... selections. They came to take sick [people] to the crematory. During each time I lived through much deathly fear. My whole method of saving myself was that I hid myself. Christian women were lying there, so I climbed over to the Christians, into their beds, and there I always had the good fortune to hide.

Q: Did the Christian women let you?

A: Yes. There was a Christian woman, a very fine one .... She was also very sick. She was already near death, that Christian woman.

Q: Why was she in the concentration camp?

A: She was there for political causes .... And ... she was not taken. Christians were not taken to the crematory, just Jews ....[Note: Epstein was mistaken on this point.] They had it much better. They received aid from the Red Cross. They received packages from home, and we nothing. We had to look on how they ate. If there was one, a kind one, she would occasionally give us, the sick, something. And that is how I was going on saving myself in the sick-ward. My sickness was very terrible to describe. Complications set in afterwards. I had many boils on the body. I had neglected scabies .... And I had nothing with which to cure myself. At one time I lay already completely dead, that the Christian women cried ... they made an outcry that I am already going to die. So there came up to me a doctor, and she brought some sort of an injection, and she gave it to me.

Q: A Jewish doctor?

A: Yes ....[Note: The SS routinely used Jewish doctors to treat fellow inmates who fell ill. This illustrates the tension that existed between the need to provide slave labor and the ultimate goal of genocide.] After that injection I became a little stronger, and I got out of bed. I nursed the other sick. Much strength I did not have, but I was already able to walk around a little. Three weeks had passed. There came an order to deliver the names of all the sick, everyone who had scabies .... Then one knew that he is for sure going to his death. And I had it, too. I was very worried, and I knew that now has come the moment that I have to go .... I did not sleep at night. I could not eat, because I knew that all my misery, all my suffering was for nothing, because now had come my end .... But it was not so. The same day when they had ordered to make the list of us, they came to that sick-ward where there were only typhus patients, and all were taken out, the entire sick-ward. Not one remained. It was on the night of Yom Kippur.

Q: What was done with them?

A: All were taken, undressed, nude, wrapped in blankets, thrown in the ... truck like sheep, shut the trucks, and driven away in the direction of the crematory. We all went and looked, so we saw how the women [on the trucks] were singing *Kol Nidrei* .... They were singing the *Hatikvah*. When they said good-by, they said, "We are going to death, and you take revenge for us." ... They are still pleading to be left. They are young. There was a girl 18 years old, and she was crying terribly. She said that she is still so young, she wants to live, they should leave her, they should give her some medicine to heal her scabies. And nothing helped. They were all taken away.

Q: How come you were not included? You also had scabies.

A: I was not yet in the line .... Everything went according to the line ....

Q: How many sick were taken?

A: Four hundred persons. An entire block ....

Q: Could the crematory be seen burning?

A: Of course! When we went out at night we saw the entire sky red [from] the glow of the fire. Blood was pouring on the sky. We saw everything. We knew. When we went to the shower hall we saw the clothing of the people who were not any more lying there. The clothing was still there. We recognized the clothing of the people who had left and returned no more .... So that we knew. It was 100 percent! We saw every night the burning crematory. And the fire was so red it was gushing forth blood towards the sky. And we could not help at all. Sometimes, when we would go out at night to relieve ourselves, we saw how illuminated ... how transports were brought with mothers and children. The children were calling to the mothers.

Q: That was in Birkenau. [Note: Birkenau was the extermination division of Auschwitz.]

A: It was to Birkenau that they brought huge transports from Hungary, from Holland, from Greece ... from all over Europe .... And all that was burned in Auschwitz. The children they burned immediately, and from a certain number of people, from thousands, a hundred might be taken out, and they were brought to the camp …. And the rest were burned …. The next morning a German doctor appeared. I became very scared. All who were in the block became scared — we were all sick from malaria — because it was said that the others were taken yesterday and us they will take today …. In the meantime he came with a list, and called out my name and another 12 Jewish names, and to that another 50 Christian women …. And he said that we who are sick with malaria, who show a positive sickness — because there were positive and non-positive …. Because on me was made a … a … a …

Q: A blood test?

A: … a blood test, and it showed that I had a positive malaria. So they told us that we were going to Majdanek, back to Majdanek …. I did not believe it. In the evening all of us were taken, 70-odd people. We were put on a truck and driven to the train. Riding on the truck all of us believed that we were going to the crematory. We had thought that it will be an open truck, and we will be able to see where we are being taken to, but ultimately it turned out to be quite different. We were taken in a closed one. But [as we were driven] past the guard we heard … "70-odd prisoners for Majdanek." … So we already knew that we were being taken to Majdanek …. We were put … on the station, we were led into a freight car, which is used for transporting cattle. We were all put in. Among [us] were many ethnic German women who had also been imprisoned there in the camp ….

Q: Because of what?

A: They were for prostitution.

Q: How did they behave, those women?

A: Very mean. Very mean. They beat so. They hit so. One can't at all imagine.

Q: [Fighting] among themselves?

A: No they beat us, us …. And upon coming into the railroad car they made such a little piece of a ghetto. They put us into a small part of the railroad car …. And for themselves they took the bigger part. And in our part we were squeezed one on top of another. We nearly crushed ourselves to death. En route two girls died. They were very weak. We had no food. And they were full of scabies …. They could not stand it any more. En route … they were taken down in the middle of the night in Majdanek, and they were dead …. We arrived there, 11 Jews …. When I was there the first time there were still 30,000 Jews …. A few days later we found out that there were Jews here. So one Jew sneaked away … and came to us. She wanted to see the Jews who had arrived. From them we learned about a most sad misfortune …. On the 3rd of November it was. At 4 in the morning there came down the entire Gestapo with many policemen, with many SS men. They surrounded the entire Majdanek camp and called out all the people. There were 23,000 people.

Q: Not only Jews, everybody ….

A: Just the Jews. All the Christians remained in the blocks…. The Jews were taken out and told to form rows of five. The music played very violently and …

Q: Was it Jewish music?

A: No. Polish music. German music …. And the people were told to go up [to the place where] the crematory had been installed. Two days before, 80 men had been taken out. And they were told to dig very large pits. And nobody knew what these pits were for …. Ultimately it turned out that those pits were for the people who had dug them …. They went up in rows of fives, children, mothers, old, young, all went up to the fifth sector [of the camp]. Coming to the graves, there stood sentries with Tommy guns and with machine guns. And they told them all to undress. Young women flung themselves at the sentries and began to plead that he should shoot them with good aim so that they should not suffer …. In the head … not in the stomach or the leg so that they should suffer …. And the sentries laughed at that and said, "Yes, yes. For you such a death is too good. You have to suffer a little." And not everyone was hit by the bullet. And from them were separated 300 women, those who had remained whom we had met. And these women had to clean up next morning — all those who remained — the shot. They were doused with gasoline and were burned.

Q: In the pits?

A: In the pits. And afterwards they had to take the clothes which everybody recognized from her mother, from her sister, from her children. They cried with bloody tears. They had to take those clothes and sort them. And everybody was thinking, "Why did I not go together with them? Why did we remain alive?" …

Q: How had they been selected?

A: They came to the square where they were standing and picked out the most beautiful women … the youngest, the healthiest women were separated …. And 55 men …. Those men were prisoners of war ….

Q: Were they Christians or Jews?

A: Jews. All Jews…. And these Jews had remained there, these 55 Jews who helped us very much — [we] the women who had returned from Auschwitz …. We were completely non-human [i.e., dehumanized]. We looked like skeletons. And they [the 55 Polish-Jewish POWs] put us on our feet. They helped us very much.

Q: What could they do?

A: They had … in the things that they sorted from the dead was very much gold, very many diamonds, whole bars of gold. This they gave away. There were Christians there …. And the Christians received food packages from home, from the Red Cross. So they [the Polish Jewish POWs] gave all that away, and they received pieces of bread, whatever one could. And with that they nourished us.

Q: Tell me, you were all searched. They looked and they searched, and one had to undress. How was it possible to find gold on the dead? …

A: A Jew had it sewn in their drawers. A Jew had it in the sole of the shoes. A Jew had it concealed in the hair. On a Jew they could never …. they searched and they searched, and they did not find …. With that the Jews would save themselves. They always had something on themselves ….

Q: And they did not hand it over to the Gestapo?

A: No. It made no difference any more. Who wanted to go to the Gestapo? We knew today we live and tomorrow we die …. It was already all the same. At that time we were not afraid of anything any more, because we knew that our turn was coming now and now we have to perish …. Later, … when we became healthier, we were transferred to the fifth sector and we lived together in one block with these 300 women ….

Q: You had recovered from the scabies?

A: Yes, I became cured, because these men took from the Christians salves which they received from the Red Cross, stole it from them and brought to us ….

Q: Why did they bring you over there? … To Majdanek, these who had positive malaria?

A: Because they … it was [just] a whim on their part. Thirty thousand they burned and 13 they led to life …. That is how it was being done by them …. And I had the luck that I was among these 13, and that I had been taken out …. And we could not believe it ourselves …. And we were in Majdanek also thinking any day we will be burned. There are no Jews. To the crematory we saw them bringing every day other … children, women …. They were brought and immediately burned, from Lublin, from all over, from the entire Lublin region. Christians ….

Q: They were not gassed?

A: Gassed first and then burned. If there was no gas, they [the SS] would shoot and then burn [them]. We even heard shots, too, because it was very near …. And we were there together with them and we lived together with them. The women told us about those tragedies. It was so frightful. They cried so terribly that it was …. They would just repeat, "Are there still Jews in the world?" We thought there were no more Jews, only we few have remained. We thought that they have already exterminated all the Jews from Europe, from all Poland. And we told them there is still a camp in Auschwitz, they are still burning Jews every day ….

Q: And then?

A: After having been eight months in Majdanek, the second time, an order came: These women, the 300, the women survivors of the action, must go to Auschwitz. And we, the 13, of whom had remained 11, go someplace else, because we have been tattooed, and they [are] not. They began crying very much …. Two days later we were led out to Plaszow …. Near Cracow, a [forced labor] camp …. They had added yet 300 women from Radom …. There were little children, too. Pregnant women were there, and they led us away to Plaszow. Arriving in Plaszow, they took away the small children. They took away the pregnant women. There was a famous hill. They were taken to the top and undressed nude. There were no crematories. They were shot, and afterwards we carried boards and made a fire, and they were all burned.

Q: You yourself carried the …

A: Yes I carried the board! We carried the boards, and we saw how they shot them. If anyone had gold teeth, they pulled the teeth out.

Q: You saw that yourself?

A: Saw myself. I had afterwards still worse [experiences]. Before leaving Plaszow …. It was on the Jewish cemetery. Where the cemetery was once … they made a camp …. We walked on the tombstones. With the tombstones they made streets. They [the SS] shot people every day at first. A Jew was pushing a barrow with stones. He struggled. So he [the guard] did not like the way he pushed it. He was instantly shot ….

Q: And then?

A: While in Plaszow, a transport was brought with small children from Krasnik. I was all alone. I had it very hard, but I remedied it a little. I went to scrub floors in the blocks. People who had [something] gave me a little piece of bread to eat. When they brought the children I took a great liking to a little girl. That little girl was from Krasnik. Her name was Chaykele Wasserman.

Q: How come children were brought without mothers?

A: The mothers had been … It was like this. They had liquidated the camp. The Russians were approaching Krasnik, so they liquidated the camp. And that child's mother had escaped, and she was shot. And that child had come alone, without a mother, to the lager. And many children — they were all without mothers, because the mothers were immediately taken away. And the children separately. And the children were … they did not have enough time to take along the mothers. They grabbed the children and ran with them. And the children were brought to Plaszow. I took that little girl. I was with that little girl for four months. That child was very dear to me. I loved it very much. That child could not go anyplace without me. I was thinking I shall live through this war. I will be very happy with such a pretty and smart little girl, because it had hurt me very much that I had lost my brother's children. And I cheered myself up a little with that child ….

Q: What did the child do there all day in the camp?

A: The child did nothing. The child went around … on the street. It was not even called to inspection. Sometimes it went to inspection, and sometimes not …. After a time, they [the guards] came and took away from us all the children, without exception. And that child was very clever. She had a very clever head on her.

Q: How old was she?

A: She was eight years old …. She hid in a latrine, that is in a privy …. All the children were taken away. People came and told me to go there, Chaykele is calling me, she cannot crawl out from the hole. And I went and pulled out the child. The child stank very badly. I … washed her up, dressed her in other clothes, and brought her to the block. And that child …

Q: You have to excuse me. When a child hides in a latrine … did the other people know when they went to the latrine …

A: No. When inspection was over [and] the children were taken away, women went to the latrine. This was a women's latrine. So the child began yelling they should call me and I should take her out …. And I was instantly called, and I pulled the child out. When I pulled her out she was overjoyed with me, and she said she was a very clever little girl. "Now I shall already remain alive." You see? … But, alas, it was not so. After a time we were … The Russians were approaching Plaszow … and we were again dragged away. I was the second time taken to Auschwitz …. We arrived in the middle of the night.

Q: And the child with you?

A: The child I took along. What will be, will be. I kept the child with me. We came there at night. All night long the child did not sleep. She did not want to eat anything. She just kept asking me, "Does gas hurt?" … If not, [then] she is not afraid. But I cried very much. I said, "Go, you little silly one. There is a children's home. There you will be." She says, "Yes, a children's home! You see, there is the crematory. It burns. There they will burn me." It was very painful for me. I could not stand it. I could not sleep. But suddenly the child fell asleep in my arms. I left the child lying on the ground and went over to some man who worked there in the shower-bath, and I pleaded with him. I lied to him. I said it was my sister's child, and he should see to help me save the child. So he said, "You know what? Tomorrow morning you will all be undressed nude, and you will all be led before the doctor. He will make such a selection. And the child ... you will hide in your rags when you will undress." And that child was very clever. She did not even take off the shoes. She hid in the rags. And I was waiting thus — it was in the morning — till the evening, till the child will come out. And in the evening I saw the child all dressed up... When they took away all the children ... the child got out from under the rags and came to me. The German doctor had left, and the child came to me.

Q: And who ... how did she wash herself and everything?

A: In the shower-bath there were Jewish women, there where the bath was. She was washed. Clothes there were very plentiful, from the many children [who] had been burned there, thousands, hundreds of thousands of children. She had been dressed very nicely. And the child came to me with great joy. "See," she says, "again I have remained alive. I shall again remain alive."

Q: And how ... you too were left [alive]?

A: I bathed and was sent out .... They beat badly. We were chased out. I waited. It was a huge transport of a few thousand people, so I waited till the last. Everybody had gone to the camp, to the block and I waited for the child to come out .... And together with the child I left for the block .... While being in the block, not long, a short time, three days, it was very bad. It was cold. They chased us out bare to inspection. There was nothing to eat .... The cold was so cutting, one could get sick. And the child, too, had to go to inspections .... The child was counted as a grown-up person, but that child had much grief. She was not numbered .... [Note: Only those who were to be kept alive were tattooed.] After the three days there came a doctor .... And he again selected women to be sent to Germany. I was taken away. And that child cried very much. When she saw that I was being taken, she cried very much and screamed, "You are leaving me. Who will be my mother now?" But, alas, I could not help any. I could do nothing with the German. I went away and left the child ....

Q: Did you ask them ... they should ...

A: I asked, so he said, "If you want to go to the crematory, you can go with the child. And if not, then go away from the child." ...

Q: And so you don't know what happened to the child.

A: I don't know anything [about] what happened to the child. I know only one thing: I left. The child said good-bye to me, and I was led away to Bergen-Belsen .... Arriving in Bergen-Belsen, there reigned a terrible hunger. People were dying ...

Q: Do you remember in which month, in what year? ...

A: The last month. In the year 1944, in winter .... I was in Bergen-Belsen three months. The hunger was so great — a terror. We went to the garbage heap and picked the peels from the turnips that were cooked in the kitchen. And if one chanced to grab a turnip ... I was very daring. I did everything. I fought strongly to stay alive. So I got out through the gate, where they were shooting, and grabbed a turnip. And a minute later they shot a girl who grabbed a turnip. I ran into the block.

Q: Did the turnip lay outside the gate?

A: No. Outside the gate there was located the kitchen ... with ... with wires so one would not be able to get near .... So I opened the gate and go in. I risked it. I knew that the moment I grab it the bullet may hit me, but the hunger was stronger than [the fear of] death .... And I went and brought such a turnip. I returned to the block. People, corpses, dead ones, assaulted me, that I should give them [some] too. I shared it with them. We rejoiced. We finished the meal and went to sleep. After having been [there] three months, a German came again, and again selected Jews. I did not know where to [turn]. But I only wanted to go on, on. It always seemed to me here it is no good, there it will be better. And again I traveled. They collected 200 Hungarian women, 300 Polish women, and we were led away to Aschersleben ....

Q: What was there?

A: There was an airplane factory .... There everything had been bombed .... There was a camp commander, a very mean one. There were foreigners .... Prisoners of war ... Dutch, French, Yugoslavian. [Note: After about two months, the camp was evacuated on foot as American forces approached.]

Q: Where did you go?

A: Very terrible was the road. On the way many were shot, those who couldn't walk. We didn't get [anything] to eat. They dragged us from one village to another, from one town to another. We covered 60, 70 kilometers a day.

Q: How many people were you?

A: Five hundred ... . Only women. Two hundred fell en route .... I stood and looked how the camp commander took out his revolver, and [to each] one who couldn't walk he said, "Come with me," took her aside and shot

her …. We endured all that till they dragged us as far as Theresienstadt ….
[Note: Theresienstadt was the model Nazi ghetto, in Czechoslovakia, about
260 km. from Aschersleben.] Arriving in Theresienstadt we were completely in tatters. From the blankets we had to cover ourselves with, we
made socks, we dressed ourselves. We were very dirty. We were badly
treated. We were beaten. They screamed at us. "Accursed swines! You are
filthy. What sort of a people are you?" … We were thinking how would they
look if they were on our level …. There were only Jews, many Jews from
Germany. There were very many old women who were mixed [intermar-
ried], Germans and Jews. They had Jewish sons, SS men …. They were
serving Hitler, and she was Jewish; the husband was a German. And that is
the reason they remained alive. All old, grey women. And all the children
with mothers had been transported to Auschwitz before …. There was very
little food. And the Germans prepared a large crematory. They had heard
that the front is again approaching. They prepared a large crematory, but
they did not have enough time to do it …. [Note: Theresienstadt was
liberated on May 8, 1945.] We heard the Russian tanks were here. And we
didn't believe it ourselves. We went out, whoever was able. There were a lot
of sick who couldn't go. We went out with great joy, with much crying ….

Q: And then?
A: But now there began a real death. People who had been starved for
so many years …. The Russians had opened all the German storehouses,
all the German stores, and they said, "Take whatever you want." People
who had been badly starved, they shouldn't have eaten …. And the people
began to eat, to eat too much, greedily …. Hundreds of people fell a day.
After the liberation, two, three days after the liberation, there had fallen
very many people. In about a month, half of the camp had fallen. And
nothing could be done about it …. There were stables full with dead. People
crawled over the dead. It stank terribly. There was raging a severe typhus.
And I, too, got sick. I lay four weeks in the hospital …

(Epstein recovered from typhus and returned to Warsaw where she married and made preparations to emigrate to Palestine.)

References

Bartov, Omer (2003). *Germany's War and the Holocaust.* Ithaca, NY: Cornell University Press.
Bauer, Yehuda (1979). *The Jewish Emergence from Powerlessness.* Toronto: University of Toronto
    Press.
Berger, Leslie (1988). "The Long-Term Psychological Consequences of the Holocaust on the
    Survivors and Their Offspring," pp. 175–221. In Randolph L. Braham (Ed.) *The Psychologi-
    cal Perspectives of the Holocaust and of its Aftermath.* Boulder, CO: Social Science Mono-
    graphs.
Binion, Rudolph (1976). *Hitler Among the Germans.* New York: Elsevier.
Boder, David (1949). *I Did Not Interview the Dead.* Urbana: The University of Illinois Press.

Browning, Christopher R. (1992). *Ordinary Men: Reserve Police Battalion 101 and the Final Solution in Poland*. New York: HarperCollins.

Browning, Christopher R. (2000). *Nazi Policy, Jewish Workers, German Killers*. Cambridge: Cambridge University Press.

Fein, Helen (1979). *Accounting for Genocide: National Responses and Jewish Victimization During the Holocaust*. New York: Free Press.

Goldhagen, Daniel Jonah (1996). *Hitler's Willing Executioners*. New York: Alfred A. Knopf.

Gutman, Yisrael, and Krakowski, Shmuel (1986). *Unequal Victims: Poles and Jews During World War Two*. New York: Holocaust Library.

Hilberg, Raul (1985). *The Destruction of the European Jews*. (Three volumes). New York: Holmes and Meier.

Lukas, Richard C. (1986). *The Forgotten Holocaust: The Poles Under German Occupation, 1939–1944*. Lexington: University Press of Kentucky.

Roth, John K., and Berenbaum, Michael (1989). *Holocaust: Religious and Philosophical Implications*. New York: Paragon House.

Rubinstein, William D. (1997). *The Myth of Rescue*. London: Routledge.

Waite, Robert G. L. (1977). *The Psychopathic God, Adolf Hitler*. New York: Basic Books.

Wyman, David (1984). *The Abandonment of the Jews: America and the Holocaust, 1941–1945*. New York: Pantheon.

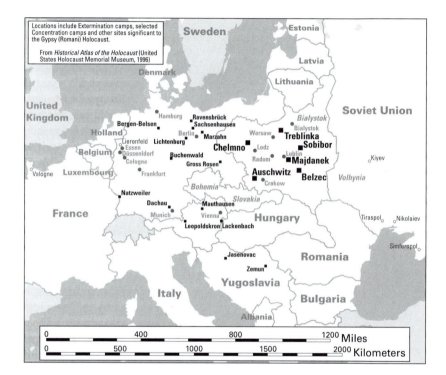

Locations include Extermination camps, selected Concentration camps and other sites significant to the Gypsy (Romani) Holocaust.

From *Historical Atlas of the Holocaust* (United States Holocaust Memorial Museum, 1996)

Sweden

Estonia

Latvia

Denmark

Lithuania

United Kingdom

Soviet Union

Holland

Hamburg

Ravensbrück

Bergen-Belsen

Sachsenhausen

Bialystok

Berlin

Marzahn

Warsaw

Bialystok

Treblinka

Lierenfeld

Lichtenburg

Chelmno

Lodz

Sobibor

Belgium

Essen

Düsseldorf

Cologne

Buchenwald

Radom

Lublin

Majdanek

Kiev

Valogne

Luxembourg

Frankfurt

Gross Rosen

Auschwitz

Belzec

Volhynia

Bohemia

Crakow

Natzweiler

Slovakia

Dachau

Mauthausen

France

Munich

Vienna

Hungary

Tiraspol

Nikolaiev

Leopoldskron

Lackenbach

Simferopol

Jasenovac

Romania

Zemun

Yugoslavia

Italy

Bulgaria

Albania

| 0 | 400 | 800 | 1200 Miles |
| 0 | 500 | 1000 | 1500 | 2000 Kilometers |

Western and Eastern European sites of Nazi Camps

CHAPTER 5

Holocaust: The Gypsies

The mass murder of between one-quarter and one-half million Roma and Sinti (Gypsies) during the Holocaust has been under-represented in current historiography about Nazi genocide. Instead, suspicion, prejudice, and stereotypes have continued to dominate historical literature about this subject.[1] Thus, Yehuda Bauer's suggestion that "the Nazis simply did not have a policy regarding the Gypsies" and that therefore Nazi persecution of Gypsies was fundamentally different from that of Jews is erroneous. Similarly, Hans-Joachim Döring's contention that Nazi policy was motivated by a combination of crime control and military security considerations, or Bernhard Streck's classification of the killing of Roma and Sinti in Auschwitz-Birkenau for epidemiological and public health reasons is equally fallacious.[2] To be sure, the "Jewish Question" loomed larger than the "Gypsy Plague" in Nazi ideology, since Roma and Sinti were socially marginal, whereas Jews were increasingly assimilated in German society and culture; the Gypsies were also far fewer in number, representing about 0.05 percent of the 1933 German population. Nevertheless, there is a striking parallelism between the ideology and process of extermination for Jews and Gypsies. Despite the similarity and simultaneity of persecution, the disparity between the vast quantity of secondary literature about Nazi Judeophobia and the limited number of studies about the fate of Roma and Sinti has inevitably influenced current historical analyses, in which Gypsies are at most an afterthought.[3]

It is clear that the persecution of Roma and Sinti on racial grounds preceded the Nazi assumption of power. Under the Second Empire and the

163

Weimar Republic, the states of Baden, Bavaria, Bremen, Hesse, and Prussia had developed laws discriminating against Gypsies and established legal stereotypes defining them as vagabonds, asocials, criminals, and racially inferior aliens. Already in 1899, Bavaria had established an "Information Agency on Gypsies" (*Nachrichtendienst in Bezug auf die Zigeuner*) that collected genealogical data, photographs, and fingerprints of Gypsies above the age of six.[4] Although under Article 108 of the Weimar Constitution, Gypsies received full and equal citizenship rights, they were nevertheless vulnerable to discriminatory legislation. The Bavarian law for "Combatting Gypsies, Vagabonds, and the Work Shy" (*Gesetz zur Bekämpfung von Zigeuner, Landfahrern und Arbeitsscheuen*) of July 16, 1926, mandated registration of all domiciled and migratory Gypsies with the police, local registry offices, and labor exchanges. A similar Prussian decree from November 3, 1927, resulted in the creation of special Gypsy identity cards with fingerprints and photographs for 8,000 Roma and Sinti above the age of six. During the last years of the Weimar Republic, arbitrary arrest and preventive detention of itinerant Gypsies — ostensibly for crime prevention — became routine. In April 1929, a national police commission adopted the 1926 Bavarian law as the federal norm and established a "Center for the Fight against Gypsies in Germany" with headquarters in Munich.[5] This agreement was renewed on March 18, 1933, with the proviso that any state could issue additional regulations.[6]

Clear lines of demarcation cannot be drawn between these Weimar legal precedents that stigmatized Roma and Sinti as habitual criminals, social misfits, vagabonds, and so-called asocials and the first Nazi measures after 1933. Initially, the Nazis developed parallel racial regulations against Jews, Gypsies, and the handicapped. Gypsies were included as "asocials" (an aggregate group including — but not limited to — prostitutes, beggars, shirkers, and any persons the police designated as "hooligans") in the July 1933 Law for the Prevention of Offspring with Hereditary Defects and in the November 1933 Law Against Habitual Criminals. The first law resulted in their involuntary sterilization,[7] while the second permitted their incarceration in concentration camps. The Denaturalization Law of July 14, 1933, and the Expulsion Law of March 23, 1934, initially implemented against *Ostjuden* (Eastern and Polish Jews), was also used to expel foreign and stateless Gypsies from German soil.

Following passage of the 1935 Nuremberg racial laws, semi-official commentaries interpreting these laws, classified Gypsies, along with Jews and Blacks, as racially distinctive minorities with "alien blood" (*artfremdes Blut*).[8] Racially mixed marriages between those of German blood and "Gypsies, Negroes, or their bastard offspring" were prohibited on November 26, 1935, in an advisory circular from the Reich Ministry of the Interior to all local registry offices for vital statistics. In the ever escalating series of interlocking Nazi regulations implementing the Nuremberg racial laws, both Gypsies and Jews were deprived of their civil rights.[9] Racial scientists compiled the official handbooks for the interpretation of the Nuremberg laws, providing the scientific justification for the regime for the later mass murder of Jews and Gypsies.

Already in 1934, the Nazi Racial Policy Office, together with the Gestapo, began to compile an "asocials catalog." The Nazi police and health bureaucracies continued and expanded the systematic registration of Gypsies as potential criminals, genetically defined, that had already begun during the Weimar Republic.[10] Thus, anthropological and genealogical registration (*Rassenbiologische Gutachtung*) identified Gypsies as "racially inferior asocials and criminals of Asiatic ancestry."[11] Moreover, Nazi social policy toward Jews and Gypsies resulted in decreased expenditures for welfare; assistance to the growing number of impoverished Jews was assigned in 1933 to the *Reichsvertretung der Juden in Deutschland* (Reich Representation of German Jews)[12] and after 1939 to the *Reichsvereinigung der Juden in Deutschland* (Reich Association of Jews in Germany),[13] whereas indigent Gypsies received progressively less financial assistance from municipal authorities.[14] These same officials subsequently interned Roma and Sinti in Gypsy camps.

A March 1936 memorandum to State Secretary of the Interior Hans Pfundtner contains the first references to the preparation of a national Gypsy law (*Reichszigeunergesetz*) and to the difficulties of achieving a "total solution of the Gypsy problem on either a national or international level." The interim recommendations in this memorandum include expulsion of stateless and foreign Gypsies, restrictions on freedom of movement and on issuing licenses for Gypsies with itinerant trades (*Wandergewerbe*), increased police surveillance, sterilization of Gypsies of mixed German and Gypsy ancestry (the so-called *Mischlinge*), complete registration of all Gypsies in the Reich, and confinement in a special Gypsy reservation.[15]

In lieu of national legislation, the Central Office of Detective Forces (*Reichskriminalpolizeiamt*, or RKPA) and the Reich Ministry of the Interior established, in early June 1936, the Munich-based Central Office to Combat the Gypsy Menace (*Zentralstelle zur Bekämpfung des Zigeunerunwesens*), which intensified harassment, coercion, and intimidation of Gypsies by the police. This Munich office served as the headquarters of a national data bank on Gypsies and represented all German police agencies with the Interpol International Center for Fighting the Gypsy Menace in Vienna.[16]

On June 6, 1936, the Reich and Prussian Ministry of Interior issued a circular containing new directives for "Fighting the Gypsy Plague."[17] The circular also authorized the Chief of the Berlin Police to direct raids throughout Prussia to arrest all Gypsies prior to the Olympic Games. Consequently, 600 Gypsies were arrested in Berlin on July 16, 1936, and marched under police guard to a sewage dump adjacent to the municipal cemetery in the Berlin suburb of Marzahn.[18] Although the presence of both sewage and graves violated Gypsy cultural taboos, Berlin-Marzahn became the largest Gypsy camp (*Zigeunerlager*). It consisted of 130 caravans condemned as uninhabitable by the Reich Labor Service; the camp was guarded by a detachment of Prussian uniformed police (*Schutzpolizei*). The hygienic facilities were totally inadequate; Marzahn had only three water pumps and two toilets. Overcrowding and unsanitary conditions were the norm; for example, in March 1938 city authorities reported 170 cases of communicable diseases.

The Gypsies at Berlin-Marzahn were assigned to forced labor. Further, the Reich Department of Health forced them to provide detailed data for anthropological and genealogical registration. In turn, this data provided the pretext for the denaturalization and involuntary sterilization of the imprisoned Gypsies. The Berlin-Marzahn Gypsy camp provided evidence of a growing interagency cooperation between public health officials and the police, essential for subsequent developments resulting in the deportation and mass murder of German Gypsies.[19] After 1939, the prisoners at Marzahn were compelled to work at forced labor in the Sachsenhausen stone quarries or to clear rubble from Berlin streets after Allied air raids. Most were deported to Auschwitz in 1943.

In spring 1936, the Reich Department of Health created the Racial Hygiene and Demographic Biology Research Unit (*Rassenhygienische und Bevölkerungsbiologische Forschungsstelle*), as its Department L3. Headed by Dr. Robert Ritter, the unit began systematic genealogical and genetic research in 1937.[20] Ritter and his associates worked in close cooperation with the Central Office for Reich Security (*Reichssicherheitshauptamt*, or RSHA) and the Reich Ministry of the Interior. Funded by the *Deutsche Forschungsgemeinschaft*, Ritter's unit was assigned to register the approximately 30,000 Gypsies and part-Gypsies in Germany in order to provide genealogical and racial data required for formulating a new Reich Gypsy law. Ritter's group aimed to show that criminal and asocial behavior was hereditary.[21]

In 1937, the anthropologist Dr. Adolf Würth, one of Ritter's associates, described the growing parallels in Nazi policy toward Jews and Gypsies:

The Gypsy question is for us today primarily a racial question. Thus, the national socialist state will basically have to settle the Gypsy question just as it has solved the Jewish question. We have already begun. Jews and Gypsies have been placed on equal footing in marriage prohibitions in the regulations for implementing the

Nuremberg laws for the Protection of German Blood. The Gypsies are not of German blood nor can they be considered related to German blood.[22]

Würth conducted genealogical and anthropological research on Gypsies in Württemberg and in 1940 supervised the first experimental deportation of 500 Roma and Sinti from the Württemberg state prison at Hohenasperg to Lublin.[23] Würth and the other practitioners of racial hygiene provided not only the intellectual infrastructure for genocide, but were also accessories in the process of mass murder. Their research was utilized by the police for implementing the segregation, sterilization, and deportation of Gypsies from the Reich.

Ritter's associates included his assistant Eva Justin, a nurse who later received a doctorate in anthropology in 1944 for her research on Sinti children separated from their families and raised in "alien" surroundings at the Catholic St. Josefspflege home in Mulfingen; after her dissertation research was completed, these children were deported to Auschwitz-Birkenau, where most were killed.[24] Ritter's other colleagues included Dr. Sophie Ehrhardt, a zoologist and anthropologist, whose research focused on East Prussian Gypsies and on Jews and Gypsies in the Lodz ghetto and the Dachau and Sachsenhausen concentration camps. Ehrhardt was subsequently appointed professor of anthropology at Tübingen University in 1942.[25]

After 1935, municipal governments and local welfare offices pressured the German police to confine a growing number of German Gypsies in the newly created municipal Zigeunerlager. These Gypsy camps were, in essence, *SS-Sonderlager*: special internment camps combining elements of protective custody concentration camps and embryonic ghettos. Usually located on the outskirts of cities, these Zigeunerlager were guarded by the SS, the *gendarmerie*, or the uniformed city police. After 1935, these camps became reserve depots for forced labor, genealogical registration, and compulsory sterilization. Between 1933 and 1939, Zigeunerlager were created in Cologne, Düsseldorf, Essen, Frankfurt, Hamburg, and other German cities. These camps evolved from municipal internment camps into assembly centers (*Sammellager*) for systematic deportation to concentration camps after 1939.[26]

In Frankfurt, for example, local officials — including Frankfurt Chief of Police Beckerle, Mayor Krebs, and representatives from the welfare office — expanded existing municipal anti-Gypsy ordinances in the spring of 1936. New measures included the following: police searches of all Gypsy residences three times a week; police checks on all Gypsy identity papers to determine whether any were stateless or foreigners, all of whom were vulnerable to expulsion; compulsory municipal genetic and genealogical registration; resettlement of all Roma and Sinti found within the city limits in the Frankfurt Zigeunerlager; prohibition on renting local camp sites to Gypsies outside the municipal Zigeunerlager; and expulsion of migrant Roma and Sinti upon arrival in Frankfurt.[27]

Additional measures in Frankfurt further increased police harassment of both domiciled and migrant Gypsies. These directives included restricting the number of new trade licenses issued to itinerant Gypsies, thereby preventing or limiting their employment as knife (or scissors) grinders, horse traders, traveling salespersons, fortune tellers, musicians, and circus performers; checking school attendance by Gypsy children, with truancy to be punished by removal to municipal juvenile facilities; and compulsory registration of all Gypsies detained or arrested by the police.[28] At the Düsseldorf Höherweg camp, the Gypsies were compelled to pay six marks monthly for inferior accommodations in barracks that did not even have electricity; they were also barred from receiving either unemployment or welfare assistance. In addition, the camp commandant mandated rigid curfews, prohibited children from playing on the grounds, and banned visits and communications from non-Gypsy relatives.[29] Similar measures were implemented in other municipal Gypsy camps.

An examination of existing historical literature about the concentration camp system before 1939 reveals that several Sinti had already been arrested and detained in the Worms-Osthofen concentration camp in 1933 and that 400 Bavarian Gypsies were deported to Dachau in July 1936. This latter arrest occurred almost simultaneously with the arrest of Berlin Gypsies and the creation of Berlin-Marzahn. An additional 1000 Gypsies "able to work" were arrested in raids on June 13 to 18, 1938, and deported to Buchenwald, Dachau, and Sachsenhausen concentration camps; women were sent to Lichtenburg concentration camp in Saxony. These 1938 arrests were authorized under an unpublished decree on "crime prevention" (*vorbeugende Verbrechensbekämpfung*) issued in December 1937. This decree extended the use of preventive arrest to all persons whose asocial behavior threatened the common good, irrespective of whether the individual had a criminal record. It was applied to migrant and unemployed Gypsies, asocials, the unemployed, habitual criminals, homeless panhandlers, beggars, and Jews previously sentenced to jail for more than 30 days (including such offenses as traffic violations). The arrests were made by the Kripo (rather than the Gestapo) and provided the expanding camp system with potential slave labor.[30]

Austrian and German Gypsies were also sent to Mauthausen and Ravensbrück prior to the outbreak of war in 1939. In summer and fall 1938, about 3000 allegedly "work shy" Roma and Sinti from the *Ostmark* (incorporated Austria) were also deported to concentration camps. Thus, 2000 male Gypsies above the age of 16 were sent to Dachau and later remanded to Buchenwald, and 1000 female Gypsies above the age of 15 were sent to Ravensbrück.[31] In 1939 and 1940, special internment camps at Maxglan/Leopoldskron in Salzburg and Lackenbach in Burgenland were created specifically for Roma and Sinti in the *Ostmark* and all German decrees and regulations against Gypsies, including genealogical and police registration, were implemented.[32]

The registration and census of Gypsies in Austria was begun in late October 1939. Similarly, a census of Gypsies was conducted in the Protectorate of Bohemia and Moravia in August 1942, after the incarceration of Gypsies in compulsory penal labor camps at Pardibice near Prague, Lety in Bohemia, and Hodonin in Moravia.

In the Netherlands, in February 1936, the Dutch Minister of Justice had already created a central Gypsy register linked to the Munich central police office and the Vienna Interpol office specializing in Gypsies. On December 30, 1937, the Police Gazette of Holland announced the opening of the Dutch Central Office for Gypsies; this office was closed in January 1939. In early 1941, a central registry for Gypsies, nomads, aliens, and the stateless was opened, and it implemented German anti-Gypsy measures for the arrest, internment, and deportation of Dutch Gypsies.[33]

Similarly in France, before the war in late 1939, Interior Minister Albert Sarraut specified that Gypsies be included among those without fixed domicile to be interned as security risks in the *camps de concentration*. The situation of French Gypsies did not improve with German occupation. The Commissariat for Jewish Affairs under Xavier Vallat in Vichy France also held jurisdiction over the fate of Gypsies as part of its responsibility for the administration of "measures for the maintenance of racial purity."[34] As in the case of French Jews, the Nazi plan — requiring the cooperation of the French police and civil service — for the identification, concentration, and deportation of Gypsies was not fully implemented before the Allied armies liberated France.

The literature about Gypsies in the pre-1939 German concentration camps is too fragmentary to permit valid generalizations, and we therefore still do not know why some Gypsies were sent to municipal internment camps while others were committed to concentration camps.

In 1938 and 1939, the Nazi ideological obsession with Gypsies became almost as strident and aggressive as the campaign against the Jews.[35] In August 1938, Gypsies were expelled, ostensibly as military security risks, from border zones on the left bank of the Rhine, and, once war had begun, they were prohibited from "wandering" in the western areas of the Reich. In May 1938, Heinrich Himmler ordered that the Munich bureau of Gypsy affairs be renamed *Reichszentrale zur Bekämpfung des Zigeunerunwesens* (Central Office to Combat the Gypsy Nuisance) and placed within the RKPA (Department V of the Central Office for Reich Security) in Berlin by early October 1938. Moreover, on December 8, 1938, Himmler promulgated a decree for "Fighting the Gypsy Plague," basing it on Ritter's anthropological and genealogical registration (*rassenbiologische Gutachtung*).

This decree recommended "the resolution of the Gypsy question based on its essentially racial nature" (*die Regelung der Zigeunerfrage aus dem Wesen dieser Rasse heraus in Angriff zu nehmen*) and mandated that all Gypsies in the Reich above the age of six be classified into three racial groups: "Gypsies, Gypsy Mischlinge, and nomadic persons behaving as Gypsies." The guidelines for implementation published in early 1939 stipulated that the RKPA assist in "the development of a comprehensive Gypsy law prohibiting miscegenation and regulating the life of the Gypsy race in German space (*im deutschen Volksraum*)."[36] Comprehensive and systematic residential and genealogical registration of Gypsies by local police and public health authorities became mandatory, and photo identity cards were to be issued to all Gypsies and part-Gypsies. The implementation of Himmler's decree also resulted in the purge of several dozen Gypsy musicians from the Reich Music Chamber in the spring of 1939, thereby effectively banning their employment as musicians.[37] The radicalization of Nazi attitudes by 1940 is also evident in a report from February 5, 1940, from Senior State Attorney Dr. Meissner of the Graz Circuit Court (*Oberlandesgericht*) to the Reich Minister of Justice in Berlin, which rejected the idea of Gypsy employment as musicians in Burgenland: "The Gypsies live almost exclusively from begging and theft. Their work as musicians is simply a cover and not genuine employment."[38]

The deportation of German Gypsies began shortly after the outbreak of war in 1939. On October 17, 1939, Reinhard Heydrich issued the so-called *Festsetzungserlaß*, prohibiting all Gypsies and part-Gypsies not already interned in camps from changing their registered domiciles; this measure was essential for implementing deportations.[39] In the second half of October, Arthur Nebe, chief of the RKPA, tried to expedite the deportation of Berlin Gypsies by requesting that Adolf Eichmann "add three or four train cars of Gypsies" to the Nisko Jewish transports departing from Vienna. Eichmann cabled Berlin that the Nisko transport would include "a train car of Gypsies to be added to the first Jewish deportation from Vienna."[40] However, the failure of the Nisko resettlement scheme at the end of 1939 precluded the early expulsion of 30,000 Gypsies from the Greater German Reich to the General Government.[41] The aborted October 1939 deportation took place belatedly in mid-May 1940, when 2800 German Gypsies were deported from seven assembly centers in the Old Reich to Lublin.[42] In Austria, the deportations to the General Government planned for the second half of August 1940 were postponed indefinitely and the Gypsies were subsequently deported to Auschwitz-Birkenau in

1943.[43] The rules concerning inclusion and exemption for Gypsies paralleled the later regulations used in Jewish transports.

The property and possessions of the deported Gypsies were confiscated and the deportees were compelled to sign release forms acknowledging the transfer of their possessions as *volks-und staatsfeindlichen Vermögens* (under the Law for the Confiscation of Subversive and Enemy Property, initially used for the seizure of assets of proscribed and denaturalized political opponents after July 1933).[44] The same confiscatory procedures were also employed during the earliest deportations of Jews, prior to the passage of the 11th Ordinance. The 11th Ordinance provided for automatic loss of citizenship and confiscation of property if a German Jew took up residence in a foreign country; deportation to the East (including to the *Ostland* and the General Government) counted as such a change of residence.[45] The deportation of Gypsies from Germany and Austria was again suspended in October 1940 because the General Government had protested the potential dumping of 35,000 Gypsies as well as the impending arrival of large numbers of German Jews.[46] Again in July 1941, the RSHA halted the deportation of East Prussian Gypsies, probably because of the invasion of the Soviet Union, noting that "a general and final solution of the Gypsy question cannot be achieved at this time." Instead, the RSHA proposed to construct a new Zigeunerlager enclosed with barbed wire in the outskirts of Königsberg.[47]

The patterns of both Gypsy and Jewish deportations reveal the evolving system of killings. Thus, as with the Jewish deportations to Lodz, the deportation of 5000 Austrian Gypsies from transit camps at Hartburg, Fürstenfeld, Mattersburg, Roten Thurm, Lackenbach, and Oberwart from November 5 to 9, 1941, dovetailed with the establishment of Chelmno (Kulmhof), where these Gypsies were killed in mobile gas vans in December 1941 and January 1942.[48] Similarly, the Gypsies incarcerated in the Warsaw ghetto were deported to Treblinka in the summer of 1942.[49] By that time, the SS *Einsatzgruppen* operating in the Soviet Union and the Baltic region had already killed several thousand Gypsies alongside Jews in massacres.[50] Thus the RSHA reported, in its "Situation Report USSR No. 153," that "the Gypsy problem in Simpferopol [had been] settled" in December 1941.[51] And in October 1947, Otto Ohlendorf, who had headed the Einsatzgruppe that operated in southern Russia and the Crimea, testified at Nuremberg that the basis for killing Gypsies and Jews in Russia had been the same.[52] In similar fashion, the Reich Commissar for the *Ostland* in July 1942 informed the Higher SS and Police Leader in Riga that "treatment of Jews and Gypsies are to be placed on equal footing (*gleichgestellt*)."[53]

Ritter's racial research estimated that 90 percent of the German Roma and Sinti were of mixed ancestry, thus Nazi measures were directed primarily against Gypsy *Mischlinge* in Germany and Austria up to 1942. In 1942, the regime dropped the distinction between part and pure Gypsies and subjected all Gypsies to the same treatment. In 1942 and 1943, when most Gypsy deportations from the Reich occurred, the Nazis also eliminated all distinctions between the treatment of Gypsies and Jews. Thus, on March 12, 1942, new regulations placed Jews and Gypsies on equal footing for welfare payments and compulsory labor.[54]

There is suggestive evidence that Hitler may have been involved in the formal decision to kill the Gypsies. On December 3, 1942, Martin Bormann wrote a letter to Himmler, protesting that the Reich Leader SS had exempted certain pure Gypsies from "the measures to combat the Gypsy plague" until additional research into their "language, rituals ...", and valuable Teutonic customs" could be completed. Bormann complained that neither the public, nor the party, nor the Führer would "understand or approve." Himmler added a handwritten note on the face of the letter about preparing data on Gypsies for Hitler. The marginalia states: *"Führer. Aufstellung wer sind Zigeuner"* ("Führer. Information who are the Gypsies").[55] Himmler met with Hitler on December 10, 1942, and six days later, responding to Bormann's pressure and probably to Hitler's order, Himmler issued the Auschwitz decree on Gypsies, which led to their deportation to and eventual murder in Birkenau.[56]

The evidence suggests that Hitler was directly involved and informed of most killing operations, and that simultaneously the administration of policy by German officials stationed outside Germany cumulatively radicalized the implementation of central policy toward German and European Gypsies.

Already on September 26, 1942, three months before Himmler's Auschwitz decree, 200 Gypsies were transferred from Buchenwald to Auschwitz and assigned to build the new Gypsy enclosure (BIIe) at Birkenau. On February 26, 1943, the first transport of German Gypsies arrived at the newly erected Gypsy "family camp" (BIIe) in Birkenau; Gypsies from occupied Europe arrived at Auschwitz-Birkenau after March 7, 1943.[57] The pattern of deporting Gypsies as a family unit was first established during the May 1940 Hohenasperg deportations to Lublin and continued in Auschwitz. The history and fate of the Gypsies in the Birkenau *Zigeunerlager* paralleled the creation and later destruction of the so-called *Familienlager* for Theresienstadt deportees in Birkenau BIIb.[58]

On August 2, 1944, the Gypsy camp at Auschwitz-Birkenau was liquidated. An earlier SS attempt to obliterate the Birkenau Gypsy camp BIIe on May 16 had failed because of armed resistance; the prisoners fought the SS with improvised knives, shovels, wooden sticks, and stones.[59] By the time Birkenau was evacuated, 13,614 Gypsies from the German Reich had died of exposure, malnutrition, disease, and brutal medical experiments; 6,432 had been gassed; and 32 had been shot while trying to escape. Thus, about 20,000 of the 23,000 German and Austrian Roma and Sinti deported to Auschwitz were killed there.[60] Finally, on April 25, 1943, both Jews and Gypsies were denaturalized and placed on an equal footing under the provisions of the 12th Ordinance to the Reich Citizenship Law, and on March 10, 1944, a circular letter from Himmler directed that the publication of restrictive decrees against Jews and Gypsies be discontinued as their "evacuation and isolation" had already been largely completed.[61]

Despite the growth of specialized monographs, the lacunae in Holocaust literature about Nazi policies toward Roma and Sinti are still vast. Future research should address the need for a comprehensive and systematic handbook listing all published and unpublished Nazi laws, ordinances, and directives against German and Austrian Gypsies, as well as similar decrees in the other countries of Axis and occupied Europe. It is also important to analyze the presence and deportation of German Gypsies to ghettos in Bialystok, Cracow, Radom, Warsaw, and Lodz. Scattered entries in Adam Czerniakow's diary recorded the presence of German and Polish Gypsies in the Warsaw ghetto in April and June 1942; parallel decrees from the city and county of Warsaw confirm the incarceration of Gypsies in the Warsaw ghetto in June 1942 and their subsequent deportation to Treblinka.[62] Although fragmentary data are available, research about Roma and Sinti resistance is still negligible.

Current literature has also ignored references to the killing of Gypsies in *Einsatzkommando* situation reports from the occupied Soviet Union, although a more systematic analysis of this material would be relatively simple.[63] Likewise, Nazi usage and language toward Gypsies requires more organized analysis, since it seems logical that the pacification and antipartisan operations in the occupied Soviet Union and Baltic, known as *Bandenbekämpfung*, included activities against Jews, Gypsies, and Communist partisans. The public language of Nazi propaganda was used both for indoctrination and intimidation, whereas the less public language of Nazi bureaucrats utilized code words and circumlocutions for deportations and killing operations. The Nazis generally described their victims in pejorative terms, transmuting objective language into terms of contempt to describe the victims that their own policies and deeds had created.[64]

Holocaust historiography during the past 40 years has emphasized anti-Semitism and the Jewish fate. Despite new sources and research during the 1980s, the older interpretations are still dominant. There are still no parallel studies about the fate of Gypsies and Jews in the major German concentration camps (Bergen-Belsen, Buchenwald, Dachau, Mauthausen, Natzweiler, Ravensbrück, and Sachsenhausen); in transit camps such as Westerbork in Holland and Malines in Belgium; in killing centers at Belzec, Chelmno, Sobibor, Treblinka, and Auschwitz-Birkenau; and in the labor camps that dotted the Reich and all of occupied Europe.[65] Furthermore, there are no comparative studies about the parallel fate of German Gypsies in concentration camps and Zigeunerlager prior to 1939. Current literature analyzing the fate of Roma and Sinti in occupied Europe is still relatively narrow, apart from several significant works about the Netherlands and Czechoslovakia.[66] The gaps in our knowledge about the Gypsy Final Solution are still vast, although significant progress has been made toward understanding the connection between Nazi ideology, German social policy, and the genocide of German and European Gypsies.

Discrimination against Sinti and Roma did not cease with the collapse of Nazi Germany in 1945. During the immediate postwar years, harassment by German and Austrian police, and housing, health, and welfare authorities was common. In Germany, Gypsy registration files created during the Nazi era along with some of the police personnel were transferred to postwar successor agencies; these compromising files disappeared and were sometimes destroyed when public disclosure of their existence proved embarrassing. Thus, for example, from the early 1950s to the mid-1970s, the *Landfahrerzentrale* (Vagrant Department) of the Bavarian police retained the Gypsy records of the Nazi Central Office to Combat the Gypsy Menace headquartered after 1936 in Munich. These records disappeared and were allegedly destroyed in the 1970s, when the nascent Sinti and Roma civil rights movement initiated inquiries about them.[67]

Prior to the 1980s, few archives and scholars were interested in documenting Nazi crimes against Roma and Sinti. The fragmentation and dispersion of German records during and after World War II hampered early recognition of the importance of the partial files of Ritter's Racial Hygiene and Demographic Biology Research Unit located in Ehrhardt's research collection at Tübingen University; it also required several years to catalog these records after they were transferred in 1981 to the German Federal Archives in Koblenz.[68]

In addition, German bureaucrats encouraged the emphasis on Jewish victimization in Holocaust historiography, since the excesses of anti-Semitism could be blamed on the pathology of Hitler and his SS followers, whereas the murder of German nationals in the so-called euthanasia killings and the killing of Sinti and Roma, both carried out by "ordinary" German bureaucrats, scientists, and policemen, implicated a far larger segment of the German population. Moreover, the focus on Nazi anti-Semitism also prevented discussion of how deeply the German scientific community was involved in the killing operations against Jews as well as against Gypsies and the handicapped.

And finally, German postwar restitution legislation and its implementation excluded most Sinti and Roma survivors, subjecting them to arbitrary and repetitive bureaucratic humiliations. Most Gypsy survivors were initially disqualified from receiving compensation as racial victims for imprisonment prior to the March 1943 Auschwitz decree. Although this date was later changed to December 1938, both dates excluded restitution for incarceration in early internment camps such as Marzahn or Lackenbach, ignored deportation to ghettos such as Radom or Bialystok after 1940, restricted claims for health disabilities caused by involuntary sterilization and medical experiments, and required minimum periods of involuntary detention in certain officially recognized camps and ghettos to qualify for meager settlements. Claims filed by Gypsy survivors for homes and businesses impounded at deportation were invariably disallowed, often after investigation by the same policemen who had previously arrested them in the Nazi era. Health claims for physical and psychological trauma were similarly disregarded. This failure of empathy with Gypsy survivors was rationalized using the language of Nazi stereotypes that defined the victims as "asocial and criminal." Despite minor improvements in both legislation and court decisions by the 1980s, hostile practices such as the involuntary denaturalization of many German Sinti survivors and the reduction of modest restitution settlements by deducting any prior welfare assistance established a flagrant pattern of official dissembling and hostility.[69]

Despite democratization and economic recovery, de-Nazification in postwar Germany and Austria remained incomplete. West German political culture included widespread amnesia to the continuities of personnel in government and academia. This continuity exemplified one aspect of the collective failure to assume political responsibility for the Nazi murder of Sinti and Roma. For example, the staff of the Racial Hygiene and Demographic Biology Research Unit in Berlin-Dahlem had little difficulty in securing employment after 1945, and they eluded all penalties during postwar judicial proceedings. Ritter taught criminal biology at the University of Tübingen from late 1944 to 1946 and was hired in December 1947 as a physician for children by the Frankfurt Health Office. Once again, Ritter hired Justin to work with him; she was employed as a psychologist at the Frankfurt Health Office. After brief investigations, judicial proceedings against Ritter and Justin as accessories in the murder of German Gypsies were discontinued.[70]

Ehrhardt continued her research and teaching as a professor of anthropology at Tübingen University, where she used the plaster casts of Gypsy heads and fingerprint data from the records of the Racial Hygiene Unit entrusted to her after the war. Judicial proceedings against her were dropped in 1985.[71] Würth became an official in the Bureau of Statistics in Württemberg-Baden from 1951 to 1970. Würth was never tried as an accessory to murder since judicial investigations of his career were discontinued. Many perpetrators were never placed on trial; for example, the physician and anthropologist Professor Otmar Freiherr von Verschuer, who had supervised and subsidized many of Josef Mengele's notorious experiments on Gypsy and Jewish twins at Auschwitz, was never investigated or indicted. After the war, he established the Human Genetics Institute at the University of Münster in 1951 and was appointed a professor at Münster in 1953.[72]

Postwar police careers revealed a similar lack of repercussions for involvement in the deportation and killing of Sinti and Roma. Thus, Josef Eichberger, who had been responsible for Gypsy deportations in the RSHA, became head of the "Gypsy Department" of the Bavarian State Police; Leo Karsten became head of the "Migrants (*Landfahrer*) Department" of the Baden State Police in Karlsruhe; and Hans Maly, a senior officer in Department VA2 (preventive measures against asocials, prostitutes, and Gypsies) of the RSHA from January to late September 1943, was later hired as head of the Bonn Kripo after 1945. Judicial proceedings were dropped against these police.[73]

In 1969–1971, during the trial of Otto Bovensiepen, the former chief of the Berlin Gestapo from March 1941 to November 1942, the statute of limitations had expired on all crimes of the Nazi period except murder. Bovensiepen was indicted for "knowingly and with base motives assisting in the deportation and killing of at least 35,000 Berlin Jews and 252 Gypsies." The trial was suspended in 1971, since Bovensiepen had suffered a heart attack and his physician testified that he would never be able to live through the trial.[74] Furthermore, after a 43-month trial, the Siegen District Court sentenced Ernst August König on January 24, 1991, to life imprisonment for murders he had committed as SS Blockführer in the Gypsy camp BIIe at Auschwitz-Birkenau.[75]

Allied tribunals of the four postwar occupation armies and the successor states (the Federal Republic of Germany, the German Democratic Republic, and the Republic of Austria) tried large numbers of Nazi criminals for crimes committed during World War II; usually specific crimes against Sinti and Roma were part of larger indictments against suspected perpetrators for participation in the *Einsatzkommandos* or crimes committed in the concentration camps.[76]

On a different but related note, it is uncommon to find explicit acknowledgment of Sinti and Roma victims in most postwar Holocaust memorials. That said, their tragic fate is explicitly recognized in monuments on Museumplein in Amsterdam, at the former Gypsy camps in Salzburg and Lackenbach, in concentration camp memorials at Bergen-Belsen and Auschwitz-Birkenau, and in new memorials at the children's home in Mulfingen, as well as at the sites of their deportation in Heidelberg and Wiesbaden.[77]

German unification and changes in the former Soviet bloc since 1990 have altered the political map of Europe. These changes are, however, still, incomplete and it is still too early for any final analysis. Nevertheless, recent developments do show that the administration of memorials in the countries of Eastern Europe and in reunited Germany will at best transform and at worst diminish the status of most Holocaust memorials. Growing popular resentment against Jews and Gypsies, hatred of outsiders, as well as the emergence of local fascist and neo-Nazi groups also bode ill for the future of these memorials.[78]

The belated recognition of the Gypsy Holocaust is still incomplete in current historiography. During the 1980s new sources and research produced interpretations that corrected many of the old imbalances by pointing to the connections between the murder of the Jews and that of the Gypsies and the handicapped. These analyses have, however, been unable so far to alter the older interpretation; prejudice and the habits of some 50 years cannot be reversed overnight.

The Gypsy Holocaust has taught us that the German health care system and the involvement of German scientists — physicians, psychiatrists, anthropologists, and geneticists — were essential to implement the mass murder of all European Gypsies alongside that of the European Jews.

These findings also provide us with a better understanding of how Nazi policy evolved. Although there is an obvious link between policy and ideology, there was no defined corpus of Nazi ideology (even other Nazi leaders did not read Alfred Rosenberg). Instead, Nazi ideology was reflected by the writings of large numbers of people, including Party functionaries, government bureaucrats, and racial scientists. In fact, policy was revealed less in ideological statements by leaders than in the day-to-day activities of middle-level management. Hitler set policy goals, but middle-level management delineated and implemented policy. Hitler was preoccupied with racial purity and was determined to cleanse the gene pool of the German nation. He demanded the exclusion of the unfit and the alien. In cooperation with racial scientists, the Nazi party and German government bureaucrats defined the groups to be excluded.

From the beginning in 1933, these bureaucrats focused on the handicapped, Jews, and Gypsies, advancing solutions for exclusion that became progressively more radical. Before the Final Solution of mass murder became feasible, these bureaucrats proposed sterilization and deportation (or emigration) as solutions. The handicapped were thus sterilized before they were killed, and this also applied to many Gypsies. Even during the war, Nazi functionaries continued to search for an easy method that would make mass sterilization of Jews possible. When emigration or expulsion was no longer feasible but before the killings commenced, the Nazis instituted the deportation of Jews and Gypsies as a means of exclusion.

Sterilization, deportation, and killings thus reflected the evolving policy of exclusion and was applied to the handicapped, Jews, and Gypsies.

Further, Party and government agencies competed for the right to implement policy. Ideologues like Julius Streicher, even Joseph Goebbels, were "outside the loop" when the policy to kill was decided and implemented. The killing of the handicapped was directed by the Führer Chancellery in cooperation with racial scientists and health care functionaries. The killing of Jews and Gypsies was directed by Heydrich (later Ernst Kaltenbrunner) as chief of the Security Police and SS Security Service. Under Heydrich's command, the Gestapo (political police) dealt with Jews, and the Kripo (detective forces) dealt with Gypsies. While it is true that the Kripo, traditionally concerned with crime prevention, tended to focus on Gypsy mobility and supposed Gypsy crime, it deferred to racial scientists for its guidelines on how to classify and exclude Gypsies. The delineation of Gypsy policy thus largely devolved on Ritter, a psychiatrist whose research in racial science centered on Gypsies, and who headed the Eugenic and Criminal Biological Research Station (*Rassenhygienische und Kriminalbiologische Forschungsstelle*) of the Reich Health Office and later the Criminal Biological Institute of the Security Police at Kripo headquarters. Both Gestapo and Kripo thus relied on racial scientists to define the condemned groups. They also needed Hitler's order, or at least his authorization, to implement a policy of mass murder. In the final analysis, the activities and records of these implementing agencies reflect policy decisions about genocide better than do public declarations, even the Führer's speeches.

The German racial theories that served as the basis for extermination were never rational or consistent. Thus in Germany, "pure" Jews were killed, but those of mixed ancestry were usually not included in killing operations, because the bureaucracy chose not to alienate Germans related to Jews. In contrast, Gypsies of mixed ancestry were the first victims, because their German relatives, usually holding low social status, posed no bureaucratic problems. And while the bureaucracy worked hard to limit the number of exempted Jews of mixed ancestry, Ritter classified 90 percent of all Gypsies as having mixed origins. Various Nazi leaders, including Himmler, had their own favorite racial theories, but none ever inhibited the relentless bureaucratic drive toward extermination. The files of Ritter's agency provide incontrovertible documentary evidence that "pure" Roma and Sinti were registered and incarcerated, thereafter deported, and eventually killed. Our growing understanding of the Gypsy Holocaust enables us to restore the complexity of this history, and perhaps this history may also provide us with a better understanding of the interaction between science and state bureaucracy with the forces of popular prejudice and racism.

Eyewitness Accounts: Holocaust — The Gypsies

The fate of the Gypsies (Roma and Sinti) in the concentration camps and killing fields of the Holocaust has been largely invisible in current historiography about Nazi genocide. Recent scholarship about the experiences of Roma and Sinti in Nazi-occupied Europe has generally been printed by an assortment of small publishers, thereby discouraging most scholars from ferreting out this diverse literature and impeding the inclusion of new data as more than an afterthought. This has resulted in a tacit conspiracy of silence about the isolation, exclusion, and systematic killing of the Gypsies, rendering much Holocaust scholarship deficient and obsolete.

Several reasons explain the disparity between the vast quantity of literature about Nazi persecution of the Jews and the limited number of studies about Nazi anti-Gypsy ideology and practice. Although the percentage of Gypsy mortality was approximately the same as the percentage of Jewish mortality in the Holocaust, the sheer weight of numbers of the Jewish victims captured immediate attention. Moreover, even in the 1940s, surviving sources about the fate of European Jews were far more numerous than those about Gypsies. Further, Jewish survivors published a substantial memoir literature, whereas Gypsy survivors were less articulate in print and more dependent on oral traditions. As each group of victims tended to write its own history of the Holocaust, the larger Jewish communities obviously dominated postwar historiography, whereas the less articulate communities of Gypsies remained largely silent and had no academic representation.

Although there is at present no comprehensive bibliography about the fate of Roma and Sinti during the Holocaust, the growing literature about this subject has been a byproduct of the European Roma and Sinti civil rights movement since the 1980s. A substantial number of these new local and regional studies include eyewitness narratives.

The following survivor narratives were selected from this published literature. They represent typical aspects of the cumulative experiences of German and Austrian Roma and Sinti men and women between 1933 and 1945. These events include the internment of German Sinti in special municipal camps after 1935, such as the Dieselstrasse camp in Frankfurt (Jakob Müller); the May 1940 deportation from Hamburg to Lublin (Lani Rosenberg); the Belzec labor camp (Lani Rosenberg); imprisonment in Sachsenhausen, Gross Rosen, and Litomerice concentration and labor camps (Hugo Franz); medical experiments on Gypsy prisoners at Natzweiler-Struthof and Neckarelz (an unnamed Sinto from Nuremberg); daily life in the Auschwitz-Birkenau Gypsy family camp, BIIe, including the May 1944 revolt and the August 1944 liquidation (Elisabeth Guttenberger and Anna P.); the 1942 killings of Gypsies at Treblinka

(Michael Chodźko); and the difficulties encountered by Roma survivors in Austria after 1945 (Maria Kohlberger, Leopoldine Papai, and Johann Breirather). All translations are by Sybil Milton.

The German Sinto, Jakob Müller, born in 1928, recounts his childhood experiences of deportation from Worms to the special municipal Gypsy internment at Dieselstrasse in Frankfurt am Main, where he was forced to live from September 10, 1940, until his family was deported to Auschwitz on March 13, 1943. His detailed description of the Dieselstrasse special camp reveals the overcrowded conditions and the special difficulties of the incarcerated Sinti children. Müller's story is published in Eva von Hase-Mihalik and Doris Kreuzkamp, *Du kriegst auch einen schönen Wohnwagen: Zwangslager für Sinti und Roma während des Nationalsozialismus in Frankfurt am Main,* ["You will also get a nice wagon to live in: Involuntary internment camps for Sinti and Roma in Frankfurt under the Nazis."] (Frankfurt: Brandes and Apsel, 1990), pp. 23–27:

> ... No reasons were given when we were picked up in Worms. We lived in a large area with many other Sinti. After surrounding the area, they arrived in our home at Kleine Fischerweide 50, located adjacent to the Nibelungen school. Screaming "Out, out, out" — we could only take the most essential items with us. We were placed on a truck that took us directly from Worms to Frankfurt. My father wasn't at home, since he was with the German air force.
>
> In 1941, my father was dishonorably discharged from the army "for racial reasons" and he too was sent to the Frankfurt camp. We arrived at the Dieselstrasse camp in Frankfurt on September 10, 1940, and were there until we were deported to Auschwitz on March 13, 1943.
>
> The Dieselstrasse camp was about 80 meters [ca. 240 ft.] long and 20 meters [ca. 60 ft.] wide. We were forced to live in abandoned moving vans. There were about 25 such vans and initially 150 to 180 persons were housed there. Many families with 8 to 12 members were forced to live in a space 7 meters [21 ft.] long by 2 meters [6 ft.] wide. They were forced to live in about 14 square meters and were crowded together in very cramped quarters.
>
> There was always roll call in the mornings; we were counted — we were, to be sure, fenced in; there was a guard booth at the exit and four policemen on rotating shifts were always stationed there
> ....
> We were allowed to attend the Riederwald school for one year, but then the local population complained about this and eventually

we were seated separately in the last row of the class. Then came the Frankfurt order that forbade Gypsy children from attending schools ....

Lani Rosenberg, a German Sinto, describes his experiences after 1938 in Hamburg and Belzec labor camp. His father and brother were initially arrested during the June 1938 raids targeting "asocials" and deported to Sachsenhausen concentration camp; in mid-May 1940 the rest of his family was arrested and deported from Germany to Lublin (in occupied central Poland). Rosenberg's account is excerpted from Rudko Kawczynski's essay, "Hamburg soll 'zigunerfrei' werden" ("Hamburg will be 'free of Gypsies'"). In Angelika Ebbinghaus, Heidrun Kaupen-Haas, Karl Heinz Roth (Eds.) *Heilen und Vernichten im Mustergau Hamburg: Bevölkerungs- und Gesundheitspolitik im Dritten Reich* ["Healing and Killing in the Model Gau Hamburg: Reproductive and Health Policies in the Third Reich"] (Hamburg: Konkret Literatur Verlag, 1984), pp. 49–50:

> The eldest in our family were arrested first. My father and older brother were arrested by the police in June 1938 at 5 A.M. In the greatest of haste, my mother asked an attorney to try to free my father and brother. Although the police had no grounds for arresting them, shrugging his shoulders the attorney reported that one couldn't do anything about it. He informed us that they had been taken to Sachsenhausen concentration camp. I wrote petitions for clemency, requesting my father's and brother's release, to Department C2 of the *Reichskriminalpolizeiamt* in Berlin and to the Führer. Eventually, I received a warning from the Hamburg-Eimsbüttel local police to stop annoying the Führer, or I too would also be arrested. Those Sinti that were still free were ordered not to leave the city limits. For starvation wages, I was compelled to do heavy physical labor.
>
> On May 16, 1940, I, my mother, and all my other siblings still in Hamburg were arrested. I asked the police why we were being arrested. They replied that we were being resettled in Poland. We were assembled together with several hundred other Gypsies and brought to a shack near the harbor. Each of us received a red number painted on our skin. The transport to Poland began several days later. We were permitted to take only some of our clothing with us. All money and items of value were confiscated.
>
> After several days travel we arrived in Poland at a place called Belzec. We were immediately received by an SS unit and were separated by age and gender. The SS took no great pains with many of the Gypsies, who were forced to dig their own graves; these Gypsies

were then shot and buried. While being beaten we were forced to run to a shack. Later we had to put barbed wire around this hut. Early every morning we had to stand for roll call. Afterwards there were more beatings, we then received our tools, and were forced to run to "work" while again being beaten. The work place was located close to the Russian border. During the first three months of arrest, many of the younger children died of starvation and disease. There was no medical care. I often witnessed how Gypsies were shot, only because they tried to get some water. Once I observed that several 8- to 12-year-old children were compelled to lie on the ground while booted SS men marched over their bodies. It is impossible to detail everything that I experienced during five years in the concentration camps, since words are inadequate to report all of it. I lost eight brothers and sisters as well as my parents under the Nazis. My father was shot someplace near Schwerin shortly before the war ended ....

Hugo Franz, head of the German Sinti organization in Düsseldorf, was a victim of German racial persecution. Franz was born in Dresden in 1913 to a family that had lived in Germany for 300 years. When Franz graduated from secondary high school (*Gymnasium*), Nazi racial laws prevented him from entering law school. He instead attended the Saxon state orchestral school and then formed his own band in Hamburg together with his three brothers; after 1939 his identity papers were confiscated and he was not permitted to accept road engagements for his band. Franz was compelled to abandon his profession as a musician and was forced to work at the Blohm and Voss copper plant. Arrested in January 1942, he survived subsequent imprisonment in Sachsenhausen, Gross Rosen, and Litomerice concentration and labor camps. His experiences are published in an interview in Jörn-Erik Gutheil et al. (Eds.) *Einer mußüberleben: Gespräche mit Auschwitzhäftlinge 40 Jahre danach* ["One of us must survive: Conversations with Auschwitz prisoners forty years later"] (Düsseldorf: Der Kleine Verlag, 1984), pp. 50-52:

At the time I was living with my parents in Hamburg. On January 7, 1942, I was arrested by the Gestapo at 5 in the morning. They told me to pack my tooth brush and other toiletries. My mother was told that I would be taken to a concentration camp ....

At the police station, I had to countersign the protective custody order for my arrest, and I was then imprisoned for about a month until a transport for Oranienburg-Sachsenhausen could be consolidated. Beatings had already started during the transport. We wondered, 'What will become of us, and where had we landed?' Everything was utterly new and strange.

We stood in the grim cold in Sachsenhausen for five hours — it was winter — and were then delivered to the Political Department. There an SS Technical Sergeant informed me that since I was a Gypsy, my transfer to this concentration camp was the end of the road for me, that it was a one-way street with no way back out. There, for the first time in my life, I saw shrunken heads like the ones made by headhunters, but these were Gypsy heads. They stood on a sideboard in the Political Department.

We were then taken to a barrack, where every hair on our bodies was shorn and shaven off. We were next taken to the bath, an ice cold shower. We were compelled to hand over all of our clothing and in return received prisoner uniforms — zebra uniforms. I wore size 39 shoes and was given size 43. By this time, we all looked a bit odd. The beating began when we arrived back in the barracks. There were already Sinti prisoners in this camp and I knew a few of them. They had connections to the clothing depot and arranged for me to get half-way decent clothing. A brown triangle had been sewn onto my prison uniform, because I had been classified an antisocial. [The inverted brown or beige triangle was the special marking used to identify Gypsy prisoners; it was frequently replaced by the more common black triangle for Roma and Sinti prisoners reclassified as "asocials" in the concentration camps.]

We were then separated into different work groups. We carried stones that were to be used in construction and had to move everything at double time. We had to carry hundred-weight sacks, two at a time. Anyone not able to do this had signed his own death warrant because SS guards kicked him mercilessly with their rubber boots. Out of a work commando of 100 men, 30 to 40 were often gone by the end of the day ....

[In mid-March 1942,] we were transferred to work in a rock quarry in Gross Rosen concentration camp; we often worked until midnight on the construction of the camp. We slept four men to a blanket. The windows had not yet been installed in our barracks, and when we awoke in the morning, there was often snow on our blankets.

Our rations were a piece of bread, which had at best 30 percent flour; the rest consisted of ground chestnuts and sawdust. Afternoons, turnips; evenings, coffee. We had to save some of our breakfast bread for evening, and we then got one cube of margarine for 60 people. The result of this bad food was dysentery. For medicine, there was carbon or chalk tablets, and this white substance had to be taken by spoon. The result was zero, nothing whatsoever. The majority of prisoners died. A transport of 5000 to 6000 prisoners was completely used up in eight weeks.

I, too, had typhus and at one point weighed only 78 pounds. A friend managed to have me transferred to the kitchen, where I peeled potatoes. There I did not have to work as hard, and I received a half-liter more to eat per day. That's how I recovered from that disease. Otherwise, typhus meant a death sentence. The crematorium could not keep up. We had mountains of ashes which were used to fertilize fields. Whenever a German prisoner died, the camp notified his relatives. These notices were, of course, pre-printed forms. They usually stated that the cause of death was due to a generally weakened condition or heart failure. For 20 marks, the family could receive the ashes of the deceased in an urn ….

At Gross Rosen, the Sinti were not housed together in a separate barracks, but you could tell who they were by their triangular marking …. As Gypsies, we could not be appointed to any prisoner posts. I was, however, the only Sinti who kept the barracks register for the *Lagerältesten* [camp elder]. It worked as follows: The block leader, a prisoner, received his assignment from the camp elder, who in turn reported to the SS. The SS appointed the prisoners to clean the barracks. The members of this work crew were responsible for order and cleanliness in the barracks, reporting to the block leader. The SS made it easy for themselves. If anything untoward occurred, punishments descended down the hierarchy; the SS would beat the camp elder, who in turn would beat the barracks elders, then the barracks elder would in turn beat the room elder, and then the room elder would beat the prisoners.

My block elder had been brought up in a juvenile care program, starting in special schools and homes and then in prison. Whenever he wanted to write home, I had to write these letters for him, but never received any benefits for doing this. A German prisoner could become a capo, a room elder, a block elder, or even a messenger to the Political Department. No Sinto could get any of these posts ….

I was in Gross-Rosen until 1943 and was then transferred to a satellite camp, a chemical plant owned by BASF at Dyhrenfurth near Breslau. There were 300 prisoners in the small camp at this factory. The factory produced poisonous gas for weapons: bombs, grenades, these were the Führer's last weapons. Many prisoners became unconscious and died while filling these weapons. We were almost blinded by our work, and tiny little pills were placed in our eyes to dilate the iris so we could continue to see. Because we worked with these weapons, we were sworn to secrecy. I was not allowed to tell any of the other prisoners anything about my work.

And because I knew these secrets, I had a double sense of despair and hopelessness that the Nazis would not allow me to survive.

When Lodz was liberated by the Russians on January 2, 1945, we were evacuated and had to march 70 kilometers in wooden clogs back to Gross Rosen. Prisoners too exhausted to survive the march were shot. The main camp at Gross Rosen was filled beyond capacity, since all the satellite camps had been reassembled at the main camp. After a brief stop at Gross Rosen, we were marched to Striegau …. I will never forget that march. Women standing along the road threw stones and other objects at us, calling us "pigs." At Striegau we were loaded onto open freight cars, but the locomotive did not arrive and we were forced to march back to Gross Rosen through the night. Two to three hundred prisoners were crammed into a barrack normally assigned to one hundred prisoners; we stood packed together like sardines in a box.

In the middle of the night, the barracks were lit up when the camp came under attack. The Russians had probably learned that the prisoners had been evacuated, but were unaware that the prisoners had been forced to return that night. We pushed the window panes out and sought safety from the shelling outside. We saw many wounded and dead lying everywhere. The next morning the transport to Striegau was reassembled. Every hundred prisoners were placed in open freight cars, seated adjacent to grenades that were tied together. We collected snow from the edge of the train car in order to moisten our lips, since we had not received any water all day. We travelled for six days in those open freight cars from Gross Rosen via Dresden to Litomerice in Czechoslovakia; the latter camp was located four kilometers from Theresienstadt. By then, there were only 13 prisoners left in my car.

We arrived at the camp, a former barracks already occupied by Czech and Polish prisoners. The bunk beds consisted of ten levels of boxes and since the lower tiers were already occupied, a weak prisoner could not climb that high. Our block elder from Gross Rosen arranged that we were sent to a small satellite camp called Elsabe. The prisoners worked 150 meters deep in subterranean mine tunnels completing tank motors for the Elsabe Company of Chemnitz …. After two months there, I learned from a guard that the tunnels were mined and would be blown up along with the prisoners to prevent these motors from falling into enemy hands ….

A German Sinto from Nuremberg, whose name is deleted to protect his privacy, narrates his ordeal with phosgene gas experiments at Natzweiler-Struthof concentration camp in the excerpt "I was a Guinea Pig," published in Jürgen Ziegler (Ed.) *Mitten unter uns; Natzweiler-Struthof: Spuren eines Konzentrationslagers* ["In Our Midst; Natzweiler-Struthof:

Traces of a concentration camp"] (Hamburg: VSA Verlag, 1986), pp. 96–98:

On March 8, 1943, our entire family was arrested. We were sent to the Nuremberg prison and then to the concentration camp at Auschwitz. Auschwitz was a nasty camp. We were frequently beaten and had to do heavy labor. The death toll was high. One day, 90 volunteers were requested for construction work in Germany. We reported since conditions couldn't be worse than here at Auschwitz.

More people reported than were selected. They took only young men who still had some strength left. We were taken from Auschwitz to Rothau in cattle cars. From there, we traveled by truck uphill to Struthof. Our transport was divided into two groups: 45 men had to share a small room with three-tier bunk beds; each bed was occupied by 2 men. We had to hand over all of our clothing and received only a night shirt and wooden shoes. We lived in this room for a while. Then the medical experiments began. By then, we regretted volunteering and said "not one of us will come out of here alive" .... Meanwhile we learned that previously at Struthof, not even 1 women among the 90 who had been subjected to medical experiments had survived.

One day we were informed that physicians would come to inoculate us. We were told that we shouldn't be afraid, since antidote shots would also be distributed. The physicians in their white coats arrived and we had to march past them with goose steps. I received an injection in my upper left arm. Everyone became ill with high fevers. One person went mad hitting his head repeatedly with his wooden clogs until he died after several days. He was not the only person to go crazy after these experiments. At first I was spared from the high fevers. The others couldn't eat anything because of high fevers. Several people died in our room. When the others were improving, I had a high fever and was bathed in sweat for several days, but I survived. We were not forced to work in the camp during these medical experiments, but were isolated and prohibited from leaving our room. The experiments lasted from fall 1943 to spring 1944. After this, we were compelled to work in the camp. We had to cart away waste from the latrines. The carts had to be pulled up the mountain ....

One day a transport for Neckarelz was assembled. [Neckarelz contained two satellite labor camps for male prisoners from Natzweiler and existed from March 21, 1944, to late March 1945.] Everyone reported for labor. Since I didn't want to remain in Natzweiler, where I feared I would die of lethal injections or be forced to participate in phosgene gas experiments, I volunteered for Neckarelz ....

We were taken to Neckarelz by train and housed in a school. The school was surrounded by barbed wire. I was, however, too weak to work. When we reported for roll call, the other prisoners assisted me. I was also carried to work in the tunnels. I tried to hide whenever I could. One day a prisoner physician who occasionally visited the school informed me: "I can no longer keep your [condition] secret and will have to send you back to Natzweiler." Since I was too weak to work loading stones onto trucks in the tunnels, I was sent back to Natzweiler. I was immediately placed in a large room with perhaps 100 other prisoners, they were ill with tuberculosis. They died like flies: in front of me, behind me, and next to me. Here I met a prisoner physician to whom I owe my life. He was French. He concluded that my illness was not that severe and that he could help me. Once I was a bit better, I was moved to another room. One day, we were informed that all Gypsies in the camp had to report. We were taken to the gas chamber in Struthof. Many of us were taken to that gas chamber. Before I entered it, an SS doctor gave me an injection .... The interior of the gas chamber had white tiles. I had previously heard that there were gas experiments on prisoners at Struthof. One of the other prisoners said to me: "If you are sent inside, you should urinate on your handkerchief, hold it to your mouth, and lie down next to the door sill." I couldn't really imagine this, but in any case I followed those instructions. When I entered, I took a towel scrap on which I had urinated, held it firmly to my nose and mouth, and placed myself as low as possible by the door sill. After a while, the door was opened and I stumbled out. Even today, I don't know how I survived. Perhaps I was lucky, perhaps it was the injection, or maybe they had used too little gas. At any rate, I emerged from the gas chamber and reentered the camp. I stayed there until late summer 1944, when the camp was evacuated to Dachau. The Americans arrived [at Dachau] on April 29, 1945, and we were liberated ....

The report by Anna P., née Schopper, born in 1926 in Dortmund, details her experiences in the Gypsy family compound BIIe at Auschwitz-Birkenau from mid-March 1943 to early summer 1944. It is excerpted in the published catalog of the Dortmund Municipal Holocaust Memorial: Günther Högl (Ed.) *Widerstand und Verfolgung in Dortmund, 1933-1945: Katalog zur ständigen Ausstellung des Stadtarchivs Dortmund in der Mahn-und Gedenkstätte Steinwache* (Dortmund: Wittmaack Verlag, 1992), p. 440.

I was deported to Auschwitz as a 16-year-old girl together with my mother and nine brothers and sisters. The journey from Dortmund lasted several days and was horrible. We were packed together in cattle cars and received almost nothing to eat and drink. We reached Auschwitz on March 14, 1943. On arrival, we were immediately forced to hand over the few things we had been allowed to take with us; they even seized our clothing and shoes. We were shaved and tattooed; I was assigned number Z 2964. Housing consisted of barracks without windows and with very few air vents. There was barely any possibility to bathe and there was never any soap. The bathrooms — simple outhouse toilets — mocked every description. It was ghastly.

I had to work on road construction crews together with other women; we hammered the pavement level and hauled stones. Frequently, we were whipped to force us to continue working.

Provisions were catastrophic. One small loaf of bread was divided into eight portions; we had to make do with one portion of bread, a small pat of margarine, and a minuscule quantity of turnip greens. For lunch we were fed turnip stock. We were always hungry and grew steadily weaker. Many died from exhaustion and illness, especially from typhus. I got sick with dysentery and felt wretched. There were no drugs. I was compelled to eat charcoal, a byproduct of the wood burning stoves in the barracks and thus perhaps survived that illness.

I later worked in the kitchen and recovered a bit. Since I was able to work, I was transferred in early summer 1944 together with my sister to a munitions plant in Zwodau/Graslitz [today respectively called Svatava and Kraslice in Czechoslovakia; the 1944 site of a subsidiary labor camp of Flossenbürg concentration camp]. It was there, totally emaciated and at the end of my strength, that I was liberated.

Elisabeth Guttenberger, a German Sintezza, was born in Stuttgart in 1926 and completed eight years of primary school there. She attributes her survival at Auschwitz to her earlier education that resulted in her assignment to a camp office. Together with four brothers and sisters, she had previously lived "in a very beautiful part of Stuttgart with many gardens and parks. My father earned his living with antiques and stringed instruments. We lived peacefully together with our neighbours." Arrested and deported to Auschwitz-Birkenau in early March 1943, she was given prisoner number Z-3991. She describes resistance by the prisoners of the Birkenau Gypsy family camp (BIIe) in mid-May 1944 and the liquidation of BIIe in early August 1944, resulting in her transfer on August 1, 1944, to Ravensbrück concentration camp. Guttenberger has told her story in many books, including H. G. Adler, Hermann Langbein, and Ella Lingens-Reiner (Eds.) *Auschwitz: Zeugnisse und Berichte*, ["Auschwitz: Testimony and Reports"], 3d rev. exp. ed. (Frankfurt: Europäische Verlagsanstalt, 1984), pp. 131–34. Her narrative was republished in German, Polish, and English languages in Auschwitz-Birkenau State Museum and Documentation and Cultural Center of German Sinti and Roma, Heidelberg (Ed.) *Memorial Book: The Gypsies at Auschwitz-Birkenau*, 2 vols. (Munich, London, New York, and Paris: K.G. Saur, 1993), 2: 1497–1503. Her published account in the *Memorial Book* has been reedited by Sybil Milton to include additional material from Guttenberger's earlier published accounts:

Gypsies, like the Jews, were persecuted for racial reasons. All Gypsies that could be found were deported to Auschwitz, without consideration for their profession or trade, whether they had fixed domiciles or not .... As a 17-year-old girl, I was arrested ... and taken to Auschwitz.

... We were arrested in March 1943. At 6 o'clock in the morning the police came and took us away in a truck. I was then 17. I was deported to Auschwitz together with my parents, four brothers and sisters, a 3-year-old niece, my 80-year-old grandmother, and many other relatives. My other grandmother came somewhat later with her daughter and nine grandchildren ....

The first impression I had of Auschwitz was horrible. It was already dark when we arrived. A huge tract of land, although one was able to see only the lights. We had to spend the night on the floor of a huge hall. Early the next morning we had to march into the camp. There, prisoner numbers were tattooed on our arms and our hair was cut off. The clothes, shoes, and the few things we still had with us were taken away. The Gypsy camp was in the Birkenau section, located between the men's camp and the prisoners' infirmary [*Häftlingskrankenbau*]. In this section were 30 barracks which were called blocks. One block served as the toilet for the entire camp. More than 20,000 Gypsies were kept in the rest of the barracks. The barracks had no windows, only air vents. The floor was made out of clay. In one barrack, where there was enough room for perhaps 200 people, 800 or more people were lodged. This way of housing so many people was a horrible martyrdom. My aunt walked next to me. We looked at each other and tears began to roll down our faces .... It was dreadful. The people sat motionless on their plank beds and just stared at us. I thought I was dreaming. I thought I was in hell.

After about 14 days, we were divided into work gangs. With many other women, I was forced to carry heavy stones for construction work in the camp. The men were forced to build the camp road. Even old men, whether they were sick or not, had to work .... Everyone was used. My father was then 61. No one paid any attention to that .... Auschwitz was a death camp.

At that time, the construction of Birkenau had not yet been finished. The worst part was the hunger. The hygienic conditions are barely describable. There was virtually no soap or facilities for washing. When typhus broke out, the sick could not be treated, because there was no medicine. It was hell. One cannot imagine anything more horrifying. First, the children died. They cried day and night for bread. Soon they all starved to death. The children who were born in Auschwitz did not live long either. The only thing the Nazis were concerned with was that the newborn were properly tattooed and registered. Most infants died several days after their births. There was no child care, no milk, no warm water, let alone powder or diapers. The older children, above the age of ten, had to carry rocks for the camp road, despite the fact that starvation caused them to die every day ….

In our labor brigade, we had to do everything while running. An SS *Blockführer* accompanied us by bicycle. If a woman tripped, because she was too frail, she was whipped. Many died from those beatings. The Blockführer in charge of the Gypsy camp was an SS Corporal [Ernst August] König; I never heard that he was tried or sentenced after the war. Even today, I could identify him immediately. [König was belatedly arraigned and indicted for murders he had committed in the Birkenau Gypsy camp and after a trial lasting nearly two years was sentenced to life imprisonment in January 1991 in the Siegen District Court. He subsequently committed suicide in prison after his appeal was rejected.]

Early morning roll calls were torture, standing at attention from 6 to 8 in the morning irrespective of weather. Everyone had to assemble for roll call, even the elderly, the children, and the sick. On Sunday, roll calls often lasted until noon, often standing in harsh heat without protective head covering. Many collapsed from heat prostration and infirmities.

After my first month in Auschwitz, a transport with 2000 Russian Gypsies arrived. These poor people were in the camp for only one night. They were sent to the crematoria and gassed the next day. Everyone, however short their stay in Birkenau, asked about the chimneys that produced smoke all night and all day. They were told that people were gassed and burned there. On the evening that the Russian Gypsies were gassed, the barracks were secured and we were forced to remain in our barracks [*Blocksperre*]. At about 9 that evening, trucks arrived at our compound and the Russian Gypsies were forcibly shoved aboard and driven to the crematoria. I secretly witnessed their departure.

I was also an eyewitness to another gassing operation. I had already been assigned to work in camp clerical office and was permitted to walk outside our barracks. The so-called sick camp [*Krankenlager*] was adjacent to our barracks. Jewish and Polish male prisoners were incarcerated there. I observed two trucks driving up to their barracks and the sick were thrown on board. Many could no longer walk and were starved skeletons. A few were naked; others had only a shirt. Before the trucks departed, a few prisoners mustered enough courage to curse their murderers.

After about a half year, I was put to work in a camp clerical office. There I had to file note cards for the transport lists, and was placed in charge of the main men's register for our camp. I had to enter the death notices brought in from the infirmary. I entered thousands of names into that book. I had been in the office for just eight days when a death notice with my father's name arrived. I was paralyzed and tears streamed down my face. At that moment, the door swung open and SS Staff Sergeant Plagge stormed in and screamed, "Why is she blubbering in the corner?" I could not answer. My friend, a clerk named Lilly Weiss, said, "Her father died." In response Plagge said, "We all have to die," and left the office ....

The Gypsies also tried to defend themselves against the liquidation of the Gypsy camp. That was a very tragic story. The Gypsies made weapons out of sheet metal. They sharpened the metal into knives. With these improvised weapons and clubs, they tried to defend themselves as best they could. I know an eyewitness, a Polish woman named Zita, who worked across from us and lived through the liquidation of the Gypsy camp. Later, she told me how the Gypsies hit out and defended themselves, because they knew that they were going to be gassed. The resisters were mowed down with machine guns ....

In 1944, about 2000 Gypsies able to perform labor were deported from our compound; about 4500 people were left behind. These were the elderly, the sick, and those no longer able to perform heavy labor. These people were "liquidated," as the SS called it, during the night of July 31 to August 1, 1944. Of the 30,000 Gypsies deported to Auschwitz, only about 3,000 survived. I know these figures because I worked in the camp office.

I lost about 30 of my relatives in Auschwitz. Both of my grandmothers died there. An aunt with ten children was there, only two children survived .... My father literally starved to death in the first few months. My older sister contracted typhus and died in 1943. Naturally, malnutrition and hunger were significant factors. Then my youngest brother died at the age of 13. He had to carry heavy rocks until he was an emaciated skeleton. My mother died of starvation several months afterwards. Auschwitz cannot be compared to anything else. To say, 'the hell of Auschwitz' is not an exaggeration ....

I left the camp ill and am still sick today. I would like to remove the prisoner number tattooed on my lower left forearm. When I wear summer clothing without sleeves, I always cover this number. I have noticed that people stare at this tattooed number and often make malicious and vicious comments, thus always reminding me of the hellish camp experiences ....

There are few survivor reports about the killing fields of occupied Poland and the Soviet Union, where Jews and Gypsies were executed in forests, drowned in local rivers, and killed inside many ghettos, labor camps, and killing centers. Several eyewitness accounts by local residents are excerpted in Polish postwar regional publications as well as in the materials assembled by postwar Polish judicial authorities. These extracts provide us with some insight about the fate of Gypsies deported from various Polish ghettos to Treblinka or killed in Polish fields and forests. The narrative by Michael Chodz´ko, a former prisoner at the Treblinka labor camp, was initially published in his article "The Gypsies in Treblinka," *Rzeczpospolita* [*The Republic*], Lublin, no. 35, September 6, 1945) and was reproduced in Jerzy Ficowski's book, *Cyganie na polskich drogach: Wydanie trzecie poprawione i rozszerzone* ["Gypsies on the Roads of Poland"], 3d rev. exp. ed. (Cracow and Wroclaw: Literary Publishing House, 1965), pp. 125–26:

In the spring of 1942, Gypsies … were locked up within the narrow walls of Jewish ghettos. The death penalty was threatened for leaving the ghetto and not wearing the armband with the letter Z [*Zigeuner,* Gypsy]. Until the fall of 1942, Gypsies were hauled off, along with Jews, to the killing centers at Majdanek, Treblinka, and others, where they were killed in the gas chambers, or else shot, and their bodies later burned. Despite the walls and barbed wire closing off the Jewish quarters, groups of Gypsies succeeded in temporarily getting outside the ghettos. The Germans sent Gypsies to the "labor camp" at Treblinka with assurances that they would like it in the camp especially organized for them in the forest …. They arrived in Treblinka to set up "their camp." The march was halted at the edge of the forest which was the place of execution and the grave for hundreds of thousands of people. Trustingly, the crowd sat down in a meadow; they were allowed to light a fire, over which they prepared hot meals. A few hours later the SS arrived, and the men were separated from the women and children. Their possessions and baggage were piled up in one big heap. The men were led off deeper into the forest …. They were forced into a pit a hundred at a time, and then machine-gunned. The Gypsies who were still alive were forced to bury those who had been shot — and who were often only wounded — before they, themselves, were pushed into the pit, and a hundred people more were deprived of their lives in the clatter of machine-gun fire. The bodies were covered with a shallow layer of earth …. When the men were taken away, the Gypsy women did not know what had happened to them, but when they heard the constant gunfire, they began to scream and wail. The Nazis at that point ceased to dissemble: they no longer spoke of a "Gypsy camp" and encouraged the soldiers to begin a brutal massacre. They seized babies from their mothers and killed the infants by bashing their heads against trees. With whips and cudgels the SS covered with blows the women who had been driven insane by the spectacle. The women threw themselves at the soldiers and tried to wrest their babies away. This scene was only brought to an end by salvos of gunfire from the surrounding SS and soldiers. The bodies of the executed women and children were later cleared by other prisoners specially brought in for that purpose; the corpses were taken to graves that had been prepared beforehand in an adjacent forest.

An Austrian Roma survivor Leopoldine Papai, then 36 years old, was interviewed in 1966 in her modest home on the outskirts of Vienna by Selma Steinmetz for a project of the Documentation Archives of the Austrian Resistance, Vienna. Excerpts from this interview were reprinted in Steinmetz's *Österreichs Zigeuner im NS-Staat* ["Austrian Gypsies under the Nazis"] (Vienna, Frankfurt, and Zurich: Europa Verlag, 1966), pp. 40–41:

My father was the village blacksmith in Holzschlag. Many Gypsies lived there in 1938. And we were permanent residents, not like now [living] at the edge of town. We were then a large family with nine children; three of my brothers were already married and had many children. My married sister also had four children, when the persecutions began. Already in 1941, they took my father, three brothers, and two sisters to Sindisdorf near Pinkafeld. Two brothers and a sister were deported to Litzmannstadt [the Lodz ghetto] and were never heard from again. My parents and my other siblings were sent back home after two days and their ration cards were returned to them.

However, the SS returned in April 1943. My father was then above the age of 60. I was still a child, only 14; my youngest sister was four years younger. We were deported in cattle cars. If our town officials had been consulted, we would certainly have been allowed to remain at home. The mayor had tears in his eyes, when we last saw him. We petitioned to be allowed to remain at home. The residents assuredly needed a blacksmith like my father. This is why we had initially been allowed to stay. But by April 1943, it was too late and no pleas would have helped. We were forced to leave.

We were sent directly to Auschwitz with a large transport and were immediately driven to heavy labor. [Steinmetz notes that the Auschwitz Calendarium of April 16, 1943, records the registration of 1847 Austrian Gypsies arriving at Auschwitz, and that Leopoldine Papai was assigned the number Z-7706.] I had to carry 10 kg. of heavy stones. I also witnessed how Jews were sent to the gas chambers. We observed how they undressed
....

My parents were killed in Auschwitz, my father died of typhus. In the fall of 1944 ... there were no longer any Gypsies in our large camp. We were told that they had all been sent to the gas chambers.

Shortly thereafter, my sister and I — together with many Jews — were sent to Ravensbrück. Many on this transport were shot, many died. After eight months, we were again deported, initially to Mauthausen and later to

Bergen-Belsen. That was the worst. There was absolutely nothing to eat there and we slept on the bare ground. The British freed us in Bergen-Belsen.

There are only 2 of us alive out of 36 family members; my sister and I .... I have lung problems because of the camps and will probably never be completely healthy.

The former Austrian political prisoner Johann Breirather wrote to the Federal Association of the Austrian Resistance and the Victims of Fascism on February 21, 1961, about the fate of his foster daughter, the Roma child Sidonie Adlersburg. Sidonie Adlersburg's tragic childhood was also narrated in a popular Austrian television dramatization entitled *Requiem for Sidonie*, directed by Karin Brandauer in 1990. This text by Sidonie's foster father is preserved in the Documentation Archives of the Austrian Resistance (DÖW), file 668:

Post Neuzeug 200, Upper Austria

Neuzeug, 21 February 1961

Dear Comrades!

Our family read in the newspapers that Franz Hofer, former Gauleiter of the Tyrol, was arraigned. I would now like to record the following:

In 1933, we accepted a foster child with dark skin from the child welfare office. Ostensibly the mother had abandoned this child, but we never learned more precise information. These are the circumstances of how we obtained this child. Her name was Sidonie Adlersburg and she was presumably of Gypsy descent.

We considered her a member of our family along with our two other children. Everyone, except for racial fanatics, was fond of this child with her amusing manner.

In the fall of 1942, we were repeatedly told by the Steyr district child welfare office that our Sidonie would be sent to a children's home. We appeared several times at the child welfare office in order to keep this child. We don't want to describe those difficult times. At the end of February 1943, the child welfare office informed us that they had ostensibly located the child's mother. The mother was in Hopfgarten in the Tyrol. On 10 March 1943, a nurse from the Steyr child welfare office took Sidonie to Hopfgarten. We were not convinced that the mother had actually been found. After the collapse of the Third Reich, I became a communal official of Sierning and, with American permission, telephoned Hopfgarten. I learned that Gypsies of all ages had been assembled and deported from Hopfgarten and that the children were deported last. This transport, which included our Sidonie, was sent to Auschwitz in Poland. After 1945 we learned from the Steyr district child welfare office that according to a nurse from Vienna, who had herself been a prisoner at Auschwitz, Sidonie Adlersburg was infected with typhus bacilli and had then been gassed. I will end my report here.

Comrades, I was a political prisoner during the years 1933–1934 and this fact is officially certified in document no. 243 issued to me by the Upper Austrian state government.

We are not screaming for revenge, but everyone responsible for the death of others should be held accountable before a court of law. If former Gauleiter Franz Hofer is responsible for the deportation of Gypsies and people of color from all of Austria, he should be placed on trial. I am enclosing a photograph [of Sidonie] for your documentation.

With fraternal greetings,

[signed] Johann Breirather

An official statement by the Austrian Roma, Maria Kohlberger, on May 3, 1948, at the Linz district administration [*Bezirkshauptmannschaft*] tells of her inability to work as a commercial exhibitor, her assignment to forced labor, and the death of most of her family in several concentration camps. Her statement reveals the failure of postwar restitution to Roma and Sinti Holocaust victims. Kohlberger's affidavit is found in the Documentation Archives of the Austrian Resistance (DÖW), Vienna, file 13457:

Ms. Maria Kohlberger, born on 25 March 1909 in Buch, Lower Austria, Austrian citizen, commercial exhibitor, residing at Ödt 34, Traun, records the following statement at the Linz district administration office on 3 May 1948:

Until 1938, I held a license as a commercial exhibitor. With the incorporation of Austria in the German Reich, this license was rescinded, since as a descendant of Gypsies I was unable to document that I was Aryan. Since that time, I was constantly under

Gestapo surveillance. I was assigned to conscript labor in the Göring armament factory, was not allowed to leave the city, and was not deported to a concentration camp, since my employers reported that I was a good worker.

My mother Cäcilie Kohlberger died in Auschwitz. My brother Julius Kohlberger, together with his three children, perished at Dachau. My sister Albine Rosenfeld died together with her eight children in Litzmannstadt (Lodz), only because they were not Aryans.

I suffered severe injury as a racial persecutee under the terms of the Victims Welfare Law (*Opferfürsorgegesetz*). All professional items were confiscated from my sister Albine Rosenfeld, who was also a licensed commercial exhibitor. I have never received restitution for all impounded articles related to the practice of my licensed trade. Police official Neudorfer at the police presidium in Linz can confirm these facts. I am therefore requesting under paragraph 4 of the Victims Welfare Law that all objects urgently needed to reestablish my business be returned to me ....

Notes

This essay is a revised and expanded version of a paper presented at the 1991 annual meeting of the German Studies Association, Los Angeles.

1. For a discussion of Gypsies in Holocaust historiography, see Sybil Milton, "The Context of the Holocaust," *German Studies Review* 13 (1990): pp. 269–83; idem, "Gypsies and the Holocaust," *The History Teacher* 24, no. 4 (August 1991): pp. 375–87; and Correspondence, *ibid* 25, no. 4 (August 1992): pp. 515–21. For a discussion of postwar trends in German historical literature about Roma and Sinti, see Michael Zimmermann, *Verfolgt, vertrieben, vernichtet: Die nationalsozialistische Vernichtungspolitik gegen Sinti und Roma* (Essen: Klartext, 1989), pp. 87–98; and Kirsten Martins-Heuß, *Zur mythischen Figur des Zigeuners in der deutschen Zigeunerforschung* (Frankfurt: Haag and Herchen, 1983).

2. Yehuda Bauer, "Holocaust and Genocide: Some Comparisons," in Peter Hayes (Ed.) *Lessons and Legacies: The Meaning of the Holocaust in a Changing World* (Evanston, IL: Northwestern University Press, 1991), p. 42; idem, "Jews, Gypsies, Slavs: Policies of the Third Reich," *UNESCO Yearbook on Peace and Conflict Studies 1985* (Paris: UNESCO, 1987), pp. 73–100; idem, "Gypsies," *Encyclopedia of the Holocaust*, 4 vols. (New York and London: Macmillan, 1990), Volume 2: pp. 634–38; Hans-Joachim Döring, *Die Zigeuner im nationalsozialistischen Staat*, Kriminologische Schriftenreihe, Volume 12 (Hamburg: Deutsche Kriminalogische Gesellschaft, 1964), pp. 19ff. and 193; Bernhard Streck, "Nationalsozialistische Methoden zur Lösung der 'Zigeunerfrage,'" *Politische Didaktik: Zeitschrift für Theorie und Praxis des Unterrichts* 1 (1981): pp. 26–37; and idem, "Die nationalsozialistischen Methoden zur 'Lösung des Ziegeunerproblems,'" *Tribüne: Zeitschrift zum Verständnis des Judentums* 20, no. 78 (1981): pp. 53–77. Two excellent critiques of Streck's misinterpretations and unambiguous use of Nazi stereotypes and linguistic usage are Joachim S. Hohmann, "Ihnen geschah Unrecht: Zigeunerverfolgung in Deutschland," *ibid* 21, no. 82 (1982): pp. 100–13; and Romani Rose, "Die neuen Generation und die alte Ideologie: Zigeunerforschung — wie gehabt?," *ibid* 21, no. 81 (1982): pp. 88–107.

3. Excellent examples are Leni Yahil, *The Holocaust: The Fate of European Jewry* (New York and Oxford: Oxford University Press, 1990), and Richard Breitman, *The Architect of Genocide: Himmler and the Final Solution* (New York: Knopf, 1991).

4. See Ludwig Eiber (Ed.) *"Ich wußte, es wird schlimm"; Die Verfolgung der Sinti und Roma in München 1933–1945* (Munich: Buchendorfer Verlag, 1993), pp. 14–16. For the development of police and psychiatric registration practices in the late 19th and early 20th centuries, see Susanne Regener, "Ausgegrenzt: Die optische Inventarisierung der Menschen im Polizeiwesen und in der Psychiatrie," *Fotogeschichte* 10, no. 38 (1990): 23–38.

5. See Eiber, *Die Verfolgung der Sinti und Roma in München,* pp. 40–45; Zimmermann, *Verfolgt, vertrieben, vernichtet;* and Joachim S. Hohmann, *Geschichte der Zigeunerverfolgung in Deutschland* (Frankfurt and New York: Campus, 1988).

6. Karola Fings and Frank Sparing, *Nur Wenige Kamen Zurück: Sinti und Roma im Nationalsozialismus* (Cologne: Landesverband Deutscher Sinti und Roma NRW and El-De-Haus, 1990), p. 3.

7. Gisela Bock, *Zwangssterilisation im Nationalsozialismus: Studien zur Rassenpolitik und Frauenpolitik* (Opladen: Westdeutscher Verlag, 1986), pp. 361–68 and 452–56. See Theresia Seible, "Sintezza und Zigeunerin," in Angelika Ebbinghaus (Ed.) *Opfer und Täterinnen: Frauenbiographien des Nationalsozialismus,* (Nördlingen: Greno-Delphi Politik, 1987), pp. 302–16.

8. Wilhelm Stuckart and Hans Globke, *Kommentare zur deutschen Rassengesetzgebung* (Munich and Berlin: C. H. Beck'sche Verlagsbuchhandlung, 1936), p. 153; Arthur Gütt, Herbert Linden, and Franz Massfeller, *Blutschutz- und Ehegesundheitsgesetz, 2nd ed.* (Munich: J. F. Lehmanns Verlag, 1937), pp. 16, 21, 150, and 226.

9. The *Reichsbürgergesetz* of September 17, 1935, reduced Jews and Gypsies to second-class citizens because of their "alien blood," and in 1942 the 12th decree to the *Reichsbürgergesetz* resulted in most German Roma and Sinti being declared stateless. Jews and Gypsies above the age of 20 also lost the right to vote in Reichstag elections on March 7, 1936. See Joseph Walk (Ed.) *Das Sonderrecht für die Juden im NS-Staat: Eine Sammlung der gesetzlichen Maßnahmen und Richtlinien — Inhalt und Bedeutung* (Heidelberg and Karlsruhe: C. F. Müller Juristischer Verlag, 1981), no. 127 on p. 156. Similarly, neither Jews nor Gypsies were permitted to vote in the April 10, 1938, plebiscite on the incorporation of Austria; this directive was issued in Vienna on March 23, 1938, ten days after the incorporation of Austria. See Dokumentationsarchiv des österreichischen Widerstandes, Vienna (hereafter DÖW), file 11151.

10. See Franz Calvelli-Adorno, "Die rassische Verfolgung der Zigeuner vor dem 1. März 1943," *Rechtsprechung zum Wiedergutmachungsrecht* 12 (December 1961): pp. 121–42; and Joachim S. Hohmann, *Robert Ritter und die Erben der Kriminalbiologie: "Zigeunerforschung" im Nationalsozialismus und in Westdeutschland im Zeichen des Rassismus* (Frankfurt, Bern, New York, and Paris: Peter Lang, 1991).

11. See Heinrich Wilhelm Kranz, "Zigeuner, wie sie wirklich sind," *Neues Volk* 5, no. 9 (September 1937): pp. 21–27.

   Heinrich Wilhelm Kranz (1897–1945), an opthamologist, had joined both the Nazi Party and Nazi Physicians' League prior to 1933. After his appointment to teach race science (*Rassenkunde*) at Giessen, he obtained, in 1938, the newly created chair for race science at Giessen University. He became the rector of Giessen in 1940. In Giessen he also headed the Race Political Office of the Gau Hessen-Nassau. In 1940–1941, together with Siegfried Koller, he published their three-volume *Die Gemeinschaftsunfähigen,* advocating sterilization, marriage prohibition, and compulsory internment in labor camps for "asocials."

   For biographical data on Kranz, see Berlin Document Center: Heinrich Wilhelm Kranz file; Michael H. Kater, *Doctors Under Hitler* (Chapel Hill and London: University of North Carolina Press, 1989), pp. 115–19; Benno Müller-Hill, *Murderous Science: Elimination by Scientific Selection of Jews, Gypsies, and Others; Germany, 1933-1945,* trans. George R. Fraser (Oxford: Oxford University Press, 1988), note 73 on p. 181; and Hohmann, *Geschichte der Zigeunerverfolgung,* pp. 115–21.

   For the antecedents of Nazi practice and ideology towards Gypsies, see *ibid,* pp. 48-84. For a brief history of Ritter's office in the *Reichsgesundheitsamt,* see *Bundesgesundheitsblatt* 32 (March 1989), special issue "Das Reichsgesundheitsamt, 1933-1945: Eine Ausstellung."

12. The *Reichsvertretung der Juden in Deutschland* (or the Reich Representation of German Jews) was created in 1933, and served as the federal umbrella organization established by Jewish organizations in Germany to represent the Jewish community vis-à-vis the German government; part of its name was changed under the Nuremberg racial laws of 1935 from "of German Jews" (*der deutschen Juden*) to "of Jews in Germany" (*der Juden in Deutschland*). In February 1939, following the dissolution of all remaining individual Jewish organizations in Germany, the *Reichsvertretung* was formally replaced by the unified *Reichsvereinigung*.

13. The *Reichsvereinigung der Juden in Deutschland* (or the Reich Association of Jews in Germany) was the compulsory association of all Jews in Germany after 1939.

14. Bundesarchiv Koblenz (hereafter BAK), R36, files 1022 and 1023: Fürsorge für Juden und Zigeuner. The institutionalized handicapped faced similar deteriorating conditions, see Angelika Ebbinghaus, 'Kostensenkung, 'Aktives Therapie' und Vernichtung." In Angelika Ebbinghaus, Heidrun Kaupen-Haas, and Karl Heinz Roth (Eds.) *Heilen und Vernichten im Mustergau Hamburg: Bevölkerungs- und Gesundheitspolitik im Dritten Reich* (Hamburg: Konkret Literatur Verlag, 1984), pp. 136–46.

15. BAK, R18/5644, pp. 215–27, containing cover letter and 6-page memorandum from Oberregierungsrat Zindel to Staatssekretär Pfundtner, "Gedanken über den Aufbau des Reichszigeunergesetzes," March 4, 1936. The document states: "Auf Grund aller bisherigen Erfahrungen muss jedenfalls vorweg festgestellt werden, daß eine *restlose Lösung des* Zigeunerproblems weder in einem einzelnen Staate noch international in absehbarer Zeit möglich sein wird." (emphasis in the original) Reproduced in facsimile in Henry Friedlander and Sybil Milton (Eds.) *Bundesarchiv of the Federal Republic of Germany, Koblenz and Freiburg*, Volume 20 of *Archives of the Holocaust* (New York and London: Garland, 1993), 20: pp. 100–06.

16. Runderlaß des Reichs- und Preußischen Ministers des Innern betr. "Bekämpfung der Zigeunerplage," June 5, 1936 (III C II 20, Nr. 8/36), in *Ministerialblatt für die Preußische Innere Verwaltung* 1, no. 27 (June 17, 1936): 783. Reproduced in facsimile in Eva von Hase-Mihalik and Doris Kreuzkamp, *Du kriegst auch einen schönen Wohnwagen: Zwangslager für Sinti und Roma während des Nationalsozialismus in Frankfurt am Main* (Frankfurt: Brandes and Apsel, 1990), pp. 43–44.

17. Staatsanwaltschaft [hereafter StA] Hamburg, Verfahren 2200 Js 2/84: Reich- und Preußisches Ministerium des Innern, Runderlaß betr. "Bekämpfung der Zigeunerplage," June 6, 1936 (III C II 20, Nr. 10/36); published in *Ministerialblatt für die Preußische Innere Verwaltung* 1, no. 27 (June 17, 1936): 785. Reproduced in facsimile in Hase-Mihalik and Kreuzkamp, *Wohnwagen*, pp. 44–45.

18. See Ute Bruckner-Boroujerdi and Wolfgang Wippermann, "Das 'Zigeunerlager' Berlin-Marzahn, 1936-1945: Zur Geschichte und Funktion eines nationalsozialistischen Zwangslagers," *Pogrom* 18, no. 130 (June 1987): pp. 77–80.

19. BAK, ZSg 142/3: Report about the Gypsy Camp Marzahn, September 1, 1936, and report by G. Stein, "Untersuchungen im Zigeunerlager Marzahn," Frankfurt, October 26, 1936.

20. See Hans Reiter, *Das Reichsgesundheitsamt 1933–1939: Sechs Jahre nationalsozialistische Führung* (Berlin: Julius Springer Verlag, 1939), pp. 356–58. See also the special issue "Das Reichsgesundheitsamt, 1933–1945: Eine Ausstellung," *Bundesgesundheitsblatt* 32 (March 1989): pp. 13–30; and *Feinderklärung und Prävention: Kriminalbiologie, Zigeunerforschung und Asozialenpolitik*, Volume 6 of *Beiträge zur nationalsozialistischen Gesundheits- und Sozialpolitik* (Berlin: Rotbuch Verlag, 1988).

21. Robert Ritter, "Die Bestandsaufnahme der Zigeuner und Zigeunermischlinge in Deutschland," *Der Öffentliche Gesundheitsdienst* 6, no. 21 (February 6, 1941): pp. 477–89; idem, "Die Aufgaben der Kriminalbiologie und der kriminalbiologischen Bevölkerungsforschung," *Kriminalistik* 15, no. 4 (April 1941): pp. 1-4; and idem, "Primitivität und Kriminalität," *Monatsschrift für Kriminalbiologie und Strafrechtsreform* 31, no. 9 (1940): pp. 197–210. See also BAK, R73/14005, containing Ritter's reports and correspondence with the Deutsche Forschungsgemeinschaft; and BAK, ZSg 149/22, similar Ritter material in the Hermann Arnold Collection.

22. Adolf Würth, "Bemerkungen zur Zigeunerfrage und Zigeunerforschung in Deutschland," *Verhandlungen der deutschen Gesellschaft für Rassenforschung, Sonderheft des Anthropologischen Anzeiger Stuttgart* 9 (1937–1938): p. 92.

23. Müller-Hill, *Murderous Science*, pp. 143–49.

24. See Reimar Gilsenbach, "Wie Lolitschai zur Doktorwürde kam," in *Beiträge zur nationalsozialistischen Gesundheits- und Sozialpolitik* 6 (Berlin, 1988): pp. 101–34; Johannes Meister, "Schicksale der 'Zigeunerkinder' aus der St. Josefspflege in Mulfingen," *Württembergisch Franken Jahrbuch* (1984): pp. 197–229; and ibid, "Die 'Zigeunerkinder' von der St. Josefspflege in Mulfingen," *1999: Zeitschrift für Sozialgeschichte des 20. und 21. Jahrhunderts* 2, no. 2 (April 1987): pp. 14–51. See also Eva Justin, "Die Rom-Zigeuner," *Neues Volk* 11, no. 5 (1943): pp. 21–24; and Justin's dissertation, *Lebensschicksale artfremd erzogener Zigeunerkinder und ihrer Nachkommen*, v. 57, no. 4 of the series *Veröffentlichungen aus dem Gebiete des Volksgesundheitsdienstes* (Berlin: Richard Schoetz, 1944).

25. Sophie Ehrhardt, "Zigeuner und Zigeunermischlinge in Ostpreußen," *Volk und Rasse: Zeitschrift des Reichsausschusses für Volksgesundheit und der Deutschen Gesellschaft für Rassenhygiene* 17 (1942): pp. 52–57. Zentrale Stelle der Landesjustizverwaltungen, Ludwigsburg (hereafter ZStL), 415 AR 314/81, Bd. 1, pp. 110–31 (Ehrhardt) and Bd. 2, pp. 332–46 (Würth): Ermittlungsverfahren der StA Stuttart gg. Sophie Ehrhardt und Adolf Würth; these interrogations are reproduced in facsimile in Henry Friedlander and Sybil Milton (Eds.) *Zentrale Stelle der Landesjustizverwaltungen, Ludwigsburg*, vol. 22 of *Archives of the Holocaust* (New York and London: Garland, 1993), 22: pp. 315–48. See also Benigna Schönhagen, Ed., *Nationalsozialismus in Tübingen: Vorbei und Vergessen* (Tübingen: Stadt Tübingen-Kulturamt, 1992), pp. 107, 110–11, 292, and 316–17.

26. For Cologne, see Karola Fings and Frank Sparing, "Das Zigeuner-Lager in Köln-Bickendorf, 1935–1958," *1999: Zeitschrift für Sozialgeschichte des 20. und 21. Jahrhunderts* 6, no. 3 (July 1991): pp. 11–40. For Düsseldorf, see Angela Genger (Ed.) *Verfolgung und Widerstand in Düsseldorf, 1933–1945* (Düsseldorf: Landeshauptstadt Düsseldorf, 1990), pp. 126–33; and Karola Fings and Frank Sparing, *"z. Zt. Zigeunerlager": Die Verfolgung der Düsseldorfer Sinti und Roma im Nationalsozialismus* (Cologne: Volksblatt Verlag, 1992). For Essen and Gelsenkirchen, see Michael Zimmermann, "Von der Diskriminierung zum 'Familienlager' Auschwitz: Die nationalsozialistische Zigeunerverfolgung," *Dachauer Hefte* 5 (1989): pp. 87–114; and idem, *Verfolgt, vertrieben, vernichtet*, pp. 18–22. For Frankfurt, see Wolfgang Wippermann, *Die nationalsozialistische Zigeunerverfolgung*, Volume 2 of the four-part study *Leben in Frankfurt zur NS-Zeit* (Frankfurt: Stadt Frankfurt am Main — Amt für Volksbildung/Volkshochschule, 1986); Die Grünen im Landtag Hessen, Lothar Bembenek, and Frank Schwalba-Hoth, Ed., *Hessen hinter Stacheldraht; Verdrängt und Vergessen: KZs, Lager, Außenkommandos* (Frankfurt: Eichborn Verlag, 1984), pp. 153–68; and Hase-Mihalik and Kreuzkamp, *Wohnwagen*. For Hamburg, see Rudko Kawczynski, "Hamburg soll 'zigeunerfrei' werden," in Ebbinghaus and others, *Heilen und Vernichten im Mustergau Hamburg*, pp. 45–53.

27. Stadtarchiv Frankfurt, Mag. Akte (Stadtkanzlei) 2203, vol. 1: Minutes of the Frankfurt City Council, March 20, 1936, concerning "Massnahmen gegen das Zigeunerunwesen."

28. Hase-Mihalik and Kreuzkamp, *Wohnwagen*, p. 42.

29. Fings and Sparing, *Die Verfolgung der Düsseldorfer Sinti und Roma*, pp. 36–37.

30. StA Hamburg, 2200 Js 2/84: Decree of the Reich and Prussian Ministry of the Interior concerning "Vorbeugende Verbrechensbekämpfung durch die Polizei," December 14, 1937, and "Richtlinien," April 4, 1938. For the raids against so-called asocials, see Wolfgang Ayaß, "'Ein Gebot der nationalen Abeitsdisziplin': Die Aktion 'Arbeitsscheu Reich' 1938," *Beiträge zur nationalsozialistischen Gesundheits- und Sozialpolitik* 6 (Berlin, 1988): pp. 43–74. For a survey of the concentration camp system, see Henry Friedlander, "The Nazi Concentration Camps." In Michael Ryan (Ed.) *Human Responses to the Holocaust* (New York and Toronto: Edwin Mellen Press, 1981), pp. 33–69; and Falk Pingel, *Häftlinge unter SS-Herrschaft: Widerstand, Selbstbehauptung und Vernichtung im Konzentrationslager* (Hamburg: Hoffmann and Campe, 1978). On camps for women, see Sybil Milton, "Women and the Holocaust: The Case of German and German-Jewish Women." In Renate Bridenthal, Atina Grossman, and Marion Kaplan (Eds.) *When Biology Became Destiny: Women in Weimar and Nazi Germany* (New York: Monthly Review Press, 1984), pp. 297–333, esp. 305–07. For the 1933 imprisonment of several Sinti in Worms-Osthofen concentration camp, see Michail Krausnick (Ed.) *"Da wollten wir frei sein!": Eine Sinti-Familie erzählt* (Weinheim and Basel: Beltz and Gelberg, 1993), p. 73.

31. The persecution of Gypsies in incorporated Austria is relatively well documented. See Selma Steinmetz, *Österreichs Zigeuner im NS-Staat* (Vienna, Frankfurt, and Zurich: Europa Verlag, 1966); Erika Thurner, *Nationalsozialismus und Zigeuner in Österreich* (Vienna and Salzburg: Geyer Edition, 1983); and Andreas Maislinger, "'Zigeuneranhaltelager und Arbeitserziehungslager' Weyer: Ergänzung einer Ortschronik," *Pogrom* 18, no. 137 (1987): pp. 33–36.

32. Dokumentationsarchiv des österreichischen Widerstandes, Ed., *Widerstand und Verfolgung in Salzburg 1934–1945*, 2 vols. (Vienna and Salzburg: Österreichischer Bundesverlag and Universitätsverlag Anton Pustet, 1991), 2: pp. 474–521; and Elisabeth Klamper, "Persecution and Annihilation of Roma and Sinti in Austria, 1938–1945, *Journal of the Gypsy Lore Society* 5, Vol. 3, No. 2 (1993):55–65.

33. B. A. Sijes, and others, *Vervolging van Zigeuners in Nederland, 1940–1945* (the Hague: Martinus Nijhoff, 1979).

34. See Michael R. Marrus and Roger O. Paxton, *Vichy France and the Jews* (New York: Basic Books, 1981), pp. 366–68.

35. See, for example, "Fahrendes Volk: Die Bekämpfung der Zigeunerplage auf neuen Wegen," *NS-Rechtsspiegel* (Munich), February 21, 1939, facsimile in Sybil Milton and Roland Klemig (Eds.), *Bildarchiv Preußischer Kulturbesitz*, Vol. 1 of *Archives of the Holocaust* (New York: Garland, 1990), Part 1, figs. 150–51; "Die Zigeuner als asoziale Bevölkerungsgruppe," *Deutsches Ärzteblatt* 69 (1939): pp. 246–47; and "Die Zigeunerfrage in der Ostmark," *Neues Volk* 6, no. 9 (September 1938): pp. 22–27. See also DÖW, file 4942: Oberstaatsanwalt Dr. Meissner, Oberlandesgericht Graz, report to Reichjustizminister, February 5, 1940.

36. Runderlaß des Reichsführer SS und Chef der Deutschen Polizei im Ministerium des Innern, December 8, 1938, betr. "Bekämpfung der Zigeunerplage," *Ministerialblatt des Reichs- und Preußischen Ministeriums des Innern* 51 (1938): pp. 2105–10. See also "Ausführungsanweisung des Reichskriminalpolizeiamts," March 1, 1939, published in *Deutsches Kriminalpolizeiblatt* 12, special issue (March 20, 1939).

37. See National Archives and Records Administration, Washington, Microfilm Publication T-70, reel 109, frames 3632755-6: Peter Raabe's remarks as president of the Reich Music Chamber published in *Amtliche Mitteilungen der Reichsmusikkammer*, May 1, 1939. The lists of expelled Gypsy musicians were published between February and December 1940. See *ibid*, frames 3632796-8, containing the list published on February 15, 1940. This material is cited in Alan E. Steinweis' *Art, Ideology and Economics in Nazi Germany: The Reich Chambers of Music, Theater, and the Visual Arts* (Chapel Hill and London: University of North Carolina Press, 1993), pp. 126–27, 132, and 205.

38. Nuremberg Doc. NG-684, copy in DÖW, file 4942.

39. StA Hamburg, Verfahren 2200 Js 2/84: RSHA Schnellbrief to Kripo(leit)stellen, October 17, 1939.

40. ZStL, Slg. CSSR, Bd. 148, pp. 55–57, and Bd. 332, pp. 289–300, 306. Some of these documents are reproduced in facsimile in Henry Friedlander and Sybil Milton (Eds.) *Zentrale Stelle der Landesjustizverwaltungen, Ludwigsburg*, vol. 22 of *Archives of the Holocaust* (New York and London: Garland, 1993), 22: pp. 71–78. See also Jonny Moser, "Nisko: The First Experiment in Deportation," *Simon Wiesenthal Center Annual* 2 (1985): pp. 1–30.

41. BAK, R18/5644, pp. 229–30: Letter from Leonardo Conti, Secretary of State for Health in the Reich Ministry of Interior, to the Central Office of the Security Police, Kripo headquarters, and the Reich Health Department, Berlin, January 24, 1940. The letter states:

It is known that the lives of Gypsies and part-Gypsies is to be regulated by a Gypsy law (*Zigeunergesetz*). Moreover, the mixing of Gypsy with German blood is to be resisted and, if necessary, this could be legally achieved by creating a statutory basis for the sterilization of part-Gypsies (*Zigeunermischlinge*). These questions were already in a state of flux before the war started. The war has apparently suddenly created a new situation, since the possibility of expelling Gypsies to the General Government is available. Certainly, such an expulsion appears to have particular advantages at the moment. However, in my opinion, the implementation of such a plan would mean that because it is expedient to do this at the moment, a genuine radicalization would not be achieved. I firmly believe, now as before, that the final solution of the Gypsy problem (*endgültige Lösung der Zigeunerproblems*) can only be achieved through the sterilization of full and part-Gypsies …. I think that the time for a legal resolution of these problems is over, and that we must immediately try to

sterilize the Gypsies and part-Gypsies as a special measure, using analogous precedents .... Once sterilization is completed and these people are rendered biologically
harmless, it is of no great consequence whether they are expelled or used as labor on
the home front.

42. Hessisches Hauptstaatsarchiv, Wiesbaden [hereafter HHStA], 407/863. See also Milton,
"Gypsies and the Holocaust," pp. 380-81; Zimmermann, *Verfolgt, vertrieben, vernichtet*, pp.
43–50; Hans Buchheim, "Die Zigeunerdeportation vom Mai 1940," in *Gutachten des
Instituts für Zeitgeschichte*, 2 vols. (Munich, 1958), 1: pp. 51ff.; and Michael Krausnick,
*Abfahrt Karlsruhe 16.5.1940: Die Deportation der Karlsruher Sinti und Roma; ein unter-
schlagenes Kapitel aus der Geschichte unserer Stadt* (Karlsruhe: Verband der Sinti und Roma
Karlsruhe e.V., 1991). The May 1940 deportation was linked to Reinhard Heydrich's
instructions to chiefs of police and district governors in Germany in the so-called *Umsied-
lungserlaß* of April 27, 1940 for the "resettlement, arrest, and deportation of Gypsies above
the age of 17 from western and northwestern border zones." See BAK, R58/473: Richtlinien
für die Umsiedlung von Zigeunern, Berlin, April 27, 1940.

43. See DÖW, file E18518: letter from Kripostelle Salzburg to the Reichsstatthalter Provincial
President Dr. Reitter, Salzburg, July 5, 1940. The Gypsies were to be imprisoned in a special
camp until deportation; there they would be registered and given medical examinations.

44. United States Holocaust Memorial Museum Archives, Record Group 7, Washington, Fojn-
Felczer collection: Ruling (*Feststellung*) of the Reich Ministry of Interior, Berlin, January 26,
1943, that Gypsies transferred to concentration camps on orders of the Reich Leader SS
were defined as enemies of the Reich and, consequently, their property and possessions
could be seized.

45. See Henry Friedlander, "The Deportation of the German Jews: Postwar German Trials of
Nazi Criminals," *Leo Baeck Institute Yearbook* 29 (1984): p. 212.

46. Werner Präg and Wolfgang Jakobmeyer, Ed., *Das Diensttagebuch des deutschen Generalgouv-
erneurs in Polen, 1939-1945* (Stuttgart: Deutsche Verlagsanstalt, 1975), pp. 93, 146–47
(March 4, 1940), 158 (April 5, 1940), and 262 (July 31, 1940). See also Friedlander, "Deportation of German Jews," p. 209.

47. StA Hamburg, Verfahren 2200 Js 2/84: RSHA Rundschreiben to Kripoleitstelle Königsberg, July 22, 1941. The fate of one East Prussian Sinti family deported to the Bialystok
ghetto is detailed in Amanda Dambrowski, "Das Schicksal einer vertriebenen ost-
preußischen Sinti-Familie im NS-Staat," *Pogrom* 12, nos. 80-81 (March-April 1981): pp.
72–75.

48. See Jerzy Ficowski, *Cyganie na Polskich Drogach* (Cracow and Wroclaw: Wydawnictwo Liter-
ackie, 1985), pp. 129–51; Lucjan Dobroszycki (Ed.) *The Chronicles of the Lodz Ghetto,
1941–1944* (New Haven and London: Yale University Press, 1984), pp. 82, 85, 96, 101, and
107; Antoni Galinski, "Nazi Camp for Gypsies," 16 pp. mimeographed paper presented at a
conference of the Main Commission for the Investigation of Nazi and Stalinist Crimes in
Poland (Warsaw, April 1983); and DÖW, files 11293, 11477, and 18518. See also Hanno
Loewy and Gerhard Schoenberner, *"Unser einziger Weg ist Arbeit": Das Getto in Lodz,
1940–1944* (Frankfurt and Vienna: Löcker Verlag, 1990), pp. 186–87.

49. Raul Hilberg, Stanislaw Staron, Josef Kermisz, Ed., *The Warsaw Diary of Adam Czerniakow:
Prelude to Doom* (New York: Stein and Day, 1979), pp. 346–47, 351, 364–68, and 375. See
the decree of the Warsaw police president "Mit den Juden auch die Zigeuner hinter
Mauern," *Nowy Kurier Warszawski* no. 131 (June 5, 1942); and Michal Chodzko, "Zigeuner
in Treblinka," *Rzeczpospolita* (Lublin), no. 35 (September 6, 1944), translated and excerpted
in Tilman Zülch (Ed.) *In Auschwitz vergast, bis heute verfolgt: Zur Situation der Roma
(Zigeuner) in Deutschland und Europa* (Reinbek bei Hamburg: Rowohlt, 1979), pp. 101–03.
See also Yad Vashem, Jerusalem, E 39: Elias Rosenberg, "Das Todeslager Treblinka" (11 pp.
typescript, written en route to Palestine, n.d. [1946?]), pp. 6–7. Rosenberg describes the
arrival of two Roma transports in Treblinka in late November 1942 and records their defiance on the way to the gas chambers, thus necessitating the use of additional German SS
and Ukrainian guards.

50. For one example, see the published judgment (sentenced to life imprisonment) against SS Lieutenant Colonel (*Obersturmbannführer*) Albert Rapp (chief of Sonderkommando 7a of Einsatzgruppe B) for killing Jews, Gypsies, and the handicapped; Landgericht Essen, March 29, 1965, 29 Ks 1/64, in *Justiz und NS-Verbrechen: Sammlung deutscher Strafurteile wegen nationalsozialistischer Tötungsverbrechen*, Ed. Adelheid L. Rüter-Ehlermann and C. F. Rüter, 22 vols. (Amsterdam: University Press Amsterdam, 1968–81), 20: no. 588, pp. 732 and 754ff. See also ZStL, Sammlung UdSSR, Bd. 245 Ac, p. 318: Extract from a 1945 Soviet report concerning the town of Elgawa, occupied on June 30, 1941, which notes that 6000 Jews were killed; 44 institutionalized psychiatric patients were shot on September 2, 1941, and an additional 440 psychiatric patients were shot and buried in a nearby forest on January 8, 1942; and 280 Gypsies were shot and killed on May 27–28, 1942.

51. Nuremberg Doc. NO-3278: "Ereignismeldungen UdSSR 153," January 9, 1942.

52. *Trials of War Criminals before the Nuernberg Military Tribunals under Control Council Law No. 10* [Green series], 14 vols. (Washington: Government Printing Office, 1950–1952), 4: p. 286.

53. Yivo Institute, New York: Berlin Collection, Occ E 3-61: Reich Ministry for the Occupied Eastern Territories to Reichkommissar Ostland, June 11, 1942.

54. StA Hamburg, Verfahren 2200 Js 2/84: Anordnung des Reichsarbeitsministers betr: die Beschäftigung von Zigeuner, March 13, 1942. The parallel law for Jews was "die Verordnung über die Beschäftigung von Juden," October 3, 1941, *Reichsgesetzblatt* 1: 675, and "die Verordnung zur Durchführung der Verordnung über die Beschäftigung von Juden," October 31, 1941, ibid 1: 681.

55. BAK, R19/180.

56. StA Hamburg, Verfahren 2200 Js 2/84: RSHA Schnellbrief betr: Einweisung von Zigeuner-mischlinge, Rom-Zigeunern und balkanischen Zigeunern in ein Konzentrationslager, January 29, 1943. The text of the December 16, 1942, unpublished decree has been lost, but the date of that December law is found in the first sentence of the January 29, 1943, Schnell-brief. Professor Richard Breitman, American University, kindly provided the information about the Himmler meeting with Hitler.

57. Danuta Czech, *Kalendarium der Ereignisse im Konzentrationslager Auschwitz-Birkenau 1939–1945* (Reinbek bei Hamburg: Rowohlt, 1989), p. 423.

58. See Milton, "The Context of the Holocaust," p. 275; and HHStA, 407/863: Richtlinien für die Umsiedlung von Zigeunern, Berlin, April 27, 1940.

59. Auschwitz-Birkenau State Museum and Documentation and Cultural Center of German Sinti and Roma, Heidelberg (Ed.) *Memorial Book: The Gypsies at Auschwitz-Birkenau*, 2 vols. (Munich, London, New York, and Paris: K.G. Saur, 1993), 2: 1547; and Czech, 774. See Elisabeth Guttenberger testimony, pp. 254–258.

60. See Benno Müller-Hill, *Tödliche Wissenschaft: Die Aussonderung von Juden, Zigeunern und Geisteskranken, 1933–1945* (Reinbek bei Hamburg: Rowohlt, 1984), pp. 68ff.

61. Walk, no. 480 on p. 397. See above, notes 9, 44, and 45. See also *Trials of War Criminals before the Nuremberg Military Tribunals under Control Council Law No. 10* [Green Series], 3: p. 713 (Nuremberg document PS 664). In 1943, German neighbors denounced the few remaining Sinti families living in Berlin-Karlshorst, see Reimar Gilsenbach, "Wie Alfred Lora den Wiesengrund überlebte: Aus der Geschichte einer deutschen Sinti-Familie," *Pogrom* 21, no. 151 (January-February 1990): pp. 13–18.

62. See above, note 49.

63. See Helmut Krausnick and Hans-Heinrich Wilhelm, *Die Truppe des Weltanschauung-skrieges: Die Einsatzgruppen der Sicherheitspolizei und des SD 1938–1942* (Stuttgart: Deut-sche Verlags-Anstalt, 1981).

64. See Henry Friedlander, "The Manipulation of Language." In Henry Friedlander and Sybil Milton (Eds.) *The Holocaust: Ideology, Bureaucracy, and Genocide.* (Millwood, NY: Kraus International Publications, 1980), pp. 103–13.

65. The first special study on Gypsy labor assignments in concentration camps is Romani Rose and Walter Weiss, *Sinti und Roma im Dritten Reich: Das Programm der Vernichtung durch Arbeit* (Göttingen: Lamuv, 1991).

66. See Donald Kenrick and Grattan Puxton, *Sinti und Roma: Die Vernichtung eines Volkes im NS-Staat*, trans. Astrid Stegelmann (Göttingen and Vienna, 1981). Although dated, this useful study is European in scope. There are few comprehensive accounts for occupied Europe. For Belgium, see José Gotovitch, "Quelques donnes relatives l'extermination des tsiganes de Belgique," *Cahiers d'Histoire de la Seconde Guerre Mondiale* 4 (Brussels, 1976): pp. 161–80. For Czechoslovakia, see Ctibor Necas, *Nad osudem ceskych a slovenskych Cikanu* (Brno, 1981); and idem, "Die tschechischen und slowakischen Roma im Dritten Reich," *Pogrom* 12, nos. 80–81 (March–April 1981): pp. 62-64. For occupied and Vichy France, see Jacques Sigot, *Un camp pour les Tsiganes…et les autres: Montreuil-Bellay, 1940-1945* (Bordeaux: Wallada, 1983); and Uwe Knödler, "Saliers 1942–1944: Ein Romalager im besetzten Frankreich," *Pogrom* 20, no. 146 (May 1989): pp. 39–40. For the Netherlands, see B.A. Sijes and others, *Vervolging van Zigeuners in Nederland 1940–1945*; and Leo Lucassen, *"En men Noemde hen Zigeuners": De Geschiedenis van Kaldarasch, Ursari, Lowara en Sinti in Nederland, 1750–1944* (Amsterdam and the Hague: Stichting beheer IISG-SDU, 1990). For Poland, see Jerzy Ficowski, *Cyganie na Polskich Drogach*, pp. 129–51; and idem, *Cyganie w Polsce: Dzieje i Obyczaje* (Warsaw: Wydawnictwo Interpress, 1989). See also David Crowe and John Kolsti (Eds.) *The Gypsies of Eastern Europe* (Armonk, NY, and London: M. E. Sharpe, 1991).

67. See Eiber, pp. 10–11 and 132–36; and Thurner, appendix XXVIII, facsimile of September 29, 1948, notice from the Austrian Federal Ministry of the Interior to all police departments recommending expulsion for "the increasing Gypsy nuisance."

68. See Eiber, pp. 136–38; Romani Rose, *Bürgerrechte für Sinti und Roma: Das Buch zum Rassismus in Deutschland* (Heidelberg: Zentralrat Deutscher Sinti und Roma, 1987), pp. 122–30; and Josef Henke, "Quellenschicksale und Bewertungsfragen: Archivische Probleme bei der Überlieferungsbildung zur Verfolgung der Sinti und Roma im Dritten Reich," *Vierteljahrshefte für Zeitgeschichte* 41, no. 1 (1993): pp. 61–77.

69. See Rose, pp. 46–67; Arnold Spitta, "Entschädigung für Zigeuner?: Geschichte eines Vorurteils." In Ludolf Herbst and Constantin Goschler (Eds.) *Wiedergutmachung in der Bundesrepublik Deutschland.* (Munich: Oldenbourg, 1989), pp. 385–401; Christian Pross, *Wiedergutmachung: Der Kleinkrieg gegen die Opfer* (Frankfurt: Athenäum, 1988); and Ingo Müller, *Hitler's Justice: The Courts of the Third Reich*, transl. Deborah Lucas Schneider (Cambridge, MA: Harvard University Press, 1991), pp. 261–69. See also the script for the film by Katrin Seybold and Melanie Spitta, *Das falsche Wort: Wiedergutmachung an Zigeunern (Sinti) in Deutschland?* (Munich: Katrin Seybold Film Productions, 1980). For Austria, see Brigitte Bailer-Galanda, "Verfolgt und vergessen: Die Diskriminierung einzelner Opfergruppen durch die Opferfürsorgegesetzgebung," *Dokumentationsarchiv des österreichischen Widerstandes Jahrbuch* (1992): pp. 16–20.

70. ZStL, 415 AR 55/82: StA Frankfurt, Verfahren gg. Robert Ritter u.a., 55 (3) Js 5582/48 (discontinued August 28, 1950); ibid, 402 AR 116/61: StA Frankfurt, Verfahren gg. Eva Justin u.a., 4 Js 220/59 (discontinued April 27, 1961); ibid, 415 AR 930/61: StA Frankfurt, Verfahren gg. Eva Justin, 4 Js 220/59 (discontinued December 12, 1960).

71. ZStL, 415 AR 314/81: StA Stuttgart, Verfahren gg. Sophie Ehrhardt u.a., 7 (19) Js 928/81 (discontinued January 29, 1982, reinstituted March 15, 1982, discontinued November 21, 1985).

72. Christian Pross and Götz Aly, Ed., *The Value of the Human Being: Medicine in Nazi Germany, 1918–1945*, transl. Marc Iwand (Berlin: Ärztekammer Berlin and Edition Hentrich, 1991), p. 38.

73. ZStL, 414 AR-Z 196/59: StA Frankenthal, Verfahren gg. Leo Karsten, 9 Js 686/57 abd 9 Js 153/59 (discontinued July 30, 1960); ibid, 415 AR 930/61: StA Cologne, Verfahren Hans Maly u.a., 24 Js 429/61, 24 Ks 1/64 (discontinued May 13, 1970).

74. StA Berlin, Verfahren gg. Otto Bovensiepen u.a., 1 Js 9/65; microfilm of the indictment at the Leo Baeck Institute Archives, New York.

75. *Memorial Book: The Gypsies at Auschwitz-Birkenau*, 2: p. 1643. König committed suicide in prison.

76. Rose, pp. 130–34; Henry Friedlander, "The Judiciary and Nazi Crimes in Postwar Germany," *Simon Wiesenthal Center Annual* 1 (1984): pp. 27–44; Jürgen Weber and Peter Steinbach (Eds.) *Vergangenheitsbewältigung durch Strafverfahren?: NS-Prozesse in der Bundesrepublik Deutschland* (Munich: Günter Olzog Verlag, 1984); and Heiner Lichtenstein, *Im Namen des Volkes?: Eine persönliche Bilanz der NS-Prozesse* (Cologne: Bund, 1984). For Austria, see Karl Marschall, *Volksgerichtsbarkeit und Verfolgung von nationalsozialistischen Gewaltverbrechen in Österreich: Eine Dokumentation, 2nd ed.* (Vienna: Bundesministerium für Justiz, 1987).

77. Sybil Milton (text) and Ira Nowinski (photographs), *In Fitting Memory: The Art and Politics of Holocaust Memorials* (Detroit: Wayne State University Press, 1991).

78. See *Pogrom* 21, no. 154 (July–Aug. 1990): pp. 11–30, containing articles on Roma in Bulgaria, Czechoslovakia, Hungary, Romania, and the former German Democratic Republic.

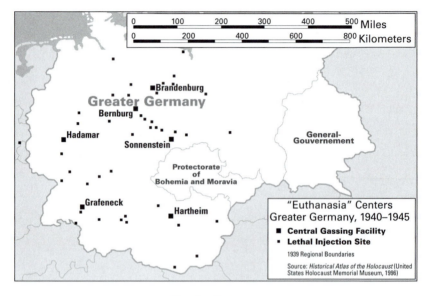

Greater Germany

CHAPTER 6
Holocaust: The Genocide of Disabled Peoples

HUGH GREGORY GALLAGHER

Aktion T-4 Euthanasie: **Summary of Program**

In the late 1930s and throughout World War II, physicians of Germany's medical establishment, acting both with and without the acquiescence of the Nazi government, systematically killed their severely disabled and chronically mentally ill patients. These people were said by their doctors to be "useless eaters" — persons with "lives not worth living."

The officially sanctioned killing program, begun in 1939, was called "*Euthanasie,*" although most of its victims were neither terminally ill nor in unbearable pain, nor were they anxious to die. The program's proponents advanced various arguments in its justification — compassion, eugenics, economics, racial purity. The official program was halted by Adolph Hitler in the summer of 1941, in the face of a rising wave of protests from disabled people, their families and friends, and religious officials. Even so, many doctors, acting largely on their own counsel, continued killing patients in hospitals and institutions throughout Germany.

Over the course of the official program and the unofficial so-called "runaway" euthanasia that followed it, more than 200,000 German citizens met their death at the hands of their physicians. The mass murder techniques developed in the euthanasia hospitals were later utilized against Jews.

Aktion T-4 Euthanasie Operation — To Whom, by Whom, How, and Why?

In the fall of 1939, upon the successful conclusion of the Polish campaign, Hitler signed an order that read, in toto, "*Reichsleiter* [Philip] Bouhler and Dr. [Karl] Brandt, M.D., are charged with the responsibility of enlarging the authority of certain physicians to be designated by name in such a manner that persons who, according to human judgment, are incurable can, upon a most careful diagnosis of their condition of sickness, be accorded a mercy death." (*U.S. Nuremberg War Crimes Trials*, 1946–1947, M887, Tape 17, Doc. 630-PS)

Hitler and Brandt together worked most carefully on the wording of the order. Brandt felt that it was impossible for a doctor to say with absolute certainty that a patient was incurable, and that, therefore, a certain leeway was required. But Hitler, who distrusted doctors after the death of his mother from cancer, did not wish to give them too much leeway; he insisted upon adding, "Upon the most careful diagnosis of their [the patients'] condition of sickness." Brandt gave this account in his testimony at Nuremberg. He emphasized repeatedly that the order was not an order to kill; it was instead an authorization to specifically designated physicians allowing them to act if, in their judgment after "the most careful diagnosis," the patient is "incurably sick." The physicians were given a license to kill; they were not directed to do so (Mitscherlich, 1962, p. 265).

Brandt and the chief of Hitler's Chancellery, Bouhler, set to work implementing the order. Bouhler's deputy, Viktor Brack, would handle administrative details, and three other men were placed in charge of policy formulation and operation. All three were physicians: Dr. med. Herbert Linden, who held the sub-Cabinet-level position of Chancellor in charge of all sanatoria and nursing homes within the Department of Interior; Professor Heyde; and his deputy Professor Nitsche, who served as the chief medical experts of the euthanasia program. Heyde had held the position of professor of psychiatry at the University of Wurzburg and was head of the University Clinic for Nervous Diseases (Amir, 1977, p. 183). The new operation was housed in an imposing Berlin villa, address *Tiergartenstrasse* 4, and for this reason the program came to be known as *Aktion T-4*.

Three corporations were set up to handle the actual operation of the program. These were given purposely vague and misleading names:

Allgemeine Stiftung fur Anstaltwesen: The "Foundation for the Care of Institutions in the Public Interest" handled the budgetary and financial aspects of the program — the costs of which were not small.

Reichsarbeitsgemeinschaft Heil-und Pflegeanstalten: The "National Group for Study of Sanitoria and Nursing Homes" was charged with the actual administration of the program — the National Group developed the selection criteria, prepared the questionnaires, provided administrative support for the review committees, and actually operated the terminal "observation institutions."

Gemeinnutzige Krankentransportgesellschaft: The "Limited Company for the Transport of Invalids in the Public Interest," which organized and operated a unique, complex system for moving tens of thousands of the sick and helpless about the countryside.

Concurrently established, although separately administered, was the "Reich Committee for Research on Hereditary and Constitutional Severe Diseases." This committee was charged with "assisting the dissolution" of mentally afflicted, severely handicapped, or "idiotic" children. The authority under which this last committee functioned was a decree issued by the Ministry of the Interior on August 1938, which in fact predated Hitler's euthanasia order.

Both before and after Hitler's order of September 1939, secret meetings were held across Germany. At these meetings, the leading psychiatrists, physicians, and medical professors were carefully briefed on the new euthanasia program. Euphemisms were used to describe the program: "Negative population policies" was mass killing; "refractory therapy cases" were disabled people targeted for killing; "specialist children's wards" were children killing centers; and "final medical assistance" was, of course, murder. There was never a doubt as to what was being discussed.

These men were told the euthanasia program was a part of the "breakthrough campaign" necessary to obtain the new medicine of the Third Reich. This held that medical attention and money should go, on a cost-benefit analysis, to those who can be brought back to full productive health, while the chronically disabled would be removed from society as, said Dr. F. Klein, "I would remove the purulent appendix from a diseased body" (Hanauske-Able, 1986, p. 271).

In both the minutes of the "Reich Committee for the Scientific Registration of Serious Illnesses of Hereditary or Protonic Origin" — a high-level physicians' committee that met regularly with the Reich Chancellory — and in the reports of the briefing meetings with rank-and-file physicians, it was fiercely argued that the radical modernization of therapeutic activity cannot be achieved without and, in fact, must go hand-in-hand with, the elimination of these "refractory therapy cases" (Aly and Roth, 1984, p. 148).

There can be no doubt the existence and operation of the euthanasia program was general knowledge within the medical community of the wartime Reich.

Aktion T-4 officials moved quickly to institutionalize the authority Hitler had given them. They appointed between 10 and 15 doctors chosen for their "political reliability" to act as Assessors. Above them were appointed review committees of Chief Surveyors made up of university professors of psychiatry and medicine.

An organizing conference was called in which the professors of psychiatry and the chairmen of the departments of psychiatry at the medical schools of the Universities of Berlin, Heidelberg, Bonn, and Wurzburg were participants. Continuing meetings of this oversight group were conducted on a quarterly basis under the direction of the professor of psychiatry at Heidelberg (Wertham, 1968, p. 168).

"The Reich Committee" oversaw the preparation of a questionnaire designed to elicit the information it regarded useful in determining which persons were "worthy of help," and which were "useless lives," candidates for "final medical assistance." An instruction leaflet was also drawn up, giving detailed directions on how the questionnaire was to be answered. Many thousands of copies were printed by the Reich Minister of the Interior. These were distributed to the long-term hospitals, sanatoria, and asylums, along with a cover letter from Dr. Conti, Chancellor of Sanatoria and Nursing Homes, stating that a form in full must be completed for each patient by the attending physician. The information was to be typewritten with three carbons. The forms should be filled out at once, explained Conti's letter, owing to "the necessity for a systematized economic plan for hospitals and nursing institutions." At the briefings, confusion had been expressed over who was to be covered by the program. This confusion was certainly not relieved by Conti's letter, the questionnaire, or the instruction pamphlet. This material does, indeed, provide a puzzling and imprecise picture of what facts were sought or for what purpose.

The pamphlet contained a list of qualifying illnesses that was so general as to be virtually all-inclusive of patients in long-term care facilities. The terms "insanity," "imbecility," "paralysis," "chronic diseases," and "senile maladies" are not narrow.

There were three full questions on the patient's work, ability, and experience — more than on any other topic. There were but two questions related to genetic theory: Did the patient have a twin? and Did he have blood relatives of unsound mind? The twin question was easy enough to answer, but the term "unsound mind" was so general as to be meaningless. No conclusions about the genetic origins of the patients' conditions could be drawn from such sketchy information.

Speaking in medical terms, the form was a trivial business. As a witness testified at the Nuremberg "Doctors Trial": "On the basis of the questionnaires it was impossible for experts or top experts to form an exact medical opinion on the physical state of the patients" (*U.S. Nuremberg War Crimes Trials*, 1946–1947, M887, Tape 17, No. 617).

The physicians of the appraisal committee reviewed the information contained in each of the questionnaires, and determined which of the patients should live and which should die. Originally, a death warrant required the approval of all members of the Appraisal committee. However, as the program came into operation, a majority of two out of three or three out of four members was usually sufficient.

The decisions of the appraising physicians were gathered and forwarded to a senior expert — usually a professor and head of a medical department at one of the major universities.

Final decisions would be made by this senior expert. Names of the patients to be killed were then routed to Linden, who worked in conjunction with the General Patient Transport Company to arrange for the pickup and carriage of the selected patients from the nationwide array of mental institutions, nursing homes, and long-term facilities to the euthanasia institutions. There were six major euthanasia institutions. *T-4* referred to them by letter. They were:

Grafeneck, in the Black Forest, southwest of Ulm
The "old jail" at Brandenberg, near the hospital at Gorden, southwest of
   Berlin
Bernberg, in central Germany
Hartheim, northwest of Linz in Austria
Sonnenstein — often called die Sonne — near Dresden in Saxony
Hadamar, in Hesse, north of Frankfurt

Throughout the life of the program — whether death came by pill, starvation, or carbon monoxide shower — it came at the hand of a physician. It was Brack's firm and oft-stated belief that "the syringe belongs in the hand of a physician" (Lifton, 1986, p. 71).

Bouhler was insistent that a way of death be found that would be not only painless, but also imperceptible to the patient. He did not want to frighten the patients, nor make them uncomfortable. These things must be "done according to his orders, and in a dignified and not a brutal fashion" (*Trials of War Criminals*, 1946–1947, I:877).

The original regulations envisioned a "conservative" program with careful review procedures. In operation, the program became a matter of killing in wholesale lots. The psychological reasons physicians were willing to participate in these killings are no doubt complex. There is, however, an aspect of the structure of the program that made it easier: There was no single point of responsibility — no place in the procedure at which it was possible to say, here is where the patients receive their death warrant; no point where it could be said, *this* physician is responsible for this patient's death.

The local practicing physicians simply filled out the questionnaires as they were required to do. The members of the assessing committee simply gave their individual opinion on each case. Nothing more would happen unless the members were in substantial agreement. The senior review physician simply went along with the committee or else expressed an objection. He was expressing a medical opinion, nothing more. Neither the assessors nor the review physicians ever saw the patient. The transportation staff was involved in transporting patients — but it was no business of theirs as to where or why the patients were being moved. The staff that ran the centers were simply doing their jobs. Even the physician whose job it was to operate the gas chamber was not responsible for the death of the patients — after all, he played no part in their selection; he knew nothing of their cases. He was only following the procedures laid down by his superiors, and carrying out the policy of his government as advised by the most eminent members of the medical profession.

Disposal of the bodies of the dead patients presented a fairly sizable logistic problem. The German nation was in an all-out war posture, and it was simply not practical to clutter up the transportation system by shipping corpses all over the landscape. It was this reason, as much as public health reasons, that caused Bouhler to insist upon immediate cremation at the major centers. Permanent furnaces were constructed at some of the sites, but other hospitals relied upon an ingenious device, a portable furnace on wheels.

Some of the centers were so mechanized as to have a conveyer belt system installed to carry the corpses from the gas chamber to the oven. As a contemporary witness wrote, "The corpses enter the furnace on a conveyer belt, and the smoke from the crematorium chimney is visible for miles" (Sereny, 1974, p. 39).

The ash remains of the deceased were gathered from the oven and placed in ceremonial urns and delivered to their families along with a letter of condolence. No effort was made to distinguish the ashes of one victim from another. The family receiving an urn assumed they were receiving the remains of their own loved one — the letters surely indicated as much — but they were not.

A guide was prepared, probably by one of the *T-4* physicians' committees, for the use of the doctors as they were preparing the fake certificates. This helped to ensure that the cause of death assigned and the medical history of the patient were internally consistent with each other and medically sound. For example, in discussing septicemia as a cause of death in the mentally ill, it was explained that these patients frequently have boils that they scratch and, "It is most expedient to figure four days for the basic illness and five days for the resultant sepsis." (Lifton, 1986, p. 74) Doctors were warned that this diagnosis "should not be used with patients who are meticulously clean"; instead, it is "preferable for young strong patients who smear readily" (Lifton, 1986, p. 74). However, the guide warned, if septicemia is used as a cause of death for the young, it should be noted that "seven to eight days have to be allowed for the illness to take effect, since their circulation is relatively more resistant" (Lifton, 1986, p. 74).

The official, centralized euthanasia program lasted from 1939 through the summer of 1941. After two years of operation, the program's existence was widely known. The churches had raised strong and vocal objections. There had been public demonstrations in opposition to the killings. The German army was deep in the Russian campaign, and Hitler had no wish for public unrest at home. Accordingly, the Führer, in a conversation with Brandt, without ceremony or discussion, verbally ordered a halt to the euthanasia program.

This did not, however, bring an end to the killing of the disabled and the insane. Physicians across Germany continued to administer "final medical treatment" to patients they considered as having "lives not worth living." The killings continued, but the decision making and the criteria used in these decisions became those of the immediate doctor, rather than the assessor committees and the review professors. The "children's campaign," by which retarded and deformed infants were put to death, proceeded unabated. The killing continued even after the war, as U.S. Army occupation forces discovered at Kaufbeuren and Eglfing-Haar (Gallagher, 1990, p. 250).

As the bombing of German cities increased, Brandt undertook to evacuate institutionalized patients to the countryside. Many of those evacuated also were killed by their physicians. On the eastern ramparts of Germany — in Danzig, Pomerania, and West Prussia — as well as in Poland, mentally ill patients were simply shot by the local SS and police forces. Operation *14 f 13* practiced wanton killing of the sick and disabled in the camps and elsewhere. What the Germans at the time referred to as "wild euthanasia" led to additional widespread, unorganized, and indiscriminate killing. As Dörner has said, "Unplanned groups and individuals were murdered: welfare wards, asocials, wayward children, healthy Jewish children, or those of mixed blood, homosexuals, political offenders, elderly wards of nursing homes, sick and healthy Eastern workers" (Dörner, 1967, p. 151).

It is not possible to tell with any accuracy how many disabled German citizens were put to death during the Nazi years. No reliable figures exist for the spontaneous killings. Figures survive for the official centralized *T-4* killings (see Table 6.1).

In the summer of 1991 unexpected verification of these figures was unearthed in the cellar of the headquarters of the *Stassi*, the former East German secret police. The medical files of these 70,000 patients, filed alphabetically, were discovered by Michael Burleigh, a Holocaust scholar from England (Horner, 1991, p. 25).

Table 6.1

Anstalt	1940	1941	Sa
A (Graf.)	9,839	—	9,839
B (Brand.)	9,772	—	9,772
Be (Bernb.)	—	8,601	8,601
C (Linz)	9,670	8,599	18,269
D (Sonnes.)	5,943	7,777	13,720
E (Hadamar)	—	10,072	10,072
	35,224	35,049	70,273

Klee, 1983.

In some of the trial documents, the figure 120,000 is given as the overall number of inmates killed in public institutions. According to Aly and Roth (1984), this number is on the low side and does not include those who died in such separate programs as the children's operation, random euthanasia, and the so-called "Brandt campaign" whereby 20,000 lost their lives (p. 162). Dr. Leo Alexander, who served with the Office of the Chief of Counsel for War Crimes at Nuremberg and who performed the major study of the euthanasia program for the court, has estimated that 275,000 persons were killed (Breggin, 1979, p. 81).

Fredric Wertham, a psychiatrist, examined hospital records and found, for example, that the Province of Brandenberg, in 1938, had 16,295 mental patients from Berlin. By 1945, there remained but 2,379 patients. In an institution called Berlin-Buch, out of 2,500 patients, 500 survived. Kaufbeuren in Bavaria had 2,000 patients at the beginning of the war, and 200 remaining at the war's end. Many mental institutions simply closed their doors because of a lack of patients. In 1939, throughout all of Germany there were some 300,000 mental patients. In 1946, there were 40,000. This is not to say that all these persons were destroyed by the German State in the course of its euthanasia operation. After all, the general German war losses were colossal (Muller-Hill, 1988). Nevertheless, it cannot be doubted that the euthanasia program swept out entire wards, cleaned out entire hospitals. It decimated the entire German population of the severely disabled and the chronically insane.

Aktion T-4 Euthanasie: Origins in History and Thought

The *Euthanasie* killing program was no Nazi aberration. Rather it was the efficient application through public policy of the theories of leading scientists and philosophers in Western society.

Darwin's theories of evolution, combined with the rediscovery of Mendelian law, encouraged Victorians in the belief that the biological world could be as knowable, as predictable as Newton's physical world. Social Darwinism and the "science" of eugenics sought to apply evolutionary and genetic principles, as understood, to human society and breeding. Eugenicists believed most human characteristics to be inherited. In W. Duncan McKim's book *Heredity in Human Progress*, which was published in 1900, heredity is blamed for, among other things, "insanity, idiocy, imbecility, eccentricity, hysteria, epilepsy, the alcohol habit, the morphine habit, neuralgias, 'nervousness,' Saint Vitus's dance, infantile convulsions, stammering, squint, gout, articular rheumatism, diabetes, tuberculosis, cancer, deafness, blindness, deaf-mutism, color blindness" (Haller, 1963, p. 42). It is, he said, "the fundamental cause of human wretchedness" (Haller, 1963, p. 42).

U.S. President Theodore Roosevelt spoke for many forward-thinking people when he said, "Someday we will realize that the prime duty, the inescapable duty, of the *good* citizen of the right type is to leave his or her blood behind him in the world; and that *we have no business to permit the perpetuation of citizens of the wrong type*" (emphasis added) (Haller, 1963, p. 79).

The impact of Darwinian theory upon German thought was no less than it had been in Britain and America. Darwin cast a long shadow over the development of national socialism and the Third Reich. Perhaps most influential was the 1920 book *The Destruction of Life Devoid of Value*, written by psychiatrist Alfred Hoche and lawyer Karl Binding. These men were professors of reputation and importance. They argued that the medical profession should participate not only in health giving, but under certain circumstances, in death making as well. With a carefully reasoned argument, defining their terms precisely, their analysis concluded that certain people should be exterminated for racial "hygienic" purposes. They argued that the retarded, the deformed, the terminally ill, and those who were mentally sound but who were severely damaged by disease or accident should be put to death. They believed that the death should be painless and expertly administered — that is, by a physician. According to their reasoning, the right to "grant death" was a natural extension of the responsibilities of the attending physician.

Hoche and Binding were widely read and vigorously discussed. One of their readers was the young Adolf Hitler, who had read a good deal on eugenics and Monism prior to his writing of *Mein Kampf*. Upon one occasion, Hitler even allowed his name to be used in advertisements for Hoche's books (Breggin, 1979, p. 81).

There were other books and articles on the subject. The romantic philosopher Ernst Haeckel's book *The Riddle of the Universe* sold well for many years. His disciple Heinrich Ziegler was a popular writer on such issues and won the important Krupp literary award. The 1920 book *Moral der Kraft* by Ernst Mann advocated that disabled war veterans kill themselves to reduce welfare costs.

An exceedingly popular movie in the Germany of the mid-30s dealt entirely with the issue of euthanasia for the disabled. *I Accuse* was the story of a young woman suffering from multiple sclerosis. In the last reel, her husband, a doctor, after lengthy soul searching, kills his wife, as a fellow physician in the next room plays softly and funereally on the piano.

Another film (title unknown) of the Nazi years illustrated the unbearable life of the insane with particularly grisly shots of defective dystonias. This was made for the use of the medical societies. The film was widely shown to physician gatherings and was shown to the Nazi Party meeting of 1935 by Dr. Gerhardt Wagner, leader of the medical delegation.

Although long lost, unedited footage of the original film was found in the basement of *Stassi* secret police headquarters in the summer of 1991 by Michael Burleigh. In the film, a "professor" posits that the "incurably mentally ill" have a "right to die": "Is it not the duty of those concerned," he asks, reasonably enough given his premise, "to help the incapable — and that means total idiots and incurable mental patients — to their right?" (Horner, 1991, p. 25).

The general devaluation of disabled lives can be seen even in Nazi schoolroom textbooks. A mathematics text, *Mathematics in the Service of National Political Education,* set the following problem: "If the building of a lunatic asylum costs 6 million marks and it costs 15,000 marks to build each dwelling on a housing estate, how many of the latter could be built for the price of one asylum?" Another asked how many marriage allowance loans could be given to young couples for the amount of money it costs the state to care for "the crippled, criminal, and insane" (Mitscherlich, 1962, p. 234; Alexander, 1949, p. 39).

When the German physicians and medical professors set up *T-4 Euthanasie,* they were instituting a program whose principles had been widely and thoroughly discussed.

Aktion T-4 Euthanasie: Impact and Response

After the war, Brandt, director of the *Euthanasie* program, and Brack, administrator of the program, were hanged at Nuremberg for war crimes and crimes committed against humanity. Many of the principal *T-4* physicians fled or disappeared. Occasionally, one surfaced and faced trial. Such trials were long, drawn out, unsatisfactory affairs, largely because of the unwillingness of one physician to testify against another.

Other principal physicians simply resumed their practice under assumed names. Their presence was known to their peers in the medical community, but was not reported. The rank and file of the German physicians, those who had been active in the program, and the rest who had raised no objection to it, continued the practice of medicine, albeit no longer killing their patients.

Over more than a half century since the *T-4* program, the German medical establishment has never acknowledged, examined, or apologized for the killings. A book summarizing accurately the *T-4 Euthanasie* evidence accumulated in the Nuremberg trials, written by a young psychiatrist, Alexander Mitscherlich, was published in 1949. It was suppressed and denounced as "irresponsible, … lacking documentation." The book was seen as an attack upon the "inviolable honor of German medicine." One reviewer said that only a "pervert" would read such a book and called its author a "traitor to his country" (Hanauske-Able, 1986, p. 272).

In 1977, the courageous Margarete and Alexander Mitscherlich wrote in the foreword to their book *Die Unfahigkeit zu trauern (The Inability to Grieve)*, "Today in many minds, there is a reluctance to accept the facts of history … . What happened in the Third Reich remains alive in our subconscious, dangerously so. It will be fatal for us to lose touch with the truth of what happened then. We must struggle to seek out the truth of that era rather than search for improved defenses to hide us from this truth."

Encouragingly, in the 1980s a new, younger generation of historians have focused their attention on the social history of the Nazi years. In the course of their studies, they have done important research on the *T-4 Euthanasie* program and associated killing — work that took too long to be published. These historians include Ernst Klee, Goetz Aly, Harl Heinz Roth, Benno Hill, and Michael H. Kater. Their work documents the known killings and continues to uncover killings hitherto unknown. The medical killing of disabled patients was widespread, indeed.

Unfortunately, however, the German medical establishment, which retains, and rightly so, much prestige in the society, has chosen to deal with the *Euthanasie* episode with what amounts to an across-the-board denial. Medical students have been expelled from medical schools for attempting to discuss the matter. It is reported (personal communication) that Dr. Hartmut M. Hanauske-Able was no longer able to practice in Germany after publishing a 1986 article on the subject in the British medical journal *Lancet*.

In Germany today, as in the United States, there is a lively, ongoing debate over questions of medical ethics: abortion, amniocentesis, tracking the genome, "right to die," euthanasia, and disability rights. Present, like Banquo's ghost, in all these discussions is the memory, expressed or unexpressed, of the medical killings of the 1930s and 1940s.

A particularly vivid example of this took place at Rehab 88, the fifth international rehabilitation trade fair, held at Karlsruhe in 1988. The person asked to give the keynote address for the professional section of the conference was Hans Henning Atrott, president of the German Society for Humane Dying. His subject was "Active Assistance for Dying: The Final Rehabilitation." It is perhaps not surprising that organizations of disabled persons were outraged that such a talk should be given at such an occasion. They protested to the conference organizers, but to no avail. As a last resort, they broke up Atrott's lecture by bursting into the hall in their wheelchairs, dressed in garbage bags, sipping from cans labeled "cyanide," and waving signs that read "useless lives" and "lives not worth living." (Gallagher, 1990, p. 270) Atrott found it all most unfortunate, telling the media that the protest reminded him of Nazi tactics. It was a return, he said, to "terror against different thinking" (Gallagher, 1990, p. 270).

In 1987, Pope John Paul II made a visit to West Germany. He made a pilgrimage to Münster Cathedral to pray at the tomb of Cardinal Graf von Galen, the bravest of the religious leaders to protest the *T-4* killing of disabled people. Later, in a meeting with disabled people, the Pope warned, "Human life should not be divided into that which is worth living and that which is not" (*New York Daily News*, 1988, p. 2).

Conclusion

Close to 200 years ago, English doctor Christopher Huffeland wrote, "If the physician presumes to take into consideration in his work whether a life has value or not, the consequences are boundless, and the physician becomes the most dangerous man in the state" (Wertham, 1968, p. 153). In *T-4 Euthanasie*, the physicians of Germany demonstrated just how dangerous.

Eyewitness Accounts: Nazi Genocide of Disabled Peoples

The victims of the *T-4 Euthanasie* program were not aware they had been selected for "final medical assistance" until too late. Without warning, they were bundled from their hospital beds into the waiting transports, taken to the killing centers, and, quite promptly, killed. It was all most efficient, and there were few escapees. The victims were chronically mentally ill, mentally retarded, and severely disabled people, struggling to survive in time of war; it is not surprising there are no memoirs. There are, however, eyewitness accounts of what went on.

What follows are accounts by those who observed the operation of the killing program. The witnesses include three parents of disabled children, a nurse, an archbishop, and a judge.

The first three accounts are taken from testimony heard in a criminal trial of three doctors in Vienna, Austria, in 1946. Austria had been part of Germany during the Nazi years and the *T-4* program took the lives of many disabled Austrians. The first witness, Leopold Widerhofer, tells how his daughter, a schizophrenic patient, survived, thanks to his efforts and those of sympathetic doctors. These doctors were taking great risks by trying to save their patients from *T-4*.

The two other Austrian accounts are those of parents whose infants were killed — one of the victims was a 4-year-old with speech difficulties and weak leg muscles; the other, a 2-year-old, also had speech difficulties. These children were not severely disabled; they were not in pain, nor were they dying. Killing them had nothing to do with euthanasia; it had a lot to do with murder.

Leo Alexander was a physician in the U.S. Army of Occupation in Germany at the end of World War II. He was one of the very first to investigate the *Aktion T-4* killing program. Included here is a verbatim statement made to him on August 5, 1945, by Amalie Widmann, a nurse who went looking for her patients who had been transferred to a killing center. Nurse Widmann's concern for her patients nearly cost her her life.

The activity at the killing centers was supposed to be secret. Soon, however, the neighborhoods surrounding the hospitals figured out what was going on. The impact of the killings on the community is vividly described in a courageous letter to the Ministry of Justice written by the Bishop of Limburg. The letter, printed here, is now in the U.S. Archives. It was a part of the evidence gathered for the "Doctors Trial," one of the Nuremberg War Crimes Trials of 1946.

The killing program, complained Henrich Himmler, head of the SS, "is a secret and yet is no longer one" (Gallagher, 1990, p. 144). It had, in fact, become something of an embarrassment. Local law officials were alarmed by the unrest and fears stirred in the community by the killing, as demonstrated in the extract printed here of an unsigned report from a provincial court to the Ministry of Justice in Berlin.

One man became the symbol of the resistance to the so-called euthanasia program. He was the Bishop of Münster, Graf von Galen, the "Lion of Münster." A man of commanding presence and unquestioned moral authority, von Galen risked his life by giving a powerful sermon decrying the killing. "Woe to humanity," he thundered from his pulpit. "Woe to the German people if God's holy command 'Thou shalt not kill' is not only transgressed but if this transgression is tolerated and carried out without punishment." Copies of the sermon were distributed under cover all over Germany — to the fury of Hitler — and had much to do with the public outcry against *T-4 Euthanasie*. The text of von Galen's sermon is included in the following collection of accounts.

Testimony of Leopold Widerhofer

This testimony was presented before the Vienna District Court (Landesgericht) in the proceedings against Dr. Ernst Illing, Dr. Marianne Türk, and Dr. Erwin Jekelius, Vienna, February 27, 1946.

A facsimile of this document is reprinted in Elisabeth Klamper (Ed.) *Dokumentationsarchiv des Österreichischen Widerstandes, Vienna,* Volume 19 of the series *Archives of the Holocaust* (New York and London: Garland, 1991), pp. 114–16.

The Defendants

Dr. Ernst Illing (b. 1904, Leipzig) was a physician who joined the Nazi party on May 1, 1933; he was the director of the Vienna City Psychiatric-Neurological Clinic for Children Am Spiegelgrund, 1942–1945, where he killed about 200 children. He was sentenced to death by the Vienna District Court on July 18, 1946.

Dr. Erwin Jekelius (b. 1905) was a physician and member of the Nazi party. He was director of the Vienna City Psychiatric-Neurological Clinic for Children Am Spiegelgrund, 1940–1942.

Dr. Marianne Türk (b. 1914, Vienna) was appointed physician at the Vienna City Psychiatric-Neurological Clinic for Children Am Spiegelgrund in August 1940. Together with Dr. Ernst Illing, she killed a total of 200 children (ca. 7 to 10 per week) under the so-called euthanasia program. She was sentenced to 10 years prison by the Vienna District Court, July 18, 1946.

The clinic Am Spiegelgrund, officially known as the Vienna City Psychiatric-Neurological Clinic for Children, was located on the grounds of Am Steinhof and was used as a children's ward for the children's euthanasia program.

Am Steinhof was the popular name for the Wagner von Jauregg Mental Hospital and Nursing Home of the City of Vienna. About 4000 patients were sent from Am Steinhof to the Hartheim euthanasia killing center.

Witness Interrogation
Hallein County Court
District Court I for Criminal Cases, Vienna II

On February 27, 1946
Beginning at 11:30 A.M.

Present:
Judge: Dr. Sandri
Secretary: Dr. Vavrovsky

Criminal Case:
Against Dr. Ernst Illing, Dr. Marianne Türk, and Dr. Erwin Jekelius regarding paragraph 134 of the Penal Code.

The witness is warned to answer the questions addressed to him truthfully to the best of his knowledge and conscience, to conceal nothing and to give testimony, in such a way that, if necessary, he can affirm it under oath.

He stipulates the following personal data:

1. First and last name: Leopold Widerhofer
2. Age: 76 years old
3. Place of birth: Waya-on-the-Enns, Upper Austria
4. Religion: Roman Catholic
5. Marital status: married
6. Occupation: retired grammar school headmaster
7. Place of residence: Vienna I, Bräunerstr. 4, currently Hallein No. 278.
8. Relationship to the defendant or to other individuals involved in the investigation: none.

My daughter, Gerta Widerhofer, was brought to the sanatorium Am Steinhof in 1933 because of schizophrenia. She remained in treatment as a psychiatric patient there.

At the beginning of August 1940, my wife and I heard a rumor during a visit to the Steinhof institution that patients at this institution were being transferred to Germany secretly at night and that they would continue to be taken away in the future. Out of concern for our daughter's life, in mid-August 1940, I personally went to see Dr. Erwin Jekelius, who was then director of the Viennese Health Office, Vienna I, Schottenring 28, in order to inquire about this. After considerable discussion, I attempted to discover whether my daughter was on the list of patients to be transferred. He denied this. I was satisfied with this.

Soon thereafter, I heard in the waiting room of the director's office of the institution Am Steinhof, that my daughter actually was on the list, and Dr. Wilhelm Podhaisky, Vienna 109, XV Baumgartnerhöhe, showed me my daughter's file, which he had already removed to his custody in order to try to save her life. This file was taken out of the records of those individuals who were to be prepared for transport; thus Dr. Podhaisky kept her file.

Dr. Podhaisky later arranged a meeting for me with the Director, Dr. Jekelius, in the waiting room of the executive offices of Am Steinhof; this would have been at the beginning of October 1940. During the nearly one hour discussion between me and the Director, Dr. Jekelius, which Dr. Podhaisky attended on behalf of the patients, Dr. Jekelius said to me twice in the presence of Dr. Podhaisky: "Your daughter must die." He tried to justify this because her disease was incurable. To my excited demand that my daughter, if she must die, would wish to die here at Am Steinhof, rather than be carried off, Dr. Jekelius replied: "Herr Direktor, you probably understand that we cannot allow our staff doctors to be implicated." I replied: "I only know that the patients will really be killed." Dr. Jekelius never responded to this.

The transports with mentally ill patients from Am Steinhof to unknown destinations continued throughout the next weeks. During this time, the two physicians from Steinhof, Dr. Unlauf and Dr. Podhaisky, routinely tried to delay the transports and they rescued my daughter by relocating her to ward 24. When this ward was evacuated at night, they moved my daughter to convalescent ward 20.

The deportations from Steinhof stopped at the end of December 1940. My daughter is still in Am Steinhof today and her condition has improved substantially.

I would also like to add, that acquaintances of mine who likewise had dependents at Am Steinhof, had already received notifications written between September and November 1940 that stated that their sick dependents, who had been transferred from Am Steinhof, had suddenly died of some disease, such as infected tonsils or pneumonia.

I would also like to state that during the subsequent months, children that were difficult to handle arrived in the vacant women's wards and that Dr. Jekelius was named director of the children's department created here.

My wife, Marie Widerhofer, never observed these matters directly, but learned of them only from my comments. She never spoke with Dr. Jekelius, nor with Dr. Podhaisky nor Dr. Umlauf. She therefore cannot testify in these proceedings based on her own observations.

Testimony of Anny Wödl

This testimony was presented before the Vienna District Court in the proceedings against Dr. Ernst Illing, Dr. Marianne Türk, and Dr. Erwin Jekelius, Vienna, March 1, 1946 [mistyped in document as 1945].

Source: DÖW E 18282 (photocopy of file Landesgericht Wien Vg 4d Vr 5442/46). A facsimile of this document is reprinted in Elisabeth Klamper (Ed.) Dokumentationsarchiv des Österreichischen Widerstandes, Vienna,

Volume 19 of the series Archives of the Holocaust (New York and London: Garland, 1991), pp. 117–119.

Gugging

Provincial Mental Hospital and Nursing Home in Lower Austria. In 1940, more than 500 of the over 1,000 patients at Gugging were deported to the Hartheim euthanasia killing center, many of them via the Niedernhart hospital.

Witness Interrogation
Vienna District Court for Criminal Offenses
District Court I for Criminal Cases, Vienna II

On 1 March 1945 [sic, actually 1946]
Beginning at

Present:
Judge: Agr. Dr. Zips
Secretary: Bürgert

Criminal Case:
Against Dr. Ernst Illing et al.

The witness is warned to answer the questions addressed to him truthfully to the best of his knowledge and conscience, to conceal nothing and to give testimony, in such a way that, if necessary, he can affirm it under oath.

He stipulates the following personal data:

1. First and last name: Anny Wödl
2. Age: 43 years old
3. Place of birth: Gutenstein
4. Religion: Roman Catholic
5. Marital status: single
6. Occupation: nurse
7. Place of residence: Vienna 9, Thurngasse Nr. 5/11
8. Relationship to the defendant or to other individuals involved in the investigation: none.

I refer to my petition on page/lines 179 through 187 of the record, which I fully uphold and add to my testimony.

I am appending the following:

I bore a handicapped child on 24 November 1934 who had difficulties walking and talking and did not develop as he should. It turned out that he understood everything, but that he couldn't speak. Also his legs were obviously too weak to carry him, so that in essence he could not walk. The doctors couldn't really determine if he actually suffered, nor could they decide the cause of his condition. I put him in the institution at Gugging when he was four years old.

I was very concerned about my child when the operation against the "incurably ill, mentally ill, and elderly" began, especially since I knew the Nazi state's position in principle about these matters. When the "operations" were carried out in Vienna, there was anxiety in the population. I was determined to appeal to Berlin in order to save my child or to stop the mechanism. I have described in detail in my petition what I achieved. The only person who really wanted to help was Dr. Trub, who was employed at Ballhausplatz.

With the exception of Dr. Jekelius, I spoke to no other physicians about this matter. In any case, Dr. Jekelius was fully aware of what was happening and it was unambiguously clear from his remarks that he totally endorsed the entire operation against "life unworthy of life" and that he was prepared to act as the Nazi state demanded. I finally realized that I could not save my child after this conversation. Therefore, I wanted at least to stop my child from being carried off somewhere. I also wanted to spare the child any further pain, if it had to die. For these reasons, I begged Dr. Jekelius, that if the death of my child could not be stopped, that it be quick and painless. He promised me this. I never learned whether he himself carried out the deed, or whether he let someone else do it and in what manner. I saw my child's corpse. I was struck by the look of pain on his face.

On the whole, an individual could not do anything to stop these "actions," as is evident in my case. Most people did not dare try anything, since it was clear that it was much too dangerous. Meanwhile, the killing operations had spread to all sanatoriums and were carried out. I do not know the details. I only know what we heard when things leaked out and what also appeared in the press.

Testimony of Emma Philippovic

This testimony was presented before the Vienna District Court (*Landesgericht*) in the proceedings against Dr. Ernst Illing, Dr. Marianne Türk, and Dr. Erwin Jekelius, Vienna, March 2, 1946.

Source: DÖW E 18282a (photocopy of file at *Landesgericht Wien*, Vg 4d Vr 5442/46). A facsimile of this document is reprinted in Elisabeth Klamper (Ed.) *Dokumentationsarchiv des Österreichischen Widerstandes, Vienna,* Volume 19 of the series *Archives of the Holocaust* (New York and London: Garland, 1991), pp. 120–21.

Witness Interrogation
Vienna District Court for Criminal Offenses
District Court I for Criminal Cases, Vienna II

On 2 March 1946
Beginning at

Present:
Judge: Agr. Dr. Zips
Secretary: Bürgert

Criminal Case:
Against Dr. Ernst Illing et al.

The witness is warned to answer the questions truthfully to the best of his knowledge and conscience, to conceal nothing and to give testimony, in such manner that, if necessary, he can affirm it under oath.

1. First and last name: Emma Philippovic
2. Age: 47 years old
3. Place of birth: Vienna
4. Religion: Jewish
5. Marital status: widowed
6. Occupation: homemaker
7. Place of residence: Vienna 5, Schönbrunnerstr.
8. Relationship to the defendant or to other individuals involved in the investigation: none.

I refer to my petition on page 202 of the document, which I wish to add to my testimony. My daughter displayed speech defects at the age of two. They subsequently intensified, eventually resulting in a complete inability to speak. But it then became better again. I do not know whether she would have become completely healthy.

I did not see my child after her death. But my husband, who has since died, did see her corpse and he told me that the girl was emaciated. I was told that the child had died from pneumonia. At that time, pneumonia was widespread. On the death certificate, which I have presented for examination, no cause of death is given. I suspect a violent death. I do not know who was responsible for this; I also do not know which doctor was in charge of the ward at the time. After all, as a Jew, I was not permitted to go there and visit my daughter.

Excerpt from Public Mental Health Practices in Germany:
Sterilization and Execution of Patients Suffering from Nervous or
Mental Disease

Reported by Leo Alexander, Major, M.C., AUS. CIOS Item 24, Medical.
Combined Intelligence Objectives Sub-Committee, G-2 Division, SHAEF
(Rear) APO 413, p. 35, August 19, 1945.

Miss Widmann stated that the first transport of patients to a killing
center left Wieslech on 19 February 1940. Among the patients were a good
many who had become endeared and attached to Miss Widmann. After
they had been taken to the killing center, Miss Widmann became unable to
take her mind off the sad fate of these patients, and she became unable to
rest day or night. She had to think about them all the time. She finally felt
that it might give her ease of mind if she could actually see what happened,
and she decided to visit the killing center in Grafeneck herself. So she
asked for a furlough, not telling anybody what she planned to do, and she
went to Grafeneck on 22 July 1940. When she got off the train at Marbach
a.d. Lauter bei Munzingen, which is the railhead for Grafeneck, the people
whom she asked for directions to Grafeneck looked at her in a peculiar
way as if there was something strange or funny about her. When she finally
arrived in front of the institution in Grafeneck, she found a sign reading:
"Entry strictly prohibited because of danger of infection." There were
heavily armed men in green uniforms, obviously police about the area.
Suddenly Miss Widmann felt gripped by an overwhelming feeling of
anxiety and she ran away over an open field crying bitterly. She sat down
and cried for a while. She then saw that she was on the premises of a stud
farm. The farmer came and asked her whether he could do anything for
her, and she told him that she wanted to go and see the institution in
Grafeneck. The farmer then told her: "Do not go there. One must not say
anything." Shortly afterwards, an SS man appeared, accompanied by other
SS men, with hounds. They took her into the building, where she was
brought before an official who asked her what she wanted. She said that
she wanted to see some of her old patients and find out how they were.
The official then stated that the patients liked it so much there that they
would never want to leave again. He then interrogated her sharply about
her antecedents and her connections with any group, if any. He then
called up Dr. Möckel. Miss Widmann added that she felt she owed her life
to Dr. Möckel because if he had not talked for her they would have killed
her. The reason why she went there was because of her deep feeling of
close relationship with her patients.

Excerpt from U.S. Nuremberg War Crimes Trials, November 21, 1946 – August 20, 1947. National Archives Microfilm Publications, M887, Doc. 615—PS.

In August 1941 the Bishop of Limburg wrote, *inter alia*:

About 8 kilometres from Limburg, in the little town of Hadamar, on a hill overlooking the town, there is an institution which had formerly served various purposes and of late had been used as a nursing home. This institution was renovated and furnished as a place in which, by consensus of opinion, the above-mentioned euthanasia has been systematically practised for months — approximately since February 1941. The fact is, of course, known beyond the administrative district of Wiesbaden because death certificates from the Hadamar-Moenchberg Registry are sent to the home communities. (Moenchberg is the name of this institution because it was a Franciscan monastery prior to its secularization in 1903.)

Several times a week buses arrive in Hadamar with a considerable number of such victims. School children of the vicinity know this vehicle and say: "There comes the murder-box again." After the arrival of the vehicle the citizens of Hadamar watch the smoke rise out of the chimney and are tortured with the ever-present thought of the poor sufferers, especially when the nauseating odours carried by the wind offend their nostrils.

The effect of the principles at work here is that children call each other names and say, "You're crazy; you'll be sent to the baking oven in Hadamar." Those who do not want to marry, or find no opportunity, say "Marry, never! Bring children into the world so they can be put into the bottling machine!" You hear old folks say, "Don't send me to a State hospital! When the feeble-minded have been finished off, the next useless eaters whose turn will come are the old people."

Excerpt from U.S. Nuremberg War Crimes Trials, November 21, 1946 – August 20, 1947. National Archives Microfilm Publications, M887, Doc. 844

The following is an extract of a letter from the Frankfurt am Main Provincial Court of Appeal to the Ministry of Justice in December of 1939.

People living near sanatoria and convalescent homes, as well as in adjoining regions, sometimes quite distant, for example throughout the Rhineland, are continually discussing the question whether the lives of incurable invalids should be brought to an end. The vans which take patients from the institutions they occupy to transit stations and thence to liquidation establishments are well-known to the population. I am told that whenever they pass the children call out: "There they go again for gassing." I hear that from one to three big omnibuses with blinds down go through Limburg every day on their way from Weilmünster to Hadamar, taking inmates to the Hadamar liquidation centre. The story goes that as soon as they arrive they are stripped naked, given a paper shirt and immediately taken to a gas-chamber, where they are poisoned with prussic acid and an auxiliary narcotic. The corpses are said to be transferred on a conveyor belt to an incineration chamber, where six are put into one furnace and the ashes then packed into six urns and sent to the relatives. The thick smoke of the incinerators is supposed to be visible every day over Hadamar. It is also common talk that in some cases the heads or other parts of the body are detached for anatomical investigation. The staff employed on the work of liquidation at these institutions is obtained from other parts of the country and the local inhabitants will have nothing to do with them. These employees spend their evenings in the taverns, drinking pretty heavily. Apart from the stories told by the people about these "foreigners," there is much anxiety over the question whether certain elderly persons who have worked hard all their lives and may now in their old age be somewhat feeble-minded are possibly being liquidated with the rest. It is being suggested that even old peoples' homes will soon be cleared. There is a general feeling here, apparently, that proper legal measures should be taken to ensure that, above all, persons of advanced age and enfeebled mentality are not included in these proceedings.

Sermon of Clemens August Graf von Galen, Bishop of Münster, August 3, 1941

Source: *Dokumente zur Euthanasie*, Ernst Klee (Ed.) Frankfurt: Fisher Tagebuch Verlag, 1985 (reprinted with permission).

Devout Christians! A pastoral message of the German bishops of June 26, 1941, which was read in all Catholic churches on July 6, says: "According to the Catholic moral code there are some commandments which need not be kept if their observance would involve great difficulties. But there are others, holy obligations of our moral consciousness which we have to fulfill even at the cost of our lives. Never, under any circumstances, may a human being kill an innocent person outside of war or in just self-defense." On July 6 I already had occasion to add to the words of this universal pastoral message the following explanation: For the past months we have heard reports from care and residential institutions for mental patients that patients who had been ill for a long time and who appear to be incurable have been removed forcibly on orders from Berlin. Relatives are being notified a short time afterwards that the corpse has been cremated and that they can claim the ashes. There is a suspicion bordering on definite knowledge that these numerous unexpected deaths among psychiatric patients are not due to natural causes but have been intentionally brought about. The philosophy behind this is the assumption that so-called unworthy lives can be terminated, innocent human beings killed if their lives have no value for the nation and the state. This is a terrible doctrine that seeks to justify the murder of innocent people and allows the killing of invalids who can no longer work, cripples, incurable patients, and the feeble elderly.

We have heard from reliable sources that lists have been made of such patients who will be removed from the care and residential institutions in the province of Westphalia and shortly afterwards killed. The first transport left the Marienthal institution near Münster in the course of the past week.

German men and women! Paragraph 211 of the criminal code is still in force. It states, "Whosoever intentionally kills a person will be punished for murder by death if he has done it with premeditation."

To protect those who intentionally kill those poor people, members of our families, from legal punishment, patients who have been designated to die are being removed from their home institutions to far-away facilities. Some illness is given as a cause of death. Since the corpse is immediately cremated neither relatives nor the criminal police can ascertain what the cause of death was. But I have been assured that neither the Ministry of the Interior nor the agency of Dr. Conti, the surgeon general, denies that a large number of psychiatric patients have been intentionally killed in Germany and will be killed in the future.

Paragraph 139 of the criminal code states, "Whosoever becomes aware of the plan for a capital offense and does not bring it to the attention of the authorities or the threatened person will be punished." When I heard of the plan to remove patients from Marienthal and to kill them, I filed the following charges by letter with the prosecutor of the court in Münster and the president of police in Münster: "According to reports a large number of patients, so-called unproductive citizens, of the provincial care institution of Marienthal near Münster have been transferred in the course of this week to the Eichberg institution to be intentionally killed as has happened in other institutions according to general belief. Since such a procedure is not only contrary to the divine and natural moral code but has to be punished by death according to paragraph 211, I herewith dutifully raise charges according to paragraph 139 of the criminal code and ask that the threatened citizens be immediately protected through prosecution of the agencies which organize the transport and the murder and that I be notified of whatever has been done." I have not received any information on intervention by the state prosecutor or the police.

I had previously lodged a protest on July 26 with the provincial administration of Westphalia which is responsible for the institutions to which patients have been entrusted for care and cure. It was in vain. I have heard that 300 persons have been removed from the residential care Wartstein institution.

Now we have to expect that these poor defenseless patients will be murdered in due time. Why? Not because they have committed a heinous crime, not because they attacked the caregiver in a way which would have forced him to defend his own life in justified self-defense. Are these cases in which killing is allowed and even necessary, besides killing of the enemy in a just war? No, these hapless patients have to die not for any of these reasons but because they have become unworthy to live — according to these opinions they are "unproductive citizens." The judgment holds that they cannot produce any goods; they are like an old machine which does not run anymore, they are like an old horse which has become lame and cannot be cured, they are like a cow which has ceased to give milk. What does one do with such an old machine? One wrecks it. What does one do with a lame horse, with unproductive cattle? No, I do not want to labor the comparison, justified and illuminating as it would be. We are not dealing with machines, or horses, or cows, whose only destiny is to serve people, to produce goods for human beings. They can be wrecked, they can be slaughtered when they can no longer serve their purpose. No, these are human beings, our fellow citizens, our brothers and sisters. Poor people, sick people, unproductive people, so what. But have they forfeited their right to live? Do you, do I have a right to live only as long as we are productive, as long as others recognize us as being productive? If the principle is established and applied that "unproductive fellow citizens" can be killed, woe to all of us when we get old and feeble. If it becomes permissible to kill unproductive people, woe to the invalids who invested and sacrificed and lost their energies and sound bones during their working careers. If unproductive fellow citizens can be eliminated by force, woe to our brave soldiers who return to their homeland severely injured, as cripples, as invalids. Once it becomes legal for people to kill "unproductive" fellow citizens — even if at presently only our poor defenseless mentally ill are concerned — then the basis is laid for murder of all unproductive people, the incurable, the invalids of war and work, of all of us when we become old and feeble.

All that is necessary is another secret decree that the procedure tested with mental patients is to include other "unproductive persons," is to be applied to patients with incurable lung disease, to the feeble elderly, the disabled workers, to severely injured veterans. Nobody would be safe anymore. Some commission can put him on the list of the "unproductive." And no police will protect him and no court prosecute his murder and punish the murderer. Who could still trust his physician? Maybe he would report the patient as "unproductive" and would be ordered to kill him? It is inconceivable what depraved conduct, what suspicion will enter family life if this terrible doctrine is tolerated, adopted and carried out. Woe to humanity, woe to the German people if God's holy command "Thou shalt not kill" is not only transgressed but if this transgression is both tolerated and carried out without punishment.

I will give you an example of what happened today. In Marienthal there was a man about 55 years old, a farmer in a village in the area of Münster — I know his name — who had been suffering from episodes of mental derangement for some years and who had been brought to the Marienthal care and residential institution. He was not really a psychiatric case; he was able to receive visitors and was always happy when his relatives came. Just two weeks ago he was visited by his wife and one of his sons who was home on leave from the front. The son dotes on his father. Saying farewell was difficult, since nobody knows if the son will return and see his father again because he may be killed fighting for his fellow citizens. The son, the soldier, will certainly not see his father again, who has meanwhile been placed on the list of "unproductive" people. A relative who wanted to visit the father this week in Marienthal was sent away with the information that the patient had been transferred on orders of the Ministry for Defense. The destination was unknown but the relatives would be informed in a few days. What will this information contain? The same as in other cases? That the person died, was cremated, and that the ashes could be claimed after payment of a fee? The soldier who fights and risks his life for fellow German citizens will not see his father again on this earth because fellow German citizens in his own country have killed him.

References

Alexander, Leo (1976). *Public Mental Health Practices in Germany: Sterilization and Execution of Patients Suffering from Nervous or Mental Disease.* Combined Intelligence Objectives Subcommittee, G2 Division, SHAEF (Rear) APO 413. U.S. National Archives.

Aly, Goetz, and Roth, Heinz (1984). "The Legalization of Mercy Killings in Medical and Nursing Institutions in Nazi Germany from 1938 until 1941." *International Journal of Law and Psychiatry,* 7(2):145–63.

Amir, Amnon (1977). *Euthanasia in Nazi Germany.* Unpublished doctoral dissertation. Albany: State University of New York at Albany.

Breggin, Peter Roger (1979). "The Psychiatric Holocaust." *Penthouse,* January, pp. 81–84.

Dörner, Klaus (April 1967). "Nationalsozialismus und Lebensvernichtung." *Vierteljahrshefte für Zeitgeschicte,* 15(2):122–152.

Gallagher, Hugh G. (1990). *By Trust Betrayed: Patients, Physicians, and the License to Kill in the Third Reich.* New York: Henry Holt.

Haller, Mark H. (1963). *Eugenics: Hereditarian Attitudes in American Thought.* New Brunswick, NJ: Rutgers University Press.

Hanauske-Able, Hartmut M. (1986). "Politics and Medicine: From Nazi Holocaust to Nuclear Holocaust: A Lesson to Learn?" *The Lancet,* August, 8501(2):271–273.

Horner, Rosalie (September 26, 1991) "Opened Files Detail Nazi Program to Kill 'Defectives'." *St. Louis Post Dispatch,* 25.

Kater, Michael H. (1987). "The Burden of the Past: Problems of a Modern Historiography of Physicians and Medicine in Nazi Germany." *German Studies Review,* X(1), pp. 31–56.

Klee, Ernst (1983). *"Euthanasie" im NS-Statt, Die "Vernichtung lebensunwerten Lebens."* Frankfurt: S. Fisher.

Lifton, Robert Jay (1986). *The Nazi Doctors: Medical Killing and the Psychology of Genocide.* New York: Basic Books, Inc.

Mitscherlich, Alexander (1962). *The Death Doctors.* (Translated by James Cleugh; Originally published in 1949.) London: Elek Books.

Muller-Hill, Benno (1988). *Murderous Science.* Oxford: Oxford University Press.

New York Daily News (1988). "Pope Condemns World War II Treatment of Handicapped." June 27, p. 2.

Sereny, Gitta (1974). *Into That Darkness: From Mercy Killing to Mass Murder.* New York: McGraw-Hill.

Trials of War Criminals Before the Nuremberg Military Tribunals Under Control Council Law No. 10, Nuremberg, October 1946–April 1947 Volumes I and II. Washington: U.S. Government Printing Office.

U.S. Nuremberg War Crimes Trials, November 21, 1946–August 20, 1947. National Archives Microfilm Publications, M887.

Wertham, Fredric (1968). *A Sign for Cain: An Exploration of Human Violence.* London: Robert Hale, Ltd.

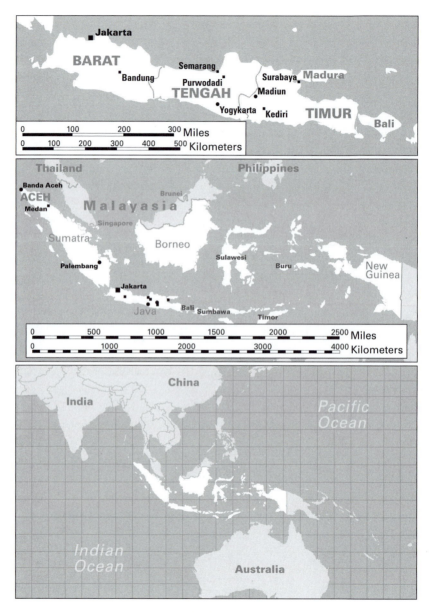

Indonesia

CHAPTER **7**

The Indonesian Massacres

ROBERT CRIBB

During the six-month period from October 1965 to March 1966, approximately half a million people were killed in a series of massacres in Indonesia. The victims were largely members of the Indonesian Communist Party (*Partai Komunis Indonesia, PKI*) which until that time had been the largest Communist Party in the non-Communist world. By 1965 it appeared to many observers inside and outside Indonesia that the Party was well-placed to come to power after President Sukarno's departure. The massacres followed an attempted coup d'etat in the Indonesian capital, Jakarta, in which the PKI was implicated, at least in the public mind, by circumstance and vigorous military propaganda, and resulted in the Party's destruction. These massacres paved the way for the accession to power of a business-oriented and military-dominated government under General Suharto.

Who Committed the Genocide?

The Indonesian killings were the work of anti-Communist army units and civilian vigilantes, drawn especially, but by no means exclusively, from religious political parties. Both groups brought to the killing a long-standing hatred of Communism.

The army's hostility dated from the years of armed struggle against the Dutch (1945–1949), when Communist influence had been strong both within army units and among independent irregular troops, or *lasykar*. The professional soldiers who soon struggled through and up into the top

235

military positions resented both Party influence in the junior ranks and the independent Communist units that challenged their monopoly of armed force. Resentment had become alarm when the crypto-Communist Defense Minister Amir Syarifuddin attempted to introduce political commissars into army units in 1946. With bitter disgust, moreover, senior officers recalled the so-called Madiun Affair of 1948, when Communist army units had declared a Soviet Republic in the East Java town of Madiun. At that time, the Indonesian Republic had been reduced by Dutch offensives to a constricted area in Central and East Java and was girding itself to resist an expected final onslaught. The uprising had been a complex affair, the product, at least in part, of anti-Communist provocation of the Communist troops, but the incident lived on in the memories of the army leadership as proof of Communist treachery (Sundhaussen, 1982).

Religious opposition to the PKI came mainly from orthodox Islam. Although Islam was statistically the religion of just under 90 percent of the population, approximately half the Muslim population belonged to a distinctive Javanese form of the religion, often called *Kejawen*, which was strongly mystical and blended with pre-Islamic beliefs. Whereas the followers of *Kejawen* often saw little to fear in Communism, pious orthodox Muslims feared that the Communists would install an atheist state, anathema to Islam, if they came to power. The Indonesian Republic had adopted belief in God, but not Islam, as one of its guiding principles in 1945, and for many Muslims even this was a barely tolerable compromise. This religious antagonism was compounded by memories of the Madiun affair, when Communist forces, briefly in control of parts of East Java, had massacred several hundred Muslims who resisted them. Among Indonesia's Christian communities, attitudes toward the PKI were more divided: Some Christians shared the Muslim anathemization of Communist atheism, while others were sympathetic to the Party's goal of social justice and indeed backed the Party's campaigns on land and other issues in some regions.

A third pole of opposition to the PKI came from the conservative wing of the secular Indonesian Nationalist Party (PNI). Although sections of the PNI were sympathetic to the left, the Party establishment was generally conservative, representing the interests of the entrenched bureaucratic elite. The PNI's electoral support had depended especially on the traditional loyalty of peasants to this elite, and the Party was threatened more than any other by the rise of PKI support in the countryside. It, thus, provided a rallying point for civilians who were opposed to the PKI but suspicious of organized Islam.

Hostility between the army and organized Islam had been strong during the years after independence, with the army taking 15 years to suppress a fundamentalist Muslim uprising called *Darul Islam*. The two, however, found themselves gradually drawn closer by their shared hostility to the prospect of the PKI coming to power. In Indonesia's first fully free elections in 1955, the Communist Party had won 16.4 percent of the national vote, making it the fourth largest party, but its influence was growing rapidly and it maintained by far the best disciplined and organized party structure in the country. Sukarno drew it into his orbit as he consolidated his political power in a system he called Guided Democracy (1959–1965), declaring communism to be part of the state ideology and sponsoring a gradual penetration of state institutions by the Party (Mortimer, 1974). In early 1965 it appeared likely that workers and peasants would be armed and trained to make up a "Fifth Force" alongside the army, navy, air force, and police, thus creating a militia that would give the PKI direct access to armed force for the first time since the revolution.

The anti-Communist coalition was broadened by a widespread and more general hostility to the PKI. This hostility stemmed partly from the Party's energetic efforts to recruit support throughout society that saw it take sides on a wide variety of issues. For each issue that won it allies, it acquired a set of enemies, and on some issues, such as the redistribution of farm land in East Java, social violence had reached high levels even before the massacres began (Walkin, 1969). In East Java, the PKI supported Hindu revivalists against the local Muslim establishment; in Hindu Bali, however, the Party vigorously denounced Hinduism and disrupted religious practice (Hefner, 1990, pp. 193–215; Cribb, 1990, pp. 241–48). The immediate reason for hatred between Communists and non-Communists, therefore, varied enormously over the breadth of the Indonesian archipelago and for many years formed one of the important obstacles to a better understanding of the massacres as a whole.

Hostility to the Party also stemmed from what were widely believed to be the circumstances of the 1965 attempted coup in Jakarta. The coup itself was an ambiguous affair that may never be fully understood. Army units from the presidential palace guard, headed by Lieutenant-Colonel Untung, abducted six senior anti-Communist generals from their homes early on the morning of October 1. This action was ostensibly an attempt to thwart a rumored right-wing coup d'etat by the generals. The generals were probably to be kidnapped, intimidated, and humiliated into abandoning their alleged coup plans. A clandestine bureau of the PKI was probably involved with the kidnappers, though the rest of the Party, except for a few leaders, was certainly unaware of the plot. The targeted generals, however, were killed, and the kidnappers announced, from Halim air force base near Jakarta, that a new Revolutionary Council had seized power. It is probable that the announcement was a panicked response to the botched kidnappings, but it was widely perceived in Indonesia, including by PKI members themselves, as the Party's attempt to seize power (Crouch, 1978, pp. 97–134).

The coup appeared to be a cynical grab for power, upsetting the uneasy balance of Guided Democracy. The killings of the generals, moreover, were the first significant political assassinations since the chaos of the war of independence; the young daughter of another general was fatally injured in cross fire. Rumors then emerged that a number of the generals had been tortured and mutilated before death by frenzied Communist women who celebrated their achievement with an orgy involving Party cadres and left-wing air force officers. (For definitive disproof of these rumors, see Anderson, 1987.) Word quickly spread, too, that Communists throughout the country had planned a similar fate for their other enemies and that holes had been dug in every district to accommodate the bodies of their victims. The stories of torture and mutilation, and those of the preparation of holes, have now been shown to be false, but they contributed greatly to the anti-Communist determination to kill.

How Was the Genocide Committed?

Although the motives driving the killers varied greatly, there was a common pattern to much of the killing itself. In each region, typically, news of the attempted coup in Jakarta was followed by a period of tense relative calm in which both sides attempted to assess what had happened. In most cases, the killings did not begin until the arrival of anti-Communist troops from outside, though there were some exceptions to this. In strongly Muslim Aceh, in northern Sumatra, and in parts of East Java, local Muslim leaders took the initiative to kill Communists within days of the coup attempt. Knowledge that the killing of Communists was sanctioned by the armed forces was enough to set the massacres off in some areas, but the army often intervened to give weapons and rudimentary training to anti-Communist vigilantes. In a few regions, the army itself conducted most of the killings, while here and there it felt obliged to dragoon unwilling local communities to help in the slaughter.

The actual killing followed two distinct patterns. In some places, the army and vigilantes organized raids on houses or villages suspected of harboring Communists. The killing was carried out mostly at night and commonly with bayonet or *parang*, the single-bladed machete of the Indonesian peasant. In some cases, entire communities closely associated with the PKI were killed, but more commonly the army and vigilantes took with them blacklists of intended victims who were taken from their villages and killed nearby. The bodies were generally dumped in rivers or caves or were buried in shallow graves. The sites of some of these graves are still known locally and avoided. Often, however, victims were first detained for weeks or months in prisons, barracks, or detention camps before being taken some distance from their homes and killed more or less secretly. At times, the bodies of the victims were mutilated. Some killers may have wished to avenge the alleged mutilation of the generals or to conceal the identity of the victims, but in some cases they had a more spiritual motive: In local belief, influenced by Islamic practice, to damage a body immediately before or after death is also to damage the soul, condemning it to lesser existence in the hereafter and limiting its capacity to return to earth to afflict its tormentors (Gittings, 1990).

Few of the victims offered significant resistance. The vast majority of Party members were as unprepared for violent conflict as their anti-Communist enemies. Indeed, some of the victims were strikingly passive. In North Sumatra victims were reported to have formed long, compliant lines at the river bank as they waited for methodical executioners to behead them and tumble the head and body into the water. There are reports from Bali that Party members went calmly to their deaths wearing white funeral clothes (Hughes, 1967, pp. 160, 181). One reason for this passivity seems to have been that Party members hoped initially that not resisting would show that they had not been involved in the Jakarta coup and they remained committed to seeking a legal path to power. In parts of Central Java, where the PKI had been strongest, there was some attempt to set up stockades in defense of Communist villages, but this was largely futile against the army. After most of the killings were over, remnants of the PKI attempted to establish a guerrilla base in the countryside of southern East Java, but this too was soon suppressed.

Why Was the Genocide Committed?

Discussion of the reasons for the Indonesian massacres, aside from considering the motives mentioned above, has focused on the unexpected ferocity of the killings in a country whose people had something of a reputation for gentleness. Most authors have argued that the killings involved something more than the political elimination of the PKI. Because it is likely that the destruction of the Party as a political force could have been achieved with many fewer deaths than actually occurred, observers have sought additional explanations for the scale of the massacre.

This issue raises questions of national psychology that are both difficult and delicate, and most attempts to explicate the event have not been convincing. Some scholars have suggested that the massacre represented a kind of collective running *amok* (*amok* being, after all, an Indonesian word). *Amok*, however, almost invariably takes place in response to projected imminent defeat and humiliation. It normally ends in the death of the *amokker* and has many of the hallmarks of an indirect form of suicide (Spores, 1988). Others have suggested that the Javanese shadow puppet play, or *wayang*, portrays the characters on the left of the puppeteer as both wrong and doomed to violent destruction, and, so, inclined Indonesians to expect the PKI to perish in a welter of blood, but this theory fails to do justice to the complexity of *wayang* philosophy (see Anderson, 1965). Other scholars have emphasized the atmosphere of fear and uncertainty that gripped Indonesia at the time, arguing that the killings were a product of panic in an environment of intense political conflict. There is evidence, too, that many of the vigilantes were drawn from the criminal underworld. They were men of violence in any case and were given the freedom to exercise violence on a massive scale during the killings. Nonetheless, it is also worth remembering that the military forces around General Suharto felt entirely uncertain of success when they launched the massacres. Communist influence had deeply pervaded Indonesian society and politics. It was so unclear who was to be trusted that the Suharto group seems to have relied on lists prepared by the United States Central Intelligence Agency to identify the senior leftists who were to be removed. In these circumstances, the scale of the killing may partly reflect the army's determination to make sure that it would prevail.

More promising is our growing knowledge of the role of the men of violence (rural and urban gangsters, enforcers, and the like) in Indonesian society and the special role that terror plays in consolidating their authority (Cribb, 1991, pp. 52–55). In the discussion below — under "Who Was Involved?" — however, we shall see that there are formidable obstacles to developing this line of analysis. However, first let us consider briefly who the victims were.

Who Were the Victims?

The killings were directed primarily against members and associates of the PKI and its affiliated organizations. The Party claimed a membership of 3 million and its affiliates another 20 million, though both figures were probably exaggerated. In the course of the killings, many private quarrels were also settled, and a significant number of non-Communists perished because of mistaken identity or association with Communists. In the politically charged atmosphere of the mid-1960s, however, many private quarrels had taken on a political dimension, and the distinction between private and political was correspondingly vague.

Few records of any kind were made or kept of the killings as they took place. The few foreign journalists who were in the country found access to the countryside very difficult and were, in any case, kept busy reporting the complex political changes taking place in national politics.

Under the long Suharto era (1966–1998), Indonesians, on the whole, remained reluctant to speak about the killings, except in very general terms. This reluctance probably stemmed from a sense of shame at the magnitude of the massacres and an unwillingness to discuss what was still a sensitive topic in a country dominated by the military (who presided over the killings in the first place).

This lack of information makes it impossible to say for certain how many people perished during the killings of 1965–1966. The death toll certainly included most of the Party leadership, including the General-Secretary D.N. Aidit. Estimates have ranged from a low of 78,000 to a high of 2 million. Today, most scholars accept a figure of between 200,000 and 500,000. The Indonesian Suharto government itself, which considered the killings to have been a necessary purge of Communist influence from society, has never seriously denied that the killings took place and indeed has publicly inclined to the higher figure (Cribb, 1990, p. 12). As we shall see in "Historical Forces and Trends" below, the Indonesian Suharto government drew some political advantage from cultivating the memory of massive killing.

The intensity of the killing varied dramatically from region to region. It was most ferocious in areas where the PKI had been on the ascendant, in the countryside of Central and East Java, in Bali, and in the plantation belt of North Sumatra; it was least prevalent in the cities, and in places such as Aceh, West Sumatra, and Madura where overwhelming community hostility to the Party had made it a minor part of the political landscape.

At the time, it was reported that Indonesia's substantial Chinese community were especially targeted as victims. The Chinese were and are deeply resented in Indonesia for their relative success in business since colonial times, and they were further encumbered in 1965 by their perceived association with the People's Republic of China. In 1959, however, Chinese traders had been expelled from rural areas, thus removing them from the regions where the heaviest killing took place. The PKI had been more tolerant of Indonesian Chinese than most other groups, and there were thus many Chinese among the Party activists who perished, but there is no evidence that the Chinese suffered disproportionately on this occasion.

Who Was Involved?

Only in a few instances does the available information permit us to identify individual killers. This is partly because those involved often kept their identities secret by wearing masks and acting at night. But it is also a result of a strong sense of communal responsibility for the massacres. This communal responsibility rests on traditional village notions of justice in which crime was seen as committed both by and against whole communities, regardless of the individual who may have carried it out or who may be charged with avenging it. Even those whose hands were never physically bloodied have consequently felt a shared responsibility for the killings.

This sense of mass responsibility was also deliberately encouraged by the army, which aimed to ensure that it did not carry the burden of blood alone. Until the massacres were well advanced, many observers inside and outside Indonesia were uncertain whether the PKI could be effectively eliminated as a political force. The army was, therefore, keen to recruit irrevocably to its side as many groups as possible, knowing that those who had joined in the bloodshed could never change sides. As the killing proceeded, participation became something of a test of anti-Communist credentials. Those who had made compromises with the leftist elements in Guided Democracy often felt that they could prove themselves only by joining with especial enthusiasm in the anti-Communist witch-hunt. This was especially so on the island of Bali (Soe, 1990).

Historical Forces and Trends

The massacres of 1965–1966 played a key role in the long-term destruction of political parties as a significant force in Indonesian public life. The nationalist movement during the closing decades of Dutch rule in the first half of the 20th century had formed itself into a series of political parties, and at independence it had seemed natural that one or more political parties should take the lead in determining the country's future. The resilience of local Party organizations was strengthened by the self-reliance they developed during the war of independence when central control was at a minimum. At a national level, however, the parties were for the most part fragile and even coincidental alliances of politicians whose power bases lay in regional, social, ethnic, or religious groups. Only in the PKI did the Party organization have a powerful base in its own right. Independent Indonesia adopted a parliamentary system in which governments were created by coalition on the floor of parliament, but this political form proved to be profoundly disappointing to many Indonesians. Coalitions were unstable, few lasting longer than a year, and politicians in general appeared to be obsessed with peddling influence and favors, rather than with determining policy in the national interest.

Sukarno's suspension of the parliamentary system and declaration of martial law in 1957, therefore, were greeted favorably by many Indonesians in the hope that an authoritarian government less beholden to sectional political interests would rule the country better. Guided Democracy's economic performance was dismal, but most observers attributed this to Sukarno's concentration on ideology and foreign affairs and to the growing influence of the PKI rather than to his authoritarian political structures. The forces who marshaled against the PKI in 1965, therefore, included many who were determined to prevent parties from ever again exercising a decisive role in Indonesian politics.

In this perspective, the massacres were less important for their elimination of one particular party than for the curse they cast on party politics in general. While believing firmly that the PKI had to be exterminated, many conservatives deeply regretted that Indonesian politics had reached such a point and they blamed the hatreds that underlay the killings not simply on the PKI but on the freedom that all parties had used to pursue their own sectional interests. In Suharto's Indonesia, therefore, the killings became a horrible warning of what might happen if populist politics were permitted. At each carefully managed national election, when the government electoral organization, called *Golkar*, won handsomely against the two permitted alternative parties, the specter of the violence of 1965–1966 was one of the forces that shepherded voters into support for the government.

Long-Range Impact

The killings eliminated the PKI as a significant political force in Indonesia. The Party has been formally illegal since March 1966, and aside from two or three attempts during the late 1960s to establish rural guerrilla bases on a Maoist model, there has been no clear sign of any PKI activity within Indonesia since that time. The Indonesian Suharto government regularly warned the public against the "latent danger" of the Party, and from time to time unexplained incidents, such as fires in public buildings, were blamed on a putative PKI underground, but it is most probable that the PKI was simply being used as a convenient scapegoat in these cases. A somewhat factionalized Party-in-exile continues to exist, based originally on Party members who happened to be abroad in October 1965 or who subsequently escaped the killings, and drawing more recently on exiled Indonesian dissidents, but it appears to have little impact in Indonesia itself.

The psychological impact of the killings on both survivors and perpetrators is difficult to assess. As mentioned above, Indonesian autobiographical writing about the killings is exceptionally sparse. In the late 1960s, a number of short stories appeared in which authors tackled various aspects of the killings (Aveling, 1975), but the topic failed to develop even as a genre in Indonesian literature. One or two anecdotes exist that describe killers who suffered horribly in later life as a consequence of their participation, but these are balanced by accounts of killers who live easily with their memories (Young, 1990, p. 80).

The memory of the killings, moreover, appears to have relatively little significance for those one might regard as survivors. This is partly because the killings appear to have been remarkably effective in eliminating those whom they targeted; that is, the active cadre of the PKI. More important, however, the relative disregard of the killings is a consequence of the fact that an even larger number of leftists were punished by detention during the years after the coup. The Indonesian government itself has put the number of detainees at one and a half million. Not all these people were held at once, and some were released after a few months, but many were kept for years, and large numbers were exiled to the isolated prison island of Buru in eastern Indonesia. Virtually all shared the experience of hunger, humiliation, and mistreatment during their detention, and they suffered from harassment and discrimination for decades after their release. It appears that this experience of suffering has overshadowed — for most of them — the briefer and more distant terror of the killing months.

The impact of the killings is perhaps seen most strongly today in the changed religious geography of parts of Java, Timor, and North Sumatra, where an estimated 2.8 million people converted to Christianity in the years immediately after 1965. These conversions were partly a consequence of the military government's insistence that all Indonesians should profess a religion. Although some Christian vigilantes were as brutal in the killings as their Muslim counterparts, the Christian churches in general took a much more active pastoral role among the families of victims and were rewarded with many converts. Conversion was also perhaps a consequence of a general spiritual crisis that the appalling level of violence presented to Indonesian society.

Responses

News of the killings reached the international press soon after they began, and, although the obstacles to effective reporting were formidable, a thin stream of news and feature articles (Kirk, 1966; King, 1966; Palmos, 1966; Turner, 1966) made available to the world community the fact that a massacre of enormous proportions was under way in Indonesia. The international response was muted — partly because attention focused on the growing power of the military in Jakarta, and partly because the non-Communist world had no wish to make an issue of events it regarded favorably. Without specifically commending the Indonesian army for its actions, the world preferred not to know the details of what was happening, though *Time* came close to commendation when it described the PKI's suppression as "The West's best news for years in Asia" ("Vengeance," 1966, p. 26).

Leftists outside Indonesia for their part were reluctant for many years to investigate the details of the killing. This was probably true for two reasons. First, leftist critics of the Suharto government, as well as other organizations such as churches and human rights organizations, generally focused on what they saw as its shortcomings — restrictions on political activity, corruption, regressive development policies, and the like — rather than on what they would regard as historical crimes. Second, the left was aware that the PKI created many enemies in Indonesian society by its vigorous espousal of contentious issues such as land reform. PKI activists were, according to circumstance, unyielding, unreasonable, and even inconsistent. Their enemies had many grudges one might regard as legitimate, even if the response was unnecessarily violent. The left, therefore, has found its analysis of the killings to be most effective when they were simply interpreted as a general "white terror" or violent conservative reaction to Communism, and the precise details of each killing were not explored.

Scholarly Interpretation

No significant observer had predicted the extent of the violence in Indonesia in 1965–1966 on the basis of a scholarly understanding of Indonesian society. For many years afterwards, scholars did not treat the massacres as a major event in Indonesian history. This was partly a consequence of the lack of information, but it reflected also a broader historiographical difficulty in blending the separate courses of local and national history into a single coherent narrative. Because the national significance of the killings cannot be explained without reference to local conditions, any more than the local significance could be discussed without reference to national events, the killings had an elusive character that has militated against close analysis.

The circumstances of Suharto's fall, however, increased the willingness of scholars to pay attention to the massacres of 1965–1966. Throughout the long years of Suharto's New Order, scholars had debated whether the spectacular economic achievements of the government — Indonesia went from being one of the poorest countries in the world to being one of the celebrated Asian economic "tigers" — justified the high levels of corruption and the continuing political repression of the military-dominated government. In 1997, however, the Indonesian economy collapsed as part of a more general Southeast Asian economic crisis, and the severity of the collapse was widely attributed to shortcomings in Suharto's policies. With the old president's economic credentials in tatters, scholars became more inclined to examine his political shortcomings and to identify the 1965–1966 massacres as the beginning of the New Order — that is, the first act in a long story of political repression — rather than as the end of Sukarno's Guided Democracy — that is, the working out of tensions generated in the struggle for independence and in the attempt to shape a workable democratic system for Indonesia.

Disregard for the killings may also be related to the character of the scholarly community that studies Indonesia. At least until recently, this community tended to be dominated by scholars who had made the study of Indonesia their life's work and who brought to their studies a deep familiarity with Indonesia and an affection for its people. Perhaps because it is hard to reconcile such widespread killings with affection for Indonesians, scholars with the experience that would enable them to examine the killings in detail have tended to look for other research topics and to focus their discussion of the events of 1965 on the attempted coup of September 30, 1965. The circumstances of the coup are themselves shrouded in uncertainty, but they at least permit scholars to identify innocent parties in a way in which the killings do not.

Insofar as historical debate exists, it focuses on the relative responsibility of the armed forces and of the vigilantes in initiating and sustaining the killings. The left on the whole gives greater emphasis to the role of the military, the right to the vigilantes, but this disagreement has never reached the level of controversy.

Current Attitudes

Interest in the Indonesian massacres revived in the late 1980s and early 1990s after two decades of neglect. A small number of previously little-known personal accounts appeared (see "Eyewitness Accounts"), and a collection of essays on the killings attempted to restore the topic to the scholarly agenda (Cribb, 1990). An important reason for this interest seemed to be a growing awareness that the survivors on both sides of the massacres were reaching old age and within a short span of time might not be around to add their testimony to the record. President Suharto, moreover, had his 70th birthday in 1991, and it was widely accepted that his period of dominance in Indonesian politics was coming to an end. Furthermore, four important local studies of the killings (Hefner, 1990; Sudjatmiko, 1992; Robinson, 1995; Sulistyo, 1997) made it possible to analyze the killings in a way that was less dependent on scattered anecdotes.

Many observers expected an upsurge of Indonesian interest in the killings after the fall of President Suharto in 1998. Indeed a number of groups did begin to investigate the killings — collecting testimonies and even excavating mass graves. The activities of these groups, however, met widespread hostility and obstruction both from the authorities and from Muslim groups. Although one might expect that the hostility would stem from fear of exposure and perhaps punishment, the resistance to opening the case of the 1965–1966 massacres seems to be driven above all by a remarkably persistent anti-Communism. Important sections of Indonesian society are deeply reluctant to allow any actions that might be seen to rehabilitate the PKI, which had been excoriated for more than three decades as Indonesia's most important source of evil. A suggestion by Indonesia's fourth president, Abdurrachman Wahid, that the ban on the Communist Party might be lifted in the name of national reconciliation met such vehement resistance that he was forced to drop the idea. In addition to those who actively reject the need for any investigation of the massacres, there is also a strong feeling in parts of Indonesian society that the country is already beset with violence and social conflict and that little good would be done by raising such an old issue.

As scholarly assessment of Suharto's impact on Indonesia takes shape, a deeper understanding of the circumstances that brought him to power becomes increasingly important.

Lessons from the Indonesian Massacres

The Indonesian killings share with those in Cambodia (see Chapter 11) an overwhelmingly political, rather than racial, orientation that distinguishes them from the other racially or ethnically motivated genocides discussed in this volume. They were an extreme example of the violence that is a part of the political process throughout much of the world. However, political motives are also not absent in many other massacres. In any case, the predominance of political considerations in the Indonesian killings reminds us that genocide does not simply occur because of racism but rather is a consequence of deep human antagonisms.

Eyewitness Accounts: The Indonesian Massacres

Three eyewitness accounts of the Indonesian killings are included herein. As the analysis above explained, the Indonesian killings have produced remarkably few direct testimonies by survivors or participants, and the first two accounts reproduced here are unique for the detail they provide: Other accounts, published and unpublished, tend to be secondhand or fragmentary.

The first account was written by an anonymous author who was a member of a left-wing youth organization in Kedurus, near Surabaya, the main city of East Java. The Brantas is Java's longest river and it enters the sea near Surabaya. The author makes clear that he would have become a victim himself had he been caught. The account was written in 1989, over 20 years after the events it describes.

The second account describes the killings in Kediri, also in East Java, from the point of view of a young man whose family was not on the Communist side but who nonetheless viewed the fate of the PKI with concern. The author, Pipit Rochijat, describes himself throughout the account as "Kartawidjaja's Son No. 2." This is due to the fact that Indonesians are often reluctant to use personal pronouns, because this can seem forward; thus, names are commonly used as a polite substitute.

Both testimonies highlight the contrast between the clandestine nature of the actual killings and the public knowledge that they were taking place. The author of the first account witnessed the murder of his old teacher and others only because he happened to be hiding near the secluded abattoir where the killings took place. The killers whom he watched took some care to conceal the identity of their victims but none at all to conceal the bodies, which were simply flung into the river. Pipit Rochijat, too, describes the way in which victims were often taken away to some secluded spot to be killed, yet bodies and parts of bodies were widely displayed. This phenomenon (contrasting with the public executions and the secret disposal of bodies employed by some repressive regimes) highlights the extent to which the killings were intended to create terror, as well as eliminating political opponents. Uncertainty about who had been killed and where and why kept the Communists and the left in general off balance, encouraging rumor and uncertainty. Unable to be sure just what the scope of the killings would be, the Communists could not judge whether it was best to fight, to flee, or to confess.

This uncertainty also emerges powerfully in the final testimony. This account is the work of an Indonesian journalist sent by his newspaper to investigate one of the last outbreaks of killing associated with the suppression of the PKI. The poverty-stricken Purwodadi region of Central Java was one of a small number of rural areas where the PKI began to develop a guerrilla strategy, and the suppression of the Party's incipient military campaign was reportedly accompanied in late 1966 and early 1969 by a wave of killings of civilians by army and home guard forces. Maskun Iskandar visited the region in early 1969 at the invitation of the Indonesian army, which denied the killings had taken place. His report was published serially in the independent newspaper *Indonesia Raya*.

Iskandar's testimony is in many ways unsatisfactory. He saw no bodies, heard little testimony except from official sources, and draws no conclusions. His account leaves the reader hanging and the fact that he visited the region as a guest of the Indonesian army would seem to cast further doubt on his credibility and on the figures he cites. To a Western reader, his report seems almost inconsequential; to an Indonesian reader, however, aware of the constraints of official censorship and unofficial controls on journalism, his report leaves little doubt that a significant massacre took place. His diffident reference to the "camps of death" at Kuwu and the "left-overs" in the camps elsewhere, for instance, would give the censor little to object to, but draw the reader's attention to ominous nomenclature. He dismisses as "useless" his questions to children about their missing parents, but reports faithfully that their eyes brim with tears. He describes the sergeant known as "007" (licensed to kill) as if he disbelieves the story, but his readers will draw their own conclusions from the nickname. When he talks casually about the risk of "losing" his notes, his Indonesian readers know immediately that he is referring to the risk of confiscation by the authorities.

Maskun's report does not tell us what happened in Purwodadi, but his writing reminds us powerfully that not all victims of genocide are able to leave oral or written testimony as their memorial. There are times in human history when neither victims, nor survivors, nor perpetrators, have preserved more than a fragmentary record of genocide. The victims at Purwodadi, whose fate is faintly recorded in Iskandar's account, stand for a much larger group, not only in Indonesia, whose destruction remains largely unrecorded.

Account 1

"By the Banks of the Brantas" was first published in Injustice, *Persecution, Eviction: A Human Rights Update on Indonesia and East Timor* (New York: Asia Watch, 1990), pp. 87–90. Reprinted by permission of Asia Watch.

Some people spoke of Pak[1] Mataim, the bicycle repairman, one of whose eyes was white. His house had been used as the local PKI secretariat, and they said he was the first person in the village to be arrested. He had been frightened out of his wits. He was taken to the police station and later detained in Mlaten.

Mlaten? Where was there a prison in Mlaten? There wasn't. That night I went to Mlaten to see for myself. In fact it was a warehouse that had become a detention center. Now the building was surrounded with a thick fence of woven bamboo, so that you couldn't see it from the outside. The police station I passed seemed empty. I kept going south, past the subdistrict military headquarters. It was guarded not just by the army but by members of the Banser.[2] Banser was also guarding the subdistrict government offices — they were everywhere.

Now every night, raids took place. Four members of my organization were arrested. They were all able to escape or perhaps they were deliberately let go. They were asked about me, and it was clear I was already on the list of those to be arrested. After that I no longer slept at home at night. More often I became a wanderer on the banks of the Brantas. I didn't have to exhaust myself finding a place to hide because there was an abattoir, surrounded by high grasses, which was completely deserted. My younger brothers knew about my hiding place, and one day brought a schoolmate to see me and warn me to get out of the city. She said I didn't need to go back to school, especially since the school was being searched and one of the people they were looking for was me.

Politics forced my transformation from student to fisherman. There were many others on the Brantas, fishing with nets or rods. Unfortunately for me, the fish I caught didn't bring in any money; I couldn't sell one.

In November, the rains began to come. The river ran muddy and fast with weeds, leaves, human limbs, and headless corpses. Fishermen vanished from the banks. I was the only one left, not to fish but to save my life. At night it was the same as before, only now I was on my own. One night I heard a rustling coming from the abattoir. I got closer and lay prone in the bushes like a snail. When I heard voices, I got frightened, but I still wanted to know what was going on. A few seconds later, I heard the engine of a car. Several Banser members got down from a Willis jeep. Some of them wore black and carried a piece of rattan about half a meter long in their left hands, while in the right they carried machetes. Then came a truck which I recognized as belonging to Pak Abu, the owner of a textile mill in Jarsongo … .

Among those wearing black were several people I knew. Pak Harun wore glasses, had a paunch, and always wore a black fez when he went out. He had a small mustache and dark skin. He was the number one man in *Nahdatul Ulama* [the national Islamic organization] in the Karangpilang subdistrict. Rejo, still young, was a member of *Ansor*, the *Nahdatul Ulama* youth wing, in Wiyung, a village to the west of Kedurus. He was large and tall, also mustached, and wore a seaweed bracelet around his right wrist. He often frequented bars.

"Is the sack ready?" Harun asked. The others said everything was ready. An oil lamp flickered over my head and forced me to lie flat, hoping that the tall grasses would obstruct their view. I didn't dare move, ignoring the ants and mosquitoes.

A man was hauled off the truck, his feet and hands bound. A plump man, he was dragged around like a banana stalk. It took three people to do it. They were only ten meters in front of me when, reaching the abattoir, they untied his feet. He was wearing a white cotton shirt with brown stripes. He looked disheveled, as though he hadn't changed clothes in days. He seemed weak — maybe he hadn't been getting enough to eat. The Petromax lamp suddenly illuminated his face, and I got a shock. It was Pak Mukdar, the elementary school principal in Kedurus. His head was bare (usually he wore a fez), and his eyeglasses were gone. Weak as he was, he was forced to stand. There were a few uniformed army sergeants and other military men, but it wasn't clear what rank the others held or what unit they were from. They asked Pak Mukdar questions, and I strained my ears to hear. I just heard murmurs; it wasn't clear whether he had answered.

"If you don't answer what we ask," said one of the military, "say your last prayers. We're going to send you to meet your maker."

The old man didn't say anything. Instead, he began to sing the song so frequently sung by PKI members, the *Internationale*. Before he could finish, he was shoved from behind by a man in black and fell flat. Maybe he fainted. With his hands still tied, his neck was hacked by Rejo, the youth from Wiyung. He finished off the unconscious, weak old man, whose hands were still tied. My teacher — such a meaningless death, in an abattoir meant for slaughtering cattle. His head was removed and put in the sack. Then they dragged his body to the river and tossed it in. It washed away slowly in front of me … .

Another body was also thrown in, also headless. I couldn't count how many headless corpses passed by me. Every time, the head was put in the gunny sack. Then I heard a shout from a voice I recognized and froze; it was Pak Mataim, our bicycle repairman who I think was illiterate. He seemed very thin, and he too was dragged along like a banana stalk. He moaned, begging for mercy, for his life to be spared. They laughed, mocking him. He was terrified. The rope around his feet was taken off, leaving his hands still tied. He cried, and because he couldn't keep quiet, they plugged up his mouth with a clump of earth.

Rejo went into action, and like lightning, his machete cut through the neck of his victim, the one-eyed, powerless, bicycle repairman. His head went into the sack. Then his hands were untied, so that it looked as though he died without first being bound. At first, his headless body disappeared beneath the surface of the water, then eventually it floated up. The next person killed was a woman; I don't know who she was.

At midday when my brother came, he told of seeing a corpse caught against a tree on the edge of the river. From the clothes and certain features of his body, they discovered it was Pak Muktar. I didn't say a word of what I'd seen. The news caused my mother to fall ill, but such news came every day from the Brantas. Our house was finally raided but I managed to slip away. Following the suggestion of a friend from school, I left the Surabaya area for Lawang, but there too the murderers were roaming around. Suheri, a young killer from the village of Bambangan, invited me to join in helping herd a young man he wanted to kill to the Purwasari forest. He was one of Suheri's own group, not a member of any organization. But Suheri wanted his wife, then a beautiful woman. He didn't get his way, though. When he went to claim his victim's spouse, the woman concerned had disappeared.

Forgive me if I don't include pictures of the places I have described here. At the very least, I hope this little account of the last moments of the many victims can become a kind of explanation for their children, wives, and even grandchildren. Because one thing is clear, not a single person has taken responsibility for all those murders, let alone officially informed the families of those killed.

Account 2

Extracted from Pipit Rochijat's "Am I PKI or non-PKI?" *Indonesia*, 40(1985). pp. 37–52. Reprinted by permission of the Cornell University Modern Indonesia Project.

The Situation during G30S 1965. Up to 1965, the [national] front was divided in two: on the one side the Communist Front, and on the other the United Nationalist-Religious Front. And their respective strengths were about evenly balanced. For some reason or other, PKI strength in the region of Kediri, Tulungagung and Blitar was especially conspicuous. Maybe there was some kind of spillover from Madiun towards Kediri.

The events of October 1, 1965, are something difficult, impossible to forget. The atmosphere was so tense, as though everyone was expecting something [catastrophic] once the takeover of power in Jakarta had been broadcast. All Kartawidjaja said to his family was: "Watch out, be very careful. Something's gone very wrong in Jakarta." Usually the doors and windows of the house were shut around 10:00 P.M., but on October 1 they were closed at 7:00. Fear seized the Kartawidjaja family, for the rumor that the PKI had made a coup and murdered the generals was already spreading. The PKI's own aggressive attitude and the way in which the generals had been killed strengthened the suspicion of PKI involvement. "Such brutal murders could only be the work of *kafirs*, i.e., the Communists," was the kind of comment that one then heard. At the same time, the Kartawidjaja family felt very thankful that General Nasution[3] had escaped with his life. The only pity was that his little daughter was beyond rescue. For almost two weeks, everything was quiet in the Kediri region. People merely stayed on the alert and tensely watchful. In State High School No. 1, too, the atmosphere was very heated. Reports that it was the PKI that had gone into rebellion spread rapidly. At every opportunity the Nationalist and Religious groups vilified the students involved with the IPPI.[4] For its part, IPPI took evasive action and rejected all "accusations." They claimed to know nothing about what had happened. They said that the events in Jakarta were a matter of the Council of Generals.

About two weeks after the events of October 1, the NU[5] (especially their Ansor Youth) began to move, holding demonstrations which were joined by the *santri* [Orthodox Muslims] masses from the pondok and *pesantren* [Islamic dormitories and schools] around Kediri. They demanded the dissolution of the PKI, and that the death of each general be paid for with those of 100,000 Communists. Offices and other buildings owned by the PKI were attacked and reduced to rubble by the demonstrators. It was said that about 11 Communists died for nothing, simply because they were foolish enough to feel bound to defend PKI property. In an atmosphere of crisis suffused with so much hatred for the PKI, everything became permissible. After all, wasn't it everyone's responsibility to fight the *kafir*? And vengeance against the PKI seemed only right, since people felt that the Party had gone beyond the pale. So, the fact that only 11 Communists had [so far] died was regarded as completely inadequate. This kind of thinking also infected Kartawidjaja's Son No. 2.

Yet there was a [strange] episode which is worth mentioning here. To the east of the Kediri municipal bus station there was a certain PKI office. Actually, it was really only an ordinary house. But in front of it there was a signboard bearing all those names smelling of the PKI; from the PKI itself through the BTI,[6] Gerwani[7] and IPPI, to the People's Youth. It so happened that when the demonstrators arrived in front of that house, they found an old man out in front getting a bit of fresh air. They asked him whether he was a member of the PKI. "No," he answered, "I'm a member of the BTI." "Same thing!" yelled a number of the demonstrators as they started beating him. He toppled over, moaning with pain. He was lucky not to be killed. But the house was demolished as a result of the rage of the masses. And, as usual, before carrying out their task, the NU masses roared "*Allahu Akbar* [Allah is Great]!" After this bloody demonstration, Kediri became calm once more. Only the atmosphere stayed tense. And this went on for about 3–4 weeks.

Wanted:[8] Communists. Once the mesmerizing calm had ended, the massacres began. Not only the NU masses, but also those of the PNI joined in. The army didn't get much involved. First to be raided were workers' quarters at the sugar factory. Usually at night ... to eliminate the Communist elements. It was done like this: a particular village would be surrounded by squads of Nationalist and Religious Youth (Muslim and Christian [Protestant], for example in Pare). A mass of Ansor Youth would be brought in from the various *pondok* and *pesantren* in the Kediri region. On average, about 3000 people would be involved. The expectation was that, with the village surrounded, no Communist elements would be able to escape.

It was pretty effective too. Each day, as Kartawidjaja's Son No. 2 went to, or returned from, State Senior High School No. 1, he always saw corpses of Communists floating in the River Brantas. The thing was that the school was located to the *kulon* [west] of the river. And usually the corpses were no longer recognizable as human. Headless. Stomachs torn open. The smell was unbelievable. To make sure they didn't sink, the carcasses were deliberately tied to, or impaled on, bamboo stakes. And the departure of corpses from the Kediri region down the Brantas achieved its golden age when bodies were stacked together on rafts over which the PKI banner proudly flew.

In those areas through which the Brantas did not wind, the corpses were, as you'd expect, buried in mass graves — as, for example, around Pare. There the Christian [Protestant] masses were very active. But then, the export of corpses down the Brantas began to bother the city of Surabaya. The rumor went round that the drinking water was filtered out of the river. And by the time they reached Surabaya, the corpses were in complete decay. After protests from Surabaya, PKI were no longer flung into the Brantas, but were disposed of in mass graves. The prepared holes were dug pretty big, and were thus capable of handling dozens of Communists at a time.

Furthermore, at one time the road leading up to Mount Klotok (to the west of Kediri city) was decorated with PKI heads.

About 1 kilometer to the north of the Ngadirejo sugar factory, you'd find a lot of houses of prostitution. Once the purge of Communist elements got under way, clients stopped coming for sexual satisfaction. The reason: Most clients — and prostitutes — were too frightened, for, hanging up in front of the houses, there were a lot of male Communist genitals — like bananas hung out for sale.

Naturally, such mass killings were welcomed by the Nationalist and Religious groups. Indeed [they felt,] the target of 100,000 Communist lives for one general's had to be achieved. It was the same for Kartawidjaja's Son No. 2 and his family. Specially when they got the word that for the Kartawidjaja family a Crocodile Hole[9] had been prepared, for use if the PKI were victorious.

This atmosphere of vengeance spread everywhere. Not merely in the outside world, but even into the schools, for example State High School No. 1. There the atmosphere was all the more ripe in that for all practical purposes the school broke down, and classes did not continue as usual. Many students did not come to school at all — like Syom, for example, a friend of Kartawidjaja's Son No. 2, who had to spend most of his time going round helping purge the Kediri region of Communist elements. Kartawidjaja's Son No. 2 saw many cases where teachers and student members of IPPI at State High School No. 1 were held up at knife point by their Nationalist and Religious comrades. With the knives at their throats they were threatened with death. They wept, begging forgiveness and expressing regret for what they had done while members of the IPPI. In the end, all the secrets came out (or maybe false confessions). Each person tried to save himself at another's expense. After all, they were human beings too, and thus still wished to enjoy life.

It was evident that the Kediri area was unsafe for Communists (strangely enough, except in one instance, they made no move to offer any resistance). So most of them tried to flee to Surabaya or sought protection at the Kediri City *Kodim* [District Military Command]. But even in jail they were not safe. Too many of them sought safety there, and the jail could not take them all in. In the end, the army often trucked them off to Mt. Klotok (the road there passed by State High School No. 1). Who knows what the army did with them there — what was clear was that the trucks went off fully loaded and came back empty. Furthermore, the *Kodim* had no objections at all if people from the Nationalist or Religious groups came to ask for [certain] Communists they needed. The *Kodim* was prepared to turn over Communist prisoners, provided those who needed them brought their own transportation (not including motorbikes, of course).

At State High School No. 1 student activity proceeded calmly. It was practically like long vacation except for continuing to assemble at school. On one occasion a teacher asked Syom, the friend of Kartawidjaja's Son No. 2, where he'd been all this time, never coming to school. And indeed, he had seldom showed up. He answered: "On tour [of inspection], sir." And people understood what he meant by "on tour." For aside from being an acronym of *turu kana-turu kene* (sleeping there, sleeping here), it also meant "busy eliminating Communists." Syom was one of the executioners. And the fame of an executioner was measured by the number of victims whose lives he succeeded in taking.

Usually, those Communists whom people had managed to round up were turned over to an executioner, so that he could despatch their souls to another world. Not everyone is capable of killing (though there are some exceptions). According to what a number of executioners themselves claimed (for Kartawidjaja's Son No. 2 had many friends among them), killing isn't easy. After despatching the first victim, one's body usually feels feverish and one can't sleep. But once one has sent off a lot of souls to another world, one gets used to killing. "It's just like butchering a goat," they'd claim. And the fact is that Kartawidjaja's Son No. 2 often stole out of the house, either to help guard the [local] PNI headquarters located in the home of Pak Salim (the driver of the school bus in the area around Ngadirejo) or to watch the despatch of human souls. This, too, made sleeping difficult. Remembering the moans of the victims as they begged for mercy, the sound of the blood bursting from the victims' bodies, or the spouting of fresh blood when a victim was beheaded. All of this pretty much made one's hair stand on end. To say nothing of the screams of a Gerwani leader as her vagina was pierced with a sharpened bamboo pole. Many of the corpses lay sprawled like chickens after decapitation.

But even though such events were pretty horrifying, the participants felt thankful to have been given the chance to join in destroying infidels. Not to mention the stories brought back by Maha, a friend of Kartawidjaja's Son No. 2, who participated in eliminating the Communists in the Pare area. He was a Christian. What he said was that the victims were taken off by truck and then set down in front of holes prepared in advance. Then their heads were lopped off with a Samurai [sword] that had been left behind by a Japanese soldier in the past. When the mission was accomplished, the holes were filled in with earth.

And among so many incidents, naturally there were a few which still remain a "beautiful" memory for Kartawidjaja's Son No. 2. For example, when the Ansor Youth surrounded a particular village to the east of the sugar factory, they went into a number of houses to clean out the Communist elements. In one house, as it happened, there were two kids living there who were listed as activists in the People's Youth. When the Ansor people knocked at the door, it was the parents of the two hunted boys who answered. "Where are your sons?" "If it's possible, please don't let my boys be killed" — such was the request of the old couple. They offered to give up their lives in their children's stead. Not merely was this offer accepted, but the exterminators also killed their two children.

Even though Kartawidjaja was hated by the PKI, on one occasion he told Kartawidjaja's Son No. 2 to go to the home of Pak Haryo, an employee who lived next door and was an activist in the SBG. Kartawidjaja told him to fetch Pak Haryo to the house and have him sleep there, bringing with him whatever clothes he needed. But since it was then pretty late at night, when Kartawidjaja's Son No. 2 knocked at the door, Pak Haryo's family made no response. Maybe they were afraid that it might be the Angel of Death come visiting. The next morning, Kartawidjaja came himself to pick up Pak Haryo. Subsequently, he was taken by Kartawidjaja to Surabaya, to be hidden there.

Naturally, helping Communists wasn't at all in line with the ideas of Kartawidjaja's Son No. 2. So he asked: "Dad, why are you of all people protecting Pak Haryo?" "Pak Haryo doesn't know a thing, and besides it would be a shame with all his kids."

Kartawidjaja was fortunate in that he was always informed about "who and who" was to lose his life. And many Communists who had once vilified Kartawidjaja now came to his house to ask for protection. On one occasion he set aside a special space in the meeting hall where people asking for his protection could overnight.

All through the purges, the mosques were packed with Communists visitors. Even the Worker's Hall was specially made over into a place for Friday prayers. As a result, many people judged that the PKI people had now become *sadar* [aware: of their past errors, of Allah's truth]. And hopes for survival became increasingly widespread. And at one of these Friday prayers, Kartawidjaja was asked to make a speech in front of all the assembled worshippers. He told them that "praying isn't compulsory. Don't force people to do it. Let those who want to pray pray. And if people don't want to, then they don't have to."

Account 3

Extracted from Maskun Iskandar's "Purwodadi: Area of death." In Robert Cribb (Ed.) *The Indonesian Killings of 1965–66*, 1990, pp. 203–13. Reprinted by permission of the Centre of Southeast Asian Studies, Monash University.

My hair, clothes, my bag were all dusty. It was a bad road from Purwodadi to Kuwu. In a few places the asphalt could still be seen, but for the rest the road was paved only with brittle stones which crushed easily. "Hard river stones are like gold in this area,"[10] said the military man who escorted us in the jeep. We proceeded slowly, seldom meeting another vehicle. I had been told that the only public transport available was an old train which ran the 62 kilometres from Semarang to Purwodadi. So here was one piece of Princen's[11] information confirmed: communications were difficult. But was the rest true? Had there been mass killings? Were conditions in the Kuwu area tense? Now that I was on my way to the area, I had to find answers to these riddles.

Before we left Purwodadi for the Kuwu area, which had been identified in press reports as the centre of the killing, the KODIM commander gave us a briefing. PKI membership in Purwodadi was estimated at 200,000, out of a population of 700,000 in 18 *kecamatan*.[12] Two hundred of the 285 *lurah* [village heads] were PKI, he told us. Out of this number, only about a thousand had been "finished off," and those were only the leaders. "If we arrested everyone who was PKI," the commander told us, "we would not know what to do with them. We do not have space to detain them and we could not simply release them because the rest of the population would not have them back." The commander of KODAM VII[13] plans to transmigrate them.

On the afternoon of March 5, I visited 4 of the 14 prison camps in Purwodadi *kabupaten*.[14] I saw 987 prisoners and it would be dishonest if I were to say that they were either fat or the reverse. The camps themselves, I was told, included former store houses which the military had borrowed from local people. So there were no terrifying iron bars, but they were secure enough. Let us take Camps I and II in Kuwu as examples. Local people call them *kamp maut*, camps of death. It is not clear to me, however, just what they mean by this. Is there some connection with those reports about Kuwu being in the grip of fear? I don't know.

Stories passing from mouth to mouth tend to get bigger. This was why my editor had sent me to get firsthand accounts. Had killings taken place without due legal process? Was it true that each *desa* [village] had to supply 75 victims a night? Was it true, as we heard, that the victims were tied up in groups of five before being shot, struck with iron bars or slaughtered without mercy? I had no success in checking these details and I got tired of hearing the same words: "I don't know," and "Perhaps." My readers, I know, want positive confirmation, not inferences from lack of information. I remembered the instructions of my editor before I left: "When you are doing this job," he said, "remember that all we are interested in is the truth. Truth may be bitter, but we are not aiming to discredit anyone or damage anyone, we have no hidden agenda, as people are inclined to allege these days."

Little children surrounded the jeep, but they did not dare come close, not like the children at the army barracks. They seemed to wonder why so many outsiders were visiting their village lately. I approached one of them and asked in low Javanese, "Do you have a sister?" He was silent. "Where is your mother?" I asked again. He remained silent, making circles in the sand with his big toe. "Is your father here?" I asked at random. The child raised his eyes. They were brimming over. Then he ran away into the narrow streets of the *kampung*. I deeply regretted asking those "useless" questions.

Back in my hotel, I attempted to sort my confused notes. The very figures I had written down of numbers killed seemed to be shaking. The names of villagers where the killings had taken place seemed to cry out. Perhaps the light in the room was too dim. The other guests in the hotel were all asleep; I had come back rather late. It was 8:00 P.M. when we left Purwodadi for Semarang accompanied by our military escort.

I noted once again what I had heard from an official source who wanted to remain anonymous. Three hundred prisoners, he said, had been killed in the *desa* Simo. Two hundred and fifty in Cerewek, two hundred in Kalisari, one hundred in Kuwu, two hundred in Tanjungsari. Was this true? "Did this really happen?" I had asked him. "It's no secret any more," he told me. "All the locals know about it. No honest man will deny it. The graves of the victims are witness to it." I asked the same questions to all those who gave me information, people who wanted to crush the PKI but did not want it done in this way. What they said was, "This kind of thing will not solve anything, not for the people who do it, not for those it is done to." When the army took me through those areas which were said to be tense, I tried to find proof. Was it true that there was a grave behind Cerewek railway station which had recently been planted with banana trees? Was there a grave in the rice fields at Banjarsari? Someone told me there were graves along the river in Tanjungsari, but our escort did not let us see any of these things. I got tired of writing down the names of villages where there were supposed to have been executions and burials. In Pakis, so my official source said, there were 100 victims; in Grobogan, 50. Outside this area my source did not have specific information, but he named villages: Toroh, Kedungglundung, Sambongbangi, Telogo, Mbogo, Banjardowo, Plosorejo, Monggot, Gundik and so on. Could any of this be proven?

Almost the whole night long, I sorted at my notes on the Purwodadi affair. I made a simple map, marking important places, places with reported killings, reported burial places, areas where there was a majority of women. I was also told that in Cerewek, Gabus and Sulur 70 percent of the population are widows. Some people even said that in Banjardowo it was hard to find a single adult male. Where could they have gone to? It was very late and water in the bathroom was dripping constantly. Some of my notes were hard to find. "It would be terrible to lose them," I thought. "After they took so much effort to compile." I thought of all the time I had spent, asking here and there, officials only, of course, and only from the KODAM and KODIM. I had even managed to talk directly to people who took active part in crushing the PKI.

I had a lot of information about the operations in Purwodadi, right from when they began, but that would take too much space. Let us start with April 5, 1968, just under a year ago. The police in Purwodadi had just arrested Sugeng, a former PKI member who conducted raids in the area. Under interrogation, he told the police that the PKI was putting together an underground organization called the People's Liberation Army [*Tentara Pembebasan Rakyat, TPR*], led by Suratin, who was still at large. Level I of the *TPR* (equivalent to the PKI's old *Comite Daerah Besar*, regional committees) was based first in Semarang, at Jl Dr. Cipto 280 and 298 [a street address]. Government forces then took over these buildings and began breaking up PKI operations with increasing success. The PKI kept up its operations, but it was shadowed ever more closely and had to change its operatives frequently. "When did the large-scale arrests begin?" I asked one of those involved. "June 27, 1968," he answered.

Hearing that date reminded me that responsibility for operations had been transferred to KODIM 0717 Purwodadi. If I am not mistaken, the headquarters had then been in Grobogan, about 4 kilometres from Purwodadi, while the investigating team had been first at Kradenan and then at Kuwu, about 5 kilometres away. I stopped writing, and tried to remember what I had noted down about Corporal S and Sergeant S. From what I had been told, both men were much feared in Kuwu. Perhaps there was some connection with the story I heard from Kuwu residents in Semarang that the sergeant was known as Agent 007. Ian Fleming's James Bond. Licensed to kill. I was surprised people could be so loose in their use of terminology. James Bond was on the side of good, but was this man? People told me that he used to summon the authorities to a ritual meal before he went out on his operations. One time he got drunk and shouted, "I am Agent 007. I have killed hundreds of people." Fortunately, an official who happened to be sitting next to him was able to stop his mouth and prevent him from saying any more.

Again I rummaged through my notes on the arrests. There was an official who told me that the arrests had gone on for a month from July 27. When the prisoners had been collected, they took 75 away each night, in two lots. Later this became less and they only took away 75 prisoners every Saturday night.

Someone walked past my room. I quickly hid the papers under the mattress and switched off the light. Then everything fell quiet again, except for the constant short cough of the night watchman. It reminded me of an incident before I had met the KODIM commander in Purwodadi the previous night, but I might come back to that. I still had not finished transcribing my notes on the arrests and killings.

According to the earliest information from Princen, two to three thousand people had been killed. This seemed very high, out of a total population of 8000 in Purwodadi *kabupaten*.[15] So I began to count. Seventy-five people a night for, say, two months, how much would that be? Now, there are 285 *desa* in Purwodadi. There cannot have been killing in all of them, so let us assume just ten, and that the killings took place once a week, not every night. This would make 8 (weeks) ∗ 10 (*desa*) ∗ 75 people = 6000 people. Impossible! What if I make it just one *desa*? That is still hundreds, still mass killings. I folded up my notes. I would return them in due course to the authorities in the form of questions.

I saw no beggars in Purwodadi. They say the *kabupaten* was once full of them, but there was now no sign of them. I asked my escort. They had been pulled in during the searches, he said; there were 43 in the camps now. Were they PKI people hiding as beggars, I wondered, or just ordinary non-Communist beggars? Another thing drew my attention. There were said to be five mad people in the camp, and none had been sent to a mental hospital. Even one mad person is a lot for a small *kabupaten*, but five? Perhaps Purwodadi is an exception. It was not clear whether these people were mad when they went into the camp or whether they became mad there. I do not know.

There are 14 women among the prisoners, perhaps Gerwani, perhaps not. I did not get a chance to ask them. But let me give details of the prison camps as I know them. There are 14 camps in Purwodadi. In the town itself, there are 411 prisoners, in Toroh 51, in Gundik 40. Ah yes, and before I forget, the total includes 127 prisoners left over from the arrests in 1965. In Godong there are 9 prisoners; in Kradenan two camps, the first with 55, the second with 67. Fifty in Sulur, seventy-two in Grobogan. The total number of prisoners, including beggars, lunatics, and women, is 987 in 14 camps. In Wirosari there are 79 prisoners, in Ngaringan 64, in Tawangharjo 36, in Pulokulon 47, in Grubug 5, in Tewoganu 33, in Kedungjati 1. In January there were four cases of illness, in February two. Some people said these were all recent arrivals, others called them "leftovers" (*sisa*). It was not altogether clear to me what the term *sisa* meant, so I did not pay much attention to it.

I put all my notes and the materials I had not yet transcribed back in my bag and closed it with a large question mark. I hope that an investigation team dedicated to upholding the law will open it.

Notes

1. Pak: an honorific meaning "father," used to address older men.
2. One of the Muslim vigilante groups active in East Java.
3. General A. H. Nasution was at the time Chief of Staff of the Armed Forces and Minister of Defense. When the *Untung* group attacked his home on the morning of October 1, the general's daughter was killed by a stray bullet.
4. The League of Indonesian High School Students, affiliated with the PKI.
5. *Nahdatul Ulama*, the main Muslim political party.
6. The Indonesian Peasants' Front, affiliated with the PKI.
7. The Indonesian Women's Front, affiliated with the PKI.
8. The word "Wanted" is in English in the original text.
9. *Lubang Buaya* (Crocodile Hole) was the name for the area, within the Halim Perdanakusumah Air Base perimeter, where the bodies of the assassinated generals were disposed of (down a disused well).
10. The collection of river stones for the paving of roads was one of the traditional obligations laid on the rural population in Java.
11. H. J. Princen, an Indonesian of Dutch descent, was and is a major human rights activist who pursued humanitarian issues both under Sukarno's Guided Democracy and under Suharto's New Order. It was he who broke news of the alleged massacres in Purwodadi.
12. District; an administrative division.
13. The regional military command for Central Java.
14. Regency; the administrative division above kecamatan.
15. Eight thousand is, of course, far too low. Earlier Iskandar gives the *kabupaten* population as 700,000.

References

Anderson, Ben (1965). *Mythology and the Tolerance of the Javanese*. Ithaca, NY: Cornell University Modern Indonesia Project.

Anderson, Ben (1987). "How Did the Generals Die?" *Indonesia*, 43:109–34.

Asia Watch (1990) *Injustice, Persecution, Eviction: A Human Rights Update on Indonesia and East Timor*. New York: author.

Aveling, Harry (1975). *Gestapu: Indonesian Short Stories on the Abortive Communist Coup of 30th September 1965*. Honolulu: University of Hawaii Southeast Asian Studies Working Paper, no. 6.

Cribb, Robert (1990). *The Indonesian Killings of 1965–1966: Studies from Java and Bali*. Clayton, Victoria, Australia: Monash University Centre of Southeast Asian Studies.

Cribb, Robert (1991). *Gangsters and Revolutionaries: The Jakarta People's Militia and the Indonesian Revolution, 1945–49*. Sydney: Allen & Unwin.

Cribb, Robert (2002). "Unresolved Problems in the Indonesian Killings of 1965–66." *Asian Survey*, July/August, 42(4):550–63.

Crouch, Harold (1978). *The Army and Politics in Indonesia*. Ithaca, NY: Cornell University Press.

Gittings, John (1990). "The Black Hole of Bali." *Guardian Weekly*, September 23, p. 22.

Hefner, Robert W. (1990). *The Political Economy of Mountain Java*. Berkeley: University of California Press.

Hughes, John (1967). *Indonesian Upheaval*. New York: McKay.

King, Seth (1966). "The Great Purge in Indonesia." *New York Times Magazine*, May 8, p. 89.

Kirk, Donald (1966). "The Struggle for Power in Indonesia," *The Reporter*, February 25, p. 38.

Mortimer, Rex (1974). *Indonesian Communism Under Sukarno: Ideology and Politics, 1959–65*. Ithaca, NY: Cornell University Press.

Palmos, Frank (1966). "One Million Dead?" *The Economist*, August 20, pp. 727–28.

Robinson, Geoffrey (1995). *The Dark Side of Paradise: Political Violence in Bali*. Ithaca, NY: Cornell University Press.

Rochijat, Pipit (1985). "Am I PKI or Non-PKI?" *Indonesia*, 40: 37–56.

Soe Hok Gie (1990). "The Mass Killing in Bali," pp. 252–58. In Robert Cribb (Ed.) *The Indonesian Killings of 1965–1966. Studies from Java and Bali*. Clayton, Victoria, Australia: Monash University Centre of Southeast Asian Studies.

Spores, John (1988). *Running Amok: An Historical Inquiry*. Athens: Ohio University Center for International Studies.

Sudjatmiko, Iwan Gardono (1992). "The Destruction of the Indonesian Communist Party (PKI) (A Comparative Analysis of East Java and Bali)." Ph.D. thesis, Harvard University.

Sulistyo, Hermawan (1997). "The Forgotten Years: The Missing History of Indonesia's Mass Slaughter (Jombang-Kediri 1965–66)." Ph.D. thesis, Arizona State University.

Sundhaussen, Ulf (1982). *The Road to Power: Indonesian Military Politics 1965–67*. Kuala Lumpur: Oxford University Press.

Time (1966) "Vengeance." *Time Magazine,* p.26.

Turner, Nicholas (1966). "Indonesian Killings May Exceed 300,000," *The Guardian,* April 7.

Walkin, Jacob (1969). "The Moslem-Communist Confrontation in East Java, 1964–1965." *Orbis,* 13(3):822–47.

Young, Kenneth R. (1990). "Local and National Influences in the Violence of 1965," pp. 63–99. In Robert Cribb (Ed.) *The Indonesian Killings of 1965–66: Studies from Java and Bali*. Clayton, Victoria, Australia: Monash University Centre of Southeast Asian Studies.

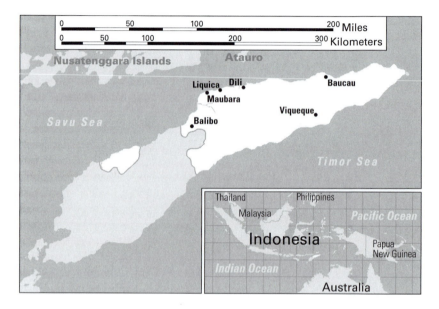

East Timor

CHAPTER 8
Genocide in East Timor

JAMES DUNN

Introduction

In 1975 Indonesian forces invaded the Portuguese colony of East Timor, which was then in the process of decolonization. The invasion provoked a spirited armed resistance, and during the subsequent five-year period, which was marked by bitter fighting in the interior and harsh oppression in occupied areas, the population of the territory underwent a substantial decline. So heavy was the loss of life that 16 years later (in 1991) the population was reported to be significantly lower than the estimate prior to the Indonesian invasion. In relative terms, therefore, the humanitarian costs of this act of forced integration reached genocidal proportions, which makes the East Timor case manifestly one of the most costly genocides in recent history.

While it should not be concluded that the Indonesian authorities embarked on a grand plan designed to bring about the systematic destruction of the Timorese people, Indonesia's occupation strategies and the behavior of the military seemed bound to achieve that end. The large influx of Indonesian settlers into the province could, in the long run, have led to ethnocide — that is, the destruction of the distinctive culture of East Timor. In the years following the invasion, however, the Timor case remained on the UN agenda, despite persistent efforts by Indonesia and its powerful Western friends. Thanks to the efforts of courageous Timorese such as Bishop Carlos Bello, by the end of the 1980s there was a growing awareness in the international community of the catastrophic consequences of this process of annexation and subjugation.

Be that as it may, until the 1990s, the international response to this very serious violation of international law was largely characterized by indifference and irresolution. Indeed, the expressions of international concern at the deteriorating humanitarian situation in the years following the invasion were so weak that Indonesian authorities had become openly defiant of world opinion. As a result, the Suharto government, despite its heavy dependence on Western economic aid, clearly did not feel the need to respond to international concerns in a positive way — that is, until the Santa Cruz massacre in November 1991.

The Santa Cruz massacre sent shock waves around the world and forced the Indonesian authorities on the defensive. Still, its concessions were of little real significance, falling well short of a concession to the demands of East Timor's leaders for the removal of the Indonesian military and for an act of self-determination. And again, thanks to accommodating reactions from officials in, among others, Washington, Paris, Tokyo, and Canberra, the Suharto government appeared to regain its determination to ignore the ongoing criticisms of its annexation of East Timor. Indonesia's agreement to the holding of a plebiscite, under UN auspices, in August 1999 was, it should be understood, an outcome attributable less to international pressures than to the fall of Suharto following the Asian economic collapse. The flexible stance adopted by President Habibie and the determined efforts of Kofi Annan, the newly appointed UN Secretary-General, were the key elements in the fortuitous sequence of events that led to East Timor's liberation in September 1999, after 24 years of occupation. As it happened, the Indonesian military persisted until the very end with its practice of indiscriminate killing and wanton destruction, until the International Forces in East Timor (INTERFET) intervention, authorized by the Security Council, forced its withdrawal from the territory.

On the other hand, events elsewhere in the early 1990s, the implications of the liberation of the Baltic States and the international rejection of Iraq's seizure of Kuwait, together with the awarding of the Nobel Peace Prize jointly to Jose Ramos Horta and Bishop Bello, served to place Indonesia's occupation of East Timor under closer scrutiny. In the event, it was not international pressure but the fall of the Suharto regime, following the collapse of the Indonesian economy, that provided the catalyst for a radical change in Indonesia's Timor policy. The new president, Habibie, began a process of negotiation with East Timorese leaders, on the one hand, and UN and Portuguese officials, on the other, which led to a UN-administered plebiscite on August 30, 1999. In spite of extreme intimidation, the outcome of the plebiscite was decisive; almost 80 percent of voters rejected Jakarta's offer of autonomy. After a period of violence, which shocked the international community, President Habibie responded to the demands of the Security Council, and the intervention of President Clinton, and ordered the withdrawal of Indonesian troops and agreed to the transfer of the former Portuguese colony to the United Nations Transitional Administration in East Timor (UNTAET), with the task of preparing the devastated country for full independence.

The Setting

The island of Timor lies at the southeastern extremity of the Indonesian Nusatenggara island group, which was named the Lesser Sundas in Dutch colonial times. It is located at the opposite end to the island of Bali, one of Asia's best-known tourist attractions. Following a long period of rivalry and conflict, Timor came to be divided into two almost equal parts by the Dutch and Portuguese colonial administrations. The partition began to take shape about the middle of the 17th century, as Portugal's colonial power in the East Indies began to weaken in the face of the more vigorous Dutch intrusion. Boundary disputes between the two colonial powers persisted until the late 19th century; that is, until the Lisbon Convention of 1893 and the subsequent signing of the *Sentenca Arbitral* in April 1913, which demarcated the borders as they exist today. The Portuguese colony of East Timor comprised the eastern half of the island, the tiny enclave of Oecussi on the north coast of West Timor, and the small island of Atauro north of Dili.

East Timor is a small country, but it is not insignificant by the standards of smallness among today's membership of the United Nations. The territory has an area of about 7300 square miles, comparable in size as well as population with Fiji and only slightly smaller in area than Israel or the state of New Jersey. On the eve of the Indonesian invasion, the Timorese population of the territory was estimated at about 680,000 people, with an annual growth rate of near 2 percent.

Portuguese navigators first reached Timor about 20 years after Columbus embarked on his epic trans-Atlantic crossing half a millennium ago. About 50 years later, their colonial rule of the area began in earnest. Therefore, for more than four centuries Portugal had been the dominant, almost exclusive, external influence in East Timor — except for a brief Japanese interregnum, from February 1942 until they surrendered to Allied forces in August 1945.

Within five years, the Dutch colony of the Netherlands East Indies was formally to become the Republic of Indonesia. Portuguese colonial rule over East Timor was restored, however, and until 1974 its colonial status was virtually ignored by the nationalist leaders of the new republic. This lack of interest persisted during the last seven years of Sukarno's presidency, when Indonesia embarked on an aggressive anticolonial policy, with Jakarta vigorously asserting its own claim for the "return" of West Irian. After that objective was secured, Indonesia launched, in 1962, a costly and futile confrontation of Malaysia, which Sukarno perceived as a British neocolonial creation.

At no stage during this period did Indonesia seek to bring any real pressure to bear on the Portuguese administration in East Timor, although the Salazar regime had by that time become the chief target of the mounting campaign for decolonization. Portugal had become the only colonial power that refused to declare its colonies non-self-governing. While Dutch colonialism in West New Guinea was denounced in vitriolic terms, the more traditional form of colonial rule then being conducted by the Portuguese in neighboring East Timor scarcely rated a mention in Jakarta.

From the early 1960s until 1965 there were occasional remarks by a few leading Indonesian political and military figures, hinting that East Timor's future lay with its big neighbor, but these statements were not taken further by the government of the time, and certainly never evolved into a formal claim or political campaign.[1] After 1965, the Suharto regime, which was keen to develop closer relations with the Western nations sharing its hostility to Communism and to attract economic assistance from them, was anxious to show that Indonesia no longer had territorial designs on the territories adjacent to it.

This policy appeared to prevail at the highest political level in Jakarta, right up to the point of Indonesia's military intervention in East Timor, with most official statements from Jakarta emphasizing East Timor's right to self-determination.[2] Certainly, at no stage, under either Sukarno or Suharto, was a claim to East Timor ever formally made by the government in Jakarta.[3]

The idea of an East Timor nation emerged spontaneously from the Portuguese colonial experience, just as Indonesia, Malaysia, Singapore, and the north Kalimantan states were shaped by British and Dutch colonial policies and rivalry. Although the two great empires of Srivijaya and Majapahit extended Java's influence to other parts of the archipelago for a period, there is no evidence that Timorese kingdoms were ever subjugated by the Javanese.

As a political concept, the notion of a nation of East Timor, even taking into account the arbitrary division of the island, is surely no less valid than the idea of an Indonesian state.

It could be said that the Indonesian nation was itself created not by a natural historical evolution but by colonial circumstances, determined by imperial and commercial rivalry in distant Western Europe. The legitimacy of the Indonesian state, it could therefore be argued, has its roots in Dutch colonial expansion and the political consensus — and dissent — it aroused, rather than in the natural evolution of a national political culture. In the world at large in 1974, events in East Timor aroused little interest. It was poor, undeveloped, remote, and unconnected to the global network of commercial and tourist communications. It possessed no apparent strategic value to any nation, with the possible exception of Indonesia. Its status was therefore of little consequence, in perceptions of national interest, other than to Portugal, Indonesia, and Australia. By the end of that year, the Portuguese themselves, with their empire now falling apart, had turned to Europe and were little interested in the fortunes of a distant colony of very little economic value.

Australia is East Timor's nearest Western neighbor, its Northern Territory coastline lying less than 400 miles to the south, across the Timor Sea. For some years after the Second World War, Canberra regarded the Portuguese colony as strategically important, but by 1962 its significance had faded in the view of the Australian political establishment. In that year, it was the assessment of the Australian government that Indonesian rule over East Timor would not pose any additional external threat and was therefore not unacceptable. Significantly, in September of 1974 Prime Minister Gough Whitlam, who was attracted to the notion that East Timor's integration with Indonesia was the best solution, conveyed that view to the Indonesian leader, President Suharto, at a meeting in Java.

Based on the strong support for decolonization and self-determination declared by Whitlam after he came into office in December 1972, the Timorese had a much more optimistic view of Australia's position. Furthermore, their idea that Australia owed a debt to East Timor, because of the extensive support Australian forces received during their commando operation against the Japanese in 1942,[4] had created an unshakable belief that Australia would help them out in the end.

While Foreign Minister Adam Malik was prepared to countenance independence for East Timor, his views were not in fact shared by Indonesia's most powerful military leaders, who had, from the very outset, different plans for East Timor's future. To be fair, it was not so much a desire for additional territory that motivated them — East Timor was, in the days before the recent off-shore oil discoveries, anything but an economic prize. One of their main concerns was that an independent East Timor would stimulate ambitions for independence among discontented nearby ethnic groups, such as the West Timorese and the Ambonese. Also, in the aftermath of the Vietnam War, Indonesia's military leadership was obsessed with the risk of Communist infiltration and insurgency. To the military, therefore, integration was the only acceptable solution for East Timor.

As it happened, the Australian government was in a position to head off Indonesia's designs on East Timor but did not do so. From their extensive intelligence monitoring of Indonesian military activities[5] they were aware, at its very inception, that a subversive operation had been put in place with the aim of bringing about integration.[6] Before the end of 1974 this operation was set up by a group of Indonesian generals, among them Lieutenant-General Ali Murtopo, Major-General Benny Murdani (a senior intelligence officer close to the president), and Lieutenant-General Yoga Sugama, then head of the intelligence services. The existence of this operation, code-named *"Operasi Komodo,"*[7] became known to U.S. and Australian intelligence agencies before the year was out. Its aim was to bring about the integration of East Timor at any cost, though preferably by nonmilitary means. Its first activities, which included a stream of clumsy propaganda vilifying the independence movement, the open backing of Apodeti, and some thinly disguised covert intelligence actions, had the effect not of dividing the two major parties, but of bringing them together.

Thus it was partly in reaction to this heavy-handed meddling that, early in January 1975, Fretilin[8] and UDT[9] formed a common front for independence. There is little doubt that Australia's accommodating stance, at the official level, strengthened the hands of the generals bent on the annexation of East Timor. Indeed, it is probable that the viability of this operation was predicated on the assumption that Australia would accept it. By the end of 1974, Indonesia was waging a strident propaganda campaign against Fretilin, in particular, and all Timorese in favor of independence in general. Fretilin was a party of the left, and the Indonesian military chiefs were quite paranoid about its activities. The Fretilin leaders were accused of being Communist and anti-Indonesian, and falsified accounts of links between them, Peking, and Hanoi were circulated. In reaction to the provocative propaganda outpourings from Jakarta, the Timorese themselves became increasingly hostile towards Indonesia.

In the first couple of months after April 1974, the Portuguese were rather indifferent towards the idea of independence for East Timor, with some military officers believing that joining with Indonesia made sense for such a small and undeveloped country. One senior official believed he had a responsibility to promote the idea of integration.[10] However, the apparent popular support for independence eventually convinced Lisbon and the colonial authorities that the Timorese were simply not disposed to merge with Indonesia. They saw themselves as being different, in terms of their culture, their languages, their political traditions, and their religions.[11] The aggressive approach of the Indonesians after August 1974 merely served to strengthen the East Timorese national consciousness, impelling the two major parties to form a coalition for independence. In the event, the Portuguese authorities commenced a decolonization program late in 1974, presenting the Timorese political elite with three options — full independence, continuing with Portugal under some new and more democratic arrangement, or integration with Indonesia.

The year 1975 proved to be a turbulent one for East Timor. As a result of political instability in Portugal, and the demoralization of the overseas administration, the decolonization program for Timor soon ran into difficulties. Political turmoil in Lisbon weakened the colonial power's administrative control, and the Indonesian generals heading Operasi Komodo exploited the deteriorating situation subtly and subversively. By mid-autumn of that year political differences had surfaced between the two major parties, and in an Operasi Komodo operation, guided by Lt. General Murtopo himself, the Indonesians sought to divide the independence movement. Their propaganda offensive against Fretilin was intensified, while the UDT leaders were invited to Jakarta — and courted. They were lectured, sometimes by Murtopo himself, on the dangers of Communist subversion, were exhorted to break the coalition with Fretilin, and were sent, at Jakarta's expense, on tours of anti-Communist political centers in Asia — to South Korea, the Philippines, and Taiwan. Furthermore, fabricated evidence of links between the Fretilin leaders, on the one hand, and Peking and Hanoi, on the other, was passed on to them.

At least two of the conservative Timorese leaders, Lopes da Cruz and Mousinho, were actually recruited by Bakin, the powerful Indonesian military intelligence agency.[12] By the middle of 1975, relations between the two Timorese parties had become so tense that talks between them broke down completely. At this time, rumors were circulated by Bakin agents that Fretilin was planning a coup and encouraging UDT leaders to act hastily and rashly. [13]

Early in August 1975, Lt. General Murtopo informed UDT leaders, who were visiting Jakarta, that his intelligence agents had uncovered a Fretilin conspiracy to launch a coup, and he encouraged them to take pre-emptive action.[14] Days after their return, these UDT leaders, with what military support they could muster, launched an abortive coup in Dili — abortive, because within three weeks the party and its followers had been overwhelmed by Fretilin. They were defeated not because of external military intervention, but because most Timorese troops, who formed the majority of the colonial military establishment, favored the left-wing party. In this brief but intense conflict[15] the Portuguese, whose administrative apparatus had been reduced to a small number of officials and fewer than 100 combat troops, withdrew to the offshore island of Atauro.[16]

The Indonesian military, their plans having backfired, would have no truck with the independence movement and ignored its overtures. *Operasi Komodo's* military commanders sought to persuade President Suharto to authorize direct military intervention, but the president, who was unenthusiastic for any moves that would prejudice Indonesia's international standing (especially in Southeast Asia and in the United States) as a nation without territorial ambitions, continued to hesitate until September when Generals Murtopo, Murdani, and Sugama (then head of Bakin) managed to secure his consent to a military operation against East Timor. They were able to assure him that the governments of greatest importance to Indonesia, among them the United States, Japan, Australia, the Netherlands, and ASEAN (Association of Southeast Asian Nations) would accommodate a military operation to secure East Timor's integration into Indonesia.

Two weeks later, Indonesia's first major military action against East Timorese territory was launched: It was carried out as a covert operation and involved an attack on the border village of Balibo. Its casualties were to include the five members of two television teams from Australia.[17]

Weeks before this assault, the victorious Fretilin leaders had sought to assuage Indonesian fears, and had encouraged the Portuguese to return and resume decolonization. But there was no response from the Portuguese, whose government in Lisbon was still in crisis. The Indonesian response was a series of military attacks over the border from West Timor. The official news agency *Antara* claimed that the "anti-Fretilin forces" had regrouped and were counterattacking.

With the Portuguese having failed to respond to their request to return and resume decolonization, the Indonesians attacking from the west, and the international community ignoring their plight, Fretilin's decision unilaterally to declare East Timor an independent republic was hardly surprising.

The Invasion and Its Aftermath

Having in a way provoked Fretilin's hasty decision unilaterally to declare East Timor independent, the Indonesians lost no time in mounting a full-scale invasion — an amphibious attack on the capital, Dili. The status of East Timor was therefore changed abruptly on December 7, 1975,[18] when a combined military and naval force, under the overall command of Major-General Murdani, moved in from the sea. From the considerable evidence accumulated over the past several decades, it is clear that the invasion and subjugation of East Timor, especially in the early stages, was carried out with scant regard for the lives, let alone rights, of the Timorese people. Not only was the act of aggression itself a violation of the UN Charter, but the brutal way it was carried out over a period of several years constitutes genocide.

In the very first days of the invasion, rampaging Indonesian troops engaged in an orgy of indiscriminate killing, rape, and torture. Large-scale public executions were carried out — women being included among the victims — suggesting a systematic campaign of terror. In some villages whole communities were slaughtered, except for young children.

Outraged by these atrocities, the small but determined Timorese army bitterly contested the advance of the invading forces, and in terrain ideal for guerrilla warfare they were able to inflict heavy losses on the attackers, until the early 1980s, denying the ABRI[19] effective control outside the main towns and administrative centers. The retaliation of the invading force to this stiff challenge to integration was the imposition of a harsh and oppressive occupation. In the areas under Indonesian control, serious human rights violations were a daily occurrence, forcing tens of thousands of Timorese to seek refuge behind Fretilin lines.

The invasion force, which was soon to amount to more than 30,000 troops, entered the Portuguese colony from the west, where East Timor adjoins Indonesia, and in landings at major towns on the north coast, such as Baucau and Maubara. Thousands of Timorese were killed in the first weeks of the invasion when, from all accounts, troops went on the rampage, no doubt in response to the unexpectedly determined Timorese resistance to the invasion. In Dili there were a number of public executions — including along the wharf area where more than 100 were reportedly shot, at Santa Cruz, at the Military Police barracks, and at Tasitolo, near the airport. Also, in the small towns of Maubara and Liquica and at other villages in the interior, Indonesian military units carried out public executions, numbering from 20 to more than 100 persons.

While conditions in the occupied areas were harsh and oppressive, indiscriminate killing, raping, and torture were even more widespread in the disputed areas. In their advance into the mountainous interior, especially where the advance was being hotly contested, the Indonesian forces killed many of the Timorese they encountered. The biggest single killing reported to the author by the Timorese driver of one of the Indonesian trucks occurred in 1975 at Lakmanan, near the western border, where invading troops returning from a stiff encounter with Fretilin turned their guns on a large temporary encampment of Timorese. One of these witnesses estimated that as many as 2000 were killed over a period of several hours.[20]

As Indonesia sought to overpower the armed resistance and to suppress opposition to integration in occupied areas, tens of thousands of Timorese were to perish up to the end of 1979. During this period, East Timor was virtually sealed off from the outside world. The International Red Cross, which had been present in strength until just before the invasion, did not regain access to the territory until the second half of 1979, almost four years after the invasion.[21]

Although initially it was the intention of most townsfolk to remain in their homes and communities, the widespread killing, the torture, and the raping committed by the invading troops resulted in the flight of a large proportion of the population into the interior, to the comparative safety of the mountain districts under the control of Fretilin. However, it was in the mountainous interior of the island that the greatest loss of life was to occur in the following three years. Most of the deaths were from famine and related diseases, but it was the harsh treatment meted out by the Indonesians that prompted the Timorese to flee to the mountains.

Because of the absence of demographic records, whether kept by the invaders or by other authorities, no precise account of the human cost of the invasion and its aftermath exists. However, recent Indonesian census statistics provide evidence that it attained genocidal proportions. Before the invasion East Timor's population was about 690,000, and growing at about 2 percent. It follows that by, for example, 1991, there should have been more than 950,000 people; but based on Indonesian statistics, in East Timor, which had been designated the 27th province of Indonesia, there were only about 740,000 people.[22] Of this number, though, as many as 140,000 were non-Timorese who had, in recent years, moved into the territory from elsewhere in Indonesia, some of them transmigrants and others opportunistic drifters. The upshot is that, in effect, the Timorese population, some 16 years after the invasion, was 12 percent less than what it was in 1975.

The annexation of East Timor had a drastic effect on all aspects of life in the community. Before the invasion, the ethnic and cultural patterns in the territory were exceedingly complex but, aside from some special characteristics, they resembled the patterns in the nearby islands of Eastern Nusatenggara.[23] The population was essentially Autronesian in character, but with a noticeable Melanesian influence. It reflected a long procession of migrations from west, north, and the east. But it would be an oversimplification to describe the territory as culturally part of Indonesia, if only because of the great ethnic and cultural diversity within this sprawling archipelagic nation. To call a Timorese "Indonesian" is rather like calling a Kurd an Iraqi or a Tibetan Chinese, labels that are imprecise and attract resentment. The Timorese were not, however, antagonistic towards people from other parts of the archipelago, at least before Indonesia began to meddle in the affairs of the island.[24] But in the past they had regarded the occasional visiting Indonesia fishing vessels with some suspicion. Perhaps this was because, unlike the Javanese or Buginese, the Timorese were not themselves a seafaring people and felt threatened by outsiders with these skills.

The rugged mountainous interior of East Timor provided excellent conditions for Fretilin's guerrilla campaign, but the resistance forces were not in a position to provide the basic needs of the tens of thousands of people who sought refuge within this territory. Food and medical supplies were inadequate, and the Timorese were subjected to constant air attacks (including, for a short period, the use of napalm). The Timorese were bombed and strafed, and once the Indonesian air force acquired Bronco anti-insurgency aircraft from the United States, these attacks intensified. In the two years following the invasion, the Timorese leaders did manage to feed the people within their lines by developing the agricultural resources available to them in the rich valleys, but according to reports from Fretilin, in 1978 these farms were subject to air attacks by AURI[25] aircraft. According to one report, chemical substances were dropped on the crops, causing the plants to die. By 1978, the food situation behind Fretilin lines was desperate, and the Timorese leaders began encouraging their people to return to Indonesian-occupied areas; the resistance forces were no longer able to feed them, nor to provide even the most basic of medical treatment.

Initially, when these "refugees" moved into occupied territory, their reception was anything but humane. Some suspected Fretilin supporters were summarily executed, while many others were beaten or tortured at the slightest provocation.[26] The refugees were forced into resettlement camps, where food and medical facilities were grossly inadequate. In 1979, the first international aid workers to enter the territory reported that the basic needs of the Timorese in these centers were being seriously neglected and that thousands were dying needlessly from famine and disease.

Reports on the grim situation in East Timor began to come out of the territory as early as the end of 1976. In that year a confidential report from Catholic Church sources depicted a scene of oppression and wanton killing. Its authors suggested that in the year since the invasion as many as 60,000 Timorese might have lost their lives.[27] Was the international community aware of this very heavy loss of life and, if so, how did it react? In fact, these early reports aroused very little international attention. East Timor was remote, little known, and without any strategic or economic importance, even to the colonial power. While the UN itself promptly condemned the invasion and called on Indonesia to withdraw its forces, its pronouncements were mostly vague and irresolute.[28]

There is a more sinister aspect to this dismal situation. When the gravity of the humanitarian situation in this territory began to unfold, East Timor could easily have been made an issue of international concern by nations like the United States or Australia if their governments had chosen to do so.[29] In the 1970s, however, Indonesia had begun to assume a new importance in the eyes of the major Western powers. It was large, Muslim, and oil-producing, and the archipelago straddled the division between the strategically important Pacific and Indian Oceans. And the Suharto regime, despite its undemocratic character, fulfilled important political conditions — it was anti-Communist, it was development-oriented, and it had created a facade of stability and harmony.

Under those circumstances, the Western governments with the greatest interest in Indonesia — that were also best placed to monitor events in East Timor — chose to play down the reports, most of them emanating from Church sources in Dili, that Indonesian military operations were inflicting heavy loss of life on the general population. In the Australian parliament, for example, these reports were repeatedly alluded to by official sources as being unproven, or ill-founded and exaggerated.

If the foreign missions in Jakarta were aware of just how serious was the humanitarian situation, they were careful not to disclose it in their public statements. In the case of the missions representing Australia, Canada, and the United States, the extent to which their diplomats were able to report on this situation was, in the experience of this writer, diminished by the tacit support that their governments had given to integration. According credibility to the reports from organizations such as the Catholic Church in East Timor would have been tantamount to admitting by implication a measure of responsibility.

Some of the reports made public could not have been honestly arrived at. For example, early in 1977 one U.S. State Department official told members of the U.S. Congress that only 2000 Timorese had died as a result of the invasion. A few weeks later another U.S. official, Robert Oakley, came up with a revised figure of 10,000, which yet another official source later qualified with the comment that many of these deaths had occurred in the fighting between Fretilin and UDT.[30] Australian official responses were delivered in a similar vein. Their statements appeared to be designed to minimize the seriousness of the situation on the ground in East Timor and, in so doing, to discredit reports that Indonesian troops were responsible for widespread death and destruction. It was a blatant attempt to deflect international criticism of Indonesian actions. Thus, in 1978, when conditions in the territory were being described as nightmarish, the Australian government led by Prime Minister Fraser felt able to take the extraordinary step of recognizing de facto the annexation.[31]

By the end of 1979, however, the devastating consequences of Indonesia's military annexation of East Timor could no longer be concealed. And so, some four years after the invasion, when Indonesian authorities finally allowed a small number of international aid workers to conduct a survey of the humanitarian needs of the province, the dimensions of the tragedy began to emerge. The human misery they encountered shocked even some officials with experience in Africa and Southeast Asia. Their estimates suggested that in the preceding four years, Timor had lost between a tenth and a third of its population and that 200,000 of the remainder were in appalling conditions in "resettlement camps," which one official, who had previously served in Cambodia, described as among the worst he had seen.[32]

These revelations should have shocked the world into demanding that Indonesia withdraw from the former Portuguese colony, but that did not happen. Not one of the major powers was prepared to press Indonesia to reconsider its seizure of the territory and to bring any real pressure to bear on the Suharto government. The best that Washington and Canberra could come up with was to urge Indonesia to admit international humanitarian relief organizations.[33] These requests, which brought some response from Indonesia, resulted in the readmission to the province of the International Red Cross, which had been forced to leave on the eve of the invasion, in the face of Indonesia's refusal to guarantee the necessary protection.[34]

It was to be more than a decade after the invasion before Jakarta could claim to exercise administrative control over most of the island. Into the late 1990s armed resistance continued, despite annual large-scale operations by Indonesian forces, who invariably outnumbered the guerrillas by more than ten to one.[35] Thanks to the intervention of international agencies, and the work of some dedicated Indonesians, material conditions in Timor improved markedly during the 1980s. However, serious human rights abuses, mostly by the Indonesian military, continued to occur throughout the 1990s. In one annual report after another issued by Amnesty International, the authorities were accused of summary executions, "disappearances," torture, and imprisonment on the grounds of conscience.[36]

Notable examples of indiscriminate killing occurred at Creras, near Viqueque, in August 1983 and in Dili in November 1991. The Creras incident was first recounted to the author by a priest from the district some months later, and its details confirmed in 2001 by a leading East Timorese, Mario Carrascalao, who in 1983 was governor of the province. He told me that shortly after the incident he went to the area and personally investigated it. According to these accounts, raping by Indonesian troops led to an attack by the Falintil (the military arm of Fretilin) on the Indonesian military unit to which the soldiers belonged, an attack that resulted in the killing of 16 Indonesian troops. In the following days, Indonesian forces, allegedly under the command of Major Prabowo Subianto (later Lieutenant-General), carried out severe reprisals against the population of the immediate region. According to Carrascalao, over 1000 people, including many women and children, were massacred.

Another case of indiscriminate killing was the Dili massacre of November 1991, which cost the lives of more than 200 young Timorese. It occurred when Indonesian troops opened fire on unarmed demonstrators, most of them students, near the Santa Cruz cemetery in Dili. The incident was widely reported in the international media, thanks to the presence of foreign observers. The Timorese were about to engage in a peaceful protest at the killing of one of their number, as well as at the forced integration of the territory. For several minutes Indonesian troops fired into the crowd of demonstrators, killing many of them. From evidence that subsequently became available, it appears that most of the killings took place after the firing had stopped. A large number of the wounded were killed in crude fashion, some of them over the next two or three days, with their bodies being secretly disposed of at a site near Tibar.

Largely in response to an international reaction, the Indonesian government set up a Committee of Inquiry (*Komisi Penjelidik Nasional*), which issued its Preliminary Report on December 26, 1991. While the report acknowledged some mistakes and lack of control, it absolved the authorities, including the military command in East Timor, from any responsibility for the massacre. While several senior military officers, including the East Timor and regional commanders, were removed from their posts, they were not formally charged with any offenses. Subsequently, nine junior-ranking soldiers and one policeman were to face court-martial, but the charges laid against them were of a relatively minor nature. None of the troops was charged with killing, and all received relatively light sentences. For the Timorese demonstrators, however, it was a different matter. More than a dozen trials were held and, although none was charged with carrying weapons or using violence, most received severe sentences ranging from six years to life imprisonment.[37]

The Santa Cruz massacre is significant not only because it occurred 16 years after the beginning of Indonesia's military action to annex East Timor. It also happened at a time when the Suharto regime, and governments friendly to it, were seeking to assure the international community that the East Timor situation was settled, and no further action against Indonesia was therefore warranted. Government officials in, for example, the United States, Canada, and Australia were insisting that indiscriminate killing, and most other forms of mistreatment, had been ended by a more enlightened regional administration.

While the humanitarian situation in the province eased in the mid-1990s, a new crisis unfolded following the collapse of the Suharto regime in May 1998, and the launching of a more conciliatory policy towards the East Timorese by his successor, Habibie. By the middle of that year, self-determination and the possibility of independence was again on the agenda. The new president began a dialogue with both Timorese leaders and senior UN officials, including Kofi Annan himself, the new UN Secretary-General, who stepped up the world body's efforts to achieve a just solution to what, at that time, was the biggest issue of its kind remaining on the agenda of the Decolonization Commission.

These new moves, and the development of a more democratic regime in Jakarta, led to two conflicting developments: on the one hand, a sharp increase in East Timorese demands for self-determination and the right to the choice of independence, and on the other, a strong reaction on the part of the Indonesian military command. These developments were of particular concern to the politically powerful Special Forces Command (*Kopassus*), which had played a leading role in the illegal seizure of the former Portuguese province, and in the subsequent administration of the territory. In the years of military operations against the Timorese resistance, many thousands of Indonesian troops had lost their lives, and the idea of giving up the territory was therefore anathema to the commanders.

In the event, senior Kopassus generals organized the establishment of a militia force, recruited from among the East Timorese minority who favored continuation of Indonesian rule. The structure of the militia was designed by Kopassus, while arms, military training, and other funding were provided from various government sources. Under these arrangements, each of the 13 districts had a militia unit. These troops were exhorted to wage a campaign of violence and intimidation against East Timorese who favored independence.

Early in 1999, President Habibie announced his readiness to agree to a plebiscite on his offer of autonomy, assuring the Timorese that the right to independence would be accepted should the offer be rejected. The militia campaign of violence was stepped up with TNI officers, who called on the paramilitary forces to attack and kill pro-independence supporters — in some cases, the militia were exhorted to kill supporters' families. What transpired was, in effect, a conspiracy by senior TNI generals aimed at preventing the loss of East Timor and at sabotaging UN efforts in support of what was regarded internationally as a much-delayed act of self-determination. These commanders may have operated independently, but clearly their operations were known to the Indonesian defense force commander, General Wiranto.

The presence of United Nations Mission in East Timor (UNAMET) after June 1999 hampered this campaign of violence but by the time the plebiscite was held in August of that year dozens of East Timorese had been killed in attacks organized or aided by the Indonesian military, and thousands more had been dislocated by the militia terror. As the plebiscite approached, the military commanders realized that, regardless of the militia operations, they were going to lose the vote. It was then that the military command devised a campaign of killing and destruction, as a punishment of the East Timorese for their disloyalty and their humiliation of the Indonesian military. The operation, designated *"Operasi Guntur"* (Operation Thunder), was launched within hours of the announcement of the results of the plebiscite (78.5 percent voted against acceptance of the autonomy). TNI troops, aided by their militia, swarmed over the province in a campaign of destruction. In less than three weeks 72 percent of all buildings and houses were destroyed or damaged, and hundreds of East Timorese were killed, many of them in massacres at Suai, at Maliana, and in the Oecussi enclave. More than 250,000 people were deported to West Timor. The casualty rate would have been much higher had not hundreds of thousands of Timorese fled to the mountains where they faced severe food shortages — a crisis, though, that was soon eased by UN and Australian emergency airdrops.

Unlike in 1975, this genocidal crime attracted an immediate global response, with the UN Security Council calling on Indonesia to end the rampage and allow for the implementation of the outcome of the plebiscite. A force composed of a coalition of the willing, led by Australia, was instructed by the UN to enter the territory immediately after its authorization by President Habibie. The nightmare of the previous weeks ended, but East Timor was left in a totally devastated state, and without the basic elements of a community infrastructure. The loss of life from this military operation is still not fully known (some of the bodies were disposed of in the deep-sea channel north of the island), but the author believes that it could exceed 2000.

The following November a UN mission with a comprehensive mandate to prepare the country for independence began its mission, ending a quarter of a century of harsh occupation. Reconstruction of the nation's destroyed towns and villages began, and after considerable delay the return of those who had been forced to go to the Indonesian part of the island was negotiated by UN authorities. The UN has been less successful in its quest to bring to justice those ultimately responsible for these atrocities. According to the findings of the International Commission of Enquiry established by CHR Resolution 1999/S-4/1, "ultimately the Indonesian Army was responsible for the intimidation, terror, killings, and other acts of violence experienced by the people of East Timor before and after the popular consultations [plebiscite]." A more damning report came from Indonesia's Human Rights Commission's special committee, implicating the military, including General Wiranto, as being responsible for these heinous actions.

The obvious answer would have been an ad hoc international tribunal but enthusiasm for such an outcome soon wilted. That was due to several reasons. First, Indonesia came under the leadership of President Wahid, a leading reformer, who insisted that Indonesia would itself establish a tribunal and bring to justice the military commanders responsible for the crimes committed. Second, Wahid encountered great difficulty in implementing his reforms, and one of the casualties was the proposed tribunal. Third, though it finally came into being some months after Megawati Sukarnoputri took office, it was a pale shadow of the intended tribunal, its terms of reference offering an escape for the generals responsible for setting up the militia. Indeed, its outcome has been a farce. The senior officer, who gave orders at the Suai massacre, has been acquitted. Other killers have not even been charged. More seriously, not one of the conspirators who planned the campaign of terror and killing has even appeared before the court — except to witness its proceedings! One senior officer was given a brief sentence, but his case is subject to an appeal.

In East Timor itself, a number of militia were captured, and after a considerable delay several were sentenced to lengthy prison terms. Unfortunately, for several months the efforts of UNTAET's prosecutors suffered from poor direction. Then, under the new management of the prosecutor-general's office, the process was expedited, but with the office no longer being a direct UN responsibility it encountered political criticism from the leaders of the newly independent state, who were anxious to avoid a confrontation with Jakarta in the first difficult years of independence. The recent indictment of a number of Indonesian military commanders attracted an angry rejection from Jakarta and a cool response from Dili.

Responsibility for the Genocide

There can be little doubt that direct responsibility for the killing in East Timor rests with the Indonesian military forces. From the outset, the invading forces had an opportunity to extend maximum protection to the noncombatant population, in accordance with the Geneva Conventions. These basic rights the invaders almost totally ignored, at huge cost to Indonesia, as it turned out.[38] A humane and disciplined occupation would have moderated the attitudes of the Timorese themselves, and the character of the resistance would have been radically different. As it turned out, the senseless killing and harsh occupation policies in general, especially under General Dading Kalbuardi, stiffened the courage, determination, and endurance of the *Falintil,* the military arm of Fretilin. Indeed, because the armed resistance was effectively isolated, and was able to attract little international support, their will to resist may have collapsed much earlier had it not been for the harsh nature of Indonesian military rule in East Timor.

From time to time it has been alleged that many of the Timorese casualties were caused by the civil war, or later internecine conflicts. In fact, between 1500 and 2000 were killed in the brief civil war of August 1975,[39] but there is no evidence that tribal conflicts occurred after Indonesia's invasion. On the other hand, it is known that the resistance forces killed several hundred collaborators over a period of ten years.

It has been argued, especially by some apologists for the Suharto regime, that none of this killing was ordered from Jakarta and that most of the blame rests with undisciplined or impulsive troops. Following the killings at Santa Cruz cemetery, for example, officials in Washington, Canberra, and certain other Western capitals responded along these lines. Yet, governments cannot be absolved of responsibility so conveniently. Even if these killings were not ordered by the government of Indonesia, it remains the final responsible authority. Moreover, the government can hardly claim ignorance of human rights abuses of this nature, because they were so frequently reported and the focus of regular protests by organizations like Amnesty International and Asia Watch.

The Suharto government's line of defense was especially facile if we consider the Santa Cruz tragedy. The Indonesian decision to set up a commission of investigation was clearly a response to international outrage, and not a spontaneous reaction to the news of the killing. In the immediate aftermath of the massacre, the reaction from Jakarta was defensive, while the military's response was dismissive, even defiant.[40] There can be little doubt that the Indonesian authorities would have reacted differently had foreign observers not been present. It may well be that no order to kill indiscriminately has ever been issued by Jakarta — even at the highest military levels. Nevertheless, it is inconceivable that the military command had been unaware of the indiscriminate killing and summary executions perpetrated by the military during those 16 years. Yet there is no evidence that, until the Santa Cruz incident, any of the perpetrators were ever placed on trial or disciplined.

It is impossible not to conclude, therefore, that such gross violations of fundamental human rights had been tolerated by the government of Indonesia. Certainly, within the military itself such killings had become acceptable behavior. In Indonesia, military and political leadership tends to merge at the top, and therefore it follows that the top-ranking responsible authorities in Indonesia had long been aware that the behavior of the military forces in East Timor had resulted in the decimation of the indigenous population.

Clearly, genocide, in the form of the destruction of a significant part of a group, can occur as the result of inhumane and irresponsible actions, without a formal intention being identified. Troops can be indoctrinated with hatred in what many might accept as the normal preparation for combat; that is, the strengthening of the soldier's will to fight. In Timor, for example, in the early weeks of the fighting some of the Indonesian forces were told they were fighting Communists, who had been the subject of hatred and indiscriminate killing after 1965, because of the PKI's alleged conspiracy to overthrow the government and set up a Marxist state.[41] And ideological hatred breeds racial hatred and intolerance. The way the annexation of East Timor was carried out inevitably provoked an irreconcilable antagonism on the Timorese side. Dislike, therefore, was mutual, causing Indonesian troops to care little about the lives of Timorese, whose language they did not speak and whose religion most of them did not share.

On the other hand, there is no evidence that the Indonesian government, or for that matter the military leadership, sought, as a matter of deliberate policy, to destroy the Timorese people as a race or ethnic group. Yet it cannot escape the charge that it was aware of the wanton human destruction, especially between 1975 and 1982, and the organized militia violence that culminated in massive destruction, wanton killing, and large-scale deportations in 1999.

There is one aspect of intention worthy of closer scrutiny. It could be argued that when it became apparent to Indonesia's highest political and military authorities that the majority of the East Timorese were opposed to integration, the Indonesian military command in the province sought to destroy the will of the people for independence. This meant destroying a key element in the Timorese identity, that is, changing their identity from that of a people seeking to shape their own political future to a radically different status, that of being a loyal component of the Indonesian state.

If they had initially aimed to achieve this end by persuasion — by winning hearts and minds — why did their invading force behave like barbarians? Why did they torture, rape, and kill indiscriminately? Was not this killing and other inhuman actions, which inevitably led to tens of thousands of deaths, part of a plan to destroy the desire for independence and the will to oppose integration?

If we accept the words of no less an authority than General Murdani,[42] the principal targets of the occupation authorities for eradication were, and, for that matter, continued to be for years to come, the independence movement leaders and their supporters. But the government's oppressive policies ensured that the vast majority of Timorese still yearned for independence if only a few of them were prepared to take up arms. If the Indonesian military had persisted with the idea that all support for independence must be eliminated, it would have placed the majority of the population at risk.

The Timor situation highlights an important dimension of the subject of this book — cultural genocide. In Portuguese times, foreigners made up only a small percentage of the population of East Timor. The largest minority was the Chinese. The Portuguese, even if we include their military, never amounted to more than a few thousand people.

By the early 1990s, outsiders — that is, people who had come from elsewhere in Indonesia after the invasion — made up one fifth of the population. In terms of power, they were not a mere minority, but the successors of the colonial power. In fact, their presence was infinitely more pervasive and had a far greater impact on Timorese society. From the latter's point of view, these intruders dominated virtually all aspects of the government of the province. In the economy, as well as in government and the military, the Indonesian role was much more powerful and commanding than was the place of the Portuguese, even under the Salazar dictatorship.

The Indonesian newcomers were very much a ruling class, dominating as they did the military and the civil government. Thousands of transmigrants moved into some of the province's best agricultural lands, in some cases displacing the indigenous inhabitants. And a flood of informal arrivals, mostly drifters seeking to exploit any economic opportunity, swelled the populations of the major towns. This massive intrusion of outsiders, and Jakarta's efforts to change Timorese ways and attitudes, was undermining the very identity of the Timorese, the least "Indonesian" of the communities of the archipelago.

Special Characteristics of the Timor Case

The case of East Timor presents a number of distinctive elements. First and foremost, it is a live issue, an issue of our time as distinct from being a lesson of history. The question of culpability for the crimes committed is still before the United Nations. It is one of the issues that had not been resolved when UNTAET's mandate ended, leaving the world body with a continuing responsibility. There has been strong pressure for the setting up of an ad hoc international tribunal, but the proposal has attracted little support from the UN Security Council, despite widespread criticism of the conduct of the Indonesian tribunal. The low level of international interest has discouraged some of East Timor's leaders from pursuing such an outcome. Hence, more emphasis has been placed on the reconciliation process than the exposure of past crimes and action against those responsible for them. Although East Timor's position has changed radically over the past ten years, this case continues to highlight the frailty of international resolve when it comes to the small and unimportant in the global power play. It is a reminder of the vulnerability of small states outside the mainstream of global political and economic interests.

While past international responses at times caused Indonesian political leaders some discomfort, they have always been able to resist such pressures. The Santa Cruz massacre illustrates this point. The official response from countries like Australia, the United States, and Japan was restrained, even nonjudgmental. Most of those governments, who were quick to denounce relatively recent cases of indiscriminate killing in Iraq and Bosnia-Herzegovina, did not resort to the same kind of blunt language in their responses to the massacre of more than 200 Timorese in November 1991.

On the whole, in its seizure of East Timor, Indonesia was able to exploit the prevailing Cold War context. Indeed, the Suharto regime's Western friends to an extent encouraged the annexation by accepting as credible Jakarta's alleged fears of Communist insurgency in the post-Vietnam years. Perhaps the most disturbing aspect of this case is that these crimes against humanity went virtually unchallenged at a time when acts of aggression and oppression were being challenged in almost every other part of the world.

Third, the annexation of East Timor could in fact have been averted, had Indonesia's Western friends acted responsibly in the 1974–1975 period. The Suharto regime's moves to annex the colony were carefully devised against the anticipated reactions of countries like Australia and the United States, whose intelligence agencies were familiar with the unfolding conspiracy. It is in this context that the genocide dimensions of the problem are profoundly disturbing. Most Western governments, especially those members of Indonesia's aid consortium, were aware, more than a decade before the Santa Cruz killing, of the genocidal impact of Jakarta's military operations in East Timor, that is, in the terms of Article II(c) of the Convention. The failure of the IGGI (Inter-Governmental Group on Indonesia) members, in particular, to take up the issue at a time when the Suharto regime was heavily dependent on Western aid was at best shameful. Ever since the anti-Communist Suharto regime came to power it had been sensitive to the concerns of major Western powers like the United States. Despite this fact, even when the extent of loss of life in East Timor became evident in the early 1980s, the continued acceptability of Indonesia rule of the former Portuguese colony was never seriously questioned.

Fourth, although the Timor case was for more than two decades before the United Nations, the problem was not effectively addressed until after the fall of President Suharto, the collapse of his regime brought about by causes unrelated to the Timor problem. East Timor is arguably the only remnant of the once-extensive European empires to have been annexed by its neighbor, with the virtual collusion of many of those nations who today regard themselves as being at the forefront of the international movement to promote universal respect for human rights, including the right to self-determination.

The Timor Case as a Contributor to Genocide Studies

The case of East Timor is a significant one, particularly as a definitive case of genocide within the terms of Article II of the UN Convention on the Prevention and Punishment of the Crime of Genocide. Although the question of the denial of the right to self-determination has now been resolved, the commission of the serious crimes committed have yet to be appropriately dealt with by the international community. The violation against the people of East Timor has some classical characteristics, in the sense that it resulted from an act of aggression by the large power next door. However, it occurred within a contemporary historical framework; that is, an extensive body of human rights principles and laws had set down protective parameters for the international community. It also occurred at a time when acts of aggression of this kind were no longer tolerated by the UN system, as the cases of the Falklands (1982) and Kuwait (1990) dramatically demonstrated.

On the other hand, the lesson of East Timor is that some things have not changed, despite the growing intolerance of the international community toward gross human rights violations involving mass killing. The East Timorese suffered from their country's remoteness, from its lack of economic and strategic importance, and conversely, from the perceived importance of the violator, today the world's largest Islamic nation, which forms a strategically and economically important division between the Indian and Pacific Oceans. However, one of the most disturbing aspects of the case is that the perpetrators of those atrocities were in practice shielded from international scrutiny by countries like Australia and the United States, which pride themselves on their commitment to human rights.

Perhaps the most disturbing aspect of the experience of East Timor is that it highlights just how difficult it is to invoke the Genocide Convention, even in circumstances where the evidence that grave violations have occurred is substantial and persistent. Indeed, the Timor case suggests that the Convention is so difficult to invoke that it is perceived by the victims and others as being virtually irrelevant as an international legal protection or recourse against this monstrous form of crime. On a number of occasions at the United Nations, Timorese representatives and their supporters examined the possibility of invoking the Convention before the International Court of Justice, but in each case experts cast doubt on this course of action. As for the governments of Australia and the United States, "genocide" is a term that has been studiously avoided, even when there have been expressions of concern at the human rights situation in Timor.

The East Timor case also brings into focus the factor of cultural genocide, which is of crucial importance when the victims of aggression are massively outnumbered, in terms of population. While this aspect is not specified in the Convention, it remains extremely important, as the Timor cases attests.

It is very likely that deliberate "Indonesianization" would have submerged Timorese culture, ultimately risking its destruction, had not unforeseen circumstances led to a radical change of policy by the Indonesian government.

Eyewitness Accounts: Genocide in East Timor

Since Indonesian troops invaded East Timor close to 30 years ago, eyewitness accounts have provided mounting evidence of gross human rights violations, including those of a genocidal character. Such testimonies have been collected by professional human rights agencies such as Amnesty International and Asia Watch and, at the time of writing, a UN Supported Truth and Reconciliation Commission. In the past, researchers, including this writer, encountered a major obstacle to the recording of these accounts — the informants invariably insisted that their identities should not be made public. A few witnesses spoke out publicly but the vast majority were extremely reluctant to be identified. Until the end of Indonesian occupation in 1999, and even in its aftermath, the reason advanced was understandable enough — fear of reprisals by the Indonesian security authorities against relatives and friends in East Timor, or against refugees remaining in West Timor under duress.

Unlike other issues of this nature, the Timor saga was not, at least for close to 25 years, a matter of past history: It was an ongoing drama. While the authorities responsible for the most serious violations may no longer have been in the territory, the regime whose policies enabled them to take place was still firmly in power. And while the way East Timor was seized had been the subject of widespread criticism, there was not a serious attempt, until 1999, by the major powers to persuade Indonesia to withdraw from East Timor and to allow a process of self-determination to take place. Indeed, for many years, there was simply not enough international pressure, nor foreign or human rights presence in Timor, to discourage retaliation and victimization against advocates of self-determination. Until very recently, in fact, accounts of harassment by security authorities of the relatives of those Timorese involved in the resistance and related activities continued to filter through to outside human rights agencies.

While the penalties may have eased in the mid-1990s, the TNI led campaign of violence, deportations, and massive destruction that occurred in 1999 demonstrated that the nature of the military-dominated administration remained unchanged. Its intolerance of opposition to integration is well recorded, including several actions by the military commander in the aftermath of the Santa Cruz incident. If anything, political oppression was intensified in 1992, especially after the appointment of Governor Abilio Osorio Soares, who had long been associated with the Indonesian intelligence network.

Between 1991 and 1999 few foreigners were able to gain free access to East Timor. In those circumstances, it was very difficult to make contact with witnesses of indiscriminate killings and torture, let alone offer some protection against reprisals from the military authorities. This problem was highlighted during the trial of Xanana Gusmao in Dili, when the defense counsel informed the court that he was having difficulty in persuading witnesses to appear on behalf of the accused. The situation changed after the UN intervention in 1999, but the massive upheaval caused by the TNI's final destructive campaign of revenge, and UN and Timorese rehabilitation priorities, led to considerable delay in addressing the atrocities perpetrated during the 24 years of Indonesian occupation. Only in 2000 were these incidents starting to be investigated.

As for the TNI perpetrators, although several of the commanders have been brought before an Indonesian tribunal in response to internal pressures, most have been acquitted. Only one officer received a light sentence, but that case was summarily dismissed by a higher court. The UN-led prosecutor-general's office in East Timor has issued a number of indictments against Indonesian officers, as well as militia members, but so far these have been ignored by the government of Indonesia. It remains a matter of grave concern that most of the indicted commanders have been rewarded with promotions, with several of them subsequently occupying responsible operations roles in TNI military actions in West Papua and Aceh.

The following are selections of accounts that were brought to the direct attention of the author in the aftermath of the invasion. Although much new material now being assembled is available, these testimonies are typical in character.

Account 1

The Invasion of Dili. Etelvina Correia was interviewed by the author some months after the invasion. She was chosen because of her clear and unhesitating account, and because she was one of the few witnesses at the scene of the killing. Following is an abbreviated version of her account.

The attack on Dili began at about 4 A.M. on December 7. Etelvina Correia was in the church, which is located in the waterfront area. Some time later paratroops began to land (some of them dropped into the water). At 7 A.M. she saw paratroops shoot a woman in the parish garage and later three women in front of the church, although their hands were raised. The Indonesian soldiers then ordered all of the people in the vicinity of the church to go inside. Next day, Etelvina and the others were ordered by troops to go to the wharf area. There 20 women — Chinese and Timorese — were taken out in front. Some of them had children who were weeping. The soldiers tore the children from the women who were then shot one by one, with the crowd being ordered to count after each execution. At 2 P.M. on the same day, 59 men, including Chinese and Timorese, were taken to the wharf and executed in the same way. Again the witnesses were ordered at gunpoint to count. They were told that these killings were in reprisal for the killing of a paratrooper near the Toko Lay shop in Dili.

Account 2

The following consists of extracts from a letter written in November 1977 by a Catholic priest in East Timor and sent to two Dominican nuns, Sister Natalia Granada Moreira and Sister Maria Auxiliadora Hernandez. Its importance is that it was written during what was probably the worst period following the invasion. At the time, East Timor was securely closed off to the outside world, and communications even to other parts of Indonesia were heavily censored. This letter was smuggled out by a person who carried it to Jakarta.

The War. It continues with the same fury as it had started. Fretilin continues the struggle, in spite of famine, lack of clothing, death, and a crisis in understanding and objectives which has surfaced lately. The invaders have intensified their attacks in the three classic ways — from land, sea and air.

Between 7 and 31 December 1975, and up to February 1976, in Dili harbour there were at anchor up to 23 warships which vomited intense fire towards Dili 24 hours a day. Daily eight to twelve helicopters and four bombers flew reconnaissance and bombing runs near Dili. Numerous tanks and armoured vehicles roamed about the territory. The Indonesian armed forces in Timor must have surpassed 50,000 (I don't know for certain). In December last year there was heavy movement of ships in Dili, discharging war materials and disembarking troops. From last September (1977) the war was again intensified. The bombers did not stop all day. Hundreds of human beings died every day. The bodies of the victims became food for carnivorous birds (if we don't die of the war, we die of the plague), villages were completely destroyed, some tribes decimated ... . And the war enters its third year with no promise of an early end in sight. The barbarities (understandable in the Middle Ages and justifiable in the Stone Age), the cruelties, the pillaging, the unqualified destruction of Timor, the executions without reason, in a word all the "organized" evil, has spread deep roots in Timor.

There is complete insecurity and the terror of arbitrary imprisonment is our daily bread (I am on the "persona non grata" list and any day I could disappear). Fretilin soldiers who give themselves up are disposed of — for them there is no prison. Genocide will come soon, perhaps by next December. Taking advantage of the courage of the Timorese, they are being urged to fight their brothers in the interior. It is they who march in front of the (Indonesian) battalions to intimidate the prey.

[Section on the position of the Church omitted]

The Political Situation. Indescribable. Sabotage and lies dominate the information sector. Integration is not the expression of the will of the people.

The people are controlled by the Indonesians and, given the character of the oppressor and the level of the Indonesian presence, it is a lamb being led to the slaughter. In the presence of such force, there is no way to resist; liberty is a word without meaning. The proclaimed liberation is synonymous with slavery. Timor is returning to the nineteen forties and anti-communism is an Islamic slogan meaning "iconoclasm." The reform of our customs means the setting up of cabarets and houses of prostitution … . In commerce, the search for basic needs dominates, and black-market is the rule. The Chinese are easily corrupted and they themselves are instruments of commercial exploitation. To travel outside of Indonesia is a dream. Mail is censored.

… Please do something positive for the liberty of the Timorese people. The world ignores us and our grief … . We are on the road to complete genocide. By the end of December the war could exterminate us. All of the youth of Timor (30% of the population) are in the forests: the Indonesian control only one or two kilometres beyond the villages. We ask all justice-loving people to save Timor, and we ask God to forgive the sins of the Timorese people … .

Timor, November 1977 [name withheld]

Account 3

The next item consists of extracts taken from a message, written in 1977, from a Timorese father to his son in Portugal, with whose whereabouts he was not familiar. Again, it is rather general, but it is one of the few firsthand written accounts of conditions in East Timor at that time.

Tell my son that for nothing on this earth should he return to Timor. I would rather die without seeing him again than to know that he had returned to this hell … .

There are very few Timorese in the streets of Dili; most of them are in the forests, dead or in prison; the cost of living is extremely high and there is a need for the most basic foodstuffs. The suffering is indescribable, as may be affirmed by the Apostolic Nuncio in Jakarta who went to Dili in the middle of October to celebrate an open-air mass. The weeping, the tears, the laments of the orphans, widows and forsaken were such that the Mass had to be interrupted for a quarter of an hour before it could continue … .

In a desperate attempt to crush by force the armed resistance which continues to exist in most of the territory, the Jakarta authorities now have sent ten more battalions to Timor. Thus, the number of Indonesian troops engaged in fighting usually cited as being over 40,000 must now be more than 50,000 ... . The increase in military operations has once more turned Timor into a place of arms and warfare. At the present time, with the beginning of the rainy season, land operations should have diminished but the constant air raids and the launching of incendiary bombs which have been systematically punishing the rural populations continue.

Account 4

Extract from a Letter from Timor also in 1977. A continuous, increasingly violent war rages in Timor. The group of villages in which I lived have been completely destroyed. There is not one soul there. I myself am in Dili and I have gone many days without eating. These are the effects of war. But there are people who are much worse off than I. I have been sick several times and at death's door for want of medication. The cost of living in Dili is very high and the salaries are very low. One sees no one else but Indonesian soldiers and Chinese on the streets of Dili. There are very few Timorese for the majority are either in the forest, dead or in jail. The luck of Timor is to be born in tears, to live in tears and to die in tears. It would, perhaps, be more appropriate to say that one does not cry for one has no more tears to shed, for Timor is no longer Timor: it is nothing but an oppressed worm ... .

Account 5

The following account was conducted by Michele Turner, a well-known Australian oral historian. The subject is a former Timorese guerrilla fighter, named Laurenco, who spent much of the early years of the occupation in the eastern sector of the island. He describes conditions in a mountain area, where many Timorese lost their lives, largely through air attacks, and the consequences of famine. (Note: Both Accounts 5 and 6 are extracts from Michele Turner's *Telling: East Timor Personal Testimonies, 1942–1992* (Sydney, Australia: University of New South Wales, 1992). Reprinted with permission.)

Our section in the east was the last to be attacked. In 1978 they started to come against us. At first we didn't resist, just watched the enemy, let them feel confident. Matebian Mountain is a big area and there were 160,000 of us, fighters and civilians, divided into small groups.

On 17 October 1978 some Indonesians got right to the bottom of Matebian Mountain and that's when we started to fight back. For those first two months, October and November, we were very successful and about 3000 Indonesians died. Then they got angry and scared to come close and started to bomb us from the air. They bombed twice a day, in the morning and in the afternoon with four black planes. Their name I know now is Broncos, but we called them scorpions because they had a tail that curves up at the back like that insect. Their bombs left a big hole about two metres deep. Then they got new supersonic planes. Our people were very frightened of those because you didn't even hear they were there until they were gone. Those supersonics would zoom along the valley so fast we couldn't shoot them.

The bombing became constant, in rotation. Three supersonics came to bomb for about forty-five minutes and then went back to reload. Half an hour later the black scorpions came, and this could go on all day. In Matebian there are a lot of caves and we hid there and only moved at night.

We knew by radio from the south zone that the Indonesians had dropped four napalm bombs there. Then they dropped two of these on us. I saw all the flames and heard people shouting and screaming. I was on another mountain but I could see well; there was a close view of it, straight across. Some of us set out straight away to help those people. By foot it took half an hour to go down and up again, and by the time we got there everything was completely burnt. We saw a whole area about fifty metres square all burnt, no grass, nothing except ash. On the rocks it was a brown reddish color and on the ground ash too, no ordinary grey ash, sort of yellow ash, like beach sand. You couldn't see where bodies had been. There was nothing except ash and burned rocks on the whole area, but we had heard those people screaming.

We could find no bones or bodies, but people near said there were about a hundred people living there who were killed by this. Those people disappeared, they were not sheltering, we never saw them again. The population was large but people were in small groups in different places and knew where each group was. The whole population was very upset — no bodies of those people left to bury. My cousin said, "If this is what they can do there is no hope for the world."

We had no food because of all the bombing and we lost radio contact. Fretilin decided they couldn't defend the people properly any more and the population should surrender, otherwise we would all be wiped out. When they announced this decision the people cried. Falintil said they couldn't force us, but this was the best thing for all. Our leader said, "You surrender and it will be better for you to get food and it will be better for us too so we can fight freely. But this doesn't mean that the war stops. We will keep fighting for our freedom and don't forget, wherever you go outside, that we are nationalists, and if ever you have a way to help us in the bush, do it." Then Falintil gave up their responsibility for the people and everyone decided for themselves to stay or go. Also the Falintil broke up into small groups to fight as guerillas.

About 2000 of us tried to stay in the mountains. We broke into three groups to escape and I was in one of these trying to get through the encirclement. In our group there were a few hundred, mostly fighters, only about a hundred ordinary people. We kept walking and walking. The Indonesians would drop some bombs, we would hide, then walk again. We were in a valley and the Indonesians were up higher. If they shot at us our fighters did not shoot back so that the Indonesians would think we were just a normal group of people walking to surrender. We had no food, the area we were going through was mostly rocks. The enemy burnt the trees and any food growing; the animals were dead.

Account 6

The following is an extract from an account by an elderly Timorese woman, named Eloise, who was in Dili when the Indonesian invasion of the capital took place in 1975. This incident was only one of a number of mass killings carried out by Indonesian troops, following their assault on Dili.

On 7 December we woke and heard this big noise of planes and saw parachutes and planes covering the light — it became dark because of them, so many. There were shots and we went inside and kept listening to more and more shooting. In the afternoon some Timorese came and told us everyone must come to surrender at headquarters. We had to get a stick and put a piece of white material on it and come. They said, "These are orders from the Indonesian people." So we went, women and children and old men and young men.

Once we got there, they divided us: the women and children and old men to one side, and on the other young boys they wanted to help carry Fretilin things — they had taken over their store and there was ammunition and food there. We watched while they took all this stuff out from the storeroom. When they finished they were coming to join us, but the Indonesians said, "No, stay there!" Then they ordered us to form a line and wait.

Then an Indonesian screams an order and we hear machine gun running through [sic] the men. We see the boys and men dying right there. Some see their husbands die. We look at each other stunned. We think they are going to kill us next. All of us just turn and pick up the children and babies and run screaming, wild, everywhere.

Notes

1. Curiously, the strongest argument for such an outcome was advanced in 1966 by an American academic, Professor Donald Weatherbee, who concluded, "In a sense, Portuguese Timor is a trust territory, the Portuguese holding it in trust for Indonesia." ("Portuguese Timor: An Indonesian Dilemma," *Asian Survey,* December 1966)

2. In June 1974, in contrast to most of his colleagues (who studiously avoided uttering the word "independence") Foreign Minister Adam Malik generously assured the Timorese of Indonesia's support for East Timor's independence. In a letter to Jose Ramos Horta, a Fretilin leader, Malik wrote, *inter alia:* "The independence of every country is the right of every nation, with no exception for the people in Timor."

3. In 1957, for example, Indonesia told the UN First Committee, in a reference to Timor: "Indonesia has no claim to any territories which had not been part of the former Netherlands East Indies. No one should suggest otherwise or advance dangerous theories in that respect."

4. Within weeks of Pearl Harbor, Australian and some Dutch forces, ignoring the protests of the Portuguese — at that time neutral — had landed in East Timor, bringing in large Japanese forces. The Timorese gave the Australians extraordinary support until their withdrawal a year later. The Japanese then imposed a harsh occupation on the local population, which cost perhaps as many as 70,000 Timorese lives.

5. Under a special agreement (UKUSA) this intelligence surveillance was shared with the United States and formed the basis of key DIA (Defense Intelligence Agency) briefings prepared for the administration in Washington.

6. The Australian relationship was not as important to Indonesia as were its links with the United States, Japan, or the Netherlands, but a firm Australian stand on the decolonization rights of the Timorese would certainly have influenced the policies of the other states and reinforced Suharto's misgivings about military intervention.

7. Named after the dragon, or giant lizard on the nearby island of Alor.

8. *Frente Revolucionaria de Timor-Leste Independente* — the Revolutionary Front for an Independent East Timor.

9. Uniao Democrata de Timor — the Timorese Democratic Union.

10. Based on remarks made to the writer by Major Metello, a senior representative of the Armed Forces Movement.

11. East Timor is predominantly Roman Catholic.

12. Based on talks in 1975 with two of those present at the meeting, Mousinho and Martins.

13. An example of the provocative disinformation role of Bakin at this point was the deliberate circulating of a story by *Operasi Komodo* agents, that a number of Vietnamese officers had been smuggled in to Timor and were training a Fretilin military force.

14. In fact, at the time, most Fretilin leaders were out of the country, so it was an unlikely eventuality.

15. The humanitarian consequences of this civil war were assessed by the International Red Cross and an Australian Council for Overseas Aid (ACFOA) mission, of which I was the leader, with the former insisting that the total loss of life was about 1500.

16. For an account of the withdrawal see Chapter 11 of *Missao Impossivel? Descolonizacao de Timor* by Mario Lemos Pires, the Portuguese governor at that time.

17. There is now ample evidence that these newsmen were shot by Indonesian troops, at least three of them having been executed some time after the force entered the village.

18. As an indication of Western complicity, U.S. intelligence was informed in Jakarta by their Indonesian opposite numbers that the attack would take place on December 6. However, American officials in Jakarta were shocked to discover that President Ford and Dr. Kissinger would be in the Indonesian capital on that day, and their hosts obligingly delayed the attack 24 hours.

19. *Angkatan Bersenjata Republik Indonesia*, Indonesian Armed Forces.

20. The Indonesian Army often used Timorese drivers, because of their familiarity with the difficult, and sometimes dangerous, road conditions in the interior.

21. The International Committee of the Red Cross (ICRC) team, under the leadership of Andre Pasquier, was forced to withdraw before the invasion when Indonesia refused to respect its neutrality.

22. In fact, in October 1989 Governor Carrascalao, in a briefing to visiting journalists, gave a much lower total figure — 659,000, which, he said, was growing at 2.63 percent annually. If this figure was correct, it gives an indication of the pace of immigration from elsewhere in Indonesia.

23. I have chosen deliberately to use the past tense, because the great upheaval caused by the invasion, especially the resettlement programs, has clearly had a significant impact on cultural and settlement patterns.

24. However, their attitudes were to an extent influenced by the hostility towards Javanese that was prevalent in Indonesian Timor, especially after the widespread killings in 1965-1966.

25. *Angkatan Udara Republik Indonesia*, Air Force of the Republic of Indonesia.

26. See *East Timor: Violations of Human Rights* (London: Amnesty International, 1985).

27. A copy of this report, *Notes on East Timor*, is held by the writer.

28. A General Assembly was followed by Security Council Resolution 384 (December 22, 1975), which was unanimously agreed to, a rare achievement at that time.

29. Of Indonesia's major trading and aid-donor partners — the United States, Japan, West Germany, Australia, and the Netherlands — only the last-mentioned showed concern at the government level.

30. Testimony of Robert Oakley in "Human Rights in East Timor and the Question of the Use of U.S. Equipment by the Indonesian Armed Forces," before Subcommittees of the Committee on International Relations, House of Representatives, 95th Congress, March 28, 1977. And letter from Edward C. Ingraham, Department of State, May 13, 1977.

31. East Timor had by that time been designated Indonesia's 27th province. Canberra waited only until 1979 before according *de jure* status to its recognition.

32. The confidential report to which the author was given access stated that, of the 200,000, about 10 percent were in such bad shape that they could not be saved.

33. In fairness, it should be noted that Australia was a major provider of financial backing for the International Red Cross mission's operations.

34. Indonesia imposed strict conditions on the admission of the ICRC, which limited its effectiveness. For example, for some years it was denied the right to carry out tracing activities. Moreover, most of its work was carried out by the Indonesian Red Cross, which was largely under military direction.

35. In fact, the last of these operations, *Operasi Senjum*, involving some 10,000 troops was carried out in the central mountain area in the middle of November 1996.

36. See in particular the annual reports published by Amnesty International, especially *East Timor: Violations of Human Rights* (London: Amnesty International Publications, 1985). Also see the publications of *Asia Watch*, especially its detailed accounts of the circumstances of the Santa Cruz massacre in Dili in November, 1991.

37. See "East Timor: The Courts-Martial" (*Asia Watch*, June 23, 1992).

38. The spirited Timorese resistance took a heavy toll on Indonesian lives; as many as 20,000 reportedly having been killed since 1975.

39. Based on the assessment of the International Red Cross mission, as conveyed to the writer some weeks after the civil war had ended.

40. Including from General Try Sutrisno, the defense forces commander, who was elected vice president of Indonesia in 1993.

41. The slaughter of more than half a million "Communists," including their families, in the aftermath of the 1965 *Gestapu* affair, most of them by the army, was perhaps the bloodiest episode in Indonesia's history.

42. In a speech to Timorese officials in Dili, in February 1990, Murdani warned that those who still sought to form a separate state "will be crushed by ABRI. ABRI may fail the first time, so it will try for a second time, and for a third time." In a reference to Fretilin and its sympathizers he said: "We will crush them all ... to safeguard the unity of Indonesian territory."

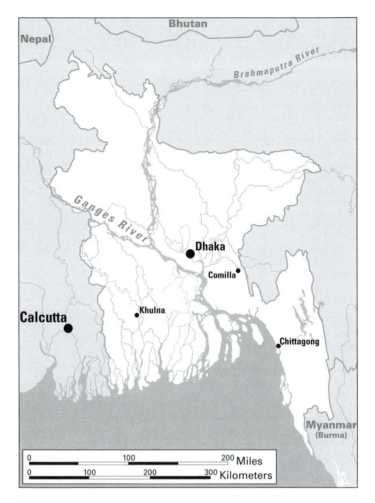

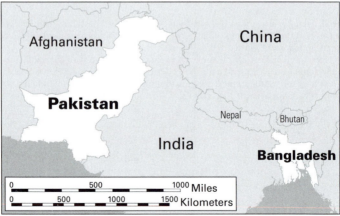

Bangladesh

CHAPTER **9**

Genocide in Bangladesh

ROUNAQ JAHAN

Introduction

The birth of Bangladesh in 1971 was a unique phenomenon in that it was the first nation-state to emerge after waging a successful liberation war against a postcolonial state. The nine-month-long liberation war in Bangladesh drew world attention because of the genocide committed by Pakistan, which resulted in the murder of approximately 3 million people and the rape of nearly a quarter-million girls and women. Ten million Bengalis reportedly took refuge in India to avoid the massacre of the Pakistan army, and thirty million people were displaced within the country (Loshak, 1971; Mascarenhas, 1971; Payne, 1973; Ayoob and Subrahmanyan, 1972; O'Donnell, 1984).

Written three decades after the genocide, this chapter addresses the following: the historical forces that led to the genocide; the nature of the genocide (why, how, and who committed the genocide); the world response; the long-range impact of the genocide on the victims; the way the genocide is remembered today; and some lessons that can be drawn from the 1971 Bangladesh genocide.

Background to the Genocide

Though the liberation war in Bangladesh lasted only nine months, the nationalist movement that preceded the war spanned the previous two

297

decades. Indeed, the seeds of the Bangladesh nationalist movement were planted very soon after the creation of Pakistan in 1947.

When India was partitioned on the basis of religion and the new state of Pakistan was established comprising the Muslim-majority areas of India, Bengali Muslims voluntarily became a part of Pakistan. But very soon it became apparent to the Bengali Muslims that, despite their numerical majority, they were being hurt in a variety of ways: Their linguistic cultural identity was being threatened by the ruling elite (which was predominantly non-Bengali) in the new state; they were being economically exploited; and they were excluded from exercising state power (Jahan, 1972).

The nationalist movement first emerged as a struggle to defend and preserve the ethnic linguistic Bengali identity of the Bengali Muslims. Though the Bengalis comprised 54 percent of Pakistan's population, in 1948 the ruling elite declared their intention to make Urdu, which was the language of only 7 percent of the population, the sole state language. Bengali students immediately protested the decision and launched a movement that continued for the next eight years until the Pakistan Constitution, adopted in 1956, recognized both Bengali and Urdu as state languages (Ahmad, 1967).

The Bengalis had to defend not only the right to practice their own language, but other creative expressions of their culture such as literature, music, dance, and art. The Pakistani ruling elite looked upon Bengali language and culture as too "Hindu leaning" and made repeated attempts to "cleanse" it from Hindu influence (Urnar, 1966, 1967, 1969). First, in the 1950s, attempts were made to force Bengalis to substitute Bengali words with Arabic and Urdu words. Then, in the 1960s, state-controlled media such as television and radio banned songs written by Rabindra Nath Tagore, a Bengali Hindu, who won the Nobel Prize in 1913 and whose poetry and songs were equally beloved by Bengali Hindus and Muslims.

The attacks on their language and culture alienated the Bengalis from the state-sponsored Islamic ideology of Pakistan and intensified their linguistic and ethnic identity that emphasized a more secular ideology and attitude.

The Bangladesh nationalist movement was also fueled by a sense of economic exploitation. Though jute, the major export earning commodity, was produced in Bengal, most of the economic investments took place in Pakistan. A systematic transfer of resources took place from East to West Pakistan, creating a growing economic disparity and a feeling among the Bengalis that they were being treated as a colony by Pakistan (Rahman, 1968; Jahan, 1972).

In the 1950s and 1960s, a group of Bengali economists carefully documented the process of economic disparity and marshalled arguments in favor of establishing a "two-economy" system. The movement toward autonomy initiated in the 1950s culminated in the famous six-point program of 1966, which not only rejected the central government's right of taxation but demanded that the power to tax and establish trade and commercial relations, including the establishment of separate accounts of foreign exchange earning, be placed in the hands of the provinces.

However, it was lack of political participation and exclusion from state power that gradually drove the Bengalis from participation, to demanding autonomy, and finally to demanding self-determination (Jahan, 1972). Constituting a majority of the population, the Bengalis expected to dominate or at least share the political power in the federal government of Pakistan. But soon after the creation of Pakistan, a small civil and military bureaucratic elite held a monopoly on government power. As a result, the Bengalis had virtually no representation in that power elite (Sayeed, 1967, 1968; Jahan, 1972).

From the beginning, the Bengalis demanded democracy with free and regular elections, a parliamentary form of government, and freedom of political parties and the media. But the ruling elite in Pakistan thwarted every attempt at instituting democracy in the country (Callard, 1957; Sayeed, 1967). In 1954, a democratically elected government in East Bengal was dismissed within 90 days of taking power. A constitution was adopted in 1956 after nine years of protracted negotiations, only to be abrogated within two years by a military coup. In 1958, just before the first nationally scheduled election, the military took direct control of the government. This was out of fear that the Bengalis might dominate in a democratically elected government.

The decade of the 1960s saw the military rule of General Ayub Khan. It was eventually toppled in 1969 as a result of popular mass movements in both wings (East and West) of Pakistan. However, after the fall of Ayub, the civil–military bureaucratic elite again regrouped and put General Yahya Khan, who was the commander-in-chief of the armed forces, in charge of the government. The Yahya regime acceded to a number of key demands of the Bengali nationalist movement, including the holding of a free democratic national election on the basis of one person, one vote. The first free democratic national elections, held in Pakistan in 1970 two decades after the birth of the country, resulted in a sweeping victory of the Bengali nationalist party, the Awami League. The election results gave the Awami League not only total control over their own province, but also a majority nationally and a right to form the federal government.

Again, though, the ruling elite in Pakistan took recourse to unconstitutional measures to prevent the Bengalis from assuming state power. On

March 1, 1971, General Yahya postponed indefinitely the scheduled March 3 session of parliament. This, in turn, threw the country into a constitutional crisis. The Awami League responded by launching an unprecedented nonviolent, noncooperation movement, which resulted in the entire administration of then East Pakistan coming to a virtual standstill. Even the Bengali civil and military officials complied with the noncooperation movement. The movement demonstrated that the Bengali nationalists had total allegiance and support of the Bengali population.

The Yahya regime initiated political negotiations with the Bengali nationalists but at the same time flew thousands of armed forces in from West to East Pakistan, thus consolidating preparations for a military action. On March 25, 1971, General Yahya abruptly broke off the negotiations and unleashed a massive armed strike against the population of Dhaka, the capital city. In two days of uninterrupted military operations, hundreds of ordinary citizens were killed, houses and property were destroyed, and the leader of the Awami League, Sheikh Mujibur Rahman, was arrested. The army also launched armed attacks in Chittagong, Comilla, Khulna, and other garrison cities. Simon Dring, a reporter with the *Daily Telegraph London*, and Michel Laurent, an Associated Press photographer, escaped the Pakistani dragnet and roamed Dhaka and the countryside. On March 28 they reported that the loss of life had reached 15,000 in the countryside. On the Dhaka University campus, 17 professors and some 200 students were killed in cold blood (Loshak, 1971, pp. 88–126).

The news of the Dhaka massacre immediately spread to the rest of the country. Instead of cowing the unarmed Bengalis into submission, which was ostensibly the intention of the Pakistani army in initiating the brutal killings, it only inflamed nationalist sentiments. Within 24 hours of the armed crackdown in Dhaka, on March 26, 1971, the independence of Bangladesh was declared from the city of Chittagong. It was announced over the radio, which was controlled by the Bengali nationalists, on the behalf of the Awami League and its leader, Rahman. The upshot of this is that a new nation was born out of what was a premeditated genocide (Jahan, 1972; Ayoob and Subhrahmanyan, 1972).

Bangladesh Genocide 1971

The genocide in Bangladesh, which started with the Pakistani military operation against unarmed citizens on the night of March 25, continued unabated for nearly nine months until the Bengali nationalists, with the help of the Indian army, succeeded in liberating the country from Pakistani occupation forces on December 16, 1971.

The atrocities committed by the Pakistan army were widely reported by the international press during 1971 (Loshak, 1971; Mascarenhas, 1971; Schanberg, 1971; Jenkins et al., 1971; Coggin et al., 1971).

From the eyewitness accounts documented during and immediately after the genocide in 1971 and 1972, as well as those published over the last 20 years, it is possible to analyze the major features of the Bangladesh genocide — how and why it was committed — as well as those who were involved (both the perpetrators and the victims).

Why Was the Genocide Committed?

The genocide in Bangladesh caught the outside observers as well as the Bengali nationalists by surprise. After all, the Bengali nationalists were not involved in any armed struggle prior to March 25, 1971. They were essentially waging a peaceful constitutional movement for democracy and autonomy. Their only crime, as U.S. Senator Edward Kennedy observed, appeared to have been to win an election (Malik, 1972). So why did the Pakistani ruling elite initiate a brutal military action?

Again, perhaps, the main reason behind the atrocities was to terrorize the population into submission. The military commander in charge of the Dhaka operations reportedly claimed that he would kill 4 million people in 48 hours and thus have a "Final Solution" of the Bengal problem (Jahan, 1972). The Pakistani military regime calculated that since the Bengalis had no previous experience in armed struggle, they would be frightened and crushed in the face of overwhelming fire power, mass killings, and destruction. But the atrocities created a completely opposite effect on the Bengalis. Instead of being cowed, they rose in revolt and chose the path of armed struggle to resist armed aggression. When news of the Dhaka massacre reached other cities and towns, human waves overran the police stations and distributed arms to people. But the initial armed resistance was short-lived, as the Bengalis lacked substantial arms and were vastly outnumbered in terms of trained soldiers. The Pakistani army was able to recapture a majority of the towns. Not surprisingly, the process was brutal and many innocent civilians were killed by the military.

Though the initial armed resistance failed, the Bengali nationalists were not prepared to give up the liberation struggle. Instead of direct confrontation, the liberation fighters chose the course of guerrilla warfare. Nearly 100,000 young men were given armed training within Bangladesh and India, and they succeeded in virtually destroying the communication and supply lines of the Pakistani army. To retaliate against the guerrillas, the Pakistani army embarked on a strategy of destroying entire areas and populations where guerrilla actions were reported. Massive killing, looting, burning, and raping took place during these "search-and-destroy" operations (Coggin et al., 1971, pp. 24-29; Jenkins et al., 1971, pp. 26-30; Malik, 1972).

The reasons behind the genocide, however, were not simply to terrorize the people and punish them for resistance. There were also elements of racism in this act of genocide. The Pakistani army, consisting mainly of Punjabis and Pathans, had always looked upon the Bengalis as racially inferior — a nonmartial, physically weak race, not interested in serving or unable to serve in the army (Marshall, 1959). General Ayub Khan's (1967) remarks about the Bengalis in his memoirs reflected the typical attitude of the Pakistan's civil military power elite:

> East Bengalis ... probably belong to the very original Indian races
> .... They have been and still are under considerable Hindu cultural
> and linguistic influence .... They have all the inhibitions of
> downtrodden races .... Their popular complexes, exclusiveness,
> suspicion and ... defensive aggressiveness ... emerge from this his-
> torical background (p. 187).

The image of the Bengalis as a nonmartial race, created by the British colonialists, was readily accepted by the Pakistani ruling elite. A policy of genocide against fellow Muslims was deliberately undertaken by the Pakistanis on the assumption of racial superiority and a desire to cleanse the Bengali Muslims of Hindu cultural linguistic influence.

How Was the Genocide Committed?

On March 25, 1971, when the Pakistani government initiated military action in Bangladesh, a number of sites and groups of people were selected as targets of attack. In Dhaka, for example, the university campus, the headquarters of the police and the Bengali paramilitia, slums and squatter settlements, and Hindu majority localities, all were selected as special targets. The Pakistani ruling elite believed that the leadership of the Bengali nationalist movement came from the intellectuals and students, that the Hindus and the urban *lumpenproletariat* were the main support-ers, and that the Bengali police and army officials could be potential leaders in any armed struggle. In the first two days of army operations, hundreds of unarmed people were killed on the university campus, and in the slums and the old city where Hindus lived. (Eyewitness accounts of killings in the Dhaka university campus are included in this chapter.)

When the news of the Dhaka massacre spread and the independence of Bangladesh was declared on March 26, spontaneous resistance was organized in all the cities and towns of the country. The Awami League politicians, Bengali civilian administration, police, army, students, and intellectuals constituted the leadership of the resistance. This first phase of the liberation war was, however, amateurish and uncoordinated and only lasted approximately six weeks. By the middle of May, the Pakistani army was successful in bringing the cities and towns under their control, though the villages remained largely "liberated" areas.

In occupying one city after another, the Pakistani army used the superiority of its fire and air power to its advantage. These operations also involved massive killings of civilians and wanton lootings and destruction of property. The leadership of the resistance generally left the scene prior to the Pakistani army's arrival. They took refuge either in India or in the villages. But, in any case, the Pakistani army engaged in killings and burnings in order to terrorize the population. Again, Awami Leaguers, students and intellectuals, civilian and army officers, and Hindus were selected as targets of attack (Malik, 1972). The army's campaign against the cities and towns not only led to massive civilian casualties, it also resulted in a large-scale dislocation of people. In fact, nearly 10 million people — Hindus as well as Muslims — migrated to India, and approximately 30 million people from the cities took refuge in the villages. Government offices, educational institutions, and factories were virtually closed.

The second phase of the liberation war (from mid-May to September) was a period of long-term planning for both the Bengali nationalists and the Pakistani government. The Bengali nationalists established a government-in-exile and undertook external publicity campaigns in support of their cause. They also recruited nearly 100,000 young men as freedom fighters who underwent military training and undertook guerrilla operations inside Bangladesh.

The Pakistan army essentially dug in their own strongholds during this period with periodic operations to rural areas to punish the villagers for harboring freedom fighters. The army also engaged in large-scale looting and raping of girls and women.

In fact, systematic and organized rape was the special weapon of war used by the Pakistan army during the second phase of the liberation struggle. While during the first phase, young able-bodied males were targeted for death, during the second phase, girls and women became the special targets of Pakistani aggression. During army operations, girls and women were raped in front of close family members in order to terrorize and inflict racial slander. Girls and women were also abducted and repeatedly raped and gang-raped in special camps run by the army near army barracks. Many of the rape victims either were killed or committed suicide. Altogether, it is estimated that approximately 200,000 girls and women were raped during the 1971 genocide (Brownmiller, 1981). (An eyewitness account of the mass rape camps organized by the Pakistani army is included in this chapter.)

All through the liberation war, able-bodied young men were suspected of being actual or potential freedom fighters. Thousands were arrested, tortured, and killed. Eventually, cities and towns became bereft of young males who either took refuge in India or joined the liberation war.

During the second phase, another group of Bengali men in the rural areas (those who were coerced or bribed to collaborate with the Pakistanis) fell victim to the attacks of Bengali freedom fighters.

The third phase of the liberation struggle (from October till mid-December) saw intensified guerrilla action and finally a brief conventional war between Pakistan and the combined Indian and Bangladeshi forces, which ended with the surrender of the Pakistani army on December 16, 1971 (Palit, 1972; Ayoob and Subrahmanyan, 1972). As guerrilla action increased, the Pakistani army also intensified its search-and-destroy operations. Several villages were destroyed during each day of this phase.

In the last week of the war, when their defeat was virtually certain, the Pakistani government engaged in its most brutal and premeditated genocidal campaign. During this period, villages were burnt and their inhabitants were killed. In order to deprive the new nation of its most talented leadership, the Pakistanis had decided to kill the most respected and influential intellectuals and professionals in each city and town. Between December 12 and 14, a selected number of intellectuals and professionals were abducted from their houses and murdered. Many of their names were later found in the diary of Major-General Rao Forman Ali, advisor to the martial law administrator and governor of occupied Bangladesh (Malik, 1972).

The victims of the 1971 genocide were, thus, first and foremost Bengalis. Though Hindus were especially targeted, the majority of the victims were Bengali Muslims — ordinary villagers and slum dwellers — who were caught unprepared during the Pakistani army's sweeping spree of wanton killing, rape, and destruction. As previously mentioned, the Pakistani ruling elite identified certain groups as their special enemies — students and intellectuals, Awami Leaguers and their supporters, and Bengali members of the armed forces and the police. However, many members of these targeted groups went into hiding or in exile in India after the initial attack. As a result, the overwhelming majority of the victims were defenseless, ordinary poor people who stayed behind in their own houses and did not suspect that they would be killed, raped, taken to prison, and tortured simply for the crime of being born a Bengali.

The sheltered and protected life of women, provided by the Bengali Muslim cultural norm, was virtually shattered in 1971. Thousands of women were suddenly left defenseless and forced to fend for themselves as widows and rape victims. The rape victims were particularly vulnerable. Though they were the casualties of the war, many of them were discarded by their own families as a way for the latter to avoid shame and dishonor (Brownmiller, 1981; Jahan, 1973).

Who Committed the Genocide?

The Pakistani government (the Yahya regime) was primarily responsible for the genocide. Not only did it prevent the Awami League and Rahman from forming the federal government, but it opted for a military solution to a constitutional crisis. In doing so, it decided to unleash a brutal military operation in order to terrorize the Bengalis. Yahya's decision to put General Tikka Khan (who had earned the nickname of "Butcher of Baluchistan" for his earlier brutal suppression of Baluchi nationals in the 1960s) in charge of the military operation in Bangladesh was an overt signal of the regime's intention to launch a genocide.

When Bangladesh was liberated, the Pakistani army surrendered; and shortly thereafter, the Bangladesh government declared its intention to hold war crime trials against the Pakistan army. Charges, however, were only brought against 193 officers (out of the 93,000 soldiers within its ranks). Bangladesh later gave up the idea of war crime trials in exchange for a negotiated settlement of outstanding issues with Pakistan. This involved the return of the Bengalis held hostage in Pakistan, repatriation of the Biharis from Bangladesh to Pakistan, division of assets and liabilities, and recognition of Bangladesh (O'Donnell, 1984).

The Pakistani military leaders, however, were not the only culprits. The political parties (e.g., the Pakistan Peoples Party [PPP]) also played an important role in instigating the army to take military action in Bangladesh. The PPP and its leader Zulfikar Ali Bhutto supported the army action all through 1971 (Bhutto, 1971; Jahan, 1973).

There were also Bengalis who collaborated with the Pakistani regime. During the second phase of the liberation struggle, the Pakistani government deliberately recruited Bengali collaborators. Many of the Islamic political groups (Muslim League and the Jamaat-e-Islami) opposed to the Awami League also collaborated with the army. Peace committees were formed in different cities and localities and under their auspices *rajakars* (armed volunteers) were raised and given arms to counter the freedom fighters. Two armed vigilante groups (Al Badr and Al-Shams) were trained and took the lead in the arrest and killing of the intellectuals during December 12 to 14, 1971. Some Bengali intellectuals were also recruited to conduct propaganda in favor of the Pakistanis.

The non-Bengali residents of Bangladesh — the Biharis — were the other group of collaborators. Many of them acted as informants and also participated in riots in Dhaka and Chittagong. Biharis, however, were also victims of Bengali mob violence.

The World's Response to the Genocide

World response to the genocide can be analyzed at dual levels — official and nonofficial. Prior to the discussion of the latter, it first must be noted that Pakistan immediately launched a propaganda campaign to deny the existence of genocide (Government of Pakistan, 1971; Bhutto, 1971).

At the official level, world response was determined by geopolitical interests and major power alignments. Officially, India was sympathetic and supportive of the Bangladesh cause from the beginning. The USSR, India's major superpower ally at the time, supported the Indian-backed cause. As a result of the USSR's support, all the Eastern Bloc countries naturally were also supportive of Bangladesh (Jackson, 1975).

Pakistan's allies were predictably opposed to Bangladesh. Islamic countries were generally supportive of Pakistan. So was China. The official policy of the United States was to "tilt in favor of Pakistan" because Pakistan was used as an intermediary to open the door to China (Jackson, 1975).

At the nonofficial level, however, there was a great outpouring of sympathy for the Bangladesh cause worldwide because of the genocide. The Western media — particularly the United States, British, French, and Australian — kept Bangladesh on the global agenda all through 1971. Well-known Western artists and intellectuals also came out in support of Bangladesh. George Harrison, the former Beatle, and Ravi Shankar, master of the sitar, held a Bangladesh concert. André Malraux, the noted French author, volunteered to go and fight with the Bengali freedom fighters. In the United States, citizen groups and individuals lobbied Congress successfully to halt military aid to Pakistan. Despite the Nixon administration's official support of the Pakistani government, influential senators and congressmen (such as Frank Church and Edward Kennedy) spoke out strongly against the genocide. Members of parliament in the United Kingdom and other Western countries were also highly critical of the Bangladesh genocide.

Both officially and unofficially, India played a critical role in mobilizing support for Bangladesh. The genocide and the resultant influx of 10 million refugees in West Bengal and neighboring states created spontaneous unofficial sympathy. The press, political parties, and voluntary organizations in India pressed Indian Prime Minister Indira Gandhi to immediately intervene in Bangladesh when the Pakistani army cracked down in March 1971. The Indian government initially refused to intervene but gave moral and financial support to the Bangladesh government-in-exile as well as the freedom fighters. It also sponsored a systematic international campaign in favor of Bangladesh. And finally, in December 1971, when the ground was well prepared, Bangladesh was liberated as a result of direct Indian army intervention (Jackson, 1975).

The world's sympathy for the Bangladesh people in the aftermath of the 1971 genocide was also demonstrated by the tremendous relief and rehabilitation efforts mounted by the United Nations and private voluntary organizations in Bangladesh. Even before the liberation of Bangladesh, large-scale relief efforts were undertaken by the world community to feed the refugees in the India-based camps. And during the first two years of the new nation's existence, "as many as 72 foreign relief groups, including UN agencies, contributed to what observers considered the largest single and most successful emergency relief endeavor of our times" (O'Donnell, 1984, p. 112). More specifically, nearly $1.3 billion of humanitarian aid was given to Bangladesh during that period.

Though the international community responded generously in giving humanitarian aid, there was very little support for the war crime trials that Bangladesh proposed to hold. The Indian army quickly removed the Pakistani soldiers from Bangladesh soil to India in order to prevent any reprisals or mob violence against them. India and other friendly countries were also supportive of a negotiated package as a way to settle all outstanding issues between Pakistan and Bangladesh, including the war crimes perpetrated. Though public opinion favoring war crime trials against the Pakistani army was high in Bangladesh, the Rahman regime finally conceded to foregoing the trials. This created a deep scar in the national psyche; indeed, the lack of a trial created a perdurable sense of betrayal and mistrust.

Long-Range Impact of the Genocide on the Victims

A major impact of the genocide was the introduction of violence in Bangladesh society, politics, and culture. Prior to 1971, Bengalis were a relatively peaceful and homogeneous community with a low level of violent crimes. They were highly faction-ridden and politicized, but differences and disputes were generally settled through negotiations, litigation, and peaceful mass movements. After the Pakistani armed attack, Bengalis took up arms and for the first time engaged in armed struggle. This brought a qualitative change in people's attitude to conflict resolution. Nonviolent means of protest and conflict resolution were largely discarded in favor of armed violence.

The genocide, looting, burning, and rapes also brutalized the Bangladeshi society. After witnessing so much violence, the people seemed to develop a higher degree of tolerance toward wanton violence.

The role of Bengali collaborators in perpetrating the genocide created deep division and mistrust in the otherwise homogeneous Bengali social fabric. After the birth of Bangladesh, the whole country appeared to be divided between the freedom fighters and collaborators. But not all collaborators were clearly identified. For example, the members of the two vigilante groups (Al Badr and Al-Shams) were never traced and punished. As a result, the feeling that the collaborators were still at large and capable of striking again created deep fear and a certain paralysis of action, particularly among the intellectuals.

In addition to these three general impacts — violence, brutalization, and mistrust — the genocide has had several long-term impacts on the different victim groups. The Hindu community has not felt safe again in Bangladesh, and after 1971 many of them decided not to return to Bangladesh. Furthermore, there has been a steady migration of young Hindus to India even after Bangladesh was liberated.

Students and youth, who became familiar with the use of arms, did not give them up after 1971. They started using sophisticated weapons in settling political scores. Continuous armed conflicts between rival student groups made the college and university campuses one of the most dangerous places in the country. That resulted in destroying the academic atmosphere and the standard of educational institutions.

The genocide and the issue of collaborators also created a deep division within the armed forces. From 1975 to 1981, the various factions of the armed forces staged numerous bloody coups and counter-coups, which resulted in the killing of virtually all the military leaders who participated in the liberation war.

The status of women was also altered as a result of the genocide. The sudden loss of male protection forced thousands of women to seek wage employment. For the first time, women entered occupations such as public works program, rural extension work, civil administration, and police work, which were not open to them before. Violence against women also became more widespread and common.

Do People Care Today?

The genocide and the liberation war has been kept alive primarily through creative arts: theater, music, literature, and painting. Furthermore, continuing well into the 1990s, many vivid eyewitness accounts of the genocide and personal diaries of 1971 were published in Bangladesh. It is interesting to note that from 1971 to 1973, it was mostly foreigners who published eyewitness accounts of the Bangladesh genocide (Mascarenhas, 1971; Malik, 1972; Payne, 1973). Bengalis themselves did not sit down to write or collect these accounts. But a decade and a half after the events, a flood of writing on the genocide began to emerge, most of it coming from ordinary citizens in Bangladesh relating their personal experiences of the genocide.

While the genocide and the liberation war have not been forgotten by the people of Bangladesh, the collaborators have been gradually "rehabili-tated" through state patronage. Since the 1975 army coup and the overthrow of the Awami League regime, many of the collaborators who had been opposed to the Awami League joined the political parties floated by the two military leaders, Ziaur Rahman (1975–1981) and Ershad (1982–1990). The two military leaders tilted the country toward Islamic ideology, allowed religious-based parties to function, and appointed a few well-known collaborators to their cabinet. The gradual ascendance of the Islamic forces in the country became even more evident when, after the 1991 election, the Bangladesh Nationalist Party (BNP) succeeded in forming the government with the support of the fundamentalist party, Jamaat-e-Islami.

The control of state power by the collaborators of the 1971 genocide finally enraged the victims of genocide to take direct political action. They launched a mass movement to eliminate the "Killers and Collaborators of 1971." A citizens' committee was convened in 1991. It was headed by Jahanara Imam, a well-known author whose son was killed by the Pakistani army in 1971. It demanded a trial of Golam Azam, the head of the Jamaat-e-Islami party for complicity in the 1971 killings. The nonpartisan civic organization galvanized the support of the intellectuals and youth. The major opposition party, the Awami League, also threw in its support. The citizens' committee organized major nonviolent protests, nationwide strikes were organized, and a public trial was held where children, wives, and other relatives of victims of genocide gave testimony against the Jamaat-e-Islami party and Azam. The genocide and the collaborators' issue, which had gradually been side-stepped since 1975, were also brought back to the center stage of the political arena.

Lessons from this Genocide

What lessons can be drawn from the 1971 Bangladesh genocide? First, once a state adopts a systematic policy of genocide against any nationality group, the nationality group, threatened with genocide, will feel stronger in the legitimacy of its claim to form its own separate state.

Second, once a policy of genocide is initiated, it is difficult to settle conflict through peaceful negotiations. The Bengalis gave up the path of constitutional struggle and political negotiations and chose the course of armed struggle after the Pakistani intention of killing several million people to arrive at a "Final Solution" became evident to the Bengalis.

Third, genocide creates a deep trauma in the national psyche. It creates fear, suspicion, and mistrust. The Bengalis are suspicious of all foreign powers including India, which helped to liberate the country. Resentment against the Indian army emerged in the weeks following the liberation of the country, and the Indian army was withdrawn within 90 days. There is not only constant fear of foreign aggression, there is also distrust about foreign agents and collaborators. The deep animosity between the freedom fighters and collaborators makes national consensus-building efforts almost impossible. Creating a civil society in Bangladesh continues to be difficult since the issue of genocide divides the nation so deeply.

Postscript

The issues of genocide and collaboration have continued to play an important role in Bangladesh politics. After the 1991 election, Jamaat-e-Islami (a fundamentalist party) gained legitimacy and strength, as the Bangladesh Nationalist Party was able to form the government with Jamaat's support. During the 1996 election campaign, the Awami League pursued a two-pronged strategy. Jamaat's ability to tilt the election outcome was not lost on the Awami League. Therefore, on the one hand, it kept Jamaat away from forming an electoral alliance with the BNP; on the other, it successfully utilized the anti-Jamaat campaign launched by the NGOs and cultural organizations whose work with education and women's empowerment had come under attack by Jamaat. In the 1996 election Jamaat lost heavily and the Awami League was returned to power after 21 years.

During the four years of the Awami League government (1996–2000), the "committee against the killers and collaborators of 1971" gained official support. The committee demanded that Pakistan formally apologize to Bangladesh for the genocide of 1971. Textbooks used in public schools and programs in state-sponsored media also started to specifically refer to the genocide committed by the Pakistanis. (In previous decades, often reference was made to genocide without specifying the name of Pakistan.) However, the Awami League lost the 2001 election when the BNP was successful in forming an electoral coalition with the Jamaat and the other Islamist parties. Thirty years after opposing the birth of Bangladesh and collaborating with Pakistan, Jamaat-e-Islami succeeded in gaining a share in state power as a partner in the BNP-led coalition. The new government immediately began rewriting the textbooks of public schools and revising the programs of state-sponsored TV and media. The prime minister of Pakistan, on an official visit to Bangladesh in 2002, finally referred to "excesses" committed by the Pakistani soldiers, but the statement fell far short of expressing apologies for the genocide of 1971.

Eyewitness Accounts: Genocide in Bangladesh

The following eyewitness accounts of the 1971 genocide depict different incidents. The first two eyewitness accounts describe the mass murders committed on March 25 on the Dhaka University campus. The first account is by a survivor of the killings in one of the student dormitories (Jagannath Hall) where Hindu students lived. The second account is by a university professor who witnessed and videotaped the massacres on the Dhaka University campus. The third and fourth eyewitness testimonies describe the mass rape of women by the Pakistanis. The fifth testimony describes the killings in the village of Bangabandhu by Rahman, the leader of the nationalist movement. The last account describes the atrocities of the non-Bengali Biharis who collaborated with the Pakistan army.

The testimonies are taken from two sources. One is a Bengali book entitled *1971: Terrible Experiences* (1989), which was edited by Rashid Haider and is a collection of eyewitness accounts. Sohela Nazneen translated the accounts from Bengali to English. The other source, *The Year of the Vulture* (1972), is Indian journalist Amita Malik's account of the genocide. In the Malik book Dhaka is spelled "Dacca," which was the spelling used in 1972.

Account 1: Massacre at *Jagannath Hall*

This testimony is from Kali Ranjansheel's "Jagannath Hall e-Chilam" ("I was at Jagannath Hall"). In *1971: Terrible Experiences* (1989), p. 5. It was translated by Sohela Nazneen. Reprinted with permission.

I was a student at the Dhaka University. I used to live in room number 235 (South Block) in Jagannath Hall. On the night of 25th of March, I woke up from sleep by the terrifying sound of gunfire. Sometimes the sound of gunfire would be suppressed by the sound of bomb explosions and shell-fire. I was so terrified that I could not even think of what I should do! After a while I thought about going to Shusil, assistant general secretary of the student's union. I crawled up the stairs very slowly to the third floor. I found out that some students had already taken refuge in Shusil's room, but he was not there. The students told me to go to the roof of the building where many other students had taken shelter but I decided (rather selfishly) to stay by myself. I crawled to the restrooms at the northern end of the third floor and took refuge in there. I could see the east, the south and the west from the window. I could see that the soldiers were searching for students with flashlights from room to room, were taking them near the *Shahid Minar* [Martyr's memorial] and then shooting them. Only the sound of gunfire and pleas of mercy filled the air. Sometimes the Pakistanis used mortars and were shelling the building. The tin sheds in front of assembly and some of the rooms in North Block were set on fire ....

After some time, about 40 to 50 Pakistani soldiers came to the South Block and broke down the door of the dining room. The lights were turned on and they were firing at the students who took shelter in that room .... When the soldiers came out they had Priyanath [the caretaker of the student dormitory] at gunpoint, and forced him to show the way through all the floors of the dormitory. During this time I was not able to see them as I left the restroom by climbing up the open window and took shelter on the sunshed of the third floor. But I could hear the cracking sounds of bullets, the students pleading for mercy and the sound of the soldiers rummaging and throwing things about in search of valuables. The soldiers did not see me on the sunshed.

… After they left, I again took refuge in the washroom. I peeked through the window and saw that the other students' dormitory, Salimullah Hall, was on fire. The northern and the eastern parts of the city were on fire too as the north and east horizon had turned red. The whole night, the Pakistani soldiers continued their massacre and destruction …. Finally I heard the call for the morning prayer.

… The curfew was announced at dawn and I thought that this merciless killing would stop. But it continued. The soldiers started killing those who had escaped their notice during the night before.

… It was morning and I heard the voices of some students. I came out of the washroom, and saw that the students were carrying a body downstairs while soldiers with machine guns were accompanying them. It was the dead body of Priyanath. I was ordered to help the students and I complied. We carried bodies from the dormitory rooms and piled them up in the field outside. There were a few of us there — students, gardeners, two sons of the gateskeeper and the rest were janitors. The janitors requested the Pakistanis to let them go since they were not Bengalis. After a while the army separated the janitors from us.

… All the time the soldiers were cursing and swearing at us. The soldiers said, "We will see how you get free Bangladesh! Why don't you shout 'Joy Bangla' [Victory to Bengal]!" The soldiers also kicked us around. After we had finished carrying the bodies, we were divided into groups. They then took my group to one of the university quarters and searched almost every room on the fourth floor and looted the valuables. Downstairs we saw dead bodies piled up, obviously victims from the night before. They also brought down the flag of Bangladesh.

… After we came back, we were again ordered to carry the dead bodies to the *Shahid Minar*. The soldiers had already piled up the bodies of their victims and we added other bodies to the piles. If we felt tired and slowed down, the soldiers threatened to kill us.

… As my companion and I were carrying the body of Sunil (our dormitory guard), we heard screams in female voices. We found that the women from the nearby slums were screaming as the soldiers were shooting at the janitors (the husbands of the women). I realized that our turn would come too as the Pakistanis started lining up those students who were before us, and were firing at them. My companion and I barely carried the dead body of Sunil toward a pile where I saw the dead body of Dr. Dev [professor of philosophy]. I cannot explain why I did what I did next. Maybe from pure fatigue or maybe from a desperate hope to survive!

I lay down beside the dead body of Dr. Dev while still holding onto the corpse of Sunil. I kept waiting for the soldiers to shoot me. I even thought that I had died. After a long time, I heard women and children crying. I opened my eyes and saw that the army had left and the dead bodies were still lying about and women were crying. Some of the people were still alive but wounded. All I wanted to do was to get away from the field and survive.

I crawled towards the slums. First I went to the house of the electrician. I asked for water but when I asked for shelter, his wife started crying aloud and I then left and took refuge in a restroom .... Suddenly I heard the voice of Idu who used to sell old books. He said, "Don't be afraid. I heard you are alive. I shall escort you to safety." I went to old Dhaka city. Then I crossed the river. The boatman did not take any money. From there, I first went to Shimulia, then, Nawabganj and finally I reached my village in Barishal in the middle of April.

Account 2: Horror Documentary

This testimony is from Amita Malik's *The Year of the Vulture* (1972), pp. 79-83.

At the professors' funeral, Professor Rafiq-ul-Islam of the Bengali Department whispered to me, "At the television station you will find that there is a film record of the massacre of professors and students at Jagannath Hall. Ask them to show it to you."

This sounded so incredible that I did not really believe it. However, I wasted no time in asking Mr. Jamil Chowdhury, the station manager of TV, whether he did, indeed, have such a film with him: "Oh yes," he said, "but we have not shown it yet because it might have dreadful repercussions." He was, of course, referring to the fact that the Pakistani army was still very much in Dacca in prisoner-of-war camps in the Cantonment, and it would have been dangerous to show them gunning down professors and students at Dacca University. The people of Dacca had shown tremendous restraint so far, but this would have been going a bit too far. However, I had it confirmed that NBC VISNEWS and other international networks had already obtained and projected the film.

"But who shot the film?" I asked in wonder. "A professor at the University of Engineering, who had a video tape recorder and whose flat overlooks the grounds of Jagannath Hall," said Mr. Chowdhury. It was therefore by kind courtesy of Dacca TV that I sat in their small projection room on January 5 and saw for the first time what must be a unique actuality film, something for the permanent archives of world history.

The film, lasting about 20 minutes, first shows small distant figures emerging from the hall carrying the corpses of what must be the students and professors massacred in Jagannath Hall. These are clearly civilian figures in lighter clothes and, at their back, seen strutting arrogantly even at that distance, are darker clad figures, the hoodlums of the Pakistan army. The bodies are laid down in neat, orderly rows by those forced to carry them at gunpoint. Then the same procession troops back to the Hall. All this time, with no other sound, one hears innocent bird-song and a lazy cow is seen grazing on the university lawns. The same civilians come out again and the pile of bodies grows.

But after the third grisly trip, the action changes. After the corpses are laid on the ground, the people carrying them are lined up. One of them probably has a pathetic inkling of what is going to happen. He falls on his knees and clings to the legs of the nearest soldier, obviously pleading for mercy. But there is no mercy. One sees guns being pointed, one hears the crackle of gunfire and the lined up figures fall one by one, like the proverbial house of cards or, if you prefer, puppets in a children's film. At this stage, the bird-song suddenly stops. The lazy cow, with calf, careers wildly across the lawn and is joined by a whole herd of cows fleeing in panic.

But the last man is still clinging pathetically to the jackboot of the soldier at the end of the row. The soldier then lifts his shoulder at an angle, so that the gun points almost perpendicularly downwards to the man at his feet, and shoots him. The pleading hands unlink from the soldier's legs and another corpse joins the slumped bodies in a row, some piled on top of the very corpses they had to carry out at gunpoint, their own colleagues and friends. The soldiers prod each body with their rifles or bayonets to make sure that they are dead. A few who are still wriggling in their death agony are shot twice until they stop wriggling.

At this stage, there is a gap, because Professor Nurul Ullah's film probably ran out and he had to load a new one. But by the time he starts filming again, nothing much has changed except that there is a fresh pile of bodies on the left. No doubt some other students and professors had been forced at gunpoint to carry them out and then were executed in turn. In so far as one can count the bodies, or guess roughly at their number in what is really a continuous long-shot amateur film, there are about 50 bodies by this time. And enough, one should think.

Professor Nurul Ullah's world scoop indicated that he was a remarkable individual who through his presence of mind, the instinctive reaction of a man of science, had succeeded in shooting a film with invaluable documentary evidence regardless of the risk to his life.

I immediately arranged to track him down and he very kindly asked me to come round to his flat. Professor Nurul Ullah is a professor of electricity at the University of Engineering in Dacca. I found him to be a quiet, scholarly, soft-spoken, and surprisingly young man with a charming wife. He is normally engrossed in his teaching and students. But he happened to be the proud possessor of a video tape recorder which he bought in Japan on his way back from a year at an American university. He is perhaps the only man alive who saw the massacre on the lawns of Dacca University on the first day of the Pakistani army crack-down.

It was fascinating to sit down in Professor Nurul Ullah's sitting room and see the film twice with him, the second time after he had shown me the bedroom window at the back of his flat which overlooked both the street along which the soldiers drove to the university and the university campus. When he realized what was happening, he slipped his microphone outside [through] the window to record the sounds of firing. The film was shot from a long distance and under impossible conditions. Professor Nurul Ullah's description of how he shot the film was as dramatic and stirring as the film itself:

"On March 25, 1971, the day of the Pakistani crack-down, although I knew nothing about it at the time, my wife and I had just had breakfast and I was looking out of my back windows in the professors' block of flats in which I and my colleagues from the Engineering University live with our families. Our back windows overlook a street across which are the grounds of Jagannath Hall, one of the most famous halls of Dacca University. I saw an unusual sight, soldiers driving past my flat and going along the street which overlooks it, towards the entrance to the University. As curfew was on, they made announcements on loudspeakers from a jeep that people coming out on the streets would be shot. After a few minutes, I saw some people carrying out what were obviously dead bodies from Jagannath Hall. I immediately took out my loaded video tape recorder and decided to shoot a film through the glass of the window. It was not an ideal way to do it, but I was not sure what it was all about, and what with the curfew and all the tension, we were all being very cautious. As I started shooting the film, the people carrying out the dead bodies laid them down on the grass under the supervision of Pakistani soldiers who are distinguishable in the film, because of their dark clothes, the weapons they are carrying and the way they are strutting about contrasted with the civilians in lighter clothes who are equally obviously drooping with fright.

"As soon as firing started, I carefully opened the bedroom window wide enough for me to slip my small microphone just outside the window so that I could record the sound as well. But it was not very satisfactorily done, as it was very risky. My wife now tells me that she warned me at the time: 'Are you mad, do you want to get shot too? One flash from your camera and they will kill us too.' But I don't remember her telling me, I must have been very absorbed in my shooting, and she says I took no notice of what she said.

"It so happened that a few days earlier, from the same window I had shot some footage of student demonstrators on their way to the university. I little thought it would end this way.

"Anyway, this macabre procession of students carrying out bodies and laying them down on the ground was repeated until we realized with horror that the same students were themselves being lined up to be shot. After recording this dreadful sight on my video tape recorder, I shut it off thinking it was all over — only to realize that a fresh batch of university people were again carrying out bodies from inside. By the time I got my video tape recorder going again, I had missed this new grisly procession but you will notice in the film that the pile of bodies is higher.

"I now want to show my film all over the world, because although their faces are not identifiable from that distance in what is my amateur film, one can certainly see the difference between the soldiers and their victims, one can see the shooting and hear it, one can see on film what my wife and I actually saw with our own eyes. And that is documentary evidence of the brutality of the Pak army and their massacre of the intellectuals."

Account 3: Our Mothers and Sisters

The following testimony is from M. Akhtaurzzaman Mondol's "Amader-Ma Bon" ("Our Mothers and Sisters"). In *1971: Terrible Experiences* (1989), p. 197. It was translated by Sohela Nazneen. Reprinted with permission.

We started our fight to liberate Vurungamari from the Pakistani occupation forces on November 11, 1971. We started attacking from West, North and East simultaneously. The Indian air forces bombed the Pakistani stronghold on November 11 morning. On November 13 we came near the outskirts of Vurungamari, and the Indian air force intensified their air attack. On November 14 morning the guns from the Pakistani side fell silent and we entered Vurungamari with shouts of "*Joy Bangla*" [Victory to Bengal]. The whole town was quiet. We captured 50 to 60 Pakistani soldiers. They had no ammunition left. We found the captain of the Pakistan forces, Captain Ataullah Khan, dead in the bunker. He still had his arms around a woman — both died in the bomb attack in the bunker. The woman had marks of torture all over her body. We put her in a grave.

But I still did not anticipate the terrible scene I was going to witness as we were heading toward east of Vurungamari to take up our positions. I was informed by wireless to go to the Circle Officer's office. After we reached the office, we caught glimpses of several young women through the windows of the second floor. The doors were locked, so we had to break them down. After breaking down the door of the room, where the women were kept, we were dumbfounded. We found four naked young women, who had been physically tortured, raped, and battered by the Pakistani soldiers. We immediately came out of the room and threw in four *lungis* [dresses] and four bedsheets for them to cover themselves. We tried to talk to them, but all of them were still in shock. One of them was six to seven months pregnant. One was a college student from Mymensingh. They were taken to India for medical treatment in a car owned by the Indian army. We found many dead bodies and skeletons in the bushes along the road. Many of the skeletons had long hair and had on torn saris and bangles on their hands. We found 16 other women locked up in a room at Vurungamari High School. These women were brought in for the Pakistani soldiers from nearby villages. We found evidence in the rooms of the Circle Officers office which showed that these women were tied to the window bars and were repeatedly raped by the Pakistani soldiers. The whole floor was covered with blood, torn pieces of clothing, and strands of long hair ....

Account 4: The Officer's Wife

This testimony is from Amita Malik's *The Year of the Vulture* (1972), pp. 141–42.

Another pathetic case is that of a woman of about 25. Her husband was a government officer in a subdivision and she has three children. They first took away the husband, although she cried and pleaded with them. Then they returned him half-dead, after brutal torture. Then another lot of soldiers came in at 8 or 9 A.M. and raped her in front of her husband and children. They tied up the husband and hit the children when they cried.

Then another lot of soldiers came at 2.30 P.M. and took her away. They kept her in a bunker and used to rape her every night until she became senseless. When she returned after three months, she was pregnant. The villagers were very sympathetic about her but the husband refused to take her back. When the villagers kept on pressing him to take her back, he hanged himself. She is now in an advanced stage of pregnancy and we are doing all that we can do to help her. But she is inconsolable. She keeps on asking, "But why, why did they do it? It would have been better if we had both died."

Account 5: The Maulvi's Story

This testimony appears in Amita Malik's *The Year of the Vulture* (1972), pp. 102–104.

On April 19, 1971, about 35 soldiers came to our village in a launch at about 8 A.M. A couple of days earlier, I had asked the Sheikh's father and mother to leave the village, but they refused. They said, "This is our home and we shall not go away." Soon after I heard the sound of the launch, a soldier came running and said, "Here Maulvi, stop, in which house are the father and mother of the Sheikh?" So first, I brought out his father. We placed a chair for him but they made him sit on the ground. Then Sheikh Sahib's *amma* [mother] was brought out. She took hold of my hand and I made her sit on the chair. The soldiers then held a sten-gun against the back of the Sheikh's *abba* [father] and a rifle against mine. "We will kill you in 10 minutes," said a soldier looking at his watch.

Then they picked up a diary from the Sheikh's house and some medicine bottles and asked me for the keys of the house. I gave them the bunch of keys but they were so rough in trying to open the locks that the keys would not turn. So they kicked open the trunks. There was nothing much inside except five teaspoons, which they took. They saw a framed photograph and asked me whose it was. When I said it was Sheikh Sahib's, they took it down. I tried to get up at this stage but they hit me with their rifle butts and I fell down against the chair. Finally, they picked up a very old suitcase and a small wooden box and made a servant carry them to the launch.

Then they dragged me up to where the Sheikh's father was sitting and repeated, "We shall shoot you in 10 minutes." Pointing to the Sheikh's father, I asked: "What's the point of shooting him? He's an old man and a government pensioner." The soldiers replied, "*Is liye, keonki wohne shaitan paida kiya hai*" ["Because he has produced a devil."]. "Why shoot me, the *imam* of the mosque?" I asked. "*Aap kiska imam hai? Aap vote dehtehain*" ["What sort of an *imam* are you? You vote."], they replied. I said: "The party was not banned, we were allowed to vote for it. We are not leaders, we are *janasadharan* [the masses]. Why don't you ask the leaders?" The captain intervened to say that eight minutes were over and we would be shot in another two minutes. Just then a major came running from the launch and said we were to be let alone and not shot.

I immediately went towards the *masjid* [mosque] and saw about 50 villagers inside. Three boys had already been dragged out and shot. The soldiers asked me about a boy who, I said, was a *krishak* [cultivator]. They looked at the mud on his legs and hands and let him go. Khan Sahib, the Sheikh's uncle, had a boy servant called Ershad. They asked me about him. I said he was a servant. But a *Razakar maulvi*, who had come with them from another village, said he was the Sheikh's relative, which was a lie. The boy Ershad was taken to the lineup. He asked for water but it was refused.

Another young boy had come from Dacca, where he was employed in a mill, to enquire about his father. He produced his identity card, but they shot him all the same. They shot Ershad right in front of his mother. Ershad moved a little after falling down so they shot him again. Finally, the boy who had carried the boxes to the launch was shot. With the three shot earlier, a total of six innocent boys were shot by the Pakistani army without any provocation. They were all good-looking and therefore suspected to be relatives of the Sheikh.

After this, the Sheikh's father and mother were brought out of the house. *Amma* was almost fainting. And the house was set on fire and burnt down in front of our eyes until all that remained was the frame of the doorway which you can still see. Altonissa, the lady with the bloodstained clothes of her son, is the mother of Tomb Yad Ali who was shot. They did not allow her to remove her son's body for burial, because they wanted the bodies to be exposed to public view to terrorize the villagers. They also shot Mithu, the 10-year-old son of this widowed lady. She had brought him up with the greatest difficulty — they never had anything to eat except *saag-bhaat* [spinach and rice]. They shot little Mithu because he had helped the *Mukti Bahini*. You can now ask the ladies about their narrow escape.

Shaheeda Sheikh, Sheikh Mujib's niece, then added that fortunately all the women were taken away to safety across the river to a neighbouring village three days before the Pakistani soldiers came. For months they had lived in constant terror of *Razakars* pouncing on them from bushes by the village pond. Beli Begum, Mujib's niece, a strikingly lovely woman, told me how she had fled from the village when seven months pregnant and walked 25 miles to safety. Pari, a girl cousin, escaped with a temperature of 104 degrees. Otherwise they would all have been killed.

Account 6: Massacre at Faiz Lake

This testimony is from Abdul Gofran's "Faiz Lake - Gonohataya" ("Massacre at Faiz Lake"), which first appeared in *1971: Terrible Experiences* (1989). It was translated by Sohela Nazneen.

I own a shop near Akbar Shah mosque in Pahartali. On November 10th, 1971, at 6 A.M. about 40 to 50 Biharis came to my shop and forced me to accompany them. I had to comply as any form of resistance would have been useless against such a large number of people.

They took me to Faiz Lake. As we passed through the gates of Faiz Lake I saw that hundreds of non-Bengalis had assembled near the Pumphouse and wireless colony. The Bengalis who had been brought in were tied up. They were huddled by the side of the lake which was at the north side of the Pumphouse. Many of the Biharis were carrying knives, swords and other sharp instruments. The Biharis were first kicking and beating up the Bengalis brutally and then were shoving their victims towards those carrying weapons. This other group of armed Biharis were jabbing their victims in the stomach and then severing their heads with the swords. I witnessed several groups of Bengalis being killed in such a manner .... When the Biharis came for me, one of them took away my sweater. I then punched him and jumped into the lake .... I swam to the other side and hid among the bushes .... The Biharis came to look for me but I was fortunate and barely escaped their notice. From my hiding place I witnessed the mass murder that was taking place. Many Bengalis were killed in the manner which had been described earlier.

The massacre went on till about 2 o'clock in the afternoon. After they had disposed of the last Bengali victim, the Biharis brought in a group of ten to twelve Bengali men. It was evident from their gestures that they were asking the Bengalis to dig a grave for the bodies lying about. I also understood from their gestures that the Biharis were promising the group that if they completed the task they would be allowed to go free. The group complied to their wish. After the group had finished burying the bodies, they were also killed, and the Biharis went away rejoicing. There were still many dead bodies thrown around the place.

In the afternoon many Biharis and [the] Pakistani army went along that road. But the Pakistani soldiers showed no sign of remorse. They seemed rather happy and did nothing to bury the dead.

When night fell I came back to my shop but left Chittagong the next day.

References

Ahmad, Kamruddin (1967). *A Social History of East Pakistan.* Dhaka: Crescent Book Store.

Ayoob, Mohammad, and Subrahmanyan, K. (1972). *The Liberation War.* New Delhi: S. Chand and Company.

Bhutto, Zulfikar Ali (1971). *The Great Tragedy!* Karachi: Pakistan Peoples Party.

Brownmiller, Susan (1981). *Against Our Will: Men, Women, and Rape.* New York: Simon and Schuster.

Callard, Keith (1957). *Pakistan: A Political Study.* New York: Macmillan.

Coggin, Dan, Shepherd, James, and Greenway, David (1971). "Pakistan: The Ravaging of Golden Bengal." *Time,* August 2, pp. 24–29.

Government of Pakistan (1972). *Summary of the White Paper on the Crisis in East Pakistan.* Islamabad: Governor of Pakistan.

Haider, Rashid (Ed.) (1989). *1971: Vayabaha Ovigayata (1972: Terrible Experiences).* Dhaka: Jatiya Shahitya Prakasheni.

Jackson, Robert (1975). *South Asia Crisis: India, Pakistan and Bangladesh.* London: Chatto and Windus.

Jahan, Rounaq (1972). *Pakistan: Failure in National Integration.* New York: Columbia University Press.

Jahan, Rounaq (1973a). "Elite in Crisis: The Failure of Mujib-Yahya-Bhutto Negotiations." *Orbis,* Summer, 17(21):575-597.

Jahan, Rounaq (1973b). "Women in Bangladesh," pp. 5–30. In Ruby Rohrlich-Leavitt (Ed.) *Women Cross Culturally: Change and Challenge.* The Hague: Mouton Publishers.

Jahan, Rounaq (1980). "Reflections on the National Liberation Movement," pp. 34–64. In Rounaq Jahan (Ed.) *Bangladesh Politics: Problems and Issues.* Dhaka: University Press.

Jenkins, Loren, Clifton, Tony, and Steele, Richard (1971). "Bengal: The Murder of a People." *Newsweek,* August 2, pp. 26–30.

Khan, Ayoob (1967). *Friends not Masters.* London: Oxford University Press.

Loshak, David (1971). *Pakistan Crisis.* New York: McGraw-Hill.

Malik, Amita (1972). *The Year of the Vulture.* New Delhi: Orient Longman.

Marshall, Charles B. (1959). "Reflections on a Revolution in Pakistan." *Foreign Affairs,* 37(2):247–56.

Mascarenhas, Anthony (1971). *The Rape of Bangladesh.* New Delhi: Vikas Publication.

O'Donnell, Charles Peter (1984). *Bangladesh.* Boulder, CO: Westview Press.

Palit, Major-General D. K. Palit (1972). *The Lightening Campaign: Indo-Pakistan War.* New York: Compton Press.

Payne, Robert P. (1973). *Massacre.* New York: Macmillan.

Rahman, Anisur (1968). *East and West Pakistan: A Problem in the Political Economy of Regional Planning.* Cambridge, MA: Center for International Affairs, Harvard University.

Sayeed, Sk. B. (1967). *The Political System of Pakistan.* Boston MA: Houghton Mifflin.

Sayeed, Sk. B. (1968). *Pakistan: The Formative Phase.* London: Oxford University Press.

Schanberg, Sidney (October 1971). "Pakistan Divided." *Foreign Affairs,* 50(1):125–35.

(n.a.) (1971). "Pakistan's Agony." *Time,* August 9, pp. 24–29.

Umar, Badruddin (1966). *Sampradaikata [Communalism].* Dhaka: Janamaitri Publications.

Umar, Badruddin (1967). *Sanskriti Sankat [Crisis in Culture].* Dhaka: Granthana.

Umar, Badruddin (1969). *Sanskntite Sampradaikata [Communalism in Culture].* Dhaka: Granthana.

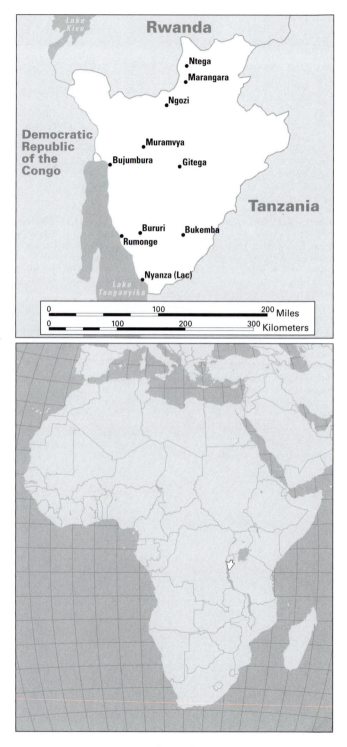

Burundi

CHAPTER 10
The Burundi Genocide

RENÉ LEMARCHAND

The first recorded case of genocide in the Great Lakes Region of Africa occurred not in Rwanda but in neighboring Burundi, 22 years before the more widely publicized 1994 bloodbath. The scale and targeting of the massacres, not to mention their purposefulness, leaves no doubt about their genocidal character. From May to July 1972 anywhere from 200,000 to 300,000 Hutu lost their lives at the hands of a predominantly Tutsi army in an orgy of killings triggered by an abortive Hutu insurrection. Though largely forgotten in the West, the events of 1972 remain deeply etched in the collective memory of the Hutu people, not only in Burundi but among the older generations of Hutu in Rwanda.

Piecing together a coherent picture of what happened before and during the killings is no easy task. Unlike what happened in Rwanda, the carnage attracted only minimal attention from the media. The few journalists who cared to investigate the massacres were denied access to the interior of the country, and their quest for credible accounts of the atrocities were restricted to official sources. No attempt was made by the government to conduct a serious investigation of the circumstances and scale of the blood-bath. Nothing comparable to Alison Des Forges' (1999) thoroughly documented inquest into the roots, mechanisms, and scale of the Rwanda genocide is available for Burundi. To this day, the search for explanations is trapped in divergent narratives. While some commentators (Tutsi) tend to impute genocidal intentions exclusively to Hutu insurgents, others (Hutu) blandly deny the existence of an insurrection, arguing against all evidence that unrest was deliberately instigated by the government in order to justify a genocidal response (Nsanze, 2003). Today the 1972 genocide has been obliterated from Burundi's official memory (Lemarchand, 2002). The only genocide officially acknowledged refers to the killings of thousands of Hutu by Tutsi in the wake of President Melchior Ndadaye's assassination in 1993. In Milan Kundera's felicitous phrase, the mass murder committed against Hutu has been "airbrushed out of history."

This calculated amnesia and obfuscation notwithstanding, certain basic facts are well established: Whereas the victims belonged overwhelmingly to the Hutu majority, the perpetrators of the genocide were for the most part drawn from the ruling Tutsi minority; the killings occurred in response to a localized, abortive Hutu-led insurgency that caused thousands of deaths among innocent Tutsi civilians; the repression and subsequent massive physical elimination of Hutu civilians were largely conducted by government troops assisted by the youth wing of the ruling party; and, in the wake of the slaughter, tens of thousands of Hutu men, women, and children fled the country, seeking asylum in neighboring states. (All of the above and much more is graphically revealed in the cables sent out to Washington by the U.S. Embassy Deputy Chief of Mission [DCM], Michael Hoyt, available from the author's collection at the University of Florida.)

The carnage has had a devastating impact on Burundi society. It has drastically reconfigured the country's ethnic map, driving a deep wedge between Hutu and Tutsi. The immediate consequence was the physical elimination of the entire pool of educated Hutu elites, and of all Hutu officers and troops, thus paving the way for the emergence of a Tutsi ethnocracy, protected by an all-Tutsi army. Unlike what happened in Rwanda, the *génocidaires* won the day. For the next 20 years all positions of influence and responsibility in the government, the administration, the army, and the economy were in Tutsi hands. Unsurprisingly, it was among the refugee community of Tanzania, the largest of all refugee communities, that the most radical, bitterly anti-Tutsi sentiments took hold of the hearts and minds of Hutu exiles. The legacy of hatred is still being felt today.

The Historical and Regional Context

The histories of Burundi and Rwanda are inseparable from each other. No attempt to understand the roots of the Burundi carnage can overlook the impact of the Hutu revolution in Rwanda (1959–1962) on the crystallization of ethnic enmities; similarly, only at the risk of greatly simplifying the dynamics of mass murder in Rwanda can one neglect the significance of the 1972 killings in Burundi (Lemarchand, 1995).

That both countries should have experienced bloodshed on such an appalling scale must be seen in the light of their shared heritage — colonial and precolonial. No other two societies on the continent had more in common in terms of size, social structure, traditional political systems, and ethnic configurations. Minute in size, deeply stratified, held together by popular allegiance to monarchical symbols, they also share strikingly similar ethnic maps. In each state the socially dominant ethnic minority, the Tutsi, held sway over the Hutu majority, representing about 80 percent of the total population (estimated at roughly 7 million in each state in 1994).

These commonalities can be easily overdrawn, however, and unless the contrasting elements are taken into account, the essential difference between the two genocides — the victimization of Hutu in one case and of Tutsi in the other — will remain obscure. Reduced to its simplest expression, where Burundi differed from Rwanda most markedly is in the greater complexity of its social hierarchies. Unlike Rwanda, where power was highly centralized and the line of cleavage between Hutu and Tutsi straightforward, in Burundi the real holders of power were a distinct category, namely the princes of the blood (*ganwa*), with the king (*mwami*) reduced to a *primus inter pares*.

Furthermore, the Tutsi were themselves divided into two groups, the lowly Tutsi-Hima, concentrated in the south of the country, and the more prestigious and status-conscious Tutsi-Banyaruguru, found predominantly in the north — again, the kingship was never identified with Tutsi rule to the extent that it was in Rwanda. Because of its greater pluralism and social complexity, Burundi was spared the agonies of a Hutu revolution before the advent of independence. Unlike what happened in Rwanda, where a revolutionary conflict pitted Hutu versus Tutsi, in Burundi preindependence politics revolved around princely factions, each drawing support from a mixed following of Hutu and Tutsi. The country crossed the threshold of independence not as a Hutu-dominated republic but as a constitutional monarchy, with a government consisting of a mixed assemblage of *ganwa*, Tutsi, and Hutu elements (Lemarchand, 1970).

Not until after independence (1962), and largely as a consequence of the demonstration effect of the Rwanda revolution, did a significant hardening of Hutu–Tutsi tensions emerge on the political horizon. The proclamation of a Hutu republic in Rwanda served as a powerful source of inspiration for many aspiring Hutu politicians; indeed, for many, Rwanda became the model polity that helped shape their vision of the future. For most Tutsi, on the other hand, republican Rwanda evoked a nightmarish scenario, to be avoided at all cost. With tens of thousands of Tutsi asylum seekers from Rwanda entering the country, each with tales of horror to tell, the message was driven home loud and clear.

A turning point in the escalation of the Hutu–Tutsi conflict came in May 1965, with the first postindependence elections to the national assembly, in which Hutu candidates scored a landslide victory, capturing 23 seats out of a total of 33. Their victory quickly proved illusory. Instead of appointing a Hutu as prime minister, the king turned to a princely figure and longtime protege of the Court (Leopold Bihumugani). Robbed of their victory at the polls, the Hutu elites reacted angrily to what they perceived as an intolerable interference. On October 18, 1965, Hutu anger broke out in an abortive coup directed at the king's palace, followed by sporadic attacks against Tutsi elements in the interior. Panic-stricken, the king fled the country, never to return. In reprisal, Tutsi units of the army and *gendarmerie* arrested and shot 86 leading Hutu politicians and army officers. After the discovery of an alleged Hutu plot in 1969, 70 Hutu personalities, civilian and military, were arrested on the grounds of conspiring against the state; 25 were meted out a death sentence, and 19 of them were immediately executed.

In the minds of those few Hutu politicians who survived the repression, recourse to force was increasingly seen as the only viable option. This hardening of attitude on the Hutu–Tutsi problem was largely shared among Hutu students at the Université Officielle de Bujumbura. In point of fact, according to reliable accounts (Kiraranganiya, 1985), the instigators of the Hutu rebellion of April 1972 were three students (Celius Mpasha, Albert Butoyi, and Daniel Ndabiruye), affiliated with the *Parti du Peuple*, known for their pro-Hutu militancy. The systematic exclusion of Hutu elements from all positions of responsibility in the government, the civil service, and the higher ranks of the armed forces was the central element behind the abortive Hutu rebellion.

But if the insurgency must be seen in the context of the growing polarization of ethnic ties, its timing draws attention to the violent intra-Tutsi squabbles and maneuverings that preceded the uprising. This growing split within the ruling oligarchy is what prompted the insurgents to exploit the situation to their advantage.

In the months preceding the slaughter, the country seemed to be tottering on the brink of anarchy. The long-simmering struggle between Tutsi-Hima and Tutsi-Banyaruguru was threatening to get out of hand (Lemarchand, 1974, 1995). The country was awash with rumors of plots and counterplots, leading to the arrest and bogus trials of scores of Banyaruguru politicians. Meanwhile, the ruling clique, headed by President Michel Micombero, and consisting principally of Tutsi-Hima from the Bururi province, saw its legitimacy plummet. Nothing could have done more to solidify Tutsi solidarities than the looming threat of a violent Hutu uprising.

The Road to Mass Murder

On April 29, 1972, like a bolt out of the blue, a violent Hutu-led insurrection burst upon the normally peaceful lakeside towns of Rumonge and Nyanza-Lac in the south. In a matter of hours terror was unleashed by

Hutu upon Tutsi. Countless atrocities were reported by eyewitnesses, including the evisceration of pregnant women and the hacking off of limbs. In Bururi, all military and civilian authorities were killed. After seizing control of the armories in Rumonge and Nyanza-Lac, the insurgents proceeded to kill every Tutsi in sight, as well as a number of Hutu who refused to join the rebels. During the first week of violence it is thought that the insurgency claimed the lives of anywhere from 2000 to 3000, most of them Tutsi. At this point, in an attempt to build a political base, some of the insurgents retreated to Vyanda, near the provincial capital of Bururi, and proclaimed a mysterious "*République de Martyazo.*" A week later government troops brought the nascent experiment to an end. By then, though, the repression had already caused untold casualties throughout the country.

Although no one knows how many were involved, the insurgents could not have numbered more than a few thousand (and not 25,000 as the government subsequently claimed). A French pilot, who flew helicopter missions on behalf of the Burundi army, put their number at 1000, "including the majority of committed or conscripted Hutu, Zairian Mulelistes in the middle, and the organizers at the top" (Hoyt, May 5, 1972). Despite the persistent reports of the presence of Mulelistes (a reference to the Congolese rebellion of 1964, said to have been instigated by Pierre Mulele) among the insurgents, questions remain as to their numbers and motives for joining the Hutu uprising.

On May 30, after proclaiming martial law, President Micombero requested immediate military assistance from President Mobutu of Zaire. With Zairian paratroopers holding the airport, the Burundi army then moved in force into the countryside. What followed was not so much a repression as a hideous slaughter of Hutu civilians. The carnage went on unabated until August. By then almost every educated Hutu element was either dead or in exile.

Exactly how many died between May and August is impossible to say. Conservative estimates put the total number of victims somewhere between 100,000 and 150,000. This is considerably less than the 300,000 claimed by Hutu opponents of the regime, and far more than the 15,000 at first cited by the Burundi authorities. However much one can disagree about the scale of the massacre, that it reflects a planned annihilation is hardly in doubt. Much of the "planning," as we now realize, was the work of the Minister of Foreign Affairs at the time, Artémon Simbananiye, assisted in his task by the Minister of Interior and Justice, Albert Shibura, and the executive secretary of the ruling *Union pour le Progrés National* (*Uprona*) party, André Yanda. All three were of Hima origins; the latter two also held key positions in the army.

For many Hutu, "*le plan Simbananiye*" is the key to an understanding of the killings. According to this master plan, conceived long before the Hutu uprising, the aim was to provoke the Hutu into staging an uprising so as to justify a devastating repression and cleanse the country once and for all of the Hutu peril. There is, in fact, little evidence of any such provocation; nor is it at all clear that any such plan existed prior to the Hutu uprising. What is beyond question, however, is that Simbananiye used the "clear and present danger" posed by the Hutu insurgency as a pretext to go far beyond the immediate exigency of restoring peace and order. As the social profile of the victims clearly shows, the ultimate objective was to systematically kill all educated Hutu elements, including civil servants, university students, and schoolchildren and, in so doing, eliminate for the foreseeable future any serious threat of Hutu rebellion. It is in this sense that one can indeed speak of a "Simbananiye plan" (Lemarchand, 1995).

The systematic targeting of educated Hutu elements is a point on which most observers agree. As Jeremy Greenland (1976) reported, "The government radio broadcasts encouraged the population to 'hunt down the python in the grass,' an order which was interpreted by Tutsi in the interior as license to exterminate all educated Hutu, down to the level of secondary, and, in some cases, even primary schoolchildren. Army units commandeered merchants' lorries and mission vehicles, and drove up to schools removing whole batches of children at a time. Tutsi pupils prepared lists of their Hutu classmates to make identification by officials more straightforward" (p. 120). In Bujumbura, Gitega, and Ngozi, all "cadres" of Hutu origins — not only local civil servants but chauffeurs, clerks, and semi-skilled workers — were rounded up, taken to the nearest jail, and either shot or beaten to death with rifle butts and clubs. In Bujumbura alone, an estimated 4000 Hutu were loaded up on trucks and taken to their graves.

Some of the most gruesome scenes took place on the premises of the university in Bujumbura, and in secondary and technical schools. Scores of Hutu students were physically assaulted by their Tutsi classmates, and many beaten to death. In a scenario that would repeat itself again and again, groups of soldiers and members of the *Uprona* youth wing, the so-called *Jeunesses Révolutionnaires Rwagasore* (*JRR*), would suddenly appear in classrooms, call the Hutu students by name and take them away. Few ever returned. Approximately one third (120) of the Hutu students enrolled at the university disappeared in such circumstances. The few Tutsi who urged restraint did so at their own peril. As Michael Hoyt (1972), then acting Deputy Chief of Mission at the U.S. Embassy, stated on May 27th, "We have reliable reports that some Tutsi urging restraint in Bujumbura on the basis that the situation has gone too far are being arrested and immediately executed" (p. 1).

Nor was the Church spared. Reporting from Bujumbura in early June, Marvine Howe (1972) noted that "12 Hutu priests are said to have been killed, and thousands of Protestant pastors, school directors and teachers"

(p. 4). No sector of society was left untouched, least of all the military. This is how Hoyt (1972) describes the extent of the purges within the army:

> The death toll in the army resulting from the execution of Hutu has risen. Recent Belgian estimates point to more than 500. About 150 Hutu were executed on the night of May 22. Forty-one on the night of May 27. Definition of Hutu has altered, however. Now one grandparent is enough to result in classifying soldiers as Hutu. Using this standard some 100 Hutu were believed to be alive in the army on May 23 (p. 2).

To impute genocidal intentions to all Tutsi would be both unfair and inaccurate. Whether intentions ultimately made a difference is another matter. In the countryside anti-Hutu violence stemmed from a variety of motives, some involving personal enmities, others rooted in crassly material calculations. The desire to appropriate the victims' property appears to have been a major inducement to violence. Again, to quote from Greenland (1976): "In countless cases, the furniture was removed from the homes of arrested Hutu, with the widows and orphans left sitting on the bare floor. The cars and lorries of wealthier Hutu became the property of those who arrested them" (p. 122).

Clearly, responsibility for the killings cannot be ascribed collectively to all Tutsi. Many paid with their lives for their determination to protect Hutu elements, and the same is true of those Hutu who, during the insurgency, took it upon themselves to shelter Tutsi civilians. The key participants in the genocide were the army and the JRR, often operating hand in hand, in groups of varying size depending on the magnitude of the task that lay ahead. "In Muramvuya," according to Hoyt (1972), "the populace was thrown into near panic by the sudden arrival of nearly 1000 JRR elements" (n.p.). In most instances, the arrests and subsequent executions were conducted by mixed teams of army men and JRR elements consisting of a dozen individuals; and where neither group could be summoned in sufficient numbers, arms were distributed to local Tutsi males with instructions to act as surrogate paramilitary groups. In an atmosphere saturated with fear, the killing of Hutu seemed to have become part of the civic duty expected of every Tutsi citizen. A number of Tutsi refugees from Rwanda accepted the assignment with little or no hesitation. Particularly in the northern region, where refugee camps were located, much of the killing was done by Tutsi refugees, perhaps as much out of revenge as out of fear that they might once again be the target of Hutu violence.

Fear of an impending Hutu-instigated slaughter of all Tutsi elements, nurtured by lingering memories of what happened in Rwanda in 1959–1962, certainly played a crucial part in transforming the repression into a genocide. That many Tutsi perceived the Hutu attacks as posing a mortal threat to their survival, there can be no doubt; nor is there any question, that many viewed the wholesale elimination of Hutu elites as the only way of dealing effectively with what they perceived as a clear and present danger — a kind of "Final Solution" to a situation that threatened their very existence as a group. In the short run, their calculation proved entirely correct: The wholesale decapitation of the Hutu elites insured peace and order for the next 16 years. But as is now becoming increasingly clear, the long-term effects of the genocide have enormously complicated the quest for a peaceful solution of the Hutu–Tutsi question. Among the new generations of Hutu elites few are willing to forget or forgive.

The Silence of the International Community

In the White Paper issued by the government in the wake of the killings, the point that comes across again and again is that the Hutu rebels had committed genocide against the people of Burundi; in putting down the rebellion, the state prevented the insurgency from taking an even bigger toll. Surprisingly, the diffusion of this inversionary discourse — aimed at shifting the onus of genocide to the insurgents — was received with little more than polite indifference by international public opinion. The unwillingness of the international community to see through the humbug of official media and take heed of the many warning signs preceding the slaughter, all wrenchingly clear, is little short of astonishing. Perhaps the most surreal of all international responses to the slaughter came from the Organization of African Unity (OAU) — now the African Union (AU) — on May 22, 1972, during the visit to Bujumbura by OAU Secretary-General Diallo Telli. "The OAU," said Telli, "being essentially an organization based on solidarity, my presence here in Bujumbura signifies the total solidarity of the Secretariat with the President of Burundi, and with the government and the fraternal people of Burundi" (Hoyt, May 22, 1972, n.p.). It is an ironic commentary on Telli's expression of solidarity with the chief organizer of the butchery that he himself was later murdered by Guinean President Sekou Touré. Then, too, the OAU appeared to be in "total solidarity" with Telli's murder.

To take the full measure of Western indifference, one can do no better than quote from the surprisingly guarded letter of the diplomatic corps delivered to President Micombero on May 30, at the initiative of the papal nuncio: "As true friends of Burundi we have followed with anguish and concern the events of the last few weeks. We are thus comforted by your appointment of groups of 'wise men' to pacify the country, and by the orders that you have given to repress the arbitrary actions of individuals and groups, and acts of private vengeance and excesses of authority" (Hoyt, May 30, 1972, n.p.). By then "excesses of authority" had sent well over 100,000 Hutu to their graves. Unsurprisingly, the only member of the diplomatic corps who refused to sign the letter, presumably objecting to its offensive wording, was the French ambassador.

Hardly more edifying was the response of the UN Secretary-General, Kurt Waldheim, to the carnage. Following the visit of a UN Special Mission to Burundi from June 22 through 28, headed by I.S. Djermakoye, Special Advisor on African Affairs, Waldheim expressed his "fervent hopes that peace, harmony, and stability can be brought about successfully and speedily, that Burundi will thereby achieve the goals of social progress, better standards of living and other ideals and principles set forth in the UN Charter" (quoted in Teltsch, 1972, p. 1). The cynicism behind such pious hopes is a devastating commentary on the role of the UN during the genocide. In 1972, as in 1994, the UN sat on its hands as hundreds of thousands of innocent Africans were being slaughtered.

Scarcely more edifying was the response of the U.S. government. In the words of a report of the Carnegie Endowment for International Peace, the official stance of the United States revealed an extraordinary combination of "indifference, inertia, and irresponsibility" (Brown et al., 1973, p. 4). The remarkably detailed reports by the U.S. Deputy Chief of Mission in Bujumbura, Michael Hoyt, sent to the State Department failed to elicit as much as a minimal expression of concern from the Secretary of State. "On May 25, 1972," according to Roger Morris, "[U.S. Ambassador] Thomas Melady routinely left the country for a new assignment. He departed with a decoration from the Burundi government, he and his home office in Foggy Bottom maintaining total silence about the horror" (Morris, 1977, p. 267). Perceptions of Burundi as an "autistic and suspicious society," to quote from a 1972 State Department policy paper (Morris, 1977, p. 267), seemed entirely consistent with the kind of benign neglect displayed by U.S. policy makers in the face of irrefutable evidence of genocide.

The Aftermath

Although the killings were intended first and foremost to crush the insurrection, there was a great deal more at stake. The underlying objectives of the Micombero government in orchestrating the huge bloodletting were: (1) to insure the long-term stability of the state by the wholesale elimination of all educated Hutu elites and potential elites (e.g., schoolchildren); (2) to transform the instruments of force — the army, the police, and the *gendarmerie* — into a Tutsi monopoly; (3) to rule out the possibility of a restoration of the monarchy (hence the killing of young King Ntare in Gitega on May 1); and (4) to create a new basis of legitimacy for the Hima-dominated state by projecting an image of the state as the benevolent protector of all Burundians against their domestic and external enemies.

On each of these counts, the Micombero government met with considerable success — at least in the short run. For the next 16 years —

until the Ntega and Marangara riots of 1988 — Burundi experienced a period of unprecedented peace. The country was virtually bereft of educated Hutu elites; the ever-present threat of another slaughter was enough to discourage all forms of protest; and the army was now a Tutsi army — and it remains so to this day.

This surface impression of a country at peace with itself was suddenly shattered in August 1988, however, with a new outburst of ethnic unrest in the northern communes of Ntega and Marangara. Triggered by the provocations of a local Tutsi notable, and fueled by rumors of an impending massacre of Hutu peasants, the rioting took the lives of hundreds of Tutsi civilians before the army moved in and unleashed another bloody repression. While some 40,000 panic-stricken Hutu fled to Rwanda, according to press reports anywhere from 20,000 to 30,000 were massacred by the army (Chrètien et al. 1989, p. 171).

Unlike what happened in 1972, the international community responded to the killings with a sense of shock. Substantial press coverage of the events, coupled with charges of gross human rights violations from the European Community, were instrumental in persuading the Burundi government to introduce major constitutional and political reforms. Even more decisive in bringing about a more liberal political climate was the U.S. Congressional hearing held in September 1988, followed by the passage of a nonbinding resolution urging the government of Burundi to conduct an impartial inquiry into the circumstances of the riots, to take steps to investigate and prosecute those responsible for the atrocities committed during and after the riots, and, most importantly, to allow the safe return to their homes of Burundi's refugee population (Lemarchand, 1991, p. 86). By driving home to the Burundi authorities that their failure to heed Congressional warnings would entail major costs in terms of economic assistance and international loans, the resolution carried important consequences. It set in motion a train of reforms culminating in 1993 with the organization of multiparty presidential and legislative elections. The decisive victory scored by the predominantly *Hutu Front des Démocrates du Burundi* (*Frodebu*) and its candidate to the presidency, Ndadaye, effectively wrested power away from the Tutsi minority, enthroning, 21 years after the genocide, representatives of the Hutu majority.

What happened next brought into sharp focus the enduring legacy of the 1972 carnage. Ndadaye's assassination, on October 21, 1993, was the work of Tutsi extremists who saw in the coming to power of a Hutu president a threat not so much to their survival as to their economic and political privileges. Having reaped for decades the benefits of unfettered control of state institutions, a transfer of power to a Hutu carried ominous implications. A return to the status quo ante by political assassination seemed all the more feasible given the profile of the army. What they did not foresee was the violent response of the Hutu community. The news of Ndadaye's assassination was greeted on the hills with an orgy of anti-Tutsi violence. Possibly as many as 25,000 Tutsi were killed by their Hutu neighbors in an uncontrolled outburst of rage — in turn, causing the army to kill at least as many Hutu in retaliation.

In today's Burundi, the 1993 killings of Tutsi is the only genocide officially acknowledged. Nothing is said of the Hutu victims of 1993, much less of those of the 1972 genocide. Yet memories of the 1972 genocide go a long way towards explaining the fury that suddenly seized the Hutu peasants as they turned against innocent Tutsi civilians. As one Hutu clergyman reported, "When we told them [*les excités*] not to spill blood, they said 'Look, since 1972 it is our blood that's being spilled! Now we hear that President Ndadaye has been killed. If they did that, that means we are next!" (Lemarchand, 1995, p. xiv) Memories of 1972 suddenly came back with an emotional charge made more potent by intimations of an impending massacre of Hutu populations.

Ndadaye's assassination unleashed the radical streak of Hutu extremism, until then held in check by the more moderate *Frodebu*. Here again, one must go back to the political legacy of the 1972 genocide: It was in the refugee camps of Tanzania that came into being the *Parti de la Libération du Peuple Hutu* (in short, *Palipehutu*) in April 1980, which soon established itself as the principal vehicle of Hutu radicalism. Though denied the opportunity to present candidates in the 1993 elections, the *Palipehutu* rank and file voted overwhelmingly for the *Frodebu*. In the weeks following Ndadaye's murder, the party went into a state of suspended animation, while many of its former members joined Leonard Nyangoma's *Conseil National pour la Défense de la Démocratie (CNDD)*, and ultimately the *CNDD's* armed wing, the *Forces pour la Défense de la Démocratie (FDD)*. Thus, if there is little question that Ndadaye's assassination was the precipitating element behind emergence of an armed Hutu rebellion, the roots of Hutu radicalism go much further back in time. Along with the thinly veiled anti-Tutsi racism that surrounds its ideology, Hutu radicalism is, in a fundamental sense, the by-product of the 1972 bloodbath.

Long before the 1994 genocide of Tutsi in Rwanda, the Burundi carnage drastically altered the country's ethnic frame. It hardened the Hutu–Tutsi fault line to an unprecedented extent, while giving rise to the mythical representations that loomed so prominently during the Rwanda genocide. Contrary to an all-too-prevalent opinion, it is not in Rwanda but among the Hutu survivors of the 1972 bloodbath that history came to be recast as myth, and in the process new identities crystallized around the terms "Hutu" and "Tutsi." No longer were these ethnic labels relatively free of moral connotations; they now carried a powerful emotional load, conjuring up an image of the Tutsi as the embodiment of moral perversity.

If there is little doubt that Ndadaye's assassination played a critical role in the sequence of events leading to the extermination of some 600,000 Tutsi in Rwanda, it is no less important to remind ourselves of the contribution of the mythologies spawned by the 1972 genocide to the scurrilous propaganda distilled through the airwaves of Radio Mille Collines (Chrétien, 1995). As the work of Liisa Malkki (1995) convincingly demonstrates, many of the same themes were already apparent in the accounts that the Hutu refugees in Tanzania gave of their own martyrdom.

As in Rwanda, where neither time nor forgiveness will dim the memories of the 1994 slaughter, for years to come Burundi's genocidal past will continue to haunt its future, shaping its destinies in ways that are as yet impossible to predict.

Eyewitness Accounts: The Burundi Genocide

Note: Oral witness accounts of the events surrounding the 1972 genocide are extremely scarce, in part because of the restrictions placed by the Burundi authorities on unaccompanied travel through the countryside — especially when the aim is to interview survivors of the genocide — and in part because of the logistical, administrative, and political difficulties involved in gaining access to refugee camps in neighboring states. Malkki is one of the very few trained anthropologists to have conducted extensive interviews with refugees in Tanzania (in Mishamo, Kigoma, and Ujiji). The following three accounts are reproduced from her doctoral dissertation, *Purity and Exile: Transformations in Historical-National Consciousness Among Hutu Refugees in Tanzania* (1995). All were recorded in 1987, in Mishamo, Tanzania.

What is particularly noteworthy about these oral "mythico-histories," as Malkki described them, is the manner in which they intersperse myth and history, thereby providing the basis for a fundamental redefinition of collective identities. As Malkki (1995) points out, "If 'history' could ever be defined as a faithful recording of facts in an absolute reality, the Hutu constitution of history would be 'realistic.' The Hutu history, however, went far beyond accurate recording. It represents not only a description of the past, nor even merely an evaluation of the past, but a subversive recasting and reinterpreting of it in fundamentally moral terms" (pp. 124–25) In short, the implication is not that every word is pure fiction, only that reality has been filtered through the prism of an exceptionally traumatic experience. The result is a set of collective representations that have become part and parcel of the vision that the refugees have of themselves and of their recent history.

It should be noted that the names of Malkki's interviewees are not available. The key reason is that their discourse carries significant political implications which could conceivably be held against them.

Account 1

The first account is a graphic description of the atrocities committed by Tutsi against Hutu. How much is invention, how much is a faithful rendering of reality is impossible to tell. Although some of the more nauseating forms of torture alluded to in the text are probably made up, they reveal a construction of social reality rooted in a horrifying experience that continues to shape the consciousness of many Hutu refugees. Recorded in Mishamo, Tanzania, in 1987.

There was a manner of cutting the stomach [of pregnant women]. Everything that was found in the interior was lifted out without cutting the cord. The cadaver of the mama, the cadaver of the baby, of the future, they rotted on the road. Not even burial. The mother was obliged to eat the finger of her baby. One cut the finger, and one said to the mother: Eat! ... Another case which I remember: they roped together *opapa* [a father] with his daughter, also in Bujumbura. They said: Now you can party! They were thrown into the lake .... My older brother, he was roped, and then he was made to roll, slide on the asphalted road behind a car. The Tutsi's intention was to equalize the population, up to 50 percent. It was a plan. My brother's body was left in the forest. If it had been left on the road, the foreigners would have seen it, and they would have written about it .... The girls [Tutsi] in secondary schools ... killed the Hutu [girls]. The Tutsi girls were given bamboos. They were made to kill by pushing the bamboo from below [from the vagina] to the mouth. It is a thing against the law of God. Our party would never do this. God must help us. During the Genocide every Tutsi had to make an action [to kill]. In the hospitals, in the Churches .... Even the sick were killed in the beds of the hospitals. The genocide lasted three months, from the 29th of April to the end of August. But the killing was started again in 1973, above all in Bukemba .... In other cases a bonfire was lighted, then the legs and arms of the Hutu were tied [informant describes how the arms, tied in the back of the body, and the legs were fastened to ground, so that a circle of captives around the fire was forced to bend backwards]. Then the fire, the heat, inflates the stomach, and the stomach is ruptured. You see, with the heat much liquid develops in the stomach, and then the stomach is ruptured. For others, a barrel of water was heated, and the people were put into it .... For the pregnant women, the stomach was cut, and then the child who had been inside — one said to the mama: Eat your child! This embryo! One had to do it. And then, other women and children, they were put inside a house, like 200, and then the house was burned. Everything inside was burned .... Others utilized bamboos, pushing them from here [anus] up to here [mouth] ....
(Malkki, 1995, pp. 183–84).

Account 2

The second account brings to light a crucial aspect of the 1972 killings: the wholesale massacre of all middle class and educated Hutu elements, down to the primary schoolchildren. It brings out the sense of deep moral indignation felt by virtually every survivor of the massacre when reflecting upon the fact that educational achievement was sufficient reason for being killed. Recorded in Mishamo, Tanzania, in 1987.

They wanted to kill my clan because my clan was educated. The clans which were educated, cultivated, they were killed. In my clan, there were school teachers, medical assistants, agronomists … some evangelists, not yet priests, and two who were in the army …. All have been exterminated. Among those who were educated, it is I alone who remains …. There are many persons who leave Burundi today because one kills everyday. The pupils, the students … It is because these are intellectuals — because if you do not study you do not have much *maarifa* [knowledge, information]. Many Hutu university people were killed. The government workers, they were arrested when they were in their offices, working. The others also in their places, for example, an agronomist, when he was walking in the fields where he works, he was arrested. Or a veterinary technician: one finds him in his place, where he works. There were medical technicians, professors …. Or the artisans in the garage, or those who worked in printing houses or in the ateliers where furniture is made. They were killed there, on the spot …. The male missionaries and the female missionaries, who were doing their work in the Churches, in the schools as professors, or in the hospitals as doctors, they were not killed on the spot. They were killed in the prison. I think that the very first who were poured into the lake were the masculine missionaries and the feminine missionaries …. If you are a student, that's a reason for killing you; if you're rich, that's a reason; if you are a man who dares to say a valid word to the population, that's a reason for killing you. In short, it is a racial hate (Malkki, 1995, pp. 193–94).

Account 3

The third account reveals the circumstances of the massacre: the helicopters hovering over bands of hapless peasants, their flight into the bush, the constant fear of being picked up by soldiers, their long march into exile, their relief upon meeting friends and relatives whom they thought had been killed, their sadness upon learning of the death of others. And then the redeeming opportunity to "talk, talk, talk about what had happened …."

We heard the guns: boom! boom! boom! boom! And then there were helicopters, and when they saw a group of men on the ground, they killed them. We left home. We went into the forest and hid ourselves in the rocks. Others, they took flight immediately, all the way to Tanzania, but we stayed three months in the rocks, from April until June. We put the children under the rocks, and then we looked around. If the soldiers were far, we went into the fields to find cassava, sugar cane, like that, to give to our children …. Then, in the night, around 8 o'clock, we began the voyage [toward Tanzania] having prayed to God that he would protect us. That was the 9th of June 1972. We walked for one day and two nights. We arrived in Tanzania … with meat from our horses, with knives and three radios, with money in our pocket [Burundi francs]. When we arrived at the frontier they said to us: "Approach, approach, dear friends!" We were fearful. We asked each other: "What? The soldiers have reached here already?" They said, "We are the soldiers of Tanzania." We did not know where the boundary was. We just walked like sheep, truly like animals. We were very tired. Our children, their feet were swollen. The Tanzanian soldiers asked, "So, what do you have?" We said, "Knives and radios …." Concerning the money we said nothing. The soldiers said: "Yes, approach." They said, "Sleep here on the sand first, near the lake." We slept perhaps two hours. Then they said, "Now we will take you to Kigoma." While we were going towards Kigoma, on the way, we thought it was just us who had come here, but we ended up being 150. But then the others said, "No, no, no, we want to return to Burundi. Here in Tanzania we will starve. We want to go home." So, 35 of us remained in Tanzania. But — sad to say — all those who returned were killed. When we arrived in Kigoma, oh, oh, oh! … we met many, many, many men, women, from all the provinces of Burundi. We even saw people from different provinces whom we had met in the Church conferences in Burundi. All of them, they were all there! We asked them, "Where is your wife?" They said, "My wife is already killed; I ran away alone." And then, "Where is the pastor of your commune?" They responded, "He, he was killed." Like this we learned the news. One said: "Many, many were killed in the area where we lived …." The majority of the people came from Bururi, near the frontier. The first thing they did was talk, talk about what had happened …. We stayed in Kigoma for eight weeks, then the trucks came to take us to the camp (Malkki, 1995, p. 209).

Account 4

This last account is from Hanne Christensen's excellent study of a Burundi refugee settlement in Tanzania, *Refugees and Pioneers: History and Field Study of a Burundian Settlement in Tanzania* (1985). Described by the author as "extracts from interviews with refugees," which were conducted in 1984, it is a composite picture of the personal traumas and sufferings many have experienced in Burundi and in exile, while at the same time conveying the sense of nostalgia felt by most refugees for their homeland.

Homeland was a beautiful place, full of gentle hills and peacefully grazing cattle. My dreams are still bound to the homeland. We left Homeland during the warfare. Our relatives were killed. My husband lost eleven brothers, I five. They were killed by guns, spears and arrows. My husband was put in jail for three months. All that time he was tied, and fellow detainees were killed in front of his eyes. He kept alive, fortunately. After the killing stopped, he was released — and we fled. I had already taken flight from our homestead. We met on the way, in a hidden place just by coincidence. I had been living in the bush for one month, and we proceeded together to the host-country. Entering a foreign country as a refugee is to suffer extreme hardship. You feel lost after having left your country. Your belongings are completely separated from you. You live in fear of starvation. You are shocked because you have witnessed the execution of others, sometimes even of your relatives and friends. You are afraid that you have become invisible to God's merciful eye. You feel totally desolate. Arriving in the area of settlement, we got scared to death. It was in the middle of nowhere. Never in our lives had we seen such thick forest, inhabited only by wild animals, snakes and big, biting flies. We slept close to one another in a big bundle in the open air under the trees, surrounded by fires. During the daylight hours we cleared the forest. We were absolutely positive that we would starve, but prayed and prayed to get courage and food (Christensen 1985, pp. 136–37).

References

Brown, Michael, Freeman, Gary, and Miller, Kay (1973). *Passing-By: The United States and Genocide in Burundi, 1972.* New York: The Carnegie Endowment for International Peace.

Chrètien, Jean-Pierre, Guichaoua, Andre, and Le Jeune, Gabriel (1989). *La Crise d'Aout 1988 au Burundi.* Paris: Karthala.

Chrètien, Jean-Pierre (1995). *Rwanda: Les medias du génocide.* Paris: Karthala.

Christensen, Hanne (1985). *Refugees and Pioneers: History and Field Study of a Burundian Settlement in Tanzania.* Geneva: United Nations Research Institute for Social Development.

Des Forges, Alison (1999). *Leave None to Tell the Story: Genocide in Rwanda.* New York and Paris: Human Rights Watch and International Federation of Human Rights.

Greenland, Jeremy (1976). "Ethnic Discrimination in Rwanda and Burundi," pp. 95–134. In Willem A. Veenhoven (Ed.) *Case Studies on Human Rights and Fundamental Freedoms: A World Survey, Vol. 4.* The Hague: Martinus Nijhoff.

Howe, Marvine (1972). "Slaughter in Burundi." *The New York Times,* June 11, pp. 1, 4.

Hoyt, Michael (1972). "U.S. Embassy Cables from Bujumbura to State Department, April 29–August 29, 1972." (Unpublished materials, available from the author's collection at the University of Florida, Gainesville; Web site: www.uflib.ufl.edu/cm/africana/fulltext.htm).

Kiraranganiya, B.F. (1985). *La vérité sur le Burundi.* Sherbrook, Canada: Editions Naaman.

Lemarchand, René (1970). *Rwanda and Burundi.* London: Pall Mall Press.

Lemarchand, René (1974). *Selective Genocide in Burundi.* London: Minority Rights Group.

Lemarchand, René (1991). "Burundi: The Politics of Ethnic Amnesia," pp. 70–86. In Helen Fein (Ed.) *Genocide Watch.* New Haven, CT: Yale University Press.

Lemarchand, René (1995). *Burundi: Ethnic Conflict and Genocide.* New York and Cambridge: Woodrow Wilson Center Press and Cambridge University Press.

Lemarchand, René (2002). "Le génocide de 1972 au Burundi: Les silences de l'histoire," pp. 551–67. *Cahiers diétudes Africaines,* No. 167, XLII–3.

Malkki, Liisa (1995). *Purity and Exile: Transformations in Historical-National Consciousness Among Hutu Refugees in Tanzania.* Chicago: University of Chicago Press.

Morris, Roger (1997). *Uncertain Greatness: Henry Kissinger and American Foreign Policy.* New York: Harper and Row.

Nsanze, Augustin (2003). *Le Burundi contemporain: L'état-nation en question.* Paris: L'Harmattan.

Teltsch, Kathleen (1972). "Killings Go on in Burundi," July 20. *The New York Times*, p. 1.

Cambodia

The Cambodian Genocide 1975–1979

BEN KIERNAN

In the first few weeks after Cambodia fell to the Khmer Rouge in April 1975, the nation's cities were evacuated, hospitals emptied, schools closed, factories deserted, money and wages abolished, monasteries emptied, and libraries scattered. Freedom of the press, movement, worship, organization, association, and discussion all completely disappeared for nearly four years. So did everyday family life. A whole nation was "kidnapped," and then besieged from within. Meals had to be eaten in collective mess halls. Parents ate breakfast in sittings, and if they were lucky their sons and daughters waited their turns outside. During the years 1975 to 1979, Democratic Kampuchea (DK) was a prison camp state, and the 8 million prisoners served most of their time in solitary confinement. One and a half million of the inmates were worked, starved, and beaten to death.

Pol Pot and His Circle

The shadowy leaders of Democratic Kampuchea gave few clues to their personal lives. In 1978, the first journalists into DK from Yugoslavia, had to ask the prime minister, "Who are you, comrade Pol Pot?" He was evasive (Pol Pot, 1978, pp. 20–21). New light on his social background suggests its importance for his political life. How little is explained by his personality, though, remains an anomaly.

The story began in a large, red-tiled, timber house on stilts overlooking a broad, brown river, downstream from the town of Kompong Thom. The river teemed with fish, its lush banks lined by coconut and mango trees.

Behind the houses along the bank stretched large ricefields. A small Chinese shop sold a few consumables.

On May 19, 1928, Pol Pot was born Saloth Sar, the youngest in a family of six boys and a girl. His parents owned 9 hectares of riceland, 3 of garden-land, and six buffalo. Pol Pot's father, Saloth, with two sons and adopted nephews, harvested enough rice for about 20 people. In later years (during the reign of the Khmer Rouge), due to their relative wealth the family would have been deemed "class enemies." But few villagers thought so then. Rich or poor, everyone tilled the fields, fished the river, cooked tasty soups, raised children, propitiated local spirits and French colonial officials, or thronged Buddhist festivities in Kompong Thom's pagoda. In 1929, a French official described Kompong Thom people as "the most deeply Cambodian and the least susceptible to our influence."

But the Saloth family were Khmer peasants with a difference. They had royal connections. Pol Pot's cousin had grown up a palace dancer, becoming one of King Monivong's principal wives. At 15, his eldest sister, Saroeung, was chosen as a consort. In 1928, his eldest brother, Loth Suong, began a career in palace protocol. In 1934, at the age of six, Pol Pot joined him.

The country boy Saloth Sar never worked a ricefield or knew much of village life. A year in the royal monastery was followed by six years in an elite Catholic school. His upbringing was strict. The girl next door, Saksi Sbong, recalls that Saloth Sar "was very serious and would not gamble or allow children to play near his home" (Kiernan, 1985a, p. 27). The palace compound was closeted and conservative, the old king a French puppet. Outside, Phnom Penh's 100,000 inhabitants were mostly Chinese shopkeepers and Vietnamese workers. Few Cambodian childhoods were so removed from their vernacular culture.

At 14, Pol Pot went off to high school in a bustling Khmer market town. But he missed World War II's tumultuous end in Phnom Penh. Youths forced his cousin, the new boy-king Norodom Sihanouk, to briefly declare independence from France, and Buddhist monks led Cambodian nationalists in common cause with Vietnamese communists. In 1948, while back in the capital learning carpentry, Pol Pot's life changed. He received a scholarship to study radio-electricity in Paris.

He wrote Suong occasionally, asking for money. But one day a letter arrived asking for the official biography of King Sihanouk. Suong sent back advice: Don't get involved in politics. But Pol Pot was already a member of the Cambodian section of the French Communist Party, then in its Stalinist heyday. Those who knew him then insist that "he would not have killed a chicken," that he was self-effacing, charming. He kept company with Khieu Ponnary, eight years his senior, the first Khmer woman to get the *baccalauréat*. The couple chose Bastille Day for the day of their wedding back home in 1956.

Most of Pol Pot's Paris student friends — such as Khieu Samphan, Ieng Sary, and Son Sen — remained in his circle long after they were overthrown from power. He had early disagreements with Hou Yuon, later a popular Marxist intellectual, who was to be one of the first victims after the seizure of power by the Khmer Rouge in 1975. But Pol Pot stood out in his choice of a *nom de plume*: the "Original Cambodian" (*khmaer da'em*). Others preferred less racial, modernist code-names, like "Free Khmer" or "Khmer Worker." Pol Pot's scholarship ended after he failed his course three years in a row. His ship arrived home in January 1953 (Kiernan, 1985a, pp. 30–32, 119–22).

The day prior to his arrival home, King Sihanouk had declared martial law to suppress Cambodia's independence movement, which was becoming radicalized by French colonial force. Pol Pot's closest brother, Saloth Chhay, joined the Cambodian and Vietnamese Communists, and took Pol Pot along. In this first contact, Vietnamese Communists began teaching him, as one of them later put it, how to "work with the masses at the base, to build up the independence committees at the village level, member by member." It seemed a patronizing slight, like his failure to quickly rise to the leadership, despite overseas experience. A former Cambodian comrade claims that Pol Pot "said that everything should be done on the basis of self-reliance, independence, and mastery. The Khmers should do everything on their own" (Kiernan, 1985a, p. 123).

In the 1960s, a group of younger, mostly French-educated communists took over the leadership of the more orthodox (pro-Vietnamese) Workers' Party of Kampuchea, which had led the struggle against French colonialism in the 1950s. In 1966, the new leadership changed the party's name to the "Communist Party of Kampuchea" and set out on their path to power by staging an uprising against Prince Norodom Sihanouk's neutralist government. After victory over Sihanouk's successor regime, that of Marshal Lon Nol, in 1975, they proclaimed the state of Democratic Kampuchea, which, as previously noted, lasted nearly four years before being overthrown by a Vietnamese invading army in 1979.

The ruling body in DK comprised the members of the Standing Committee of the Central Committee of the Communist Party of Kampuchea (CPK). The leaders with maximum national power and responsibility for the genocide about to be perpetrated were those based in Phnom Penh and not those specifically responsible for a particular geographic area of the country. The former were known as the "Party Center." The Party Center was comprised of the following individuals: Saloth Sar (alias Pol Pot), secretary-general of the CPK since 1962, and prime minister of DK; Nuon Chea, deputy secretary-general of the Party since 1960, and president of the Representative Assembly of DK; Ieng Sary, who was ranked number 3 in the Party leadership since 1963 and was one of DK's deputy prime ministers (responsible for foreign affairs); Son Sen, number 11 in the Party in 1963 and a deputy prime minister of DK (for defense and security); Khieu Samphan, a Party member since the 1950s who became DK's president; Ieng Thirith, wife of Ieng Sary and DK minister of social action; and Yun Yat, wife of Son Sen and DK minister of culture. Khieu Ponnary, older sister of Ieng Thirith and childless wife of Pol Pot, was a provincial Party official and president of the Women's Association of Democratic Kampuchea, but reportedly suffered insanity around 1975. (Pol Pot remarried in Thailand after his overthrow and had two children.)

Two other figures were longtime members of Pol Pot's group. Though they held regional posts in 1975, they increasingly assumed responsibility for the implementation of genocidal policies throughout the country: Mok, number 9 in the Party in 1963, was Party secretary of the key Southwest Zone and later chief of the general staff of the Khmer Rouge armed forces, and Ke Pauk, Party secretary of the Central Zone of DK, later became undersecretary-general of the Khmer Rouge armed forces.

The Mechanics of Power

The late 20th century saw the era of mass communications, but DK tolled a vicious silence. Internally and externally, Cambodia was sealed off. Its borders were closed, all neighboring countries militarily attacked, use of foreign languages banned, embassies and press agencies expelled, local newspapers and television shut down, radios and bicycles confiscated, mail and telephones suppressed. Worse, Cambodians had little to tell each other anyway. They quickly learned that any display of knowledge or skill, if "contaminated" by foreign influence (normal in modern societies), was a folly in Democratic Kampuchea. Human communications were reduced to daily instructions and orders.

The CPK Center, known as *Angkar Loeu* (the high organization), began its purges in the 1960s by assassinating Party figures assumed to be too close to Vietnam's Communists. In the early 1970s, before taking power at the national level, the Center organized the arrest and "disappearances" of nearly 900 Hanoi-trained Khmer Communists who had come home from North Vietnam to join the insurgency against Lon Nol's regime. They had accounted for half the Party's membership in 1970. Then the Center gradually exerted its totalitarian control over the population by replacing autonomous or dissident Zone administrations and Party Committees with Center-backed forces commanded by loyalist Zone leaders Mok and Ke Pauk. By 1978, purges had taken the lives of half of the members of the

Party's Central Committee, although there is no evidence that this body had ever officially met.

Democratic Kampuchea was initially divided into six major zones, and 32 regions, each of which in turn comprised districts, subdistricts, and villages. One aim of the CPK Center was to build larger and larger units at the local level, abolishing village life altogether in favor of "high-level cooperatives" the size of a subdistrict. At the other end of the hierarchy, the Center set about reducing the autonomy of the zones by bringing them under its own direct control.

The most common pattern was for Mok's or Ke Pauk's forces to undermine a zone from below, first purging the district, subdistrict, and village committees, then regional ones, before finally picking off the severely weakened zone Party leadership. Another tactic was to carry out purges through the regional security forces (*santesok*) in a direct chain of command from the Center, bypassing the zone leadership. Those arrested were taken to the nerve center of the system, the national security service (*santebal*) prison in Phnom Penh, code-named Office S-21, now preserved as the Tuol Sleng Museum of Genocide. Up to 20,000 people, mostly suspected CPK dissidents and regional officials, were tortured and killed there from 1976 to 1979. Chief of the *santebal*, Kaing Khek Iev, alias Deuch, reported directly to Son Sen, who was the Center official responsible for security.

The entire process began in the insurgent zones before victory. In 1973, with Center backing, Mok emerged supreme in a factional battle for control of the Southwest Zone Party Committee, executing his senior and rival, Prasith, who had been number 7 in the 1963 Party hierarchy. The poorest region, renamed the Western Zone, was assigned to another rival, Chou Chet, who was eventually executed in 1978. After victory in 1976, Ke Pauk's forces carried out a violent purge of cadres loyal to his executed predecessor, Koy Thuon, in the Northern Zone, now enlarged and renamed the Central Zone. In 1977, Mok's Southwest Zone forces and administrators carried out a similar purge of the Northwest Zone, eventually arresting the Zone Party Secretary, Nhim Ros, number 8 in the 1963 Party hierarchy. On the other side of the country, Mok also took over two of the five regions of the Eastern Zone. Finally, a May 1978 conventional military suppression campaign commanded by Son Sen, Ke Pauk, and Mok overran the rest of the Eastern Zone and abolished its Party Committee. Zone Secretary So Phim, number 4 in the Party hierarchy since 1963, committed suicide.

The Center's struggle for total control was complete. But it had sown the seeds of its own overthrow. Surviving officials of the Eastern Zone went into rebellion, and in late 1978 they crossed the border and requested the Vietnamese military assistance that eventually brought DK to an end.

The Ideology of Genocide

Along with Stalinist and Maoist models, an underlying theme of the political worldview of the Pol Pot group was a concern for national and racial grandiosity. Their disagreements with Vietnamese Communists in Paris in the early 1950s concerned the symbolic grandeur of the medieval Khmer temple of Angkor Wat and their sensitivities over the small size of Cambodia's population. In their view, Cambodia did not need to learn or import anything from its neighbors. Rather, they would recover its pre-Buddhist glory by rebuilding the powerful economy of the medieval Angkor kingdom and regain "lost territory" from Vietnam and Thailand. Democratic Kampuchea treasured the Cambodian "race," not individuals. National impurities included the foreign-educated (except for Pol Pot's Paris-educated group) and "hereditary enemies," especially Vietnamese. To return Cambodians to their imagined origins, the Pol Pot group saw the need for war, and for "secrecy as the basis" of the revolution (Boua et al., 1988, pp. 214, 220). Few of the grass-roots, pragmatic Cambodian Communists could be trusted to implement such plans, which Pol Pot kept secret from them, just as he never admitted to being Saloth Sar.

The Party Center, with its elite, urban background, French education, and a racial chauvinism little different from that of its predecessor (the Lon Nol regime), inhabited a different ideological world from that of the more moderate, Buddhist-educated, Vietnamese-trained peasant cadre who made up the mass of the Party's membership. The acknowledged lack of a political base for its program meant that tactics of "secrecy" and violence were considered necessary. These tactics were used first against suspected Party dissidents, and then against the people of Cambodia as a whole. Given the sacrifices from the population that the nationalist revival required, the resistance it naturally provoked, and the regime's preparedness to forge ahead "at all costs," genocide was the result.

Who Were the Victims? Who Was Involved?

Genocide against a Religious Group

Pol Pot's government tried to eradicate Buddhism from Cambodia. Eyewitnesses testify to the Khmer Rouge massacres of monks and the forcible disrobing and persecution of survivors. Out of a total of 2680 Buddhist monks from 8 of Cambodia's 3000 monasteries, only 70 monks were found to have survived in 1979 (Boua, 1991, p. 239). There is no reason to believe these eight monasteries were atypical. If the same death toll applied to the monks from all the other monasteries, fewer than 2,000 of Cambodia's 70,000 monks could be said to have survived.

A CPK Center document dated September 1975 proclaims:

Monks have disappeared from 90 to 95 per cent … . Monasteries …
are largely abandoned. The foundation pillars of Buddhism … have
disintegrated. In the future they will dissolve further. The political
base, the economic base, the cultural base must be uprooted (cited
in Boua, 1991, p. 235).

This clear evidence of genocidal intent was carried through. As
Chanthou Boua (1991) points out, "Buddhism was eradicated from the
face of the country in just one year" (p. 227). By early 1977, there were no
functioning monasteries and no monks to be seen in Cambodia. In 1978,
Yun Yat claimed that Buddhism was "incompatible with the revolution"
(Jackson, 1989, p. 191). The Cambodian people, she said, had "stopped
believing" and monks had "left the temples" (Jackson, 1989, p. 191). She
added: "The problem gradually becomes extinguished. Hence there is no
problem" (Jackson, 1989, p. 191).

Genocide against Ethnic Groups

The largest ethnic minority groups in Cambodia before 1970 were the
Vietnamese, the Chinese, and the Muslim Cham. Unlike most other
Communist regimes, the Pol Pot regime's view of these and the country's
20 other national minorities, who had long made up over 15 percent of the
Cambodian population, was virtually to deny their existence. The regime
officially proclaimed that they totaled only 1 percent of the population.
Statistically, they were written off.

Their physical fate was much worse. The Vietnamese community, for
example, was entirely eradicated. About half of the 450,000-strong
community had been expelled by the United States-backed Lon Nol
regime in 1970 (with several thousand killed in massacres). Over 100,000
more were driven out by the Pol Pot regime in the first year after its victory
in 1975. The ones who remained in Cambodia were simply murdered.

In research conducted in Cambodia since 1979 it has not been possible
to find a Vietnamese resident who had survived the Pol Pot years there.
However, eyewitnesses from other ethnic groups, including Khmers who
were married to Vietnamese, testify to the fates of their Vietnamese
spouses and neighbors. What they witnessed was a campaign of systematic
racial extermination.

The Chinese under Pol Pot's regime suffered the worst disaster ever to
befall any ethnic Chinese community in Southeast Asia. Of the 1975
population of 425,000, only 200,000 Chinese survived the next four years.
Ethnic Chinese were nearly all urban, and they were seen by the Khmer
Rouge as archetypal city dwellers, and as prisoners of war. In this case, they
were not targeted for execution because of their race, but like other

evacuated city dwellers they were made to work harder and under much more deplorable conditions than rural dwellers. The penalty for infraction of minor regulations was often death. This basically constituted systematic discrimination predicated on geographic or social origin.

The Chinese succumbed in particularly large numbers to hunger and to diseases like malaria. The 50 percent of them who perished is a higher proportion even than that estimated for Cambodia's city dwellers in general (about one-third).

Further, the Chinese language, like all foreign and minority languages, was banned, and so was any tolerance of a culturally and ethnically distinguishable Chinese community. This, in essence, constituted being destroyed "as such" (Kiernan, 1986b).

The Muslim Chams numbered at least 250,000 in 1975. Their distinct religion, language and culture, large villages, and autonomous networks threatened the atomized, closely supervised society that the Pol Pot leadership planned. An early 1974 Pol Pot document records the decision to "break up" the Cham people, adding: "Do not allow too many of them to concentrate in one area." Cham women were forced to cut their hair short in the Khmer style, not wear it long as was their custom; then the traditional Cham sarong was banned, as peasants were forced to wear only black pajamas. Ultimately, restrictions were placed upon religious activity.

In 1975, the new Pol Pot government turned its attention to the Chams with a vengeance. Fierce rebellions broke out. On an island in the Mekong River, the authorities attempted to collect all copies of the Koran. The villagers staged a protest demonstration, and Khmer Rouge troops fired into the crowd. The Chams then took up swords and knives and slaughtered half a dozen troops. The retaliating armed forces massacred many and pillaged their homes. They evacuated the island, and razed the village, and then turned to a neighboring village, massacring 70 percent of its inhabitants.

Soon after, the Pol Pot army forcibly emptied all 113 Cham villages in the country. About 100,000 Chams were massacred and the survivors were dispersed in small groups of several families. Islamic schools and religion, as well as the Cham language, were banned. Thousands of Muslims were physically forced to eat pork. Many were murdered for refusing. Of 113 Cham *hakkem*, or community leaders, only 20 survived in 1979. Only 25 of their 226 deputies survived. All but 38 of about 300 religious teachers at Cambodia's Koranic schools perished. Of more than a thousand who had made the pilgrimage to Mecca, only about 30 survived. (Kiernan, 1988)

The toll goes on. The Thai minority of 20,000 was reportedly reduced to about 8,000. Of the 1800 families of the Lao ethnic minority, only 800 families survived. Of the 2000 members of the Kola minority, "no trace … has been found" (Kiernan, 1990b).

Genocide against a Part of the Majority National Group

Finally, of the majority Khmers, 15 percent of the rural population perished in 1975–1979, and 25 percent of the urban population. Democratic Kampuchea initially divided its population into the "old citizens" (those who had lived in Khmer Rouge Zones before the 1975 victory) and "new citizens" (those who had lived in the cities, and were the last holdouts of the Lon Nol regime). All cities were evacuated in April 1975. The next year, however, the "new citizens" were rebaptized "deportees," and most failed to even qualify for the next category, "candidates," let alone "full rights citizens," a group to which only favored peasant families were admitted. But not even they were spared the mass murders of the 1977–1978 countrywide purges.

The most horrific slaughter was perpetrated in the last six months of the regime, in the politically suspect Eastern Zone bordering Vietnam. The author interviewed 87 survivors in the Eastern Zone: In just 11 villages, the Khmer Rouge carried out 1663 killings in 1978. In another community of 350 people, there were 95 executions in 1978; 705 executions occurred in another subdistrict, 1950 in another, 400 in another. Tens of thousands of other villagers were deported to the northwest of the country. En route through Phnom Penh they were "marked" as easterners by being forced to wear a blue scarf, reminiscent of Hitler's yellow star for Jews (Kiernan, 1989b), and later eliminated en masse.

A total 1978 murder toll of over 100,000 (more than one-seventeenth of the eastern population) can safely be regarded as a minimum estimate (Kiernan, 1986a). The real figure is probably much higher (see Table 11.1).

The Historical Forces at Work

Rural conditions were better in prerevolutionary Cambodia than in neighboring countries like Vietnam or even Thailand. Land was more equitably distributed, and most peasant families owned some land. However, rural debt was common, and the number of landless tenants or sharecroppers increased from 4 percent of the farming population in 1950 to 20 percent in 1970 (Kiernan and Boua, 1982, p. 4). Thus, alongside a landowning middle peasant class, a new class of rootless, destitute rural dwellers emerged. Their position was desperate enough for them to have nothing to lose in any kind of social revolution.

The gap between town and countryside has been cited as a precondition for the Khmer Rouge's march to power. Unlike the countryside, the cities were not predominantly Khmer, but included large populations of ethnic Chinese and Vietnamese. Nor was the urban manufacturing sector very significant, producing few consumer goods for the countryside. Many peasants saw cities as seats of arbitrary, even foreign, political and

TABLE 11.1   Approximate Death Tolls under Pol Pot, 1975–1979

Social group	1975 pop.	Numbers perished	%
"New Citizens"			
Urban Khmer	2,000,000	500,000	25
Rural Khmer	600,000	150,000	25
Chinese (all urban)	430,000	215,000	50
Vietnamese (urban)	10,000	10,000	100
Lao (rural)	10,000	4,000	40
TOTAL New citizens	3,050,000	879,000	29
"Base Citizens"			
Rural Khmer	4,500,000	675,000	15
Khmer Krom	5,000	2,000	40
Cham (all rural)	250,000	90,000	36
Vietnamese (rural)	10,000	10,000	100
Thai (rural)	20,000	8,000	40
Upland minorities	60,000	9,000	15
TOTAL Base citizens	4,840,000	792,000	16
Cambodia	7,890,000	1,671,000	21

economic power. But none of this, of course, explains why the Pol Pot regime also turned against the peasantry in such large numbers.

Another factor was the rapid expansion of education in Cambodia in the 1960s, after long neglect of education under French colonial rule. A generation gap separated peasant parents from educated youth, who were often unable to find work after graduating from high school and drifted into political dissidence. The Khmer Rouge in the 1960s recruited disproportionately among schoolteachers and students.

Other historical forces at work included the increasing repression by the Sihanouk regime, which drove the grass-roots left into dissidence, enabling the French-educated Khmers of elite background, led by Pol Pot, to harness these home-grown veterans of the independence struggle to its plans for rebellion in 1967–1968; and conflict between the Vietnamese and Chinese Communists over Cambodia gave Pol Pot's faction Chinese support and valuable maneuverability against the orthodox pro-Vietnamese Khmer Communists (Kiernan, 1985a). And although it was an indigenous political phenomenon, Pol Pot's regime would not have come to power without the massive economic and military destablization of Cambodia by the United States, beginning in 1966.

On March 18, 1969, the U.S. Air Force began a secret B-52 bombardment of Vietnamese sanctuaries in rural Cambodia (Shawcross, 1979a, pp. 21-23, 31). Exactly one year later, Prince Norodom Sihanouk was overthrown by the U.S.-backed general, Lon Nol. The Vietnam War spilled across the Vietnam–Cambodia border, Sihanouk swore revenge, and a new civil war tore Cambodia apart.

The U.S. bombing of the countryside increased from 1970 until August 15, 1973, when the U.S. Congress imposed a halt. Up to 150,000 Cambodians had been killed in the American bombardments. Nearly half of the 540,000 tons of bombs fell in the last six-month period. Hundreds of thousands of peasants fled into the cities, to escape first the bombing and then the imposition of Khmer Rouge power. In the ashes of rural Cambodia arose the CPK regime, led by Pol Pot.

Pol Pot's forces had profited greatly from the U.S. bombardment. Contemporary U.S. government documents and peasant survivors reveal that the Khmer Rouge used the bombing's devastation and massacre of civilians as recruitment propaganda, and as an excuse for their brutal, radical policies and their purge of moderate and pro-Vietnamese Khmer Communists and Sihanoukists (Kiernan, 1985a, 1989a). By 1975 they had national power.

The Long-Range Impact on the Victim Groups

The population of Cambodia totaled around 6.5 million in 1979. The survivors thus emerged from the Pol Pot period nearly 3.5 million fewer than the 1980 population that had been projected in 1970 (Migozzi, 1973, p. 269). Not all of the difference is attributable to the Pol Pot regime; much is the result of the American war and aerial bombardment of the populated areas of Cambodia from 1969–1973, and of projected population growth that was unrealized due to instability, population displacement, and harsh living conditions throughout the 1970s. But 1.5 million deaths are attributable to the Khmer Rouge regime (Table 11.1, and Kiernan, 1990a).

The Cambodian population remains severely affected by psychological trauma. Post-traumatic stress syndrome is a general problem, including illnesses such as psychosomatic blindness, which has been diagnosed among survivors living in the United States.

International Responses and Current Status of the Cambodian Genocide Issue

On December 6, 1975, eight months after the Khmer Rouge takeover, U.S. President Gerald Ford and U.S. Secretary of State Henry Kissinger visited Southeast Asia. Ford told Indonesia's President Suharto: "The United States intends to continue a strong interest in and influence in the Pacific, Southeast Asia, and Asia. As a whole, we hope to expand this influence." Continuing, Ford said: "The unification of Vietnam has come more quickly than we anticipated. There is, however, resistance in Cambodia to the influence of Hanoi. We are willing to move slowly in our relations with Cambodia, hoping perhaps to slow down the North Vietnamese influence although we find the Cambodian government very difficult." Kissinger then explained Beijing's similar strategy: "The Chinese want to use Cambodia to balance off Vietnam. We don't like Cambodia, for the government in many ways is worse than Vietnam, but we would like it to be independent. We don't discourage Thailand or China from drawing closer to Cambodia" (Burr and Evans, 2001). For such geopolitical reasons, while the Cambodian genocide progressed, Washington, Beijing, and Bangkok all supported the continued independent existence of the Khmer Rouge regime.

In January 1979, the Vietnamese army invaded Cambodia, driving out the Khmer Rouge. A much less repressive regime was established with Hun Sen, first as foreign minister, and then as prime minister from 1985 onward. Vietnamese troops withdrew in 1989, after training a new Cambodian army that succeeded in defending the country on its own. But most of the international community embargoed the new government and continued to recognize the "legitimacy" of the defunct Pol Pot regime, voting for it to occupy Cambodia's UN seat for another 12 years. Therefore, until 1989, the Khmer Rouge flag flew over New York, and until 1992 Pol Pot's ambassador ran Cambodia's mission there. No Western country voted against the right of the government-in-exile dominated by the Khmer Rouge to represent their former victims in international forums (Kiernan, 1993, pp. 191–272).

Independent commentators often followed suit. In 1979 British journalist William Shawcross, author of *Sideshow*, a good study of the pre-1975 U.S. intervention and wartime destruction of Cambodia, hung the label of "genocide" on the Khmer Rouge's opponents. He alleged that Hanoi's invasion to topple Pol Pot meant "subtle genocide" (Shawcross, 1980, pp. 25–30) by enforced starvation, and warned of "2 million dead by Christmas" (Shawcross, 1979b, n.p.). Fortunately, he was very wrong. In his second book, *The Quality of Mercy*, Shawcross conceded that "there is no evidence that large numbers of people did 'starve to death' at the hands of the Vietnamese or their Cambodian allies" (Shawcross, 1984, p. 370). He also noted, "For the overwhelming majority of the Cambodian people the invasion meant freedom" (Shawcross, 1984, p. 78). Nevertheless, most Western governments portrayed the Vietnamese invasion as the cause of the Cambodian problem.

In the decade after Pol Pot's overthrow, many reputable legal organizations also dismissed proposals to send delegations to Cambodia to investigate the crimes of the DK regime. The International Commission of Jurists, the American Bar Association, and LawAsia all refused such opportunities to report on what the UN's Special Rapporteur on genocide, Benjamin Whitaker, described in 1985 as genocide, "even under the most restricted definition."[1]

A few voluntary organizations around the world pressed on, unaided by major human rights groups. These included the U.S. Cambodia Genocide Project, which in 1980 proposed a World Court case (Stanton, 1993); the Australian section of the International Commission of Jurists, which in January 1990 called for "international trials" of the Pol Pot leadership for genocide; the Minnesota Lawyers International Human Rights Committee, which in June 1990 organized a one-day mock trial of the Khmer Rouge following the procedures of the World Court, with testimony by a dozen victims of the genocide; the Washington-based Campaign to Oppose the Return of the Khmer Rouge, supported by 45 U.S. organizations, a former Cambodian prime minister, and survivors of the Khmer Rouge period; Yale University's Cambodian Genocide Program; and the NGO Forum, an international body of private voluntary agencies working in Cambodia.

At the first Jakarta Informal Meeting of Southeast Asian diplomats, on July 28, 1988, the Indonesian chairman's final communique noted a regional consensus on preventing a return to "the genocidal policies and practices of the Pol Pot regime" (Vatikiotis, 1988, p. 29). But the November 3, 1989, United Nations General Assembly resolution watered this down to "the universally condemned policies and practices of the recent past." A February 1990 Australian proposal referred only to "the human rights abuses of a recent past" (Australian Department of Foreign Affairs and Trade, 1990, pp. v–7). The five permanent members of the Security Council (the United States, the UK, France, the USSR, and China) emasculated this formulation in August 1990, vaguely nodding at "the policies and practices of the past" in the peace plan they drew up and imposed on Cambodia in late 1991.

In June 1991, the co-chairs of the Paris International Conference on Cambodia, Indonesia and France, accepted Phnom Penh's proposal that the final Agreement stipulate that the new Cambodian Consitution should be "consistent with the provisions of … the UN Convention on the Prevention and Punishment of the Crime of Genocide" (*Indochina Digest,* June 7, 1991). But the great powers rejected it; reference to the Genocide Convention disappeared from the Agreement.

In Western countries, public pressure on governments mounted. One result was the British government's disclosure on June 27, 1991, that despite repeated denials, its elite SAS military teams — from 1983 to at least 1989 — had trained forces allied to the Khmer Rouge (Pilger, 1991b, 1991c; *Asia Watch*, 1991, pp. 25–27, 59). The UN Subcommission on Human Rights, which the previous year had quietly dropped from its agenda a draft resolution condemning the Pol Pot genocide, now passed a resolution noting "the duty of the international community to prevent the recurrence of genocide in Cambodia" and "to take all necessary preventive measures to avoid conditions that could create for the Cambodian people the risk of new crimes against humanity" (UN Subcommission on Human Rights, 1991). For the first time, the genocide was acknowledged "in an official international arena" (Jennar, 1991). *The New York Times* (1991) called on Washington to publish its "list of Khmer Rouge war criminals and insist on their exclusion from Cambodian political life," and for their trial before "an international tribunal for crimes against humanity" (n.p.). Pol Pot, Ieng Sary, and Mok announced that they would not stand in UN-sponsored elections, but would campaign for Khmer Rouge candidates (*Indochina Digest*, August 30, 1991). They continued to lead the organization from the shadows.

In September 1991, diplomats revealed that "Western nations want the former head of the notorious Khmer Rouge to leave his nation, quickly and quietly," and that the United States had approached China for help in ensuring this "or at a minimum, making sure he remains in a remote part of Cambodia." Khieu Samphan retorted that Pol Pot had no plans to leave Cambodia. U.S. pressure on China and the Khmer Rouge remained verbal. Washington's material policy involved pressure on Hanoi, "to see that Vietnam holds Hun Sen's feet to the fire" (U.S. Deputy Assistant Secretary of State Kenneth Quinn quoted in Pilger, 1991d, pp. 10–11).

In October 1991, U.S. Assistant Secretary of State Richard Solomon said Washington "would be absolutely delighted to see Pol Pot and the others brought to justice for the unspeakable violence of the 1970s." He blamed Hun Sen for the Agreement's failure to include provision for a trial: "Mr. Hun Sen had promoted the idea over the summer months of a tribunal to deal with this issue. For reasons that he would have to explain he dropped that idea at the end of the negotiations" (quoted in *Indochina Digest*, November 1, 1991). The facts show, however, that the United States had never supported the idea of a trial from the time it was broached in June 1986 by Australia's Foreign Minister Bill Hayden, and that the United States and China had forced Hun Sen to drop the demand (Kiernan, 1991a).

In Paris on October 23, 1991, as the Agreement was signed, U.S. Secretary of State James Baker stated: "Cambodia and the U.S. are both signatories to the Genocide Convention and we will support efforts to bring to justice those responsible for the mass murders of the 1970s if the new Cambodian government chooses to pursue this path" (Shenon, 1991, p. A16). Australia's new Foreign Minister Gareth Evans, who had balked at his predecessor's proposal for legal action against the Khmer Rouge, now said: "We would give strong support to an incoming Cambodian government to set in train such a war crimes process" (Murdoch, 1991, p. 1).

The struggle to bring the Khmer Rouge leaders to justice began to bear fruit after the 1993 UN-sponsored elections, when they killed peacekeepers from Bangladesh, Bulgaria, Japan, and China. Following the UN's withdrawal, in 1994, the new Cambodian coalition government outlawed the Khmer Rouge insurgency, which began to fragment (Kiernan, 2002). In August 1996, Pol Pot's former deputy Ieng Sary defected to the government, bringing the military units under his command. Sary received a "pardon" for his opposition to Phnom Penh since 1979; he also retained autonomous authority over Pailin province. Other Khmer Rouge leaders jockeyed for similar deals. In June 1997, fearing further betrayal, Pol Pot murdered Son Sen. In the jungle of northern Cambodia, as the last military forces loyal to Pol Pot abandoned their base, they drove their trucks over the bodies of their final victims: Son Sen, his wife Yun Yat — the DK minister of culture — and a dozen of their family members. Mok turned in pursuit, arrested Pol Pot, and subjected him to a show trial in the jungle for the murder of Son Sen. But in March 1998, former deputy commander Ke Pauk led a new mutiny against Mok, and also defected to the government. The next month, as the various factions slugged it out, Pol Pot died in his sleep. It is possible that he may have committed suicide in order to evade capture. U.S. officials had been negotiating to take custody of Pol Pot at the Thai border.

In December 1998, the top surviving Khmer Rouge leaders — Nuon Chea, former deputy party secretary, and Khieu Samphan, former DK head of state — surrendered to the government. Cambodian troops captured Mok in March 1999. And the next month, Kang Khek Iev, alias Deuch, the former commandant of Tuol Sleng prison, was discovered by a British journalist (Dunlop, 1999). He, too, was quickly arrested by Hun Sen's police. Phnom Penh prosecutors announced that Deuch and Mok would be charged with genocide, and that both Nuon Chea and Khieu Samphan would be summoned to testify and would also be charged with genocide. Despite the deaths of Son Sen, Pol Pot, Ke Pauk (who died in 2002), and Mok (2006), five or more DK leaders remain liable to prosecution. But the specific nature of any charges remains to be determined.

Cambodia's two prime ministers, Hun Sen and King Sihanouk's son Norodom Ranariddh, had appealed in 1997 to the UN to establish an international tribunal to judge the crimes of the Khmer Rouge. In response, the UN created a Group of Experts to examine the evidence, including the documents collected by Yale's Cambodian Genocide Program and its now-independent offshoot, the Documentation Center of Cambodia. The UN experts concluded in 1999 that the Khmer Rouge should face charges "for crimes against humanity and genocide" (United Nations, 1999, pp. 19–20, 57). They reported that the events of 1975–1979 fit the definition of the crime outlawed by the United Nations Genocide

Convention of 1948. In their view, the Khmer Rouge regime had "subjected the people of Cambodia to almost all of the acts enumerated in the Convention. The more difficult task is determining whether the Khmer Rouge carried out these acts with the requisite intent and against groups protected by the Convention." The experts' response to this challenge was affirmative:

> In the view of the group of experts, the existing historical research justifies including genocide within the jurisdiction of a tribunal to prosecute Khmer Rouge leaders. In particular, evidence suggests the need for prosecutors to investigate the commission of genocide against the Cham, Vietnamese and other minority groups, and the Buddhist monkhood. The Khmer Rouge subjected these groups to an especially harsh and extensive measure of the acts enumerated in the Convention. The requisite intent has support in direct and indirect evidence, including Khmer Rouge statements, eyewitness accounts, and the nature and numbers of victims in each group, both in absolute terms and in proportion to each group's total population. These groups qualify as protected groups under the Convention: the Muslim Cham as an ethnic and religious group; the Vietnamese communities as an ethnic and, perhaps, a racial group; and the Buddhist monkhood as a religious group.
>
> Specifically, in the case of the Buddhist monkhood, their intent is evidenced by the Khmer Rouge's intensely hostile statements towards religion, and the monkhood in particular; the Khmer Rouge's policies to eradicate the physical and ritualistic aspects of the Buddhist religion; the disrobing of monks and abolition of the monkhood; the number of victims; and the executions of Buddhist leaders and recalcitrant monks. Likewise, in addition to the number of victims, the intent to destroy the Cham and other ethnic minorities appears evidenced by such Khmer Rouge actions as their announced policy of homogenization, the total prohibition of these groups' distinctive cultural traits, their dispersal among the general population, and the execution of their leadership.[2]

From 1999 to 2006, the UN negotiated with the Cambodian government and established a joint tribunal in Phnom Penh to ensure legal accountability for the Khmer Rouge's crimes. In 2007, the Cambodian and international co-prosecutors of the new Extraordinary Chambers in the Courts of Cambodia (ECCC) alleged that the defunct CPK regime had committed "crimes against humanity [and] genocide." The ECCC assumed custody of the imprisoned S-21 commandant Deuch, and also jailed, pending trial, four surviving leaders of the CPK "Party Center": Nuon Chea, Khieu Samphan, Ieng Sary, and Ieng Thirith.

Varying Interpretations

Interpretations of the nature of the Pol Pot regime have varied widely and controversially, even among Marxists and neo-Marxists. Its enemy and successor regime, for instance, quickly claimed that Pol Potism had been a case of Maoism exported to Cambodia by China's leaders in the 1970s. Indeed, official Chinese publications praised the Khmer Rouge rule as "the period of economic reconstruction" (Guangxi People's Publishing House 1985; Kiernan, 2002). And the pro-Chinese neo-Marxist Samir Amin (1981) had initially welcomed Democratic Kampuchea, as "a correct assessment of the hierarchy of contradictions" (p. 150) in Cambodia, and as a model for African socialists to follow because of its "rapid disurbani-sation" (p. 147) and its economic autarchy. Amin (1981) dismissed the claim that it was "an insignificant peasant rising" (p. 147). But in a 1981 reflection, Amin preferred to identify a Cambodian combination of Stalin-ist orthodoxy with what he now called "a principally peasant revolution": "The excesses, which today cannot be denied, are those which we know from the entire long history of peasant revolts. They are of the same nature and represent the same character" (pp. 4, 8–9).

In 1984, the historian Michael Vickery took up this very theme as a reason to reject Democratic Kampuchea, because, he argued, "national-ism, populism and peasantism really won out over communism" (1984, p. 289). In Vickery's view, Democratic Kampuchea was no Stalinist Com-munist regime, but "a victorious peasant revolution, perhaps the first real one in modern times" (1984, pp. 289–90, 66).

Amin's contribution is his analysis of Cambodian society as a relatively undifferentiated peasant society, similar to others in South Asia and Africa, and quite unlike China and Vietnam with their powerful landlord classes. His sympathy with the Khmer Rouge was based on their innova-tiveness in adapting a Communist strategy to these particular conditions. However, he later conceded, "this success itself has been the origin of the tragic difficulties," including "the well known excesses and shortcomings" (1981, pp. 4, 8–9).

But Vickery, in explaining the outcome of the Cambodian revolution, denies the very existence of the Stalinist vanguard attractive to Amin. He sees the Pol Pot leadership, not as significantly influenced by foreign Com-munist models, but "pulled along" by "the peasant element" (Vickery, 1984, p. 287). Vickery's approach combines an influential postwar intellec-tual trend in Southeast Asian historiography with a 1970s revisionist trend evident in the historiography of Hitler's Germany. I will examine each in turn.

In his path-breaking 1955 work *Indonesian Trade and Society*, J.C. Van Leur remarked that European historians of premodern Southeast Asia tended to see the region as outsiders, "from the deck of the ship, the ramparts of the fortress, the high gallery of the trading house" (p. 95). Yet, Van Leur (1955) argued, at least until the 19th century the European impact on Southeast Asia had been minimal and superficial: "The sheen of the world religions and foreign cultural forms is a thin and flaking glaze; underneath it the whole of the old indigenous forms has continued to exist" (p. 95).

Vickery (1998) applies this analysis to Hinduism in early Cambodian history, stressing the "Indic facade" on the indigenous culture of the pre-Angkor period. He also applies it to Communism in modern times. In *Cambodia 1975–1982*, he writes that "foreign relations and influences are very nearly irrelevant to an understanding of the internal situation" (Vickery, 1984, p. xii). He later explains: "We need investigations into autonomous development rather than superficial diffusionism, a change in emphasis which has become common in most of the social sciences and has led to important advances in the last 30 years" (Vickery, 1988, p. 17). Thus, in Vickery's view, "the only way to account for the apparent similarities between DK and the programme of Sendero Luminoso" [the Peruvian Maoist guerrilla movement] is as cases of "convergent social and political evolution out of similar backgrounds" (Vickery, 1988, p. 17). So the Cambodian and Peruvian parties' common adherence to and study of "Marxism-Leninism-Mao Zedong Thought" is seen as meaningless, if not a dangerously misleading "facade."

But in my view, DK ideology was not purely indigenous. It was an amalgam of various intellectual influences, including Khmer elite chauvinism, Third World nationalism, the French Revolution, Stalinism, and some aspects of Mao Zedong's "Great Leap Forward" — which DK claimed to outdo with its own "Super Great Leap Forward." The motor of the Pol Pot program was probably Khmer racist chauvinism, but it was fueled by strategies and tactics adopted from unacknowledged revolutionary models in other countries. Such syncretism is historically common in Southeast Asia, and it suggests that in an important sense the Khmer Rouge revolution was *sui generis*.

Vickery combines his argument for the primacy of the indigenous with a separate one. This is that the peasantry as a mass dominated the Cambodian revolution and took it in a direction the Pol Pot leadership could not have "either planned or expected .... It is certainly safe to assume that they did not foresee, let alone plan, the unsavory developments of 1975–79. They were petty bourgeois radicals overcome by peasant romanticism ..." (Vickery, 1988, p. 17; Vickery, 1984, p. 287). Now this argument is not unlike Hans Mommsen's analysis of Nazi Germany.

Mommsen believes, for instance, that Hitler did not plan the extermination of the Jews early in his career, but that Nazi policy was formed on an ad hoc basis over time and under the pressure of developing circumstances. It was a case of "cumulative radicalization." Mommsen's argument is that Hitler was no freak aberration, and that German history and society more broadly are also implicated in the genocide of the Jews. Similarly, Vickery considers DK an illustration of what happens when a peasantry assumes power: "It now appears fortunate that those who predicted a predominance of agrarian nationalism over Marxism in China and Vietnam were mistaken" (Vickery, 1984, p. 290).

The Pol Pot regime, then, was made up of "middle-class intellectuals with such a romantic, idealized sympathy for the poor that they did not imagine rapid, radical restructuring of society in their favour would lead to such intolerable violence" (Vickery, 1988, p. 14). But, Vickery claims, these Khmer Rouge leaders simply discovered that "it would have been impossible to hold the support of their peasant army," unless political enemies were "punished" and a departure made from the 1917 Bolshevik model of maintaining a "normal administration" and urban "privilege" (Vickery, 1988, pp. 14, 20, 5). And when the urban populations were deported to the countryside, "the majority base peasants" of Cambodia allegedly participated "with some glee" in the persecution of "their class enemies" (Vickery, 1989, p. 47). "The violence of DK was first of all — because it was such a complete peasant revolution — the victorious revolutionaries doing what peasant rebels have always wanted to do to their urban enemies …. [It] did not spring forth from the brains of Pol Pot or Khieu Samphan" (Vickery, 1984, p. 286; Vickery, 1988, p. 17).

A major problem with this analysis is lack of evidence. Vickery's *Cambodia 1975–1982* contributes much to our knowledge of the Khmer Rouge, but he did not consult peasant sources seriously. Among the 90 or more interviewees Vickery presents in his survey of DK, only 1 is a peasant. This interviewee hardly supports the notion of a peasant revolution, reporting "that they were fed well, but overworked and subject to 'fierce' discipline" (Vickery, 1984, p. 112). A family that Vickery (1984) describes as "half peasant–half urban," although "most of them by 1975 had long since ceased doing field work," all survived DK, but they "said that their many cousins, aunts, uncles, etc., … had perished, mainly of hunger and illness, although they were peasants … . In the opinion of the survivors, DK mismanagement had simply been so serious that not even peasants could survive" (p. 106).

Nearly all Vickery's oral testimony in fact comes from male urban evacuees he met in refugee camps in Thailand in 1980. His account of DK's Southwest Zone, which he correctly calls "the 'Pol Pot' zone par excellence," is based on the testimony of four former students, a former

French teacher, a former Lon Nol soldier and a medic, an agricultural engineer, "a girl from the 'new' people," and "an attractive, well-educated woman of the former urban bourgeoisie" (Vickery, 1984, pp. 98, 91, 97). These ten accounts offer unconvincing documentation of a key zone in a "peasant revolution." The few inside accounts in the book include corroboration, already noted, of an initial order to "kill urban evacuees indiscriminately." This order went out to both the Southwest and the Northwest Zones (Vickery, 1984, p. 98, 112). It clearly emanated from the central government — indeed from the very "brains of Pol Pot and Khieu Samphan."

This was probably the first major controversy in the historiography of the Cambodian revolution: the question of central control. Anthony Barnett (1983) argued that DK was "a highly centralized dictatorship" (p. 212). He also stressed its Stalinism, and its creation of "a nation of indentured labourers" (pp. 211–29). But Serge Thion (1983) contended that it was "a bloody mess," "riddled" with factional and regional divergence, so that "the state never stood on its feet" (p. 28). "Stalin, at least, was a realist. Pol Pot ... was and is an unimaginative idealist, a forest monk, lost in dreams" (Thion, 1993, p. 168). David P. Chandler (1991) also followed Vickery, asserting: "Under the regime of DK, a million Cambodians, or one in eight, died from warfare, starvation, overwork, misdiagnosed diseases, and executions. *Most of these deaths, however, were never intended by DK.* Instead, one Cambodian in eight fell victim to the government's utopian program of total and rapid social transformation...." (italics added) (p. 1)

Barnett was closest to the truth. Despite its millenarian tone, Pol Potism was not a centrifugal or a peasant ideology but a centralizing one (Kiernan, 1983, pp. 136–211). Understating the death toll of 1.7 million, Chandler (1991) also fails to adduce evidence that the regime "never" intended "most" of the deaths, and skims the issue of how many were intentional (p. 271). He does suggest (without citing a source) that in 1978, "perhaps a hundred thousand Eastern Zone people were killed," but is vague in attributing responsibility and explains it as an evacuation that "degenerated into a massacre" (Chandler, 1991, p. 271), suggesting it was unintended despite the deliberate marking of victims in Phnom Penh itself (Kiernan 1989b, 1991b). The regime was able to plan such mass murders precisely because of its concentrated power. It has been noted that the Khmer Rouge leadership not only succeeded in conscripting a massive labor force to turn Cambodia's landscape into a checkerboard of irrigation works, they even communalized people's breakfasts. The regime's intent was clear and was successful.

Chandler also overlooks the second major controversy, the case for genocide. He briefly notes the abolition of religion (Chandler, 1991, pp.

263–65), but not the ban on minority languages and cultures nor the enforced dispersal of ethnic communities, and he offers no estimates of any death toll among either Buddhist monks or minorities. He concedes that "the party seems to have ... discriminated against the Chams, a Muslim minority unsympathetic to the revolution" — a false imputation until the genocide began in 1975. He avers that DK, as he puts it, treated the Chinese "poorly," but that China may have helped protect them. And he notes that a Central Committee directive ordered the execution of ethnic Vietnamese residents in Cambodia. Yet Chandler concludes: "By and large, the regime *discriminated* against enemies of the revolution rather than against specific ethnic or religious groups" (italics added) (Chandler 1991, p. 285). He reveals no basis beyond DK's own for regarding these victims as "enemies of the revolution."

Nevertheless, there is scholarly agreement that the Khmer Rouge committed crimes against humanity. Eventually, a consensus on the genocide also emerged. Legal authorities Steven Ratner and Jason Abrams (1997) write in *Accountability for Human Rights Atrocities in International Law* that "the existing literature presents a strong *prima facie* case that the Khmer Rouge committed acts of genocide against the Cham minority group, the ethnic Vietnamese, Chinese, and Thai minority groups, and the Buddhist monkhood. While some commentators suggest otherwise, virtually every author on the subject has reached this conclusion" (p. 244).

Meanwhile new evidence has continued to accumulate. The archive of 50,000 pages obtained by the Cambodian Genocide Program in 1996 includes a vast amount of secret correspondence and other documents from the highest levels of the Khmer Rouge regime, including its security organ, the *santebal*. (Note: This archive has been microfilmed by Yale University's Sterling Library Southeast Asia Collection.)

Since 1997, the CGP's Web site (www.yale.edu/cgp) has cumulatively published the Cambodian Genocide Data Bases, which now include over 19,000 biographical records of Khmer Rouge figures from Pol Pot down to local district chiefs, 5,000 photographs of victims, and 3,000 catalogue records on Khmer Rouge-era documents, many of them digitally displayed. These and other primary materials ensure that scholarly research and debate will long continue on the nature of the genocidal practices of the Pol Pot regime.

Eyewitness Accounts: The Cambodian Genocide — 1975–1979

Oral accounts of the Cambodian experience under the Khmer Rouge regime were difficult to collect after 1975, when that regime established itself and immediately closed the country to outside visitors (except for occasional short guided tours by foreign diplomats). Along with the broadcasts of the official DK radio station, the accounts of refugees who managed to flee to Thailand, Laos, or Vietnam were nevertheless the major source of information reaching the outside world. In 1979, after the Vietnamese destruction of the Khmer Rouge regime, Cambodia was opened to journalists and researchers, and many more refugees also found their way to foreign countries. Thousands of refugees and others who remained in Cambodia have now told their stories of the 1975–1979 years, and some literate Cambodians have published books on their experience. But relatively few have been published in English, and even fewer narrate the experiences of the Khmer peasant majority, of ethnic minorities, of women, or of children. The accounts that follow have been chosen to fill that gap.

These testimonies were collected by Ben Kiernan and Chanthou Boua in 1979 and 1980, in the immediate aftermath of the overthrow of the Khmer Rouge. Kiernan, then a graduate student in Southeast Asian History at Monash University, Melbourne, Australia, was conducting his dissertation field research on 20th century Cambodia. One of the interviews took place in a Cambodian village, one in a Lao refugee camp in Thailand, and two in a Buddhist monastery inside Thailand. The interviews were conducted in Khmer without an interpreter and in the absence of any person exercising authority over the interviewees. The conversations were tape-recorded and translated as accurately as possible by Kiernan and Boua. The details recounted are reasonably typical of hundreds of other interviews recorded by Kiernan in 1979–1980 and do not conflict with anything known from other sources about Cambodia in the 1970s, though the mass of material is for logistical reasons difficult to corroborate on all specific points.

Account 1: "The Chams Are Hopeless" by Nao Gha

Nao Gha, a minority Cham Muslim woman, was interviewed by Kiernan in her village in Takeo province on August 26, 1980. The translation from the Khmer is by Kiernan.

I am 45 years old. I was born in Smong village, Smong subdistrict, Treang district, Takeo province. I first met the Khmer Rouge in 1972–73, when they came here. In 1973, they called all of us Chams to the mountains. We went to Kampot province, to Ang Krieu in Angkor Chey district. We spent a year there. They still treated us well, let us work and fend for ourselves. They spoke well to us. They called us "deported base people" [*neak moultanh phniaer*]. They did not persecute us. Our leaders were chosen from among us Chams. In 1974 they sent us back home. Everyone came back from Angkor Chey, over 100 families, but religion was no longer allowed.

In 1975, after liberation, the persecution began. Some Chams came from Phnom Penh to live in a nearby Cham village. We had to work on irrigation non-stop, day and night. Killings of Khmers began in 1975. In 1976–77 they killed someone every one or two months, for small infringements.

Then in 1976 they dispersed the Chams. The ten villages of Chams in this area were all dispersed, for instance to Samrong, Chi Khma, and Kompong Yaul subdistricts. We were not allowed to live together. Our village was also dispersed. They burnt our village down. Four to eight families were sent out to each of eight villages. I went with five families to Kantuot village, in Tralach subdistrict. There I had to grow dry season rice, far away, and would return to the village only after seven months.

Our Cham leaders were dismissed in 1976, and replaced by Khmers. We were not allowed to speak Cham. Only the Khmer language was allowed. From 1977, they said: "There are no Vietnamese, Chinese, Javanese [Chams and Malays] — only the Khmer race. Everyone is the same."

No Cham women joined Pol Pot's revolution. A few men had but the Pol Pot regime did not trust us. They did not let us do anything; they did not let us into their kitchens. When we went to eat [in the communal mess halls established in 1976] we could only go to the tables, we weren't allowed to go into their kitchens or anything. They were afraid we would poison the food or something. They hated us. They brought up the issue of the Chams being "hopeless." Soeun, the district chief of Treang [and son-in-law of the Southwest Zone commander Mok], said this several times in meetings of people from the entire district, beginning in 1977 and also in 1978. He also said at every meeting that the Chams had "abandoned their country to others. They just shouldered their fishing nets and walked off, letting the Vietnamese take over their country." [Soeun was referring to the 17th-century Vietnamese takeover of the kingdom of Champa, after which many of the Chams fled central Vietnam and settled in Cambodia. On this, Nao Gha volunteered the following comment:] I don't know anything about that. It happened long ago. I don't know which generation it was when the Vietnamese invaded and they shouldered their fishing nets and ran off to live in another country. I don't know, I don't know which generation that was.

All the Chams were called "deportees," even the base people. [In DK those who had lived in the Khmer Rouge areas before the 1975 victory were called "base people," or "people of the bases." They were distinguished from the urban evacuees, or "deportees." The Cham base people were denied this status; after being dispersed, they too were called "deportees."] The Khmers were called "full rights" and "candidate" people. We were called "minority" and were all classified as "deportees." Deportees were the most numerous, followed by candidates. The full rights people were relatives of cadres. The deportees, the candidates, and the full rights people all ate together, but lived separately and held separate meetings.

They met in one place and studied politics; and the other two categories had meetings elsewhere.

1977 and 1978 were years of hard work and the greatest persecution. 1978 was the year of hardest work, night and day. We planted from 4 A.M. to 10 A.M., then ate a meal. At 1 P.M. we started again, and worked until 5 P.M., and then from 7 to 10 P.M. There was some education, for young children to learn the alphabet. It was about one hour per day, from 12 to 1 P.M.

There was not enough food, and foraging was not allowed. Rations consisted of yams and *trokuon* [a leafy Cambodian water vine]. Twice a month in 1978 we were forced [against their religious beliefs] to eat pork on pain of execution. People vomited it up. My three brothers died of starvation in 1976, 1977, and 1978. My other relatives are still alive. Of the five families with whom I went to Kantuot village, one person died of illness. In four other villages, one or two others were killed for refusing to eat pork. They were accused of being holy men [*sangkriech*] in the old society. There was starvation in Samrong subdistrict, mostly in 1977, and one or two killings. In 1978 they killed four entire families of Chinese in my village. I don't know why. Also in 1978, they killed our former Cham leaders who had joined the Khmer Rouge but had been dismissed in 1976.

Account 2: "They Did Nothing at all for the Peasants" by Thoun Cheng

Thoun Cheng, a Cambodian refugee who fled the Pol Pot regime in June 1977, was interviewed in the Khmer language by Boua and Kiernan at the Lao refugee camp at Ubon Ratchathani, northeast Thailand, on March 13 and 14, 1979. His story has been arranged in sequence by Boua and Kiernan, with occasional editorial comments in brackets.

I was born in 1957 in the village of Banteay Chey, in Chamcar Loeu district, Kompong Cham province, Cambodia. My father was a carpenter, but with the help of just his family, he also worked his 6 hectares of *chamcar* [garden farmland] growing pineapples and bananas. My mother died when I was small; I had three older brothers.

During the 1960s, Banteay Chey was populated by about 3200 ethnic Khmers, who mostly worked *chamcar,* and about 400 Chams, who grew rice. There were four Buddhist *wats* [Buddhist pagodas] and one Muslim mosque. Land was unevenly distributed: an elderly landlord owned 30 hectares in the village and an unusually large holding of 770 hectares in other parts of the district, including one large pineapple plantation. Poor farmers usually owned from 1 to 3 hectares.

I studied in primary school in the village; my education was interrupted by a three-year stay with relatives in the town of Kompong Cham, and six months in Phnom Penh.

The overthrow of Prince Norodom Sihanouk in 1970 was greeted with some disappointment by the villagers of Banteay Chey. I remember some of them traveling to Kompong Cham to take part in protest demonstrations. Soon after, fighting took place in the area between troops of the new Lon Nol Government and revolutionary Khmer Rouge claiming loyalty to the Prince. The Lon Nol troops retreated and were not seen in the area again.

As Banteay Chey itself was free of fighting, my relatives from Kompong Cham, a bus driver and his family, came to live in the village in 1970.

The war put an end to supplies of medicine to the village. Schools were closed, too, and I never got the opportunity of a secondary education. So from 1970, I made furniture and tilled the soil with my father.

Vietnamese Communist troops began making frequent visits to Banteay Chey. They paid for supplies that they needed and did not mistreat villagers. We first saw indigenous Khmer Rouge troops (who spoke like people from Kompong Cham) when they entered the village in 1972 and left again without causing upset. They lived in the forest and visited the village frequently over the next three years; life went on as before. The Khmer Rouge never stayed in or recruited from Banteay Chey and were busy fighting the Lon Nol troops all the time.

In 1973, the Vietnamese stopped coming; in the same year, the village had to withstand three months of intense bombardment by American B-52s. Bombs fell on Banteay Chrey three to six times a day, killing over 1000 people, or nearly a third of the village population. Several of my family were injured. After that, there were few people left to be seen around the village, and it was quiet. Food supplies remained adequate. Later, in 1973, the Khmer Rouge temporarily occupied most of Kompong Cham City and evacuated its population to the countryside. Seventy-four people from the town came to Banteay Chey and took up a normal life there. Some of the evacuees had died of starvation and bombardment by Lon Nol planes along the way.

The Khmer Rouge victory in April 1975 and their evacuation of Phnom Penh city brought 600 more people to Banteay Chey. The newcomers were billeted with village families. Relatives of ours, a couple and their three children, and one single man, stayed in my father's house. They had set out on foot from Phnom Penh 15 days earlier and arrived tired and hungry, although unlike some others they had not lost any of their family members along the way. [The single man, Kang Houath, was eventually to escape from Cambodia with Cheng. Houath took part in one of the interviews with Cheng in Ubon. He said that some village people along the way had given the evacuees food, and others had exchanged food for clothes and other goods offered by the Phnom Penh people. The bulk of the people travelling the roads at the time, however, were former peasants who had taken refuge in Phnom Penh during the war and had been instructed or allowed to return to their villages by the Khmer Rouge, Houath added.] In return for food and shelter, the new arrivals in Banteay Chey helped the locals in their work in the fields.

Also in April 1975, Khmer Rouge troops came to live in the village. It was not long before they began imposing a very harsh lifestyle on the villagers. Everybody was now obliged to work in the fields or dig reservoirs from 3 or 4 A.M. until 10 P.M. The only breaks were from noon till 1 P.M. and from 5 to 6 P.M. [This compared to an average 8-hour day worked by the *chamcar* farmers in the preceding years.] One day in ten was a rest day, as well as three days each year at the Khmer New Year festival. Land became communal.

Also from 1975, money was abolished and big houses were either demolished, and the materials used for smaller ones, or used for administration or to house troops. The banana trees in the *chamcar* were all uprooted on the orders of the Khmer Rouge and rice planted in their place. Production was high, although some land was left fallow and rations usually just consisted of rice porridge with very little meat. After the harvest each year, trucks would come at night to take away the village's rice stores to an unknown destination.

In 1975, the Khmer Rouge also began executing rich people, although they spared the elderly owner of 800 hectares. They also executed college students and former government officials, soldiers, and police. I saw the bodies of many such people not far from the village. Hundreds of people also died of starvation and disease in the year after April 1975, when medical supplies were lacking.

At this time, the Khmer Rouge, led by "friend Sang," claimed that they were "building Communism"; they occasionally mentioned a Communist Party, although its local (and national) members were unknown to us. The soldiers did not work in the fields but mounted an armed supervision over those who did; nonmilitary members of the Khmer Rouge worked unarmed alongside the villagers. There were no peasant organizations formed or meetings held about work; every decision concerning the work to be done and how to do it was made by the supervisors, with no participation on the part of the workers.

There was a large number of Khmer Rouge troops in the village, in the hundreds; they lived separately from the people in a big hall which no one else was allowed to visit. I never chatted with any of the soldiers in the two and a half years I lived with them in Banteay Chey.

Everyone, including my father, disliked the Khmer Rouge in Banteay Chey — the work was simply too hard, the lifestyle too rigid, and the food too inadequate. The Khmer Rouge occasionally claimed to be on the side of the poor, the peasants, but they did nothing at all for them. On the contrary, sometimes they said: "You were happy during the war, now is the time for you to sacrifice. Whether you live or die is not of great significance."

I managed to hide two radios buried in the ground. The batteries were precious so I listened to the radio only once or twice a month. Traditional village music was banned; the Khmer Rouge theatre troupes that visited the village about once in three months were the only form of entertainment.

In the April 1976 elections, only the very big people [i.e., the leading officials] voted in Banteay Chey. Also, by that stage, the *wats* and the mosque in Banteay Chey were empty. Saffron-robed Buddhist monks were nowhere to be seen. The Muslim Chams were obliged to eat pork on the occasions it was available; some adamantly refused, and were shot.

During 1976–1977 most of the Khmer Rouge leaders in the village changed six times. More than 50 Khmer Rouge were executed in these purges. Sang's position was finally assumed by Friend Son.

Then, from January 1977, all children over about 8 years of age, including people of my age [20 years], were separated from their parents, whom we were no longer allowed to see although we remained in the village. We were divided into groups consisting of young men, young women, and young children, each group nominally 300-strong. The food, mostly rice and salt, was pooled and served communally. Sometimes there was *samlor* [Khmer-style soup].

The Khmer Rouge soon began attacking the Vietnamese Communists in speeches to these youth groups. These speeches were propaganda.

Also in early 1977, collective marriages, involving hundreds of mostly unwilling couples, took place for the first time. All personal property was confiscated. A new round of executions began, more wide-ranging than that of 1975 and involving anyone who could not or would not carry out work directions. Food rations were cut significantly, leading to many more deaths from starvation, as were clothing allowances. Three sets of clothes per person per year was now the rule. Groups of more than two people were forbidden to assemble.

1977 was easily the worst year of all. Many people now wanted to escape, although they knew it was very dangerous. My mind was made up when it became clear that I would remain unable to see my father and brothers. It was June 1977.

Houath, a neighbor, one other man, and I took three baskets of dry rice. [Cheng did not say how this was acquired.] Avoiding everyone along the way, we headed north and east for Thailand. Laos was closer but I had heard on the radio that Laos was "building Communism" too and I didn't want to go there. As it turned out, however, the four of us lost our way to Preah Vihear province and hit the Lao border at Kompong Sralao.

Although Khmer Rouge troops were thinned out because of the conflict with Vietnam, we were spotted by soldiers who fired immediately, killing two of my companions. Houath and I were separated but arrived safely in Laos, where we met up again in a local jail on the banks of the Mekong.

I noticed that the Lao soldiers behaved differently from the Khmer Rouge I knew. They asked questions first, before apprehending people they suspected, whereas the Khmer Rouge were much more inclined to shoot suspects on the spot. I also gained the impression that living conditions in Laos were considerably better than in Cambodia.

Houath and I spent a total of 37 days in two Lao jails. I was given rice to eat, much more than I had had for a long time in Banteay Chey. I was not ill-treated, but when I was told that Vientiane was being asked for instructions whether to send me back to Cambodia, I escaped with Houath, and we fled to Thailand on 8 September 1977.

I spent another ten months in a Thai jail, before being transferred to the Ubon refugee camp.

Account 3: Peasant Boys in Democratic Cambodia by Sat and Mien

These are accounts of the experiences of two teenage Cambodian peasant boys (Sat and Mien) during 1975–1978. Boua and Kiernan interviewed them in a Buddhist *wat* near where they were tending their new master's horses, in Thailand's Surin province, on March 7, 12, and 19, 1979. The text includes every detail recounted by the boys, translated and arranged in sequence by Boua and Kiernan. Occasional points added appear in brackets.

"They Were Killing People Every Day" (Sat). I was born in 1966 in the village of Lbaeuk, Kralanh district, Siemreap province, Cambodia. The village is a long way from Siemreap town, and I have never been there. My father, Kaet, was a rice farmer. He had married again after my mother died. I had five brothers and sisters; I was the third oldest.

In the years 1975 and 1976, they were killing people every day. Killings took place at some distance from the village. I heard that victims were bound and then beaten to death. They were usually people found to be fishing illegally or who had failed to inform the Khmer Rouge of all their activities. Also during 1975–76, food was scarce in the village; rice porridge with banana stalks was the usual meal.

I can't remember when the Khmer Rouge first came from Oddar Meanchey province and took rice from the people of Lbaeuk. They soon began ordering the demolition of half a dozen big houses in the village, and the building of a large number of smaller ones to house the villagers. Many of the new houses became flooded in the subsequent rainy seasons.

They were built in a circle around the outskirts of the village; to provide communal dining facilities, a large "economics hall" [*kleang setakec*] was constructed in the now empty centre of the village.

The Khmer Rouge recruited a large number of volunteers in Lbaeuk, mostly youths about 20 years old. They were attracted by the much larger food rations that Khmer Rouge received, and by the fact that they did not have to work, and could kill people. On some occasions Khmer Rouge members who had committed some transgression were executed by their fellows.

The village *wat* was also demolished; several people were killed in an accident that occurred in the process. The large statue of Buddha from inside was thrown in a nearby stream. The local Khmer Rouge leader had given orders for this to be done, without giving a reason; he was obeyed out of fear. From that time on, monks were no longer seen around the village.

The year 1976 was worse than 1975. By now, no one in Lbaeuk dared complain or question the regime. My father was temporarily jailed by the Khmer Rouge. I don't know the reason.

In 1977, all young children no longer breast-feeding were taken from their parents and cared for permanently by female members of the Khmer Rouge. The reason given was to enable the mothers to work more effectively. Boys of my age [11] and older were taken together to a forest locality called Lbaeuk Prey. There were over 100 boys in all. Our task was to plant rice, supervised by about 20 armed Khmer Rouge in their early twenties. We worked there for five months, during which time more than 20 of us were taken away to a nearby mountain top. I never saw them again. I believe they were killed.

They were boys who had not worked hard or had missed work or played games, and had ignored three warnings to this effect. [More minor infringements of the rules, Sat says, were punished with a spell breaking rocks to make roads.] Or, they were people who didn't reply when asked what were their parents' occupations.

Morale was low among the young workers. Laughing was permitted, but there was no singing while we worked and no dancing or other entertainment afterwards. Every night there were meetings, in which we boys were urged to work harder; there were no political speeches or discussion at these meetings, and nationalism was mentioned only in the context of the Vietnamese "attempt to take over our land." There were no references to China.

Other tasks we performed were removing weeds from the rice fields and making fertilizer. The job I preferred was tending crops such as watermelons, cucumbers, and other vegetables. I was able to spend a lot of time doing this because I was ordered to. Khmer Rouge leaders on bicycles and with guns [both possessions were a sign of office] occasionally inspected my work. I was never allowed to eat any of the fruits of my labor, all of which were carted away by truck; I don't know where. The food rations I received varied from rice porridge with salt, to rice porridge with fish.

At night we were obliged to mount guard duty. I was taught how to use a gun but never considered becoming a Khmer Rouge soldier when I was older.

Many of us missed our parents badly. Some of us cried with grief at times; the Khmer Rouge would then beat them with sticks until they stopped crying. One month after commencing work at Lbaeuk Prey, we were permitted to visit our parents in Lbaeuk. Some of the parents broke into tears on seeing their sons. My father told me he had now been assigned the task of catching fish for the village communal dining hall; he was forbidden to use any of his catch for his or his wife's consumption. My brothers and sisters had all been taken elsewhere and were not at home. After this visit, which lasted several hours, I returned to Lbaeuk Prey and never saw my family again.

In late 1977, all the boys from Lbaeuk Prey were taken in trucks to Samrong in Oddar Meanchey province. As before, the workers there were all teenage boys. I do not know where the teenage girls from my village had been taken.

In Samrong we began building a road that was to go to Preah Vihear [through hundreds of kilometers of uninhabited forest]. We were told that the road would be used to transport food and supplies. We all worked at the rate of 2 or 3 meters of road per day, using locally made buckets to shift the earth; some boys threw up the soil, while others packed it down into a road surface. By the time I left this site five months later, no vehicles had yet been seen on the road.

There was nothing enjoyable about this experience. We boys were not taught to read or write or to sing any songs; we were never shown any radios, books, or magazines, although I noticed that some of the Khmer Rouge had such things.

Later we boys were taken to a place in the forest called Ken, also in Oddar Meanchey province. We were again put to work building a road. We worked from 6 A.M. to 10:30 A.M., had a short lunch break and then worked until 6 P.M., when we had another short break and a wash and then worked until 10 P.M. There were no rest days. The work was so exhausting that some of the boys fell down unconscious at the work site.

Then, early in 1979, a Khmer Rouge leader arrived on a bicycle and announced that the Vietnamese were in Kralanh. We were told to walk to nearby Paong; when we arrived we were led towards the Thai border on foot for three or four days, carrying our own food and sleeping when tired.

I crossed into Thailand. However, one group of boys came across some Thai tanks; never having seen such things, they ran frightened back into the jungle, where they were killed by Khmer Rouge soldiers.

Now, I am not allowed to walk around or talk to people.

When I become an adult, I want to live with other people.

"The Khmer Rouge Leader Was a Kind, Easygoing Person" (Mien). I was born in 1965 in the village of Samlaeng, Roang subdistrict, Preah Vihear province, Cambodia. My parents, who were rice farmers, called me Daung.

[In early 1970, troops of the new Lon Nol regime retreated from Preah Vihear and from that point the province was under undisputed Communist control.] During the next few years, Vietnamese Communist troops passed through Samlaeng, on one occasion, provoking a lot of interest but no hostility. They didn't steal anything from or harm the villagers; after paying for what they wanted, they moved on.

Also during the war, Samlaeng was bombed "many times" [by U.S. or allied aircraft] over a long period. I don't know if any of the people were killed.

In 1975 [after the Khmer Rouge captured and evacuated Phnom Penh], a number of people arrived in Samlaeng on foot after walking from Phnom Penh. Some people had died along the way; the villagers helped the newcomers settle in to their new environment.

During 1975–76, life went on as before. My parents were happy during this period. Khmer Rouge troops lived in the village but did not cause any upset; I never heard any mention at all of any actual or suspected executions. Food supplies were adequate.

Then, in 1976, the revolution began. Its purpose was "to build up the country," I was told. The entire village was now obliged to eat in a communal dining hall. Rations were tight — usually only rice porridge. In late 1976, I heard that a Phnom Penh evacuee had disappeared from the village and was thought to have been executed. This was the only such case I knew of while living in Samlaeng.

In 1977, myself and three other village boys my age were taken away from our parents. The Khmer Rouge who escorted us away said that they would come back later to take away the other boys in the village, in groups of four at a time. I was taken to Samrong in Oddar Meanchey province, joining a work group of about 30 boys, the oldest of whom was 17. Our job was to clear the forest for *chamcar*, or garden farmland. Each morning we got up at 4 A.M. and worked around the house we lived in, tending fruit and vegetable crops, until 6 A.M. Then we would go into the forest and work there until 10 A.M. when we ate our lunch. This consisted of a carefully rationed bowl of rice porridge, sometimes with salt, sometimes with *samlor*. It was not tasty but I was always hungry and would eat it all. At 6 P.M. we would stop working in the forest and return to our houses. Every night we boys were assigned a small plot of land to tend near the houses we lived in. When we finished this task to the satisfaction of the overseers we were allowed to go to sleep.

While living with my parents, I had only been accustomed to doing household chores, and I found it difficult to adjust to the new lifestyle. The work was not enjoyable; each boy was allocated an area of forest to clear and we worked some distance from each other. We were not taught to sing songs or dance, or to read or write. I was never allowed to visit my parents again.

Nevertheless, the leader of the Khmer Rouge where I worked was a kind, "easygoing" person who never got angry and did not physically mistreat the children. The Khmer Rouge leader was about 30 years old.

After many months at Samrong, all the boys were sent to a place called Phnom Phtol, or Phnom Seksor. There we spent a few months looking after herds of water buffaloes. In early 1979, with Vietnamese troops approaching the area, we were told to go to Paong; we crossed the border into Thailand, followed by a large number of Khmer Rouge soldiers and children, not long after.

Notes

1. "Report to the Economic and Social Council," United Nations, July 2, 1985, 4/SUB, 2/1985/ 6, at 10 n. 17. "We agree with that assessment," the U.S. Department of State conceded in 1989.
2. S. Heder and B. Tittemore portray the UN experts as hesitant on the genocide issue: "They cautioned that it might be a 'difficult task' to prove that the CPK carried out acts 'with the requisite intent' to destroy such ethnic and religious groups 'as such'." "Seven Candidates for Prosecution: Accountability for the Crimes of the Khmer Rouge," War Crimes Research Office, American University, 2001, p. 14, n. 24.

References

Amin, Samir (1981). "The Lesson of Cambodia." *Conference on Kampuchea*, Tokyo, May–June, pp. 4, 8–9.

Asia Watch/Physicians for Human Rights (1991). *Land Mines in Cambodia: The Cowards' War*. New York: AW/PHR.

Australian Department of Foreign Affairs and Trade (1990). *Cambodia: An Australian Peace Proposal*. Canberra: ADFAT, pp. v–7.

Barnett, Anthony (1983). "Democratic Kampuchea: A Highly Centralized Dictatorship," pp. 212–29. In David. P. Chandler and Ben Kiernan (Eds.) *Revolution and Its Aftermath in Kampuchea: Eight Essays*. New Haven, CT: Yale Council on Southeast Asia Studies.

Boua, Chanthou, et al. (1980). "Bureaucracy of Death: Documents from Inside Pol Pot's Torture Machine." *New Statesman*, May 2, pp. 669–76.

Boua, Chanthou; Chandler, David P.; and Kiernan, Ben (Eds.) (1988). *Pol Pot Plans the Future: Confidential Leadership Documents from Democratic Kampuchea, 1976–77*. New Haven, CT: Yale University Southeast Asia Studies Council Monograph No. 33.

Boua, Chanthou (1991). "Genocide of a Religious Group: Pol Pot and Cambodia's Buddhist Monks," pp. 227–40. In P.T. Bushnell, V. Schlapentokh, C. Vanderpool, and J. Sundram (Eds.) *State-Organized Terror: The Case of Violent Internal Repression*. Boulder, CO: Westview.

Burr, W., and Evans, M.L. (Eds.) (2001). "Text of Ford-Kissinger-Suharto Discussion, U.S. Embassy Jakarta Telegram 1579 to Secretary State, December 6, 1975." In *East Timor Revisited: Ford, Kissinger and the Indonesian Invasion, 1975-76*. Washington: National Security Archive.

Chandler, David P., and Kiernan, Ben (Eds.) (1983). *Revolution and its Aftermath in Kampuchea: Eight Essays*. New Haven, CT: Yale University Southeast Asia Studies Council Monograph No. 25.

Chandler, David P. (1985). "Cambodia in 1984: Historical Patterns Reasserted?" pp. 177–86. *Southeast Asian Affairs 1985*. Singapore: Heinemann.

Chandler, David P. (1991). *The Tragedy of Cambodian History*. New Haven, CT: Yale University Press.

Cohen, Nick (1991). "Oxfam Activities Censured as too Political." *Independent*, May 10. London: n.p.

Dunlop, Nic (1999). "KR Torture Chief Admits to Mass Murder." *Phnom Penh Post*, April 30–May 13:1, 10.

Evans, Richard J. (1989). *In Hitler's Shadow*. New York: Pantheon.

Jackson, Karl (Ed.) (1989). *Cambodia 1975–1978: Rendezvous with Death*. Princeton, N.J.: Princeton University Press.

Indochina Digest (June 7, 1991), No. 91–23.

Indochina Digest (August 30, 1991), No. 91–35.

Indochina Digest (November 1, 1991), No. 91–44.

Jennar, Raoul (1991). *The Cambodian Gamble*. Jodoigne, Belgium: European Center for Far Eastern Research.

Kiernan, Ben, and Chanthou, Boua (Eds.) (1982). *Peasants and Politics in Kampuchea, 1942–1981*. London: Zed Books.

Kiernan, Ben (1983). "Wild Chickens, Farm Chickens, and Cormorants: Kampuchea's Eastern Zone under Pol Pot.," pp. 136–211. In David Chandler and Ben Kiernan (Ed.) *Revolution and Its Aftermath in Kampuchea*. New Haven, CT: Yale Council on Southeast Asia Studies.

Kiernan, Ben (1985a). *How Pol Pot Came to Power: A History of Communism in Kampuchea, 1930–1975*. London: Verso.

Kiernan, Ben (1985b). "Kampuchea and Stalinism," pp. 232–49. In Colin Mackerras and Nick Knight (Eds.) *Marxism in Asia*. London: Croom Helm.

Kiernan, Ben (1986a). *Cambodia: Eastern Zone Massacres*. New York: Columbia University, Centre for the Study of Human Rights, Documentation Series No.1:101.

Kiernan, Ben (1986b). "Kampuchea's Ethnic Chinese under Pol Pot: A Case of Systematic Social Discrimination." *Journal of Contemporary Asia*, 16(1):18–29.

Kiernan, Ben (1986c). "William Shawcross, Declining Cambodia." *Bulletin of Concerned Asian Scholars*, 18(1):56–63.

Kiernan, Ben (1988). "Orphans of Genocide: The Cham Muslims of Kampuchea under Pol Pot." *Bulletin of Concerned Asian Scholars*, 20(4):2–33.

Kiernan, Ben (1989a). "The American Bombardment of Kampuchea, 1969–1973." *Vietnam Generation*, Winter, 1:1:4–41.

Kiernan, Ben (1989b). "Blue Scarf/Yellow Star: A Lesson in Genocide." *Boston Globe*, February 27, p. 13.

Kiernan, Ben (1990a). "The Genocide in Cambodia, 1975–1979." *Bulletin of Concerned Asian Scholars*, 22(2):35–40.

Kiernan, Ben (1990b). "The Survival of Cambodia's Ethnic Minorities." *Cultural Survival*, 14(3):64–66.

Kiernan, Ben (1991a). "Deferring Peace in Cambodia: Regional Rapprochement, Superpower Obstruction," pp. 59–82. In George W. Breslauer, Harry Kreisler, and Benjamin Ward (Eds.) *Beyond the Cold War*. Berkeley: Institute of International Studies, University of California.

Kiernan, Ben (1991b). "Genocidal Targeting: Two Groups of Victims in Pol Pot's Cambodia," pp. 207–26. In P.T. Bushnell, V. Shlapentokh, C. Vanderpool, and J. Sundram (Eds.) *State-Organized Terror: The Case of Violent Internal Repression*. Boulder, CO: Westview Press.

Kiernan, Ben (1992). "The Cambodian Crisis, 1990–1992: The UN Plan, the Khmer Rouge, and the State of Cambodia." *Bulletin of Concerned Asian Scholars*, 24(2):3–23.

Kiernan, Ben (Ed) (1993). *Genocide and Democracy in Cambodia: The Khmer Rouge, the United Nations, and the International Community.* New Haven, CT: Yale Council on Southeast Asia Studies.

Kiernan, Ben (1996). *The Pol Pot Regime: Race, Power and Genocide in Cambodia under the Khmer Rouge, 1975–1979.* New Haven, CT: Yale University Press. (Second edition with new Preface, 2002.)

Kiernan, Ben (2002). *The Pol Pot Regime: Race, Power and Genocide in Cambodia under the Khmer Rouge, 1975-1979, 2nd edition.* New Haven, CT: Yale University Press.

Kiernan, Ben (2000). "Bringing the Khmer Rouge to Justice." *Human Rights Review*, 1(3):92–108.

Kiernan, Ben (Ed.) (2002). "Conflict and Change in Cambodia." Special Issues of *Critical Asian Studies*, 34(4).

Leopold, Evelyn (1991). "Western Nations Want Former Cambodian Leader to Leave Country." September 22. Reuter Cable, UN (NYC).

Migozzi, Jacques (1973). *Cambodge: faits et problémes de population.* Paris: Centre National de la Recherche Scientifique.

Murdoch, Lindsay (1991). "Evans Backs Pol Pot Trial." *Melbourne Age*, October 24, p. 1.

Mysliwiec, Eva (1988). *Punishing the Poor: The International Isolation of Kampuchea.* Oxford: Oxfam.

The New York Times (1991). "Sighted in Cambodia: Peace." August 28, Editorial Page, p. A20.

Pilger, John (1991a). "In Defence of Oxfam." *New Statesman and Society*, May 17, p. 8.

Pilger, John (1991b). "West Conceals Record on Khmer Aid." *Sydney Morning Herald*, August 1, n.p.

Pilger, John (1991c). "Culpable in Cambodia." *New Statesman and Society*, September 27. n.p.

Pilger, John (1991d). "Organised Forgetting." *New Statesman and Society*, November 1, n.p.

Pol Pot (1978). Interview of Comrade Pol Pot … to the Delegation of Yugoslav Journalists in Visit to Democratic Kampuchea. March 23. Phnom Penh: Democratic Kampuchea, Ministry of Foreign Affairs.

Ratner, Steven, and Abrams, Jason (1997). *Accountability for Human Rights Atrocities in International Law: Beyond the Nuremberg Legacy.* Oxford: Clarendon Press.

Shawcross, William (1979a). *Sideshow: Kissinger, Nixon and the Destruction of Cambodia.* New York: Pocket Books.

Shawcross, William (1979b). *Sunday Telegraph*, September 26, n.p.

Shawcross, William (1980). "The End of Cambodia." January 24, *New York Times Review of Books*, 26(21 and 22):25–30.

Shawcross, William (1984). *The Quality of Mercy: Cambodia, Holocaust and Modern Conscience.* London: André Deutsch.

Shenon, Philip (1991). "Cambodian Factions Sign Peace Pact." October 24, *The New York Times*, p. A16.

Stanton, Gregory (1993). "The Khmer Rouge Genocide and International Law," pp. 141–61. In Ben Kiernan (Ed.) *Genocide and Democracy in Cambodia.* New Haven, CT: Yale Council on Southeast Asia Studies.

Thion, Serge (1983). "The Cambodian Idea of Revolution," pp. 10–33. In David P. Chandler and Ben Kiernan (Eds.) *Revolution and its Aftermath in Kampuchea: Eight Essays.* New Haven, CT: Yale Council on Southeast Asia Studies.

Thion, Serge (1993). "Genocide as a Political Commodity," pp. 163–90. In Ben Kiernan (Ed.) *Genocide and Democracy in Cambodia.* New Haven, CT: Yale Council on Southeast Asia Studies.

United Nations Subcommission on Human Rights (1991). "1991/8 Situation in Cambodia" — UN Subcommission on Human Rights Resolution, August 23, 1991. Cited in Raoul Jennar's *The Cambodian Gamble.* Jodoigne, Belgium: European Center for Far Eastern Research, 1991, pp. 35–36.

United Nations (1999). General Assembly, Security Council, A/53/850, S/1999/231, March 16, Annex, *Report of the Group of Experts for Cambodia Established Pursuant to General Assembly Resolution 52/135.* New York: UN.

Van Leur, J.C. (1955). *Indonesian Trade and Society.* The Hague: W. Van Hoeve.

Vatikiotis, Michael (1988). "Smiles and Soft Words." *Far Eastern Economic Review*, August 11, pp. 28–29.

Vickery, Michael (1984). *Cambodia 1975–1982*. Boston: South End Books.

Vickery, Michael (1988). "Violence in Democratic Kampuchea: Some Problems of Explanation." Paper distributed at a conference on State-Organized Terror: The Case of Violent Internal Repression, November, East Lansing: Michigan State University.

Vickery, Michael (1989). "Cambodia (Kampuchea): History, Tragedy and Uncertain Future." *Bulletin of Concerned Asian Scholars*, 21(2–4):35–58.

Vickery, Michael (1990). "Comments on Cham Population Figures." *Bulletin of Concerned Asian Scholars*, 22, p. 1.

Vickery, Michael (1998). *Society, Economics and Politics in Pre-Angkor Cambodia: The 7th–8th Centuries*. Tokyo: Centre for East Asian Cultural Studies for UNESCO.

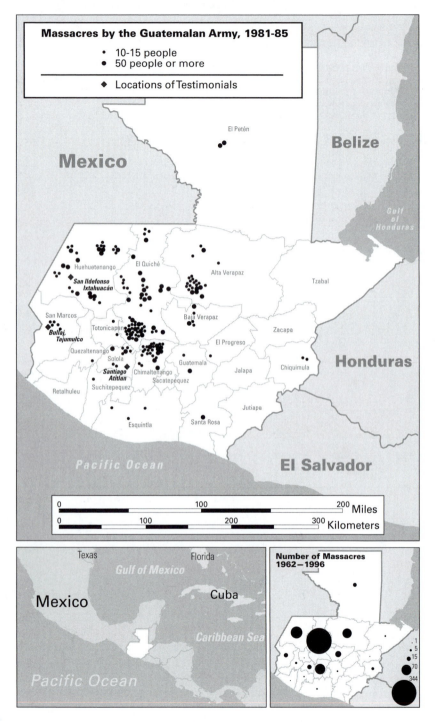

Massacres by the Guatemalan Army, 1981-85

- 10-15 people
- 50 people or more

◆ Locations of Testimonials

El Petén

Belize

Mexico

Gulf
of
Honduras

Huehuetenango   El Quiché   Alta Verapaz   Tzabal

San Ildefonso
Ixtahuacán

San Marcos   Baja Verapaz

Bullaj,
Tajumulco   Totonicapán   Zacapa

Quezaltenango   El Progreso   Honduras

Solola   Guatemala

Santiago   Chimaltenango   Jalapa   Chiquimula
Atitlan   Sacatepéquez

Retalhuleu   Suchitepéquez

Jutiapa

Esquintla   Santa Rosa

Pacific Ocean   El Salvador

| 0 | | 100 | | 200 | Miles |
| 0 | 100 | 200 | 300 | | Kilometers |

Texas   Florida   **Number of Massacres
1962 – 1996**

Gulf of Mexico

Mexico   Cuba

Caribbean Sea

Pacific Ocean

.1
5
15
70
344

Guatemala

CHAPTER 12

Guatemala: Acts of Genocide and Scorched-Earth Counterinsurgency War

SUSANNE JONAS

There is no more painful chapter in the history of modern Guatemala than the events of 1980–1983 and their sequel in the mid-1980s. At the human level, it is a tale of wholesale slaughter and acts of genocide by the counterinsurgent state security forces, carrying out extra-judicial violence without any facade of legal constraints. That these genocidal acts were almost unknown in many Western countries, certainly in the U.S., is a testament to the great silence about Guatemala during the most brutal years. It was an indifferent, at times complicitous silence The victims were overwhelmingly Mayan indigenous civilians living in Guatemala's western highlands or *altiplano*. At that time, Mayan peoples (in over 20 sub-groups) constituted well over half of Guatemala's population of 8 million.

Background: Heightened Identity Awareness and Resistance in the Mayan Highlands

Structural transformations of the 1960s–1980s changed the overall situation of Guatemala's indigenous highlands populations in their class definition and profoundly affected their self-conceptions and identities as indigenous; here lay the basis for the widespread Mayan uprising in the late 1970s and early 1980s. (For a much more detailed account see Jonas, 1991, and sources cited there.) Economic growth followed by economic crisis broke down the objective barriers that had kept the

Mayas relatively isolated in the highlands. This was greatly intensified by the economic and political crises of the 1970s and 1980s (including a major earthquake in 1976), when growing numbers of Mayas were forced to migrate to the Southern Coast as seasonal laborers, and to Guatemala City in search of jobs. These changes and displacements brought them into increased contact with the *ladino* (non-Maya), Spanish-speaking world. Rather than "ladinizing" or acculturating the Mayas, however, this experience reinforced their struggle to preserve their indigenous identity, although in new forms—as Guatemalan Jesuit priest/anthropologist/activist Ricardo Falla (1978) put it, to discover "new ways of being Indian." As will be seen below, these factors explain why Guatemala's Mayan peoples became one of the powerful social forces driving the insurgency of the 1970s and 1980s—and the principal victims of the army's response.

In the countryside, structural contradictions—the crisis in subsistence agriculture, compounded by the massive 1976 earthquake—uprooted and displaced thousands of indigenous peasants, causing them to redefine themselves in both class and cultural terms. As producers, they were being semiproletarianized as a seasonal migrant labor force on the plantations of the Southern Coast, meanwhile often losing even the tiny subsistence plots of land they had traditionally held in the highlands. The combination of their experiences of being evicted from their own lands and their experiences as a migrant semiproletariat radicalized large numbers of highlands Mayas. Even the more developmentalist influences were contradictory, in that they raised hopes and expectations in the 1960s, only to dash them in the 1970s. The clearest examples of this dynamic were those peasants who received land from the government's colonization programs in the 1960s, only to have it taken away again in the 1970s, as the powerful army officers grabbed profitable lands in colonization areas.

Culturally, throughout the 1960s and 1970s, highlands Mayan communities were being transformed and redefined, as they "opened up" to contact with the *ladino* world. Increased contact had the paradoxical effect of reinforcing their defense of their ethnic/cultural identity, as expressed in their languages, customs, community and religious practices, claims to land and other rights, and their overall worldview. These elements of their identity became a factor in mobilizing their resistance to the *ladino*-dominated state. Politically as well, "reformist" parties such as the Christian Democrats came into indigenous communities, raising expectations of change—only to leave those hopes unfulfilled for most people. Meanwhile, indigenous organizations were defined by the government as "subversive" and excluded from the minimal forms of political expression that other sectors were permitted.

Furthermore, increased army repression against indigenous communities—incursions into villages, shooting indiscriminately, sometimes massively, and other forms of attack—had contradictory effects. Rather than terrorizing the Mayas into passivity, by the late 1970s it stimulated hundreds, later thousands, of them to take up arms (or seek to do so) as the only available means of self-defense against state violence. All of these paradoxical experiences of the 1970s coincided with the transformation of grassroots organizations of the Catholic Church, the rise of Christian Base Communities, and the gradual emergence of a "Church of the Poor." This was expressed most concretely by village priests interacting with their communities, but they eventually influenced the official Church hierarchy (*Conferencia Episcopal Guatemalteca*) to shed earlier conservative positions and alliances, and align itself with social justice movements. These new religious currents became central to the radicalization of the indigenous highlands, and led the army to identify actors representing the Catholic Church (including some bishops) as part of the "subversive" movement.

By 1978, these various strands were woven together in the emergence of the *Comité de Unidad Campesina* (CUC) as a national peasant organization, including both peasants and agricultural workers, both Mayas and poor *ladinos,* but led primarily by Mayas. From the viewpoint of the army and business elites, CUC was by definition a "subversive" organization. CUC came into the limelight after a major army massacre at Panzós, Alta Verapaz in May 1978 (see Grandin, 2004), and the January 1980 massacre at the Spanish embassy in the capital, where Guatemalan security forces burned alive 39 indigneous protesters from the town of Nebaj, Quiché—including Vicente Menchú, father of the 1992 Nobel Laureate Rigoberta Menchú. In February 1980, CUC staged a massive strike of workers on the Southern Coast sugar and cotton plantations; from the viewpoint of landowners and the army, this strike was their worst nightmare come true.

Also important in the growth of a politicized indigenous movement was a change in the stance of Guatemala's revolutionary armed insurgents vis-à-vis the Maya population. The leftist movement, which by its own definition was fighting for a socialist revolution, had begun in 1960, operating in eastern Guatemala, primarily a *ladino* (non-Mayan) area. The movement (*Fuerzas Rebeldes Rebeldes*, FAR) had undergone a strategic defeat during the army's massive counterinsurgency campaign of 1966–1968, with U.S. military forces and advisers directly training the Guatemalan army (see below). That campaign, directed primarily against unarmed civilians, also introduced the phenomena of death squads and "disappearances" to Guatemala—indeed via Guatemala, to all Latin America. The late 1960s saw the consolidation of the counterinsurgency state that was to dominate Guatemala for decades.

These events of the late 1960s led to a broad reevaluation of strategy and goals by the insurgents, and an organizational recomposition within the movement from 1968 through the early 1970s, following several splits from the FAR. Most important, the insurgents concluded that they had to rectify having virtually ignored the indigenous population during the 1960s. By the time of their resurgence in the early 1970s, two of the three major organizations, *Ejército Guerrillero de los Pobres* (EGP) and *Organización del Pueblo en Armas* (ORPA) spent several years being educated by the indigenous population (about Mayan languages, customs, and rights struggles) and organizing a political support base primarily in the western highlands before renewing armed actions later in the 1970s.

The guerrilla armed uprising reached its height in 1980–1981, gaining 6–8,000 armed fighters and 1/4–1/2 million active collaborators and supporters (Adams, 1988, p. 296), and operating in many parts of the country. By the early 1980s, entire Mayan highlands communities were turning to the insurgents for arms, to defend themselves from army incursions and massacres—although in reality, the insurgents were totally unprepared to provide these communities with the means to defend themselves, and subsequently lost support from these communities. The new wave of armed struggle was taken very seriously by Guatemala's elites and army as heralding a possible seizure of power by the insurgents. In early 1982, the various guerrilla organizations united in the *Unidad Revolucionaria Nacional Guatemalteca* (URNG), overcoming years of sectarian divisions. Even as unity was proclaimed, however, and even as the revolutionary movement achieved its maximal expression during 1980 and 1981, a change in the balance of forces between the insurgents and the army began during the second half of 1981, as the army initiated an unprecedented counteroffensive against the civilian support base of the insurgents.

The "Guatemala Solution": Total War at the Grassroots, Acts of Genocide, and Crimes Against Humanity

To those of us who have studied this history in detail on the basis of interviews and primary documents, what is most striking is the unity and single-minded determination of all those involved in the campaign against "*la subversión.*" Inherent within this vision was the assumption that a scorched-earth counterinsurgency war was necessary to establish "social peace." Within this context, human rights crimes, including massacres and acts of genocide, were simply beside the point, since the Mayan population was viewed as "subversive" by definition.

The stepped-up military counteroffensive was initiated in mid-1981 under the leadership of Gen. Benedicto Lucas, brother of military

President Romeo Lucas García (1978–1982). The campaign began in Guatemala City, with a fall 1981 lightening swoop against the urban infrastructure of the guerrilla organizations, as well as urban popular movements.

The major thrust of the counterinsurgency campaign, however, was the scorched-earth war in the highlands which began in 1981, but became even more brutal in 1982–1983 under the regime of Gen. Efraín Ríos Montt (who took power through a military coup in March 1982, and was displaced by another coup in August 1983). As the army openly acknowledged, the goal was literally to "drain the sea" in which the guerrilla movement operated and to eradicate its civilian support base in the Mayan highlands. The principal techniques included depopulation of the area through "scorched earth" burnings of entire villages, and massacres and large-scale forced relocations of the village inhabitants. Entire sectors of the Maya population became military targets, leading many scholars to identify these policies as genocidal. Falla (1984) called it genocide "in the strict sense," because it involved massacres of people such as the elderly and children who did not yet have the use of reason and therefore could not be considered guerrilla collaborators: "The ideological bridge is the concept that guilt and crime are transmitted biologically. It is racist" (p. 116).

The dozens of scholars who reached the same conclusions about the genocidal nature of these policies were joined by national, international, and inter-governmental human rights organizations in judging that the army's policies *were systematically directed to destroy some ethnic sub-groups in particular, as well as the Mayan population in general.* In addition, the U.N. General Assembly overwhelmingly passed resolutions in 1982 and 1984 condemning the Guatemalan regimes responsible for these policies; the U.N. Human Rights Commission assigned Special Rapporteurs on Guatemala for many years, and hearings were held by the U.N. Committee for the Prevention of Discrimination and Protection of Minorities. In 1984, Pope John Paul II denounced the Guatemalan regime. (In addition to my own interviews and specific sources cited in the references for this essay, numerous reports were issued by organizations such as Amnesty International and Americas Watch.)

The statistics are staggering: some 440 villages were entirely destroyed, according to the army's own figures. In the period 1981–1983 alone, 100,000–150,000 (primarily Mayan) unarmed civilians were killed. There were over one million displaced persons (1 million internal refugees, 200,000 refugees in Mexico). Accompanying these massive population displacements was the deliberate destruction of huge areas of the highlands (burning of forests, etc.) to deny cover to the guerrillas, and to assure that the region could never again serve as a theater for revolutionary operations. The environmental devastation was irreversible, even modifying climate and rainfall patterns (Perera, 1989).

According to participants in the war (from the insurgent side) subsequently analyzing the 1981–1983 period, the goal of the genocide and scorched-earth policies went beyond elimination of the insurgents' support base and the material base of the local economy. The deeper objective was to "fracture the very bases of the communal structure and of ethnic unity, destroying the factors of reproduction of culture and affecting the values on which it rests . . . understanding that the possibilities of survival and reproduction of the indigenous culture are directly linked to the prospects for revolution . . ." (*Opinión Política* [OP] #2 and #3, 1985). As one indicator, many Mayas in the highlands subsequently stopped wearing *traje* or traditional dress. In short, the very *identity* of the indigenous population was at stake; in this sense, the war took on the character of an assault by the *ladino* state against the Mayan civilian population. Further, the scorched-earth policy had the goals of destroying all forms of economic autonomy in the Mayan communities (Smith, 1990)—and of "provoking such a degree of communal impoverishment as to destroy this form of peasant organization and place the producers at the mercy of capitalist economic laws . . ." (OP, 1985). It was, in short, the most violent form of proletarianization—through military means.

A striking example of village massacres has been recounted by Ricardo Falla (1984) in his 1983 testimony at the Permanent People's Tribunal in Spain:

> The best-documented massacre under the [1982–1983] Ríos Montt regime was perpetrated by the army at the totally indigenous village-farm of San Francisco in Nentón, Huehuetenango on July 17, 1982. An estimated 352 people were killed, of whom we have 302 names, 220 of them with the person's age and/or parentage. This village [is] . . . not far from the northern border of Huehuetenango with Chiapas, Mexico.
>
> The survivors have been interviewed by the Christian Committee of the Diocese of San Cristóbal de las Casas in August 1982, by myself [Ricardo Falla] at the beginning of September 1982, by members of the Guatemalan Committee for Justice and Peace, and by Alan Riding, a reporter from the *New York Times* for an article published on October 12, 1982. On different dates, to different interviewers, the two main survivors have given absolutely consistent versions of the events.
>
> The pattern of the massacre, as in other massacres, was as follows. The soldiers separated the men off to one side, telling

them that there was going to be a meeting, and locked them up in the courthouse of the village-farm. The soldiers then rounded up the women from their various homes and locked them up at another location along with their children, both those having the use of reason and those not yet having it (the survivors make this distinction very clearly).

At about 1:00 p.m., the soldiers began to fire at the women inside the small church. The majority did not die there, but were separated from their children, taken to their homes in groups, and killed, the majority apparently with machetes. It seems that the purpose of this last parting of women from their children was to prevent even the children from witnessing any confession that might reveal the location of the guerrillas.

Then they returned to kill the children, whom they had left crying and screaming by themselves, without their mothers. Our informants, who were locked up in the courthouse, could see this through a hole in the window and through the doors carelessly left open by a guard. The soldiers cut open the children's stomachs with knives or they grabbed the children's little legs and smashed their heads against heavy sticks.

Some of the soldiers took a break to rest, eating a bull—the property of the peasants—that had been put on to roast. Then they continued with the men. They took them out, tied their hands, threw them on the ground, and shot them. The authorities of the area were killed inside the courthouse.

It was then that the survivors were able to escape, protected by the smoke of the fire which had been set to the building. Seven men, three of whom survived, managed to escape. It was 5:30 p.m.

The massacre continued, and when about six people were left, the soldiers threw grenades at them, killing all but two. Since it was already night, these two escaped through the window, covered with blood but uninjured. One of them was shot, the other lived. He is the surprise witness of this horrible deed. It is said that he arrived in Chiapas, Mexico, at 11 a.m. the following day, but because he had such a darkness in his soul, he did not even notice that it was daytime (pp.112–114).

Institutionalization of the Counterinsurgency Apparatus

The next phase of the counterinsurgency campaign, from 1983 to 1985 (under the military regime of Gen. Oscar Mejía Víctores), was also violent and devastating for the highlands Mayas. The most obvious goal was to consolidate military control over the population through a series of coercive institutions. Among these were:

(a) mandatory, involuntary paramilitary "civilian self-defense patrols" (PACs), designed to force villagers to participate in the eradication of the guerrilla movement, and generally to eliminate political activity in opposition to the government. Anyone who refused service was fined or, much worse, treated as a "subversive" himself. At one point, the PACs involved one million peasants—one eighth of the entire population, *one fourth of the adult population*;

(b) rural resettlement camps known as "model villages," concentrated in "development poles"—in essence, forced resettlement camps in which every aspect of people's lives was subject to direct military control; and

(c) Inter-Institutional Coordinating Councils, which centralized administration of development projects at every level of government (local, municipal, provincial, national) under military control. This created a military structure parallel (superior) to that of the civilian administration—a striking example of the militarized state. All of these institutions were subsequently legalized in the new Constitution of 1985, which provided the juridical framework for the elected civilian governments, beginning in 1986.

The purposes of the PACs went far beyond having auxiliary paramilitary forces, or even a captive labor force to construct roads and other infrastructure needed by the army. The goal was "to construct new and massive forms of counterrevolutionary local power; . . . to compromise a growing number of people in repressive activities, creating indestructible barriers between them and the rest of the civilian population—and irreversible levels of compromise of the patrol members with the army" (*Opinión Política*, 1985), even in carrying out massacres of fellow-villagers. Villages and ethnic groups were turned against each other, in an attempt to create "civil war" (Arias, 1985, p. 117). One anthropologist who observed PAC operations closely was struck by

> . . . the degree of guilt and shame that people had internalized as a result of their participation in the civil patrol system. Apparently people had such guilt because the army entered the region like an angry father, accusing the Mayas of being rebellious children who were responsible for the civil damage and strife created by the guerrilla movement. In its early stages, the army presented the formation of the civil patrols to the Mayas as a way of extricating

themselves from any association with the guerrillas. During this period, when the civil patrols were being formed, the army forced Mayas to go on *rastreos* (hunts for guerrillas) and sometimes to stone or machete to death fellow villagers who were suspected or accused of being "subversives." Many of those who refused to participate in these acts or who tried to escape from civil patrol duty were punished by local authorities or sent to the regional army base for pushishment. . . . (Davis, 1988, p. 28)

The Development Poles were the major institution for the army's policies of population reconcentration from their original villages, following massacres and village destructions. These were intended, in the first instance, to deprive the revolutionaries of their support base; but longer range, to centralize the new forms of counterinsurgent local power. These settlements, designed according to a military logic, brought the displaced populations under total army control. Particularly since the war had destroyed local supplies of food, firewood, etc., the displaced became dependent upon the army for food, as well as for work, shelter and other "benefits," in a program called "Beans and Guns" (later "Shelter, Work and Tortillas"). This was a striking example of the systematic use of hunger as a weapon of social control.

Architects of these programs—including civilian counterinsurgents, those who, in the army's words, "had the vision to get involved" in the army's pacification programs—insist that they had a political as well as a military goal: to overcome the historic alienation between the state apparatus and the population by (forcibly) "winning it over" to the army's side, to create a real social base "among the people." According to one army document (cited in Manz, 1988, p. 18), military officers sought to mirror structures of the *Ejército Guerrillero de los Pobres* (EGP), in order to mobilize the population against the EGP. Military authorities even described the PACs as instruments of "participation"—as if they involved voluntary activity. In reality they were the product of extreme coercion, with resisters becoming targets of repressive retaliation.

Such coercion has been at the core of the relationship of the *ladino* army to the Mayan population since the nineteenth century: "The military came to see rural Guatemala as its particular preserve, and reveled in its dominant position there. Any attempt to alter that position and organize peasants or rural workers into independent associations" was, therefore, an intolerable challenge (Handy, 1986, p. 407). In this sense, the genocide of the early 1980s was a logical extension of pre-existing Mayan/*ladino* relations (Adams, 1988, pp. 283–284). At the root of this system of institutionalized violence lay the fear of an indigenous uprising or "coming down from the highlands" (Arias, 1985, p. 115); the uprising of the early 1980s came closer than any other experience to realizing that great fear.

Genocide Revisited: The Post-war Truth Commission or "Historical Clarification Commission" (CEH)

Among the most controversial underlying issues of the Guatemalan Peace Accords negotiated over the course of six years (1991–1996) to end the 36-year war was justice for the victims of the war. (For a complete account of the negotiation of the Peace Accords and the subsequent struggles for their implementation, see Jonas, 2000). The issue of justice for the victims, including investigations of the massacres in the highlands, was addressed in several accords, the main one being the June 1994 Truth Commission Accord. Despite many weaknesses built into that Accord (e.g., not naming individual names, not automatically having judicial consequences), the Truth Commission (formally, "Historical Clarification Commission" [*Comisión de Esclarecimiento Histórico*], CEH) itself was constituted and began functioning with great energy on July 31, 1997, six months after the signing of the Peace Accords on December 29, 1996. The Commission was headed by German human rights expert Dr. Christian Tomuschat, who had previously served as the U.N.'s human rights monitor (Rapporteur) on Guatemala; the other members were two moderate Guatemalans, indigenous educator Otilia Lux de Cotí, and *ladino* lawyer Alfredo Balsells Tojo, both highly respected across the spectrum of Guatemala's organized social movements and political parties.

During the next year, the CEH took testimony from 9,000 war victims, who came forward in large numbers to tell their stories—as had been the case with the report authored by the Catholic Church Archbishop's Office of Human Rights (ODHA), entitled *Guatemala: Nunca Más* ("Never Again"). (The major coordinator of that report, Auxiliary Bishop Juan Gerardi, was brutally assassinated two days after the report's release in April 1998; this became Guatemala's highest profile post-war political crime.) In May 1998 the CEH conducted a public forum to get input from civil society organizations, including testimony from "binational" Guatemalan individuals and communities living in the United States. The Commission also sought written documentation from all domestic and foreign players in the war; while getting cooperation from the former insurgents of the *Unidad Revolucionaria Nacional Guatemalteca* (URNG), it ran into stone walls in attempting to gain access to Guatemalan army documents.

The CEH received an extension of its mandate in order to fully prepare its report, "Memory of Silence," which was finally presented on

February 25, 1999, to a packed audience of 10,000. No one—not even the many interviewees, human rights groups, and analysts who had contributed to sections of the report—was prepared for the magnitude and scope of its findings. Among the highlights of the Report were the following:

- Both the magnitude and proportionality of the crimes were even more overwhelming than previously known: The long debate over the number of people killed during the 36-year war was put to rest, as the CEH Report—like the 1998 report of the Catholic Church's Archbishop's Office—concluded that over 200,000 had been killed or "disappeared" during the course of the 36-year civil war (1960–1996). State forces were found to have committed 626 massacres, the URNG 32. Of the total atrocities documented, *93% had been carried out by state security forces and paramilitary groups linked to them (e.g., PACs)*; the URNG was responsible for 3%; and the remaining 4% was carried out by unidentified "other" forces.
- Although the entire war (1960–1996) was marked by acts of extreme brutality and cruelty, it was primarily during the "scorched earth" war in the indigenous highlands (1981–1983) that state forces committed *acts of genocide, as defined by international law (indiscriminate extermination of indigenous groups as such, elimination of entire Maya communities, including babies)*; furthermore, these were carried out as part of state policy, not simple "excesses." This particular finding was central, given that genocide was excluded from the 1996 amnesty accord and therefore, according to the CEH, could (i.e., should) be prosecuted.
- Rape and sadistic acts of sexual assault and torture against women were routine and systematic—part of soldiers' instructions; in an interview, Tomuschat called this the most "frightening" part of the Report.
- As with the army, responsibility for URNG atrocities was attributed to the top leadership, and could not be dismissed as "excesses" or "errors" by rogue elements.
- The Report made a strikingly harsh indictment of U.S. policy, beginning with its active involvement in developing the counterinsurgency capabilities and policies of the Guatemalan army during the 1960s. During the 1970s–1980s dirty war, the U.S. government directly and indirectly supported some of the Guatemalan state's illegal operations (although with some ambivalence under the Carter administration, 1977–1980). During the 1980s, the U.S. government was fully aware of the massacres and other atrocities during that period of "scorched-earth" warfare and did nothing to

stop them; in fact, it indirectly enabled and signaled approval of their actions (see below).

On the basis of its findings, and in order to begin meeting the massive challenges of reconciliation, the Report made far reaching recommendations for major obligations to be undertaken by the two parties. By far, the bulk of these obligations fell on the governmental side, but successive governments, beginning with the one that had signed the Accords, under President Alvaro Arzú (1996–1999), have rejected them directly or indirectly and considered them non-binding. Above all, the government explicitly rejected the CEH finding that acts of genocide had been committed by state security forces.

Despite the government's refusal to implement its recommendations, the Truth Commission Report has remained alive in numerous ways. In the popular imagination, the CEH Report, together with the ODHA Report, will go down in history as the authoritative interpretation of the war. Reacting to the government's stance, a broad range of civil society organizations formed a multi-sector coalition to maintain public pressure on the government, and to insist that the report's recommendations were binding. Even years later (as of 2007), domestic and international efforts are targeting war criminals from the scorched-earth war years—if not successfully, at least keeping the issues alive and central to Guatemala's political agenda. In short, genocide and crimes against humanity remain an open wound in Guatemala—but for that very reason, an open and ongoing campaign for justice to the unarmed civilian victims exists.

The U.S. Role: Not Simply By-Stander, but Enabler

Many treatments of genocide omit the Guatemalan case altogether—one of the most celebrated being the Pulitzer-Prize winning book by Samantha Power (2002), in which Guatemala does not even appear in the index. Additionally, it is most common to portray the U.S. role as failing to act in time to prevent genocide (a sin of omission). In the Guatemalan case, however, the U.S. government, under most administrations during the second half of the twentieth century, did not fail to act, but rather was a major enabler of systematic repression and eventually, in the 1980s, acts of genocide.

The active U.S. role began with the decisively-documented 1954 Cold War anti-Communist intervention by the Central Intelligence Agency (CIA), to overthrow the democratically elected, nationalistic government of Jacobo Arbenz (1951–1954). During the mid- to late 1960s (1966–1968), the U.S. government responded to Guatemala's leftist insurgency (formed in 1960) by directly re-training and transforming the Guatemalan army into a disciplined, counterinsurgency "killing machine," accompanied by death squads, etc. U.S. responsibility was documented at the time by U.S. participants (e.g., in *Time* magazine, 1/26/68, p. 23); it was definitively confirmed when a 1968 memo by then-U.S. Ambassador Viron Vaky surfaced (decades later), expressing regrets about the U.S. role in establishing the Guatemalan counterinsurgency state.

During the genocidal phase of the war in the early 1980s, the United States under the Reagan administration, which was constrained by Congressional human rights legislation from sending direct military aid to Guatemala, found many indirect ways to signal its approval for the army's scorched-earth war. To cite just a few examples: in 1981, the administration sent top envoy/adviser General Vernon Walters to Guatemala to let the Guatemalan regime know that it was seen as a "friend"—and subsequently in Washington, to lobby for a renewal of U.S. military aid. Assistant Secretary of State Thomas Enders, and even President Reagan himself, defended the regime of Gen. Ríos Montt as "improving human rights," even as the latter presided over the genocidal policies of 1982–1983. In late 1982, Reagan (unsuccessfully) lobbied Congress to stop giving him a "bum rap" and to renew U.S. military aid, while accusing U.S.-based human rights organizations of spreading "disinformation" about Guatemala.

Perhaps the most compelling statement about U.S. responsibility in the Guatemalan case came from a public admission by U.S. President Bill Clinton—despite his administration's ongoing collaboration with the Guatemalan army. Three weeks after the release of the CEH Report, during his (pre-scheduled) March 1999 trip to Guatemala, Clinton made the historic gesture of acknowledging responsibility for U.S. actions and complicity with human rights crimes in Guatemala over the previous forty years. Meeting with an assemblage of Guatemalan civil society organizations, Clinton stated, "For the United States, it is important that I state clearly that support for military forces or intelligence units which engaged in violent and widespread repression of the kind described in the [Truth Commission] report was wrong, and the United States must not repeat that mistake. We must, and we will, instead, continue to support the peace and reconciliation process in Guatemala" (March 16, 1999).

EYEWITNESS ACCOUNTS

Genocide Committed by the Ríos Montt Regime in Guatemala

The following eyewitness accounts are based on testimony delivered at the Permanent People's Tribunal (a spin-off from the earlier Bertrand Russell Tribunal) held in Madrid in January 1983. The accounts were originally published in Spanish by the Instituto de Estudios Políticos para América Latina y Africa (IEPALA) in *Tribunal permanente de los pueblos: Sesión Guatemala* (Madrid: IEPALA, 1988). They were translated and published in English in 1984, in the volume co-edited by Susanne Jonas, Ed McCaughan and Elizabeth Sutherland Martínez, *Guatemala: Tyrany on Trial* published by Synthesis Publications (no longer in existence), San Francisco, pp. 82–86, 87–92, 100–106, 130–133, 154–161.

Testimony of Guillermo Morales Perez (Indian Peasant)

My name is Guillermo Morales Pérez, and I am here as a witness for my people in Guatemala. My residence is Bullaj, Tajumulco, department of San Marcos. I live between two villages: Monte Cristo and Bullaj. Today I am going to tell everything that is happening in Guatemala under President Ríos Montt.

As a witness I am going to testify before the public and the members of the jury as to how we have spent the months of 1982. When Ríos Montt became President, he announced that he was going to be demo-cratic, but how long did the democracy of Ríos Montt last? Only 20 days, no more. After 20 days, he began to massacre, kidnap, and torture, according to the radio, and we heard that our brothers were being kidnapped and tortured.

The army entered the village of Bullaj the first time quietly, volun-tarily, with affection, and what did they do? They deceived the people, they deceived us, they did what Ríos Montt ordered. He sent his army to trick us, and what happened when they entered? They killed two men. On May 15, 1982, the army entered and killed two men, dragging them out of their homes. The army men do not love their brothers, they think of us as animals. It's the same as when we go to kill a chicken. The army men no longer have mercy for Christians; they no longer have sympathy; they only think of us as animals. But it is they who have become animals, these government employees, this government, because it is the govern-ment that has declared a law to kill us for being peasants.

The army returned on July 20, and what did they do to us? They committed an injustice, because they came to the edge of these two villages, surrounded them, and started firing bullets to kill all the people who lived in the two villages. They succeeded in entering the village, and they set up camp. And out of fear, we fled. We went about 50 meters away from the houses because while we were inside, they had continued to fire at us. We left at night, without cover, dragging the children along. Women, 25 and 30 years old, pregnant, crept out of their houses. Others had just given birth only two days before. Even in their situation, they had to leave their homes, and they were very bitter, what with the bullets and all. Filled with fright, we had to leave, with the army on top of us, and we, what could we respond with? We are nobody, and they called us guerrillas.

And what type of guerrillas are we if we have nothing, if we only work in the fields? Our struggle is to work enough to be able to feed and maintain our families and to live through the year. Because if we do not work, we cannot live. The condition of the land where we live is bad. We don't have 300 or 1,000 *cuerdas*; we have scarcely one, five, or 10 *cuerdas* [one *cuerda* is the equivalent to 350 square meters—Eds.]. There is nowhere to put any livestock, or any other type of animal. We don't have that possibility. Thus, we can only work the land; it's the only way we can earn a living. . . .

The shooting lasted from July 20 to July 22, almost three days. Then we returned to our houses. We proclaimed that we had not committed any crime because all we do is work in the fields. This is what we did. But what did they do? The set up camp in the village of Bullaj; we remained in our homes and continued working. On July 24 they began to bombard, bombard, bombard. They shot bullets all over, it was a noise like one hears when it rains on the coffee trees, like one hears in the *charunales* [trees that are used to provide shade for the coffee trees—Eds.]. We heard the shots very well, and they fell like a light rain. We ran away in fright, in terror, because we had never heard so many shots before.

Two more men were killed: Marcos Cash, 65 years old, and Luciano Chávez, 35 years old—they killed them, they hung them up. This evil army hung them, they knifed them in the neck, and at the same time they stuck them in their sides. They did all this the way they wanted, just like killing an animal to eat. This is what they did to our brothers.

We ran from the fear that we felt, with this constant bombardment that lasted two more days, July 24 and July 25. The following day, July 26, they camped in the village again. On July 27, they began burning all the houses. They burned the houses, they burned everything that was inside them—clothes, beds, our personal documents, money—all these things were burned. And at the same time, they ate all the animals, and what they could not eat, they shot full of holes. It lasted almost seven days, ending on August 2. From July 20 to August 2, 1982, 45 houses in all were burned. During this period, 300 or more army soldiers were in the village.

They returned November 24. And they returned in another way, trying to deceive us again. What did they do? They entered the village without making any noise, they came without firing a shot, very quietly, and we trusted them. Perhaps they were not going to do anything. Perhaps everything was over. Because according to what Ríos Montt said on the news, everyone was supposed to return to their homes and to rebuild them. The army was not going to continue burning; he said, "I repent for having burned your homes." In a note sent to the mayor of the Tajumulco he said, "Rebuild your homes, don't be afraid of the army, when they come, they will come in peace, they will not repeat their acts."

We felt safe and trusting, because we really felt that we had not committed any crime. We thought that we had not wronged Ríos Montt; we only claimed our rights to live well with what we earn from our own work. What did the army do on November 24 in the village of Monte Cristo? That afternoon, around 4:00 p.m., they divided up to go to the houses of the village, and captured four families, little boys and girls, teenagers, old men and women. They took them to where the army was camped and brought them before their commander. What did the commander of the army say? "Kill these lazy good-for-nothings, because they are with the guerrillas." They were then killed with machetes and knives, without using firearms. They cut off the head and arms of one of the women; they left her without head and arms, and they cut open her chest with a knife. Her name was Luisa Martín. And in this manner, they finished off all members of the four families, 18 people in all. The names of the dead people are: Joaquín Martín, Emiliano Martín, Juventino Hernández, Felipe Chávez, Jesús Ramos, Lucía Martín, Chavela Martín with three children, María Ramos, Esperanza Ramos, Oracio Martín and four other children from two to five years of age.

The following day, they continued burning houses and robbing whatever they found, things that the people had worked for. There were around 150 soldiers who entered the village on November 24 and 25.

We have heard the news that Ríos Montt wants to end the war with "Beans and Guns." There in our village, we see very clearly what the army does—bombard, shoot, burn houses, kill people, and destroy all the food supplies in the village. We have never seen this offer of beans that the news speaks of. . . .

So many of our friends and family have died, and in addition to this, Ríos Montt has given orders for the creation of groups to patrol under his orders. On December 23, these patrols killed Santiago López, 55 years old; Rafael Chávez, 35 years old; and Rosalía Chávez, a 14-year-old girl. What did they do to this girl? They raped her and then killed her. They killed her 10 meters inside the Mexican border, but they took her out again and buried her 10 meters inside the Guatemalan border. This is what the patrol did under orders from the army. . . .

The landowners have also acted in an evil way toward us. They give us a task which takes two days to do, and we only earn one *quetzal*, 50 *centavos*. Meat with bone is one *quetzal* for half a kilo, and pure meat costs one *quetzal*, 65 *centavos* for half a kilo. To be able to buy this half kilo of meat, we must work for two days. In reality, we do not eat any meat, and our families eat only a little tamale with salt. We cannot eat anything else the way the rich people can: milk, meat, eggs, vegetables, avocados—all the things that are at the market, that the land produces.

The rich people have all of this. And they have us like slaves, like animals, like beasts of burden, and they ride us. We carry them on our backs and give the rich man what he wants—we do everything.

Our personal dignity is dominated; and because of the lack of schooling and food, our children are the way they are, like me, with little schooling, even to explain this message I am giving. The majority of the country is also like this. We have no teachers, and at the same time, we do not have enough time to learn. There is much injustice in Guatemala. This is what I came to testify here in this country of Spain, so you will help us, because we can no longer stand the situation in Guatemala. Just as we are together here today, all together, we are brothers. We believe in this brotherhood and for this reason we plead for help and aid, to help our Guatemala be healed, that we may live in freedom and tranquility, and that we may all live together as brothers. Thank you.

Testimony of Regina Hernández (Guatemalan Committee for Justice and Peace, Refugee Program)

My name is Regina Hernández, and I am a member of the Guatemalan Committee for Justice and Peace (Comité Pro-Justicia y Paz de Guatemala). I have come before the Permanent People's Tribunal to give testimony about the displaced persons, or refugees, inside Guatemala. Before leaving Guatemala, I spent several months with these refugees, sharing their life and anguish.

They are the survivors of massacres perpetrated by the army in the villages in the highlands of Guatemala. They are those who managed to escape when their houses and crops were burned. Many of them witnessed the murders of their parents, brothers and sisters, spouses, and children.

Some are entire villages or communities who scattered to hide in the mountains when they heard that the army was near, to avoid being massacred like neighboring villages.

Others discovered earlier that the army was approaching, and because of the terror sown by the soldiers wherever they go, these people preferred to seek refuge in the capital or in other regions of the country, with the idea of returning to their villages when things settled down.

Others are families who have some relative or relatives connected with the opposition or "people's organizations" in Guatemala, and are thus "guilty by association."

The majority have no place to go and continually flee from one place to another. In their letter celebrating Holy Thursday, the bishops of Guatemala calculated the number of these refugee or displaced persons inside the country as more than one million. They also said that more houses have been destroyed by the current repression than were destroyed in the earthquake of 1976. The number of refugees has grown, because the repression—instead of decreasing—has become more acute.

HOW THE DISPLACED PERSONS LIVE

The conditions of our lives are very bad. If once we lived in misery, under inhuman conditions, today our situation is worse—it is indescribable. We try to survive by imitating little wild animals, fleeing constantly in self-defense like hunted rabbits or deer. But the difference is that we are people, and it is difficult for us to move around—the colors of our clothes, especially the *huipiles* [traditional blouses, known for their beauty—Eds.] of the native women, make us targets, and we travel from place to place in groups of hundreds and sometimes thousands.

There are families with five or six children, small children who must be carried. To see a woman with one child on her back and one at her waist is very sad. Children who can walk carry a few clothes or a little food.

You fall and scramble up again. You hurt yourself on the thorns along the path, and then salty perspiration runs down into these cuts. This burns, as you can imagine! Then, when you decide to rest a little, the mosquitoes and flies crowd around to suck up your blood.

It is incredible how the children tolerate this without crying. What they can't stand is knowing that the army is near. I remember when we were in a small village and it was rumored that the soldiers were corning. All the children began to shout with fear and anguish.

When we found a place away from the soldiers, we would sit down to eat and share whatever we were able to bring along. We were so hungry that a cold corn tortilla and a little salt (if we had any) tasted wonderful. When we ran out of tortillas, we would go a day with only half a glass of corn meal mixed with water; this was all we had for the whole day.

We would also search for herbs we recognized and eat the leaves. This was during the winter, the season when the herbs grow. Sometimes all we had was a raw ear of corn that we found in those places where the crops had not been destroyed by the army. In the mountains, the refugees eat anything to survive.

Imagine what disease you find in these places where everything is lacking, where we must sleep exposed to the rain and wear our clothes wet until they dry out again. So many children have died of diarrhea, measles, pneumonia! If they don't die at the hands of the army, they die from disease.

So we move on, in growing numbers. In the mountains there are places that resemble the settlements constructed after the earthquake, where you find 1,500 to 2,000 families, places where you might eat only tortillas once or twice a day. Sometimes you wait a long time before getting to taste a little salt. There are places where people have gone to the extreme of drinking their own urine, because the rivers might be poisoned. We have also quenched our thirst with the dew that forms on the leaves of the plants.

Nevertheless, in the middle of all the anguish and terror that the army causes us, we try to encourage and inspire each other, to cheer each other up. One time we organized a little party, with guitars and violins, sharing with each other some of what we had left. We do this to have a few joyful moments and not to go crazy from anguish.

It's during these times that we live the Gospel—with deeds, not only with words. When we get to a place, we look around and check to see that everyone has arrived, that someone has not gotten lost along the way, that none of the children are missing. We all worry about each other. If we plan to stay in a spot for some time, we share what we have brought along to eat, and the few blankets or plastic covers that we managed to carry along to cover us at night. This is how we celebrate our faith, by sharing everything: sorrow, grief, suffering, and joy.

THE FEAR OF MODEL VILLAGES

All the things our people need are, for the government, a means of pressure to force us to turn ourselves in. They trick the international press into believing that the government is a savior, regrouping people and offering them "shelter, food, and work." But you don't know how much sorrow there is in the hearts of the people that the government has relegated them to living in "model villages." How can people agree with a government that has murdered their families and burned everything they had? If they are living in these "model villages," it is because they are there under threat. Men must be part of the civilian patrols; if they don't do it, they are killed.

DAYS OF ANGUISH IN CHIMALTENANGO

I would like to tell you what happened on July 16, 17, and 18, 1982, when the army entered the village of San Martín Jilotepeque in the department of Chimaltenango. They entered the village on July 16, at 11:30 a.m., accompanied by civilian patrols. That day I was with a friend who had asked me to come to her house. We couldn't get there, because in the road we met all these people running away from the soldiers. It began to pour down rain that afternoon. We ran from the village and regrouped in a village nearby, with about 400 others, while the soldiers went from house to house, killing chickens to eat and trying on the men's clothes. The soldiers had also gotten wet in the rain and they were nonchalantly changing their clothes.

Meanwhile, in the next village, we got an enormous pot and prepared food for the children. We couldn't sleep because of the shots we heard throughout the night. The next day the soldiers approached the village where we were staying and all of us had to flee again. I remember the dawn of July 17, when we heard the cry, "Run, the soldiers are coming!" The children began to cry, terrorized, but after we started walking, they calmed down some. Each person carried his belongings, his poncho, some tortillas, corn meal, or whatever he could find. Each child who could walk also carried something.

The people of three villages came together in one place. We were resting when we again heard shots nearby. Once again we fled. Finally we came to another place farther away, where we found more people from other villages. There we rested again and shared what we had. We ran out of water and ate dry corn meal. We became nauseated from the lack of water. There were too many of us, so we decided to divide up into smaller groups. Each group went to a different village where we knew there were no soldiers. But in all this activity, families got divided up. In my group, there was a child carrying his mother's clothes and a poncho, while his mother went off in a second group carrying their tortillas. Her oldest child was in a third group, and the father—with the rest of the ponchos—went with yet a fourth group. I also saw a little girl about five years old who had lost her parents. But there we were!

We found a little orange tree loaded with oranges. We picked them all. They were very acidic, but they helped a lot. After a long walk—all day long—we came to another place about 9:00 p.m., and slept there. At this place they gave us hot tortillas, water, and a little salt.

On July 18 at 5:00 a.m., we were all up and ready to go. We washed with the dew from the plants. We found yucca and some other food and we each ate a little. We gave the leftover tortillas to the children. We were busy doing all this when we heard shots. We had to run again. Minutes later we saw the soldiers come running down a road. We had separated into groups of 20. What hurt me the most was seeing the old people with their canes, but thank God we managed to get away. From a distance, we saw the village burn.

When we heard that the soldiers had left our village, we returned home. We got there at 4:00 p.m. It was so sad, watching families find their houses and possessions reduced to ashes!

HELP FOR THE REFUGEES

All this suffering has forced me to leave my country to seek help. We need your help to cry out and denounce what is happening in Guatemala, where they try to smother our cries with massacres. We need your help to survive and to resist this war.

Inside Guatemala, the service that I performed for my people was to bring them a little medicine, some food and clothes that I got from my friends. By sharing I have learned much from them. This little assistance meant risking my life; I knew that if I was found delivering these things, I would disappear forever. Many times I have been on the edge of death, sometimes from bullets and sometimes from flames, when they set fire to the forests. I have had to cross burning forests, practically suffocating from smoke inhalation.

What sadness! In Guatemala, the assassins of the Ríos Montt regime can go everywhere. And we, who have not stained our hands with blood, who have only tried to help, to defend ourselves, and to survive, must travel oh so carefully, hiding as if we were thieves. We are certain that someday there will be justice and that peace will come to Guatemala, with the help of all the people of the world.

The Committee for Justice and Peace has made a promise to bring help to 11 departments of Guatemala. It is one of the urgent tasks that we as Christians must undertake now, in this moment of struggle for our liberation.

Testimony of Juan Velázquez Jiménez (Indian Peasant and Mineworker)

My name is Juan Velázquez Jiminéz from the municipality of San Ildefonso Ixtahuacán, department of Huehuetenango. I come as a representative of the people of Guatemala to tell what is happening with the Ríos Montt government. But before that, I would like to speak of what has made my people famous: the problems of the mines at San Ildefonso Ixtahuacán, and the four-day march to the capital of Guatemala that my people made to hold a demonstration.

Work in the mine began when the government signed a 40-year contract with a gringo man [ie., foreign—Eds.] named René Abularach. The people protested with a demonstration saying that they did not want the mine. A lawyer came, but the government showed no respect to him. Then the army troops began to arrive at the mine. The army had no respect for the people, but instead began to beat and slaughter them. The municipal mayor was immediately informed of what the army was doing but the mayor did not come, out of fear of the army. Later, the army arrested 15 men from the village, whom they took away. They also took prisoner a priest and a catechist and brought them by truck to the Huehuetanango department seat.

The army charged that the priest was guilty because he was giving guidance to the people. The priest responded that the people were only seeking their rights. The soldiers told the priest that he should not get involved in politics and let him go. The other men were struck, beaten, and kicked, and then were allowed to return to their village.

Later the gringos came to work in the mine and extracted tons of minerals in trucks. The people did not want the mine to continue because it was dangerous for the community. People thought that the community was going to cave in because the miners dug tunnels under people's homes. Tunnels were dug 4 kilometers under people's houses and some of the land in the community did cave in. Then, many people left to go to other, more faraway towns: to Cuilco, Ixcán, and La Costa. We were afraid, thinking that the whole town was going to cave in at once. We also did not want the mine because the lifeblood of the land, a very valuable mineral called tungsten, was being taken to another country.

People formed a union and went to demonstrate at the capital, walking on foot. For four days, they walked to the capital to demonstrate against the mine. Later, the same problems with Mr. Abularach continued. He claimed that the mine was not worth anything, while he was really trying to keep the miners from unionizing.

Now I would like to continue telling about what is going on with the Ríos Montt government. On May 6, 1982, the soldiers left Huehuetenango, and arrived in my town of San Ildefonso Ixtahuacán at noon. Along the road, they grabbed one of my brothers, took off his shirt and his pants, and left him naked. The soldiers tied him up and stuck him in a car. A red truck was in front and two olive green trucks were in back. They arrived at a crossroads where the trucks remained. They also left my brother there tied up in the car, with five soldiers to watch him.

Later, the soldiers arrived at a church where we were having a celebration. They started kicking us around and made us leave. At the celebration there were 45 adults and our children. The soldiers then gathered us together in the basketball court. Later, more soldiers arrived and surrounded the whole village. They began to drag people out of their homes until 10:00 p.m. Then they put us in a school, locked us up and told us to stay there while they ate, saying they were exhausted because of us. They locked the door real well and went to eat.

When they got back, the soldiers began to talk to us: "Now we sure did catch you today, you subversive thieves, you disgraceful Indians, you savages." We answered, "We are not stealing. We are celebrating the word of God." The second lieutenant said, "There is no God here who will bless you." They grabbed a 22-year-old peasant, and the second lieutenant told him: "All of you are bums and gossips. You are the teachers of all the subversive people here." Then one of the soldiers threw a lasso around the peasant's neck, and they hung him right there from a beam in the school. But the rope broke and the peasant fell to the ground. The second lieutenant kicked him, told him to get up, and then they tied him up again. They hung him again, and beat him all over until he died. Then the soldiers laid his body down.

The second lieutenant asked, "Where are the catechists?" The soldiers grabbed two of them and then three more people. Outside the school, the soldiers began to fire their guns, and those soldiers who were inside the school began to steal watches and money from the people. Then the soldiers took the dead man's body from the school and they brought some bombs inside, saying to us, "Be careful that you don't leave, because you will die." They grabbed 11 people from among those at the school, and took them to prison. My brother, whom they had left in the truck, also was killed. Five soldiers remained at the school, but then they left, with us locked inside. We stayed there crying. At 7 a.m. we broke down the doors of the school, and went home.

The soldiers went to Cuilco but later they returned to Huehuetenango, to the settlement called Laguneta, Aldea Alta in the municipality of San Ildefonso Ixtahuacán. I was working in the cornfields when they came. There were two peasants from the village of La Cumbre Papal, going to work in Chiapas. The soldiers grabbed them and searched their bags; they took away some hats that the peasants had, and then the soldiers tied them up by the neck. Five soldiers pulled at them from one side, and five soldiers from the other. The peasants were left there dead, tied to a tree. The soldiers cut off a piece of flesh from their legs, pants and all, and they left it hanging on a stick. They did that to both of these men.

Then they climbed up on a building and began to shoot. I was trembling with fear. When they arrived at the village of La Cumbre, they began to burn houses. I went to Laguneta and there I found a municipal employee. I told him that the soldiers had already killed two peasants. "We are not aware of it," said the employee. This happened on June 12, 1982. On June 13, 20 of us got together and went to see the bodies of the dead men. We took off the rope, dug a hole, and we buried them. And this I saw with my own eyes, because it is not good to tell lies.

On June 15, 1982, I was buying medicine in San Ildefonso Ixtahuacán when the airplanes went over. There were two in front and one behind, another two and then one, two and then one. There were a lot of planes and I was not able to count them all. I counted only eight. That day they went to bomb Nentón and San Pedro Necta, in the department of Huehuetenango. On the 16th, they were still bombing. The next day, one of my cousins arrived who had escaped death in the bombings; he was crying. Many people were killed in the bombings. There were many children killed, my cousin said.

On August 18, 1982, the soldiers came to organize civilian patrols in the village of Akjel, in the municipality of San Ildefonso Ixtahuacán. They ordered the assistant mayor to convene the people. When people arrived, the second lieutenant began talking, saying that by order of the Efraín Ríos Montt government, they were going to organize the civilian patrols. People asked him, "What are these civilian patrols for?" The second lieutenant answered, "To take care of the people so that the guerrillas don't come in." Then people asked: "Well, what are these patrols going to defend themselves with?" He answered, "You are going to carry machetes, rope, and a piece of wood. And if there are a lot of guerrillas, you are going to ring bells, sound horns, and yell, so that people come to grab the subversives."

People then said to the second lieutenant, "Second lieutenant, but we have to work on the farm. How are we going to eat?" He answered, "If you do not want to patrol, then you are subversives. You are going to respect the law, because it comes from the government. And if you don't respect the law that I have announced to you, I will kill your entire village." Then he showed us some bombs, and told us: "Here are your avocados, we are going to use them on your family." The people became very frightened and they agreed to patrol under the barrels of the soldiers' guns.

The second lieutenant said that the patrols had to receive identification cards that he himself, and the commander of the San Ildefonso patrols, would issue. On November 3, people from the village presented themselves in town and 100 identification cards were given out. The second lieutenant announced that all youth of 18 years old or over would have to go away to serve in the army. He also said that every patrol group had to bring its flag and identification cards when it was patrolling. "If you don't carry your flag and your identification cards, then you are guerrillas, and the army will kill you." That is how the civilian patrols in my town were organized.

On October 5th, I went to sell some oranges and bananas to the village of La Cumbre Papal. The civilian patrols were there, together with the soldiers. The soldiers asked for my papers, and told me that

I had to go with them to the village of Papal. While I was in the village, the soldiers removed a man named Juan Ordoñez from his house, and another neighbor, and they set both of their houses on fire. The houses were made of straw. As the houses were burning, they threw both men, who were tied up very tightly, into the fire. And then they took me down farther, and we ran into two children who were eating corn on the cob in their homes. One ran off and hid in the *tamascal* [a steam bath used by the Indians—Eds.], and the other, a five-year-old, stayed inside the house. The soldiers set the house on fire, and burned it down with the child inside. The dead child was left in the house. The other child who had hidden in the *tamascal* was also killed. The soldiers then began to burn the other houses in the village. I could not count them all. I counted at least 20 houses that were burned by the soldiers. Then they let me return to my home.

In the month of November, a white pickup truck arrived. When it came to the Sevillaj bridge near the Cuilco mound, it stopped in front of Sr. José Lopez's house. Soldiers from the truck set his house on fire and then they machine-gunned Sr. Lopez, who was 60 years old, and all of his family. They killed a total of 10 people in that house. There was not one single person from José Lopez's family left. Then they forced the civilian patrol, who were accompanying the soldiers, to bury the dead in 6-foot ditches.

Throughout Guatemala, in various places and towns, our people cannot stand so much repression any more. People find dead bodies thrown at the side of the road. We find dead bodies without heads, without hands, without legs. We do not want anymore killing. We cannot stand Ríos Montt's repression, his misery, any more. We cannot work, we cannot do business, we cannot eat, because of everything that Ríos Montt is doing. And now we peasants want Ríos Montt to resign. We cannot stand him any more. I hope that you ladies and gentlemen can help us so that this Ríos Montt government will resign, along with his army, which is finishing us all off in Guatemala.

Testimony of Juan José Mendoza (Indian Community Leader)

A high point of this testimony was the story, which follows, of a community organization in the well-known tourist town of Santiago Atitlán, whose population of about 25,000 spoke Maya-Tzutuhil—Eds.

. . . In Santiago Atitlán, a group of Atitecos who had suffered and knew the pain and suffering of their people organized in 1966. They were catechists of the Catholic Church. With the help of the parish priest,

Father Ramón Carlin (a missionary from Oklahoma, USA), they began a campaign to teach reading and writing to the population. In 1970, with 300 members, we organized the Radio Association of the Voice of Atitlán. All the villages on the banks of Lake Atitlán participated; together we would seek a just and humane life.

We organized groups to teach reading and writing. We organized cooperatives: handicrafts, agriculture, and savings and loans offices. We began programs of health information and adult education, cultural programs and religious programs preaching the Christian gospel. We had a radio station to transmit the programs to all neighboring villages. Peasant children, young people, women, men, and the elderly participated. We all respected the sacred right to life of our relatives and neighbors; we shared our grief and our suffering as well as our happiness. All of the members of the Radio Association of the Voice of Atitlán voluntarily worked together to bring happiness and well-being to the lives of our oppressed people. Then, for trying to come out of our life of misery, the hatred of the government and the wealthy landowners destroyed us.

In June 1980, the army set up camp in the village of Cerro de Oro, eight kilometers from the town of Santiago Atitlán, with seven truckloads of soldiers, 50 soldiers in each truck. They interrogated the villagers of Cerro de Oro, to find out who were the collaborators in the Radio Association of the Voice of Atitlán and who were the influential people of the village. But the villagers did not give any information. So the army moved their camp to Cantón Panabaj, two kilometers from the village of Santiago Atitlán, on September 5.

On September 30, at 7:30 p.m., a paramilitary squad in a red car, coming from the department of Sololá, kidnapped the catechist Juan Ixbalán on a public street of the town of Santiago Atitlán. On October 10 they kidnapped another catechist, Manuel Coché. They tied his hands, beat him up, and dragged him from his house. Then the army forced the population to attend a meeting on October 15, at 11:00 a.m. They announced that the army had been sent by the government of Lucas García to protect and take care of the town of Santiago Atitlán. The people were prohibited from walking on the streets after 7:30 p.m., were forced to return from their work in the fields early in the day, and were forbidden to go very far from the town.

On October 24, at 4:30 p.m., the army and the national police surrounded the building of the Radio Association of the Voice of Atitlán, leaving after half an hour. But at 1:30 a.m., on the 25th, a group of soldiers, dressed in civilian clothes and well armed, kidnapped Gaspar Culan Yataz, director of the Radio Association; he was beaten savagely and shot in the head. His wife and daughter were also beaten. The soldiers carried the unconscious Mr. Gaspar to the camp; nothing more was heard of him.

The building of the Association was searched and plundered by the army on November 12. They stole radios and office machines, destroyed doors and windows. They hid a bag of firearms inside the building. The following day, Father Francisco, who had been the parish priest of Santiago Atitlán since 1969, told the mayor what had happened. The mayor callcd the army and, together with the army, he entered the building. The colonel ordered the soldiers to search the building, and they found the sack containing firearms. The colonel told those present that the Association had used arms and that they were accomplices of the subversives.

Four members of the Association were kidnapped on November 15, and savagely tortured. Three were buried in Chimaltenango in graves marked "XXX." The body of the youngest was found by his relatives, whose names are Nicolás Ratzan Tziná, Juan Pacay Rujuch, Diego Sosof Coché, and Esteban Ajtzip R. We had to hide in the ravines and hills and could not work. Many of our houses were ransacked, we were victims of persecution. Ever since the kidnapping of the director, we have had to abandon our work as the Radio Association of the Voice of Atitlán. . . .

The murderous army was always looking for ways to terrorize the population of Santiago Atitlán. In September 1981 there was new persecution of ex-members of the Radio Association of the Voice of Atitlán. The army sent letters to every one of the ex-members telling them to give themselves up at the camp. If they did not turn themselves in, their houses would be burned, their families would be killed, and they would be prosecuted according to the law of the army. To save their families, 15 ex-members of the Association turned themselves in.

They were held in the camp for 15 days. They were threatened and forced by the Minister of National Defense to declare to the international and national press and to Guatemalan television that they were collaborators or members of the subversives and that all of them had gone to the camp to seek refuge and ask for protection by the army. On November 18, the army gave the interview to the press and television in the camp of Panabaj, Santiago Atitlán; they also forced many people to go to the camp and pretend to be subversives seeking shelter and refuge in the camp. All of these lies hide the crimes of the Lucas Garcia regime from the eyes of the world.

In the face of this difficult situation, many of us had to flee to Mexico at the end of November 1981.

Following the coup d'etat of March 23, 1982, Mendoza returned to Guatemala hoping to find more peace but instead found even greater insecurity. He came to live in the community of Nahualá where the following incident took place: an example of the Guatemalan people's indestructible defiance.—Eds.

The military commander had received an order from the army saying that the civilian patrol should not go out at 7:00 p.m., as was the custom, but should wait until 10:00 p.m. for that night only. However, the civilian patrol disobeyed the military commander and went out at 7:00 p.m. At that moment, the army was about to kidnap someone.

A group of well armed soldiers dressed in civilian clothes passed by, accompanied by a person with his head covered who was going to point out the house where the kidnapping would take place. The civilian patrolmen recognized the voice of the hooded person, and when the two groups met, a member of the civilian patrol unhooded the person. At that point, the soldiers machine-gunned the civilian patrolmen and also killed the hooded person. But members of the civilian patrol had prevented the kidnapping and unmasked the army as the author of the kidnappings and massacres of the indigenous population.

Testimony of Carmelita Santos (Indian Catechist)

My name is Carmelita Santos. I am an indigenous catechist and a member of the Guatemalan Committee for Justice and Peace.

I present my testimony to this People's Tribunal in the name of my Guatemalan brothers and sisters who are unable to lift up their voices today, and who suffer under the military dictatorship of General Efraín Ríos Montt. I wish to speak in the name of all the men, women, children, and elderly people of my country, so that the world will know about the terrible injustices that we suffer there, and so that our right to live on this earth as people and as children of God will be recognized.

MY WORK AS A CATECHIST

I work in communities, talking to the people about God, and the people like that. I also teach people how to sing. People like to sing or to shout, because they fill their lungs with air and it makes them happy.

In 1970 and 1972, some good priests came here, who were honestly committed to helping their brothers in need. They weren't like the ones before them, who only talked to the "ladinos" in the village. They took care of us all. They came to our village to evangelize us but on seeing our communal lands where we all ate the same corn, they were the ones who were evangelized. When there was happiness, we all shared in it. And we all shared the same sorrows.

The priests wanted to improve our plight, but because we were many, two priests alone could not carry out improvements for all. The best thing they did was to set up schools, to train cornmunity leaders. These schools were established in various regions of Guatemala, since the priests could not cover every town. They and the nuns would visit each school, and then return two weeks or a month later. Those of us who were trained were called catechists, or community leaders.

The catechist works with the community, spreading the Word of God, allowing everyone to participate. The Word of God leads us to organize and make our demands together, because we will not be listened to on an individual basis. We organized a demonstration, protesting our oppression by the rich. But they said: "What's going on? The down-trodden Indians are acting up. Those who open their mouths will be killed."

HEALTH EDUCATION

The nuns taught us the importance of hygiene. When children have rashes or intestinal parasites or diarrhea, it's because of bad health conditions. But there are even worse problems in villages like Canchún Chitucán, where there is no water because it sank after the earthquake. There is hardly enough to drink. Where could the people go? A priest said: "Let's dig a well."

But the religious people's love for the poor and their total devotion were not well-received by the rich. Neither they, nor the police, nor the judges, nor the soldiers like it when someone is concerned about the poor. They accused the priest of being a "guerrilla chief" and tried to capture him and kill him, but he managed to escape. He had to leave the country.

THE CHURCH, THREATENED AND PERSECUTED

First they threaten the community leader. If he doesn't leave immediately, he is kidnapped during the night and killed in the ravine. This has been done to catechists and to people who have listened to their sermons. Now we cannot hold our masses, or recite the rosary or the Novena of the Sacred Heart of Jesus, because we are being watched. In our village there are two strange men; they are not from the village, but they appear and disappear in the evenings.

Who persecutes the Christians? The big judges, paid by the governor or the ex-governor of Salamá; the soldiers stationed in the town of Rabinal; the national police; an employee of the city who is a friend of the soldiers or the national police; or a military cornmander.

This happened during the time of Lucas García, who said that there was freedom for the Church but who really persecuted it. They watched the villages and took away our leaders, killing them one by one. Oh! But Lucas went too far, and it was known that he was an assassin. The rich say that there was a change in government. They put in Ríos Montt, saying that he was "better," but he has the same heart as Lucas, and sharper nails. He's "democratic" but he's smarter than Lucas. Oh! "The envoy of God," Ríos Montt calls himself. Is he like God, powerful and merciful with the poor?

TESTIMONY OF THE COMMUNITIES SUFFERING IN THE GENOCIDE CARRIED OUT BY THE RÍOS MONTT GOVERNMENT

Ríos Montt shows his power to the poor. When he took over, he ordered his soldiers to eliminate from the map of Rabinal, Baja Verapaz, several villages that no longer had inhabitants. The people there had been slaughtered by soldiers and 10 commando squads from Xococ: Río Negro, Camalmapa, Canchún, Buena Vista, and the village of Chichupac, where there were only about 20 survivors. . . . In each of these villages there had been 300, 400, 500 or more inhabitants, not counting children. I say this because I have been in these communities many times, singing, praying, and celebrating the Word of God, or we would dance to the *son* of San Pablo or Rabinal. It hurts me that my people have left me alone. And I say this because I burn inside from the injustice of Rios Montt against my poor people of Rabinal and against all the other poor people of the indigenous regions of Guatemala. Let them kill me for speaking the truth. I am not afraid.

Ríos Montt says that he is governing in the name of God. For those who believe in him, he is a Christian and belongs to an evangelical sect. But the repression got much worse for the poor with the arrival of Ríos Montt.

1. *Plan de Sanchez, July 18, 1982*

It was Sunday. Before, no one would go to the town to do their shopping. But that day, July 18th, in various villages—Concul, Irchel, Xeciguan, Chiac, and the whole village of Plan de Sánchez—the people decided to come with their baskets on their heads, filled with *macuy*, and *chiquiboy* [foods—Eds.] to sell and exchange for corn. Women came with chickens, or baby pigs, to trade for food to feed their families. Other women from the mountains brought cheeses to exchange for corn from Rabinal. Some merely wanted to go to Sunday mass. It was around 10 a.m. The soldiers stationed there had mortars and began to fire bombs on the villages around the town of Rabinal. Then a helicopter flew over us and dropped more bombs. There were two little planes, very high up, some distance from the helicopter, and we had the impression that they were watching over the helicopter.

When everyone saw this, and heard "boom! boom! boom!," they all got up. Some were crying because they had left their children in their village, children of 3 or 4 years who were too little to run away. Others said, "Mine are 8 and 10 years old; maybe they've run to the ravine." "But what about the elderly, who can't run?" So they decided to go to the villages.

But down the path, a village called Plan de Sánchez was surrounded by soldiers who would not let the people go by, telling them to wait for the captain, who was going to tell them something. Some, seeing the crowd from a distance, returned to the town. Others hid in the ravines and the hillside. Meanwhile, the soldiers were searching the houses in Plan de Sánchez, taking away the good clothing and the valuable old jewelry, stealing it all. Then they set the houses on fire and rounded up the children and the old people, all in one group.

In the afternoon, they began raping the women and torturing the men. What terrible screams could be heard two mountains away! Then they piled everyone up, poured fuel on them, and set fire to the people. Women, old people, and children were turned to ashes. One of the burning people managed to escape, and ran around like a cat until she finally fell into the ravine. The soldiers howled when they saw this naked person doing that; it was just a joke for Ríos Montt's soldiers.

Then they piled up the dead bodies and went to get Lorenza, the woman who had survived the fire. They sat her in the middle of all the bodies, they cut her lips, and made her watch the soldiers as they placed the burnt children at their dead mothers' breasts and the men's heads between the women's legs.

Lorenza was a preacher in the village, along with Narcisa. They belonged to the church choir and gave sermons. Narcisa had been burnt alive. But Lorenza had survived, and the soldiers asked her if she believed in God. "Let's see if He saves you!" they shouted. Lorenza, lying in agony, heard but remained quiet.

On Monday, July 19th, the soldiers went down to their barracks, taking with them some pigs, chickens, clothes, and jewelry from the dead people's homes. Some of the villagers managed to sneak down and bury some of the dead, and they found Lorenza dying. Jacinto, Lorenza's father, came and took his daughter to the health center. But the soldiers caught on immediately and they captured Jacinto and Lorenza. They said, "Hand over that shit, let's burn it some more." And Jacinto yelled that he would not hand over his daughter to the soldiers. At last he managed to get into the health center. A nurse wanted to help, but a soldier stopped her from doing anything. He took a needle out of his bag and gave Lorenza an injection. She died, leaving behind a baby girl 11 months old. In just one afternoon, 225 men, women, babies, and elderly people were killed, all burnt to death.

2. The Siege of the Church

One day we were working in my village. I can't remember the exact date, but it was a bit before what happened in Plan de Sánchez. In the afternoon a group of soldiers entered, shouting, "Well, well, what's going on with the Indians? Yours is a happy life. Why are you quiet? Where are the *marimbas,* your drums and *chirimía*? Eli? Go on with your customs, go to the chapel, celebrate the Word of God. Sing, and pray for peace." They told us a date, and said they would return, to see if we had done what they told us. We all asked each other, "Should we do it? My God, would they kill us during the mass? Maybe we shouldn't." "But they'll kill us anyway if we don't," said someone else. "Just yesterday they bombed a village." So we decided to do what they had said.

We took the *marimbas,* but played only one song, because almost all of us cried when we heard our song. We began the celebration of the Word of God, and we sang. When we had finished, our chapel was completely surrounded by soldiers.

The captain entered and came to us. "Well, folks, we want peace," he said. "But if you make trouble, we have this for you," and he showed us a big rifle in his hand. "This is for you if there's trouble." Our Bibles were on the altar. And he went up to the altar, took the Bibles and set them on fire. (For the soldiers, the Bible is subversive literature. Many people have buried theirs.) He took a hymnal, opened it and read a song which says:

> It is not enough to pray.
> Many things are needed
> for there to be peace.

The captain was furious, and he shouted, "Subversives! It's true, we have to kill all the Indians. And it doesn't matter if they are all gone. Don't worry, the village won't be empty—we can bring foreigners to live in your villages. There are plenty of people in the world!" I wanted to answer him, but I knew I would have been killed on the spot. I said to myself, "No foreigner could live in our village. We have no beds in which to sleep, all we eat is corn, we have no nearby water, no baths, no latrine, no electricity. No foreigner could live in our villages." And I wanted to answer, "They could not stand to live like we do, and work so hard. But riches do not fall from the sky, as my mother says, so we must work hard." I was so angry, but I didn't say a word, thank God.

The captain had a notebook, with a list of names in it, and he began to call out the names of all the members or Delegates of the Word of God.

They were all poor peasants. When they heard their names being called, they humbly stood up, took off their hats and said "Here, I am here." They didn't understand why their names were being called. Quickly, the soldiers stood behind each person who answered. There were many men, each one with a soldier behind him. Some people thought maybe they were being called to form a commission. Some of the women had packed lunches, and went up to their husbands to tell them to take the food with them. The soldiers got very angry and almost kicked the women out. Then the men were taken outside. Their hands were tied and they were lined up below a pole near the chapel. The children cried out to their fathers, wanting to go with them, but the soldiers dragged the children away without pity. "Do you want us to kick you?" they asked. But the children did not understand what the soldiers were saying, and they continued crying. The mothers consoled their children.

The soldiers took the men down to a creek. They tied them with a rope around their necks and hung them from the trees, beating them with sticks and branches. At first, we heard screams, but little by little the voices grew fainter because the ropes cut off the men's breathing. Night fell, and the men had not died. The soldiers stayed, sitting there shouting and laughing. Who knows what they were laughing about. Maybe Judas knows. This is the story of Christians from the base communities and how they were killed. That day, 32 men died.

Jesus preached and helped the needy. He was persecuted to death, nailed to a wooden cross. Jesus still suffers today on the heavy cross of Guatemala, from the terrible repression by Ríos Montt. The Christian base communities represent Jesus, and they are killed, dragged out of their churches for celebrating the Word of God.

3. Chichupac, April 19, 1982

On the 18th of April, soldiers entered the village of Chichupac, telling the people not to be afraid. "We are defending the country," they said. "You must trust us. We want to talk to you in a group. The government we have now is good. We will return tomorrow, but we want everyone to gather together in the church. If you have old people who are sick, take them to church tomorrow, because we will bring two doctors with us. If they have problems with their lungs, or a toothache, they will be cured tomorrow. Take the children as well: we will bring them toys to make them happy."

Some people believed the soldiers, and they went to church. Many soldiers arrived and they passed out used plastic toys. There was no doctor.

After the toys were handed out, the soldiers did not respect the statue of Christ that the catechists had put on the altar. They began to destroy the statue with their machetes. The people were surrounded and could not leave the church. Then the soldiers called out people's names, including children, and took them to the clinic nearby. All the names were of people who had learned how to read and write. (During the time of Lucas García, all peasants had been ordered to learn how to read. People signed up to learn, and the catechists signed up to teach, but the soldiers killed them. One catechist was killed while carrying a notebook with the names of the people who were studying, including the names of children who could not go to school but who had signed up to learn.)

The women were raped before the eyes of the men and the children in the clinic. The men and the boys had their testicles cut off. Everybody's tongues were cut out. Their eyes were gouged out with nails. Their arms were twisted off. Their legs were cut off. The little girls were raped and tortured. The women had their breasts cut off. And the soldiers left them all there in the clinic, piled up and dying. Those who were not on the list were prohibited from burying the victims. I only remember that 15 children were killed. I cannot remember how many adults were killed. A woman who was there told me all this . . .

References and Sources Cited

NOTE: This chapter is based primarily on knowledge gained through direct interviews conducted with a wide range of Guatemalans (and others involved), from virtually all political persuasions and social strata, over the course of several decades (since 1967). With a few exceptions, the following list of written sources is primarily from the 1980s, during the historical period discussed in this chapter; and it includes almost exclusively sources actually cited in the chapter. Unfortunately, considerations of space preclude an all-inclusive list of the 1980s literature—or of current scholarship that is interpreting and reinterpreting the historical era chronicled here, and that constitutes a vibrant new genre of scholarship.

Adams, Richard (1988). "Conclusions: What Can We Know about the Harvest of Violence?" in Robert Carmack (Ed.) *Harvest of Violence*. Norman: University of Oklahoma Press, pp. 274–291.

Americas Watch, reports on Guatemala (almost yearly throughout the 1980s).

Amnesty International, reports on Guatemala (almost yearly throughout the 1980s).

Arias, Arturo (1985). "El movimiento indigena en Guatemala: 1970–1983," in Daniel Camacho and Rafael Menjivar (Eds.) *Movimientos Populares en Centroamerica*. San Jose: EDUCA.

Comisión para el Esclarecimiento Histórico (CEH) (1999). *Guatemala: Memory of Silence*. Guatemala: CEH.

Davis, Shelton (1988). "Introduction: Sowing the Seeds of Violence," in Robert M. Carmack (Eds.) *Harvest of Violence*. Norman: University of Oklahoma Press, pp. 3–38.

Falla, Ricardo (1984). "We Charge Genocide," in Susanne Jonas, Ed McCaughan and Elizabeth Sutherland Martinez (Eds.) *Guatemala: Tyranny on Trial*. San Francisco: Synthesis Publications, pp. 112–119.

— (1978). *Quiché Rebelde*. Guatemala: Editorial Universitaria.

Grandin, Greg (2004). *The Last Colonial Massacre.* Chicago Ill.: University of Chicago Press.

Handy, James (1986). "Resurgent Democracy and the Guatemalan Military," in *Journal of Latin American Studies,* Vol. 18 (November), pp. 383–408.

Jonas, Susanne (1991). *The Battle for Guatemala: Rebels, Death Squads and U.S. Power.* Boulder, CO: Westview Press.

— (2000). *Of Centaurs and Doves: Guatemala's Peace Process.* Boulder, CO: Westview Press.

Manz, Beatriz (1988). *Refugees of a Hidden War: The Aftermath of Counterinsurgency in Guatemala.* New York: State University of New York.

Oficina de Derechos Humanos del Arzobispado de Guatemala (ODHA) (1998). *Guatemala: Nunca Más.* Guatemala: ODHA.

Opinión Política (OP) (1985) Número 2 (Enero-Febrero) y #3 (Marzo-Abril). Guatemala/Mexico. (This was the analytical publication of a group of dissidents who had split from the EGP in 1984.)

Perera, Victor (1989). "A Forest Dies in Guatemala," in *The Nation* (November 6).

Power, Samantha (2002). *"A Problem from Hell:" America and the Age of Genocide.* New York: Basic Books.

Schirmer, Jennifer (1998). *The Guatemalan Military Project.* Philadelphia: University of Pennsylvania Press.

Smith, Carol (Ed.) (1990). *Guatemalan Indians and the State: 1540–1988.* Austin: University of Texas Press.

United Nations General Assembly and Commission/Subcomission reports and resolutions, as referred to in text.

Twenty and Twenty-First Century Cases of Genocide of Indigenous Peoples

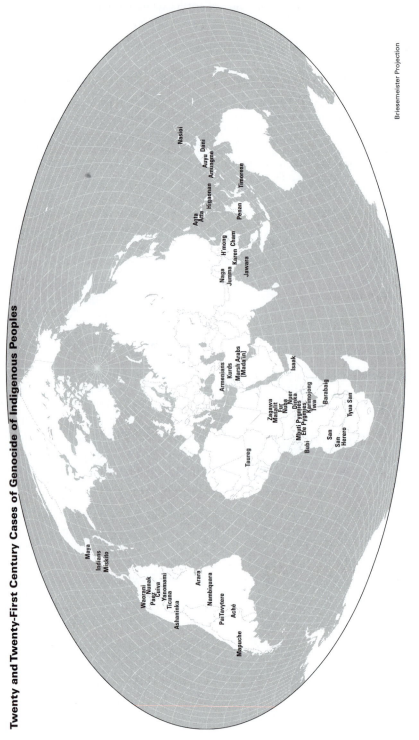

Briesemeister Projection

Indigenous Peoples

CHAPTER 13

Physical and Cultural Genocide of Indigenous Peoples

ROBERT K. HITCHCOCK AND TARA M. TWEDT

Introduction

The indigenous peoples in the world today have been described as "victims of progress" (Bodley, 1999) and who as a people have had to face "colonization, genocide, and a constant struggle for cultural and physical survival" (Independent Commission on International Humanitarian Issues, 1987, p. xi). Indigenous peoples are small-scale—and sometimes large-scale—societies that frequently have been dealt with harshly by the governments and citizens in the states in which they live. Some see them as being particularly vulnerable to genocidal acts because of their small group sizes, cultural distinctiveness, occupation of remote areas, and relative technological and organizational simplicity (Kuper, 1985, p. 301; Burger, 1987, p. 38; Amnesty International, 1992a, pp. 61–62).

Variously referred to as aboriginals, native peoples, tribal peoples, Fourth World peoples, or "first nations," these populations have suffered from vicious mistreatment, discrimination, and lack of equal opportunity in employment for centuries. This was especially true from the time of colonial expansion into Africa, Asia, the Pacific, and the Americas (International Labour Organization (1953); Wolf, 1982; Wilmer, 1993; Heinz, 1988; Howard, 2003). As Burger (1987) notes, "When the indigenous population did not encounter direct genocide, they faced instead enslavement, forced labor, and menial work" (p. 38). Over the past 500 years, literally millions of indigenous peoples have had to cope with destruction of their life ways and habitats, disease, dispossession, and exploitation (Clay, 1984; Maybury Lewis, 1997, 2002; International Work Group for Indigenous Affairs 1988; Hitchcock, 1999; Hitchcock and Koperski, 2008).

Substantial numbers of indigenous peoples have been the victims of gross violations of human rights. These violations have ranged from extrajudicial executions of individuals and torture to intentional starvation and from large-scale massacres of entire groups to, as previously mentioned, genocide. According to the International Work Group for Indigenous Affairs (1988), a conservative estimate of the annual deaths of indigenous peoples by violent means in the 1980s was around 30,000 (p. 1). Through 2008, indigenous peoples continued to face threats in numerous countries. In the Philippines, for example, at least 26 indigenous rights activists were killed in government crackdowns on members of opposition groups (Stidsen, 2007a, p. 11). There were also killings of indigenous people in numerous other countries, including Bangladesh, Brazil, India, Indonesia, Kenya, and Russia (Stidsen, 2007b).

In many cases worldwide, these deaths are attributable directly to state actions and to the unwillingness of non-indigenous agencies and individuals to assess the impacts of their policies on indigenous societies. A critical problem is that although international human rights standards pertaining to indigenous peoples exist, these standards frequently are ignored at the local, national, and international levels.

Several major factors have been responsible for the threats to the lives and well-being of indigenous peoples in the twentieth and early twenty-first centuries. The first is competition for resources, both on the part of states and transnational corporations (Gedicks, 1993, 2001; Hitchcock, 1994, 1997). The second factor is that a number of indigenous groups have sought self-determination in the face of efforts on the part of governments to assimilate them. The third factor is the opposition on the part of some indigenous groups to the plans and policies of political elites and development agencies. A major concern of indigenous peoples in 2007 was the tendency of governments to criminalize indigenous groups, designating some of them as terrorists. The "war on terrorism" which intensified after the events of September 11, 2001, has seen indigenous and minority groups around the world exposed to greater risk and increased human rights violations (Minority Rights Group, 2007; Stidsen, 2007b).

Genocides of indigenous peoples occur, as Kuper (1985) notes "in the process of struggles by ethnic or racial or religious groups for power or secession, greater autonomy, or more equality" (p. 155). Many indigenous groups have suffered from the depredations of governments, private companies, and individuals bent on taking their land and resources—forcibly or through quasilegal means such as treaties and agreements

(DeLoria, 1969, 1985; Burger, 1987, 1990; Durning, 1992, pp. 21–23; Amnesty International, 1992a, pp. 34–41; Hitchcock, 1994; Bodley, 1999; Wishart, 2001).

Indigenous populations frequently have been denied the right to practice their own religions and customs and/or to speak their own languages by nation-states, a process described as "cultural genocide" or "ethnocide" (Kuper, 1981, pp. 31, 41; Burger, 1987, p. 31; Heinz, 1988, p. 75; Chalk and Jonassohn, 1990, pp. 9, 23). For purposes of this chapter, ethnocide will be distinguished from genocide as it refers to the destruction of cultures rather than people per se. Ethnocide ultimately may have a significant impact on the well-being of indigenous societies since it sometimes results in people becoming so dispirited as to lack the desire to survive.

This chapter, then, centers on issues relating to the physical and cultural genocide of various indigenous peoples. We deal first with the question of the characteristics of indigenous peoples. Next, we focus on the issue of the definition of genocide as it relates to indigenous populations, and we examine the various indigenous peoples as victim groups. We follow with a discussion of the contexts in which genocides of indigenous groups occur, and we conclude with some recommendations for ways to protect indigenous peoples from the horrors of genocide.

Who Are Indigenous Peoples?

No single agreed-upon definition of the term "indigenous peoples" exists. According to the Independent Commission on International Humanitarian Issues (1987), four elements are included in the definition: (1) pre-existence, (2) non-dominance, (3) cultural difference, and (4) self-identification as indigenous (p. 6). The term "indigenous peoples" is usually used in reference to those individuals and groups who are descendants of the original populations residing in a country. In the majority of cases they are ethnic minorities. In some cases, the term "indigenous" applies to non-European groups residing in regions that were colonized by Europeans. The term "indigenous peoples" is also used to apply to local populations who lived in a place before a state system incorporated them (Perry, 1996, p. 8).

There are different approaches among analysts to the issue of terminology regarding indigenous peoples. The International Labour Organization (1953) uses the phrase "tribal and indigenous peoples" (pp. 3–5), while the World Bank and the United Nations prefer "indigenous peoples" (Martinez Cobo, 1987; World Bank, 2005a). As the World Bank's (2005a) Operational Directive 4–10 on Indigenous Peoples notes, no single definition is appropriate to cover the diversity present in these populations (p. 1).

Indigenous peoples generally possess ethnic, economic, religious, or linguistic characteristics that are different from the dominant groups in the societies where they exist. In many cases, they tend to have a strong sense of cultural identity and social solidarity, which many group members attempt to maintain (Niezen, 2003). Most indigenous peoples prefer to reserve for themselves the right to determine who are and are not members of their groups (Ewen, 1994; Anaya, 1996; Perry, 1996).

Nearly forty percent of the world's countries (72 of 191) contain peoples defined as indigenous. Estimates of the numbers of indigenous peoples vary widely, but generally range between 350,000,000 and 700,000,000 (Soefestad, 1995; Maybury-Lewis 1997; Stidsen, 2007a, p. 10). Together, indigenous peoples comprise about 6–10 percent of the world's total population, depending on the way figures are calculated (Hitchcock and Koperski, 2008). Table 1 contains an estimate of the numbers of indigenous peoples around the world. Some of these groups live on borders and as such are essentially transboundary in nature, which is seen as a threat by some states concerned with border security. The approximately 100,000 San, for example, are found in six countries of southern Africa (Angola, Botswana, Namibia, South Africa, Zambia, and Zimbabwe) (Suzman, 1991), while the 60,000–100,000 Saami are found in Norway, Sweden, Finland, and Russia (Lehtola, 2004). Indigenous peoples usually are minorities, but in some states they make up the majority of the population, as is the case in Papua New Guinea (87 percent), Bolivia (77 percent), and Guatemala (55 percent). Indigenous peoples represent some 10 percent of Latin America's population and are the largest disadvantaged group on the continent.

TABLE 13.1 Estimated Numbers of the World's Indigenous Peoples with Examples of Some Indigenous Groups and Their Population Sizes

Region	Number of Groups	Overall Population
North America (2 Countries)	250	328,667,927
Indians (Canada) (613 bands)		1,000,000
Indians (United States) (515 Tribes)		2,851,000
Inuit (Canada)		47,000
Central America (8 Countries)	370	147,338,108
Kuna		58,000
Miskito (Nicaragua)		170,000
Zapotec (Mexico)		545,000
South America (14 Countries)	561	371,274,004
Ache (Paraguay)		1,800
Arhuaco (Colombia)		9,000
Mapuche (Argentina, Chile)		1,710,000

Quechua (Bolivia, Ecuador, Peru)		8,889,298
Shipibo (Peru)		25,000
Yanomamo (Brazil, Venezuela)		24,700
Yora (Peru)		850
Russia	105	143,420,309
Khanty (3 Tribes)		21,500
Saami		1,775
Tribes of Siberia (30 Tribes)		199,900
Udege		1,920
Eastern Asia (7 Countries)	82	1,538,099,417
Ainu (Japan)		25,000
Bouyei (China)		3,157,700
Thao (Taiwan)		400
Melanesia (5 Countries)	1,000	7,398,902
Papuans (312 Tribes)		2,209,000
South-East Asia (10 countries)	1,400	571,337,070
Dayak (Borneo, Indonesia)		3,000,000
Orang Asli (Malaysia)		133,000
Hill Tribes (Thailand)		923,257
Penan (Malaysia)		12,000
South-Central Asia (14 Countries)	820	1,594,572,436
Adivasis (India)		89,500,000
Chakma (Bangladesh)		260,000
Australia and New Zealand	210	4,127,726
Aboriginals (Australia)		517,000
Maori (New Zealand)		310,000
Africa (54 Countries)	2.000	887,223,445
Batwa (Pygmies) (8 Countries)		400,000
Bushmen (San) (6 Countries)		107,100
Hadza (Tanzania)		1,350
Maasai (Kenya, Tanzania)		1,359,000
Tuareg (6 Countries)		3,500,000
Grand Total	6,798	6.5 billion people
Indigenous peoples		650,000,000,000

Note: This table contains estimates of the numbers of ethnolinguistic groups, as presented in *Ethnologue* (www.Ethnologue.com). Estimates of population sizes of indigenous peoples are notoriously difficult to obtains, data presented here are approximate. The information is drawn from a variety of sources, including national censuses, statistical surveys, research reports, and from such organizations as the United Nations Statistical Division, United Nations Unrepresented Nations and Peoples Organization, the World Factbook 2005, www.geohive.com, International Mission Board, www.PeoplesGroups.org, Survival International (www.survival-international.org), the International Work Group for Indigenous Affairs (www.iwgia.org), Cultural Survival (www.cs.org), Amnesty International (www.amnesty.org), Human Rights Watch (www.hrw.org), Antislavery International (www.antislavery.org), the International Labour Organization (www.ilo.org), Minority Rights Group International (www.minorityrights.org) and the World Bank (www.worldbank.org). Note that this table does not include some countries in Asia and the Pacific such as East Timor, which became an independent country on August 31, 2007. The total number of countries is 191.

Particular problems arise in defining people as indigenous in Africa and Asia. In many parts of Africa it is difficult to establish antecedence since a variety of populations have moved in and out of local areas over time. Most African countries are multiethnic entities that contain a sizable number of different societies. Nigeria, for example, has at least 500 ethnic groups within its borders (Gordon, 2003). However, African governments are reluctant to disclose what percentage of their population is indigenous, taking the position, as Botswana has, that all the people in the country (with the exception of Europeans and Asians) are indigenous (see the Botswana government website, www.gov.bw). Individual Africans, on the other hand, frequently identify themselves as members of specific tribal or ethnic groups, which they tend to see as indigenous.

Even if some people claim to be indigenous, the countries where they live may not recognize them as aboriginal. The government of India, for example, maintains on the one hand that no indigenous groups exist within the country, but, on the other hand, the Indian government designates tens of millions of its citizens as "tribals" (Adivasis, "Scheduled Tribes") (Bhengra, Bijoy, and Luthui, 1998).

African and Asian countries tend to take one of two different positions on the issue of indigenous populations: (1) they claim that there are no indigenous peoples whatsoever within their boundaries, or (2) they state that all groups in the country are indigenous (Martinez Cobo, 1987, p. 5; Sanders, 1989, pp. 417–418). Some countries, such as Botswana, prefer not to differentiate specific groups as targets of assistance, in part because they do not wish to be seen as practicing a kind of apartheid or separation on the basis of ethnic identification, as was seen in neighboring South Africa until 1994 (Saugestad, 2001; Hitchcock, 2002). On the other hand, there are states that do not want to admit to having indigenous peoples, in part, because they do not want to have to respond to queries or submit to investigations by the United Nations, the International Labour Organization, and other agencies on behalf of indigenous peoples. Some of them, such as Kenya, Tanzania, and the United States also do not want to meet new demands of indigenous populations for compensation for losses of land or natural resources.

Indigenous peoples are united in their desire to maintain their identities and to seek better standards of living and fair treatment. In some cases, these desires have led to efforts on their part to resist the attempts of states or other groups to change them. Some ethnic groups have been successful in their attempts to seek self-determination and sovereignty, as seen, for example, in the case of the people of East Timor, which became the world's newest nation on August 31, 2007.

While there is tremendous diversity among the world's indigenous peoples, they tend to have a number of socioeconomic features in common. Many indigenous peoples have strong ties to the land and its resources. Their economies are sometimes subsistence oriented, producing goods for domestic use, although many of them do engage in market activities and raise cash through sales of goods and services. Some indigenous peoples derive a fairly significant portion of their diet and material requirements from hunting and gathering. Others are pastoralists (herders) who graze their domestic animals in savannas, deserts, temperate zones, and mountain environments. The vast majority of indigenous peoples are farmers who not only raise crops but also engage in various off-farm activities and rural and urban wage sector employment. Although many of these groups occupy remote areas, they are not isolated.

Some analysts suggest that contemporary indigenous groups are among the world's most disadvantaged populations (Heinz, 1988; Maybury-Lewis, 1997, 2002; Bodley, 1999). A large percentage of the world's indigenous people live below the poverty line. In Namibia, for example, 60 percent of the San were below the poverty datum line (Suzman, 2001, p. 8) while 95 percent of the Batek of Malaysia have incomes below $200 per year (Kirk Endicott, personal communication, 2007). Infant mortality rates among them tend to be high while health and nutritional standards generally are low. Unemployment rates are high, with some American Indian groups experiencing a 50 to 70 percent unemployment rate.

Many members of indigenous groups do not own land, and most groups have experienced dispossession or reductions in their ancestral territories. Educational and literacy levels generally are low, and languages are disappearing at a rapid rate, in part because of government policies aimed at acculturation and teaching of national languages (Nettle and Romaine, 2000; Skutnabb-Kangas, 2000). At the same time, some indigenous peoples and their supporters such as the Lacandon Maya of Chiapas and Ju/'hoansi San in Namibia have started schools with curricula geared to their specific needs (Hays, 2007; Jill Gnade, personal communication).

Racism is a fact of life for indigenous peoples throughout the world. They are usually at the bottom of the socioeconomic scale of the countries where they live, and they are marginalized politically and legally. Indigenous groups have had difficulty getting redress for crimes committed against them, and they have often been treated negatively by courts when they have been charged with illegal activities. Often, the sentences they receive are more severe than those meted out to non-indigenous individuals (Amnesty International, 1992b). Members of indigenous communities tend to be overrepresented in the prisons of states such as Australia, Canada, and Botswana. Sometimes charges against indigenous groups are trumped up in order to remove them from lands that others covet, as was the case with the Triqui Indians in Mexico in 1984–1985 and with the Penan in Malaysia in 1988–1989 (see www.survival.org). Many indigenous leaders argue that they have had to pay a terrible price for their interaction with non-indigenous societies.

Genocides among Indigenous Peoples

Many researchers, human rights workers, and journalists deem the ways in which indigenous peoples have been dealt with in the twentieth century to be genocide (Lewis, 1969, 1974, 1976; Munzel, 1973, 1974, 1985; Arens, 1976, 1978; Clay, 1984; Barta, 1987; Legters, 1988; Tatz, 1991, 2003; Hitchcock, 1999; Jaimes, 1992; Totten, Parsons, and Hitchcock, 2002; Barkan, 2003; Daes, 2005; Rensink, 2006). It is clear from a critical review of the literature on indigenous peoples that most writers use a fairly broad definition of the concept of genocide. While some researchers see genocide as a set of acts committed with the intent to destroy groups in whole or in part, as defined by the United Nations Convention on the Prevention and Punishment of the Crime of Genocide, others extend the concept to include such actions as intentional prevention of ethnic groups from practicing their traditional customs; forced resettlement; denial of access to food relief, health assistance, and development funds; and destruction of the habitats utilized by indigenous populations.

Sometimes victim groups label actions against them as genocidal in order to seek public recognition of the problems they are facing or to bring about greater condemnation of the actions of perpetrators. Defining genocide too narrowly, on the other hand, could have the effect of allowing authorities to overlook actions that are destructive and which eventually could result in the extinction of indigenous populations. As Totten, Parsons, and Hitchcock (2002) point out, if we are to develop sound conventions and warning systems to prevent genocide from occurring, then we need to have a comprehensive understanding of what does and does not constitute genocide (pp. 76–78).

Genocide, in the eyes of a number of social scientists, is the deliberate and systematic destruction of a racial, political, social, religious, or cultural group by the state (Chalk and Jonassohn, 1990; Horowitz, 2002; Gellately and Kiernan, 2003). One problem with this approach, however, is that it may not cover those acts that are committed by settlers and miners in the Amazon, or private companies involved in the implementation of development projects. Clearly, in order to cover the diversity existing in cases of annihilation of indigenous peoples, it is necessary to use a definition that incorporates the full array of target groups and perpetrators and which specifies intent.

Fein (1990) defines genocide as "sustained purposeful action by a perpetrator to physically destroy a collectivity social reproduction of group members, sustained regardless of the surrender or lack of threat offered by the victim" (p. 24). This definition is useful in that it excludes single massacres and is aimed at physically destroying group members selected on the basis of their being part of a collectivity.

It is important to note that genocide is by no means a simple or unified phenomenon. Genocide represents systematic efforts to destroy collectivities, many of which are minorities. Cases of physical genocide include those in which the killing of members of a collectivity threatens the survival of the group as a whole. In practice, however, genocidal acts usually do not result in total annihilation of the population. Groups that have been subjected to genocidal treatment often end up being victimized in other ways as well; they are sometimes raped, enslaved, deprived of their property, and forcibly removed to new places. Some groups have died out as a result of indirect impacts of genocide, including starvation and disease.

Chalk and Jonassohn (1990) use the term "genocidal massacre" in reference to those cases in which a combination of genocide and ethnocide was employed (p. 26). In these instances, "There is no intent to kill the entire victim group, but its disappearance is intended" (p. 26). The distinction between physical and cultural genocide is by no means clear-cut. According to Chalk and Jonassohn (1990) assimilation policies on the part of the United States, combined with differential legal treatment of Indians, had major impacts on the well being of Native Americans (pp. 195–203). In the Americas, Australia, South Africa, and other settler societies, most indigenous peoples suffered and died from disease, starvation, and related physical and cultural stresses (Wolf, 1982; Barta, 1987; Bodley, 1999, pp. 38–41, 78–93; Tatz, 1991, 2003; Brantlinger, 2003; Daes, 2005).

While the U.S. government generally did not openly espouse extermination policies, it did engage throughout its history in cultural modification programs that led to the destruction of Indian societies. It is not surprising, therefore, that American Indian writers tend to describe American government policy as genocidal in intent (see, for example, DeLoria, 1969, 1985). Most non-Native Americans would reject the suggestion that they are part of a genocidal society (for a discussion of this concept, see Barta, 1987, pp. 237–240). The fact is, though, that while the U.S. government employed ethnocide as its major indigenous peoples' policy, it was always ready to resort to genocide if it was deemed desirable (DeLoria, 1969, 1985; Legters, 1988; Chalk and Jonassohn, 1990, p. 203; Jaimes, 1992). Examples of genocidal actions against Native American populations include the massacre of Cheyenne and Arapaho at Sand Creek in eastern Colorado in November, 1864 (Hoig, 1961; Carroll, 1973; Rensink, 2006), the killings of over 200 Minnecojou and Hunkpapa Sioux at Wounded Knee in December, 1890 and the systematic extra-judicial killings of dozens of Oglala Lakota in and around the Pine Ridge Reservation in South Dakota in the 1970s (Weyler, 1982; Matthiessen, 1983; Crow Dog and Erdoes, 1990, pp. 115–116).

Forced relocation, education of Native American children in Euro-American concepts rather than Native American ones, destruction of the subsistence economies of indigenous groups, and imposition of new forms of sociopolitical organization all were implemented by American governmental agencies (Thornton, 1987). It was not until 1924 that Native Americans even received U.S. citizenship rights, and it was another decade before the government lifted its ban on Native Americans' practice of traditional religious activities (Amnesty International, 1992a, p. 7). Native Americans in the U.S. today are still seeking religious freedoms, which have been compromised by a series of court decisions.

Cultural genocide takes place under conditions of state imposition of educational programs, modernization efforts, and nation building. Throughout the world, indigenous peoples have been coerced or cajoled into giving up their cultural traditions. Sometimes this is done in the name of "national reconciliation" after decolonization. States as diverse as Turkey, Somalia, and Russia have required their citizens to learn national languages. Even countries with positive human rights records, such as Botswana, have implemented national educational systems that fail to instruct indigenous students in their own customs and languages (Biesele and Hitchcock, 2000).

Ethnocide also occurs in situations where non-native religious organizations promote their views and seek actively to discourage the practice of indigenous traditions (Palmer, 1992). It is important to note, however, that although ethnocidal policies are practiced widely, they have not led invariably to cultural disintegration. A cultural resurgence or a kind of ethnogenesis process is occurring among sizable numbers of indigenous peoples in many parts of the world (Burger, 1990; Durning, 1992, pp. 37–46; Bodley, 1999, pp. 145–169; Reed, 2003; Jackson and Warren, 2005; Stidsen, 2007b).

Genocides of indigenous peoples in the twentieth century have occurred in a number of different contexts, ranging from those where there is competition over resources and land to multiethnic settings with socioeconomic stratification and cleavages among the various groups. In the past, a significant proportion of the genocides of indigenous peoples occurred during the course of colonial expansion, a process seen in the twentieth century primarily in the movements of settlers, companies, and government agencies into frontier zones. The expansion of miners and settlers into the interior of Brazil, for example, led to the destruction of a number of groups, some of whom were killed by Indian agents of the government's Indian protection agency (Davis, 1977; Price, 1989). An invasion of Yanomami land by miners, with the apparent complicity of the government and the army, resulted in killings and environmental devastation (American Anthropological Association, 1991; Albert, 1992, 1994; Chagnon 1993a–c; Sponsel, 1994, 1997). Indian agents, settlers, and miners have also been responsible for both purposeful and accidental introduction of diseases, which had a terrible impact on tribal populations.

"Indigenous peoples are killed simply for who they are," according to Maya human rights activist and anthropologist Victor Montejo (n.d., p. 2). Indigenous peoples increasingly are protesting the human rights abuses they suffer at the hands of governments, development agencies, and multinational corporations. They note that they face many forms of persecution. Organized political killings and "disappearances" of indigenous leaders and members of opposition groups are common in countries such as Guatemala and Peru (Menchu, 1984; Carmarck, 1988; Manz, 1988; Warren, 1998; Stoll, 1999; Sanford, 2003; Jackson and Warren, 2005). In South and Southeast Asia, the Amazon Basin, the Middle East, Africa, and the Pacific, entire communities of indigenous peoples have been massacred (Anti-Slavery Society, 1984; Burger, 1987; Gurr and Scaritt, 1989; Tatz, 1991; Maybury-Lewis, 1997; Daes, 2005; Stidsen, 2007b; Hitchcock and Koperski, 2008; Survival International, www.survival-international.org).

In Brazil, more than eighty Indian tribes that came in contact with the national society were destroyed between 1900 and 1957, and as a result the indigenous population dropped from approximately a million to less than 200,000 (Davis, 1977, p. 5).

As far back as 1984, Clay noted that "There probably have been more genocides, ethnocides, and extinctions of tribal and ethnic groups in this century than any in history" (p. 1). From the standpoint of indigenous peoples' survival, the twentieth century was brutal.

Indigenous peoples have been the victims of genocidal and ethnocidal acts in part because of the ways in which they have been perceived by dominant societies. In many cases, members of indigenous communities have been described as "primitives," "subhuman," "savages," "vermin," or "nuisances." In fact, they have been subjected to these and other negative stereotypes for generations. The images of indigenous peoples have reinforced the tendencies on the part of governments to establish destructive and oppressive racial policies. Efforts on the part of states to vilify indigenous groups are frequently preconditions for genocidal action. This is especially true in those situations where nation-states are concerned about the possibility of indigenous groups supporting opposition movements, as was the case, for example, in Guatemala (Menchu, 1983; Montejo, 1987; Carmarck, 1988; Manz, 1988; Stoll, 1999; Wilkinson, 2002; Sanford, 2003).

It is extremely difficult to obtain reliable information on genocidal actions and/or outright genocides of indigenous peoples. There are several reasons for this. First, most contemporary indigenous groups that are victimized tend to be located in remote places or in conflict zones where it is difficult to gain access. Second, most governments and agencies that come in contact with indigenous groups tend to downplay or deny the severity of their treatment of those peoples. Third, some of the indigenous groups that have been the victims of genocidal acts have members who do not read or write; consequently, written records of what happened to them are rare. Fourth, while members of indigenous groups speak their own languages, they do not necessarily speak national languages that people doing interviews tend to speak; the result is that translation becomes something of a problem. Not surprisingly, there are relatively few first-person accounts of genocide of various indigenous peoples (Totten, 1991, pp. 311–319).

In the twentieth century, indigenous groups disappeared at an unprecedented rate (Clay, 1984, p. 1; Durning, 1992, p. 9). This loss of cultural diversity was a product of both physical and cultural extinction. Table 2 contains a summary of twentieth-century and early twenty first century cases of physical genocide of various indigenous peoples.

The reports from which the data are drawn include the *Urgent Action Bulletins* (UAB) of the indigenous peoples' advocacy organization Survival International, reports by other non-government organizations, published sources, and personal communications. It is evident from the data presented here that a variety of indigenous peoples in a number of different countries were the victims of genocidal actions. Indigenous hunter-gatherers, who Kuper (1981) saw as victimized groups that are perpetually at risk, have been particularly hard hit (p. 158). The treatment of foraging societies is extremely difficult to monitor, in part because they tend to be mobile and in a number of cases avoid contact with outsiders (Totten, Parsons, and Hitchcock, 2002; Castillo, 2004). Because of the tendency of hunter-gatherers to have fewer links with the larger society and their small numbers, the plight of these groups often

TABLE 13.2 Twentieth and Twenty First-Century Cases of Genocide of Indigenous Peoples

Group Name	Country	Date(s)
Africa		
Barabaig	Tanzania	1990–92
Bubi	Equatorial Guinea	1969–79
Dinka, Nuer	Sudan	1983–2002
Efe Pygmies	Congo (DRC)	1994-present
Fur, Zagawa, Masalit	Sudan	2003-present
Herero	Namibia	1904–07
Isaak	Somalia	1988–89
Karimojong	Uganda	1979–86
Mbuti Pygmies	Congo (DRC)	1994-present
Nuba	Sudan	1991–2002
San	Angola	1975–2002
San	Namibia	1912–1915
Tuareg	Mali, Niger	1988–95
Twa	Rwanda	1994
Tyua San	Zimbabwe	1982–83
Asia		
Agta	Philippines	1988
Amungme	West Papua	1997
Armenians	Turkey	1915–18
Atta	Philippines	1987
Auyu	West Papua	1989
Cham	Kampuchea	1975–79
Dani	New Guinea	1988
Higaonan	Philippines	1988
H'mong	Laos	1979–86
Jawara	India (Andamans)	1987–2001
Jumma	Bangladesh	1977–1997
Karen	Myanmar (Burma)	1988-present
Kurds	Iraq	1987–2003
Marsh Arabs	Iraq	1991
Nasioi	Bougainville	1990–91
Penan	Malaysia	1986–89
Timorese	East Timor	1975–2002
Central America		
Indians	El Salvador	1980–92
Maya Indians	Guatemala	1964–96
Maya Indians	Mexico	1994–1999
Miskito	Nicaragua	1981–86
Latin America		
Ache	Paraguay	1952–76
Ashaninka	Peru	1986

(*continued*)

TABLE 13.2—*continued*

Group Name	Country	Date(s)
Aya Ache	Guatemala	1982–85
Arara	Brazil	1992
Cuiva	Colombia	1967–71
Mapuche	Chile	1986
Nambiquara	Brazil	1986–87
Nunak	Colombia	1991
Paez	Colombia	1991
Pai Tavytere	Paraguay	1990–91
Ticuna	Brazil	1988
Waorani	Ecuador	1986–92
Yanomami	Brazil	1988–89, 1993
North America		
Indians	Canada	16th–19th centuries
Indians	United States	15th–19th centuries

Note: Data obtained from Survival International (www.survival-international.org), the International Work Group for Indigenous Affairs (www.iwgia.org), Cultural Survival (www.cs.org), Amnesty International (www.amnesty.org), Human Rights Watch (www.hrw.org), Minority Rights Group International (www.minorityrights.org), Antislavery International (www.antislavery.org), the United Nations (www.un.org), the United Nations Childrens Fund (www.unicef.org), the Permanent Forum on Indigenous Issues of the United Nations (www.unfpii.org), the World Bank (www.worldbank.org) and the annual United States Country Reports on Human Rights. See also Gedicks (1993, 2001); Bodley (1999); Hitchcock (1999), Totten, Parsons, and Hitchcock (2002:67, Table 3.1), and Hitchcock and Koperski (2008).

goes unnoticed (Kuper, 1981, p. 158; Kuper, 1985, pp. 201–202; Hitchcock, 1985, pp. 457–459).

Some indigenous groups have been deemed, by the governments of the states in which they live, as terrorists or as being involved in liberation movements, an argument that is sometimes used by nation-states to justify genocidal actions. In the Philippines, for example, members of indigenous groups on Mindanao and Luzon have been attacked because of alleged support for liberation groups, and Adivasis have been discriminated against, attacked and killed in India due to their being considered primitives, uncivilized, and subhuman (Stidsen, 2007b, pp. 314–320, 398–406).

It is important to note that warfare undertaken to exterminate an enemy can be (and has been) carried out by indigenous groups, although it is much less common among indigenous and tribal peoples (Krech,

1994, p. 14; Douglas Bamforth and Raymond Hames, personal communications). Examples in the twentieth century include the Bay region of Somalia in the early 1990s and the Democratic Republic of Congo in the latter part of the 1990s. There is also archaeological evidence that indicates the destruction of entire groups of indigenous peoples by other indigenous groups (Willey, 1990; Krech, 2002, pp. 14–15).

Typologies of Genocide Relating to Indigenous Peoples

Researchers have developed numerous typologies of genocide that include categories relevant to indigenous peoples as victim groups (Dadrian, 1975; Kuper, 1981, pp. 46–54, 88, 158; Kuper, 1984, pp. 32–33; Kuper, 1985, pp. 151, 200–202, 211–212; Smith, 1987, pp. 23–25, 30–32; Chalk and Jonassohn, 1990, pp. 22–29, 195–222, 412–414; Fein, 1990, pp. 28–30, 79–91). Of the five categories of genocide identified by Dadrian (1975), one of them, which he calls *utilitarian genocide,* aims at obtaining control of economic resources. Examples of this kind of genocide against indigenous groups include the Ache of Paraguay and the Indians of Brazil.

Smith (1987) sees genocide as an aspect of (1) war, and (2) development, and he notes that in the past genocide appeared in a variety of contexts, including conquest, religious persecution, and colonial domination. He distinguishes five different types of genocide, one of which, like Dadrian (1975), he calls *utilitarian genocide* (Smith, 1987, pp. 23–25). This kind of genocide, according to Smith, occurred especially in the sixteenth- to nineteenth-century period when colonial societies came in contact with indigenous peoples in the Americas, Australia, Tasmania, and Africa (1987, p. 23). It has continued in the twentieth century as the Indians of Paraguay, Brazil, and Peru have been destroyed, as Smith puts it, "out of cold calculation of gain, and, in some cases, as sadistic pleasure" (1987, p. 23). The basic objectives of twentieth century genocides of indigenous peoples have been, according to Smith, Indian land, resources and labor (1987, p. 25).

Like some other analysts of genocide, Smith rejects the hypotheses of population surplus and political crisis as being primary causes of the destruction of indigenous peoples, arguing instead that "They are being killed because of a combination of ethnocentrism and simple greed" (1987, p. 25). He goes on to suggest that the basic motivation behind utilitarian genocide is that some people, according to the perpetrators' world view, must die "so that others might live well" (1987, p. 25). Smith adds that one of the reasons that this kind of genocide claims fewer lives today than in the past is because earlier genocides were so effective and contemporary indigenous populations are so small (1987, p. 25). In his view, genocidal actions against indigenous peoples are not simply accidental or unpremeditated events but are acts perpetrated purposely to achieve economic objectives.

Chalk and Jonassohn (1990) classify genocides according to the motives behind them (p. 29). They distinguish four types of genocide that set out to accomplish various goals: (1) to eliminate a real or potential threat, (2) to spread terror among real or potential enemies, (3) to acquire economic wealth, and (4) to implement a belief, theory, or ideology. The genocide most relevant to indigenous peoples is that aimed at acquiring economic wealth. That said, genocides also occur in order to terrorize indigenous peoples into subservience (Chalk and Jonassohn, 1990, pp. 29, 36–37). Substantial numbers of killings and deaths of indigenous peoples due to disease and starvation occurred in the context of European expansion into the Americas, Africa, Asia, and the Pacific and were a result of campaigns by frontier settlers (Thornton, 1987). Sometimes these actions were opposed by governments, but, as Chalk and Jonassohn (1990) note, efforts to protect indigenous peoples were feeble at best (pp. 36–37).

An equivalent category to the utilitarian genocide suggested by Dadrian (1975) and Smith (1987) and that of genocide aimed at acquiring economic wealth suggested by Chalk and Jonassohn (1990) is what Fein (1984, pp. 8–9) refers to as developmental genocide. This type of genocide generally is preceded by the movement of development agencies, governmental organizations, or individuals into frontier zones where indigenous groups reside and make their living. There is, of course, significant variation in the ways in which encroaching individuals and agencies have dealt with local peoples. In some cases the outsiders have attempted to negotiate with local people; in other cases, they have taken their land and resources away from them without their permission; and in still other cases they have tried to annihilate them (Fein, 1984, p. 8; Bodley, 1999, pp. 12–92).

Harff (1984) and Gurr and Harff (1992), on the other hand, differentiate between genocides and politicides, the former referring to extreme repression aimed at destroying groups defined on the basis of their membership in particular ethnic, religious, national, or racial groups, and the latter referring to victims defined in terms of their political position (e.g., classes or political organizations opposed to the state or dominant group). Politicides, they contend, are more numerous and just as deadly as genocides (Gurr and Harff, 1992, p. 169).

Worldwide, a number of indigenous peoples are caught up in conflicts between governments and local insurgent organizations. In South America, Asia, the Pacific, and Africa, many of the instances of genocide of indigenous peoples have occurred in the context of armed conflicts in which either the government forces or the opposition groups or both have targeted local people for their support of one side or the other or solely for being in the region where military actions occur. In some cases, as in the Ituri Forest region of the Democratic Republic of Congo, indigenous peoples, in this case the Mbuti Pygmies, were targeted by groups involved in fighting in the region (Bergner, 2003; Human Rights Watch, 2003a).

It is possible to distinguish specific types of genocide involving indigenous populations. The first type, which can be termed *socio-economic genocide,* comes about in the context of colonization or exploitation of resources in areas occupied by indigenous groups (this can also be described as *developmental genocide*). The perpetrators of socioeconomic genocides range from government organizations established ostensibly to assist indigenous peoples to settlers who receive subsidies from the state and from large landowners to peasant farmers. Multilateral development banks such as the World Bank and the Inter-American Development Bank have been responsible for the destruction of indigenous populations through funding projects in the Chittagong Hills of Bangladesh (Anti-Slavery Society, 1984; Mey, 1984; Chittagong Hill Tracts Commission, 1991), the Chixoy Dam area of Guatemala (Johnston, 2005, 2006), and the islands of Sumatra, East Timor, Sulawesi, and Kalimantan of Indonesia where the Transmigration Program, a large-scale resettlement effort, was implemented (Burger, 1987, pp. 142–147; Bodley, 1999, p. 91; Gedicks, 2001). Survival International, Environmental Defense, the Sierra Club, the Natural Resources Defense Council, and other non-government organizations have attacked the World Bank for what they perceived as the Bank's failure to undertake comprehensive social and environmental impact assessments and to implement adequate compensation and resettlement programs (see, for example, Survival International, 2000). It should be noted, however, that the World Bank has made efforts to improve its policies regarding indigenous peoples. Between 1992 and 2005 the World Bank financed 449 projects involving indigenous peoples, and it had put in place a set of standards and regulations regarding the treatment and participation of indigenous peoples in project activities (World Bank, 2005a, b; Dan Aronson, personal communication, 2007).

A second type of genocide where indigenous peoples are victims is *retributive genocide,* in which actions are taken against collectivities that are perceived as threats or as representing opposition to state ideology and interests. This kind of genocide occurs in contexts in which (1) there is civil conflict, or (2) there are challenges to the legitimacy and authority of a dominant class or group. Indigenous peoples in a number of countries have been the victims of retributive genocide in the twentieth century, including the Hereros and San of Namibia, the Maya of Guatemala and Mexico, the Nuba of Sudan, the Kurds of Iraq, the Nagas of India, and various groups in Malaysia, Indonesia, and the Philippines (Gurr, 2000; Minority Rights Group International, 2007; Stidsen, 2007b; Gordon, n.d.). Data on these and other cases have been provided by governments and non-government organizations, opposition groups, anthropologists, and indigenous people themselves. This information has sometimes resulted in further investigations into the treatment of indigenous groups (see, for example, American Anthropological Association, 1991; Chittagong Hill Tracts Commission, 1991). The problem, however, is that the findings of these investigations have not always led to improvements in the situations facing indigenous populations.

It is useful, as Kuper (1984) points out, to draw a distinction between "domestic" genocides, those arising from international divisions within a society, and genocides resulting from international warfare (p. 32). The majority of the genocides perpetrated against indigenous peoples fall into the category of domestic genocides. Chalk and Jonassohn (1990, p. 18) suggest that it is often new states or regimes that try to impose ideological conformity that are especially likely to commit genocide. Fein (1984) points out that the structural relationships most conducive to genocide are ones based in ethnic stratification in which state power is not constrained effectively by internal or external checks (p. 6). The victims of genocide are often those who are not fully incorporated into the state system, middleman minorities, or opposition groups, as shown, for example, in the results of the work in the Minorities at Risk Study of the Center for International Development and Conflict Management at the University of Maryland (Gurr, 2000). In Africa, indigenous peoples have been subjected to genocidal and ethnocidal treatment in a number of states in the late twentieth and early twenty first centuries (see Table 3).

A recent case of genocide in Africa is the on-going conflict in the Darfur region of western Sudan, where Fur, Zaghawa, Masalit, and other African groups have been subjected to mass murder, rape, aerial and ground attacks, destruction of villages, crops, and livestock, ethnic cleansing, and efforts to prevent the distribution of food, medicines, and other relief supplies. (See Samuel Totten, "The Darfur Genocide," this volume Chapter 17, for a detailed discussion of that particular genocide.)

Secretary of State Colin Powell and the U.S. House of Representatives declared the events in Darfur as constituting genocide in June, 2004. United Nations Security Council Resolution 1593 referred the situation in Darfur to the International Criminal Court (ICC). Currently, there is a UN/African Union Hybrid (AU) peace-keeping force in Sudan, but

TABLE 13.3 Cases of Genocide in Africa Involving Indigenous and Tribal Peoples in Africa

Country	Population (July, 2007 estimate)	Conflict Period(s)	Number(s) of Victims	Population Below the Poverty Line	Indigenous Group(s)
Namibia	2,055,080	1904–1907, 1912–1915, 1965–1990, 1999–2002	65,000 (Herero) 13,000 (San)	34.9%	Herero, San
Rwanda	9,907,509	1963–64, 1994	5,000–14,000 500–800,000	51.7%	Hutu, Tutsis, Twa (Pygmies)
Somalia	9,118,773	1977–78, 1988–91, 1992–93	100,000, 60,000, 500,000	81%*	Isaaq, Hawiye, Eyle (Gabooye)
Sudan	39,379,358	1952–1972 1983–2004 2003-present (Darfur)	100–500,000 30–50,000, 2 million at risk	40%*	Nuer, Dinka, Shilluk, Nuba, Maban
Uganda	30,262,610	1971–79 1979–82, 1997-present	100–500,000 50–200,000 10–20,000	37.5%	Bakonjo, Twa (Pygmies), Acholi
Zimbabwe	12,311,143	1982–83, 2001-present	2,000–20,000, a few hundred	56.1%	Ndebele, Tyua San (Amasili)

Note: The data presented herein were obtained from the World Factbook (2007), United Nations Human Development Report (2006), Uppsala / PRIO Armed Conflict Data Set version 4 – 2006. The population below the Poverty Datum Line is calculated as the percentage of those people living below $1 per person per day.
* Estimate made from previous figures – no current number available.

it is under-funded and under-equipped. A number of international organizations are monitoring the situation in western Sudan, including the International Crisis Group, Human Rights Watch, and Amnesty International. Nevertheless, the killings, ethnic cleansing, rapes, and destruction of communities continue unabated as the government of Sudan continues to maintain that the situation in Darfur is an internal matter.

Ecocide, the purposeful and systematic destruction of ecosystems by states, agencies, or corporations, is a problem that many indigenous peoples in various parts of the world have also faced. For example, the Ogoni and other indigenous and minority groups in the Niger Delta of Nigeria have claimed that the government of Nigeria and transnational corporations including Shell and ExxonMobil have been complicit in allowing oil spills and the dumping and burning of toxic substances (Sachs, 1995, 1996). Similar claims have been made about the actions of the Brazilian and Venezuelan governments and the gold miners (*garimperos*) who use mercury in gold processing in the area occupied by the Yanomamo in northern Brazil and southern Venezuela (Sponsel, 1994). The former government of Iraq under Saddam Hussein had also been accused of ecocidal actions in the destruction of the marshes of southern Iraq and attacks on the Marsh Arabs (Ma'dan) and other groups in the period following the Gulf War of 1991 (Human Rights Watch, 1992; Partow, 2001). The Iraqi's drained the marshes in retaliation for the Marsh Arabs' rebellion against Saddam Hussein during the Gulf War. Turkey and Syria contributed to the draining of the marshlands as well by holding water back from the rivers entering Iraq. As Human Rights Watch (2003b) reported:

> Prior to their destruction, the marshlands (*al-ahwar*) had covered an area of up to 20,000 square kilometers around the confluence of the Tigris and Euphrates rivers in southern Iraq. . . . Together, these wetlands formed a series of interconnected permanent marshes and lakes covering an area of some 8,800 square kilometers, extending to some 20,000 kilometers when large tracts of dry or desert land were seasonally inundated. The marshlands were once home to several hundred thousand inhabitants, the Ma'dan, a people whose unique way of life had been preserved for over 5,000 years (p. 3).

Indigenous groups in southeast Asia have argued that the use by the United States of herbicides (e.g. Agent Orange) in Vietnam in the 1960s and 1970s and chemical weapons in Laos in the 1970s was ecocidal and genocidal in intent (Andrew Gray, personal communication). Efforts to conserve land and species have also led to a growing number of "invisible refugees" around the world, some of whom see themselves as victims of "coercive conservation" (Hitchcock, 1997). It has also been argued that the destruction of bison on the Great Plains in the nineteenth century was aimed specifically at destroying the peoples who were dependent on this species for their survival (Matthiessen, 1991, p. 16).

Protection of Indigenous People and Prosecution of Perpetrators

Human rights organizations have argued that specific cases of genocide should be worked up through the collection of evidence and then prosecuted to the fullest extent of the law. The former can be accomplished in part through the application of archaeological and forensic techniques aimed at determining the causes of death and identities of individuals, as was done, for example, in the case of the Kurds killed during the Anfal Campaign of the Iraqi government and army in 1988 (Middle East Watch and Physicians for Human Rights, 1988; Whitley, 1994; Goldberg, 2002). Subsequently, that evidence, as well as other types, should be presented to international tribunals and courts (e.g. the International Criminal Court) and state-level courts and institutions that can try cases of human rights violations.

Organizations established at the national level to provide assistance to indigenous peoples have been relatively unsuccessful in ensuring the long-term survival of the people they are charged with protecting. Beyond that, some organizations have actually been involved in harming groups of indigenous peoples. The National Foundation for the Indian (FUNAI) in Brazil, for example, has engaged in pacification programs and has facilitated the process whereby Indians have been removed from their lands (Davis, 1977; Bodley, 1999, pp. 68, 84; Albert, 1992; Amnesty International, 1992c; Rabben, 1998, pp. 87–95). In the Philippines, the tribal peoples' agency known as the Presidential Assistant on National Minorities (PANAMIN) was involved from 1968 to 1984 in carrying out resettlement and development programs, some of which had devastating effects on indigenous peoples (Hydman, 1992, pp. 67–68). FUNAI, PANAMIN, and other national indigenous peoples' organizations have sometimes worked closely with international development agencies and multinational corporations in their efforts to establish projects that have had deleterious social and environmental impacts. Some of these projects have been accompanied by the intentional killings of indigenous residents of the areas being developed (Survival International, 1990, 1991, 1992, 1996, 2005; Gedicks, 1993, 2001; Hitchcock 1997, 1999). Responses of indigenous groups to intensified pressure and genocidal actions ranged from peaceful protests and appeals to governments and pleas to human rights agencies for help to the establishment of grass-roots political movements and armed resistance (Burger, 1987; Durning, 1992; Neitschmann, 1994; Maybury-Lewis 1997, 2002; Jackson and Warren, 2005).

Given the prevailing attitudes toward indigenous peoples, it is not surprising that in the vast majority of instances those responsible for killing them were never brought to justice. The phenomenon of impunity, or tacit protection from prosecution, is one of the crucial factors contributing to the continuing pattern of genocidal acts and human rights violations against indigenous peoples (p. 71). After several centuries of genocide, it was only in the latter part of the 1980s that the Brazilian government actually brought federal charges of genocide against individuals. In 1988, five men were accused of intending to "exterminate or eliminate an ethnic group or race" in their murder of a number of Xacriaba Indians (Chalk and Jonassohn, 1990, p. 414). Other countries in Latin America (Colombia, Bolivia) and Southeast Asia (Malaysia) have also considered trying people for these crimes.

Very few cases of human rights violations against indigenous people by agents of governments have resulted in punishment of the offenders. For the most part, agents of governments accused of genocide of indigenous peoples have been quick to deny the charges. For example, when accused of genocidal acts against the Ache Indians of Paraguay, the country's defense Minister argued that, by definition, genocide was not perpetrated. In doing so, he made the assertion that: "Although there are victims and victimizer, there is not the third element necessary to establish the crime of genocide—that is 'intent,' therefore, as there is no 'intent,' one cannot speak of genocide" (quoted in Lewis, 1976, p. 63).

A similar defense was presented by the Permanent Representative of Brazil to the United Nations in 1969, who argued that crimes committed against Brazilian indigenous populations could not be seen as genocide because (1) they never eliminated Indians as an ethnic or cultural group, and (2) the actions were committed for "exclusively, economic reasons" and therefore lacked "the special malice or motivation necessary" to be characterized as genocide (United Nations Human Rights Communication No. 478, September 29, 1969, cited in Kuper, 1984, p. 33). Taken to its logical extreme, this argument would mean that practically none of the actions against indigenous peoples that are obviously genocidal in nature could be described as genocide.

Over the past several decades, efforts have been made by a wide variety of agencies, nongovernmental organizations, and individuals to promote the interests of indigenous peoples and to educate the public about their situations (Sanders, 1989; Swepston, 1989; Burger, 1990; Bodley, 1999, pp. 174–201; Jackson and Warren, 2005). These efforts have included the documentation of human rights abuses, working directly with individuals and groups whose rights have been violated to try to obtain legal redress, bringing pressure to bear on governments and agencies involved in activities deleterious to indigenous peoples, and providing funds and technical assistance to indigenous groups seeking to improve their lives. The work of these organizations has been constrained, however, by lack of funds and political support.

The activities of indigenous peoples' rights organizations have not been without controversy. In the 1970s, for example, the London-based non-government organization Survival International stated that the government of Paraguay had committed genocide against the Ache Indians (Arens, 1976, 1978; Smith and Melia, 1978; Survival International, 1988a, 1993). Some of the documentation of the human rights violations against the Ache was also published by another indigenous support group, the International Work Group for Indigenous Affairs (Munzel 1973, 1974). These allegations of massive human rights violations against the Ache were rejected not only by the governments of Paraguay, the United States, Britain, and West Germany, but also by Cultural Survival, an American indigenous peoples' support organization (Maybury-Lewis and Howe, 1980). The denial of the occurrence of genocide of the Ache was based in part upon a definitional question relating to whether or not there had been a "planned or conscious effort on the part of the government of Paraguay to exterminate, molest, or harm the Ache Indians in any way" (Survival International, 1993, p. 5). Intent, of course, can be inferred from the actions on the ground. As far as could be ascertained, over 100 Ache were killed. Government officials made various comments about the Ache needing to be done way with, and such comments were recorded by researchers.

Clearly, definitional issues are of major importance in the discussions concerning physical and cultural genocide. Equally as clear is the fact that the protection of indigenous groups from genocide would be enhanced if there were greater cooperation and coordination among the various organizations involved with indigenous peoples' welfare.

What the Genocides of Indigenous Peoples Have Taught Us

Many countries have made rhetorical commitments to enforce laws with respect to freedom of association, access to fair and impartial judicial procedures, and elimination of discriminatory minorities. In practice, however, numerous countries have engaged in repressive actions against their citizens. Most states, along with the United Nations, have been reluctant to criticize individual nations for their actions on the pretense that this would constitute a violation of sovereignty. They have also tended to accept government denials of genocides at face value. As a result, genocidal actions continue.

In the twentieth century dozens of indigenous peoples were the victims of physical and cultural genocide. The lack of teeth behind the rhetorical commitment to the protection of indigenous peoples' rights has been, and continues to be, a tremendous problem. If the gross violations of human rights of indigenous peoples are to be stopped, then efforts must be made to enforce existing international human rights law and to impose sanctions on those countries, institutions, agencies, and individuals responsible for genocidal actions. Attempts must also be made to develop genocide early warning systems and to determine the preconditions for genocide (Kuper, 1985, pp. 218–219; Chalk and Jonassohn, 1990, p. 4).

A major lesson learned from the experiences of indigenous peoples harmed by development projects is that detailed social and environmental impact assessments and careful consultations with local people must be carried out prior to the implementation of any projects. It is also evident that development agencies must provide for the legal protection of the lives and assets of people affected by projects. Failure to do so should result in the cutting off of all financial support for those agencies.

The protection of indigenous peoples from genocide at the international level has generally been ineffective. Few cases of genocide against indigenous peoples have been brought before the Commission on Human Rights of the United Nations. Those who have brought complaints to the United Nations have learned that the international agency does not provide redress for alleged human rights violations. In addition, they have discovered that the United Nations does not have the capacity or, according to some, the commitment, to provide direct protection from perpetrators of human rights violations. If this is to be effective, however, substantial efforts will need to be made to gain detailed knowledge of the situation on the ground before such interventions are attempted; and thus, that is a second major lesson learned.

There have been investigations by forensic anthropologists, medical doctors, and lawyers of cases where genocides and massive human rights violations were alleged to have occurred, as seen, for example, in cases ranging from Argentina and Guatemala to Rwanda and Sri Lanka (Koff, 2005). While these investigations have had positive impacts in terms of documenting tragedies and providing information to survivors about what happened to relatives and friends, the evidence obtained has yet to be brought forward in trials of people accused of genocide, war crimes, and massive human rights violations. Thus, the third lessoned learned is that follow-through on cases of genocide is crucial.

There are a number of different ways in which indigenous peoples and organizations working with indigenous groups can address issues of genocide and massive human rights violations. One way is to educate the public about genocide in general and genocides of indigenous peoples specifically. Incorporating information on indigenous peoples' genocides in curricula of schools, colleges, and universities is crucial, as is making such information available on websites and in materials distributed to international agencies, governments, non-government organizations, and the public at large.

It would be very useful if coordination among groups promoting indigenous peoples rights was enhanced. Efforts need to be made to bring together indigenous peoples and indigenous advocacy groups to discuss genocides and human rights with an eye toward coming up with recommendations on genocide prevention, early warning systems, monitoring systems, and ways to deal with genocides and massive human rights violations once they occur.

There are cases where indigenous groups and their supporters have sought legal redress against companies that have pursued policies that have caused destruction of indigenous peoples and their habitats (Gedicks, 2001; Joseph, 2004). Examples of such actions include those of the Waorani of the Oriente region of Ecuador, who sued Texaco (now Chevron Texaco) in federal court in Los Angeles under the Alien Claims Torts Act of 1789. The case was filed in 1993 by an Ecuadorian-born, Massachusetts-based international human rights lawyer named Christobal Bonifaz. It was dismissed in 1996, and again in 2001 on jurisdictional grounds. Mr. Bonifaz then brought the case to Ecuador. In 2006, it was re-filed in San Francisco, California and is still pending (Stephens, 2007, p. A18).

In 2006, local people in Myanmar brought legal action against Unocal, an American oil company, also under the Alien Claims Torts Act (Baue, 2006). It resulted in a settlement in March 2005, and constituted the first case in which a major multinational corporation paid cash to the people who brought the lawsuit. Efforts to change the behavior of UNOCAL were recommended by stockholders, leading to UNOCAL giving up its activities in Burma. Various indigenous peoples have also called for stockholder action against companies involved in corporate and environmental crime.

Not only should legal cases against corporations be pursued, in the opinions of some indigenous peoples, but so should legal redress be sought against individuals such as the chief executive officers (CEOs) of transnational corporations, an example being the CEOs of Union Carbide for the Bhopal, India disaster and of Total, the French oil company, for its involvement in slave labor in Myanmar. It has also been recommended by some indigenous peoples' spokespersons that members of the public should divest themselves of holdings in companies that engage in actions that lead to human rights violations and environmental destruction. In addition, the pursuit of legal cases against corporations has led to greater awareness of social responsibility on the part of transnationals.

There are numerous other ways that indigenous peoples can protect themselves from genocides and human rights violations. One strategy is to develop indicators for indigenous peoples' well-being that indigenous groups and non-government organizations working with them can monitor (see Taylor, 2004). A second strategy is to provide training to indigenous community-based organizations and communities in human rights and conflict resolution. Provision of education and literacy programs will also go a long way towards facilitating indigenous groups' recording of their own histories, obtaining testimonies, and collecting materials that can be disseminated in order to increase awareness of the wide array of human rights issues facing indigenous peoples. Yet another strategy for indigenous organizations and anthropologists is to conduct detailed demographic studies, as was done, for example, by Hill and Hurtado (1995) on the Ache of eastern Paraguay, in order to determine mortality rates and causes of death among indigenous peoples.

Indigenous organizations, local leaders, and advocacy groups all maintain that it is necessary to have security rights—that is, those rights involving protection of the person. Some indigenous groups have sought to protect themselves through capacity-building of local institutions and working out agreements with local police and militaries. Another strategy employed by indigenous peoples has been to gain recognition of indigenous peoples' rights at the international level and through the courts. On September 13, 2006, the United Nations General Assembly passed the Declaration on the Rights of Indigenous Peoples. Only four states voted against the declaration: Australia, New Zealand, Canada, and the United States. The issue now for indigenous peoples and their supporters around the world will be to ensure that the principles enshrined in the Declaration on the Rights of Indigenous Peoples are implemented. Indigenous peoples have had some success in gaining state recognition of land and resource rights in Australia (Young, 1995; Taylor, 2004), Canada (Anaya, 1996, p. 131), New Zealand (Wishart, 2001), and South Africa (Chan, 2004; Chennels and Du Toit, 2004). Obtaining greater civil and political rights, especially the right to participate in decision-making and policy formulation, however, remain a yet-to-be realized goal for most indigenous peoples.

The failure to prevent genocide of indigenous peoples is the result of a combination of factors, including government inaction, bureaucratic inefficiency, and lack of enforcement of international human rights law, racism, and outright greed. Experience has taught us that genocide cannot be prevented unless the perpetrators perceive that the costs of their actions will outweigh the benefits. Without efforts to document cases of genocide and to impose penalties on those governments and agencies responsible, killings and disappearances will be commonplace occurrences not just for indigenous groups but for many of the world's peoples.

EYEWITNESS ACCOUNTS

Physical and Cultural Genocide of Various Indigenous Peoples

It is exceptionally difficult to obtain reliable and detailed information on genocides of indigenous peoples. This is particularly true when it comes to locating first-person accounts of genocides involving such groups. One reason for this situation is that many contemporary indigenous groups who have been subjected to genocidal treatment tend to live in out-of-the-way places which are often inaccessible for environmental or political reasons. Documentation of genocidal events against indigenous communities is also rare since those groups residing in remote locations tend to be illiterate or have limited exposure to educational opportunities. Concomitantly, language proficiency of individuals visiting the indigenous communities is often limited at best.

Gathering data on genocides of indigenous peoples is also difficult because in many cases the gross violations of human rights are ongoing. Individuals are reluctant to talk for fear of reprisals. It is not uncommon for people to express deep concern that those responsible for the genocidal acts would retaliate against them and their families for their having revealed what transpired. They therefore are often unwilling to provide information such as their names, identities of relatives, places of residence, and any other data that could be used to determine who they are.

During the course of interviews of indigenous people who have been the victims of atrocities, we found that individuals often address the topic of violence only indirectly or in careful terms. Some of them emphasize that they find it extremely difficult to put into words all that had happened. They describe their experiences in culturally appropriate ways, which means that one has to be reasonably familiar with the languages and cultures of the societies of which they have been a part in order to get at the full meaning of what they are saying.

One of the difficulties faced by anthropologists and others investigating genocidal acts is that most of the existing accounts are not from indigenous groups but rather come from the government, the military, or other agencies who have come in contact with these groups. The problem with these reports is that they are often not based on first-person testimony, and are not as detailed or accurate as ones collected by independent investigators focusing specifically on genocidal acts. In addition, government and military reports sometimes purposely overlook events. There is also the chance of bias on the part of government authorities and military officials who may wish to downplay the severity of the issues.

Fortunately, indigenous peoples themselves are recording their experiences and telling their stories more often now than was the case in the past. This is sometimes done in autobiographical form, as can be seen in the example of Victor Montejo, a Guatemalan Quiche Maya Indian and anthropologist who described an attack on a village, Tzalala, where he was serving as a teacher in September, 1978 (Montejo, 1987). Guatemala, like some other countries in Central and South America, Africa, Asia, and the Pacific where indigenous people exist, saw oppression, genocidal massacres, and massive human rights violations over a 30 year period in the twentieth century.

One type of oral testimony obtained from indigenous peoples consists of statements made to investigators, some of whom are human rights workers such as those from African Rights, Amnesty International, Human Rights Watch, International Crisis Group, the International Work Group for Indigenous Affairs, Survival International, or Cultural Survival. An advantage of these oral histories is that they sometimes are obtained not long after the genocidal events occurred, thus ensuring that the effects of gradual memory loss are minimized, and in this way reducing the chances that subsequent reports have influences on individual perceptions.

Another type of oral testimony on genocides of indigenous peoples is that obtained during the course of interviews designed to get other kinds of information such as life histories of individuals. In such cases, the genocide is not the subject of the discussion and is only alluded to in passing. Once genocidal actions are mentioned, additional details are sought. The difficulty in these situations is that so little is known of the general context in which the genocide occurred that is not easy to ask appropriate and detailed questions. Under these kinds of conditions, it is hard to assess the validity of the testimony provided.

The oral testimonies presented here have been chosen to illustrate the types of information available on genocides of various indigenous peoples. The accounts are drawn from Bangladesh, Somalia, and Zimbabwe. The first account is taken from the Chittagong Hill Tracts Commission (*"Life Is Not Ours"*: *Land and Human Rights in the Chittagong Hill Tracts, Bangladesh: The Report of the Chittagong Hill Tracts Commission, May 1991*). The second set of first-person accounts is drawn from a report by Africa Watch (*Somalia: A Government at War with Its Own People. Testimonies about the Killings and Conflicts in the North*, Washington, D.C. and New York: Africa Watch, 1990). The third oral testimony is one obtained by Robert Hitchcock from a Tyua San man in Western Zimbabwe in June 1989.

Account 1: The Tribal Peoples of the Chittagong Hill Tracts, Bangladesh

The Chittagong Hill Tracts in southeastern Bangladesh, near the border with India and Myanmar (Burma), contain over a dozen distinct tribal peoples, known in South Asia as Adivasi and to themselves collectively as Jummas. Since the founding of the nation-state of Bangladesh in 1971, the peoples of the Chittagong Hills have had to cope with Bangladesh government efforts to pacify and control the region, which has involved counter-insurgency operations, the resettlement of people to protected villages, engagement in land reform and development efforts, and the encouragement of outsiders (Bengali settlers from the plains of Bangladesh) to establish homes and farms in the hills.

The peoples of the Chittagong Hill Tracts are socially, culturally, and linguistically distinct from the majority Bengali population of Bangladesh. Most of the Chittagong tribal peoples are not Moslems but rather Buddhists, Hindus, Christians, or animists (those practicing indigenous religions) and have been the targets of religious and cultural oppression. Their traditional agricultural practices involving shifting cultivation (also known as *swidden,* or slash and burn, horticulture) have been criticized by the Bangladesh government, which has attempted to transform the land use and tenure system in the Chittagong Hills. The construction of a hydroelectric dam at Kaptai on the Karnafuli River in the Chittagong Hills in the early 1960s saw 100,000 people displaced and over 40 percent of the arable land in the region inundated. The Bangladesh government has encouraged the development of commercial plantations for coffee, cocoa, and spices, mostly owned by outsiders; timber concessions have been granted to companies and individuals; and the rate of deforestation in the Chittagong Hills has expanded considerably (Mey, 1984; Chittagong Hill Tracts Commission, 1991; Roy, 2000).

Today the Chittagong Hills have some 600,000 residents, approximately 1% of the total population of Bangladesh. The various indigenous groups, such as the Chakma (Saksa), Mru, Marma, and Tripura, have their own traditions, social systems, forms of leadership, and belief systems and see themselves as distinct from each other. At the same time, they identify themselves as indigenous to the areas where they reside, and they claim customary rights over the land and its resources. Bangladesh government initiatives to reform the land tenure system have met with stiff resistance. The indigenous peoples of the Chittagong Hills have formed political parties, one of which, the Jana Samhati Samiti (JSS), the

People's United Party, has an armed wing, the Shanti Bahini (Peace Forces). The Shanti Bahini, which carried out attacks on government military forces, often in response to massacres and the burnings of villages, was outlawed in both Bangladesh and India.

The peoples of the Chittagong Hills have attempted to negotiate with the Bangladesh government for autonomy for the region, recognition of local peoples' land rights, the establishment of its own legislature, and land recognition of traditional tribal authorities. There has also been a strong desire among the tribal peoples of the Chittagong Hills for the cessation of settlement by outsiders in the hills. The Bangladesh government has responded with increased pressure on the Chittagong Hills population, engaging in military operations where local people were killed, their homes and farms burned, women were raped, people were forcibly relocated, and temples, churches, and traditional sacred sites destroyed. Sizable numbers of tribal peoples were displaced internally in Bangladesh, while others fled across the borders into Burma and India as refugees. International human rights groups decried what was occurring in the Chittagong Hills, and delegations were sent by organizations such as Amnesty International to investigate the situation.

The Chittagong Hill Tracts Commission is an independent body established to investigate allegations of human rights violations in southeastern Bangladesh. In November 1990, it received permission to visit the region and to conduct interviews of local people, which were carried out in 1990–1991.[1] The testimonies cover a wide range of subjects, from mass murder, disappearances, and rape to destruction of property, involuntary relocation, and religious oppression. Attacks on temples and worshippers were described by individuals, as seen in this testimony from a Marma monk about an incident that took place in Mani Gram, Khagrachari, in June, 1986:

> I was in Man Gram temple. On 12 June 1986 we tried to celebrate a function in the temple. All of a sudden some troops came and said, "What are you doing?" We replied, "We are going to wash our God." The soldiers said, "You cannot wash God because this is a Muslim state. You cannot worship the Lord Buddha; you have to abandon this religion and become Muslim." We refused to do so. Then the soldiers caught us and tied our hands and started to pour water on our heads. I was the only monk there, the others were villagers, numbering around 20. All of us were tied in pairs and the soldiers started pouring water and when they were not satisfied by pouring water they started kicking us with their boots. The water was not just water but it was mixed with green chilies. When we were tied up they stood with bayonets over us so we

would not struggle. My skin started burning and most of us were injured as I was. I had cuts and sores on my legs. We were tied up in the afternoon and they started to burn the houses of the village, which we could see. We were tied up from eight in the morning to four in the afternoon, a total of eight hours. The soldiers untied us. At about five o'clock they set fire to the temple and we went in to hiding in the jungles. The settlers were not with the soldiers when they tied us up, but were there when the village was burnt. There is a river called Chengi. After coming to the river we went hiding into the deep jungle. After four days trekking all through the jungle, I reached the border of Tripura and Karbook camp. In that lot were around 450 people. Before 12 June there was no other incident. The only reason for the attack was religion. If we became Muslim we could stay safe. I know one Marma who was my friend called Uchmang. He was threatened that if he did not become a Muslim he would be harmed with his relatives. He was forcibly converted. He came from a different village, Mahalchair in Khagrachari District.

Another testimony comes from a monk in a refugee camp in Tripura about an incident that took place in Panchari in the Chittagong Hills in 1986:

One day 13 of us went to market. I was not a monk then. The Bangladesh Rifles and settlers caught us and out of thirteen, nine were killed and four of us escaped. The reason was that we were not Muslims. They wanted us to be Muslims to take Islam. It was in the market itself and some of the people were also caught up from around. Among the people whom they caught was my wife. They cut her with *daos* (long knives)—some of the marks on her neck are still there. She is in Karbook (relief camp). This took place in the market itself on market day, Wednesday. The others ran away. They also tried to cut me with *daos* on the neck. Luckily my shirt collar was thick and I escaped from being killed. As they killed the others, they shouted, "Oh, Chakmas, will you not now become Muslim? If you refuse we will kill you now."

Account 2: The Isaaks of Somalia

In 1988, the army of the government of Somalia attacked villages in the northern part of the country with the aim of destroying members of the Isaak clan, one of several clans in Somalia which they blamed for participating in rebellious actions against the state. The justification for these acts was state security.

The Somalia case illustrates a kind of "autogenocide" not unlike that in Cambodia perpetrated by the Khmer Rouge. The genocidal actions in Somalia, like those in Cambodia, were aimed specifically at exterminating members of one's own ethnic group (Africa Watch, 1990, pp. 1–2). Prior to the outbreak of fighting in northern Somalia, members of the Isaak clan disappeared, some at the hands of the Somalia National Security Service and paramilitary forces whose task was to root out dissent.

An estimated 50,000 to 60,000 people, the majority of them Isaaks, died during the 1980s, most of them in the period between 1988 and early 1990. Civilians were targeted along with suspected insurgents. The Somalia government forces carried out sweeps of both urban and rural areas, and both massacres and extrajudicial executions occurred. Camel and goat-keeping pastoral nomads were victimized by the Somalia government due to the suspicion they were providing economic support to the insurgents. The following oral testimonies were obtained from several people in the months following the 1988 attacks by Africa Watch and in 1990 by Robert Hitchcock.

The first oral testimony is from a woman named Monda Ahmed Yusuf, who lived in the Tuurta Turwa district of Burao in northern Somalia. She was interviewed by Africa Watch in London, England, on July 2, 1989.

> Shelling with long-range weapons started on Sunday. It hit a neighbor's house. The Abdirahman family of seven people. Six of them died instantaneously. The only survivor was a little girl who had been sent to fetch sugar. The mother had just had a baby.
>
> They were after civilians. Their scouts would direct them to those areas where civilians were concentrated and then that spot would be shelled. On Monday, the shelling intensified. Two houses behind ours belonging to my uncle were hit. Luckily, one was empty as the family had congregated in the other house. It hit that house, too, and his daughter, niece and sister-in-law were wounded. Our side was particularly targeted as it was one of the areas the SNM entered when they first came into town. When the bombing started, the sight of the dying, the wounded and the collapse of houses was too much to bear.

The second testimony is that of Khadija Sugal, who described how government forces intentionally separated Isaak clanspeople from non-Isaaks.

> If they [Somali government forces] had made any distinctions between SNM[2] fighters and civilians, there wouldn't have been so

many casualties and there wouldn't have been so much suffering. What they wanted, to put it simply, was to wipe us out. A hail of bullets came at you from every direction. As we fled Burao, my wife was hit by a bullet and badly wounded. My mother-in-law died when a bomb hit their house. My mother's niece was also killed. So many people have died . . ., including so many members of my own extended family. Only God can count the numbers.

The third oral testimony on Somalia is that of Jama Osman Samater, who had been a political prisoner from 1982 through 1988:

I had just come out from the mosque from Friday prayers when I heard the news of the SNM attack on Burao. It was lunchtime. At 2:30 a whistle blew, announcing a curfew. I went home. The next morning I learned that many businessmen and elders had been arrested. I saw soldiers herding people into cars. They were confiscating all vehicles, including taxis, because when the SNM attacked Burao, taxi drivers had helped the SNM. When they couldn't find the keys quickly enough, they punctured the tires and broke the windows. I understood immediately the gravity of the situation. The soldiers were looting food and medicines from the shops and loading them onto cars. The Gulwadayaal[3] were assisting the soldiers.

As a former political prisoner, I was in danger of being re-arrested. I had to disguise myself. I went into the back of our shop, shaved my head and dressed as a nomad. As I left, I saw two other men arrested. They were "Guun," and Abdillahi Khalif, "Ku Cadeeye," both elders. I don't know what happened to them.

I went towards my house. As I was about to board the bus, one of our shop assistants told me not to go home. Soldiers had just come to the shop looking for me and they must be on their way to the house. I went to hide at a neighbor's. That night, soldiers and NSS[4] officers went to my house. They took all valuables. One of my little sons screamed "faqash" at them and they slapped him across the ears. We learned later that his eardrum burst. I stayed a second night at a neighbor's house. Then, a friend and I hid ourselves in a big rubbish bin on the outskirts of Hargeisa for an entire day. The next night, the SNM attacked Hargeisa and we came back to town. On our way back, we passed a house near a military checkpoint belonging to Yusuf Elmi Samatar and saw soldiers and a tank on the move. We learned that eighteen civilians, who had fled the city center and taken shelter there, had been killed. They were robbed of everything and some of the women were raped.

We stayed in Hargeisa until June 8. My wife, mother, six children, two sisters and their children gathered in one house. After a few days, the shelling started. It was relentless. They shelled homes, even when no one was in the house. The objective was to ensure that no one escaped alive and no house left to stand. Volleys of artillery were being fired from every direction. There was burning everywhere. In front of my sister's house, a wooden house was hit and eight people, mostly women and children, perished. The shock was so overwhelming that we soon lost any sense of fear.

I realized that my suffering in prison was nothing compared to this. In prison, my pain had affected just me. Here everyone was a victim. The shelling did not discriminate. There were even dead animals, dogs and goats, everywhere. The first dead bodies I saw were two or three traders of Asian origin who had lived in Somalia for generations. I went to hide in a mosque. I couldn't walk fast as there were so many dead bodies on the road.

The fourth testimony is that of Khadra Muhumed Abdi, who spoke to Africa Watch in London on June 2, 1989:

On the Friday, I came to our hotel (Oriental Hotel), unaware at the time, of the SNM attack on Burao. I learned that businessmen and elders were being rounded up. As a former political prisoner, I was nervous. NSS officers came to look for me. I escaped through a back door and hid in a store next door. Later, I asked a young boy to fetch me a taxi and I went to hide in my aunt's house in Dumbuluq district. I was afraid to go home for fear that they would be waiting for me.

The morning after the SNM attack on Hargeisa, I could see our district, Radio Station area, burning. It seemed as if the whole city was on fire. The government was going around with loudspeakers saying that "Four lice-ridden bandits on a suicide mission entered the town and we have now driven them away." They insisted that everything was back to normal and urged people to return to their homes. Unfortunately, many people believed them and were killed.

It was clear that the war was going on whatever the government said. I could not run because of the disability in my leg. [She limps on one leg.] My mother and my two children joined us on the third day of the fighting. A part of our house had collapsed and they tried to hide in the undamaged section. They left when it was no longer safe to stay there. A neighbor gave them shelter but the children had no milk and food was scarce.

We stayed another twelve days in my aunt's house. Soldiers came and took everything we had. What they couldn't take with them, such as trunks, they destroyed. When he sensed our tension, one of them turned around and said to me, "If I hear one word out of you, I will make you carry the heads of your children after I have cut them off." Fortunately, I made the two boys (one was a year and three months and the other was two years and three months) wear dresses, so they thought they were girls. If they had recognized them as boys they would have shot them at once. We knew of so many boys, including babies, who had been killed. A neighbor of my aunt's, known as "Cirro," had five sons and two nephews in the house. Because of their ages, he wouldn't let them out of the house. When they ran out of food, he went to buy it himself. When he came back, all seven boys were dead, their throats slit. In that same neighborhood, in a house belonging to Abdillahi Ibrahim Aden, soldiers heard them listening to the BBC. They killed four boys with bazookas.

The shelling wouldn't cease, so we hid in another house. We tried to escape between the compounds of the 24th and the 11th sector of the army. We went to the dry-river bed, about 100 of us, but were driven away by soldiers. Then we tried to escape through a place called Meegaga but turned back when we saw soldiers again. Everyone then just fled, escaping in whatever way they could. I couldn't walk fast, let alone run, because of my foot. One of my cousins and I got lost. We hid in a hut and were found by another cousin who had come to look for us. I couldn't go on. My leg hurt too much. My cousins found a donkey cart for me. We reached Qool after three days. We found thousands of other people there. I had no idea what had happened to my children and mother.

The final testimony is that of Abdi Mohamed, who Robert Hitchcock interviewed in London in July 1990. Mr. Mohamed had gone to visit relatives in the countryside southeast of Burao in Toghdeer Region. His relatives, who were nomads, had been attacked from the air, their camp bombed and strafed by Somali government planes. They had also found their main water points poisoned, and most of their camels had died from thirst. His testimony indicates the degree to which pastoral nomads were victimized by the Somali government.

Several months before the army attacked Burao [May 27, 1988], I went to see my children who had been staying in the area outside Ainabo. Two of my sons had been arrested by soldiers and accused of being members of the Somali National Movement. The soldiers said that they and other nomads were giving food to the SNM. They beat them very badly in prison but my sons told the soldiers nothing. When they got out they sent word to me in Burao to join them. As I traveled there, I saw many *barkad* [water reservoirs] that had been blown up by the army. One of the soldiers on the truck said that the army destroyed the reservoirs to punish the Isaaks for helping the SNM. They also killed the camels and cattle of people so that they had to move in to the cities to get food. Land mines were placed around the *barkad* to keep people away.

When I got to my sons' camp I found that some of my relatives had been killed. They were shot by the army after some soldiers were hurt by a mine on one of the roads. At night I could hear explosions and gunshots. In the morning we would sometimes find the bodies of people and livestock in camps that had been destroyed by the soldiers. Some of the bodies were burned. I will never forget the smell.

There were so many people killed, nearly all of them Isaaks. The government in Mogadishu wanted to destroy the Isaaks ever since 1982 when a state of emergency was declared.

Account 3: The Tyua of Western Zimbabwe

The Tyua San (Amasili, Bushmen) of western Zimbabwe and north-eastern Botswana are an agropastoral and fishing people who are former foragers (Hitchcock, 1995). Numbering approximately 2,500 in the Tsholotsho and Bulalima Mangwe Districts in western Zimbabwe and 7,000 in northern Botswana, the Tyua were affected by dispossession as a result of land being set aside for white settlers, the establishment of national parks and game reserves, the imposition of hunting laws that prevented them from obtaining wildlife legally, and forced resettlement into "protected villages" during the Zimbabwean War of Independence (1965–1980). Today, many Tyua work on the farms and ranches of other people, including Tswana, Kalanga, and Ndebele and they sell handicrafts, meat, salt, and beer to earn extra income.

In the early 1980s after Zimbabwe achieved its independence, tensions continued to be felt, particularly in Matabeleland, where one of the major groups of freedom fighters, the Zimbabwe African Peoples Liberation Army, the military wing of the Zimbabwe African Peoples Union (ZAPU), had its primary base of support. Some of the former guerrillas felt that they had not been treated appropriately by the new government, and tensions erupted into conflict in late 1980 and early 1981. Some of the former guerrillas returned to the bush and began what turned into a low-level insurgency. Beginning in 1982 and continuing into the mid-1990s, the Zimbabwe government carried out counterinsurgency operations against what they termed "dissidents." These operations included military attacks on villagers in western Zimbabwe, kidnappings of suspected terrorists, torture and murder of detainees, a wide range of atrocities against the civilian population, and restriction of the movement of food into the area (Africa Watch, 1989; Catholic Justice and Peace Commission and Legal Rights Foundation, 1997).

The man who described some of these and other events occurring in the 1982–1985 period was an elderly Tyua who had been imprisoned during the Zimbabwe war for independence. Subsequently, he was detained by the new government on suspicion of having supported the dissidents. The interview was conducted by Robert Hitchcock in Tsholotsho, Zimbabwe, on June 26, 1989. The man requested that his name not be used.

I was living in western Tsholotsho just south of Hwange.[5] I used to live in the game reserve but we were forced to leave by the whites. My father hunted elephants there but he was arrested and put in prison. I helped my mother and brothers and sisters by collecting salt at Sua. But then the war came[6] and the Selous Scouts[7] came to our village and beat us up. My brother was shot as we watched. They kept saying. "You are Bushmen. You should not support the black people."[8] I was glad when Smith[9] lost the war and we got a new government. I voted in the elections. I thought that everything would be good with a new government. The Bushmen would be treated like other people, not flogged with sticks like we were by the white farmers.

Then the killings began. At first it was white people, part of Smith's army, who came to Tsholotsho and shot people. I saw my best friend taken away by the soldiers in a truck. I never saw him again. Many people were taken away. The soldiers came at night. Sometimes they shot people in their beds. They were after Ndebele and Bushmen. They called us dissidents. But we were just people trying to make a living.

At that time the drought was very bad. There were no crops in the fields, and the wild fruits were very few. Even elands[10] were dying in the bush. Then the government said we could not get food. They stopped the trucks from coming to the stores. We were very hungry, and children and old people died of starvation. People even ate their skin blankets and shoes.

It was then that the soldiers in red hats[11] came to my village. They said that we should send women to help them carry water. Later we learned that the women had been raped. Two of the women from our village were shot by the soldiers. The army people would come to Tsholotsho and say that we were dissidents. They pointed to people and they were taken away. Later we heard they had been killed and their bodies dumped into old mines. There were many places where the bodies were left. We would sometimes find them when we were looking for lost cattle.

My close friend Khunou was arrested by the soldiers. They said he had robbed stores and stolen cattle. I told them that he was innocent, but they said, "He is just a Bushman. Bushmen are animals." That night they shot him. His wife and children fled to Botswana after the soldiers burned their houses and killed their chickens.

I was arrested by the soldiers in red hats and taken to an army base. They did not give us food or water. They tortured me by putting my head in water and hitting me on the backside. They kept calling me a "dumb Bushman." Some of the people in the camp with me died from the beatings.

Many innocent people died because of the army. We were just trying to make a living like we always have. But they felt we were just Bushmen. I wondered then why I voted for this government.

Notes

1   Chittagong Hill Tracts Commission (1991). *"Life Is Not Ours": Land and Human Rights in the Chittagong Hill Tracts, Bangladesh. The Report of the Chittagong Hill Tracts Commission, May 1991.* Copenhagen: International Work Group for Indigenous Affairs and Amsterdam, The Netherlands: Organizing Committee, Chittagong Hill Tracts Campaign. The first testimony is on p. 97, the second on p. 99.

2   The Somali National Movement, an opposition organization composed mainly of Isaaks, one of several Somali clans that was formed to fight the government forces of President Siad Barre in northern Somalia.

3   The Gulwadayaal, also known as Victory Pioneers, were paramilitary forces, established in the early 1970s, who worked directly for President Siad Barre. They had extraordinary legal authority over and above the Somali police and could charge people with crimes and make arrests.

4   National Security Service, the national security organization of the government of the Somali Democratic Republic.

5   Hwange, formerly Wankie National Park, the largest national park in Zimbabwe.

6   The Zimbabwe war for independence, which lasted from 1965 to 1980. The time period that he is referring to is the mid-to late 1970s.

7   Elite troops of the Rhodesian military.

8   The black people they were referring to belonged to the Zimbabwe African National Union, ZANU, which was made up of Ndebele, Kalanga, Tonga, and other groups and was headed by Joshua Nkomo.

9   Ian Smith, the then Prime Minister of Rhodesia.

10 *Taurotragus oryx*, large antelopes that move in herds up to about 50 animals each and which are highly prized by Tyua and other San (Bushmen) for food because of their high fat content.

11 The members of the Fifth Brigade, a North Korea-trained military unit that was under the Prime Minister's office rather than the regular Zimbabwe Army. It was this brigade that was said to have been responsible for the killings of as many as 20,000 people in western Zimbabwe in 1982–1983.

Acknowledgments

Support of the research upon which this paper is based was provided by the U.S. National Science Foundation, the Ford Foundation, the International Work Group for Indigenous Affairs (IWGIA), Hivos, the U.S. Agency for International Development (USAID), the Danish International Development Authority (DANIDA), and Rotary International. We wish to thank the indigenous and other peoples and individuals to whom we spoke in the process of compiling and analyzing the data. Israel Charny provided useful insights on genocide issues. We also wish to thank Adrianne M. Daggett for her editorial suggestions and recommendations for improvement of the chapter.

References

Abdul Joshua Ruzibiza, RWANDA: L'HISTOIRE SECRETE (Editions du Panama, Paris: 2005), with Preface and notes by Claudine Vidal, and postface by Andre Guichaoua.

Africa Watch (1989). *Zimbabwe, A Break with the Past? Human Rights and Political Unity.* New York and Washington, D.C.: Africa Watch Committee.

Africa Watch (1990). *Somalia: A Government at War With Its Own People. Testimonies about the Killings and the Conflict in the North.* New York: Human Rights Watch.

African Rights (1995). *Facing Genocide: The Nuba of Sudan.* London: African Rights.

African Rights (1996). *Rwanda: Killing the Evidence: Murders, Attacks, Arrests, and Intimidation of Survivors and Witnesses.* London: African Rights.

Albert, Bruce (1992). "Indian Lands, Environmental Policy and Military Geopolitics in the Development of the Brazilian Amazon: The Case of the Yanomami." *Development and Change* 23(1): 35–70.

Albert, Bruce (1994). "Gold Miners and Yanomami Indians in the Brazilian Amazon: The Hashimu Massacre," pp. 47–55. In Barbara Rose Johnston (Ed.) *Who Pays the Price? The Sociocultural Context of Environmental Crisis.* Washington D.C. and Covelo, CA: Island Press.

American Anthropological Association (1991). *Report of the Special Commission to Investigate the Situation of the Brazilian Yanomami, June, 1991.* Washington, D.C.: American Anthropological Association.

Amnesty International (1992a). *Human Rights Violations Against Indigenous Peoples of the Americas.* New York: Amnesty International.

Amnesty International (1992b). *United States of America: Human Rights and American Indians.* New York: Amnesty International.

Anaya, S. James (1996). *Indigenous Peoples in International Law.* New York: Oxford University Press.

Anti-Slavery Society (1984). *The Chittagong Hill Tracts: Militarization, Oppression, and the Hill Tribes.* Indigenous Peoples and Development Series, No. 2. London: Anti-Slavery Society.

Arens, Richard (1976). "Introduction," pp. 1–16. In Richard Arens (Ed.) *Genocide in Paraguay.* Philadelphia, PA: Temple University Press.

Arens, Richard (Ed.) (1976). *Genocide in Paraguay.* Philadelphia, PA: Temple University Press.

Arens, Richard (1978). *The Forest Indians in Stroessner's Paraguay: Survival or Extinction?* Survival International Document Series, No. 4. London: Survival International.

Barkan, Elazar (2003). "Genocides of Indigenous Peoples: Rhetoric of Human Rights," pp. 117–139. In Robert Gellately and Ben Kiernan (Eds.) *The Specter of Genocide: Mass Murder in Historical Perspective.* New York: Cambridge University Press.

Barta, Tony (1987). "Relations of Genocide: Land and Lives in the Colonization of Australia," pp. 237–251. In Isidor Walliman and Michael N. Dobkowski (Eds.) *Genocide and the Modern Age: Etiology and Case Studies of Mass Death.* Westport, CT: Greenwood Press.

Baue, Bruce (2006). "Win or Lose in Court: Alien claims Torts Act Pushes Corporate Respect for Human Rights." *Business Ethics,* Summer, 34(1):12–13.

Bergner, D. (2003). "The Most Unconventional Weapon." *The New York Times Magazine,* October 28, pp. 48–53.

Bhengra, Ratnaker, C.R. Bijoy, and Shirreichon Luithui (1998). *The Adivasis of India.* London: Minority Rights Group International.

Biesele, Megan and Robert K. Hitchcock (2000). The Ju/'hoansi San under Two States: Impacts of the South West African Administration and the Government of the Republic of Namibia. In Peter Schweitzer, Megan Biesele, and Robert K. Hitchcock (Eds.) *Hunters and Gatherers in the Modern World: Conflict, Resistance, and Self-Determination.* Pp. 305–326. New York and Oxford: Berghahn Books.

Bodley, John (1999). *Victims of Progress.* Fourth Edition. Mountain View, California: Mayfield.

Brantlinger, Patrick (2003). *Dark Vanishings: Discourse on the Extinction of Primitive Races 1800–1930.* Ithaca, NY: Cornell University Press.

Burger, Julian (1990). *The Gaia Atlas of First Peoples: A Future for the Indigenous World.* New York and London: Anchor Books (Doubleday).

Carmarck, Robert M. (Ed.) (1988). *Harvest of Violence: The Maya Indians and the Guatemalan Crisis.* Norman: University of Oklahoma Press.

Carroll, John M. (Ed.) (1973). *The Sand Creek Massacre: A Documented History.* New York: Sol Lewis.

Castillo, Beatriz Huertas (2004). *Indigenous Peoples in Isolation in the Peruvian Amazon.* Copenhagen: International Work Group for Indigenous Affairs.

Catholic Justice and Peace Commission and Legal Resources Foundation (1997). *Report on Massacres and Atrocities in Matabeleland, Zimbabwe 1982–87.* Harare: Catholic Justice and Peace Commission and Legal Resources Foundation.

Chagnon, Napoleon A. (1993a). "Anti-Science and Native Rights: Genocide of the Yanomami." *Human Behavior and Evolution Society Newsletter* 2(3):1–4.

Chagnon, Napoleon A. (1993b). "Covering Up the Yanomamo Massacre." *The New York Times,* October 23, p. 13.

Chagnon, Napoleon A. (1993c). "Killed by Kindness? The Dubious Influence of the Salesian Missions in Amazonas." *Times Literary Supplement,* December 24, 1993, pp. 11–12.

Chalk, Frank and Kurt Jonassohn (1990). *The History and Sociology of Genocide: Analyses and Case Studies.* New Haven, CT: Yale University Press.

Chan, T.M. (2004). 'The Richtersveld Challenge: South Africa Finally Adopts Aboriginal Title.' In Robert K. Hitchcock and Diana Vinding (Eds.) *Indigenous Peoples Rights in Southern Africa,* pp. 114–133. Copenhagen, International Work Group for Indigenous Affairs.

Chennels, Roger and Aymone du Toit (2004). "The Rights of Indigenous Peoples in South Africa. In Robert K. Hitchcock and Diana Vinding (Eds.) *Indigenous Peoples' Rights in Southern Africa.* Pp. 98–113. Copenhagen, Denmark: International Work Group for Indigenous Affairs.

Chittagong Hill Tracts Commission (1991a). *"Life Is Not Ours": Land and Human Rights in the Chittagong Hill Tracts, Bangladesh. Report of the Chittagong Hill Tracts Commission.* Copenhagen and London; International Work Group for Indigenous Affairs and Anti-Slavery International.

Chittagong Hill Tracts Commission (1991b). *"Life is Not Ours": Land and Human Rights in the Chittagong Hill Tracts, Bangladesh: The Report of the Chittagong Hill Tracts Commission 1991.* Copenhagen: International Work Group for Indigenous Affairs.

Chittagong Hill Tracts Commission (1992). *"Life is Not Ours": Land and Human Rights in the*

Chittagong Hill Tracts, Bangladesh. An Update of the May 1991 Report. Copenhagen: International Work Group for Indigenous Affairs.

Chittagong Hill Tracts Commission (1994). *"Life is Not Ours": Land and Human Rights in the Chittagong Hill Tracts, Bangladesh: Update 2.* Copenhagen: International Work Group for Indigenous Affairs.

Chittagong Hill Tracts Commission (1997). *"Life is Not Ours": Land and Human Rights in the Chittagong Hill Tracts, Bangladesh: Update 3.* Copenhagen: International Work Group for Indigenous Affairs.

Chittagong Hill Tracts Commission (2000). *"Life is Not Ours": Land and Human Rights in the Chittagong Hill Tracts, Bangladesh: Update 4.* Copenhagen: International Work Group for Indigenous Affairs.

Chowdhury, Akram H. (1989). "Self-Determination, the Chittagong, and Bangladesh," pp. 292–301. In David P. Forsythe (Ed.) *Human Rights and Development: International Views.* New York, NY: St. Martin's Press.

Clay, Jason (1984). "Genocide in the Age of Enlightenment." *Cultural Survival Quarterly* 12(3):1.

Crow Dog, Mary, and Richard Erdoes (1990). *Lakota Woman.* New York: Grove Weidenfeld.

Dadrian, Vahakn N. (1975). "A Typology of Genocide." *International Review of Modern Sociology* 5(2):201–212.

Daes, Erica-Irene A. (2005). "Indigenous Peoples," pp. 508–516. In Dinah L. Shelton, (Ed.) *Encyclopedia of Genocide Crimes against Humanity.* Detroit, MI: Thomson Gale.

Davis, Shelton (1977). *Victims of the Miracle: Development and the Indians of Brazil.* Cambridge: Cambridge University Press.

DeLoria, Vine, Jr. (1969). *Custer Died for Your Sins.* New York: Macmillan.

DeLoria, Vine, Jr., Ed. (1985). *American Indian Policy in the Twentieth Century.* Norman, OK: University of Oklahoma Press.

Durning, Alan Thein (1992). *Guardians of the Land: Indigenous Peoples and the Health of the Earth.* Washington, D.C.: WorldWatch Institute.

Erni, Chris (2006). *Strategy and Work Priorities for IWGIA's Asia Program.* Copenhagen, Denmark: International Work Group for Indigenous Affairs.

Ewen, Alexander, Ed. (1994). *Voice of Indigenous Peoples: Native People Address the United Nations.* Santa Fe: Clear Light Publishers.

Falla, Ricardo (1994). *Massacres in the Jungle: Ixcan, Guatemala, 1975–1982.* Boulder, CO: Westview Press.

Fein, Helen (1984). "Scenarios of Genocide: Models of Genocide and Critical Responses," pp. 3–31. In Israel W. Charny (Ed.) *Toward the Understanding and Prevention of Genocide: Proceedings of the International Conference on the Holocaust and Genocide.* Boulder, CO: Westview Press.

Fein, Helen (1990). Special Issue: Genocide: A Sociological Perspective. *Current Sociology* 38(1):1–126.

Gedicks, Al (1993). *The New Resource Wars: Native and Environmental Struggles Against Environmental Corporations.* Boston, MA: South End Press.

Gedicks, Al (2001). *Resource Rebels: Native Challenges to Mining and Oil Corporations.* Cambridge, MA: South End Press.

Gellately, Robert and Ben Kiernan (Eds.) (2003). *The Specter of Genocide: Mass Murder in Historical Perspective.* New York: Cambridge University Press.

Goldberg, Jeffrey (2002). "The Great Terror." *The New Yorker,* March 25, 2002, pp. 52–75.

Gordon, Robert J. (1985). "Conserving Bushmen to Extinction in Southern Africa: The Metaphysics of Bushman Hating and Empire Building,". In Marcus Colchester (Ed.) *An End to Laughter? Tribal Peoples and Economic Development,* pp. 28–42. London: Survival International.

Gordon, Robert J. (1988). "The Rise of the Bushman Penis: Germans, Genitalia, and Genocide." *African Studies* 57(1):27–54.

Gordon, Robert J. (2003). 'Introduction: *A Kalahari Family.*' *Visual Anthropology Review* 19(1–2):102–113.

Gordon, Robert J. (in press) "Hidden in Full View: The 'Forgotten' Bushman Genocides of Namibia." *Genocide Studies and Prevention.*

Gordon, Robert J. and Stuart Sholto Douglas (2000). *The Bushman Myth: The Making of a Namibian Underclass.* Second Edition. Boulder, CO: Westview Press.

Gurr, Ted Robert (2000). *Peoples Versus States: Minorities at Risk in the New Century.* Washington, D.C.: The United States Institute of Peace Press.

Gurr, Ted Robert and James R. Scaritt (1989). "Minorities Rights at Risk: A Global Survey." *Human Rights Quarterly* 11(3):375–405.

Gurr, Ted Robert and Barbara Harff (1994). *Ethnic Conflict in World Politics.* Boulder: Westview Press.

Harff, Barbara (1984). *Genocide and Human Rights: International Legal and Political Issues.* Denver: Graduate School of International Studies.

Hays, Jennifer (2007) *Education, Rights, and Survival for the Nyae Nyae Ju/'hoansi: Illuminating Global and Local Discourses.* Ph.D. Dissertation, State University of New York at Albany.

Heinz, Wolfgang (1988). *Indigenous Populations, Ethnic Minorities, and Human Rights.* Berlin: Quorum Verlag.

Hill, Kim and A. Magdalena Hurtado (1995). *Ache Life History: The Ecology and Demography of a Foraging People.* New York: Aldine de Gruyter.

Hitchcock, Robert K. (1985). "The Plight of Indigenous Peoples." *Social Education* 49(6):457–462.

Hitchcock, Robert K. (1994). "International Human Rights, the Environment, and Indigenous Peoples." *Colorado Journal of International Environmental Law and Policy* 5(1):1–22.

Hitchcock, Robert K. (1995). "Centralization, Resource Depletion, and Coercive Conservation among the Tyua of the Northeastern Kalahari." *Human Ecology* 23(2):169–198.

Hitchcock, Robert K. (1997). "Indigenous Peoples, Multinational Corporations, and Human Rights." *Indigenous Affairs* 1997/2:6–11.

Hitchcock, Robert K. (1999). "Indigenous Peoples, Genocide of," pp. 349–354. In Israel W. Charny (Ed.) *Encyclopedia of Genocide, Volume II, I–Y,* Santa Barbara, CA: ABC-CLIO.

Hitchcock, Robert K. (2002). 'We Are the First People': Land, Natural Resources, and Identity and in the Central Kalahari, Botswana. *Journal of Southern African Studies* 28(4):797–824.

Hitchcock, Robert K., Sam Totten, and William S. Parsons (2002). 'Confronting Genocide and Ethnocide of Indigenous Peoples: An Interdisciplinary Approach to Definition, Intervention, and Advocacy.' In Alexander Labhan Hinton, (Ed.), *Annihilating Difference: The Anthropology of Genocide,* pp. 43–53. Berkeley, CA and London: University of California Press.

Hitchcock, Robert K. and Thomas Koperski (2008). "Genocides of Indigenous Peoples," pp. 577–617. In Dan Stone (Ed.) *Historiography of Genocide.* New York and London: Palgrave.

Hoig, Stan (1961). *The Sand Creek Massacre.* Norman: University of Oklahoma Press.

Horowitz, Irving Louis (2002). *Taking Lives: Genocide and State Power.* Fifth Edition, Revised. New Brunswick, NJ: Transaction Books.

Howard, Bradley Reed (2003). *Indigenous Peoples and the State: The Struggle for Native Rights.* DeKalb, Illinois: Northern Illinois University Press.

Human Rights Watch (1992) *Endless Torment: The 1991 Uprising in Iraq and Its Aftermath.* New York: Author.

Human Rights Watch (2003a) *Covered in Blood: Ethnically Targeted Violence in Northern DRC.* New York: Author.

Human Rights Watch (2003b). *The Iraqi Government Assault on the Marsh Arabs.* New York: Author.

Hyndman, David (1994). *Ancestral Rain Forests and the Mountain of Gold: Indigenous Peoples and Mining in New Guinea.* Boulder, CO: Westview Press.

Independent Commission on International Humanitarian Issues (1987). *Indigenous Peoples: A Global Quest for Justice.* London: Zed Press.

International Labour Organization (1953). *Indigenous Peoples: Living and Working Conditions of Aboriginal Populations in Independent Countries.* Geneva: International Labour Organization.

International Work Group for Indigenous Affairs (1988). *IWGIA Yearbook 1987: Indigenous Peoples and Development.* Copenhagen: IWGIA.

Jackson, Jean and Kay B. Warren (2005). "Indigenous Movements in Latin America: Controversies, Ironies, New Directions." *Annual Review of Anthropology* 34:49–73.

Jaimes, M. Annette (Ed). (1992). *The State of Native America: Genocide, Colonization, and Resistance.* Boston: South End Press.

Johnston, Barbara Rose (2005). *Chixoy Dam Legacy Issues Study. Volume 1: Executive Summary Consequential Damages and Reparation: Recommendations for Remedy. Volume 2: Document Review and Chronology of Relevant Actions and Events. Volume 3: Consequential Damage Assessment of Chixoy River Basin Communities.* Santa Cruz, CA: Center for Political Ecology, March 17, 2005. http://www.centerforpoliticalecology.org.

Johnston, Barbara Rose (2006). "Banking on Violence? Guatemalan Genocide and U.S. Security." *CounterPunch,* August 19/20. Accessed at: www.counterpunch.org/hohnston08192006.html

Joseph, Sarah (2004). *Corporations and Transnational Human Rights Litigation.* London: Hart Publishing.

Kazmi, Sayyed Nadeem and Stuart M. Leiderman (2004). "Twilight People: Iraq's Marsh Inhabitants." *Human Rights Dialogue: Environmental Rights.* Accessed at: www/Carnegiecouncil.org/viewMediaphp.

Koff, Clea (2005). *The Bone Woman: A Forensic Anthropologist's Search for Truth in the Mass Graves of Rwanda, Bosnia, Croatia, and Kosovo.* New York: Random House.

Krech, Shepard (1994). Genocide in Tribal Society. *Nature* 371 (1729):14–15.

Kuper, Leo (1981). *Genocide: Its Political Use in the Twentieth Century.* New Haven, CT: Yale University Press.

Kuper, Leo (1982). *International Action against Genocide.* Minority Rights Group Report 53. London: Minority Rights Group.

Kuper, Leo (1984). "Types of Genocide and Mass Murder," pp. 32–47. In Israel W. Charny (Ed.) *Toward the Understanding and Prevention of Genocide: Proceedings of the International Conference on the Holocaust and Genocide.* Boulder, CO: Westview Press.

Kuper, Leo (1985). *The Prevention of Genocide.* New Haven, CT: Yale University Press.

Kuper, Leo (1991). "When Denial Becomes Routine." *Social Education* 55(2):121–123.

Kuper, Leo (1992). "Reflections on the Prevention of Genocide," pp. 135–151. In Helen Fein (Ed.) *Genocide Watch.* New Haven and London: Yale University Press.

Leary, John D. (1995). *Violence and the Dream People: The Orang Asli in the Malayan Emergency, 1948–1960.* Athens: Ohio University Press.

Legters, Lyman H. (1988). "The American Genocide: Pathologies of Indian–White Relations." *Policy Studies Journal* 16(4):768–777.

Lehtola, Veli-Pekka (2004). *The Saami People: Traditions in Transition.* Fairbanks: University of Alaska Press.

Lewis, Norman (1969). "Genocide—From Fire and Sword to Arsenic and Bullet, Civilization Has Sent Six Million Indians to Extinction." *Sunday Times Magazine* [London], February, 1969.

Lewis, Norman (1974). *Genocide: A Documentary Report on the Conditions of Indian Peoples.* Berkeley, California: Indigena and the American Friends of Brazil.

Lewis, Norman (1976). The Camp at Cecilio Baez. In Richard Arens (ed.), *Genocide in Paraguay,* pp. 58–68. Philadelphia: Temple University Press.

Manz, Beatrice (1988). *Refugees of a Hidden War: The Aftermath of Counterinsurgency in Guatemala.* Albany, NY: State University of New York Press.

Martinez Cobo, Jose R. (1987). *Study of the Problem of Discrimination Against Indigenous Populations. Volume V: Conclusions, Proposals, and Recommendations.* New York: United Nations.

Matthiessen, Peter (1983). *In the Spirit of Crazy Horse.* New York, NY: Viking.

Maybury-Lewis, David (1997). *Indigenous Peoples, Ethnic Groups, and the State.* Boston, MA: Allyn and Bacon.

Maybury-Lewis, David (2002). "Genocide against Indigenous Peoples," pp. 43–53. In Alexander Labhan Hinton (Ed.) *Annihilating Difference: The Anthropology of Genocide.* Berkeley and Los Angeles: University of California Press.

Maybury-Lewis, David and James Howe (1980). *The Indian Peoples of Paraguay: Their Plight and Their Prospects.* Cultural Survival Special Reports, No. 2. Cambridge, MA: Cultural Survival Inc.

Menchu, Rigoberta (1984). *I, Rigoberta Menchu, An Indian Woman of Guatemala.* Edited and Introduced by Elisabeth Burgos-Debray. London: Verso Editions.

Mey, Wolfgang (Ed.) (1984). *Genocide in the Chittagong Hill Tracts. IWGIA Document No. 51.* Copenhagen, Denmark: International Work Group for Indigenous Affairs.

Middle East Watch and Physicians for Human Rights (1988) *Chemical Genocide in Iraq.* New York: Middle East Watch and Boston: Physicians for Human Rights.

Middle East Watch (1992). *Endless Torment: The 1991 Uprising in Iraq and Its Aftermath.* New York: Middle East Watch.

Middle East Watch and Physicians for Human Rights (1992). *Unquiet Graves: The Search for the Disappeared in Iraqi Kurdistan.* Washington, D.C., New York, and Somerville, MA: Middle East Watch and Physicians for Human Rights.

Middle East Watch and Physicians for Human Rights (1993). *The Anfal Campaign in Iraqi Kurdistan: The Destruction of Koreme.* New York: Human Rights Watch and Physicians for Human Rights.

Minority Rights Group International (2007). *World Directory of Minorities 2007.* London: Minority Rights Group International.

Montejo, Victor (1987). *Testimony: Death of a Guatemalan Village.* Willimantic, CT: Curbstone Press.

Montejo, Victor (n.d.). "Testimony of Violence in Guatemala: A Mayan Indian Account." Unpublished manuscript. University of California, Davis. Department of Native American Studies.

Munzel, Mark (1973). *The Ache Indians: Genocide in Paraguay.* IWGIA Document No. 11. Copenhagen: International Work Group for Indigenous Affairs.

Munzel, Mark (1974). *The Ache: Genocide Continues in Paraguay.* Copenhagen: International Work Group for Indigenous Affairs.

Munzel, Mark (1985). The Manhunts: Ache Indians in Paraguay. In Willem A. Veenhoven, (Ed). *Case Studies on Human Rights and Fundamental Freedoms: A World Survey, Volume 4,* Pp. 351–403. The Hague: Nijhoff.

Niezen, Ronald (2003) *The Origins of Indigenism: Human Rights and the Politics of Identity.* Berkeley and Los Angeles: University of California Press.

Neitschmann, Bernard (1994). "The Fourth World: Nations Versus States. In George J. Demoko and Willian B. Wood (Eds.) *Reordering the World: Geopolitical Perspectives on the 21st Century,* Pp. 225–242. Boulder, Colorado: Westview Press.

Nettle, D. and S. Romaine (2000). *Vanishing Voices: The Extinction of the World's Languages.* Oxford: Oxford University Press.

Palmer, Alison (1992). "Ethnocide," pp. 1–6. In Michael N. Dobkowski and Isidor Wallimann (Eds.) *Genocide in Our Time: An Annotated Bibliography with Analytical Introductions.* Ann Arbor, MI: The Pierian Press.

Partow, Hassan (2001). *The Mesopotamian Marshlands: Demise of an Ecosystem.* Geneva: United Nations Environment Program.

Perry, Richard J. (1996). *From Time Immemorial: Indigenous Peoples and State Systems.* Austin, TX: University of Texas Press.

Price, John (1989). *The Nambiquara and the World Bank.* Seattle: University of Washington Press.

Rabben, Linda (1998). *Unnatural Selection: The Yanomami, the Kayapao, and the Onslaught of Civilization.* Seattle, WA: University of Washington Press.

Reed, Richard (1997). *Forest Dwellers, Forest Protectors: Indigenous Models for International Development.* Boston, Massachusetts: Allyn and Bacon.

Rensink, Brenden (2006) Native American History, the Holocaust, and Comparative Genocide: Historiography, Debate, and Critical Analysis. M.A. Thesis, Department of History, University of Nebraska-Lincoln.

Roy, Chandra Raikumari (2000). *Land Rights of the Indigenous Peoples of the Chittagong Hill Tracts, Bangladesh.* Copenhagen, Denmark: International Work Group for Indigenous Affairs.

Sachs, Aaron (1995). *Eco-Justice: Linking Human Rights and the Environment. WorldWatch Paper 127.* Washington, D.C.: WorldWatch Institute.

Sachs, Aaron (1996). "Upholding Human Rights and Environmental Justice," pp. 133–151. In Lester Brown (Ed.) *State of the World 1996.* Washington, D.C.: WorldWatch Institute.

Sanders, Douglas (1989). "The UN Working Group on Indigenous Populations." *Human Rights Quarterly* 11(3):406–433.

Sanders, Douglas (1991). "Collective Rights." *Human Rights Quarterly* 13:368–386.

Sanford, Victoria (2003). *Buried Secrets: Truth and Human Rights in Guatemala.* New York: Palgrave Macmillan.

Saugestad, Sidsel (2001). *The Inconvenient Indigenous: Remote Area Development in Botswana, Donor Assistance, and the First People of the Kalahari.* Uppsala: The Nordic Africa Institute.

Skutnabb-Kangas, T. (2000) *Linguistic Genocide in Education—or Worldwide Diversity and Human Rights?* Mahwah, NJ: Lawrence Erlbaum Associates.

Smith, R.C. and B. Melia (1978). "Genocide of the Ache-Guayaki?" *Survival International* 3(1):8–13.

Smith, Roger W. (1987). "Human Destructiveness and Politics: The Twentieth Century as an Age of Genocide," pp. 21–38. In Isidor Walliman and Michael N. Dobkowski (Eds.) *Genocide and the Modern Age: Etiology and Case Studies of Mass Death.* Westport, CT: Greenwood Press.

Sponsel, Leslie (1994). "The Yanomami Holocaust Continues," pp. 43–46. In Barbara Rose Johnston (Ed.) *Who Pays the Price? The Sociocultural Context of Environmental Crisis.* Washington D.C. and Covelo, CA: Island Press.

Sponsel, Leslie (1997). "The Master Thief: Gold Mining and Mercury Contamination in the Amazon," pp. 99–127. In Barbara Rose Johnston (Ed.) *Life and Death Matters: Human Rights and the Environment at the End of the Millennium.* Walnut Creek, California: AltaMira Press.

Stephens, Bret (2007). "Amazonian Swindle." *The Wall Street Journal*, October 20, p. A18.

Stidsen, Sille (2007a). "Editorial," pp. 10–15. In Sille Stidsen (Ed.) *The Indigenous World 2007.* Copenhagen: International Work Group for Indigenous Affairs.

Stidsen, Sille (Ed.) (2007b). *The Indigenous World 2007.* Copenhagen: International Work Group for Indigenous Affairs.

Stoll, David (1993). *Between Two Armies in the Ixil Towns of Guatemala.* New York: Columbia University Press.

Stoll, David (1999). *Rigoberta Menchu and the Story of All Poor Guatemalans.* Boulder, CO: Westview Press.

Survival International (1988a). *Paraguay: World Bank Project Threatens Forest Indians.* Urgent Action Bulletin, UAB/PGY/2. London: Survival International.

Survival International (1990). *Ecuador: Oil Companies Force 700 Waorani off Their Land.* Urgent Action Bulletin, March 1990. London: Survival International.

Survival International (1991). *Indonesia: Paper Companies to Fell Tribal Forests.* Urgent Action Bulletin, April 1991. London: Survival International.

Survival International (1992). *Ecuador: Dallas Oil Company to Invade Waorani Land.* Urgent Action Bulletin, July 1992. London: Survival International.

Survival International (1993). *The Denial of Genocide.* London: Survival International.

Survival International (1996). *Mobil Threatens Uncontacted Indians in the Peruvian Amazon.* Urgent Action Bulletin, June 1996. London: Survival International.

Survival International (2000). *The EU and the World Bank: European and World Bank Policies—A Betrayal?* Urgent Action Bulletin, October 2000. London: Survival International.

Survival International (2005). *Rio Pardo. Brazil: Un-contacted Tribe Faces Genocide.* Urgent Action Bulletin, June 2005. London: Survival International.

Suzman, James. (1991) *An Introduction to the Regional Assessment of the Status of the San in Southern Africa.* Windhoek: Legal Assistance Centre.

Suzman, James (2001b). *An Assessment of the Status of San in Namibia.* Windhoek, Namibia: Legal Assistance Center.

Synott, John P. (1993). "Genocide and Cover-up Practices of the British Colonial System Against Australian Aborigines, 1788–1992." *Internet on the Holocaust and Genocide* 44–46:15–16.

Tatz, Colin (1991). "Australia's Genocide: They Soon Forget Their Offspring." *Social Education* 55(2):97–98.

Tatz, Colin (2003). *With Intent to Destroy: Reflecting on Genocide.* London and New York: Verso.

Taylor, John (2004). *Indigenous Peoples and Indicators of Well-Being: An Australian Perspective. Center for Aboriginal Economic Policy Research Working Paper No. 33.* Canberra: Center for Aboriginal Economic Policy Research, Australian National University.

Thornton, Russell (1987). *American Indian Holocaust and Survival: A Population History Since 1492*. Norman, OK: University of Oklahoma Press.

Totten, Samuel (1991). "Introduction," pp. xi–lxxv. In Samuel Totten (Compiler/Ed.) *First Person Accounts of Genocidal Acts Committed in the Twentieth Century: An Annotated Bibliography*. Westport, CT: Greenwood Press.

Totten, Samuel (2004). "The Intervention and Prevention of Genocide: Where There Is the Political Will, There is a Way," pp. 469–490. In Samuel Totten, William S. Parsons, and Israel W. Charny (Eds.) *Century of Genocide: Critical Essays and Eyewitness Accounts*. Second Edition. New York and London: Routledge.

Totten, Samuel, William S. Parsons, Jr. and Robert K. Hitchcock (2002). "Confronting Genocide and Ethnocide of Indigenous Peoples: An Interdisciplinary Approach to Definition, Intervention, Prevention, and Adequacy," pp. 54–91. In Alexander Labhan Hinton (Ed.) *Annihilating Difference: The Anthropology of Genocide*. Berkeley and Los Angeles: University of California Press.

Warren, Kay B. (1998). *Indigenous Movements and Their Critics: Pan-Maya Activism in Guatemala*. Princeton, NJ: Princeton University Press.

Weyler, Rex (1982). *Blood of the Land: The Government and Corporate War against the American Indian Movement*. New York: Vintage Books.

Whitley, Andrew (1994). "The Remains of Anfal." *Middle East Report* (July–August), pp. 8–11.

Wilkinson, Daniel (2002). *Silence on the Mountain: Stories of Terror, Betrayal, and Forgetting in Guatemala*. New York: Houghton Mifflin.

Willey, P. (1990). *Prehistoric Warfare on the Great Plains*. New York: Garland.

Wilmer, Franke (1993). *The Indigenous Voice in World Politics: Since Time Immemorial*. Newbury Park, California and London: Sage Publications.

Wishart, David J. (2001). "Belated Justice? The Indian Claims Commission and the Waitangi Tribunal." *American Indian Culture and Research Journal* 25(1):81–111.

Wolf, Eric (1982). *Europe and the People without History*. Berkeley and Los Angeles: University of California Press.

World Bank (2005a). "Operational Directive 4–10: Indigenous Peoples." In *World Bank Operational Manual*. Washington, D.C.: World Bank.

World Bank (2005b). "Bank Procedures 4–10: Indigenous Peoples." In *World Bank Operational Manual*. Washington, D.C.: Author.

Young, Elspeth (1995). *Third World in the First: Indigenous Peoples and Development*. London: Routledge.

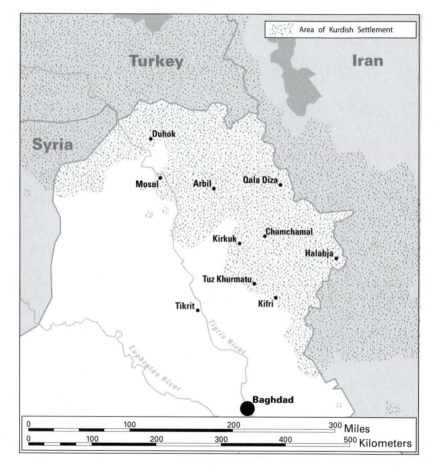

Iraqi Kurdistan

CHAPTER 14

The *Anfal* Operations in Iraqi Kurdistan

MICHIEL LEEZENBERG

Introduction

The 1988 *Anfal* ("Spoils") operations conducted by the Iraqi regime against part of its Kurdish population are among the best-documented cases of genocide. Ostensibly a counterinsurgency measure against Kurdish rebels, they in fact involved the deliberate killing of large numbers of noncombatants. Captured documents prove the regime's genocidal intent: they make abundantly clear that the government aimed at killing Kurdish civilians as such. Estimates of the number of civilian casualties vary from 50,000 to almost 200,000; the number of displaced or otherwise affected persons is far greater. Over 1000 Kurdish villages were destroyed in the operations, as were their livestock and orchards. The operations are characterized by an unusual degree of bureaucratic organization, centralized implementation, and secrecy. But because they are documented not only by eyewitness and survivor testimonies, but also by a vast number of captured Iraqi government documents, they provide one of the strongest and most unambiguous legal cases for a genocide tribunal.

Prior to the 2003 Iraq war, the chances for prosecution of the perpetrators were slim. The war itself was legitimized by Iraq's alleged (and as it turned out, imaginary) threat of weapons of mass destruction, rather than by its *actual* use of such weapons in the 1980s. Following the invasion and subsequent overthrow of the Baath regime, almost all

461

senior government members went into hiding; in due course, however, most of them were captured, notably those held to bear primary responsibility for the *Anfal* operations: former Iraqi president Saddam Hussein and his cousin, Ali Hasan al-Majid.

Although there is abundant and publicly accessible documentary evidence on the *Anfal*, little substantial research has been published since the publication of the Human Rights Watch 1995 report, *Iraq's Crime of Genocide*. Below, the factual account of the operations themselves is largely based on this indispensable study.

The Course of the Operations

In spring 1987, Iraq's predicament was bleak. In the first Gulf War, its enemy Iran appeared to be regaining momentum; in March, Iran had reopened its Northern front, in collusion with Iraqi Kurdish guerrillas. Moreover, in the course of 1987, the major Iraqi Kurdish parties, including the Kurdistan Democratic Party (KDP), headed by Massoud Barzani, and the Patriotic Union of Kurdistan (PUK), headed by Jalal Talabani, decided to join forces, ending their long-standing differences and years of infighting. The Kurds' tactical alliance with Iran posed a new threat to the Iraqi regime, which reacted by implementing increasingly drastic counterinsurgency measures. On March 29, Hussein promulgated decree no. 160, making Ali Hasan al-Majid director of the Baath Party's Directorate of Northern Affairs, which was responsible for the autonomous Kurdish region in Northern Iraq. Al-Majid, until then the director of General Security, was granted sweeping powers over all civilian, military, and security institutions of the region. He wasted no time in making use of them. In April, he ordered the first attacks, including chemical bombardments, not only against the PUK mountain headquarters but also against the Kurdish villagers and villages that could provide them with shelter and supplies. In this campaign alone, at least 703 Kurdish villages were destroyed.

After a few months, however, these operations were discontinued, possibly because the Iraqi army was too preoccupied with Iranian offensives. But al-Majid's June 1987 directives give a clear indication of what was to come. His document 28/3650, dated June 3, imposed both a total blockade and a shoot-on-sight policy on the areas outside government control: "The armed forces must kill any human being or animal present within these areas." Document 28/4008 of June 20 provides a standing order for the summary execution of all (male) captives: "Those between the ages of 15 and 70 shall be executed after any useful information has been obtained from them." These documents reaffirmed, and probably reinvigorated, standing Iraqi policies that had been in place since the late 1970s. Note: Both documents are reproduced in *Bureaucracy of Repression: The Iraqi Government in Its Own Words* (Human Rights Watch/Middle East, 1994).

The next organizational step towards *Anfal* was the nationwide census that was held on October 17, 1987. According to Human Rights Watch, this census was (at least in the Kurdish North) less a registration of population data than a sweeping government directive that not only identified the target population of the future operations, but also indiscriminately marginalized and criminalized it. All traffic to and from areas outside government control was forbidden, and relatives of alleged saboteurs were expelled from government-held areas. All individuals who consequently failed to participate in the census were stripped of their citizenship and were considered deserters or saboteurs who deserved the death penalty. It has not yet, however, been established beyond doubt precisely where these forbidden zones outside government control were located, how they were defined, and whether they coincided with the areas where the *Anfal* did in fact take place. At the time, only a few stretches of land in inaccessible mountain areas and along the border with Iran were wholly out of government reach.

The *Anfal* operations proper did not start until February 1988; presumably, by then, the Iraqi regime felt that Iranian pressure had eased sufficiently to allow for the redeployment of large numbers of troops in the North. They were conducted on a much larger scale and were of a much more systematic character than the spring 1987 operations: several army divisions participated in them, together with personnel of general intelligence and the Baath Party—and with Kurdish irregulars.

The first *Anfal* operation, starting February 23, was primarily directed against the PUK headquarters near the Iranian border, but also against the surrounding villages. Most villagers, however, appear to have escaped into Iran or to the larger cities of the Kurdish region in Iraq. Thus, whether by accident or design, the first *Anfal* does not appear to have involved the large-scale disappearance of civilians. This, however, was to change in the following operations.

In the following months, seven further operations were carried out, systematically targeting the different areas that had remained under Kurdish control. They typically involved the surrounding of the target area, which was then exposed to massive shelling and air attacks, including the use of chemical weapons. Apparently, these attacks were intended primarily to destroy the morale of the villagers and guerrillas (who had long become used to conventional bombardments). Next, with the target population dislodged, government forces would gradually encircle it and mount a massive ground attack by army troops and irregulars, or alternatively have the irregulars persuade the villagers to surrender.

The Kurdish captives were first brought to local collection points, mostly by Kurdish irregulars; subsequently, government personnel took them to centralized transit camps at military bases near Kirkuk, Tikrit, and Duhok. Here, they were divided by age and gender, and stripped of their remaining possessions. The vast majority of captured adult men were loaded onto windowless trucks and taken to execution sites in central Iraq. Several people, however, survived these mass executions. All of them report having seen rows of trenches dug by bulldozers, each holding hundreds of corpses. It is more than likely that tens of thousands of Kurdish male civilians were massacred in this way, merely on account of their Kurdish ethnicity and of their living in an area declared out of bounds by the regime.

Unknown numbers of women, children, and elderly are also suspected to have been massacred. More typically, however, women were left alive and relocated. There also is credible testimony that many younger women were sold off as brides, or rather into virtual slavery, to rich men elsewhere in Iraq, but also in Kuwait and Saudi Arabia. These reports were corroborated by a December 1989 document, which the Kurds claimed to have captured from Kirkuk's Directorate of Intelligence following the 2003 ousting of Hussein's regime. The memorandum to the Baghdad General Directorate of Intelligence, marked "Top Secret," states that a group of girls aged between 14 and 29 have been captured during the *Anfal* operations, and have been "sent to the harems and nightclubs of the Arab Republic of Egypt." (Note: A copy of the document and a partial translation can be found at www.kurdmedia.com/news.asp?id=4057.)

Many elderly captives were initially resettled in the Nuqrat al-Salman concentration camp in Southern Iraq. In the appalling living conditions there, up to 10 percent of the inmates may have died in the space of a few months. Often, corpses would be refused a proper burial and were left exposed in the summer heat (see Account 5 below).

On August 20, 1988, a cease-fire between Iran and Iraq came into effect. The Iraqi army now had its hands free to finish its campaign against the Kurdish insurgents. On August 25, it initiated the Final *Anfal*, directed against what remained of the traditional KDP strongholds in the Badinan region bordering on Turkey. This area was not entirely sealed off, however, and over 60,000 Kurds managed to escape to Turkey. Following this exodus, substantial eyewitness reports about the Iraqi regime's continuing chemical attacks against its Kurdish civilians reached the international community, along with earlier journalistic reporting on the Halabja attack (see below). Press coverage led to some minor and inconsequential protests by Western governments. Among others, the U.S. government failed to act on reports published by one of its own officials—U.S. Senate Foreign Relations Committee member Peter Galbraith. In international forums like the UN Security Council, the Iraqis avoided condemnation by cleverly manipulating remaining Cold War cleavages and existing fears of Iran.

The violence against the Kurdish civilian population did not end with the successful completion of the Final *Anfal*. Numerous refugees were lured back by the September 6 announcement of a general amnesty for all Iraqi Kurds, but many of them disappeared upon returning. The fate of the returning members of minority groups like the Yezidis and Assyrian Christians deserves particular mention. Unbeknown to themselves, these groups had been excluded from the amnesty by the government, which considered them Arabs rather than Kurds. Upon returning to Iraq, they were separated from the Muslim Kurds; many of them, including women, children, and elderly, were taken to unknown destinations and never seen again.

After the amnesty, the surviving deportees were brought back to the North and simply dumped on relocation sites near the main roads, surrounded by barbed-wire fences. Unlike the victims of most earlier deportations, they were not provided with any housing, construction materials, food, or medicine (let alone financial compensation), but just left to their own devices.

In the spring of 1989, al-Majid resigned as the Baath Party's Northern Bureau chief. To all appearances, the Kurdish insurgency had been solved once and for all. The major Kurdish parties had been thoroughly demoralized, and indeed discredited, by the government's brutal actions and faced fierce internal criticism because of their tactics, which had left the civilian population exposed to the Iraqi onslaught. Virtually the entire surviving rural Kurdish population had been violently pacified and relocated in easily controlled resettlement camps.

In these operations alone, an estimated 1200 Kurdish villages were destroyed. The number of civilian casualties has been variously estimated: Kurdish sources, based on extrapolations from the numbers of villages destroyed, at first spoke of some 182,000 people killed or missing. Human Rights Watch made a more conservative estimate of between 50,000 and 100,000 civilian dead. And during the spring 1991 negotiations between the Kurds and the government, the director of the operations, al-Majid, himself at one point exclaimed: "What is this exaggerated figure of 182,000? It could not have been more than a hundred thousand!"

Antecedents and Characteristics of the *Anfal*

Evidence

The *Anfal* operations formed the genocidal climax of the prolonged conflict between the successive Iraqi regimes and the Kurdish nationalist movement. But the extent of the atrocities at first escaped public notice. The most notorious event of this period, the widely publicized attack on Halabja in March 1988, was not part of the *Anfal* proper, although it reflected the same policies. The full scale and bureaucratic nature, and indeed full horror, of the operations did not become widely known until the aftermath of the 1991 Gulf War. In the popular uprising against the Iraqi regime, literally tons of documents from various government institutions were captured that provided ample, if partly indirect and circumstantial, evidence of the 1988 genocide. Although many questions remain unanswered, these documents, supplemented by the testimony of numerous eyewitnesses, provided ample evidence in the genocide trial against Saddam Hussein and his aides, which opened in August 2006.

The authenticity of these documents has been contested by the Iraqi government, but it is extremely unlikely that they are forgeries. They not only form a complex network of interlocking texts of a highly bureaucratic nature, but, in many cases, they closely match the testimony provided by eyewitnesses and survivors. References to government actions are often quite indirect or opaque; thus, few documents openly refer to mass executions or chemical weapons. Even internal documents usually euphemistically speak of "special attacks" and "special ammunition" when referring to chemical warfare, or of "return to the national ranks" when talking about surrender to government forces.

Organization and Implementation

Taken together, the testimony and the documentary evidence provide detailed insight into the chain of command and into the motives of the perpetrators. Among the personnel participating in them were the first, second, and fifth army divisions; General Security; and numerous members of the Baath Party, in particular those associated with the Northern Affairs Bureau, as well as irregular troops mostly provided by Kurdish tribal chieftains. The command was firmly in the hands of al-Majid, who acted as the head of the Baath Party's Northern Bureau, and who overruled all other authorities. It appears to have been the regional Baath Party apparatus, rather than the intelligence services, the police, or the army, that was at the heart of the operations. In all likelihood, the firing squads too consisted first and foremost of Party members.

There are significant differences in the execution of the successive operations. In the first *Anfal,* few noncombatants were "disappeared". In later operations, adult males were taken to mass execution sites far away from the Kurdish region. In the Final *Anfal,* captured men were often executed on the spot. Likewise, only in the operations in the Kirkuk region do women and children appear to have been executed. It is not clear whether such variations reflect an escalating logic of violence, a differentiated reaction to the degree of resistance encountered, or simply the whims of local field commanders.

The documents not only show a high degree of secrecy surrounding the operations, but also an extreme concentration of power, and the bureaucratic structure that made them possible. There are indications, for example, that military intelligence did not know precisely what was going on and that lower army officers on various occasions balked at the standing order to execute all captives. Among the Kurdish population at large, and also among Arab civilians and even among some government officials, there were a few but significant episodes of resistance or support for the victims. In the third *Anfal,* the local population of Chamchamal rose up in revolt against the deportation of villagers. During the fifth, resistance of the *peshmergas* (Kurdish guerrillas) turned out to be so strong that two further operations against the same area were mounted, keeping government forces occupied for over three months.

Especially in Arbil, the local urban population, at times at great personal risk to themselves, made a prolonged effort to help the deported villagers. Several survivors of the executions, notably Taymur ʿAbdallah from Kulajo near Kifri and Ako Izzedin Sayyid Ismael from Warani near Tuz Khormatu, were harbored by Iraqi army personnel or Arab tribesmen. (Note: For fragments of Taimour <Abdallah's testimony, see Account 3 below; for Ismael's story, see www.globeandmail.com/servlet/story/RTGAM.20030403.unolen0405/BNStory/International.) Unlike many other cases of genocide, then, the *Anfal* operations were made possible far less by mobilizing latent or open ethnic hatred among the population at large than by a highly efficient, centralized, and secret organization within the state apparatus.

In the operations, the Kurdish irregular troops, or *jash* ("donkey foal") as they are disparagingly called among Kurds, have played an important but ambiguous role. Formed in the early 1980s, as a means of relieving the Iraqi army in the northern countryside, numerous *jash* leaders, in fact, maintained contacts with the Kurdish insurgents. For many Kurds, enlisting as an irregular was a convenient means of escaping active front duty in the war with Iran (and of making a living). Other tribal leaders siding with the government, however, had their own accounts to settle with either the Kurdish parties, or with tribes and villages in nearby areas.

The Kurdish irregulars appear to have had a subordinate status among the personnel involved in the operations. They had a better knowledge of the mountainous territory than the regular security forces, and they could more easily persuade the population to surrender; but not all of them were wholly reliable in the implementation of al-Majid's orders.

It is unlikely that all irregular troops were equally well informed about the operations' true character. Apparently, many of them had merely been told to help in the rounding up of villagers for the purpose of relocation, and many also made a genuine effort to help the captives. Others, however, participated with glee in the rounding up of civilians and the looting of their possessions. In some cases, acts of clemency were simply bought by bribes. A better appreciation of the role of the *jash* is hampered to some extent by the fact that after the 1991 uprising in the North, all (powerful) government collaborators were granted a general amnesty by the Iraqi Kurdistan Front, and most of them continued to wield considerable power under the new Kurdish rulers.

Historical Forces and Trends Leading to the Genocide

As said, the *Anfal* operations were the result of highly centralized and secret government policies rather than widespread ethnic antagonisms that could easily be manipulated or mobilized for political purposes. Apart from the general repressive measures against the Kurds taken from the 1970s onwards, there are two well-documented precedents, or parallel cases, showing the Iraqi regime's readiness to resort to the killing of Kurds as such: the 1983 disappearance of Barzani clansmen and the 1988 chemical attack against Halabja. The background of both involves not only the armed Kurdish insurgency, but also the Iraqi war against Iran. After the 1975 collapse of the Kurdish front, hundreds of thousands of Kurdish villagers had already been deported to relocation camps or *mujamma'at*—their traditional dwellings having been destroyed and declared forbidden territory.

Thousands of members of the Barzani clan had been deported to Southern Iraq in 1976. In 1981, they had been relocated in the Qushtepe *mujamma'a* just south of Arbil; and then, in 1983, after Iran had captured the border town of Haj Omran with the aid of KDP guerrillas, the Iraqi government took its revenge on the Barzani clan. According to the then-speaker of the KDP, Hoshyar Zebari (at present Iraq's foreign minister), over 8,000 men were taken from the Qushtepe camp and never seen again; the remaining women were reduced to a life of abject poverty. Thus, government policies not only aimed at the physical elimination of

Kurds associated with disloyal elements, but also aimed at the symbolic destruction of the honor of both the male and female members of the proud Barzani tribe.

It is the March 16, 1988, chemical attack against the town of Halabja, in which an estimated 5,000 Kurdish civilians died a gruesome death, rather than the Anfal, that has entered collective memory as a symbol of the Iraqi repression of the Kurds. The attack was captured, if not symbolized, in the indelible image of a Kurdish father clutching his infant son, both killed by poison gas, shot by the Turkish-Kurdish photographer Ramazan Öztürk. Although the Halabja attack was not part of the *Anfal* operations proper (which only targeted rural areas, not cities), it, as previously noted, certainly follows the same destructive logic. It was prompted by the Kurdish-Iranian occupation of the city as an attempt to ease the pressure on the PUK headquarters, which at the time was bearing the brunt of the first *Anfal* operation. The chemical attack does not appear to have had any clear strategic aim, however; rather, it was in all likelihood meant as a warning or conducted as an act of revenge. After the attack, nothing happened to Halabja for several months. It was not until July 1988 that Iraqi troops reoccupied the city, which they then proceeded to demolish. The remaining population was relocated to "New Halabja" *mujammaʿa*, a few miles down the road.

The *Anfal* operations cannot simply be explained away as a drastic form of counterinsurgency; but, characterizing the mind-set that made them possible is no easy task. The question of whether, and how far, the *Anfal* operations were driven by racist animosity has not yet adequately been answered; but this question does not, of course, minimize in any way their criminal character. Racism does not appear to be a predominant feature of either Iraqi society, Baathist ideology, or the perpetrators' personalities. Although there have been, and are, occasional ethnic tensions among the different segments of the Iraqi population, there is relatively little grassroots racial hatred between Kurds and Arabs in Iraq. Even after the 2003 war, whatever tensions there were between Kurds, Arabs and Turkomans in the North paled in comparison with horrendous violence between Sunnis and Shiites in Baghdad; and this violence was mostly the work of urban gangs and militias, rather than of the population at large.

In official Baathist discourse, categories of loyalty, treason, and sabotage (which, ultimately, are of a Stalinist inspiration) are much more prominent than ethnic or racial terms; the latter appear to have been rather flexible items, given the Baath regime's at times rather arbitrary and voluntaristic way of creating and dissolving ethnic identities by bureaucratic fiat. And when overtly racist language was used, this typically concerned Iranians and Jews rather than Kurds. Baathist ideology is of an undeniably Arab nationalist character, but it has always been ambivalent as to the inclusion of Iraq's sizable Kurdish population. There are indications, however, that in the course of the 1980s, emphasizing one's Kurdish or other non-Arab ethnicity was in itself increasingly becoming a criminal offence, if not an act of treason. For example, smaller ethnic groups, like Yezidis, Christians, and Shabak, were forcibly registered as Arabs, and when they changed their ethnicity to "Kurdish" in the 1987 census, al-Majid had them deported and their villages destroyed.

It is even questionable whether al-Majid himself can be simply labeled a racist. On tape recordings of meetings with senior Party officials he can be heard speaking in a coarse and derogatory manner of Kurds, but his remarks hardly betray any generic hatred of Kurds as an inferior race; rather, he speaks of saboteurs and of uneducated villagers who "live like donkeys." Whatever such personal motives and animosities, official discourse consistently proclaimed both Kurds and Arabs as equal parts of the Iraqi people or nation, on condition of their political loyalty.

Religious considerations do not appear to have been a prime motivating or legitimating factor either. The name *Anfal*, or "Spoils," which comes from the eighth sura of the Quran, has little specifically religious significance here; rather, it appears to refer primarily to the right granted to the Kurdish irregulars involved in the operations to loot the possessions of the captured civilians. The Baath Party, which had ruled Iraq since 1968, is largely secular and was (and is) inspired more by 20th century ideologies and practices of Nazism and Stalinism than by any specifically Islamic tradition.

Of the violent and indeed murderous character of Baathist rule in Iraq, however, there can be no doubt at all. After the conclusion of the *Anfal* operations, only 673 Kurdish villages still stood in the whole of Iraqi Kurdistan. Over the years, the regime had demolished 4,049 villages. State violence had increasingly turned towards Kurdish cities. In June 1989, the city of Qala Diza, with a population of close to 100,000, which had not been targeted in the *Anfal* and was itself a site of relocation camps, was evacuated and destroyed. It is impossible to tell where this continuing process of repression and destruction would have led if it had not been interrupted by the 1990 Gulf Crisis and the ensuing war and uprising.

Responses to the *Anfal*

The Iraqi regime made a strong effort to keep the true nature of the operations entirely secret, or at least to maintain strict control over the flow of information. Throughout much of 1988, Iraqi radio proudly broadcast news of the "heroic *Anfal* campaigns," allegedly directed against saboteurs and collaborators of Iran; but these reports carefully avoided reference to the use of chemical weapons, the deportations and executions of civilians, and the razing of villages that accompanied the operations. On several occasions, victims of chemical attacks were dragged out of the nearby hospitals and disappeared; this may have been a form of collective punishment, but it is more likely that the regime was attempting to eliminate all eyewitnesses at this stage.

Despite several substantial investigations by journalists, academics, and parliamentary committees, the extent of international knowledge of, and indeed complicity in, Iraq's crimes still awaits assessment. Various European companies continued to supply Iraq with ingredients for chemical weapons, even at a time when its use of such weapons against the Iranian army was well documented. In the United States, the Reagan and Bush Sr. administrations actively supported Iraq with military advisors, equipment, and atropin (a familiar antidote to mustard gas), and blocked international diplomatic initiatives against Iraq. It is by now certain that the then U.S government had detailed knowledge about the campaign of destruction, of its scale, and of Iraq's systematic use of chemical weapons against its own civilians. Meiselas (1997) reproduces a Joint Chiefs of Staff document from the National Security Archives, dated August 4, 1987, which already speaks of a campaign coordinated by al-Majid, in which 300 villages had been destroyed, and of "the ruthless repression which also includes the use of chemical weapons" (pp. 312–13). Likewise, former U.S. military intelligence officer Rick Francona (1999), who served as a military advisor to the Iraqi regime in 1987 and 1988, asserts that his government was well aware of Iraq's use of chemical agents (in particular, nerve gas), not only against Iranian soldiers but also against its own civilians, but wished to prevent an Iranian victory at any price (cf. Hiltermann, 2007).

Interpretations of the *Anfal*

What little substantial research has been carried out on the *Anfal* operations seems to waver on how to qualify the attitude of the government that was responsible for them. As noted above, labels like "racist" or "fascist" have been used by Kurdish nationalist and foreign analysts; local Islamist voices point to the *Anfal* as evidence of the infidel (*kafir*) character of Hussein's regime. Such terms do not appear very helpful, however, in characterizing the animus that drove the operations. One thing seems clear, though: the *Anfal* operations were not the culmination of any pervasive or long-standing ethnic antagonisms between Kurdish and Arab population groups in Iraq, but the result of centralized and secretive government policies. Regarding the finer points of the character and significance of the *Anfal*, too little detailed information is available at present to allow for anything more than informed guesses.

Current Interest in the *Anfal*

The story of how the Iraqi regime managed to get away with these crimes remains to be told. From 1988 to the present, though, the moral and legal significance of the *Anfal* operations has tended to be overruled by political interests. In 1988, Iraq enjoyed near-impunity on the international stage because of its war with the universally disliked Iran, and because of the strategic and economic interests in Iraq of both Western and East Bloc countries. Following the 1991 uprising, massive and detailed evidence of the *Anfal* became available; this included captured government documents, eyewitness accounts, and forensic evidence. For years, Human Rights Watch tried in vain to have a genocide case against Iraq opened at the International Court of Justice, but no country was willing to initiate legal proceedings—which was probably due, in part, to a fear of jeopardizing their chances both on Iraq's potentially lucrative market and in the Arab world at large. In the United States, a campaign to have Hussein indicted for genocide and crimes against humanity, largely on the basis of the captured *Anfal* documents, was initiated in the late 1990s, but it was pursued erratically and appeared to reflect changing U.S. policies towards Iraq (not to mention domestic political rivalries) rather than any concern for the victims.

The U.S.-led war against Iraq in 2003 was legitimated primarily by Iraq's alleged possession of weapons of mass destruction, and hardly if at all by Iraq's actual use of those weapons against its own population. Moreover, the fact that some members of the George W. Bush (2000–2008) administration in the U.S. had in the 1980s actively supported the Iraqi regime, precisely when it committed its worst atrocities, made this administration's moral arguments for war less convincing.

The *Anfal* Trials

Information about the *Anfal* and about Iraq's use of chemical weapons had been gathered, at times at great personal risk, by the likes of the Kurdish researcher Shorsh Rasool, the British journalist Gwynne Roberts and the American diplomat Peter Galbraith; but it was the capture by Kurdish guerrilla forces of some 18 metric tones of documentary evidence in 1991 that provided the most compelling evidence for both the extent of and the genocidal intent behind the *Anfal* operations. It is unclear how much further material has been captured from the archives of government ministries, security agencies, and Party offices in the chaotic aftermath of the 2003 invasion, and in whose hands these documents are at present. Especially the archives of the security office in Kirkuk, which appears to have been the *Anfal*'s nerve center, would seem crucial, both for legal proceedings and for further research into the precise conduct and character of the operations.

In August 2003, Ali Hasan al-Majid was arrested; in December of the same year, Saddam was captured by American troops in cooperation with local forces. Following some legal wrangling as to when, where and how trials against these and other members of the former Baath regime should be held, it was decided to have them stand trial in Iraq itself, even though the country's judiciary was hardly prepared for such a massive and complicated operation. In October 2005, court proceedings against Saddam Hussein were initiated. The first trial centered exclusively around an isolated incident, the massacre of 148 Shiite men in reprisal for an assassination attempt against Saddam during a visit to the village of Dujail. Although minor in comparison with numerous other accusations, the Dujail case was relatively well supported by documentary evidence and eyewitness testimony, and promised a speedy condemnation.

In August 2006, the *Anfal* trial started against Saddam Hussein, Ali Hasan al-Majid, and several other defendants. Court proceedings were often tumultuous, and even involved the removal of the chief judge for alleged bias in favor of Saddam; but numerous survivors got a chance to testify against the former dictator. Although Saddam rarely denied the testimony brought against him outright, he repeatedly complained that he had not been given a chance to respond to the charges. He did not get to hear the documentary evidence, however: in the Dujail trial, the death penalty had been demanded, and Saddam Hussein was executed in December 2006; all remaining charges against him in the *Anfal* trial were dropped. Subsequently, in June 2007, Ali Hasan al-Majid was condemned to death, together with two others, for genocide, war crimes, and crimes against humanity.

International human rights organizations bemoaned the fact that Saddam was executed before he could properly be called to account for his role in the *Anfal* operations. The *Anfal* trials had many other flaws, not least the fact that they were conducted under continuing American occupation, which technically rendered them void under international law. Although there are few if any outright denials of the *Anfal*'s genocidal character, the murderous violence that emerged in post-2003 Iraq has likewise tended to distract attention from the enormity of the Baath regime's crimes. Because of these and other flaws, there is the risk that the *Anfal* trials may be remembered internationally, and especially in the Arab world, as a case of victor's rather than victim's justice.

There is some significant international judicial corroboration of the genocide claim, however. In December 2005, the Dutch merchant Frans van Anraat, who had sold chemicals to Iraq during the 1980s, was sentenced to 15 years for complicity in war crimes, in particular the March 1988 attack against Halabja. Although Van Anraat himself was cleared of genocide charges, the court ruled that the Halabja attack did in fact constitute an act of genocide. The international juridical implications of this ruling may be considerable.

Van Anraat's condemnation is only an isolated case, however; there are many other individuals, companies and government officials in numerous countries who still have much to answer for. Thus, in *A Poisonous Affair*, Joost Hiltermann deplores the fact the Reagan and Bush Sr. administrations have never been called to account for their tacit approval, if not active encouragement, of Iraq's use of chemical weapons. The full extent of international complicity in Saddam's numerous crimes is still far from adequately known, and may never be known in full; but to uncover this complicity in more detail, a sustained and concerted international effort will be necessary.

EYEWITNESS ACCOUNTS

As of yet, there is little available about the *Anfal* in the way of eyewitness evidence in Western languages. Important works, like Ziyad Abdulrahman's *Tuni Merg* (*Dungeon of Death*) and Shorsh Resool's *Dewlety Iraq u Kurd* (*The Iraqi State and the Kurds*), are available only in Kurdish. The main source for published accounts is, once again, Human Right Watch's *Iraq's Crime of Genocide* (1995), from which Accounts 2 and 5 below have been taken. In the future, further testimony that has served as the basis for this report may be made public. Other eyewitness accounts appear in Kanan Makiya's *Cruelty and Silence* (1993), especially the lengthy (and excruciating) interview with Abdallah, at first believed to be the sole survivor of the execution squads. (See Accounts 1 and 3.) Account 4 was recorded by the author and has not previously been published.

Account 1: The Chemical Attacks

This account by Abdallah Abdel-Qadir al-Askari, who survived the attack on Guptepe (or "Goktepe" according to HRW), provides a sense of the horrors of the chemical attacks. From Makiya's *Cruelty and Silence* (p. 135). Note: For additional testimony from al-Askari, see Human Rights Watch, *Iraq's Crime of Genocide*, 1995, pp. 118, 142, 154–5, 156–7.

On the evening of May 3 [1988] the situation in my village, Guptapa, was not normal. We had heard that the regime was preparing a chemical attack, but we didn't know when they would strike. It felt like there were unusual army maneuvers. Late in the afternoon with my brother-in-law and two friends—both teachers like myself—I climbed from our farm, which is on lower ground, to the highest point of the village. We wanted to see what was going on. Two inspection planes flew over. They threw out flares to determine the direction of the wind. Then another group of planes came, we think about 18 of them. The explosions were not very loud, which made me guess they were chemical bombs. When we raised our heads, we saw the sandy brown and grey clouds billowing upward. My background as a chemist left me in no doubt this was a chemical attack.

We climbed to the highest spot possible even though the wind was taking the gas away in the opposite direction. From there I shouted down to the people in the village: "This is a chemical attack! Try to escape! Come up the hill, come up here!" A lot of people did come to where we were and were saved. But a lot remained in the areas affected by the chemicals.

We discussed what to do. I thought we should wait ten or fifteen minutes, then go down. If we went at once, we too would be in danger and unable to help the others. But my friends wouldn't listen. So, we went down to the back of the village where the gases had not permeated and a lot of people were gathered. Some were very disturbed; one man shouted at me, "You have lost everybody; they are all killed. They have been bombing your house." This made me worried; I wanted to go back to my house but we hadn't waited long enough. Only three minutes had passed of the time I had fixed in my mind as the minimum.

The poison used in Guptapa in my opinion wasn't a single gas; it was composed of several gases. The combination affects the muscles, making them rigid and inflexible. In two minutes it can kill a person.

Finally I could run to my house. It was 20 minutes before sunset. When I got there it was entirely dark, but I found a small flashlight. First I put on a gas mask to protect myself. Then I went to the shelter which I had prepared for just such an eventuality. My wife knew that this was where the family should hide in case of chemical attack. Nobody was there. I became really afraid—convinced that nobody had survived. I climbed up from the shelter to a cave nearby, thinking they might have taken refuge there. There was nobody there, either. But when I went to the small stream near our house, I found my mother. She had fallen by the river; her mouth was biting into the mud bank.

All the members of my family had been running toward this stream because I had told them that water is good against chemical weapons. By the time they reached the stream, a lot of them had fainted and fallen into the water. Most of them had drowned. I turned my mother over; she was dead. I wanted to kiss her but I knew that if did, the chemicals would be passed on. Even now I deeply regret not kissing my beloved mother.

I continued along the river. I found the body of my 9-year-old daughter hugging her cousin, who had also choked to death in the water. Then I found the dead body of another niece, with her father. I continued along the stream. I found a woman who wasn't from our family and heard a child groan under her. Turning the woman over, I found the child; the water had almost reached him. I took the boy's clothes off, took him inside, and bundled him up in other clothes.

Then I went around our house. In the space of 200 to 300 square meters I saw the bodies of dozens of people from my family. Among them were my children, my brothers, my father, and my nieces and nephews. Some of them were still alive, but I couldn't tell one from the other. I was trying to see if the children were dead. At that point I lost my feelings. I didn't know who to cry for anymore and I didn't know who to go to first. I was all alone at night.

I saw one of my brothers: his head was tilted down a slope. My wife was still alive beside him, and my other brother was on the other side. My two daughters, the 6-month-old baby and the 4-year-old, were both dead. I tried to move them, to shake them. There was no response. They were both dead. I just knew they were dead.

My brothers and my wife had blood and vomit running from their noses and mouths. Their heads were tilted to one side. They were groaning. I couldn't do much, just clean the blood and vomit from their mouths and noses and try in every way to make them breathe again. I did artificial respiration on them and then I gave them two injections each. I also rubbed creams on my wife and two brothers. After injecting them, I had a feeling they were not going to die.

Our family has 40 members. I mean, it did. Now, of that big family we have only 15 left. Twenty-five of the beloved people of our family are dead. Among those were my five children.

Account 2: The Transit Camps

After being gathered at local camps, deportees were taken to centralized camps further south in Iraq. Here, they were primarily in the hands of the security forces or the Party apparatus. From Human Rights Watch, *Iraq's Crime of Genocide*, 1995, pp. 147.

On the first morning, they separated the men into small groups and beat them. Four soldiers would beat one captive. The other prisoners could see this. About 15 or 20 men were in each group that was taken a little way off to be kicked and beaten with sticks and [electric] cables. They were taken away in the early morning and returned in the afternoon. The soldiers did not gather the men by name, but just pointed, you, and you, and so on. They were Amn from Tikrit and Kirkuk—butchers, we know them. When one group of beaten men returned, they took another and beat them. That night, I was in a group of ten or twelve men that was taken out and blindfolded with our hands tied behind us. They took us in three or four cars to somewhere in Tikrit. We drove around all night, barely stopping. They asked me no questions. The captured men could not talk to one another. Everyone was thinking of his own destiny. Of the ten or twelve they took out that night, only five returned.

The next night, when I was back in the hall, Amn came and asked for men to volunteer for the war against Iran. Eighty men volunteered. But it was a lie; they disappeared. A committee was set up by Amn to process the prisoners, who were ordered to squat while the Amn agents took all their money and put it in a big sack. They also took all our documents. The Amn agents were shouting at us to scare us. "Bring weapons to kill them," said one. "They are poor, don't shoot them," said another. And another: "I wish we had killed all of them."

Later that night the Amn came back and took all the young men away. Only the elderly remained. The young men were taken away in Nissan buses, ten or more of them, each with a capacity of 45 people. Their documents had already been taken. They left nothing but the clothes on their backs.

Account 3: The Execution Sites

This account comes from the extraordinary testimony of Taimour Abdallah, who was taken to an execution site near the Saudi border, but managed to escape, albeit wounded. Although he did not speak any Arabic, he found refuge with a Shiite Arab family, and eventually managed to return to the Kurdish-held North. From Makiya's *Cruelty and Silence* (1993), pp. 185, 191–92, 195.

Note: Part of his testimony also appears in Gwynne Roberts' 1992 BBC television documentary, "The Road to Hell," which was aired in the United States as "Saddam's Killing Fields." See Chapter 9 ("The Firing Squads") in Human Rights Watch, *Iraq's Crime of Genocide*, 1995, pp. 160–74. See also the story of another *Anfal* survivor, Ako Izeddin Sayyid Ismael from Warani near Tuz Khormatu (*The Globe and Mail*, April 3, 2003) (full text at www.fas.harvard.edu/~irdp/reports/taimour.html).

Q: What happened when you reached the prison of Topzawa in Kirkuk?

A: When we arrived, they put women and children in one hall and the men in another.

Q: In which group did they put you?
A: I was with my mother and my sisters.

Q: Did you see your father again after being separated?
A: I saw him once more in Topzawa and then I didn't see him again.

Q: What was happening when you saw him?
A: They were taking off his clothes except for the underclothes. They manacled his hands and then they put all the men in the lorries and drove them away.

Q: After that you never saw your father again?
A: No. [p. 185]

Q: What happened next?
A: ... Just before reaching the place of the shooting, they first let us off the lorries and blindfolded us and gave us a sip of water. Then they made us go back inside. When we arrived, they opened the door, and I managed to slip aside my blindfold. I could see this pit in the ground surrounded by soldiers.

Q: Were your hands tied?
A: No.

Q: When they opened the door of the lorry, what was the first thing you saw?
A: The first thing I saw was the pits, dug and ready.

Q: ... How many pits did you see?
A: It was night, but around us there were many.

Q: Four or five holes?
A: No, no, it was more.

Q: More than five, six, seven holes?
A: Yes, yes.

Q: Describe your pit.
A: The pit was like a tank dugout. They put us in that kind of a hole.

Q: They pushed you directly off the truck into the pit?
A: Yes.

Q: How high was it? One meter? Two meters? Could you stand up inside?
A: It was high.

Q: How high?
A: Up to the sash of a man.

Q: How many people were put inside?
A: One pit to every truck.

Q: And how many people were on a truck?
A: About 100 people.

Q: Was it just a massive hole?
A: It was rectangular.

Q: Was it cut very precisely by a machine?
A: By bulldozers as you would make a pit for a tank. [pp. 191–2]

Q: . . . Did you look into the soldier's face?
A: Yes.

Q: Did you see his eyes?
A: Yes.

Q: What did you see? What could you read in his eyes, in the expression on his face?
A: He was about to cry, but the other one shouted at him and told him to throw me back in the pit. He was obliged to throw me back.

Q: He cried!
A: He was about to cry.

Q: How far away was the officer who shouted?
A: He was close to him.

Q: The soldier who pushed you back into the hole, was he the one who shot you the second time?
A: Yes. This soldier shot me again after he received the order from the officer who was standing beside the pit. When he shot me the second time I was wounded here [he points] (p. 195).

Account 4: Deportations to Nuqrat al-Salman

This is the testimony of a 78-year-old man, originally from a village in the Qaradagh area, who had been resettled in Takiya *mujamma'a* near Chamchamal. From author's interview, Takiya *mujamma'a*, spring 1992; previously unpublished.

In our village alone, six people were executed on the spot by government troops; in the neighbouring village, they shot 18 people. When they took us away from our village, we were not allowed to take anything with us—not even cigarette paper. After half a year, about 500 of us, mostly the sick and the elderly, were allowed to return. Here I have the document from the camp, saying that I am allowed to go back together with my wife and daughter. At the bottom, they have added "We have done what we had been told to do" in handwriting. Of another family of nine from our village, only the parents and a young daughter have returned. There is no news about the other six. Nobody knows what has happened to the children. They say that the truck drivers who brought them away have all been shot. Nobody knows whether there are still people in the Nuqrat al-Salman camp today, but they cannot possibly be alive after four years in that heat. People were too weak, too tired and too hungry even to bury their dead. I've heard that sometimes corpses were left lying exposed, only to be eaten by stray dogs.

Now, we are in the Takiya *mujamma'a*, but we have nothing to live from. There is one cow here, but it is not ours; we can only use its milk. We are too old to work now, and all our belongings have been stolen by the government. After the 1991 uprising, the government in reprisal stopped the supply of cheap foodstuffs here. We are still afraid of them; the day before yesterday, they shelled the *mujamma'a* with their artillery fire. They can come back anytime they like. The *peshmergas* can't defend us against their heavy arms and armoured cars. Some people tried to return to their villages near the front lines, but their houses have been bombed again soon after they had been rebuilt.

Account 5: Ali Hasan al-Majid

From Human Rights Watch, *Iraq's Crime of Genocide*, 1995, p. 254. Note: Tape dated May 26, 1988, but according to HRW more likely from 1987.

Jalal Talabani asked me to open a special channel of communication with him. That evening I went to Suleimaniyah and hit them with the special ammunition. That was my answer. We continued the deportations. I told the *mustashars* that they might say that they like their villages and that they won't leave. I said I cannot let your village stay because I will attack it with chemical weapons. Then you and your family will die. You must leave right now. Because I cannot tell you the same day that I am going to attack with chemical weapons. I will kill them all with chemical weapons! Who is going to say anything? The international community? Fuck them! The international community and those who listen to them.

... This is my intention, and I want you to take serious note of it. As soon as we complete the deportations, we will start attacking them everywhere according to a systematic military plan. Even their strongholds. In our attacks we will take back one third or one half of what is under their control. If we can try to take two thirds, then we will surround them in a small pocket and attack them with chemical weapons. I will not attack them with chemical weapons for just one day, but I will continue to attack them with chemicals for 15 days. Then I will announce that anyone who wishes to surrender with his gun will be allowed to do so. I will publish 1 million copies of this leaflet and distribute it in the North, in Kurdish, Sorani, Badinani and Arabic. I will not say it is from the Iraqi government. I will not let the government get involved. I will say it is from here [the Northern Bureau]. Anyone willing to come back is welcome, and those who do not return will be attacked again with new, destructive chemicals. I will not mention the name of the chemical because that is classified information. But I will say with new destructive weapons that will destroy you. So I will threaten them and motivate them to surrender. Then you will see that all the vehicles of God himself will not be enough to carry them all. I think and expect that they will be defeated. I swear that I am sure we will defeat them.

References

Fischer-Tahir, Andrea (2003). *"Wir gaben viele Märtyrer:" Wiederstand und kollektive Identitätsbildung in Irakisch-Kurdistan.* Unrast Verlag.

Francona, Rick (1999). *Ally to Adversary: An Eyewitness Account of Iraq's Fall From Grace.* Annapolis, MD: US Naval Institute Press.

Galbraith, Peter (2006). *The End of Iraq.* New York: Simon & Schuster.

Hiltermann, Joost (2007). *A Poisonous Affair: America, Iraq, and the Gassing of Halabja.* New York: Cambridge University Press.

Human Rights Watch/Middle East (1994). *Bureaucracy of Repression: The Iraqi Government in Its Own Words.* New York: Author.

Human Rights Watch/Middle East (1995). *Iraq's Crime of Genocide: The Anfal Campaign Against the Kurds.* New Haven, CT: Yale University Press.

Makiya, Kanan (1993). *Cruelty & Silence: War, Tyranny, Uprising, and the Arab World.* New York: W.W. Norton.

Meiselas, S. (1997). *Kurdistan in the Shadow of History.* New York: Random House.

WEBSITES:

http://www.hrw.org/reports/1993/iraqanfal/
Human Rights Watch site from which the original 1993 report and other documents on the *Anfal* can be downloaded.

http://bbcnews.com/
BBC news archive featuring timelines of Saddam Hussein's and Ali Hasan al-Majid's trials, background information on the *Anfal*, and much more about post-war Iraq.

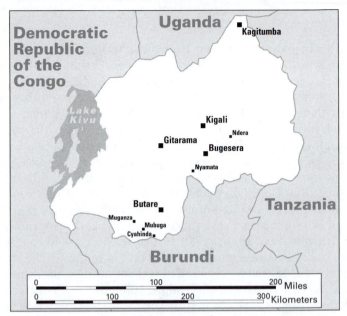

Rwanda

CHAPTER 15

The 1994 Rwanda Genocide

RENÉ LEMARCHAND

Since April 1994 Rwanda has become a synonym for one of the worst genocides of the 20th century. An estimated half a million people, mostly Tutsi, were killed in the course of a carnage that claimed twice as many victims in one month as the Bosnian civil war in two years. To this must be added almost as many deaths caused by military engagements, cholera, dysentery, famine, and sheer human exhaustion.

As much as the appalling scale of the bloodletting, it is the element of planned annihilation that gives the Rwanda killings their genocidal quality. The parallel with the 1972 genocide in Burundi immediately comes to mind (see Chapter 10, "The Burundi Genocide"). Although the threats to the ruling ethnocracies—the Hutu in Rwanda, the Tutsi in Burundi—came from identifiable groups of armed opponents, in the end entire civilian communities became the targets of ethnic cleansing (i.e., large-scale ethnic massacres)—the Hutu in Burundi, the Tutsi in Rwanda. In both states, the enemy was demonized, made the incarnation of evil, and dealt with accordingly; in both instances, the killings were planned and orchestrated from above, and owed little or nothing to a supposedly spontaneous outburst of anger from below.

Where Rwanda differs from Burundi is not just that the "rebels" happen to be Tutsi, but Tutsi refugees, or sons of refugees, who were driven out of the country in the wake of the 1959–1962 Hutu-led revolution. Few would have imagined that 30 years later the sons of the refugee diaspora in Uganda would form the nucleus of a Tutsi-dominated

politico-military organization—the *Front Patriotique Rwandais* (FPR)—
that would successfully fight its way back into the country and defeat an
army three times its size. Fewer still would have anticipated the price of
their victory. Between the FPR invasion on October 1, 1990, and the fall
of the capital (Kigali) on July 4, 1994, the killings wiped out one tenth of
Rwanda's population of 7 million.

Seen in the broader context of 20th century genocides, the Rwanda
tragedy underscores the universality—one might say the "normality"—
of African phenomena. The logic that set in motion the infernal machine
of the Rwanda killings is indeed no less "rational" than that which presided over the extermination of millions of human beings in Hitler's
Germany or Pol Pot's Cambodia. The implication, lucidly stated by
Helen Fein (1994), is worth bearing in mind: "Genocide is preventable
because it is usually a rational act; that is, the perpetrators calculate the
likelihood of success, given their values and objectives" (p. 5).

Mythologies

It is imperative to explode the myths surrounding the Rwanda genocide.
Contrary to the image conveyed by the media, there is nothing in
the historical record to suggest a kind of tribal meltdown rooted in
"deep-seated antagonisms," or "long-standing atavistic hatreds." Nor
is there any evidence in support of the "spontaneous action from
below" thesis. From this perspective, the killings are largely reducible
to a collective outburst of blind fury set off by the shooting down of
President Juvenal Habyarimana's plane on April 6, 1994. However widespread, both views are travesties of reality. What they mask is the political
manipulation that lies behind the systematic massacre of innocent
civilians.

It is not my intention to dispose of one myth by promulgating
another—the fantasy of a precolonial society where Hutu and Tutsi lived
in an eternally blissful harmony. Precolonial Rwanda was unquestionably
one of the most centralized and rigidly stratified societies in the Great
Lakes Region. Representing approximately 85 percent of a total population estimated at 2 million at the turn of the century, the Hutu peasants
were clearly at the bottom of the heap, socially, economically and politically; but if power, status, and wealth were generally in Tutsi hands, not
every Tutsi was powerful and wealthy.

Inequality was inscribed in the differential treatment accorded to each
group, and within each group. Nonetheless, Hutu and Tutsi shared the
same language and culture; the same clan names, the same customs, and
the symbols of kingship served as a powerful unifying bond between
them. Nor was conflict necessarily more intense or frequent between

Hutu and Tutsi than between Tutsi and Tutsi. Much of the historical evidence suggests precisely the opposite (Vidal, 1991).

Although the potential for conflict existed long before the advent of European rule, it was the Belgian colonial state that provided the crucible within which ethnic identities were reshaped and mythologized. The result was to drastically alter the norms and texture of traditional Rwanda society. It was the colonial state that destroyed the counter-vailing mechanisms built around the different categories of chiefs and subchiefs, thus adding significantly to the oppressiveness of Tutsi rule. It was the colonial state that insisted on individuals carrying an identity card specifying their ethnic background, a practice perpetuated until 1994, when "tribal cards" often spelled the difference between life and death. It was with the blessings of the colonial state that Christian missionaries began to speculate about the "Hamitic" origins of the kingdom, drawing attention to the distinctively Ethiopian features, and hence the foreign origins, of the Tutsi "caste" (Linden, 1977). Indirect rule, synonymous with Tutsi rule, found added legitimacy in the Hamitic lucubrations of Christian clerics; and, they eventually provided the ideological ballast of the Hutu revolution, before reappearing in 1994 in the form of a violently anti-Tutsi propaganda.

The Legacy of Revolution

After decades of unrelenting support of Tutsi rule, Belgian policies underwent a radical shift in the mid-1950s (Lemarchand, 1970). Partly in response to pressure from the UN Trusteeship Council, and partly as a result of the arrival in Rwanda of a new generation of Catholic mission-aries, imbued with the ideals of Christian Democracy, a sustained effort was made to extend educational opportunities to an increasing number of Hutu elements. This radical policy shift provoked immediate resist-ance from the custodians of Tutsi supremacy—i.e., chiefs, subchiefs, and Tutsi intellectuals generally—while prompting educated Hutu elements to press their claims for social reform upon the trusteeship authorities.

Ethnic violence suddenly erupted in November 1959, in the form of a Hutu *jacquerie* directed against Tutsi chiefs. Hundreds of people were killed on both sides of the ethnic fault line. Though quickly brought under control by the intervention of Belgian troops, the rural uprising marked the first phase of a revolutionary process culminating in January 1961 with a Hutu-led, Belgian-assisted coup that formally abolished the monarchy and led to the proclamation of a de facto republican regime under Hutu rule. By the time Rwanda acceded to independence on July 1, 1962, some 200,000 Tutsi had been forced into exile, the majority seeking asylum in Uganda, Burundi, and Zaire. Not until 32 years and a million deaths later would the destiny of Rwanda be once again entrusted to Tutsi hands.

The Hutu revolution constitutes a critical element in the background of the genocide: by forcibly displacing tens of thousands of Tutsi from their homeland—now in a homeless limbo and determined to go back to their country, by force if necessary—the revolution planted the seeds of the refugee-warrior militancy that led to the creation of the FPR in 1990 (Reyntjens, 1993). By the same token, to the extent that the Hutu revolution came to be identified with a "democratic," "anti-feudal" mass movement, its enemies could only be described in opposite terms, as feudal counter-revolutionaries bent upon restoring minority rule. It is not by accident that, during the killings, the Tutsi were collectively identified by Hutu ideologues with the "Feudo-Hamitic" enemy.

The Ideology of Genocide

The root cause of the Rwanda genocide lies in the extent to which collective identities have been mythologized and manipulated for political advantage. Today Hutu and Tutsi are not just ethnic labels; rather, they are social categories that carry an enormous emotional charge. Tutsi are seen by many Hutu as culturally alien to Rwanda, their presence traceable to "Hamitic invaders from the north" who used ruse and cunning—gifts of cattle and beautiful women—to enslave the unsuspecting Hutu agriculturalists. Only the Hutu—that is, the Bantu people, as distinct from the Hamites—qualify as authentic Rwandans. That such portrayals are at odds with every shred of evidence available is immaterial. The point is that they are critical elements in the cognitive map of Hutu ideologues. The Hamitic frame of reference is central to an understanding of the ideology of genocide. This is where the legacy of missionary historiography—evolving from speculation about cultural affinities between Hamites and Coptic Christianity to politicized dogma about the Ethiopian origins of the Tutsi—contributed a distinctly racist edge to the discourse of Hutu politicians.

Already the ideological stock-in-trade of Hutu revolutionaries in the 1950s, official references to the Hamitic peril gained renewed salience in the wake of the FPR invasion. The attack on Kagitumba on October 1, 1990, suddenly gave ominous credibility to the image of the Tutsi as an alien invader: Did they not invade the country from the north, like their forefathers, this time with arms and ammunition provided by Uganda? Is it not the case that many of the soldiers enlisted in the ranks of the FPR were born in Uganda, and that its leaders had close ties with President Museveni of Uganda, whose Hima origins are sufficient proof of his Hamitic sympathies? And, with characteristic cunning, did they not try to dupe President Habyarimana into accepting the Arusha Accords, which, if implemented, would have posed a mortal threat to the democratic heritage of the Hutu revolution?

What emerges from the incitements to violence distilled by Radio Mille Collines and other vectors of Hutu propaganda is an image of the Tutsi as both alien and clever—not unlike the image of the Jew in Nazi propaganda. His alienness disqualifies him as a member of the national community; his cleverness turns him into a permanent threat to the unsuspecting Hutu. Accordingly, nothing short of physical liquidation can deal with such danger.

The Road to Apocalypse

With the birth of several opposition parties in 1991, a whole new set of actors entered the political arena, adding an entirely new dimension to the security threats posed by the FPR invasion. For the first time since the Hutu revolution of 1959, the circumstances were ripe for a strategic alliance between the enemies from within and those from without.

Predictably, this convergence of external and internal threats generated intense fears within the ruling party, the *Mouvement Revolutionnaire National pour le Developpement* (MRND). At stake was not just the monopoly of power exercised by the party leadership, or even the structure of Hutu domination, but the political survival of a regime entirely controlled by northern Hutu elements. It is worth remembering in this connection that during much of the First Republic (1962–1973), power lay in the hands of Hutu politicians from the south-central regions; not until the coup of July 1973, instigated by Major-General Juvenal Habyarimana, and the proclamation of the Second Republic (1973–1994), did the northerners emerge as the dominant force in the government, the administration, the Party, and the army.

Given the nature of their ethno-regional underpinnings, and shared resentment of northern Hutu rule, it is hardly surprising that the three major opposition parties—the ethnically mixed *Parti Liberal* (PL), the *Parti Social Democrate* (PSD), and the *Mouvement Democratique Republicain* (MDR)—should have been perceived by MRND hard-liners as potential allies of the FPR, and therefore as presumptive traitors: the PL because of its mixed Hutu—Tutsi membership, the PSD and MDR because they drew much of their support from the Hutu masses of the south-central regions.

In this three-cornered politico-military struggle, the Tutsi civilian populations became political pawns. Courted by the PL, solicited for cash and food (and sometimes threatened) by the FPR, thoroughly distrusted by the MRND, a good many Tutsi ended up joining hands with the FPR because they felt they had no other option. Official suspicions that every Tutsi, by ethnic definition, harbored pro-FPR sympathies created the conditions of a self-fulfilling prophecy. The wholesale slaughter of hundreds of Bagogwe (a Tutsi subgroup) in northern Rwanda in January 1991, followed by the cold-blooded murder of thousands of Tutsi civilians in the Bugesera region in March 1992, set off a pattern of localized ethnic cleansing that went on almost uninterruptedly in the months preceding the genocide.

Anti-Tutsi violence increased in proportion to the magnitude of the threats posed by the FPR, but also as a result of the organizational steps taken to counter such threats. Reference must be made here to the massive recruitment and training of Hutu militias. Known in Kinyarwanda as *interahamwe* ("those who stand together"), they were ostensibly organized to protect civilians against FPR attacks; their real function, however, was to serve as a paramilitary force trained to provide auxiliary slaughterhouse support to the police, the *gendarmerie*, and the regular army. While the interahamwe came to be identified with the MRND, another group, the *impunza mugambi* ("the single-minded ones"), linked up with an even more fanatically anti-Tutsi party, the *Coalition pour la Defense de la Republique* (CDR). On the eve of the genocide the militias claimed a total membership of 50,000.

Most of the militias were recruited from among the vast pool of Hutu internally displaced persons (IDPs) driven from their homes by the advance of the FPR in the north. On the eve of the genocide about 1 million of the IDPs were registered in the whole of Rwanda, living in 40 IDP camps, for the most part in extremely harsh conditions. The IDPs, according to James Gasana (2000), who once served as minister of defense in the Habyarimana government, "were explicitly targeted by the FPR rebellion, expelled from their homes and continuously shot at in the camps to force them to move farther into the government-controlled zone. Families were separated and scattered—health centers were overwhelmed, mortality increased; suspension of schooling and lack of occupation for the young led to increased delinquency and crime" (p. 12). It is hardly a matter of coincidence that among the scores of young thugs manning the checkpoints in the capital, the vast majority were recruited among the IDPs of the Nyacinga camp, near Kigali. Seething hatred of every Tutsi in sight is what lay behind the scenes of mayhem in Kigali, Butare, and Gikongoro.

By 1992 the institutional apparatus of genocide was already in place. It involved four distinctive levels of activity or sets of actors:

1. The so-called *akazu* ("little house" in Kinyarwanda), consisting of Habyarimana's wife (Agathe), his three brothers-in-law (Protais

Zigiranyirazo, Seraphim Rwakumba, and Elie Sagatwa), and a sprinkling of trusted advisers. This core group was directly responsible for planning and orchestrating the genocide.

2. The rural organizers: recruited among communal and prefectoral personnel—i.e., *prefets, sous-prefets, bourgmestres, conseillers communaux*, etc.—and numbering anywhere from 300 to 500. They supplied the middle-level cadres in charge of engineering and supervising the killings in the communes.

3. The militias (*interahamwe*), often operating in tandem with the police and the *gendarmerie*, formed the ground-level operatives in charge of doing the actual killing. Many also played a key role in "persuading" (at gunpoint) Hutu civilians to kill their Tutsi neighbors. Although the term came to designate a variety of self-appointed killers, the core group has been described as "forming up to 1 or 2 percent of the population; they killed out of conviction; they were trained to kill, they often smoked hashish and are thought to have killed between 200–300 people each" (Physicians for Human Rights, 1994, p. 11).

4. The presidential guard, numbering approximately 6,000 and recruited exclusively among northerners, were trained specifically to assist civilian death squads. The systematic killing of opposition figures, Hutu and Tutsi, in the days immediately following the crash of the presidential plane, on April 6, 1994, was essentially the work of the presidential guard.

The sociological profile of the killers reflects the diversity of their social and institutional ties. Especially noteworthy, however, is the number of intellectuals and professional people who participated in the slaughter. Despite many exceptions to the rule, one cannot fail to notice the number of journalists, medical doctors, agronomists, teachers, university lecturers, and even priests who were identified by survivors as accomplices in the massacre of innocent civilians. At the other end of the social spectrum were the hundreds and thousands of landless Hutu peasants and unemployed city youth whose prime motivation for killing was to steal their victims' property, their land, their furniture, their radio, or what little cash they happened to carry.

What set in motion the wheels of this infernal machine was complex, a sequence of events that began with the Arusha Accords conference in Tanzania (June 1992–August 1993) and ended with the shooting down of President Habyarimana's plane in April 1994.

Although compromise was the very essence of the power-sharing formula hammered out at Arusha—whereby the FPR would have as many seats in the transitional government and legislature as the MRND, and would contribute 40 percent of the troops and 50 percent of the officer corps to the new Rwandan army—for the hard-liners within the party and the *akazu*, this was tantamount to betrayal. By instigating ethnic violence on a substantial scale in several localities, MRND/CDR extremists had every intention to derail the peace process. The wanton killing of innocent civilians thus became the quickest way of eliminating all basis for compromise with the FPR.

The decisive event that played directly into the hands of the extremists and sounded the death knell of the Arusha Accords, however, was the assassination of Burundi President Melchior Ndadaye on October 21, 1993. As the first popularly elected Hutu president in the history of Burundi, his election brought to a close 28 years of Tutsi hegemony, and this after a transition widely described by outside observers as "exemplary" (Lemarchand, 1994). His death at the hands of an all-Tutsi army had an immediate and powerful effect on the Hutu of Rwanda. The message came through loud and clear: "You simply cannot trust the Tutsi!" With Ndadaye's death vanished what few glimmers of hope remained that Arusha might pave the way for a lasting compromise with the FPR.

The shooting down of Habyarimana's plane, on April 6, 1994, on a return flight from a regional summit in Dar-es-Salaam, must be seen as the critical turning point in the sequence of events leading to the blood-bath. On board were not one but two Hutu presidents, Habyarimana and Cyprien Ntaramyira of Burundi, thus bringing to three the number of Hutu presidents killed in six months. Among other passengers killed in the crash were Burundi ministers Bernard Ciza and Cyriaque Simbizi, Major General Déogratias Nsabimana, Rwanda's Chief of Staff, Juvénal Renzaho, presidential advisor and former ambassador to Germany, Colonel Elie Sagatwa, the president's brother-in-law and special counselor, Major Thaddée Bagaragaza, head of the presidential guard, and Dr. Emmanuel Akingeneye, Habyarimana's personal physician.

Despite continuing speculation by some analysts of an *akazu*-sponsored plot intended to eliminate the "moderates," there is growing evidence to suggest that Kagame was indeed the central actor behind the crash. (Editor's note: There, in fact, continues to be speculation that various actors might have planned and carried out the downing of the plane. Among those under suspicion are: the akazv, the French government and the Rwandan Patrivtie Force. In regard to the alleged involvement of France see Linda Melvern's 2008 article, "The Perfect Crime?", in prospect.) Debate and disagreements persist between those who stubbornly adhere to the view that *akazu*-linked extremists committed the deed to rid the country of a president turned too liberal (such as

Linda Malvern and Gérard Prunier, among others) and those who point to Kagame as the chief villain. Those holding the anti-Kagame brief note that he has steadfastly refused to allow an international commission to investigate the matter, and that among the victims of the crash were some of the key supporters of the *akazu*, such as Sagatwa, Renzaho and Nsabimana. None could be described as moderates. Even more revealing are the detailed testimonies offered by former FPR officers and defectors, most notably Abdul Ruzibiza's account of how he and other members of the crack unit known as the Network Commando went about the task of preparing the ground for the shooting down of the presidential plane (Ruzibiza 2005). Ruzibiza's disclosures fully corroborate the findings of the French investigating magistrate Jean-Louis Bruguière in his brief on behalf of the three French crew members who died in the crash.

It is important to add that there were compelling political reasons for Kagame to render null and void the road map established at the Arusha conference. Seen from the perspective of the electoral calendar drawn at Arusha, it is easy to see why Kagame might have found it imperative to chart an alternative course, even if it meant planning Habyarimana's murder: with general elections scheduled to take place 22 months after the inauguration of the Broadly Based Transition Government (BBTG) there could be little doubt that the FPR would end up the loser; meanwhile with only 5 cabinet seats out of 21 in the BBTG the FPR was in no position to introduce an amendment to the Arusha provisions. The only way to prevent the nightmare scenario of a defeat at the polls was to either scrap the Arusha accords or seize power. Shooting down Habyarimana's plane would have allowed Kagame to score on both counts.

Descent into Hell

The news of Habyarimana's death spread instantly throughout the land, ushering a climate of intense fear and uncertainty. For Hutu extremists the exigencies of security, indeed survival, called for an immediate response. The decision to apply the full force of genocidal violence against all Tutsi as well as every Hutu suspected of Tutsi sympathies stemmed from a straightforward rational choice, dictated by the logic of survival: Either we kill them first, or else we'll be killed. Thus framed, the logic of the "security dilemma" left no alternative but to annihilate the enemies of the nation, the Tutsi.

In practice, setting in motion the wheels of the killing machine turned out to be a far more complex and difficult task than has been assumed by most commentators. Recent research into the dynamics of violence at the local level shows just how central to the whole genocidal process were the intra-Hutu struggles for power between moderates and extremists (Straus, 2006). In a number of communes, efforts to tip the scales on the side of the hard-liners met with considerable local resistance. As Scott Straus (2006) conclusively demonstrates, the genocide was by no means the sudden, irresistible, uniformly orchestrated butchery that some might imagine; it came about as "a cascade of tipping points, and each tipping point was the outcome of local, intra-ethnic contests for dominance (among Hutu)" (p. 93). Furthermore, as Straus (2006) shrewdly observes, the protracted struggles for supremacy that went on in many communes makes it all the more probable that a more deter- mined stance on the part of the international community would have prevented the worst from happening.

In Kigali, the killing of opposition figures, Hutu and Tutsi, began a few hours after the crash, on the basis of pre-established lists. The first to be targeted were moderate Hutu politicians affiliated with the MDR and PSD, and the Tutsi leadership and rank-and-file of the PL, including its president, Lando Ndasingwa. At this stage, little attention was paid to ethnic criteria. Anyone suspected of FPR sympathies was seen as traitor. Included in this category were Prime Minister Agathe Uwilingiyimana, the president of the Constitutional Court, the minister of labor and social affairs, and countless other lower ranking officials.

Opposition figures were disposed of in a matter of hours. Doing away with hundreds of thousands of Tutsi civilians—and thousands of Hutu in the Gitarama and Butare prefectures—proved a more difficult undertaking. Where local authorities refused to yield to the murderous injunctions coming from Kigali (as in Butare, where the *prefet* managed to keep things relatively peaceful for ten days after the slaughter began in Kigali), they were the first to be killed when the *interahamwe* showed up.

Forty-eight hours after the crash, the carnage began to spread through the countryside, causing thousands of panic-stricken Tutsi to flee their homes. Some were sheltered by Hutu neighbors, others tried to flee to FPR-controlled areas, and still others sought refuge in churches or went into hiding in neighboring swamps. The worst massacres occurred in churches and mission compounds, as in Nyamata, Musha, Karubamba. In Musha, 40 kilometers north of the capital, where some 1200 Tutsi had sought refuge, the militias went to work at 8:00 A.M. on April 8; not until the evening was the "job" (*akazi*) done.

Throughout the carnage, "the militias were exhorted by the privately owned Radio Mille Collines, which continued to broadcast messages such as 'The enemy is out there—go get him!' and 'The graves are only half full!' " (Richburg, 1994, p. 4) In a number of localities, Hutu were ordered by the militias to kill their Tutsi neighbors; failure to comply meant a death warrant for themselves and their families.

The methods used by the militias are described with clinical precision in a report by Physicians for Human Rights (1994): "The *interahamwe* used the following methods of killing: machetes, *massues* (clubs studded with nails), small axes, knives, grenades, guns, fragmentation grenades, beatings to death, amputations with exsanguination, live burials, drowning, or rape. Many victims had both their Achilles tendons cut with machetes as they ran away, to immobilize them so that they could be finished off later" (p. 11).

When death has been dispensed so massively and cruelly, one wonders whether the wounds will ever heal. The legacy of horror casts a long shadow on the capacity of Rwandan society to rise from its own ashes. And it raises problematic questions about the chances of national reconciliation: Can justice and accountability erase the haunting memories of the past? Can the RPF soldiers be prevented from dispensing a more brutal form of justice in dealing with returning refugees suspected of participating in the genocide? How can Tutsi hegemony meet both the exigencies of security and the demands of the Hutu majority for a meaningful participation in the economic and political life of the country?

Postgenocide Rwanda: The Quest for National Reconciliation

In seeking answers to these questions it is important to recall how the new Rwanda authorities interpret the root cause of the genocide, how they estimate the rate of of participation in the killings, and how best to mete out punishment. While all three are closely related to the goal of national reconciliation, in practice they raise major obstacles in the way of a viable *modus vivendi* between Hutu and Tutsi.

Despite considerable evidence to the contrary, official interpretations of the genocide are reducible to one single overriding variable: interethnic hatreds. Hence the need to drastically alter Rwanda's social map. In practice, this means that at the stroke of a pen ethnic identities have been legislated out of existence. In today's Rwanda, there are no longer Hutu, Tutsi and Twa, but only Banyarwanda—the "people of Rwanda"— and anyone suspected of encouraging "divisionism" by making loaded references to ethnic labels is liable to legal sanctions. Article 13 of the constitution deals explicitly with "revisionism, denial and trivialization (*banalisation*)" of the genocide: all are punishable by law; Article 33 further stipulates that "the propagation of ethnic, regional and racial discrimination or any other form of division is punishable by law." The rationale behind this legislation is straightforward: since ethnic enmities lie at the root of the carnage, the path to peace lies in the elimination of ethnicity from political discourse.

Given that these legal restrictions are ostensibly designed to exclude Hutu parties from participating in the political life of the country, it should come as no surprise that President Paul Kagame ran virtually unopposed in the 2003 presidential and parliamentary elections, winning 95 per cent of the vote. The next largest vote getter, MDR leader Faustin Twagiramungu, a Hutu, managed 3.7 per cent of the vote. While the Hutu have been given cosmetic representation in the government (with 13 out of 18 ministerial portfolios) this does not detract from the fact that they are being denied all legitimate avenues for making their voices heard. The banning of the main opposition party, MDR, on the eve of the elections, along with the dissolution of the principal human rights group, the League for the Promotion and Defense of Human Rights (Liprodhor) and four other civil society organizations on the grounds that they allegedly supported genocide ideas, bears testimony to the extensiveness of human rights abuses committed under the pretense of attempting to prevent "divisionism."

Another key assumption relates to the presumed massive participation of Hutu in the killings, officially estimated at three million, meaning in effect that "the entire adult Hutu population at the time of the genocide participated in it" (Straus, 2006, pp. 115, 116). Although the figure of 175,000 to 210,000 is closer to the mark (see Straus, 2006, p. 117), official estimates of Hutu participation help explain why so many were arrested on the flimsiest grounds in the days following the genocide, as well as the extreme suspicion surrounding the Hutu population in general, and the sustained efforts made to ensure the full control of the ruling RPF at every level of government.

Although decentralization lies at the heart of Rwanda's reconciliation strategy, the dominant position of the RPF at the communal and district levels makes a mockery of the notion that "decentralization (will) enhance the reconciliation of the people of Rwanda via the empowerment of the local populations." Local elections were held in March 1999 and March 2001, respectively, at the sector and district levels. The 154 communes were transformed into 91 districts, each consisting of a district council of 20 people indirectly elected by an electoral college made up of representatives of the sectors included in the district. Both were accompanied by widespread irregularities and political manipulation. Widely criticized in the sector elections was the queuing system which denied the voters the secrecy of their ballots. With the sector representatives largely under RPF control, there was little mystery about the political complexion of the electoral colleges in charge of electing district representatives.

What is known in Rwanda as "grassroots consensual democracy" rules out electoral party competition. Local elections are expected to reflect "the consensus of the people." But if the latest sector and district polls are any index, the government spares no effort to ensure that the candidates are pro-RPF sympathizers. Both in 1999 and 2001, as reported by local observers, the electors were in no doubt as to which candidates they were expected to elect. Decentralization became—for all intents and purposes—an exercise in facilitating the penetration of the RPF in the rural sectors.

Much the same purpose has been served by "villagization" policies, involving the massive relocation of rural populations. What is officially labeled the "national habitat policy" is ostensibly designed to "resolve the problem of land scarcity by redistributing the land." At the core of this initiative is a major effort to reorganize rural life by moving people away from their hillside compounds into villages. Over the last few years, hundreds of thousands of peasant families have been forcefully expelled from their homes and moved into villages (*imidugudu*). While doubts have been raised about the economic benefits of villagization, most observers would agree that the immediate result has been to greatly facilitate the political control of Hutu peasant families.

Decentralization has also been a key feature of the reform of the judicial system through the introduction of grass-roots tribunals known as *gacaca*, after the traditional councils that once handled local disputes The immediate objective of the reform is to shift the jurisdiction of the courts to *gacaca* tribunals so as to deal more effectively with the huge backlog of cases involving accusations of genocide. Ultimately, the aim is to bring impunity to an end and thus promote reconciliation among local communities.

The process began with twelve "pilot" tribunals in June 2002; by 2005, the system was implemented on a nation-wide basis, reaching out from districts to sectors and cells. Sitting as judges were some 260,000 *inyan-gamugayo* ("persons of integrity") elected by their local communities. Integrity, however, is no substitute for legal training. Despite the lack of systematic assessments, the consensus of opinion among knowledgeable observers is that the experiment has fallen short of its stated objectives. In the words of Eugenia Zorbas (2007), "the lack of provisions for the defense of alleged perpetrators, the poor training of judges, the failure to respect the principle of 'double jeopardy' and the fact that only crimes of genocide (i.e. Hutu crimes) are allowed to be discussed are among the main sources of concern for *gacaca* observers" (p. 26).

For the most part, the hearings unfold in a climate of fear—fear of taking a stand in defense of the accused, fear of giving testimony that might be held against them, fear of retribution by the families of the accused, fear of violating the pact of silence (*ceceka*) by which Hutu sometimes agree not to give testimony against another Hutu. The flight to Burundi of some 4,000 Hutu involved in *gacaca* proceedings in 2006 speaks volumes for the perception that many Hutu have of the tribunals as yet another trap set by Tutsi authorities. Their suspicions are not unfounded. According to Human Rights Watch, the *gacaca* courts have issued a very large number of sentences, frequently involving the maximum of 30 years in jail, with the result that by 2007 the prisoner population was at its highest level since the genocide, roughly 90,000 leaving out the population held in the *cachots* (lock-ups) (cited in Zorbas, 2007, p. 27). In short, if the aim of the experiment was to reduce the number of detainees and promote reconciliation, the net result has been exactly the opposite.

Scarcely more impressive is the record of the Arusha-based International Criminal Tribunal for Rwanda (ICTR). Although the Rwanda authorities voted against it, the ICTR came into existence by a resolution of the UN Security Council in 1998 for the purpose of promoting national reconciliation, peace-keeping and the fight against impunity. Rwandan national courts were given concurrent jurisdiction with the ICTR, but the latter has priority to select and bring to trial Hutu suspects; since 2007 Rwandan domestic courts are no longer free to mete out capital punishment, and thus life imprisonment is the maximum sentence given at the ICTR and Rwandan National Courts.

Among the shortcomings of the ICTR that were identified by the International Crisis Group (ICG) in 2001 were the lack of professionalism of some judges, and the extreme slowness and the high cost of the proceedings. With more than 800 employees, three trial chambers presided over by nine judges, and an annual budget of around $100 million, the performance of the ICTR has been the target of scathing criticism from journalists, scholars and advocacy groups. Its record speaks for itself: by mid-2002 only nine verdicts had been issued; as of October 2007, 27 defendants out of a total of 33 accused of genocide crimes have been tried, five of whom were acquitted, 27 cases are on appeal, while nine detainees are still awaiting trial. A number of key suspects have been extradited to Arusha, notably Théoneste Bagosora, Ferdinand Nahimana and Joseph Nzizorera, but only one (Nahimana) has been tried and found guilty. Meanwhile, the ICTR has yet to offer a coherent explanation for what happened in 1994. In the words of the ICG : "The ICTR has still not been able to shed light on the design, mechanism, chronology, organization, and financing of the genocide, nor has it answered the key question: Who committed the genocide?" (ICG, 2001, p. 1).

Nor did the ICTR succeed in its attempt to bring to trial current Rwandan army officers guilty of committing war crimes. As is by now clear, tens of thousands of innocent Hutu civilians were murdered by

Kagame's army before, during and after the genocide. According to the Gersony report, long held confidential by the UN High Commission for Refugees (UNHCR), anywhere from 20,000 to 40,000 Hutu civilians were killed by FPR soldiers in 1993 and 1994 (Des Forges, 1999, p. 726). But this is a fraction of the total number of Hutu killed by FPT units in Rwanda and eastern Congo. Since the ICTR mandate is restricted to crimes committed in 1994 it has no authority to initiate legal proceedings against human rights violations committed by the FPR from 1995 to 1997.

The efforts of former ICTR Prosecutor Carla Del Ponte to include such crimes in the ICTR's agenda were effectively thwarted by the decision of the UN Security Council to remove her from her post. As Del Ponte's former spokesperson Florence Hartman makes clear, this would not have happened without the strongest pressures brought to bear on the UN Secretary General by the Bush administration, ever anxious to take the defense of its Rwandan ally (Hartmann, 2007). Kagame's plea won the day. His troops, Kagame said, were "under no obligation to render accounts to the justice system of an international community which allowed the massacre of Tutsi" (Hartmann, 2007, p. 26). In sum, the justice of the ICTR, like that of the *gacaca*, is the victor's justice, hardly the kind conducive to reconciliation.

National reconciliation seems even less promising when one considers the repressive character of the regime. The Kagame government is a thinly veiled military ethnocracy, which rules through fear, assassination and intimidation. All dissenting voices have been silenced through the ever-present threat of being accused of "divisionism." Wealth and power are the privileges of the Tutsi oligarchs within the army and the government. The "premise of inequality"—the phrase once used to describe the texture of the Rwanda monarchy—has returned with a vengeance.

The ICG summed up the political climate at the close of 2002 in terms that have lost none of their pertinence:

> The political parties have either been dismantled or forced to accept the consensus imposed by the RPF [Rwandan Patriotic Front], the independent press has been silenced, and civil society forced to exist between repression and coercion. The RPF wields almost exclusive military, political and economic control and tolerates no criticism or challenge to its authority. The opposition has been forced into exile, and anti-establishment speeches relegated to secrecy. In the name of unity and national reconciliation, the various segments of Rwanda society are subjected to a paternalistic and authoritarian doctrine and cannot express themselves freely (International Crisis Group, 2002, p. 1).

The absence of a significant political overture is a source of immense frustration not just for Hutu; among Tutsi, the survivors of the genocide, numbering some 150,000, are not the least resentful of their growing marginalization. Meanwhile, the selective homage paid to the victims of the genocide through the annual ritual of commemorative ceremonies makes it abundantly clear to the Hutu that they are collectively seen as perpetrators. Symbolic memory thus reflects the pattern of exclusion inscribed in the new political dispensation. How to restore the impulses of truthfulness, civility and democratic governance will remain the central issue faced by the new Rwanda in the years to come; only then will the prospects for national reconciliation—as distinct from grudging mutual tolerance—enter the realm of the possible.

EYEWITNESS ACCOUNTS

Unlike the events surrounding the 1972 genocide in Burundi, a number of eyewitness accounts of the horrors surrounding the Rwanda genocide are available from a variety of sources. Journalists, human rights activists, and members of the clergy have collected a rich harvest of firsthand testimonies. Nowhere, however, are the human dimensions of the cataclysm conveyed in more chilling detail than in the London-based African Rights publication, *Rwanda: Death, Despair and Defiance* (Omaar, 1994). Except for Account 3, excerpted from a report by Physicians for Human Rights (1994), all of the testimonies below are drawn from the African Rights report.

Account 1

The following account addresses the critical role played by local government authorities—*bourgmestres*, communal counselors, *prefets*, and *sous-prefets*—in organizing the killings in the countryside. It draws from the testimonies of Antoine Mugambira, from the Kivu commune (Gikongoro prefecture), and Francois Nzeyimana, from the Muganza commune, also in Gikongoro.

We were attacked by *interhamwe*, CDR [the *Coalition pour la Defense de la Republique*], MDR-Power [Hutu hard-liners in the MDR], and MRND [the *Mouvement Revolutionnaire National pour le Developpement*]. Among those who led the attack were a certain Mukama, a soldier, together with the *bourgmestre* of the commune Kivu. They set fire to houses, destroyed our property and ate our cows. We fled to Muganza parish. When we arrived there we met many other people from

Muganza. . . . We were with white nuns who said, "Fight those people because they are killers." The second day they came back with four soldiers, reservists from Ngara and two from Nyabimata. They shot at us and left us with fourteen wounded and six dead. That was on Saturday. On Sunday, we fled again, to Cyahinda. Soldiers shot at us. *Interahamwe* too. We fought them one day, the day we arrived there.

Two of my children were killed, Nkusi and Muhire. I know the killer. He was a soldier, Mukama. He had a gun; he is the one who shot many people. They would shoot at a hundred or two hundred people. . . . It is all former soldiers who killed us. Those who fell over were beaten up with clubs or hacked to death.

In the night we decided to flee to Burundi. On the Mubuga side we saw many dead bodies, for example children on top of their dead mothers. . . . When we arrived in a place called Kukibuga, in a market place called Kugisenyi, we saw more than 300 people who had been killed with their children. They were piled up.

With other peasants we fled together at Muganza and we put up some fight against the killers by throwing stones at them but later they brought guns and shot indiscriminately. So many people were killed. Some fled to Cyahinda but there was burning and killing, so some are dead.

The killers included the *bourgmestre* called Juvenal Muhitira, helped by some local police. One of the policemen was called Mukama, another one was called Ngenzi and [there were] others who were armed. Others who killed my parents were *gendarmes* who were supposed to be protecting them. They were led by Damien Biniga who was the *sous-prefet*. I saw more than 15 dead bodies in all when I took my brother to the parish. We tried to take the worst off for treatment but the white doctors and nurses had fled themselves. When we went to the Nahihi commune, the local people threw spears and stones at us. The *gendarmes* drove us into the forest and many people were killed. We were about 400 people when we entered the forest but only 45 got out (Omaar, 1994, pp. 366–8).

Account 2

Nothing is more revealing of the extent of the moral breakdown engendered by the genocide than the wholesale desecration of churches. More people were killed in churches and church compounds than in any other site. Among many others, the churches of Ntamara, Nyarabuye, and the Centre Christus in Kigali became the scene of incredible cruelties. The first testimony, by Josianne Mukeshimana, a 15-year-old school girl, recounts what happened in Ntamara; the second, by a 13-year-old girl named Makuramanzi, describes the scene after she survived the massacre at Nyamata.

The day after the President died, houses started burning in our commune. Refugees began streaming in from other areas. We panicked as we saw *interahamwe* following people everywhere. The second day we left home and went to look for protection in the church of Ntamara. But we were not to find any protection in the church.

About five days after we had been there, there was an attack against the church. When we saw them coming, we closed the doors. They broke the doors down and tore down some of the bricks in the back wall. They threw a few grenades through the holes where the bricks had been. But most people who died were killed by machetes. When they came in, they were obviously furious that we had closed the doors. So they really macheted the refugees. The attackers were *interahamwe* but they were not from our sector. They were ordinary villagers from somewhere else. They surrounded the church to knock down anyone who escaped.

In a fury, those [*interahamwe*] inside really desecrated the church, destroying the statues. They told us: "We are destroying your church!" People could not leave. But it was also intolerable to remain in one's position as the macheting continued. So like the mad, people ran up and down inside the church. All around you, people were being killed and wounded.

Eventually I decided to drop down among the dead. I raised my head slightly; an *interahamwe* hurled a brick at me. It hit me just on top of my eye. My face became covered with blood which was useful in making them think I was even more dead. I tried to stop breathing so they would really believe that I was dead. The macheting continued all round me.

Once they thought most people were dead, they paid more attention to looting the dead. Most of them left. But one of them was not satisfied with his loot. He remained in the church. . . . He came to search my pockets and discovered that I was alive. He threatened to kill me unless I paid him. I said I had no money. He took my watch. In the meantime the other attackers were calling out to him, warning him that he might be killed if he delays any longer. He left.

I tried to get up but it was in vain. I was very weak from my injuries and there were so many bodies everywhere that you could hardly move. A few children, perhaps because they were unaware of the dangers, stood up. I called one of the children to help me. She was a girl of about nine. She replied that she could not help me because they had cut off her arms. I struggled and managed to sit up. But what I could not do was to stand up. I tried and tried but just could not do it. Finally I saw a young woman I knew, a neighbor. I called out to her. At first she did not answer. I insisted and finally she responded. When I looked closely I saw she too had had her arms cut off.

By now I don't know if what I am feeling and seeing is real life or a nightmare. I asked her if it was real life. She tried to get someone else to help me but could not find anyone. Eventually I forced myself to get up and out of the church. When I got out I got so scared that I returned to the church in spite of the dead bodies. I spent the night there with all the corpses around me (Omaar, 1994, pp. 3, 488–9).

Account 3

Next to churches, hospitals became a prime target for the massacre of civilians. The search for, and subsequent killing of, wounded survivors of previous massacres were frequent occurrences at the Centre Hospitalier in Kigali, at the Caraes Psychiatric Hospital at Ndera, and the Butare Hospital. On April 23, militias and soldiers from the Rwandan army killed 170 patients and medical personnel at the Butare Hospital. Dr. Claude-Emile Rowagoneza was present at the hospital when the massacre began on April 21. This is his testimony.

The massacres were delayed until April 20. That day everyone was asked to stay at home except those working in the hospital. Medical staff were transported to the hospital. Nurses had to walk and many were stopped at the checkpoint, asked to show their identify cards, and killed if they were Tutsi. There were 35 doctors at the hospital, of which 4 were Tutsi. Because of the danger, all four Tutsi stayed at the hospital as did some nurses. Drs. Jean-Bosco Rugira and Jean-Claude Kanangire are known to have been killed, and the fate of Dr. Isidore Kanangare, who was hiding in the hospital and may have been evacuated by the French, is unknown.

In mid-May, injured soldiers from the Kanombe barracks started being brought to Butare Hospital and no more civilians were being admitted. They also started deciding who were Tutsi on the basis of their features, looking at the nose, height, and fingers because the identity cards were no longer accurate. Some of the doctors at the hospital risked their lives by helping threatened staff by hiding and feeding them. . . .

When the patients' wounds had healed, some of the doctors—the "bad" doctors—expelled the Tutsi even though everyone knew they would be killed outside. At night, the *interahamwe* and the soldiers came in but these doctors were colluding willingly. If people refused to go, they were taken out at night. They could be seen being killed by the *interahamwe* waiting at the gates. Later the prime minister came down to Butare—apparently the educated people in Butare asked him to come—and while here he had a meeting with medical staff. They all said peace had returned and told the patients that it was safe to return home. They wanted those who were remaining here to go. Those who did were then killed. . . .

No one knew who my family were. We had good neighbors who said my family were Hutu. My wife was taken twice by *interahamwe* but neighbors insisted that she was Hutu. We have a 6-month-old daughter. My sister, mother, and father fled to Burundi but all my aunts and uncles and in-laws were killed except for my mother-in-law. In other words, more than 40 of my relatives were killed.

I spent my time hiding in a toilet at the hospital. Eventually I left the hospital and stayed with another friendly Hutu doctor who took me to another Hutu friend who hid me in his toilet. . . . On July 2, there was general panic as the FPR arrived. That night I moved from his friend's house to my own home (Omaar, 1994, pp. 27–8).

Account 4

Attempts by the perpetrators of genocide to dehumanize their victims took many forms. Particularly horrible were the methods used to force members of the same family to kill their immediate relatives. The following account by a 24-year-old Tutsi, Venuste Hakizamungu, tells how he was forced by a group of *interahamwe* to kill his own brother, Theoneste Ruykwirwa, suspected of FPR sympathies.

When the killings started, our family was not aware that Tutsi were the target. Therefore, we had had no time to plan our escape. Trouble began in another part of our sector, at Nyagasambu, but soon spread to our *cellule*. In both *cellules* people were chased by *interahamwe* who had been brought in from Bugesera. They assembled everyone in a group. When it came to our family, Hutu residents from both *cellules* tried to pass us off as Hutu by saying that "there was no tutsiship in our family." Those neighbors who we thought were trying to defend us told us to escape to a neighboring village. We left. We realized later that they were not trying to defend us. There was pressure on them to kill us and they did not want to kill us themselves. So they sent us to be killed to another village. . . .

My brother Theoneste went to the nearest village. But the people there refused to kill him. . . . The next day he came home and went straightway to a roadblock surrounded by *interahamwe*. He told them to kill him themselves and end the story there. These *interahamwe* brought him back to the house. They told us that he had to be killed in order to prove that the whole family were not agents of the FPR. They left him in the house, knowing that he would not try to escape. During this time messages were coming in every hour, urging our family to kill Theoneste. The whole family was threatened with death unless we killed Theoneste. He begged us to kill him, saying that the only alternative was death for the whole family and a very cruel death for him. . . .

After these four days, about 20 *interahamwe*, armed with machetes, hoes, spears, and bows and arrows, came to the house. They stood over me and said: "Kill him!" Theoneste got up and spoke to me. "I fear being killed by a machete; so please go ahead and kill me but use a small hoe." He himself brought the hoe and handed it to me. I hit him on the head. I kept hitting him on the head but he would not die. It was agonizing. Finally I took the machete he dreaded in order to finish him off quickly. The *interahamwe* were there during the whole time, supervising what they called "work." When Theoneste was dead they left. The next day I buried him. And I escaped immediately afterwards (Omaar, 1994, pp. 344–5).

Account 5

The rape of women and girls constitutes yet another form of dehumanization. Many of the victims were subsequently killed. One of the few survivors is a 17-year-old girl, named Louise. This is how she described her ordeal.

They came back for me. They were three delinquents. As they came towards me, they were discussing how they were going to kill me. But then one of the thugs recognized me, saying, "But she is the daughter of so and so. He is a rich man." They said I should give them money since my father is well off. I confessed I had no money. They continued to discuss ways of killing me.

Then one of them suggested that they should rape me instead. The three of them raped me in turns. Each having finished, he walked away. As the last one finished, a new group of *interahamwe* arrived. They ordered the man who raped me last to rape me again. He refused. Then they threatened to burn both of us alive unless he raped me again. So he raped me again.

When he was through, the new group of *interahamwe* beat me up. Then they said, "OK let's go. We want to show you where you are going to go." They threw me into the pit latrine. The man who pushed me pushed me so hard that instead of falling in I fell across. He dragged me back by the legs and I fell in upright, on top of my aunt. I could still hear the thugs talking. One of them said I might still be alive and suggested throwing a grenade in. Another commented, "Don't waste your grenade. A kid thrown that deep cannot be alive." They left.

I tried to climb out. But I had bled so much I was feeling dizzy. I felt I had no strength left in me. I kept falling down. Finally I collapsed. . . . When somebody came to take me out of the pit, I didn't know who it was. I realized I was out of the pit when I regained consciousness. I saw a soldier standing next to me . . . (Omaar, 1994, p. 425).

References

Ball, Howard (1999). *Prosecuting War Crimes and Genocide: The Twentieth Century Experience.* Emporia, KS: University Press of Kansas.

Des Forges, Alison (1999). *Leave None to Tell the Story: Genocide in Rwanda.* New York: Human Rights Watch.

Fein, Helen (1994). "Patrons, Prevention and Punishment of Genocide: Observations on Bosnia and Rwanda," p. 5. In Helen Fein (Ed.) *The Prevention of Genocide: Rwanda and Yugoslavia Reconsidered: A Working Paper of the Institute for the Study of Genocide.* New York: The Institute for the Study of Genocide.

Hartmann, Florence (2007). *Paix et Chatiment.* Paris: Editions Flammarion.

International Crisis Group (2001). *International Criminal Tribunal for Rwanda: Justice Delayed, Africa Report No. 30.* June 7. Nairobi/Arusha/Brussels: Author.

International Crisis Group (2002). *Rwanda at the End of the Transition: A Necessary Political Liberalisation, Africa Report No. 53.* November 13. Nairobi/Brussels: Author.

Lemarchand, René (1970). *Rwanda and Burundi.* London: Pall Mall.

Lemarchand, René (1994). *Burundi: Ethnocide as Discourse and Practice.* Washington and Oxford: Woodrow Wilson Center Press and Oxford University Press.

Linden, Ian (1977). *Church and Revolution in Rwanda.* Manchester: Manchester University Press.

Omaar, Rakiya (1994). *Rwanda: Death, Despair and Defiance.* London: African Rights.

Physicians for Human Rights (1994). *Rwanda 1994: A Report of the Genocide.* London: Author, p. 11 (typescript).

Reyntjens, Filip (1993). *L'Afrique des Grands Lacs en Crise.* Paris: Karthala.

Richburg, Keith (May 9, 1994). "In Rwanda, 'Highly Organized' Slaughter." *International Herald Tribune,* p. 4.

Straus, Scott (2006). *The Order of Genocide: Race, Power and War in Rwanda.* Ithaca and London: Cornell University Press.

Vidal, Claudine (1991). *Sociologie des Passions.* Paris: Karthala.

Zorbas, Eugenia (2007). *Reconciliation in Post-Genocide Rwanda: Discourse and Practice.* Ph.D Dissertation in Development Studies, London School of Economics and Political Science, University of London.

Bosnia and Herzegovina

CHAPTER 16

Genocidal Violence in the Former Yugoslavia: Bosnia Herzegovina and Kosovo

MARTIN MENNECKE*

For most Europeans, the term "genocide" used to be limited to the historical experience of World War II, Stalinist crimes and the Holocaust —or to events happening in places far away, coming only as close as the evening news or refugees seeking asylum. This illusion long-ago and/or of peacefulness was abruptly dashed when a series of atrocious conflicts unfolded during the 1990s in the Balkans. With the multi-ethnic, federal republic of Yugoslavia dissolving into several wars of secession, with more than two million people displaced and tens of thousands killed, the terror of genocide came back to haunt Europe. First, intense fighting ensued in Croatia, turning the country into a scene of numerous war crimes and making tens of thousands of refugees homeless. Later, the struggle for independence gained a new dimension in Bosnia and Herzegovina where numerous armed factions fought each other and civilians. The war in Bosnia and Herzegovina escalated quickly into large-scale crimes, including what euphemistically was dubbed the "ethnic cleansing" of large parts of the Bosnian Muslim population[1] and the largest massacre committed in Europe since World War II, the killing of more than 7,000 Bosnian Muslim boys and men at Srebrenica. Finally, in 1999, fighting broke out in Kosovo, where Serb armed forces tried to

* The author would like to express his deep gratitude to the late Eric Markusen, a great friend and mentor, who co-authored an earlier version of the section concerning Bosnia for the second edition of this book.

suppress the growing wish for independence. Yet again, a part of the Former Yugoslavia was engulfed in terror against civilians and the suffering of countless refugees.

At the time of writing, in June 2008, the atrocious conflicts that led to the dissolution of the Former Yugoslavia and that brought the horrors of war back to Europe in some way already seem distant history. New conflicts such as the one in Darfur, Sudan, have ensued and attract attention. This being said, all the entities that once formed the Federal Republic of Yugoslavia and its people are still marked by the traumatizing experiences of the 1990s. Whether living as internally displaced persons in Bosnia and Herzegovina, whether having returned to one's hometown or whether now living somewhere else in Europe or North America, all remember the atrocities they witnessed and suffered. The wars also continue to play a visible role in daily politics, be they the ongoing trials of former high profile politicians and military officers at the International Criminal Tribunal for the Former Yugoslavia (ICTY) in The Hague; or attempts by Croatia, Bosnia and Herzegovina and Serbia to gain membership of the European Union; or the tensions still surrounding Kosovo which on February 17, 2008 declared its independence from Serbia. Against this background, both scholars and students of genocide studies continue to wrestle with the question of how this all could come about; that is, how could genocidal violence emerge once again in Europe?

The Fall of Yugoslavia—Wars in Croatia and Bosnia and Herzegovina

Yugoslavia's descent into war and genocidal violence began in 1991, when the republic of Slovenia and then the republic of Croatia declared their independence, with the Republic of Bosnia and Herzegovina following in 1992. While the war in Slovenia, where very few Serbs lived, lasted only ten days and resulted in fewer than 50 deaths, the conflicts in Croatia and Bosnia were vastly more deadly and destructive.

In Croatia, Serbs constituted twelve percent of the population, and many of them feared that their status and security in an independent Croatia would suffer significantly. Assisted and armed by the Serb-dominated federal government in Belgrade, the capital of Yugoslavia, Croatian Serb military forces temporarily occupied approximately 33 percent of the territory in Croatia. The conflict lasted seven months and included—on all sides—the deliberate destruction of towns and cities, massacres of defenseless civilians, and the forcible removal of an ethnic group from its territory. This sort of campaign came to be known as "ethnic cleansing"—a term that tells little of the horror inflicted upon the affected civilians.

All in all, between ten thousand and twenty thousand people were killed; more than 200,000 people fled the country; and more than 300,000 became internally displaced. Efforts by international negotiators helped bring the war to an end in December 1992, without, however, challenging the "Republic of Serbian Krajina" that had been erected by the Croatian Serbs on the territory they had seized. UN peacekeepers were deployed and the war zone remained divided until late summer 1995, when Croatian military forces, in a massive offensive dubbed "Operation Storm" (or "Oluja"), retook the Serb-controlled territory. Today, some of the military leaders behind "Operation Storm" stand indicted before the ICTY and Croatian courts as responsible for "ethnic cleansing," a scorched earth campaign that led to the looting and burning of tens of thousands of Serbian homes and the unlawful killing of more than 100 civilians. "Operation Storm" is said to have forced more than 150,000 Croatian Serbs to flee their homes, an operation that constituted the single largest act of "ethnic cleansing" during the entire war in Bosnia (Prosecutor v. Gotovina et al., 2007, paras. 28–36; Bjelajac and Zunec, 2006, pp. 32ff.).

The war in Bosnia and Herzegovina (Yugoslavia's most ethnically diverse republic, with then approximately 44 percent Bosnian Muslims, 31 percent Serbs, and 17 percent Croats) began only a few months after the war in Croatia ended. It was a complex, vicious conflict that lasted more than three years and resulted in the death of approximately 100,000 people, including many civilians.[2] Among the armed factions engaged in the conflict were Bosnian Serbs, Bosnian Muslims, Bosnian Croats, regular army and paramilitary forces from Croatia and Serbia, foreign mercenaries, United Nations troops, and NATO soldiers. As in Croatia, but on a much larger scale, atrocities were perpetrated widely and by all ethnic groups. These crimes included rape; massacres; the obliteration of villages, towns, and cities; and "ethnic cleansing," when both Bosnian Serbs and Bosnian Croats attempted to remove each other and Bosnian Muslims from areas they claimed for themselves.

In March 1992, shortly after the Bosnian referendum for independence (which was boycotted by most Bosnian Serbs), the residents of the capital city of Sarajevo were subjected to an ordeal that lasted until the war ended in December 1995. Part of the city was controlled by Bosnian Serb forces, who also occupied most of the mountains surrounding it. The part of the city not controlled by the Serbs was essentially cut off from the outside world, and its inhabitants suffered from deprivation of food, water, heat, and other necessities. Only the provision of humanitarian aid by the United Nations, which was frequently halted by the Serbs, kept the population from starving. From their positions above Sarajevo, units of the Yugoslav army pounded the city with artillery, and snipers killed men, women, and children. Mosques and other cultural monuments were specifically targeted for destruction.

In this context, it is important to reiterate that all ethnic groups committed war crimes. For example, Bosnian Muslim forces also engaged in sniping and artillery attacks against the Serb section of Sarajevo (although on a far lesser scale than the Serbs) and committed raids on Serbian villages outside Srebrenica (see, for example, Prosecutor v. Oric, 2006, paras. 579ff.). Likewise, Croatian forces attacked both Bosnian Muslim and Serb civilians, for example, during the aforementioned "Operation Storm," as well as in the Lasva Valley and the Medak Pocket (see Prosecutor v. Blaskic, 2000, paras. 341ff.). Accordingly, the prosecutor at the ICTY has initiated proceedings against members of all ethnic groups, including soldiers and officers from all warring factions (for an overview of the cases see the website of the Tribunal at http:// www.un.org/icty/glance-e/index.htm). The majority of the indictments, however, is directed against Serbs, reflecting the fact that the Serb and Bosnian Serb forces were responsible for the (by far) highest number of criminal offenses. This assessment is shared by scholars studying the conflict (see, for example, Bringa, 2002, p. 199; Mennecke and Markusen 2003, pp. 293ff. with further references) and non-governmental organizations such as Human Rights Watch (Human Rights Watch, 2001).

The level and kind of atrocities committed in Bosnia and the "safe areas" (Bosnian Muslim enclaves meant to be protected by UN peacekeepers) distinguishes the Bosnian war from the other Yugoslav wars and warrants a more detailed description.

Campaigns of Violence and "Ethnic Cleansing" in Bosnia and Herzegovina

In April 1992, Bosnian Serb forces began an "ethnic cleansing" campaign against Muslims living in eastern and western Bosnia. Paramilitary units from Serbia started attacking cities along the border between Serbia and Bosnia, including the communities of Bijeljina and Zvornik. In a number of cases, regular army forces from Yugoslavia struck the target cities with artillery before the paramilitaries attacked. Many defenseless civilians— often non-Serbs identified as intellectuals, professionals, or political leaders—were murdered. The rest were driven from their homes, which were then systematically looted and destroyed. In Zvornik, trucks were brought in to collect corpses, which were then dumped in hidden sites (UN Commission of Experts, 1994, Annex 4). This campaign of terror was implemented wherever Serbs believed they had the "right" to territory occupied by non-Serbs. By mid-June 1992, Serb forces controlled two thirds of Bosnia and Herzegovina. In the course of the war, more than half of Bosnia's multi-ethnic population of 4.4 million people had been displaced. An estimated 1.3 million were internally displaced; another half a million had fled to neighboring countries; and some 700,000 had sought refuge in Western Europe.

Detention Camps and Sexual Violence

In the course of their "ethnic cleansing" campaigns, the Bosnian Serbs also established numerous detention camps, where non-Serbs were confined under inhumane conditions. Among the cases of the ICTY are several that are based on massive crimes committed in Bosnian Serb detention camps. In addition to being overcrowded and underfed, numerous inmates were frequently beaten or tortured. Some were subsequently murdered.[3] As in other acts of terror throughout the war, non-Serbs perceived to be leaders in their communities were often subjected to special cruelty, presumably part of an effort to "decapitate" the leadership and weaken resistance by the undesired ethnic groups (Klarin, 2002b).

Sexual abuse against Bosnian Muslim and other non-Serb women was practiced on a widespread and systematic basis by Serb military, para-military, and police forces and took many forms.[4] Girls and women were raped as an instrument of spreading terror during the process of "ethnic cleansing," often in front of family members in their private homes or in the open in front of other villagers. Gang rape was common, as was sexual assault of female prisoners in detention camps. There were numerous cases where girls and women were held captive for weeks and months, used as sex slaves and later sold as if they were cattle to other soldiers or killed (see, for example, Prosecutor v. Kunarac et al., 2001). According to a study by Beverly Allen (1996), thousands of rapes took place, ordered and authorized by Serb officials, and in many cases with the explicit purpose of impregnating the women. While the International Criminal Tribunal for Rwanda (ICTR) has classified certain instances of rape as acts of genocide (Prosecutor v. Akayesu, 1998, paras. 507 and 731–733), the ICTY has not included sexual violence in its deliberations of the crime of genocide. In principle, however, sexual violence committed with the intent to destroy a particular group can fall under the legal definition of genocide both as "causing serious bodily or mental harm to members of the group" and as "imposing measures intended to prevent births within the group" (see also Schabas, 2000, pp. 162–165 and 174–175).

UN Safe Areas and the Fall of Srebrenica

In the spring of 1993, the UN Security Council declared that Sarajevo, Goradze, Srebrenica, and three other Bosnian Muslim enclaves in

Serb-controlled territory were to be "safe areas," protected by a contingent of UN peacekeepers in order to provide shelter for the thousands of refugees who had fled already "cleansed" areas (see the resolutions by the UN Security Council in UN Doc. S/Res. 819, 824 and 836, 1993). This move was in itself controversial, as it seemed to acknowledge the "ethnic cleansing" of the adjacent areas. In fact, these areas soon became obstacles to international efforts to broker a peace agreement. The international community could not officially support any proposal handing the enclaves over to the Serbs via negotiations, as this could have been viewed as legitimating "ethnic cleansing" and rewarding aggression. At the same time, it was evident that the Bosnian Muslim enclaves could not continue to exist permanently in the midst of what had become Serbian territory without receiving external help. This constellation and the little trust the local Bosnian Muslim army units had in the small contingents of UN peacekeepers led to another problem, i.e. the lack of demilitarization of the safe areas. In addition, the safe areas developed into places of extreme suffering, as the refugees were subjected to frequent shelling, as well as shortages of food, medical supplies, and other necessities caused by Serb refusal to allow UN aid convoys to reach the areas (Ingrao, 2005).

In this situation, the Bosnian Serbs committed the largest massacre in Europe since World War II. It took place in the safe area of Srebrenica, where approximately 40,000 people had eked out a bare existence, many since the spring of 1992. Encountering no significant resistance from either the members of the remaining units of the Bosnian Muslim army (the Army of the Republic of Bosnia and Herzegovina), who instead tried to flee the town into Muslim-controlled areas, or the tiny contingent of some 400 Dutch UN soldiers responsible for protecting the safe area, the Bosnian Serbs entered Srebrenica on July 11, 1995.

On July 13, women, children, and elderly people were put on buses and driven to the front line, to Muslim-controlled territory. Within 30 hours, the Bosnian Serb army deported more than 20,000 people from the enclave—but not the "battle-age" men. Instead, between July 13 and 19, more than 7,000 boys and men, mostly civilians, were systematically slaughtered in a carefully planned operation. Thousands were carried on buses to execution sites where they were murdered with automatic weapons and machine guns. After the mass shooting, killers walked among the corpses, looking for survivors, who they then shot with their pistols. After the slaughter, trucks were brought in to collect the bodies and haul them to mass graves.

The so-called safe area of Srebrenica had fallen without a single shot fired by its international protectors; in fact, the UN soldiers observed the deportations and supplied the fuel for the buses used by the Bosnian Serb army. A few days later, after the news about the events of Srebrenica began to spread in the international community, the Bosnian Serbs took another safe area, Zepa—again, without encountering any serious international opposition. This safe area fell on July 25, two weeks after the Serbs had announced their plan to conquer it. Up to 2,000 men of fighting age were in danger of experiencing the same fate as their compatriots in Srebrenica, but the Croatian offensive in the Krajina forced the Serbs to withdraw troops from Zepa (see the report of the UN Secretary-General, *The Fall of Srebrenica*, 1999, paras. 394ff.).

Essential Factors behind the Conflict

Some international observers, including political leaders who wanted to avoid direct forms of intervention, suggested that "ancient hatreds" stemming from centuries of conflict in the region were responsible for the outbreak of war and its barbarity. For example, in her Pulitzer Prize-winning exposé of what she calls U.S. President Bill Clinton's administration's "ungainly wiggle campaign to avoid calling the events [in Bosnia] genocide," Samantha Power (2002) quotes Clinton's Secretary of State Warren Christopher as follows: "The hatred between all three groups is almost unbelievable. It's almost terrifying, and it's centuries old. That really is a problem from hell" (pp. 298, 303). The logics of the "ancient hatreds" argument implied that the parties to the conflict had to "fight it out" and that international intervention could not stop the bloodshed.

However, there is a strong consensus among scholars of the region that the existence of any ancient hatreds was greatly exaggerated and in any case did not cause the war. Recalling the break-up of the Ottoman Empire and its violent repercussions on the Balkans and in particular the gruesome inter-ethnic killings committed during and shortly after World War II, it was perhaps somewhat naive to claim that "[s]ignificantly, all three communities in Bosnia-Herzegovina lived for centuries in relative harmony" (Cigar, 1995, p. 13). At the same time—and in stark opposition to the aforementioned stereotypes suggesting "ancient hatreds"—it is important to remember that after World War II, under the leadership of Josef Tito (who ruled from 1945 until his death in 1980), ethnic politics and the revival of animosities from the past were discouraged. The official slogan of the Communist government was "Brotherhood and Unity"; and indeed, despite the massive physical, social, and psychological traumas experienced by millions of Yugoslavs during World War II, "relative harmony" was largely restored in Europe's most ethnically diverse nation. In some cases, this only meant co-existence; in other communities, mutual mistrust persisted and, in still others, different ethnic groups lived together peacefully. This became, for example, evident in the high level of intermarriage among Serbs, Croats, and Muslims during Tito's regime (see Bringa, 2002, pp. 217f.).

Rather than "ancient hatreds," the wars of Yugoslav secession, and the Bosnian conflict and its atrocities in particular, reflect a cluster of factors including growing economic instability, the rise of nationalistic leaders after Tito's death, the deliberate revival and exploitation of historical traumas from World War II, and the conflict in Croatia that preceded the war in Bosnia. Each is briefly addressed below.

Economic Instability in the 1980s

For much of Tito's 35-year reign, Yugoslavs enjoyed the highest standard of living and the greatest freedom to travel of any Communist nation. Hundreds of thousands spent extended periods of time in Germany and other Western European countries as "guest workers," earning very good salaries, which enabled many to buy homes and cars in Yugoslavia.

However, during the 1980s, Yugoslavia began to experience economic problems. Its productivity declined due to mismanagement and technical obsolescence in many industries, and loans from international lenders that had helped support Yugoslavia's growth and standard of living had created a massive national debt. After Tito's death in 1980, unemployment increased, and many Yugoslavs worried about their economic futures. In 1984, when the attention of the world was directed to Yugoslavia as Sarajevo hosted the Winter Olympics, observers were increasingly pessimistic about Yugoslavia's future. For example, Robin Alison Remington (1984) described the Yugoslav economy as being "on the brink of collapse" and warned that Yugoslav politicians would be "trapped by the politics of scarcity for the foreseeable future" (pp. 370, 373).

The Downfall of the Old Yugoslavia—the Rise of Nationalistic Leaders

As the national economic conditions deteriorated, tensions within and among the constituent republics developed and escalated. In 1981, less than a year after Tito's death, armed confrontations occurred between Kosovo Albanians and Serbs in the Yugoslav province of Kosovo. By 1986, prominent academics published a lengthy memorandum in Belgrade in which they described what they deemed the deteriorating and threatened state of the Serbian nation. The memorandum called on Serbia to "assess its own economic and national interests" and to wake up from its "four decades of passivity" to save the federal republic of Yugoslavia (Serbian Academy of Arts and Sciences, 1986). Despite the latter reference to Yugoslavia as a whole, the memorandum was widely perceived as an open turn from the Yugoslav experiment of pan-Serbianism (Naimark, 2001, pp. 149f.). Moreover, the relatively rich republics of Slovenia and Croatia increasingly resented the fact that tax monies they contributed to the federal government in Belgrade were being invested in what they perceived as pro-Serbian projects and services. Furthermore, the end of the Cold War weakened institutions that traditionally had represented the inter-ethnic Yugoslavia such as the Yugoslav National Army or the Communist party. Tone Bringa (2002) emphasizes therefore the failure to deal with the transition of authority and Tito's legacy as key reasons for the down-fall of the old Yugoslavia (pp. 206ff.).

Tito's death indeed created a dangerous political vacuum. No leader emerged to replace his commitment to discouraging ethnic politics and to promoting "Brotherhood and Unity," instead, just the opposite occurred. In May 1989, Slobodan Milosevic became president of Serbia as the "true defender" of Serb identity and the Serbian nation. He quickly consolidated power by purging the government and Yugoslav military of potential critics or rivals and assuming control of the powerful Serbian secret police. The Milosevic regime also took control of the media in Serbia, particularly television, and turned them into propaganda tools in order to inflame tensions between Serbs and other ethnic groups, both in Serbia and other republics. As it became clear that Slovenia and Croatia were moving toward independence, Milosevic and his agents began to provoke, organize, and arm Croatian Serbs, who then began violent resistance against the Croatian government as it pushed for independence; the former eventually seized nearly one-third of Croatian territory.

In 1990, Franjo Tudjman was elected president of the Croatian republic. He had been a general in Tito's Partisans during World War II and a major-general in the postwar Yugoslav National Army, but had been imprisoned by Tito during the 1970s and 1980s for advocating Croatian nationalism and separatism. Tudjman, the leader of the right-wing, nationalistic Croatian Democratic Union (*HDZ*), quickly instituted changes in the Croatian constitution that greatly increased his presidential powers and pushed through laws that were openly discriminatory against the Serbian minority in Croatia. Like Milosevic, Tudjman exploited the Croatian media to arouse tensions between Serbs and Croats.

Exploitation of Historical Traumas

In April 1941, when the government in Belgrade refused to accept occupation by the Nazis, Belgrade was heavily bombarded by German planes, forced to surrender, and placed under German military occupation.

During the atrocious years of occupation and civil war that followed, three major armed factions emerged within Yugoslavia: the Chetniks, the Partisans, and the Ustasha.

The Chetniks espoused Serbian nationalism and fought in small, local groups to defend the old Yugoslav monarchy against Germans, Italians and their allies. Also the better organized, multi-ethnic (but predominantly Serb) Partisans, under the leadership of Tito, fought for three years against the Axis forces. Their goal, however, was to create an independent Socialist state on the territory of Yugoslavia. Given these very different goals the Chetniks and the Partisans soon—in addition to fighting against the occupying forces—engaged in a bloody civil war against each other. The Chetniks later partly started to collaborate with the Axis powers, but eventually lost the war against the Partisans who gained the support of the Allies. Finally, the Croatian "Ustasha" regime of Ante Pavelic ruled the so-called Independent State of Croatia, which at that time included large parts of Bosnia and parts of Serbia, as well as Croatia. Pavelic enthusiastically allied with Hitler and patterned his regime after Nazi Germany, from the official policy of racism to the details of uniforms. The Independent State of Croatia willingly co-operated with the Nazi regime on the "Final Solution" against Jews and Gypsies, but went beyond it, launching a campaign of genocide against Serbs in "greater Croatia." The Ustasha, like the Nazis, established concentration camps and death camps. The most infamous of them was Jasenovac, in which captured Serbs were worked to death, starved, tortured, and killed. Between 1941 and 1945, more than 180,000 Serbs were deported, approximately 250,000 forcibly converted to Catholicism from Orthodox Christian faiths, and more than 300,000 murdered (Lampe, 2000, pp. 210–214). Also in this war, however, horrible crimes were committed by all sides. Thus, some historians assert that the Chetniks committed genocide against the Bosnian Muslims; leaving the label aside, some large-scale massacres are well documented. Another aspect of Yugoslavia's complicated history under World War II is that there existed an SS division composed of Bosnian Muslim volunteers (Benson, 2004, pp. 79f.).

When World War II ended, over one million Yugoslavs were dead. More than half of these are believed to have died as part of the Yugoslav civil war. Even if exact numbers remain a matter of contention, it is estimated that 52 percent of the total war victims were Serbs, 19 percent Croats, 10 percent Bosnian Muslims, and the remainder from other groups (Benson, 2004, p. 77).[5] The victorious Partisans added to the toll by executing tens of thousands of Ustasha and Chetniks after the end of the war in 1945. The war-time leader of the Partisans, and subsequent president of Yugoslavia, Tito, suppressed commemoration of this dark chapter in Yugoslav history, labeling all the dead as "victims of fascism." The official memory did not distinguish between the different wrongs and responsibilities and silenced individual stories of suffering. Milosevic later used the government-controlled Serbia media to revive memories of the brutality meted out to the Serbs during World War II in order to suggest to Serbs that genocide against them was possible once again (for examples see Prosecutor v. Milosevic et al., 2002, pp. 10216ff.; MacDonald, 2002, pp. 138–140). Graphic documentaries of the Ustasha genocide—including many photographs of mutilated corpses—were broadcast on Serbian television. Even mass graves of Serb victims of the Ustasha were exhumed and the bones ceremoniously reburied. Provocative, propagandistic books and articles on the genocide were also published. Additionally, academics were sent into areas of Croatia with high populations of Serbs to lecture on the atrocities of the past.

At the same time that Milosevic was resurrecting traumatic memories of Serb victimization under the Ustasha, Croatian President Tudjman instituted steps to "rehabilitate" the Ustasha regime (see generally MacDonald 2002, pp. 98ff. and 132ff.). In an important speech in February 1990, Tudjman referred to the Independent State of Croatia as "an expression of the historical aspirations of the Croatian people" (quoted in Stitkovac, 1999, p. 155). His government also renamed streets and squares after leaders of the genocidal regime and selected, for the official insignia of the newly independent nation, a coat of arms very similar to that of the former Ustasha government. Tudjman, an academic historian, also published a book in which he denied that the Ustasha regime had been guilty of genocide and drastically lowered the estimates of Serbs killed by the Ustasha. These actions, combined with new laws disadvantageous to Serbs in Croatia, fanned the flames of fear and anger.

The Croat–Serb War of 1991

The war in Croatia also contributed to the atrocious nature of the war in Bosnia. All major factions—the Yugoslav National Army, Croatian forces, and Croatian Serb forces—engaged in widespread and systematic atrocities and war crimes and thereby accelerated the escalating, reciprocal brutalization. In particular, the sieges of Dubrovnik and Vukovar, the execution of some 200 Croatian prisoners of war at Ovcara, and the aftermath of "Operation Storm" stand out as appalling crimes committed during the war in Croatia. The practice of "ethnic cleansing," as noted above, began in Croatia when Serbs forced Croats from homes and villages, and vice versa. Some of the paramilitary units that later massacred Bosnian Muslims and destroyed their homes had begun their work in Croatia. Thousands of Croatian Serbs who had been "cleansed" from Croatia fled, as refugees, through Bosnia en route to relatives and refugee camps in Serbia, further frightening and angering Bosnian Serbs.

Thus, not "ancient hatreds," but a combination of factors, including the deliberate exploitation of the traumas of the recent and more distant past by two skillful, power-driven leaders helped push Yugoslavia and, more specifically, Bosnia and Herzegovina into atrocious conflict.

International Responses to the Conflict: "Safe Areas" and UN Peacekeeping

From the moment the fighting broke out in Bosnia, the international community came under growing pressure in the media and from international human rights organizations to design a policy to stop the "ethnic cleansing" and bloodshed. In Europe and the United States, in particular, pictures of emaciated inmates detained behind barbed wire and hundreds of thousands of people being deported or fleeing their homes revived memories and images of World War II. Aware of these historical connotations, U.S. President Bill Clinton said, at the time, "If the horrors of the Holocaust taught us anything, it is the high cost of remaining silent and paralyzed in the face of genocide" (quoted in Power, 2002, p. 275). However, recalling the disastrous pictures of the failed U.S. intervention in Somalia, no government—including, and particularly, the United States—was ready to get involved in what was deemed an unpredictable and costly military intervention into the war raging in Bosnia. The main focus of the international community was to deploy international mediators that were to bring the warring parties to the negotiation table (Burg and Shoup, 1999, pp. 189ff.). Other measures that were taken—such as the international arms embargo against Bosnia and the establishment of the ICTY—seemingly demonstrated engagement, but were in reality insufficient.

UN Peacekeeping Operations

Another, parallel track was pursued under the framework of the United Nations which itself came to play a central role in the international efforts to reduce the suffering and bring the conflict to an end. In addition to other UN agencies responding to the refugee crisis, the UN Security Council authorized the deployment of UN peacekeeping forces—bringing nearly 40,000 soldiers from 39 different nations to Bosnia and Croatia. Their ability to protect endangered civilians and provide humanitarian assistance was, however, severely hampered by restricted rules of engagement, limited resources, and interference from the warring parties, but also by a lack of political will to apply the military means available. Thus, for example, they proved unable to prevent Bosnian Muslim forces from conducting raids from inside the safe areas on surrounding Serbian villages. The governments that had sent the peacekeeping troops, and their commanders on the ground, also proved unwilling to utilize the NATO air power to defend the safe areas against Serb attacks. Due to a lack of political will both in the United States and the European Union—and despite a mandate "to deter attacks" on the safe areas—the UN and its member states did not prevent such attacks and, as a result, several thousand people were killed in and around these areas.

At the same time, the international community maintained the UN arms embargo on Bosnia—which applied to all parties, but in fact only cemented the military advantage of the Serbs and, by implication, that of the Bosnian Serbs.[6] The cessation of hostilities between Croatia and Bosnian Muslims in 1994 (after diplomatic pressure from the West), along with increased U.S. military assistance in 1995, changed the course of the war. Following the Srebrenica massacre and another deadly mortar attack on Sarajevo, NATO initiated on August 30, 1995, air strikes against the Bosnian Serbs. Ultimately, U.S.-led negotiations in Dayton, Ohio, ended the conflict in Bosnia in November 1995 and paved the way for more than 60,000 international troops that formed the NATO-led Implementation Force (IFOR) sent to Bosnia to maintain the cease-fire. One year later, IFOR was transformed into the Stabilization Force (SFOR) which still had a size of around 31,000 troops. Today, there are still approximately 2,200 international troops under the framework of the European Union Force (EUFOR) left in Bosnia to oversee the implementation of the Dayton Agreement.

Questions of Responsibility—Official Reports on the Role of the United Nations and Individual States

The atrocious crimes committed in the Balkans—in particular, emerging reports about the massacres in Srebrenica and instances of mass rapes— led to harsh public criticism in numerous Western countries. How could such crimes be allowed to happen in Europe and, more so, in the presence of Western peacekeepers? Many felt that the international response to the suffering of the Bosnian Muslims during the conflict had been entirely inadequate (Cushman and Mestrovic, 1996). The question of political responsibility for this failure was evident and could not be ignored. Conspiracy theories also started to gain ground, including, for example, accusations that the Western powers or the Bosnian Muslim leaders had accepted the takeover of safe areas such as Srebrenica as a prerequisite to a future peace agreement.[7] Both the United Nations, the

Netherlands (which had peacekeepers stationed in Srebrenica), and other countries instituted inquiries into why things had gone that wrong.

In 1999, at the United Nations, U.N. Secretary-General Kofi Annan presented a comprehensive report reviewing the safe area policy and its failure at Srebrenica and Zepa. In its conclusion, the report criticizes, amongst others, the UN member states for not having done more to implement the different resolutions of the UN Security Council, and criticizes the Dutch battalion at Srebrenica—and the UN institutions involved in the area—for mishandling the available information prior to the massacre (UN Secretary-General (1999), *Report on the Fall of Srebrenica*, paras. 467ff.).

In November 2000, a commission of the French parliament began investigations into the events surrounding Srebrenica and the role of the French troops deployed to Bosnia. This was of particular interest, as there had been allegations of the French accepting the fall of Srebrenica in return for the release of French UN soldiers held hostage by the Bosnian Serbs. In the final report, the parliamentary committee of the *Assemble Nationale* (2001) rejected that there had been a tacit French approval of the "ethnic cleansing" in the safe areas. At the same time, the French inquiry acknowledged that Srebrenica also constituted a failure of France based on manifest errors of some of the French military officers involved at the time.[8]

Most comprehensive were the Dutch efforts to shed light on the fall of Srebrenica—understandably so, given the particular role of the Netherlands: it had been a Dutch battalion that had turned over the safe area and with it thousands of refugees to the Bosnian Serbs; it is Dutch officers who can be seen exchanging courtesies with the Bosnian Serb general Ratko Mladic on photographs and video footage. Ultimately, several official inquiries were instituted in the Netherlands, culminating in a 3500-plus-page report published in spring 2002 by the Netherlands Institute for War Crime Documentation (NIOD; the report is available at www.srebrenica.nl). Requested by the Dutch government in 1996, the report mainly represents a historical account of the facts and, by and large, excuses the Dutch soldiers as under-equipped peacekeepers who had been deployed to a site where there was no peace to keep. NIOD, though, confirmed that some of the earlier Dutch investigations into the role of the Netherlands in regard to Srebrenica had turned into attempts to cover up the role of government officials and politicians. Furthermore, the NIOD report criticizes the government responsible for sending the Dutch troops in the early 1990s for misjudging the situation on the ground.

As a response to this critique, the sitting Dutch cabinet jointly resigned in April 2002. Taking into account that only two of the acting ministers had been part of the government responsible for the deployment of the Dutch battalion, this decision stands out as going beyond the sheer rhetorical recognition of political responsibility. Although other international and national bodies have acknowledged a shared responsibility for mishandling the safe areas and in particular Srebrenica, only in the Netherlands has this resulted in personal consequences. It should be noted, however, that this move came many years late and only a few weeks prior to national elections. In summer 2002, the Dutch parliament initiated yet another report, this time under the auspices of a parliamentary commission that interviewed some 40 political and military officials. The final report, a 1600-page document, was presented on January 27, 2003, and provides for a detailed and candid critique of the Dutch decision-making process regarding Srebrenica. Its findings confirm that both the Dutch government and the United Nations mishandled the situation and bear the political responsibility for the lack of protection of the Muslim civilians at Srebrenica.

On the basis of the numerous international and national reports on the fall of Srebrenica and UN peacekeeping in Bosnia, it seems safe to conclude that the failure of the international community to protect the citizens of Bosnia was based on a combination of an unwillingness to become engaged, the mishandling of relevant information, and the ruthlessness of the warring parties, particularly the Bosnian Serbs' military and paramilitary units.

The International Criminal Tribunal for the Former Yugoslavia

Already while the conflicts were raging in the former Yugoslavia, some Western governments raised the question of criminal responsibility for those committing massive violations of human rights. In a step of major significance for the development of international criminal justice, the UN Security Council in May 1993 adopted a binding resolution establishing the International Criminal Tribunal for the Former Yugoslavia (ICTY)—marking the first international effort to address atrocity crimes since trials were held in Nuremberg and Tokyo after World War II. In light of the fact that most of the gross violations of human rights in the twentieth century have gone unpunished, the establishment of the ICTY, whose mandate was to investigate war crimes, crimes against humanity, and genocide committed in the Yugoslav wars since 1991 proved to be of truly historical significance (for general information on the tribunal see www.un.org/icty). The new tribunal also paved the way for further international criminal tribunals to come. In particular, the establishment of the ICTY helped to finalize the negotiations at the United Nations vis-à-vis the creation of a permanent international criminal court as successor to the Nuremberg Trials. These negotiations had been dragging on, temporarily suspended by the Cold War, since the 1950s. Ultimately, the ICTY was joined by the International Criminal Tribunal for Rwanda (ICTR) and the International Criminal Court (ICC), which were established in 1994 and 1998, respectively.

The ICTY was placed in The Hague and is composed of three Trial Chambers and one Appeals Chamber (which the ICTY shares with the ICTR) with a total of about 1,100 staff, representing over 80 nationalities. The maximum sentence the ICTY can hand down is life imprisonment. As of June 2008, the Tribunal had issued 161 indictments against persons allegedly responsible for serious violations of international humanitarian law in the Former Yugoslavia. The Tribunal has concluded proceedings against 113 persons: nine were acquitted, 55 sentenced, thirteen were sent back to national courts in the Former Yugoslavia to be tried there, and 36 died before their case could be concluded or had their indictments withdrawn. Of the remaining 50 persons, 47 are currently in some phase of their trial at the ICTY while three are at large. This includes those bearing the superior responsibility for the mass executions at Srebrenica and other crimes committed in Bosnia: the former political leader of the Bosnian Serbs, Radovan Karadzic, and Ratko Mladic, the general in command at Srebrenica. The tribunal as such has no police and is dependent on UN member states to arrest and surrender suspects. Despite a U.S. reward to pay five million US dollars for information leading to their arrest—as well as a threat by the European Union (EU) that Serbia will not be allowed to join the EU before Karadzic and Mladic are turned over to The Hague—Karadzic and Mladic are still at large.

In 2003, the UN Security Council decided that the ICTY (as well as the ICTR) was to design a so-called "completion strategy" and to conclude its work by 2010. This decision came mainly as a result of a certain tribunal-fatigue among major states in the Security Council and was also linked to the immense costs incurred by the international ad hoc tribunals for the Former Yugoslavia and Rwanda. Currently, there are international negotiations concerning what to do with Karadzic and Mladic if they are arrested after the ICTY has closed down, as well as where to place the enormous archive of the tribunal, which consists of a rich collection of witness testimonies, expert statements, video footage, photographs, and so on.

While there is no doubt that the ICTY's contribution to the development of international criminal law and justice has been seminal, there are different opinions on how much it so far has contributed to the restoration of peace and reconciliation in the region (see, for example, Orentlicher, 2008; Barron, 2007; Allcock, 2005). The number of actual cases completed is considered low compared to the money and time invested in the judicial process. Furthermore, from the very beginning various individuals mostly from Serbia have insinuated that the ICTY has an anti-Serb bias and was a political creation of the Western powers—a conspiracy theory that was also advanced by Slobodan Milosevic.

Problems and criticism aside, it is important to remember that it was the ICTY, as a result of its indictments, that removed major war criminals such as Karadzic and Milosevic from the political scene. Additionally, the ICTY has created an indisputable record of the major atrocities committed during the Yugoslav wars which will help future generations to formulate a common history of the wars—something which notably was missing after the traumatizing events of World War II. Above all, the ICTY was at the time the only means to bring some measure of justice to the countless victims of atrocity crimes and to prosecute the main perpetrators—neither Bosnia, Croatia, or Serbia were in the 1990s or the early 2000s capable of trying their own former or sitting state officials and military officers.

Transitional Justice Efforts in Bosnia and Herzegovina

Transitional justice is a term describing the process through which a given society addresses a violent past. This process is increasingly perceived as a necessary step towards rebuilding the rule of law, bringing about reconciliation, and moving towards a transition to democratic governance. Transitional justice often involves any of the following instruments or a combination thereof: international or national criminal prosecutions, truth commissions, vetting, and reparations. The exact choice depends on a variety of factors, including the degree of interest the international community takes in the matter, the political will of the national elite, and, of course, the availability of resources. In the case of Bosnia, the international community focused for (too) many years on the establishment and running of the ICTY.

When the warring parties under the supervision of the international community signed the Dayton Agreement to conclude the conflict, it was clear that the ICTY would only be able to prosecute the major war criminals. Low and mid-level perpetrators would eventually have to face national criminal courts. In principle, there are many reasons for bringing justice home to the societies of the victims—and the perpetrators. The ICTY—being situated in The Hague, conducting its proceedings in English and French and prosecuting only a minority of the actual perpetrators—remained for many people in the Balkans a remote institution that meant little vis-à-vis their personal attempts to come to terms with the past. That said, international efforts to initiate national proceedings raised a number of new problems. For example, there proved to be a strong bias among judges and prosecutors in the region for only prosecuting "the other side," i.e. Croatian trials for trying alleged Serb war criminals and vice versa. Moreover, the national institutions experienced severe difficulties in providing witnesses with the requisite protection. For a number of years, therefore, the lack of political will and a lack of qualified personnel in Croatia, Serbia and Bosnia hindered progress on this front.

A real turning point in terms of transitional justice came in early 2005 with the establishment of the War Crimes Chamber in Sarajevo in Bosnia and Herzegovina. With the help of the international community, this Chamber's task was to handle the most serious war crimes cases in Bosnia. In fact, the ICTY has begun to transfer cases to the War Crimes Chamber so as to empty its docket in order to meet its deadline for shutting down operations. Similar special chambers have been opened in Croatia and also in Serbia. This is a very positive development and has already led to a number of trials, including, in Serbia (re., the Ovcara massacre); in Croatia (the Medak Pocket); and in Bosnia (Srebrenica). There remain, however, substantial problems. For example, it has proven difficult to transmit the message and significance of these trials to the general public. In addition, the new special chambers do not mend the fact that the lower courts in all three countries still lack the will, resources, and expertise to conduct war crimes trials—and this is where the main bulk of the cases will have to be heard by the War Crimes Chamber. Around 10,000 people living in Bosnia alone are suspected of having committed war crimes during the 1990s (for more information on domestic criminal prosecutions in Bosnia, Croatia and Serbia see the numerous reports on the topical website of Human Rights Watch at http://hrw.org/doc/?t=justice_balkans and the websites of the relevant regional missions of the Organization for Security and Co-operation in Europe at http://www.osce.org/).

In regard to other transitional justice measures, the Balkans have not yet seen much development (Freeman, 2004, pp. 6–14). Vetting efforts concerning the army, police, and judiciary in Bosnia have attracted mixed reviews and are still ongoing. In terms of reparations and restitution there has not been a comprehensive government scheme for individual victims. Still, in an important decision in March 2003, the Bosnian Human Rights Chamber ordered the Bosnian Serb Republika Srpska to pay approximately 3 million Euros as a collective compensation award to the foundation overseeing the Srebrenica memorial and cemetery at Potocari (Selimovic et al. v. Republika Srpska, 2003). In June 2007, ten survivors and the Mothers of Srebrenica Foundation, representing approximately 6,000 surviving relatives, launched a law suit in a Dutch court before The Hague against the Netherlands and the United Nations over the actions of the Dutch UN peacekeepers in July 1995. The plaintiffs seek a judicial declaration spelling out the responsibility of the Netherlands and the United Nations for what happened to the Bosnian Muslims at Srebrenica and individual compensation (Fejzic et al. v. The State of the Netherlands and the United Nations, 2007; see also Clifford, 2007). It is important to note that the Dutch government continues to pay annually about 20 million US Dollars in aid to Bosnia, a third going directly to projects related to rebuilding Srebrenica; the surviving victims, however, have not yet received any compensation.

The process of establishing the truth about the events of the Yugoslav wars and the atrocities committed in Bosnia in particular has been a cumbersome one. Over the years there have been numerous attempts to establish a Truth Commission for Bosnia, but this idea has not yet materialized—initially, because of opposition from the ICTY (which feared overlap between such a commission and its own work), and later due to domestic politics. In the Serb entity of Bosnia and Herzegovina, Republika Srpska, the first official attempt at documenting the truth about Srebrenica ended in blatant denial. Aiming at presenting the "whole truth," a 132-page government report claimed that most victims at Srebrenica had been Serbs and that the other casualties were 2,000 Bosnian Muslim soldiers who had declined Mladic's offer to disarm and instead fought against the Bosnian Serb troops. The report contends that "the number of Muslim soldiers who were executed by Bosnian Serb forces for personal revenge or simple ignorance of the international law . . . would probably stand at less than 100" (Documentation Centre of Republic of Srpska, 2002, p. 34). International pressure and the afore-mentioned decision of the Bosnian Human Rights Chamber resulted in the establishment of a new commission at the end of 2002, which was to write a second, truthful report about the fate of those still missing in the aftermath of Srebrenica. Initially, the commission failed to obtain access to critical information due to obstructionism on part of the Bosnian Serb authorities, but the Office of the High Representative in Bosnia, an international administrator in charge of supervising the implementation of the Dayton Agreement, sacked several high level officials, and the commission's report was published in June 2004. In this report, some nine years after Srebrenica, the government of Republika Srpska finally acknowledged the mass executions as historical truth and helped to locate 32 unknown mass graves (Republika Srpska, 2004).

Suing Serbia—Accountability as a State

There was one more, high profile case concerning reparations for the atrocities and damages suffered by the victims during the conflict in Bosnia. Early in the conflict, in March 1993, the government of Bosnia and

Herzegovina attempted to address the "ethnic cleansing" and massive crimes committed against its civilian population outside the framework of international and national *criminal* courts by instituting proceedings against the government of Yugoslavia (which later was renamed Serbia and Montenegro) before the International Court of Justice (ICJ), the highest judicial organ of the United Nations. Different from the ICTY, the ICJ does not address the criminal responsibility of individuals, but focuses exclusively on questions of state conduct; that is, whether a state has violated rules of international law, such as the prohibition against genocide as it is set forth in the UN Genocide Convention. Therefore, the lawsuit, technically speaking, concerned nothing but the civil liability of an abstract entity—that is, the state Serbia.

Almost fourteen years after Bosnia had asked the ICJ to act "immediately . . . in order to avoid further loss of life," on February 26, 2007, the ICJ finally delivered its long awaited judgment.[9] The enormous delay was due both to successful litigation tactics by Serbia, as well as repeated requests by both parties to extend the time limit for submitting written pleadings. In its 175 page judgment, the Court determined that the massacres at Srebrenica in July 1995 constituted genocide, while the other crimes, including atrocities committed at detention camps, gross instances of sexual violence and the "ethnic cleansing" campaign, did not meet the legal definition of genocide. Notably, the ICJ agreed completely with the relevant case-law of the ICTY. With a view to Serbia's responsibility for the genocide at Srebrenica, the Court found that Serbia did not have the degree of direct control over the Bosnian Serb forces at Srebrenica, which international law requires if Serbia was *to be held legally responsible* for the genocide. The Court did find, however, that Serbia, given its close relations to the Bosnian Serbs, could have done more to prevent the genocide at Srebrenica and because of that violated the legal duty to prevent genocide—a duty that never before had been recognized under international law. Furthermore, the Court concluded that Serbia had violated its duty to punish those responsible for Srebrenica (Case, Bosnia v. Serbia and Montenegro (2007), paras. 425ff.). This made Serbia the first nation to have been found in violation of the UN Genocide Convention since its adoption in 1948. Nonetheless, the ICJ ultimately rejected Bosnia's claim for compensation.

The Bosnian Serbs and Serbia felt great relief that they had not been found legally responsible for the genocide, and immediately asserted everyone needed to move on.[10] Bosnian Muslims were very disappointed with the judgment. It was viewed as too little, too late. In particular, the decision not to label the conflict as a whole constituting genocide caused strong reactions and did not correspond to the victims' own perception. In the days following the judgment, there were angry demonstrations against the decision in Bosnia (see, for example, Reuters, February 27, 2007). Survivors from Srebrenica and local politicians called upon the international community to at least abolish the status of Republika Srpska, as it was deemed unbearable that Srebrenica as the site of genocide should remain part of the Bosnian Serb entity. Nothing came of the request.

As is so often the case with institutions of international criminal justice, little was done to put the comprehensive judgment into plain words or to elucidate its complex legal findings for the affected society. In fact, the judgment and other relevant material were only made available in French and English, the Court's two official languages. Without an outreach strategy in place, nobody was informed that the case was limited to the framework provided by the UN Convention on the Prevention and Punishment of Genocide (UNCG) and that the judges could not issue any findings as to whether Serbia was responsible for war crimes and crimes against humanity committed in Bosnia. The judgment has led to intense discussions among international law experts, particularly in regard to whether the Court was right in not finding Serbia *legally* responsible for Srebrenica. Former ICTY president Antonio Cassese (2007) called the judgment a "judicial massacre" and criticized the Court for establishing an "unrealistically high standard of proof for finding Serbia to have been legally complicit in genocide" at Srebrenica. On the other hand, the judgment undoubtedly is of great significance in that it was the first time it was held that states (and not only individuals) can violate the UNCG and that there is a legal (not solely ethical) duty to prevent genocide (Mennecke and Tams, 2007). For many survivors, however, the judgment remains yet another example of the international community failing Bosnia. In that regard, the president of a local non-governmental organization commented bitterly, "let Bosnia's blood and ashes rest on the hands of all those who made such a judgment" (quoted in Jelacic, 2007).

Genocide in Bosnia and Herzegovina?

Besides questions of political responsibility and legal accountability there is one more question that has occupied tribunals, scholars and victims alike: that is whether the conflict in Bosnia and Herzegovina as such, beyond the massacres at Srebrenica, could be characterized as genocide. The debate on this issue has been intense and at times polemical—and it is far from concluded.

Very early on in the conflict, the Prosecutor at the ICTY expressed the view that the crimes committed by Bosnian Serb forces in Bosnia and Herzegovina indeed should be labeled genocide (Prosecutor v. Karadzic and Mladic, Indictment, 1995). The judges at the tribunal disagreed, however, with this approach and dismissed the genocide charge in a number of proceedings, including cases against former detention camp guards and commanders (Prosecutor v. Jelisic, 1999 and 2001; Prosecutor v. Sikirica et al., 2001) and leading politicians (Prosecutor v. Stakic, 2003; Prosecutor v. Plavisic, 2003; see also Mennecke and Markusen 2003, pp. 310ff.). In fact, only one single case has led to a conviction for genocide before the Tribunal. On August 2, 2001, Bosnian Serb General Radislav Krstic was found guilty of genocide for his role in the mass executions at Srebrenica, constituting the first genocide conviction by an international tribunal outside Rwanda (Prosecutor v. Krstic, 2001). Notably, Krstic was ultimately only found guilty for complicity in genocide (Prosecutor v. Krstic, 2004). In a subsequent decision, the Appeals Chamber confirmed that the Bosnian Serb troops had committed genocide at Srebrenica, but found that other officers of the Bosnian Serb Army such as Vidoje Blagojevic did not act with specific genocidal intent (Prosecutor v. Blagojevic, 2007). At the time of writing, the Tribunal is hearing a joint case against seven high ranking Bosnian Serb military officers in which the Prosecution is trying to prove their respective role in the genocidal massacres at Srebrenica (Prosecutor v. Popovic et al., 2006).

Why has the ICTY held that only the mass executions at Srebrenica constitute genocide? The answer lies in the legal definition of genocide pursuant to which the perpetrator has to act with "the intent to destroy in whole or in part" a group protected under the Genocide Convention. According to the judges, only the evidence presented in regard to Srebrenica showed that there was specific genocidal intent to destroy a protected group in whole or in part. The ICTY judges found that in other cases the crimes in question aimed at terrorizing the civilian population and ultimately at removing all non-Serbs from what was considered Serb territory, but did not entail the intent to destroy a specific group in whole or in part.

The question of genocide was also taken up before other international and national courts and tribunals. Most recently, the ICJ was confronted with this matter. As mentioned before, the ICJ ruled on February 26, 2007, that the mass executions at Srebrenica constituted genocide, but confirmed (along with the ICTY) that the other crimes committed during the conflict in Bosnia did not meet the legal definition of genocide. A number of prominent international lawyers have sharply criticized the judgment in this regard (see Cassese, 2007, and Scheffer, 2007b, pp. 125–129). Conversely, the leading authority on genocide under international criminal law, William Schabas (2007), has always held the view that the atrocities committed in Bosnia could not be labeled genocide under international law (pp. 111–114). Only at the national level can one find courts that have put forward a different view on the character of the conflict in Bosnia and Herzegovina as a whole. In Germany, for example, the Federal Constitutional Court has confirmed lower court convictions on the crime of genocide that were not related to Srebrenica (German Federal Constitutional Court, 2000).

Outside the legal community the picture is more ambivalent. On the one hand, a number of well-researched and often cited monographs on the wars in the Former Yugoslavia do not refer to the conflict in Bosnia and Herzegovina as a whole as genocide (see, for example, Lampe, 2000; Naimark, 2001; see also Burg and Shoup, 1999, p. 14). Other scholars and numerous journalists writing about Bosnia and Herzegovina speak of genocide and do so with great verve (see, for example, Cigar, 1995; Fein, 2000; Power, 2002; Lemarchand, 2003). Some proponents of using the term genocide towards the conflict in Bosnia and Herzegovina have sharply criticized the legal discourse for its (alleged) "inability, as yet, to match reality authentically" (Charny, 2005, p. ix). Similarly, the aforementioned judgment of the ICJ has been rejected as a "travesty of justice" as a result of its engaging in judicial "hair-splitting" that has "made the definition of genocide so restrictive that the phenomenon of genocide effectively disappears altogether" (Hoare, 2007, n.p.). Another observer has called the judgment an "exercise in denial" and "perverse" (Shaw, 2007, n.p.). This being said, it seems easier to renounce the findings of the ICJ and the ICTY than to present a detailed and thoughtful argument as to why the conflict in Bosnia should be characterized as genocide.

Genocide in Kosovo?

Before the Yugoslav wars began in Slovenia in 1991, the autonomous province of Kosovo had been viewed as the most likely location for an outburst of ethnic violence. In contrast to the other Yugoslav republics, where the various groups had—with the important exception of World War II—lived together in relative peace, Kosovo had for a long time been the site of ethnic tensions, particularly following (and not long after) Tito's death in 1980. It was also Kosovo that brought the international spotlight back to Former Yugoslavia. In the late 1990s the province became the site of frequent discrimination and isolated acts of violence against the Kosovo Albanians and of the deadly attacks against Serb police officers committed by the so-called Kosovo Liberation Army (KLA), an armed separatist movement. Eventually these hostilities escalated into a comprehensive "ethnic cleansing" by the Serbs, which prompted an armed intervention by NATO starting in March 1999. The military intervention raised a number of complex questions, above all because of its questionable legality under international law as well as the crimes committed against the civilian population in Kosovo.

Background to the Conflict in Kosovo

Kosovo had, throughout the twentieth century, seen numerous, often, bloody changes of power and affiliation, both internally and externally. In the 1990s, under Milosevic, the situation escalated to a new dimension of civilian suffering (see on this and the following, Pavlovic, 2005).

Under the Yugoslav Constitution of 1974, Kosovo was, unlike Serbia and Croatia, not a republic, but an autonomous province. While Kosovo was predominately populated by Kosovo Albanians (more than 80 percent of the population) and steered by a multi-ethnic regional government, there were growing tensions in the 1980s between the majority and the Kosovo Serb minority. In 1981, province-wide demonstrations by Kosovo Albanians shocked the Communist leadership in Belgrade as they seemed to represent an outbreak of Kosovo-Albanian nationalism. The response was brutal; police forces from all over Yugoslavia were brought to Kosovo where a state of emergency was declared. Hundreds of Kosovo Albanians were arrested, tried and imprisoned. At the same time, Kosovo Serbs, who were overrepresented in the highest positions in the public and private sector (52 percent), felt increasingly harassed by the Kosovo Albanian majority. Thousands of Serbs left Kosovo for other parts of Yugoslavia, reinforcing a demographic trend (there was also a very high birth rate among Kosovo Albanians) which alarmed Serbs inside and outside Kosovo. It was against this background that the earlier mentioned 1986 Memorandum by the Serb Academy of Arts and Sciences spoke of the "unremitting persecution and expulsion of Serbs from Kosovo" and of "an open and total war . . . on the Serbian people . . . [which] has been going on now longer than the entire national liberation war fought in this country from April 6, 1941, to May 9, 1945" (n.p). The Memorandum condemned the passivity of the sitting government in face of this "physical, political, legal and cultural genocide of the Serbian population in Kosovo" (Serbian Academy of Arts and Sciences, 1986).

The already tense situation, with nationalist camps on both sides, escalated further when Milosevic came to power in the late 1980s (Naimark, 2001, pp. 142ff.). Milosevic, of course, did not create nationalism among the Kosovo Serbs; he took advantage of it, realizing what a powerful tool it was to galvanize people to his way of thinking. Milosevic skillfully played on the fact that Kosovo traditionally obtained a special role in Serbian ideology and public memory. It did so because of a historic battle at Kosovo Polje in 1389 when the Serb prince Lazar and his forces lost a hopeless, but—according to common perception among Serbs—heroic battle to the Ottoman army. Upon a visit to Kosovo in April 1987, Milosevic addressed a crowd of several thousand Kosovo Serbs who protested against what they perceived as discrimination and a lack of protection by the Kosovo authorities. It was here that Milosevic spoke the sentence "no one has the right to beat you" which gained him heroic status. Two years later, Milosevic was back to mark the 600th anniversary of the aforementioned battle at a massive rally where he evoked the battle's legendary meaning and the "memory of Kosovo heroism" for the express purpose of uniting the Serbs. In the coming years, Milosevic built upon this nationalist platform and responded to what he and other Serbs perceived as the marginalization of the Kosovo Serbs (Independent International Commission on Kosovo, 2000). In doing so, he introduced a series of harsh, anti-Albanian measures including the revocation of Kosovo's status as an autonomous province and the replacement of all Kosovo Albanian policemen with Serb police forces. Additionally, all Albanian language media centers were closed down and thousands of Kosovo Albanians were removed from public employment and education posts. As a result, the tensions between Kosovo Albanians and Kosovo Serbs increased considerably.

The international community, however, chose to refrain from interfering in this explosive situation. The decision not to present an outline for the future of Kosovo at the Bosnian peace talks in Dayton, Ohio, in November 1995, proved to be a detrimental omission, as it weakened the position of moderate Kosovo Albanian leaders such as Ibrahim Rugova and radicalized certain Kosovo Albanian factions. Soon after, by 1997, the KLA, began to commit attacks primarily on Serb police forces, but also on Kosovo Albanian "collaborators." By 1998, the tensions had escalated to armed conflict. As part of that process, the KLA established prisons camps where Serbs and non-Serb "collaborators" were detained under inhumane conditions, tortured and, in some cases, killed (see, for example, Prosecutor v. Limaj et al., 2005). As a consequence, many Kosovo Serbs and Roma were intimidated and fled their villages.

The Serb response towards the Kosovo Albanian opposition and the increasing number of attacks by the KLA was frequently indiscriminate and disproportionate, even if officially aimed exclusively at KLA fighters and their strongholds. In a campaign that started to resemble the war in Bosnia, Serb forces attacked villages, killed and brutalized inhabitants, and burned down houses in order to force them to leave. By the end of 1998, approximately 3,000 Kosovo Albanians had been killed and more than 300,000 expelled from their homes (Power, 2002, p. 465). In early 1999, the Serb campaign to create a Serb majority in Kosovo by means of "ethnic cleansing" continued, only temporarily put on hold when international negotiations or the presence of international observers required it.

In the course of the conflict, approximately 800,000 of the roughly two million Kosovo Albanians fled the province to neighboring countries, while several hundred thousands more became internally displaced persons. The number of Kosovo Albanians killed continues to be unclear. Estimates given by non-governmental organizations range between 5,000 and 30,000 victims, while Milosevic in his eventually aborted trial was only charged with the responsibility for the murder of more than 900 Kosovo Albanians (Prosecutor v. Milosevic, 1999, para. 66 and annexes). A detailed statistical study of the conflict suggests a total number of 9,000 to 12,000 killings were perpetrated (Ball et al., 2002, pp. 5f.). The figure of more than 100,000 victims, which was indirectly suggested by NATO officials and Western politicians when trying to justify the military intervention that started in March 1999, seems to be greatly exaggerated.

The Response of the International Community to the Kosovo Crisis

The international community seriously turned to the Kosovo issue only in the fall of 1998. In October of that year, the Serbs and Kosovo Albanians agreed to a verification mission by the Organization for Security and Cooperation in Europe (OSCE) in order to establish an enduring truce. Sent originally as an impartial, mutually accepted observer, the OSCE mission was soon perceived by the Serbs as biased towards the Kosovo Albanians since the KLA was not hindered from taking advantage of the international presence when it renewed its military activities.

It was in this context that the OSCE mission brought the "massacre of Racak"—in which Serb forces had allegedly cold-bloodedly executed 45 villagers on January 15, 1999—to the attention of the international media.[11] Despite Serb efforts to explain the deaths as resulting from battles between KLA and police units, this news became a turning point in the hitherto reluctant public debate on armed humanitarian intervention in Kosovo. Even with the international pressure growing, however, the Serb government refused to sign an agreement brokered by the multinational Contact Group at Rambouillet, France, in February and March 1999. The Serbs mainly did so because the agreement would have required the almost complete withdrawal of the Yugoslav army from Kosovo and the concomitant presence of a strong NATO force in Kosovo to supervise the implementation of the accords. In addition, an annex to the agreement envisaged unrestricted access for NATO forces throughout

Yugoslavia and opened the possibility for a future referendum on Kosovo's independence (see the agreement with appendix B, Article 8 [concerning NATO's rights of access], and chapter 8, Article I, para. 3 [concerning the future status of Kosovo], at http://www.usip.org/library/pa/kosovo/kosovo_rambtoc.html).

Western politicians subsequently overcame their inhibitions against applying military means because they feared that they yet again were, as in Bosnia, manipulated by the Milosevic regime (Power, 2002, pp. 446–448). On March 24, 1999, NATO launched, without the prerequisite mandate of the United Nations Security Council, a 78-day-long bombing campaign against Serbia and its troops deployed in Kosovo. The legality of this intervention under international law remains to this day contentious among international lawyers (see, for example, Independent International Commission on Kosovo, 2000). Given the use of controversial weaponry such as cluster bombs and the considerable damage reportedly caused to civilian targets, the NATO air campaign also raised concerns about possible violations of international humanitarian law. As a consequence, the Office of the Prosecutor at the ICTY initiated a study of the NATO air campaign which concluded that there was not sufficient evidence suggesting that NATO had committed any of the crimes under the Tribunal's jurisdiction (ICTY, 2000, *Report to the Prosecutor*, for a critical analysis of the report see Benvenuti, 2001).

In Kosovo itself, the NATO air strikes initially only served to reinforce and speed up Serbian attempts to expel Kosovo Albanians from the region. The intervening Western governments had hoped that, after a few days of bombing, Milosevic would return to the negotiation table, but they misjudged how the Serbs would react to the NATO air campaign. At the same time, NATO governments did not send in ground troops, as they wanted to minimize the risk of their own casualties. Only in the end did NATO succeed in forcing Belgrade to withdraw its forces from the province and secure the return of Kosovo Albanians who had been expelled from their homes. A tragic, and insufficiently known side effect of this return of the Albanians was that the local Kosovo Serb and Roma population became victims of acts of revenge and new "ethnic cleansing"; more than 200,000 Serbs fled Kosovo after the armed fighting ended in June 1999, and several hundred Serbs and Roma were killed (Human Rights Watch, 1999b).

The day after the NATO air strikes ended, on June 10, 1999, the UN Security Council established the United Nations Mission in Kosovo (UNMIK) and turned the former Serb province into a UN protectorate. Up to 47,000 international Kosovo Protection Force (KFOR) troops, over 4,000 international police officers, and 16,000 UN administrative staff were originally sent to Kosovo to attempt to keep the fragile peace and to help with the rebuilding of the ethnically riven society (for general information see KFOR's and UNMIK's websites at www.nato.int/kfor and www.unmikonline.org). Similar to the High Representative in Bosnia, the Special Representative of the UN Secretary General in Kosovo held ultimate legislative and executive authority. Since 1999 there have been substantive setbacks, particularly in terms of reconciling the Kosovo Albanians and Kosovo Serbs. In March 2004, the inter-ethnic tensions escalated with, up to that point in time, the worst incident of open violence against the Kosovo Serbs and Roma minorities. The riots left 19 dead and nearly 700 injured. Kosovo Albanian mobs also destroyed hundreds of private houses, thirty-two Orthodox churches and monasteries, and forced more than 4,000 Kosovo Serbs and Roma to flee from their homes (Human Rights Watch, 2004). The psychological impact of these riots and KFOR's failure to protect the minorities was devastating and hindered many refugees from returning to Kosovo. The response of the Kosovo justice system has been weak and inappropriate. As of this writing, 16,000 international (KFOR) troops remain in Kosovo to help UNMIK and the Kosovo government stabilize the situation.

Parallel to this peace building effort under the UN mission, international efforts were undertaken to hold those bearing the greatest responsibility for the crimes committed in Kosovo accountable. The ICTY set the tone by indicting the then still acting Serb president, Slobodan Milosevic, and some of his closest aides for their role in Kosovo *before* the conflict was brought to an end (Prosecutor v. Milosevic et al., Indictment, 1999). Indictments against additional high ranking Serb generals and top politicians followed (Prosecutor v. Milutinovic et al., 2006). The ICTY also heard two cases involving former KLA leaders, including one against former prime minister Ramush Haradinaj (Prosecutor v. Limaj, 2005; Prosecutor v. Haradinaj et al., 2008).[12] Following the rise of new inter-ethnic tensions in February 2000, the UN administration introduced mixed panels composed of international and Kosovar judges to try both low- and mid-level war criminals and those accused of more recent incidents of ethnic violence. The internationalized courts helped to overturn the anti-Serb bias that characterized many earlier decisions by Kosovo Albanian courts, but, at the same time, this solution encountered a series of substantial problems. In part, this was because there was not sufficient international commitment to seriously address the issue of war crimes. There were also few qualified jurists in Kosovo and problems with the protection of witnesses continued to persist.

The Question of Genocide as Regards Kosovo

The question as to whether the situation in Kosovo constitutes genocide or not began to garner international attention in late 1998 and early 1999. In the United States, for example, a heated debate ensued among political decision-makers; supporters of a NATO intervention in the government and Congress tended to invoke the genocide label while others rejected this classification and the explicit attempts to draw parallels to the Holocaust (Steinweis, 2005, pp. 281ff.). In Europe, the German Defense Secretary Rudolf Scharping stated that "genocide is starting" (quoted in Associated Press, 1999), and his British counterpart George Robertson declared that "[t]hese [NATO] airstrikes have one purpose only: to stop the genocidal violence" (quoted in Dunne and Droslak, 2001, p. 35). In addition, numerous human rights groups such as Physicians for Human Rights (1999, pp. 12–13), the International Helsinki Federation (1999) and the Gesellschaft für bedrohte Völker (Society for Threatened Peoples) (1999) issued reports that Milosevic was committing genocide against the Kosovo Albanians.[13] The media was featuring pieces as in the British *Guardian* newspaper titled "So is Milosevic guilty of genocide?" (Jordan, 1999)—and answering in the positive.

What was conspicuously lacking from the various statements speaking of genocide was a careful analysis of the situation on the ground and an informed application of these facts to the UN Genocide Convention or any other recognized social science definition of genocide. In light of the news and pictures emerging from Kosovo, one may, at first, at least to some extent, be inclined to excuse this somewhat generous use of the term "genocide" by non-experts. This is particularly so when taking into account that the Kosovo crisis constituted yet another chapter in the series of atrocious Yugoslav wars which earlier in Bosnia had escalated into the genocidal massacres at Srebrenica. There was a sense of asserting "not again!" and understandably so. At the same time, especially with regard to the aforementioned references to the Holocaust, it is necessary to underscore that the term "genocide" (as well as the historical experience of the Holocaust) will be diluted, if it is applied to situations which do not meet the strict requirements of the UN Genocide Convention.

Critics of the NATO intervention in Kosovo promptly argued that the term "genocide" and references to the Holocaust were used to galvanize the support of the general public (Steinweis, 2005, pp. 284–285). There is no doubt that the label "genocide" helped to smooth the way for the armed intervention. It is important to note that NATO, due to Russia's opposition could not obtain the requisite authorization by the UN Security Council to act on its desire to bomb Serb positions in Kosovo.

Consequently, there were heated discussions as to the legality of an armed intervention without such a mandate—and it is here the genocide label helped to convince decision-makers that regardless of the question of *legality* an intervention nonetheless was *legitimate* and needed. Such a practice, of course, opens the door for misuse. Furthermore, the focus on the term "genocide" seems misplaced. Other massive human rights violations, such as crimes against humanity, deserve similar concern and can demand and justify armed intervention by the international community as well. Thus, to overly (if not exclusively) focus on genocide is not in the interest of all victim groups. Moreover, in regard to the issue of intervention, international law does not distinguish between genocide and international crimes such as ethnic cleansing or other crimes against humanity. Any of these atrocity crimes can give rise to an intervention by the UN Security Council; and any of these crimes can trigger the evolving notion of a "responsibility to protect." The debate over using and overusing the term "genocide" has recently also come to the forefront of genocide studies. David Scheffer's welcome proposition of focusing on preventing and stopping all atrocity crimes—i.e. international crimes including war crimes, crimes against humanity and genocide—plays an important role in this regard (Scheffer, 2007a; see also Mennecke, 2007).

Somewhat surprisingly, genocide scholars have not, for the most part, shed much new light on the question as to whether the Serb crimes committed against the Kosovo Albanians in 1999 constituted genocide or not. Instead, there prevails in the field of genocide studies a striking readiness to label the Serb crimes in Kosovo "genocide," or at least to call Kosovo a case of "prevented genocide" without scrutinizing all elements of the legal or other definitions of genocide. One example for this trend can be found in a recent textbook on genocide in which the author notes the "ethnic cleansing" campaign by which the Serbs tried "to empty the territory of ethnic Albanians through selective acts of terror and mass murder," but also speaks of the "Serbs' genocidal strategies" and "genocide in Kosovo." At no point, however, does the author explain why Kosovo was a genocide (Jones, 2006, pp. 220–226). Similarly, on the website of the non-governmental organization Genocide Watch, Kosovo figures in the category of "specific genocides," but no further documentation as to why Kosovo belongs on this list is provided (www.genocidewatch.org).

Also on the legal front, the question of genocide was up for review. Significantly, the prosecutor at the ICTY decided not to indict anybody for the crime of genocide vis-à-vis the events in Kosovo. This was true for Milosevic, who was indicted in May 1999 for war crimes and crimes against humanity committed against the Kosovo Albanians, and it was also true in regard to the case against Milosevic's closest aides (Prosecutor v. Milutinovic et al., 2006). The only genocide conviction related to the Kosovo conflict was rendered in January 2001 by a local district court in Mitrovica, Kosovo. This decision, however, was immediately criticized by the mission of the Organization for Security and Co-operation (OSCE) in Kosovo as inconsistent with the evidence heard in court (OSCE, 2002a). In fact, the decision was later reversed by one of the aforementioned internationalized panels. The UN-supervised Supreme Court of Kosovo agreed with the district court that there had been "a systematic campaign of terror including murders, rapes, arsons and severe maltreatments" of Kosovo Albanians, but also found that "the exactions committed by Milosevic's regime cannot be qualified as criminal acts of genocide, since their purpose was not the destruction of the Albanian ethnic group in whole or in part but its forceful departure from Kosovo" (cited in OSCE report, 2002b, p. 49). The fact that hundreds of thousands of Kosovo Albanians were deported by the Serbs via trains and trucks to the border of Albania or Macedonia speaks against an intent to *destroy* the group (see, also, Schabas, 2001b, pp. 294–296). In addition, no reports have yet established that the Serb paramilitary forces singled out—as the ICTY held the Bosnian Serbs had done at Srebrenica—an "emblematic" part of the Kosovo Albanians for extermination (Prosecutor v. Krstic, 2004, paras. 8ff.). Instead, the evidence presented before the ICTY so far confirms that war crimes and crimes against humanity were committed against the Kosovo Albanians and, to a far lesser extent, against the Kosovo Serbs and Roma.

Living with the Scars

Whether war crimes, crimes against humanity or genocide, any conflict involving atrocity crimes leaves the affected community in a state of deep distress and trauma. There will be bystanders,[14] victims, collaborators, perpetrators, and possibly perpetrators who themselves have become victims at some point of the conflict, and vice versa. The process of reconciling these different actors and of those of various ethnic, political or other groups becomes even more challenging if the atrocity crimes were not committed as part of an inter-state conflict, but took place within one and the same society, in some cases pitching neighbor against neighbor. The whole notion of reconciliation in the aftermath of atrocity crimes is a challenging one. Along with other objectives such as rebuilding the rule of law and instituting democracy, any post-conflict effort is difficult and protracted—not to mention prone to setbacks. Bosnia and Kosovo are no exceptions in this regard, both being sites of internal (and international) conflicts between different groups within the same society. In fact, they can (and do) serve as examples of the fact that even in

Europe, with the substantive financial and political support from various international organizations such as the United Nations, the OSCE, and the European Union, the re-building of a post-conflict society remains a Herculean task.

At first blush, one may look upon the aforementioned statement as unnecessarily pessimistic with regards to Bosnia, as there indeed are a number of developments indicating that Bosnia is making progress towards becoming a stable, peaceful state and an active participant at the international level. For example, more than one million refugees have returned to their homes since the signing of the Dayton Agreement in late 1995. Significantly, more than 400,000 people returned to municipalities where they are, in terms of ethnicity, in the minority.[15] Another sign of progress is that around half of Bosnia's 500,000 war-damaged homes have been rebuilt. Some 200,000 property disputes have been resolved peacefully. Furthermore, the number of UN peacekeepers has been reduced from more than 60,000 in the mid-1990s to less than 2,200 today. Moreover, the mandate of the High Representative of the international community in Bosnia is phasing out, which means that Bosnia will win back a great deal of sovereignty and responsibility over its own affairs. At the international level, Bosnia has entered into the so-called Stabilization and Association process preparing the country for a future membership of the European Union. Also, Bosnia was in 2007 voted for two years into the UN Human Rights Council.

These positive developments, however, cannot hide the fact there are a number of persisting problems—some of which may well remain as permanent scars on Bosnia and the lives of her citizens. At the political level, the scars of the war in the 1990s are impossible to overlook. Bosnia is composed of two "entities" established at Dayton: the Bosnian Muslim-Croat Federation, which occupies 51 percent of the territory of Bosnia and Herzegovina, and Republika Srpska, the Serb entity that occupies the other 49 percent. Thus, Bosnia's internal set-up "recognizes" the logic of the "ethnic cleansing" campaigns carried out during the war; it even places Srebrenica as the execution site of more than 7,000 Bosnian Muslim men in the land of the Bosnian Serbs.[16] Srebrenica remains a troubled, and also physically battered place. Approximately 6,600 houses were destroyed during and just after the war; by the end of 2005, despite substantive international aid, only 1,500 had been reconstructed. Prior to the war, about 37,000 people lived in Srebrenica, 73 percent of them Bosnian Muslims and 23 percent Bosnian Serbs; today, some 6,000 Serbs and 4,000 Muslims live there. Moreover, the economic situation in the municipality is very poor with few outside investors and a high rate of unemployment.

The relations between the Bosnian Muslim-Croat Federation and

Republika Srpska—which are compelled to work together in the multi-ethnic presidency of Bosnia and Herzegovina—have been difficult and continue to complicate numerous important projects such as the establishment of a joint police force and constitutional amendments (International Crisis Group, 2007, pp. 9ff.). The splits running through Bosnia and Herzegovina do not only show as political and administrative borders on the map. Bosnian Muslims, Croats and Serbs have also moved and changed their lives as a response to the war and the atrocity crimes committed throughout the early 1990s. For example, prior to the war, Sarajevo was home to more than 520,000 people and of these about 50 percent were Bosnian Muslims, 30 percent ethnic Serbs, 7 percent ethnic Croats and 13 percent considered themselves as Yugoslavs or belonged to minority groups. Today, even if the exact numbers remain controversial, it is clear that the situation has changed drastically; Sarajevo's population has shrunk to around 400,000 and is dominated by Bosnian Muslims (nearly 80 percent). The few remaining ethnic Serbs (ca. 11 percent) live separated in what they call "Serb Sarajevo." Refugees are still welcome to return, but those who do often sell their apartment in order to move to a place where the majority is of their own ethnicity. Furthermore, Bosnia is also struggling with segregated schools where children take "national subjects" in which they learn the respective versions of "national history," leading to *de facto* discrimination and further separation. At elections, ethnic groups largely vote for parties of their own ethnicity. For future generations of Bosnians, it seems, Tito's slogan of "brotherhood and unity" will be little more than a historical reminiscence.

Despite the work of the ICTY and organizations such as the International Commission on Missing Persons (see http://www.ic-mp.org/home.php), thousands of Bosnians still do not know the whereabouts of missing family members. It is likely that some will never receive this information. At Srebrenica, close to the former base of the Dutch UN peacekeepers at Potocari, a burial site has been established for those victims of the 1995 mass executions whose remains were found in one of the numerous mass graves in the region and which could be identified. In 2007, Potocari also became the site of a memorial called the Srebrenica Memorial Room (see http://www.potocarimc.ba/). Every year in July, there is a commemoration ceremony to mark the anniversary of the fall of Srebrenica and to bury newly identified victims, bringing together tens of thousands of Bosnian Muslims and a small number of representatives from the international community. In the beginning, the Bosnian Muslims could only visit Potocari under the protection of a strong police force as Bosnian Serbs would throw stones at their buses and harass them on their journey. Eventually, the situation improved, but different opinions as to what and who to commemorate remain. In July 2005, for example, some Bosnian Serbs erected a seven-meter high cross in Kravica to mark the killing of some 40 Serbs by Bosnian Muslim forces in January 1993. The cross is placed at a highly visible spot which is along the main route that many of the buses bringing Bosnian Muslims to Potocari have to pass by. Kravica is also the place where during July 1995 an estimated 1,000 Bosnian Muslim men and boys were taken to be executed.

In the case of Kosovo, the question of the province's final status became the key concern for the international community. Following the end of the NATO air campaign in June 1999 there were numerous rounds of negotiations on this issue, first conducted by the Contact Group (composed of France, Germany, Italy, Russia, the United Kingdom and the United States), later aided by UN Special Envoy and former Finnish President Martii Ahtisaari. The Kosovo Albanians argued that nothing but independence should be the ultimate response to the crimes against humanity committed against them in 1999; Serbia and the Kosovo Serbs, conversely, pointed to the provocations of the KLA as the actual reason behind the conflict and the fact that all relevant UN resolutions have underscored the importance of recognizing Serbia's territorial integrity. In spring 2007, UN Special Envoy Ahtisaari presented his final proposal according to which Kosovo would gain a limited form of independence, under the supervision of the United Nations and with considerable autonomy to the Kosovo Serbs. Not surprisingly, the Kosovo Albanians accepted this proposal, while Serbia (and Russia) rejected it. When it became clear that no agreement could be reached on the Ahtisaari proposal, the United States as well as key EU states such as Germany, France and the United Kingdom gave the green light for the creation of an independent Kosovo. On February 17, 2008, the Kosovo Assembly adopted a declaration of independence. By June 2008, only 43 states (out of 192 UN members) had recognized Kosovo, underscoring how controversial and divisive this move was. Beyond Serbia and Russia—which of course consider the recognition of Kosovo as independent state a violation of international law—also EU member states such as Spain do not recognize Kosovo. Serbia has announced that it will ask the UN General Assembly to request the ICJ for an advisory opinion stating that the recognition of Kosovo's independence by the United States and others constitutes a violation of Serbia's sovereignty and international law.

In the meantime, fears that Kosovo's independence could lead to a *de facto* partitioning of the province, have materialized. The Kosovo Serbs in the northern part have protested strongly, in part violently, against this development and are currently beyond the reach of the new

Kosovo government and pose intricate challenges to both UNMIK and the European Union. This came as no surprise, as also prior to independence, Kosovo was marred by strong tensions between its Kosovo Serb minority and the Kosovo Albanian majority. More than 200,000 Kosovo Serbs had left their homeland during and after the NATO intervention in 1999; others followed later as a result of their disillusionment vis-à-vis the prospects of their status in a future Kosovo. Only about 15,000 returned, but they had little freedom of movement as they were isolated in small enclaves under the protection of KFOR peacekeeping forces. Occasionally, there were attacks on Kosovo Serbs, and frequently they were exposed to low-intensity harassment. According to a UNDP survey conducted prior to independence, more than 70% of the Kosovo Serbs were worried and anxious due to their ethnicity and fear for their safety and economic situation (UNDP, 2007b, p. 3).

Such inter-ethnic problems also persisted at the political level. For the last several years Kosovo Serb representatives refused to take part in the work of the Kosovo Assembly, and in November 2007 the Kosovo Serb population largely followed a call from Belgrade to boycott the elections. This non-relationship carried over to other entities as well; for example, the university in the Kosovo Serb enclave of Mitrovica has no official communication with the Kosovo ministry for education. The Advisory Committee to the European Framework Convention on the Protection of National Minorities concluded that "the reality in Kosovo remains disconcertingly far from [the agreed] laudable norms and plans. Hostility between Albanians and Serbs is still very tangible, a situation which also harms the protection of other communities in Kosovo, of which the Roma are in an especially difficult situation" (Advisory Committee, 2006, p. 3). A comprehensive NGO report put it even more bluntly: the Minority Rights Group speaks of "segregation" and asserted that the "situation of minorities today in Kosovo is the worst in Europe," arguing that "Kosovo has achieved [minority] rights only on paper . . . something has gone very wrong" (Minority Rights Group, 2006, pp. 6 and 28). It is indeed difficult to envisage the final status of the Kosovo Serbs in Kosovo. With a view to the newly gained independence of Kosovo as well as persisting claims by some Kosovo Serbs to be annexed to Serbia some observers have warned that Kosovo may serve as a precedent and inspire, if not provoke, other ethnic groups in- and outside Europe to copy these strategies (cf. Kuperman, 2005).

Overshadowed by the tensions surrounding the final status of Kosovo as independent nation, the international public has given much less attention to the question of whether the protracted and expensive rebuilding of Kosovo's society through international peacekeepers, police forces, and administrators has been a success. The international organizations (with the interesting exception of KFOR) have lost sympathy with the Kosovo Albanians. The approval ratings of UNMIK, for example, have continuously gone down from 65 percent in 2002 and have for the last two years been around 30 percent (UNDP, 2007b, p. 1). Both Kosovo Albanians and Kosovo Serbs are concerned with the enduring economic crisis, frustrated over the high rates of unemployment (remaining at around 45 percent) and complain about corruption, including that of representatives of international organizations (UNDP, 2007b, pp. 2–3). In November 2007, the annual progress report by the EU Commission stated that "corruption is still widespread and remains a major problem ... undermining a proper functioning of the institutions in Kosovo" (UNDP, 2007b, p. 13). Another persisting problem is the trafficking of women and under-aged girls for the purpose of forced prostitution. During the initial years following the establishment of UNMIK and KFOR it was the international presence which generated an unseen escalation of the sex trade. Instances of rape, sexual abuse, and even organized trafficking involving international staff became known. Surveys showed that in 2002, foreigners still stood for some 80 percent of the sex industry's income (Amnesty International, 2004, pp. 47ff.)—which, understandably, worsened the image of the international community in Kosovo.

Since Kosovo's newly gained independence, there are also still a number of shortcomings in the political system of the region which strongly underscore the need for long-term involvement of the international community. For example, Kosovo's judicial system still lacks a constitutional court and suffers from an increasing backlog of cases: as of November 2007, there were only eight war crimes trials underway and 48 under investigation. A backlog of 50,000 civil law cases and over 36,000 criminal law cases are still pending (Commission of the EU, *Progress Report*, 2007, pp. 11f.). The EU supports the build-up of the new Kosovo government by a 3,000 staff strong civilian mission called European Union Rule of Law Mission in Kosovo (EULEX).

Conclusion

Eric Markusen, one of the pioneers of genocide studies[17] and the co-author of an earlier version of this essay, wrote in the previous edition of this anthology that he believed, "based on a definition that combines the UN Genocide Convention with criteria developed by genocide scholars such as Helen Fein—as well as multiple visits to all sides of the conflict and the ICTY during and after the war—that the Bosnian Serbs and, on a smaller scale, Bosnian Croats did commit genocide" (Mennecke and Markusen, 2004, p. 429). Our co-authored text continued noting that "[g]enocide scholars, applying their own definitions rather than the one entailed by the UN Genocide Convention, will in no way be bound by the final verdict of the ICTY or other legal institutions. This is particularly so in the light of the well-known criticisms of the legal definition. . . . At the same time, genocide scholars will have to confront the fact that for the first time in history there is a legal body meticulously assessing the character of a conflict on the basis of a legal definition. The ICTY will make its final assessment after having heard and cross-examined thousands of survivors and expert witnesses and having analyzed tens of thousands of relevant documents, files and videos from the Balkan and other relevant countries. While law does not define reality, the work of the ICTY and other legal institutions should be scrutinized closely by any scholars interested in Bosnia and genocide" (ibid., p. 430).

The present author submits that this statement has retained its significance. In fact, to analyze and assess the legal proceedings on the atrocity crimes committed during the war in Bosnia has become even more important since the ICTY was not able to conclude the case against former Serb president Slobodan Milosevic (Prosecutor v. Milosevic, 2004, paras. 117ff.). Also, the ICJ in its aforementioned genocide case chose to limit itself to citing and confirming the ICTY's findings without putting the relevant case-law through a critical analysis (Mennecke and Tams, 2007, pp. 73f.). Significantly, Bosnia did not succeed in convincing the judges of the ICJ that Serbia should hand over the war-time records of its Supreme Defense Council. Serbia claimed that such a step would violate its national security. Critics have thus accused the Court of failing to scrutinize what may have been crucial evidence vis-à-vis Serbia's genocidal intent (see, for example, Sadovic, 2007; Simons, 2007). Obviously, all this only underscores that there is more research to be done on the question of genocide.

Future debates on the question of genocide should reach beyond calling genocide the "crime of crimes" and lead to informed and serious discussion, with respect for diverse interpretations—and not be reduced to polemics. In regard to this very issue, international law specialist and genocide scholar William Schabas (2001b) commented as follows:

> [r]egrettably, most discussions . . . usually degenerate, in short order, into accusations of "revisionism." Insistence upon giving the term "genocide" a precise and rigorous scope is said by some to further injure the sensibilities of the victims. Implied analogies are made with the repulsive and discredited work of those who deny the truth of the Holocaust . . ., making genuine discussion difficult. Of course, these innuendos are all wrong, because the debate is not about the truth of what happened. . . . Rather, it is about the characterization of the atrocities committed, and

atrocities they most certainly were. This debate is not about whether the crimes ... actually took place; it is only about whether they are most properly described as crimes against humanity, rather than "genocide" (pp. 288f.).

This being said, there remains important research to be done *beyond* the question of genocide. For example, the role of foreign mercenaries fighting on the side of the Bosnian Muslim army has not been sufficiently described yet. Also, the ongoing trial against the nationalist Serb politician Vojislav Seselj will hopefully provide interesting insights into the effects of hate speech and propaganda on the evolution of the Yugoslav wars (Prosecutor v. Seselj, 2007). Seselj is still actively involved in Serb politics and will, like Milosevic, defend himself so that the question of the impact of international criminal justice in the Balkans will be back on the agenda (cf. Orentlicher, 2008). Finally, the future trials of Ratko Mladic and Radislav Karadzic, if they ever are brought to The Hague,[18] will provide for further proceedings to be examined closely.

In 1999, when Kofi Annan presented the UN report on the fall of Srebrenica, he declared that "the tragedy of Srebrenica will haunt our history forever" (UN Secretary-General, 1999, *Report on the Fall of Srebrenica*, para. 503). The truth is that international memory and the length of time that the international community can focus its interest and concern on one conflict are limited. It seems there are too many conflicts, and life must go on. Consequently, this very recent period of European history is increasingly reduced to one commemoration per year, during which the international community officially takes note of the anniversary of the fall of Srebrenica. Other than this single occasion, this region of southeastern Europe, its people and their sufferings, are about to sink back into anonymity and oblivion. Be that as it may, it remains vitally significant, in fact critical, to remember and learn about Srebrenica, but also about less prominent crime sites such as Omarska, Foca, Celebici and Visegrad (Vulliamy, 2007). Otherwise we will not be able to understand why the rebuilding of the region, and the trust among the people,[19] takes so long. Paddy Ashdown, the former High Representative in Bosnia, was right when he concluded that "the miracle in Bosnia is how much has been done in ten years. . . . We have lost touch with how long time it takes. . . . Healing is always measured in decades" (quoted in Wilkinson, 2005). It is to be hoped for Bosnia and the other affected societies in the Balkans that decision-makers in governments and international organizations will keep this truth in mind. Indeed, the international community will need to continue its support for many years to come in order to further stabilize the region and the prospects for lasting peace.

Notes

1 The Former Yugoslavia was a multi-ethnic federation, including amongst other groups Serbs, Croats, and Bosnian Muslims. The latter were recognized by the Yugoslav constitution as a nation so that the term "Bosnian Muslim" did not refer to the religious affiliation, but to the "nationality" of a person. Starting with the war in the early 1990s, some Bosnian Muslims referred to themselves as "Bosniaks" to express their political aim of conserving Bosnia and Herzegovina as an entity and to downplay the religious undertones of the term "Bosnian Muslims" which was utilized in war propaganda. Today, the term "Bosniaks" has become officially recognized by the state of Bosnia and Herzegovina and is used in many, but not all, international reports. For the remainder of this chapter, we will in accordance with the language used by the International Criminal Tribunal for the Former Yugoslavia retain the term "Bosnian Muslims." For a more comprehensive discussion of the complicated history of the different terms and various groups residing in the Former Yugoslavia see Burg and Shoup, 1999, pp. 18ff.

2 The number of victims of the war in Bosnia and Herzegovina remains the object of great controversy, in particular among scholars and citizens of the region. In 2005, the non-governmental Research and Documentation Centre (RDC) in Sarajevo produced, after several years of research, a report listing the names of all known victims from all ethnic groups, which subsequently was confirmed by a team of international experts. As of June 2007, the Centre had established the personal data of more than 97,000 victims (of which more than 57,000 were soldiers and more than 64,000 were Bosnian Muslims, respectively) and estimated that the final result would not reach far beyond 100,000 dead. See the website of the RDC at www.idc.org.ba.

3 Among the cases of the International Criminal Tribunal for the Former Yugoslavia are several that are based on massive crimes committed in Bosnian Serb detention camps. See, Prosecutor v. Nikolic (Susica Camp), IT-94-2-S, Trial Chamber, Judgment, December 18, 2003; Prosecutor v. Krnojelac et al. (KP-Dom Foca Camp), IT-97-25, Trial Chamber, Judgment, March 15, 2002; and Prosecutor v. Kvocka et al. (Omarska, Keraterm and Trnopolje Camp), IT-98-30/1-T, Trial Chamber, Judgment, November 2, 2001. Bosnian Croat and Bosnian Muslim forces also established such camps, even if not as many. See, for example, the "Celebici Camp Case" on a prison camp near Konjic in central Bosnia where Serb detainees were killed, tortured, sexually assaulted, beaten, and otherwise subjected to cruel and inhumane treatment, Prosecutor v. Mucic et al., IT-96-21, Trial Chamber, Judgment, November 16, 1998.

4 Rape and other forms of sexual abuse of women (and to a lesser extent of men) are common features of war, and all sides in the Bosnian conflict perpetrated such atrocities; there is, however, a general consensus that the vast majority of the perpetrators were Serbs and that the vast majority of victims were Bosnian Muslims. See, for example, the *Final Report of the UN Commission of Experts* (1994), para. 251, and Naimark, 2001, p. 167.

5 It should be noted that the Yugoslav Jews and Roma suffered proportionally the most grievous losses at the hands of Nazi Germany, its allies and the Croat Ustasha regime. Four out of five Yugoslav Jews perished (ca. 57,000) and one third of the Roma population (ca. 18,000) were exterminated. See, Benson, 2004, pp. 77–78.

6 The arms embargo was imposed by the UN Security Council in Resolution 713 (1991)—before Yugoslavia dissolved. In the case against Serbia concerning alleged violations of the Genocide Convention before the International Court of Justice, Bosnia argued that this resolution effectively kept Bosnia from stopping the ongoing genocide. For an interesting discussion of the legal duty to prevent genocide, and the role of the Security Council and individual states therein, see Lauterpacht (1993), paras. 84–107.

7 For an example of such conspiracy theories, see the transcripts of the now aborted Milosevic trial, where the former Serb president contended that the fall of Srebrenica and the related executions were set up by the Muslim leadership (Prosecutor v. Milosevic, Transcripts, September 27, 2002, 10309ff.).

8 A French general, Bernard Janvier, had been in charge of the UN peacekeeping operations in Bosnia when Srebrenica fell. It was also a French General, Philippe Morillon, who, in 1993, famously promised the population of Srebrenica that they were "now under

protection of the UN forces" (UN Secretary-General *Report on the Fall of Srebrenica*, 1999, para. 38), and thus, presumedly, had nothing to fear.

    The original report by the committee established by the French Parliament, the Rapport D'Information Sur Les Événements de Srebrenica, is available at http://www.assemblee-nationale.fr/11/rap-info/i3413-01.asp. For further information and a critical evaluation of the French proceedings, see the special website provided by the French non-governmental organization *Médecins Sans Frontières* at http://www.paris.msf.org/srebrenica.

9   Application instituting Proceedings, Bosnia and Herzegovina v. Yugoslavia (Serbia and Montenegro), 20 March 1993, para. 137. All the relevant material—the application by Bosnia and Herzegovina, the written and oral proceedings including expert witness testimonies, and the final judgment with its separate and dissenting opinions—can be accessed at the website of the International Court of Justice at http://www.icj-cij.org.

10   It should be mentioned though that Serbia's president, Boris Tadic, called upon the Serb parliament and the people of Serbia to accept the judgment and to condemn the genocide of Srebrenica (Reuters, February 26, 2007).

11   On January 15, 1999, a group of approximately 45 Kosovo Albanians was shot by Serb forces in the village of Racak. What is disputed is whether these men were civilians that were massacred on the spot or whether they at least in part were KLA soldiers that were killed when fighting against the Serb forces. The issue also came up during the Milosevic trial, but was not clarified before the proceedings ended due to Milosevic's death. The Racak incident also figures in the ongoing trial of former Serb president Milutinovic and other Serb politicians and generals (Prosecutor v. Milutinovic et al., Indictment, 2006, para. 75). On Racak see also Klarin, 2002a.

12   The widely publicized case against Haradinaj is currently under appeal. On April 3, 2008 the Trial Chamber had ruled that the former prime minister could not be found guilty based on the evidence presented by the Prosecution. At the same time, the judges emphasized that many prosecution witnesses, despite of protective measures, had expressed great fear to give testimony (Prosecutor v. Haradinaj et al., Judgment, 2008, paras. 22–28).

13   It should be noted that not all human rights groups agreed to calling Kosovo a genocide. Human Rights Watch (1999a) and Amnesty International (1999), for example, harshly criticized the Serb conduct and called on the International Criminal Tribunal for the Former Yugoslavia to investigate possible war crimes, but stopped short of labeling it genocide.

14   Many of the Dutch peacekeepers who, in 1995, could not halt the fall of the safe zone remain deeply marked by their experiences. Many left the service, some suffered post-traumatic-stress and an unknown number committed suicide. In the Netherlands, the soldiers were often served up as scapegoats and portrayed as having failed in their duty; in December 2006, the Dutch government attempted to ameliorate this situation by presenting the soldiers with an insignia. Even though they did not receive a medal of honour, this move outraged survivors and the Bosnian Muslim leadership in Bosnia. In October 2007, a group of former Dutch peacekeepers visited Srebrenica, which again caused strong and mixed reactions (Dzidic, 2007; Boyle and Roknic, 2006).

15   During the war in Bosnia, about two million people became refugees. With more than one million having returned to their homes, the remaining people are believed to be spread out over the Balkans and other countries. While around 100,000 live in Serbia and Croatia, an additional 300,000 are still displaced within Bosnia itself. The remaining half-a-million refugees are thought to have established a new life elsewhere in the world. Information on the return of refugees to Bosnia and Srebrenica in particular can be found at the website of the UN Refugee Agency at www.unhcr.org.

16   This constellation—Srebrenica forming part of Republika Srpska which in turn forms part of Bosnia and Herzegovina—also influenced the earlier mentioned lawsuit of Bosnia against Serbia before the International Court of Justice. Bosnian Serb politicians tried to obstruct this case, amongst others, by filing an application with the Bosnian Constitutional Court to stop the lawsuit. The Bosnian Serbs saw little to gain from a case that was aimed at establishing that Serbia had committed genocide in Bosnia, as it was obvious that this also would affect the political and possibly legal standing of Republika Srpska. The strange situation of Bosnia entailed the somewhat absurd possibility that the International Court of

Justice ultimately would rule in favour of Bosnia and sentence Serbia to pay reparations for her involvement at Srebrenica—and these reparations would then partly benefit Republika Srpska, the entity that was established as a result of the crimes committed at Srebrenica. When the Court in February 2007 ruled that Srebrenica had been the site of genocide committed by Bosnian Serb forces, survivors from Srebrenica demanded (without success) that the town be given a special, internationalized status and separated from Republika Srpska.

17   See Markusen (2002), "My Path to Genocide Studies."

18   The former spokesman for the International Criminal Tribunal for the Former Yugoslavia has recently given new life to long-standing rumours that the United States together with other Western powers in the 1990s struck a deal with Mladic and Karadzic—offering amnesty in turn for them leaving Bosnian Serb politics (McKenna and Dzidic, 2007). It seems doubtful whether such a deal, if it ever had been struck, would continue to hinder the United States and others in arresting these two leading figures of the Bosnian war.

19   In 2007, the United Nations Development Programme (UNDP) published a comprehensive survey on how the population of Bosnia views the rebuilding of its society. The results provide interesting reading in regard to understanding the current political situation in Bosnia. For example, responding to the question whether one generally can trust most people, only 7 percent answered in the positive while 93 percent chose "you have to be very careful." According to the researchers behind the survey, the scope of this lack of social trust was surprising even compared to other transitional societies.

References

Advisory Committee to the European Framework Convention on the Protection of National Minorities (2006). *Opinion on the Implementation of the Framework Convention for the Protection of National Minorities.* ACFC/OP/I(2005)004.

Allcock, John B. (2005). *The International Criminal Tribunal for the Former Yugoslavia.* The Scholars' Initiative—Confronting Yugoslavia's Controversies. Available at http://www.salzburgseminar.org/ihjr/si/si/Team_10_Full_Text_Report.pdf.

Allen, Beverly (1996). *Rape Warfare: The Hidden Genocide in Bosnia-Herzegovina and Croatia.* Minneapolis: University of Minnesota Press.

Amnesty International (1999). *Amnesty Welcomes Milosevic Indictment.* EUR 70/81/98, May 27, 1999. Available at www.amnesty.org.

Amnesty International (2004). *"So Does It Mean We Have the Rights?" Protecting the Human Rights of Women and Girls Trafficked for Forced Prostitution in Kosovo.* EUR 70/010/2004. Available at http://web.amnesty.org/library/Index/ENGEUR700102004.

Andelman, David. A. (1980). "Yugoslavia: The Delicate Balance." *Foreign Affairs*, 58(4):835–52.

Assemblée Nationale (2001). "Rapport D'Information Sur Les Événements de Srebrenica." Available at http://www.assemblee-nationale.fr/11/rap-info/i3413-01.asp.

Associated Press (1999). "NATO Calls Serb Assault 'Genocide'." March 28, 1999. Available at http://www.usatoday.com/news/index/kosovo/koso092.htm.

Ball, Patrick, Betts, Wendy, Scheuren, Fritz, Dudukovich, Jana and Asher, Jana (2002). *Killings and Refugee Flow in Kosovo March–June 1999.* Available at http://shr.aaas.org/kosovo/icty_report.pdf.

Barron, Daniel (2007). "Yugoslav Tribunal Takes International Justice from Theory to Practice". *IWPR Tribunal Update 514.* Available at www.iwpr.net.

Benson, Leslie (2004). *Yugoslavia: A Concise History.* Hampshire: Palgrave Macmillan.

Benvenuti, Paolo (2001). "The ICTY Prosecutor and the Review of the NATO Bombing Campaign against the Federal Republic of Yugoslavia." *European Journal of International Law*, 12(3):503–530.

Bjelajac, Mile and Zunec, Ozren (2006). *The War in Croatia (1991–1995).* The Scholars' Initiative—Confronting Yugoslavia's Controversies. Available at http://www.salzburg seminar.org/ihjr/si/si/Team_7_Full_Text_Report.pdf.

Boyle, Katherine, and Roknic, Aleksandar (2006). "Dutch Peacekeepers to Return to Srebrenica." *IWPR Tribunal Update 476.* Available at www.iwpr.net.

Bringa, Tone (2002). "Averted Gaze: Genocide in Bosnia-Herzegovina," pp. 194–225. In Alexander

L. Hinton (Ed.) *Annihilating Difference: The Anthropology of Genocide*. Berkeley: University of California Press.

Brudholm, Thomas (2008). *Resentment's Virtue—Jean Améry and the Refusal to Forgive*. Philadelphia, PA: Temple University Press.

Burg, Steven L., and Shoup, Paul S. (1999). *The War in Bosnia-Herzegovina: Ethnic Conflict and International Intervention*. Armonk, NY: M.E. Sharpe.

Calic, Marie-Janine (2005). *Ethnic Cleansing and War Crimes, 1991–1995*. The Scholars' Initiative—Confronting Yugoslavia's Controversies. Available at http://www.salzburg seminar.org/ihjr/si/si/Team_4_Full_Text_Report.pdf.

Case Concerning the Application of the Convention on the Prevention and Punishment of the Crime of Genocide, Bosnia v. Yugoslavia (Serbia and Montenegro), Judgment, International Court of Justice, February 26, 2007.

Cassese, Antonio (2007). "A Judicial Massacre." *Guardian*, February 27, 2007.

Charny, Israel W. (2005). "Foreword," pp. vii–xi. In Samuel Totten (Ed.), *Genocide at the Millennium—A Critical Bibliography*. Volume 5. New Brunswick, NJ: Transaction Publishers.

Cigar, Norman (1995). *Genocide in Bosnia: The Policy of "Ethnic Cleansing."* College Station: Texas A&M University Press.

Clifford, Lisa (2007). "Srebrenica Survivors Sue Dutch and UN." *IWPR Tribunal Update 505*. Available at www.iwpr.net.

Commission of the European Union (2007). *Kosovo under UNSCR 1244 2007 Progress Report*. Available at http://ec.europa.eu/enlargement/pdf/key_documents/2007/nov/kosovo_progress_reports_en.pdf.

Cushman, Thomas, and Mestrovic, Stjepan G. (eds.) (1996). *This Time We Knew: Western Responses to Genocide in Bosnia*. New York: New York University Press.

Documentation Centre of the Republic of Srpska (2002). *Report about Case Srebrenica (The First Part)*. Available at http://www.institusb.org/pdf_dokumenti/Srebr_eng1.pdf.

Dunne, Tim, and Droslak, Daniela (2001). "Genocide: Knowing What It Is that We Want to Remember, or Forget, or Forgive," pp. 27–46. In Ken Booth (ed.) *The Kosovo Tragedy, The Human Rights Dimensions*. London: Frank Cass Publishers.

Dzidic, Denis (2007). "Fury as Dutch Soldiers Return to Srebrenica." *IWPR Tribunal Update 523*. Available at www.iwpr.net.

Eltringham, Nigel (2004). *Accounting for Horror: Post-Genocide Debates in Rwanda*. London: Pluto Press.

Fein, Helen (2000). "Civil Wars and Genocides: Paths and Circles." *Human Rights Review*, 1(3):49–61.

Fejzic et. al. v. The State of the Netherlands and the United Nations, Writ of Summons, District Court, The Hague, June 4, 2007. Available at http://www.vandiepen.com/media/srebrenica/pdf/srebrenica-writ_of_summons.pdf (website of the Dutch law firm Van Diepen Van der Kroef which represents the plaintiffs).

Freeman, Mark (2004). *Bosnia and Herzegovina:: Selected Developments in Transitional Justice*. International Centre for Transitional Justice. Available at http://www.ictj.org/images/content/1/1/113.pdf.

German Federal Constitutional Court, 2 BvR 1290/99, Decision, December 12, 2000, available at http://www.bundesverfassungsgericht.de/entscheidungen/rk20001212_2bvr129099en.html.

Gesellschaft für bedrohte Völker (1999). *Genozid im Kosovo*. Available at http://www.gfbv.ch/pdf/02-99-014.pdf.

Hoare, Marko Attila (2007). "The International Court of Justice and the Decriminalization of Genocide." *Bosnia Report*, vol. 55–56, January–July 2007. Available at http://www.bosnia.org.uk/news/news_body.cfm?newsid=2255.

Human Rights Watch (1999a). *Policy Statement on International Law in the Kosovo Conflict*. Available at http://www.hrw.org/campaigns/kosovo99/intlaw.shtml.

Human Rights Watch (1999b). *Abuses Against Serbs and Roma in the New Kosovo*. Available at http://www.hrw.org/reports/1999/kosov2/.

Human Rights Watch (2001). *The Milosevic Case: Questions and Answers—Is There an Anti-Serb Bias at the Tribunal?* Available at www.hrw.org/press/2001/08/milo-q&a-0829.htm.

Human Rights Watch (2004). *Failure to Protect: Anti-Minority Violence in Kosovo, March 2004*. Available at http://hrw.org/reports/2004/kosovo0704/kosovo0704.pdf.

Independent International Commission on Kosovo (2000). *The Kosovo Report*. Available at http://www.reliefweb.int/library/documents/thekosovoreport.htm.

Ingrao, Charles (2005). *The Safe Areas (1992–1995)*. The Scholars' Initiative—Confronting Yugoslavia's Controversies. Available at http://www.salzburgseminar.org/ihjr/si/si/Team_6_Full_Text_Report.pdf.

International Criminal Tribunal for the Former Yugoslavia (1995). *Press Release, CC/PIO/026-E*, The Hague, November 16, 1995.

International Criminal Tribunal for the Former Yugoslavia (2000). *Final Report to the Prosecutor by the Committee Established to Review the NATO Bombing Campaign Against the Federal Republic of Yugoslavia*. June 13, 2000. Available at http://www.un.org/icty/pressreal/nato061300.htm.

International Crisis Group (2007). *Ensuring Bosnia's Future: A New International Engagement Strategy*. Washington, D.C.: Author.

International Helsinki Federation for Human Rights (1999). *Genocide and Ethnic Cleansing in Kosovo*. Available at http://www.ihf-hr.org.

Jelacic, Nerma (2007). "Dismay and Jubilation of Hague Court Judgment." *Balkan Insight*, February 26, 2007. Available at www.birn.eu.com.

Jones, Adam (2006). *Genocide—A Comprehensive Introduction*. London and New York: Routledge.

Jordan, Sandra (1999). "So is Milosevic Guilty of Genocide?" *Guardian*, April 4, 1999.

Kaufman, Stephen (2007). "United States Sees Ruling as Opportunity for Healing." *USINFO*. Available at http://usinfo.state.gov/.

Kuperman, Alan J. (2005). "Suicidal Rebellions and the Moral Hazard of Humanitarian Intervention." *Ethnopolitics*, 4(2):149–173.

Klarin, Mirko (2002a). "Tribunal Judges Restrict Racak Evidence." *IWPR Tribunal Update 268*. Available at www.iwpr.net.

Klarin, Mirko (2002b). "Courtside: Brdjanin." *IWPR Tribunal Update 287*. Available at www.iwpr.net.

Lampe, John R. (2000). *Yugoslavia as History: Twice There Was a Country*. Cambridge: Cambridge University Press.

Lauterpacht, Elihu (1993). Separate Opinion, Case Concerning Application of the Convention on the Prevention and Punishment of the Crime of Genocide, Order of 13 September 1993, International Court of Justice, ICJ Reports 1993, pp. 407–448.

Lemarchand, René (2003). "Comparing the Killing Fields: Rwanda, Cambodia, and Bosnia," pp. 141–173. In Steven L. B. Jensen (Ed.), *Genocide: Cases, Comparisons, and Contemporary Debates*. Copenhagen: The Danish Center for Holocaust and Genocide Studies.

MacDonald, David Bruce (2002). *Balkan holocausts? Serbian and Croatian Victim-centred Prosecutor v. Propaganda and the War in Yugoslavia*. Manchester: Manchester University Press.

Markusen, Eric (2002). "My Path to Genocide Studies," pp. 295–311. In Samuel Totten and Steven Jacobs (Eds.), *Pioneers of Genocide Studies*. New Brunswick, NJ: Transaction Publishers.

McKenna, Brendan and Dzidic, Denis (2007). "Hartmann Doubts West's Will to Catch Suspects." *IWPR Tribunal Update 526*. Available at www.iwpr.net.

Mennecke, Martin (2007). "What's in a Name? Reflections on Using, Not Using and Overusing the 'G-Word'." *Genocide Studies and Prevention*, 2(1):57–72.

Mennecke, Martin, and Markusen, Eric (2003). "The International Criminal Tribunal for the Former Yugoslavia and the Crime of Genocide," pp. 293–359. In Steven L. B. Jensen (ed.), *Genocide: Cases, Comparisons, and Contemporary Debates*. Copenhagen: The Danish Center for Holocaust and Genocide Studies.

Mennecke, Martin, and Markusen, Eric (2004). "Genocide in Bosnia and Herzegovina," pp. 415–447. In Samuel Totten, William S. Parsons and Israel W. Charny (Eds.), *Century of Genocide: Critical Essays and Eyewitness Accounts*, 2nd edition. New York and London: Routledge.

Mennecke, Martin, and Tams, Christian J. (2007). "The Genocide Case Before the International Court of Justice." *Security and Peace*, 25(2):71–76.

Minority Rights Group (2006). *Minority Rights in Kosovo under International Rule*. Available at www.minorityrights.org.

Naimark, Norman M. (2001). *Fires of Hatred—Ethnic Cleansing in Twentieth Century Europe.* Cambridge, MA: Harvard University Press.

Netherlands Institute for War Documentation (2002). *Srebrenica, a "Safe" Area—Reconstruction, Background, Consequences, and Analyses of the Fall of a Safe Area.* Amsterdam: Boom Publishers.

Orentlicher, Diane (2008). *Shrinking the Space for Denial: The Impact of the ICTY in Serbia.* Available at http://www.justiceinitiative.org/db/resource2?res_id=104091.

Organization for Security and Co-operation in Europe, Mission in Kosovo (2002a). "OSCE calls for Review of Kosovo Genocide Conviction," January 19, 2001. Available at http://www.osce.org/kosovo/item_1_5679.html.

Organization for Security and Co-operation in Europe, Mission in Kosovo (2002b). *Kosovo's War Crimes Trials: A Review.* Available at http://www.osce.org/documents/mik/2002/09/857_en.pdf.

Pavlovic, Momcilo (2005). *Kosovo under Autonomy (1974–1990).* The Scholars' Initiative—Confronting Yugoslavia's Controversies. Available at http://www.salzburgseminar.org/ihjr/si/si/Team_1_Full_Text_Report.pdf.

Perriello, Tom, and Wierda, Marieke (2006). *Lessons from the Deployment of International Judges and Prosecutors in Kosovo.* International Centre for Transitional Justice. Available at http://www.ictj.org/static/Prosecutions/Kosovo.study.pdf.

Physicians for Human Rights (1999). *War Crimes in Kosovo—A Population-Based Assessment of Human Rights Violations Against Kosovar Albanians.* Available at http://physiciansforhumanrights.org/library/documents/reports/war-crimes-in-kosovo.pdf.

Power, Samantha (2002). *"A Problem from Hell": America and the Age of Genocide.* New York: Basic Books.

Prosecutor v. Jean Paul Akayesu, Case No. ICTR -96-4-T, Trial Chamber, Judgment, September 2, 1998.

Prosecutor v. Vidoje Blagojevic, Case No. IT-02-60, Judgment, Appeals Chamber, May 9, 2007.

Prosecutor v. Tihomir Blaskic, Case No. IT-95-14-T, Judgment, Trial Chamber, March 3, 2000.

Prosecutor v. Rasim Delic, Case No. IT-04-83-T, Amended Indictment, July 14, 2006.

Prosecutor v. Ante Gotovina et al., Case No. IT-06-90-PT, Joinder Indictment, March 6, 2007.

Prosecutor v. Ramush Haradinaj et al., Case No. IT-04-84, Judgment, Trial Chamber, April 3, 2008.

Prosecutor v. Goran Jelisic, Case No. IT-95-10-T, Trial Chamber, Judgment, December 14, 1999.

Prosecutor v. Goran Jelisic, Case No. IT-95-10-A, Appeals Chamber, Judgment, July 5, 2001.

Prosecutor v. Radovan Karadzic and Ratko Mladic, Case No. IT-95-5-I, Initial Indictment, July 24, 1995.

Prosecutor v. Radislav Krstic, Case No. IT-98-33-T, Trial Chamber, Judgment, August 2, 2001.

Prosecutor v. Radislav Krstic, Case No. IT-98-33, Appeals Chamber, Judgment, April 19, 2004.

Prosecutor v. Dragoljub Kunarac et al., Case No. IT-96-23-T, Trial Chamber, Judgment, February 22, 2001.

Prosecutor v. Fatmir Limaj et al., Case No. IT-03-66, Trial Chamber, Judgment, November 30, 2005.

Prosecutor v. Slobodan Milosevic et al., Case No. IT-99-37, Initial Indictment, May 24, 1999.

Prosecutor v. Slobodan Milosevic et al., Case No. IT-02-54, Transcripts, September 26–27, 2002.

Prosecutor v. Slobodan Milosevic, Case No. IT-02-54, Decision on Motion for Judgment of Acquittal, June 16, 2004.

Prosecutor v. Milan Milutinovic et al., Case No. IT-05-87, Third Amended Joinder Indictment, June 21, 2006.

Prosecutor v. Naser Oric, Case No. IT-03-68-T, Trial Chamber, Judgment, June 30, 2006.

Prosecutor v. Biljana Plavisic, Case No. IT-00-39 & 40/1, Trial Chamber, Judgment, February 27, 2003.

Prosecutor v. Vujadin Popovic et al., Case No. IT-05-88, Second Consolidated Amended Indictment, June 14, 2006.

Prosecutor v. Vojislav Seselj, Case No. IT-03-67, Reduced Modified Amended Indictment, March 29, 2007.

Prosecutor v. Dusko Sikirica et al., Case No. IT-95-8, Trial Chamber, Judgment on Defence Motions to Acquit, September 3, 2001.

Prosecutor v. Milomir Stakic, Case No. IT-97-24, Trial Chamber, Judgment, July 31, 2003.

Remington, Robin Alison (1984). "The Politics of Scarcity in Yugoslavia." *Current History*, 83(496):370–374.

Republika Srpska, The Commission for Investigation of the Events In and Around Srebrenica Between 10th and 19th July 1995 (2004). *The Events In and Around Srebrenica Between 10th and 19th July 1995*. Available at http://www.vladars.net/pdf/srebrenicajun2004engl.pdf.

Reuters (2007). "President Tells Serbia: Condemn Srebrenica Massacre." February 26, 2007.

Reuters (2007). "Bosnian Muslims Protest Against UN Court Ruling." February 27, 2007.

Ronayne, Peter (2005). "Genocide in Kosovo," pp. 55–74. In Samuel Totten (ed.), *Genocide at the Millennium: Genocide—A Critical Bibliographic Review*. Volume 5. New Brunswick, NJ: Transaction Publishers

Sadovic, Merdijana (2007). "Could Key Records Have Altered ICJ Ruling?" *IWPR Tribunal Update 492*. Available at www.iwpr.net.

Schabas, William A. (2000). *Genocide in International Law*. Cambridge: Cambridge University Press.

Schabas, William A. (2001a). "Was Genocide Committed in Bosnia and Herzegovina? First Judgments of the International Criminal Tribunal for the Former Yugoslavia." *Fordham International Law Journal*, 25(1):23–53.

Schabas, William A. (2001b). "Problems of International Codification—Were the Atrocities in Cambodia and Kosovo Genocide?" *New England Law Review*, 35(2):287–302.

Schabas, William A. (2007). "Genocide and the International Court of Justice: Finally, a Duty to Prevent the Crime of Crimes." *Genocide Studies and Prevention*, 2(2):101–122.

Scheffer, David (2007a). "Genocide and Atrocity Crimes." *Genocide Studies and Prevention*, 1(3):229–250.

Scheffer, David (2007b). "The World Court's Fractured Ruling on Genocide." *Genocide Studies and Prevention*, 2(2):123–136.

Selimovic et al. v. Republika Srpska, Decision on Admissibility and Merits, Case No. CH/01/8365, Human Rights Chamber for Bosnia and Herzegovina, March 7, 2003. Available at http://hrc.ba.

Serbian Academy of Arts and Sciences (1986). *Memorandum*. Available at http://www.trepca.net/english/2006/serbian_memorandum_1986/serbia_memorandum_1986.html.

Shaw, Martin (2007). "The International Court of Justice: Serbia, Bosnia and Genocide," February 28, 2007. Available at http://www.opendemocracy.net/globalization-institutions_government/icj_bosnia_serbia_4392.jsp.

Simons, Marlise (2007). "Serbia's Darkest Pages Hidden from the World Court." *International Herald Tribune*. April 8, 2007.

Steinweis, Alan E. (2005). "The Auschwitz Analogy: Holocaust Memory and American Debates over Intervention in Bosnia and Kosovo in the 1990s." *Holocaust and Genocide Studies*, 19(2):276–289.

Stitkovac, Ejub (1999). "Croatia: The First War," pp. 153–173. In Jasminka Udovicki and James Ridgeway (eds.), *Burn This House: The Making and Unmaking of Yugoslavia*. Chapel Hill, NC: Duke University Press.

UN Commission of Experts on Grave Breaches of the Geneva Conventions (1994). *Final Report of the Commission of Experts on Grave Breaches of the Geneva Conventions and Other Violations of International Humanitarian Law Committed in the Territory of the Former Yugoslavia Established Pursuant to Security Council Resolution 780 (May 27)*. United Nations Document S/1994/674. New York: United Nations.

United Nations Development Programme (2007a). *The Silence Majority Speaks—Snapshots of Today and Visions of the Future of Bosnia and Herzegovina*. Available at http://www.undp.ba/?PID=7&RID=413.

United Nations Development Programme (2007b). "Fast Facts." *Kosovo Early Warning Report*. No. 18. Available at http://www.kosovo.undp.org/repository/docs/Fast_Facts-18_Eng.pdf.

UN Secretary-General (1999). *Report of the Secretary-General Pursuant to General Assembly Resolution 53/35, The Fall of Srebrenica. November 15*. 54th Session, UN GA Doc. A/54/549, available at www.un.org/peace/srebrenica.pdf.

Vulliamy, Ed (2007). "Bosnia's Reckoning: The Painful Road to Reconciliation." *Bosnia Report*. Available at http://www.bosnia.org.uk/news/news_body.cfm?newsid=2288.

Wilkinson, Ray (2005). "Remembering Srebrenica." *UNHCR News*. Available at http://www.unhcr.org/news/NEWS/42ce70314.html.

WEBSITES

http://hrw.org/doc/?t=justice_balkans (website of the non-governmental organization Human Rights Watch on transitional justice efforts in the Balkans).

www.genocidewatch.org (website of the non-governmental organization Genocide Watch).

www.ic-mp.org (website of the International Commission on Missing Persons).

www.icj-cij.org (website of the International Court of Justice).

www.idc.org.ba (website of the Bosnian non-governmental Research and Documentation Centre).

www.nato.int/kfor (website of the Kosovo Protection Force KFOR).

www.osce.org (website of the Organization for Security and Co-operation in Europe).

www.paris.msf.org (website of the French non-governmental organization Médecins Sans Frontières).

www.potocarimc.ba/ (website of the Srebrenica Memorial Room).

www.un.org/icty (website of the International Criminal Tribunal for the Former Yugoslavia).

www.unhcr.org (website of the UN Refugee Agency).

www.unmikonline.org (website of the United Nations Interim Administration Mission in Kosovo, UNMIK).

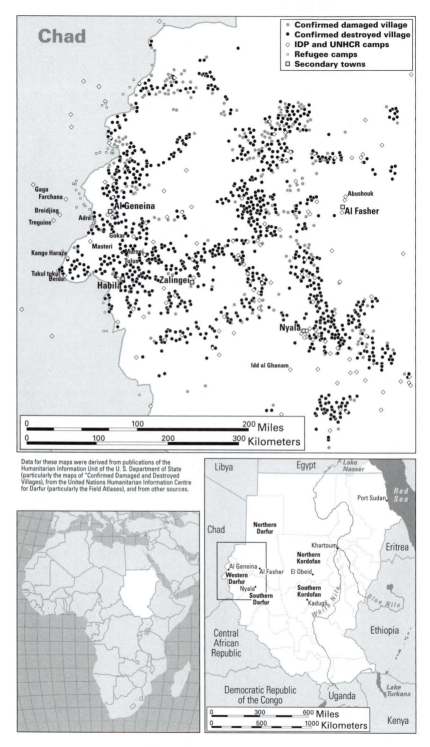

Data for these maps were derived from publications of the
Humanitarian Information Unit of the U. S. Department of State
(particularly the maps of "Confirmed Damaged and Destroyed
Villages), from the United Nations Humanitarian Information Centre
for Darfur (particularly the Field Atlases), and from other sources.

Darfur Region of Sudan

CHAPTER 17

The Darfur Genocide

SAMUEL TOTTEN

Introduction

The mass killing of black Africans of Darfur, Sudan, by Government of Sudan troops and *Janjaweed*[1] (Arab militia) constitutes the first acknowledged genocide of the twenty-first century (2003 to present).[2] Unlike the other genocidal events addressed in *Century of Genocide*, this genocide continues unabated to this day (December 2007) against the few remaining black African villages in Darfur and against internally displaced persons camps that dot the Darfur landscape. Although the process of killing (bombings from airplanes, automatic weapons fire, stabbings, the torching of people, the poisoning of wells, and chasing the victim population out into forbidding deserts without water or food) has remained constant over the years, the "progress" of the killing has ebbed and flowed as the Government of Sudan has turned the spigot of violence on and off according to its wiles in its game of brinkmanship with the international community. To date, it is estimated that well over 250,000 people have been killed and/or perished as a result of "genocide by attrition" (meaning, via starvation, dehydration, and unattended injuries).

Darfur, a region in west Sudan, is comprised of three states (Northern Darfur, Western Darfur, and Southern Darfur). The three-state region is roughly the size of France, and shares borders with Libya, Chad, and the Central African Republic. The vast majority of the people of Darfur, both the so-called "black Africans" and the Arabs, are Muslim.

555

Darfur is one of the most under-developed and isolated regions of Sudan, the latter of which constitutes one of the 25 poorest countries in the world. More specifically, over 90 percent of Sudan's citizens live below the poverty line, barely eking out an existence.

While much of the Darfur region consists of large swaths of burning desert (except during the rainy season when *wadis* swell with water), it also has lush grasslands where herds graze and areas where crops are cultivated. Up until recently, the most productive land was largely occupied by sedentary farmers and cattle owners who tended to be non-Arabs. At certain times of the year, though, the pasture land was used by the nomads to graze the herds, as a result of mutual agreement between the sedentary black Africans and Arab semi-nomadic and nomadic peoples. This resulted in a symbiotic relationship of sorts; that is, while the Arabs' animals were allowed to feed and be watered, the herds fertilized the ground owned by the black Africans, thus renewing the soil for subsequent growing seasons.

When conflicts erupted in the not too distant past amongst individuals and/or groups (be it among individuals in the same village, different black African tribal groups, or between black Africans and Arabs), the disagreements were generally resolved by the intervention and mediation of local leaders (*umdas* or *sheiks*). While neither conflict nor violence were uncommon, it rarely resulted in wholesale violence that went on for months, let alone years. When called for, some sort of "blood money" was paid to the victim, be it for kin who were killed, animals stolen, or for some other transgression. The handing over of the blood money by the "guilty party" to the "victim" generally settled the grievance, and life went on as usual.

Notably, there was a certain amount of intermarriage amongst and between the various peoples of Darfur, including non-Arabs and Arabs. Thus, different groups of people cohabited as neighbors, friends, and even relatives—and not as sworn enemies due to ethnic, racial, or any other type of classification/category.

Who Is Committing This Genocide?

Both Government of Sudan (GOS) troops and the so-called *Janjaweed* (Arab militia) are the actors carrying out the actual killing, mass and gang rape, and the wholesale destruction of black African villages. Ample evidence indicates that the vast majority of the attacks against black African villages from 2003 onward have been undertaken, in tandem, by GOS troops and the *Janjaweed*. In most cases, the attacks have involved bombings by GOS aircraft, followed by a ground attack involving hundreds of *Janjaweed* on camels and horses and four-wheel vehicles (some mounted with machine guns) carrying both GOS troops and *Janjaweed.*

The *Janjaweed* comprises semi-nomadic and nomadic Arab herders. Many had previously fought in one or more of the wars in the region, a good number serving as mercenaries. Increasingly, it should be noted, many Arab herders have been forced—upon the threat of death to themselves and harm to their families—to join in the attacks against the black Africans. It is also significant to note, and recognize, that many Arab herders are not involved in the attacks, are not members of the *Janjaweed,* and do not necessarily support—and may, in fact, look askance at—the actions of the GOS and *Janjaweed.* In this regard, Julie Flint's (2004) observations are significant:

> It cannot be stated too often that the majority of Arab tribes in Darfur have refused to join the government war in Darfur, despite blandishments, threats and inducements that range from sacks filled with cash to cars to development programs and homes in the capital, Khartoum
>
> In Darfur, the Rizeigat, Beni Halba, Habbaniya, Taaisha, Mahariya, Beni Hussein, Misseriya, and Maaliya tribes, to name only some of Darfur's Arab tribes, have all chose either to cast their lot in with the African neighbors or to endeavourer to remain neutral (p. 1).

The Sudanese government readily admits that its troops responded to attacks on government facilities (including military bases) by black African rebels, but it has claimed, time and again, that the *Janjaweed* is responsible for the subsequent and sustained scorched earth attacks against the black Africans and that it (the government) does not have the means to rein them in as they (the *Janjaweed*) are loose cannons. Such assertions are disingenuous, at best; again, ample evidence exists that the vast majority of the attacks on the black African villages have been carried out by both GOS troops and the *Janjaweed* (Human Rights Watch, 2004a; Physicians for Human Rights, 2005; U.S. State Department, 2004).

There is also evidence that the GOS purposely hired the *Janjaweed* to join GOS troops in carrying out the attacks because GOS military troops were already overstretched in their war in southern Sudan and thus did not have enough soldiers available to address the crisis in Darfur (Human Rights Watch, 2004b).[3] Concomitantly, since many of the soldiers in the GOS military were black African, the GOS didn't trust the latter to carry out attacks on their own people's villages.

Who Are the Victims?

As previously mentioned, the victims of the genocide in Darfur are various black African tribal groups in Darfur. The main groups that have been attacked are the Fur, Massalit, and Zaghawa. That said, like many, if not most, of the issues surrounding the Darfur crisis, the composition of the population of Darfur is a complex one. Indeed, although "African" and "Arab" are common terms used in describing and, at least in part, explaining, the conflict, neither term does justice to the diversity of ethnic groups that make up Darfur nor to "the nuanced relationships among ethnic groups" (Human Rights Watch, 2004a, p. 1 of "The Background").

There are many, in fact, who claim that there is virtually no difference between the so-called black Africans of Darfur and the Arab population (Mamdani quoted in Sengupta, 2004, p. 1; De Waal, 2004a; De Waal, 2004c). Mamdani (2004), for example, asserts that ". . . all parties involved in the Darfur conflict—whether they are referred to as 'Arab' or as 'African'—are equally indigenous and equally black" (p. 2). He has also stated that "from the cultural point of view, one can be both African and Arab" (Mamdani, 2004, p. 2). Such individuals assert that all the people are black (and not necessarily "light" as the Arabs are sometimes purported to be), and that since all live in Africa they are all African. In this regard, Alex De Waal (2004a), an expert on Sudan, has asserted that "characacterizing the Darfur war as 'Arabs' versus 'Africans' obscures the reality. Darfur's Arabs are black, indigenous, African Muslims—just like Darfur's non Arabs, who hail from the Fur, Massalit, Zaghawa and a dozen smaller tribes" (p. 1). More specifically, De Waal (2004b) asserts that

> The Zaghawa . . . are certainly indigenous, black and African: they share distant origins with the Berbers of Morocco and other ancient Saharan peoples. But the name of the "Bedeyat," the Zaghawa's close kin, should alert us to their true origins: pluralize in the more traditional manner and we have "bedeyiin" or Bedouins. Similarly, the Zaghawa's adversaries in this war, the Darfurian Arabs, are "Arabs." In the ancient sense of "Bedouin," meaning desert nomad . . ., Darfurian Arabs, too, are indigenous, black and African. In fact there are no discernible racial or religious differences between the two: all have lived there for centuries (n.p.).

Many also assert that there has been so much intermarriage between various groups (and there are scores upon scores of various tribal groups within the three-state region of Darfur) that it is almost impossible to definitively state whether a person is from one tribe (or ethnic group) or another. Some also assert that "where the vast majority of people [in Darfur] are Muslim and Arabic-speaking, the distinction between 'Arab' and 'African' is more cultural than racial" (UN Office for the Coordination of Humanitarian Affairs, 2003, n.p.; IRIN, 2007, p. 2). Mamdani has asserted that "the real roots of combat are not racial or ethnic but political and economic" (quoted in Hill, 2006). Some have also noted that certain individuals who have, over time, attained a certain amount of wealth have actually chosen to become "Arab."

That said, both the perpetrators and the victims, themselves, *do make a distinction between* those who are purportedly "Arab" and those who are purportedly "black African." One major report after another (Human Rights Watch, 2004a; Physicians for Human Rights, 2005; U.S. State Department, 2004) that includes first-person testimony by the internally placed persons (IDPs) and refugees from Darfur contains vast amounts of information in regard to the aforementioned distinctions made by the very people involved in the crisis. For example, in its report, *Darfur Destroyed*, Human Rights Watch (2004a) reports that "Especially since the beginning of the conflict in 2003, members of the Zaghawa, Fur, and Massalit communities have used these terms [black Africans and Arabs] to describe the growing racial and ethnic polarization in Darfur, perceived to result from discrimination and bias emanating from the central government" (p. 1, "The Background").

Furthermore, such testimony also includes ample evidence that the *Janjaweed* frequently scream racial epithets at their black African victims. The same is true in the scores of testimony this author has collected in interviews in refugee camps in Chad with survivors of the genocide. More specifically, one black African IDP and refugee after another has commented on how the *Janjaweed* (and, for that matter, GOS soldiers) screamed such epithets as slave, slave dogs, and *zurega* (which is roughly the equivalent of "nigger") at them during the attacks on their villages. All are considered extremely derogatory and vile by the victims.

Other comments that the perpetrators have spewed at the black Africans are: "You are not a real Sudanese, you're black. . . . We are the real Sudanese. No blacks need stay here"; "We are going to cut off your roots"; "The President of Sudan ordered us to cleanse Darfur of the dirty slaves so we can have the beginning of the Arab Union" (quoted in Totten, 2006, p. 98). Emily Wax (2004), a *Washington Post* correspondent in Africa, reported that as a 22-year old black African woman was grabbed and about to be raped by six *Janjaweed*, they spat out: "Black girl, you are too dark. You are like a dog. We want to make a light baby" (p. 1). Wax (2004) also reported that another young woman who was raped by militiamen was told, "Dog, you have sex with me. . . . The government gave me permission to rape you. This is not your land anymore, *abid* [slave], go" (p. 2).

Why Is This Genocide Being Committed?

The causes of any genocide are extremely complex, and the Darfur genocide is no exception. No act of genocide is ever the result of a single factor; indeed, genocide results from a synergy of trends, issues, and events that influence the thinking and actions of potential perpetrators who, ultimately, intend to extirpate, in one way or another, those it perceives as enemies, dangerous and/or loathsome in some way (and thus "outside their universe of obligation"). In the case Darfur (2003–present), the issues/events that combined to make genocide possible were the following: extreme drought; increased desertification; Arab supremacism; authoritarianism; extreme nationalism; an ever-increasing bellicosity in the region (within Sudan, Darfur and beyond its borders); and the disenfranchisement of black Africans at the hands of the Sudanese government.

Extreme Drought and Desertification

Since the early 1970s, numerous droughts (including the "great drought" of 1984–1985), resulted in ever-increasing desertification within the Darfur region. Tellingly, a result of a severe drought in the 1970s, sections of the Sahara Desert reportedly crept south by as much as 60 miles.

The desertification of the land in Darfur, accompanied by fierce stand storms, resulted in a dramatic decline in the yield of produce, loss of pastureland, and a loss of livestock. All of the latter, along with famine (some caused by nature, some by man—and some lasting much longer than those of the past), increased tensions over land usage and access to water and, ultimately, resulted in ever-increasing conflict and violence between the nomadic/semi-nomadic Arab groups and the sedentary/farming group of non-Arabs..

Exacerbating the situation was the fact that drought affected other countries in the region as well, and nomads from Chad and Libya migrated to Darfur in extremely large numbers in search of grazing land, which put further pressure on the scant resources available.

Not only did nature force nomadic groups to sweep lower south to locate sustenance for their herds, it also resulted in their grazing their herds for longer than usual. At one and the same time, farmers became evermore protective of their land. Some even resorted to putting up fences and establishing fees for land and water usage. What constituted protective efforts by the sedentary peoples/farmers were perceived by the nomads as being stingy and unfair.

Arab Supremacism

Arab supremacism is an ideology that preaches, promotes, and sustains—in certain situations, at all cost—the notion that Arab beliefs and way of life are superior to all others. In that regard, it is an ideology that perceives all those who are not Arab as inferior. In Sudan, this has led to both the demonization and disenfranchisement of certain groups. Essentially, and, ultimately, it calls for Arab dominance in all aspects of life—culturally, politically, economically, judicially, and socially.

The origins of Arab supremacism "lay in the Libya of Colonel Gaddafi in the 1970s" and "the politics of the Sahara" (Flint and De Waal, 2005, p. 50). Gaddafi, in fact, fantasized about establishing an "Arab belt" across Africa. To accomplish this goal, he created, with his oil riches, various mechanisms, including the *Faliq al Islamiyya* (Islamic Legion), which recruited Bedouins from Mauritania to Sudan; the *Munazamat Da'awa al Islamiyya* (Organization of the Islamic Call), which fostered Islamic philanthropy and evangelization; and sponsored the Sudanese opposition National Front, including the Muslim Brothers (or Muslim Brotherhood) and the *Ansar* (the *umma*'s military wing).

Any mention of Arab supremacism and Sudan is incomplete if it neglects to comment on the role of Hassan Abd al Turabi—an Islamist, former law professor at the University of Khartoum, and a government official under Jaafar Nimeiri and then Omar al Bashir. Turabi was a major figure for decades in the Muslim Brotherhood, which originated in Eygpt and had been active in Sudan since 1949. The group's primary goal in Sudan was to "institutionalize Islamic law" (Mertz, 1991, n.p.). In 1964, Turabi became the Secretary-General of the Muslim Brotherhood, which was the year that the Brotherhood established its first political party. Turabi was closely involved with the Islamic Charter Front, which proposed that Sudan adopt an Islamic Constitution. The latter basically established that those Sudanese who were not Muslim would, from that point forward, be considered and, treated, as second-class citizens.

Over time, the Brotherhood established a close relationship with young Darfurians, convincing the latter that the Brotherhood's headlong push for the establishment of Islamic law was positive and that, as an organization, it was bereft of the prejudice and discrimination that was so rife within the Sudanese government when it came to ethnic and tribal differences. Understandably, these same young people came to trust and support Turabi.

Beginning as a peaceful civilian movement, the Brotherhood gradually morphed into a powerful and radical rebel group. More specifically, following a *coup d'état* in 1969, in which Colonel Jaafar Nimeiri became prime minister of Sudan, Turabi's Islamist Party was dissolved. Immediately, though, the Islamists began planning its own rebellion. The planned rebellion, however, was quashed by the Sudanese military in March 1970. The combined effort of the Sudanese air force and ground troops resulted in the deaths of hundreds of Islamists fighters. Many survivors sought exile in Libya, where they established military-like camps in preparation for a later attempt to dislodge the Nimeiri (who eventually became president) government. As Flint and De Waal (2005) note, "Their [the Islamists'] plan [while undergoing training] was an armed invasion of Sudan from bases in Libya, crossing Darfur and Kordofan to storm the capital. [Ultimately,] in July 1976, the Ansar-Islamist alliance very nearly succeeded . . . but the army counterattacked and the rebels were defeated" (pp. 22–23).

Turabi, a master at Machiavellian politics, found a way to disassociate himself from the failed invasion and to ingratiate himself with Nimeiri. In fact, Turabi became so close to Nimeiri that he became his attorney-general in 1977. At one and the same time, in his quest to establish an Islamic state, "[Turabi] infiltrated Islamist cadres into the armed forces, including elite units such as the air force" (Flint and De Waal, 2005, p. 23).

Always intent on imposing his Islamist vision on Sudan, Turabi, in 1983, led the way in implementing *sharia* (Islamic law) in Sudan. The imposition of *sharia* resulted in a slew of amputations and hangings. Due to a combination of disgust and fear at the brutality meted out by the government as a result of its *sharia*-induced legislation and actions, Nimeiri was overthrown in 1985. Parliamentary rule was subsequently reinstated. Almost immediately, Turabi helped to establish the National Islamic Front (NIF), a political party that was controlled by the Muslim Brotherhood.

For a short while, Sudan returned to parliamentary rule. However, in 1989, with Turabi in the shadows but playing an integral role as a power broker, the military overthrew the elected government, and Omar al Bashir was installed as president of Sudan. As Sudan entered a period of increased turbulence, Turabi is said to have virtually served as the real power behind the scenes.

In the early 1990s, the Sudanese Islamists began to inculcate Islamist thought throughout Sudan. At the forefront of the effort were Turabi and Ali Osman Mohamed Taha, an ardent Islamist and an on again, off again government figure. As part and parcel of this effort, Turabi, in 1990, had established the Popular Arab Islamic Conference (PAIC), which was basically a regional organization for political Islamist militants. In his position as secretary-general of PAIC, Turabi induced the Sudan government to create "an-open door policy for Arabs, including Turabi's Islamist associate Osama bin Laden, who made his base in Sudan in 1990–1996" (Human Rights Watch, 2002, p. 1). In order to accomplish their goals, "Islamist cadres were dispatched to foment a new Islamist consciousness in every village. Islamist philanthropic agencies were mobilized to open schools and clinics, and to support the Popular Defence Forces. A raft of programmes aimed at building an Islamic Republic was launched" (Flint and De Waal, 2005, p. 28). Ultimately, though, Turabi concluded that if he was to succeed in gaining power through the elective process, he needed to part ways with the Brotherhood. That was true, for the Brotherhood perceived Islamism and Arabism as one and the same, and many of those residing in Darfur were not Arab; and since Turabi believed he needed the votes of those in the West who were not Arab, he, calculatingly, cut his ties with the Brotherhood.

In 1999, Turabi set out to become the major power in Sudan. But, once again, his grand plans came to naught. Not only did Ali Osman break with Turabi as a result of looking askance at Turabi's ploys, schemes, and intrigues, but al Bashir—not about to be pushed aside—announced a state of emergency and removed Turabi from office (thus, wiping out Turabi's powerbase within the government). The ramifications were immense for Darfur: "The Bashir-Turabi split lost Darfur for the government, but made it possible to make peace in the South" (Flint and De Waal, 2005, p. 41).

Authoritarianism

For nearly twenty years (1989–present), Sudan has been under the authoritarian rule of Omar al Bashir. His government controls virtually every aspect of Sudanese life. And when al Turabi was a power behind the scenes, it meant that the Islamists were, like puppeteers, largely directing all aspects of Sudanese life. Those living in what is commonly referred to as the "peripheries" in Sudan (that is, those areas far from Khartoum, the "center" or powerbase in Sudan), were (and are) perceived and treated as second class citizens.

As soon as the new al Bashir government, with its Islamist focus, took power in 1989, it began dictating what was and was not acceptable in the way of behavior, dress, speech, and assembly (or association) with others. Furthermore, individuals were arrested for any and all dissent, people "disappeared" into secret prisons, torture was meted out regularly and viciously, and the judicial system answered only to al Bashir and his cronies.

Disenfranchisement

First, it is important to note that Darfur is not only one of the poorest regions in Sudan but one of the poorest regions in all of Africa. Second, a single region of Sudan, the North (where Khartoum, the capital, is located), which comprises just over five percent of the population of the country, virtually controls all of Sudan. Put another way, it controls the wealth of the nation and it controls the politics of the nation. Almost all of those who hold major posts within the country have come from the North. Indeed, all of the presidents and prime ministers have come from the North, along with the vast majority of those who head-up important positions dealing with development, the infrastructure of the country, and banking. It is also the seat of advanced education in the nation Third, for years on end, the black Africans of Darfur have requested the establishment of more schools, medical facilities, and roads—all of which are minimal in number, sorely under-funded, or, as is true in the case of roads, largely nonexistent. Fourth, most, if not all, of the black Africans' requests for assistance and largely fell on deaf ears in Khartoum.

For many years, the black Africans of Darfur decried the hegemony of the North, as well as the fact that they (those residing in the West) have suffered prejudice, discrimination, and disenfranchisement. Numerous examples of such disenfranchisement could be cited, but three shall suffice. First, "infant mortality in the West (at 122.5 boys and 104.2 girls dying per 1000 births) is strikingly different from infant mortality in the North (100.1 boys and 88.8 girls per thousand births)" (Cobham, 2005, n.p.). This difference is undoubtedly due in large part to the fact that adequate medical facilities and qualified medical personnel are available in the North but not in the West. According to the Justice and Equality Movement (2000), a rebel group that issued the so-called *Black Book* that delineated the facts of disenfranchisement in Darfur, "The entire State of Western Darfur has two medical specialists in the field of obstetrics and gynaceology, one in Geneina and the other in Zalengay. They are to serve a population of 1,650,000 aided by [a] few medical students who visit the area for training and for escaping mandatory military service" (p. 53).

Second, "water development is currently reserved for the ever-expanding capital Khartoum. The rest of the country is left out, dying of thirst as well as diseases like malaria, kalazar, bilharsiasis, and other water-borne diseases" (Justice and Equality Movement, 2000, p. 41).

Third, the development of the country (the construction of roads, bridges, water systems, hospitals, schools) is largely limited to the North. Even those other areas that have seen development largely benefit those who are from the North. As for the West, "the entire Western region now lacks a single developmental scheme which could support one province for a single week" (Justice and Equality Movement, 2000, p. 5).

In May 2000, *The Black Book* (whose complete title is *The Black Book: Imbalance of Power and Wealth in Sudan*) mysteriously appeared in Khartoum. Copies were handed out outside major mosques following Friday prayers. Many are said to have even been placed, brazenly, on the desks of key Sudanese officials, including that of al Bashir. As photocopies of the book were "spontaneously" produced, *The Black Book* began to appear throughout the country and abroad. *The Black Book*, was dedicated, in part, to ". . . the Sudanese people who have endured oppression, injustice and tyranny."

The Black Book argues that ever since Sudan's independence those who control the political and economic power within the Sudanese government (frequently referred to as "the elite," or, variously, "the ruling elite"), and by extension, the entire country, are from northern Sudan. More specifically, it asserts that the vast majority of posts in the government, the judiciary, the military, and the police all come from the North (and primarily from three tribal groups, the Shaygiyya, Ja'aliyiin and Danagla), and/or are appointed by the "centre" or the ruling elite. It also states that the "peripheries" of the country (those in the West, South and East) have been purposely denied fair representation in the government, and have been forced to lead a life of impoverishment. In the authors' introduction, it is asserted that at the turn of the millennium, Sudan remains "steeped in poverty, illiteracy, disease and lack of development" (Justice and Equality Movement, 2000, p. 1).

De Waal (2004b) argues that *The Black Book* essentially "condemned the Islamist promise to Darfur as a sham. *The Black Book* was a key step in the polarization of the country along politically constructed 'racial' rather than religious lines, and it laid the basis for a coalition between Darfur's radicals, who formed the SLA, and its Islamists, who formed the other rebel organization, the Justice and Equality Movement" (p. 8). *The Black Book* may have constituted a key step in the polarization of the country along politically constructed "racial" lines, but it was hardly the first or *the* major step. In light of the ongoing attacks since the early 1990s by various Arab groups (nomads, semi-nomads and then, collaboratively, by Arab herders and GOS troops) against black African villages, it seems obvious that the "racial divide" was certainly evident, and being acted up, many years prior to the appearance of *The Black Book*. In that regard, it seems that *The Black Book* was more the messenger versus the instigator of the polarization along "racial lines."

Ever-Increasing Insecurity and Bellicosity in the Darfur Region

Beginning in the early to mid-1990s, Arab herders began carrying out attacks against entire villages of sedentary black African farmers. Over time, such attacks began to involve both GOS troops and the Arab herders working in tandem. While vicious, such attacks were certainly not as systematic as the scorched-earth attacks that became increasingly common in 2003 and beyond. Such attacks have ebbed and flowed over the years, up to today.

The initial increase in violent conflict within the region was due to a host of issues. For example, in the 1980s, the GOS, under President Nimeiri, abruptly replaced the tribal councils, the traditional bodies that helped solve and bring an end to conflicts, with government oversight of the region. Nimeiri, however, failed to provide adequate resources to the regional government offices in order to carry out their work, and, as a result, the offices and expected services largely became hollow shells

Making matters even more volatile, since riverine Arabs held the vast majority of positions in the government posts (including those as police and court officials), the black Africans of Darfur were automatically put at a distinct disadvantage. That is, disputes that were once dealt with, for the most part fairly and equitably, by traditional authorities and/or a combination of the latter and governmental authorities, were now handled by officials partial to the Arab sector of the population.

Furthermore, as certain groups of nomads increasingly bought into the beliefs of Arab Supremacism, they began to act as if they were superior to the black Africans.[4] Along with the huge influx of weapons into Darfur (resulting, in part, due to the various wars in the region, three of which were the Libya/Chad conflict, the prolonged war in southern Sudan, and the Eritrean separatist war with Ethiopia (1961–1993)), more and more herders began carrying weapons. This was likely done as a means of protection, but also because they had become accustomed to carrying them as a result of their having fought in one or more of the violent conflicts in the region. Ultimately, the GOS also provided such groups with weapons with the expectation that the Arab herders would, in various cases, serve as their proxies in dealing with the black Africans. As the Arab herders increasingly engaged in conflicts with the black Africans over land and water usage, they (the Arabs) made it known that they were ready and willing to use their weapons. Thus, with the difficulties presented by the droughts and desertification of pasture land, the influence of Arab Supremacism, and the Arab herders' experiences as mercenaries, it is not surprising that many of the Arab nomadic groups became increasingly cavalier and aggressive in their use of the sedentary people's lands in the early to mid-1990s.

Not only did the Arab nomads purposely neglect to seek permission to use the land, but they refused to apologize for trespassing when confronted by the black African farmers. And when confronted by the farmers, it was not uncommon for the nomads to threaten the lives of the farmers—and, in many cases, they carried out their threats.

Out of fear and anger over the constant assaults and attacks on their villages and a lack of protection from local and regional governmental authorities, along with the gradual realization that the Arab marauders had tacit approval from the local government officials to do as they wished, the black Africans began to form self-defense groups "on a tribal basis as opposed to based on local communities" (Fadul and Tanner, 2007, p. 301).[5]

The Initial Rebel Attacks and the Response by the Government of Sudan

By the early 1990s, traditional dispute resolution approaches were proving to be inadequate. Arab nomadic attacks against black Africans were becoming more brazen, more frequent, more vicious and more costly in terms of lost lives and destroyed villages, farm land, and orchards. In August 1995, for example, Arab raiders attacked and burned the non-Arab village of Mejmeri in West Darfur, stealing 40,000 cattle and massacring twenty-three civilians. By late 1998, more than 100,000 non-Arab Massalit had fled to Chad to escape the violent attacks (Flint and De Waal, 2005, p. 69).

A great many of the attacks on villages were not one-time affairs. In fact, in the early to late 1990s, some villages were attacked up to three to four and more times. In certain cases, African villages were partially burned down by the marauders; in others, villages were utterly destroyed. Almost always, the villages were pillaged and then the black Africans' herds were stolen. Black Africans were often forced out of their villages only to be chased down in the desert and beaten and/or killed.

Desirous of remaining on their land, the black Africans more often than not returned to their villages once the marauders had left, rebuilt those sections destroyed, and carried on with life. However, as these attacks continued unabated, the black Africans began to look askance at the government. In light of the way the black Africans were being treated (a frustrating combination of being ignored and/or ill-treated by the government), it is not surprising that the following statement/critique of the Sudanese government made it into *The Black Book*:

> *Conditions for accepting the authority of the ruler/ governing power:*
> The authority must demonstrate its commitment to maintain

sovereignty of land against foreign intruders; treat its citizens equally; afford them peace and protection; guarantee dignified life; spread freedom and dignity, and must enable its citizens to fully participate in conducting their public affairs. All that is to take place within an environment that is conducive for participation of all without religious, ethnic, skin colour and gender discrimination.

The state authority cannot implement that without commitment to its national laws that regulate and divide powers among different state organs. Most important here is the separation between state powers, and in particular the political, the judicial and the legislative (Justice and Equality Movement, 2000, p. 6).

In 2001 and 2002, before the current conflict became widely known to the outside world, a rebel movement comprising non-Arabs in Darfur emerged. The first rebel group to appear called itself the Sudanese Liberation Movement/Army (SLM/A), and on March 14, 2003, it issued the following political declaration: "The brutal oppression, ethnic cleansing and genocide sponsored by the Khartoum government left the people of Darfur with no other option but to resort to popular political and military resistance for purposes of survival. This popular resistance has now coalesced into a political movement known as the Sudan Liberation Movement and its military wing, the Sudan Liberation Army (SLM/SLA)" (The Sudan Liberation Movement and Sudan Liberation Army, 2003, pp. 1–2). Within a relatively short period of time, the group splintered, and from the split emerged a rebel group that called itself the Justice and Equality Movement (JEM). According to Flint and De Waal (2005), within JEM there are "two main tendencies that dwarf all others: one is tribal, the other Islamic" (p. 89).

In addition to providing local security for the black African villagers of Darfur, the two rebel groups issued protests against the economic and political marginalization of Darfur. The aforementioned *Black Book*, the brainchild of the leaders of JEM, was one such protest; indeed, it constituted the most detailed critique of the government to date, as well as the protest that reached the greatest and most diverse audience (from the top officials of the country all the way to the illiterate population who learned about the contents of *The Black Book* as a result of having it read to them). Members of both rebel groups came primarily (but by no means exclusively) from three non-Arab tribes—the Fur, Massalit, and Zaghawa—that had been attacked for years by nomadic Arab groups and GOS troops.

By late 2003, a flood of black Africans had either been forced from their homes as a result of GOS and *Janjaweed* attacks or had left out of sheer fear. By September 2003, the United Nations (UN) reported that some 65,000 refugees from Darfur had fled to Chad.[6] By December 9, 2003, the United Nations estimated that there were up to 600,000 internally displaced people (IDP) in Darfur as a result of the attacks on the black Africans' villages. In November 2004, *Médecins Sans Frontières* (Doctors Without Borders) estimated that some 1.8 million Darfurians had been displaced from their homes, with 200,000 of them in refugee camps in Chad (*Médecins Sans Frontières*, 2004, p. 1).

At one and the same time, the leaders of both rebel groups seemingly followed the ongoing peace negotiations between the GOS and the rebel groups in southern Sudan and realized that armed insurrection in the south had eventually led to important concessions by the GOS, including power-sharing and access to major economic resources. Whether such knowledge was the catalyst or trigger for the rebel initial attacks against the government only the leaders of SLM/A know for sure.

Popular account has it that the GOS, alarmed by the rebel attacks and with its own military forces stretched thin by the north–south civil war, decided to recruit, train, and equip Arab militias (the so-called *Janjaweed*) to help suppress what it purportedly perceived as a black African rebellion in Darfur.[7] Any government whose military bases and/or other government facilities are attacked is going to retaliate and attempt to suppress future attacks. Governments will either arrest the perpetrators or, if the situation degenerates into violence, shoot and then apprehend them, or, kill them outright. What the GOS did, however, was something vastly different and, ultimately, criminal. Using the argument that it believed that black African villagers were harboring rebels, the GOS (along with the *Janjaweed*) began attacking village after village after village of black Africans. Thus, instead of solely tracking down and attacking the black African rebel groups, the GOS and *Janjaweed* began carrying out a widespread and systematic scorched earth policy against non-Arab villagers. In doing so, the GOS troops and the *Janjaweed* slaughtered men and boys (including infants), raped, mutilated and often killed females, looted household goods and animals, and then burned the homes and villages to the ground (Physicians for Human Rights, 2005; UN Commission of Inquiry into Darfur, 2005; U.S. State Department, 2004). The attacks comprised bombings by aircraft, helicopter gunships, and four wheel vehicles with *dushkas* (mounted machine guns), as well as hundreds of *Janjaweed* on camels and horses. In a report of its findings, the UN Commission of Inquiry on Darfur (2005) stated that ". . . the large majority of attacks on villages conducted by the [*Janjaweed*] militia have been undertaken with the acquiescence of State officials" (paragraph 125). As previously mentioned, the attacks led to the forcible displacement of, at first, tens of thousands, then hundreds of thousands and, ultimately (or at least through today, December 2007) over two-and-a-half million people in Darfur alone (and more than another 250,000 in Chad). All constituted early warning signals that something was vastly wrong in Darfur.

As early as spring 2002 (May 1, to be exact), a group of Fur politicians complained to Sudanese President Omar al Bashir that 181 villages had been attacked by Arab militias, with hundreds of people killed and thousands of animals stolen (Flint and De Waal, 2005, pp. 77–78).

In what Flint and De Waal call a "pivotal point" in the conflict between the black African rebels and the GOS troops, the SLA and JEM forces struck the government air force base at el Fasher on April 25, 2003. In doing so, they killed at least 75 people, destroyed several airplanes and bombers, and captured the base's commander (Flint and De Waal, 2005, pp. 99–100). In quick succession, numerous other attacks were carried out. In fact, "The rebels were winning almost every encounter—34 out of 38 in the middle months of 2003. [At this point in time, the GOS purportedly] feared it would lose the whole of Darfur . . ." (Flint and De Waal, 2005, p. 101).

Between 2003 and today, the GOS has repeatedly denied that its troops have taken part in the scorched earth actions against the black Africans of Darfur. Furthermore, while the rest of the world asserts that at least over 250,000 have been killed in Darfur over the past four years (with certain activist organizations claiming that the number is closer to 400,000 or more), the GOS asserts that just 9,000 have been killed, mostly as a result of rebel actions. Ample evidence, though, from a broad array of sources (e.g., the black African survivors of the attacks, African Union troops deployed in Darfur as monitors, numerous humanitarian organizations working in the IDP camps, numerous human rights organizations, including Human Rights Watch, Physicians for Human Rights, and Amnesty International, and the investigations conducted by the United States in 2004 and the UN in 2004 and 2005 respectively) have provided evidence that clearly and definitively refutes the GOS' denials.

By late 2003, various NGOs (nongovernmental organizations) and the UN scrambled to help the IDPs and the refugees flooding across the Sudan/Chad border, and began getting the word out about the escalating carnage in Darfur. Finally, in December 2003, Jan Egeland, UN Under-Secretary for Humanitarian Affairs, asserted that the Darfur crisis was possibly the "worst [crisis] in the world today" (United Nations, 2004, p. 1). That same month, Tom Vraalsen, the UN Security General's Special Envoy for Humanitarian Affairs for Sudan, claimed that the situation in Darfur was "nothing less than the 'organized' destruction of sedentary African agriculturalists—the Fur, the Massaleit and the Zaghawa" (quoted in Reeves, 2003, p. 1).

In early 2004, one activist organization after another in the United States, Canada, and Europe began rallying around the Darfur issue, variously decrying the lack of action to halt the atrocities against the black Africans of Darfur, preparing and issuing reports, calling on the United Nations, the U.S. Government and/or the European Union to be proactive in addressing the crisis, and issuing calls for citizen action. On June 24, 2004, the United States Holocaust Memorial Museum (USHMM) took the extraordinary measure of shutting down normal operations for 30 minutes to focus attention on the ongoing crisis in Darfur. U.S. Senators Sam Brownback and Jon Corzine, U.S. House of Representative Donald Payne, as well as a Holocaust survivor and a member of the Darfurian community-in-exile, came together in a special program in the USHMM's Hall of Witness to highlight and discuss the unfolding conflict in Darfur. On the same day, the U.S. House of Representatives unanimously declared that the situation in Darfur constituted genocide.

On June 30, 2004, U.S. Secretary of State Colin Powell visited a refugee camp for IDP camps and a refugee camp in Chad. While visiting the IDP camp, Abu Shouk, where malnutrition was rife among the 40,000 or so black Africans, Powell said: "We see indicators and elements that would start to move you toward a genocide conclusion but we're not there yet" (quoted by the BBC, 2004, p. 2).

In July and August 2004, the United States—in a joint effort involving the U.S. State Department, the Coalition of International Justice (CIJ), and the United States Agency for International Aid (USAID)—sent a team (the Atrocities Documentation Team or ADT) of twenty-four investigators to Chad to conduct interviews with Sudanese refugees from the Darfur region of Sudan for the express purpose of collecting evidence to help ascertain whether genocide had been perpetrated by the GOS and the *Janjaweed*. The ADT, which was the first ever official field investigation of a suspected genocide by one sovereign nation into another sovereign nation's actions while the killing was underway, conducted more than one thousand interviews with Darfurian refugees in camps and settlements on the Chad side of the border with Sudan. Evidence collected by the ADT led U.S. Secretary of State Colin Powell, on September 9, 2004, in a hearing before the U.S. Senate's Foreign Relations Committee, to publicly accuse the GOS of genocide. This was the first time that a government ever accused another government of genocide during an ongoing conflict.

Ultimately, the U.S. State Department presented the findings of the ADT in an eight-page report, "Documenting Atrocities in Darfur." The analysis of the data collected in the 1,136 interviews by the ADT revealed "a consistent and widespread pattern of atrocities in the Darfur region of western Sudan" (U.S. State Department, 2004, p. 1). The data also suggested a "close coordination between GOS [Government of Sudan] forces and Arab militia elements, commonly known as the Jingaweit [*Janjaweed*]" (U.S. State Department, 2004, p. 2). Furthermore, the data indicated that there was a clear "pattern of abuse against members of Darfur's non-Arab communities, including murder, rape, beatings, ethnic humiliation, and destruction of property and basic necessities" (U.S. State Department, 2004, p. 3).

Sixteen percent of the respondents witnessed or experienced rape. Significantly, the report suggests that the rapes are probably "under-reported because of the social stigma attached to acknowledging such violations of female members of the family" (U.S. State Department, 2004, p. 7). What makes the under-reporting even more probable is the fact that all of the interpreters and half of the investigators on the team were males, and that many female victims were not inclined to mention such assaults in the company of males (strangers or otherwise).

During the course of his report on the ADP findings to the Senate Foreign Relations Committee on September 9, 2004, Powell remarked that the findings did not mean that the United States needed to do anything other than what it had already done. What that meant was this: while the U.S. had called on the GOS to cease and desist its ongoing attacks, submitted and supported various resolutions at the UN Security Council, applied sanctions against Darfur, and provided hundreds of millions of dollars for humanitarian aid and material/resource assistance to the African Union contingent on the ground in Darfur, it was not about to carry out an intervention in Darfur.

With that said, under Chapter VII of the UN Charter, the United States referred the Darfur matter to the United Nations. Subsequently, on September 18, 2004, the UN established the UN Commission of Inquiry into Darfur (COI), whose express purpose, as outlined in UN Security Council Resolution 1564, was to conduct its own investigation into the Darfur crisis. The COI conducted its inquiry in December 2004 and January 2005, and submitted its report to the Security Council in late January 2005. In its final section, "Conclusions and Recommendations," the COI report states: ". . . the Commission concludes that the Government of the Sudan and the *Janjaweed* are responsible for a number of violations of international human rights and humanitarian law. Some of these violations are very likely to amount to war crimes, and given the systematic and widespread pattern of many of the violations, they would also amount to crimes against humanity" (UN, 2005, para 603). While many scholars agreed with the conclusions of the COI, others were taken aback that—based on the COI's own findings—it had not concluded that genocide had been perpetrated (see, for example,

Fowler, 2006, pp. 127–139; Stanton, 2006, pp. 181–188; Totten, 2006, pp. 199–222).

Talk, Talk and More Talk by the International Community

Between 2004 and today, the UN Security Council issued over twenty resolutions vis-à-vis the ongoing crisis in Darfur. The resolutions addressed a host of issues, including but not limited to the following: the need by the GOS to halt the ongoing indiscriminate attacks on black African civilians and the forced displacement of hundreds of thousands of the latter; the need for the perpetrators of the atrocities in Darfur to be brought to justice without delay; concern over the GOS' failure to meet its obligations in ensuring the security of the civilian population of Darfur; disappointment regarding the constant cease-fire violations by all actors; the threat to issue various types of sanctions; the issuance of actual sanctions, including the freezing of certain actors' assets (including those of GOS officials, *Janjaweed* leaders, and a leader of a rebel group); and the referral of the Darfur conflict to the International Criminal Court (ICC), along with the names of alleged perpetrators of various atrocities.

The results of the resolutions were, at best, mixed. Some were acted on, but most were not. Various resolutions were revised time and again, along with ever-increasing threats, but largely to no avail due to a dearth of action. Tellingly, in July 2006, a senior Sudanese government official was quoted as saying that "The United Nations Security Council has threatened us so many times, we no longer take it seriously" (cited in Nathan, 2007, p. 249).

After considerable debate, compromise, and dithering, the United States and the UN Security Council finally imposed some sanctions on Sudan. For example, on April 25, 2006, the UN Security Council passed a resolution imposing sanctions against four Sudanese individuals, all of whom have been accused of war crimes in Darfur. Those sanctioned: were Gaffar Mohamed Elhassan, an ex Sudan air force commander; Sheikh Musa Hilal, a *Janjaweed* militia leader; Adam Yacub Shant, a rebel SLA commander; and Gabril Abdul Kareem Badri, a rebel National Movement for Reform and Development field commander. All four were to be subject to a ban on foreign travel, and any assets they had in banks abroad were to be frozen.

As for the United States, in May 2007, President George W. Bush ordered the imposition of sanctions that prevents 31 Sudanese companies (many of them oil related) and three individuals (two high-level government leaders and a black African rebel leader) from doing business in the United States or with U.S. companies.

Realpolitik was at the center of the dithering, the watering down of certain sanctions, and the decision not to follow through on numerous resolutions and threatened sanctions. More specifically, various members of the Permanent Five in the UN Security Council (the United States, Great Britain, France, the Russian Federation and China) have vested interests in Sudan and wanted to protect them.[8] China, for example, has an enormous petroleum deal with Sudan, and engages in significant weapons sales to it; Russia also has a major arms deal with Sudan; and the United States has, off and on, taken advantage of GOS' offers to help shut down terrorist cells within Sudan and prevent potential terrorists from traveling through Sudan on their way to Afghanistan and Iraq to battle the United States in the latter's efforts to, respectively, capture Osama Bin Laden (terrorist mastermind of the September 11, 2001 attacks on the World Trade Center in New York City and the Pentagon in Washington, D.C.) and to stabilize Iraq following the U.S.'s overthrow of dictator Saddam Hussein, which resulted in internecine conflict that has ripped the fabric of Iraq apart. Already engaged in two separate wars in two Muslim states, Afghanistan and Iraq, the United States was not about to intervene in another Muslim state, Sudan, especially when the latter issued warning after warning that any and all interveners not invited in by the GOS would face an all-out war.

In June 2004, Sudan allowed the African Union (AU) to deploy a small ceasefire monitoring team in Darfur comprised of representatives from the AU, the GOS, two (later, three) rebel groups, along with the European Union, the UN and the U.S. From a tiny force of 300 troops, the force slowly increased to—and eventually leveled off at (up through December 2007)—about 7,000 troops. "As violence against civilians continued, the African Union Mission in Sudan (AMIS) force's mandate was expanded in October 2004 to protecting 'civilians whom it encounters under imminent threat and in the immediate vicinity, within resources and capability' " (Human Rights Watch, 2007a, p. 5). The new mandate, though, for all intents and purposes constituted little more than a paper tiger. The AU had neither the resources nor the capability to truly protect anyone, let alone themselves.

Between 2003 and the end of 2007, the international community worked in various, though hardly effective, ways to bring the Darfur crisis to a close; and as it did, it continually decried the GOS troops' and *Janjaweed*'s attacks on innocent civilians and the GOS' support of the *Janjaweed* and its murderous behavior, and called on the GOS to reign in the *Janjaweed*. As previously stated, the GOS vigorously and disingenuously protested the validity of the accusations made by the international community, but, periodically, also made lukewarm promises to bring the situation under control. Such promises, though, were quickly broken. In most cases, however, the GOS blithely ignored the international community's requests, demands and threats.

When it became obvious that the AU troops were outmanned and outgunned, various calls were issued by various actors to insert UN troops into Darfur. Initially, the AU adamantly rejected the offer, asserting that it wanted to operate an all-African operation. As for Sudanese President Omar al Bashir, he was vociferous in his rejection of the suggestion. Time and again, he asserted that any force that entered Sudanese territory without an invitation from the Government of Sudan would not only be a violation of Sudan's sovereignty, but would be perceived and treated as an enemy invasion. On February 26, 2006, for example, al Bashir asserted, and then warned, that "We are strongly opposed to any foreign intervention in Sudan and Darfur will be a graveyard for any foreign troops venturing to enter" (quoted in *Sudan Tribune*, 2006, p. 1).

Finally, after immense international pressure, Sudan, in mid-June 2007, agreed to allow the deployment of a special force into Darfur, the UN/AU Hybrid (UNAMID) force. Ultimately, that was followed, on July 31, 2007, by the passage of UN Security Council Resolution 1769 which authorized a combined AU/UN Hybrid force for deployment in Darfur. The resolution called for "the immediate deployment of the United Nations Light and Heavy Support packages to the African Union Mission in the Sudan (AMIS) and a [AU/UN] Hybrid operation in Darfur [UNAMID], for which back-stopping and command and control structures will be provided by the United Nations. . . . [The] UNAMID . . . shall consist of up to 19,555 military personnel, including 360 military observers and liaison officers, and an appropriate civilian component including up to 3,772 police personnel and 19 police units comprising up to 140 personnel each." In addressing the mandate of the UNAMID, the resolution asserted that: "Acting under Chapter VII of the Charter of the United Nations: . . . UNAMID is authorized to take the necessary action, in the areas of deployment of its forces and as it deems within its capabilities, in order to: (i) protect its personnel, facilities, installations and equipment, and to ensure the security and freedom of movement of its own personnel and humanitarian workers; (ii) support early and effective implementation of the Darfur Peace Agreement, prevent the disruption of its implementation and armed attacks, and protect civilians, without prejudice to the responsibility of the Government of Sudan." Although the hybrid force is tentatively scheduled for deployment in December 2007/January 2008, as late as December 2007 there were reports that few nations had committed troops to the new hybrid force and few countries had offered support in the way of providing needed vehicles, planes, and other materiel, let alone the resources (gas and oil) to help maintain such.

Talk, Talk and More Talk About Peace

In early September 2007, U.N. Secretary General Ban Ki-moon asserted that a new round of peace talks, which were to begin on October 27, 2007, in Libya, must be "a final settlement of this issue" (quoted in the *International Herald Tribune*, 2007, p. 1). At best, that seemed wishful thinking. As the *International Herald Tribune* (2007) noted, "Darfur has a history of peace talks—their sheer numbers a testimony to their lack of success. . . . Since fighting began in 2003 between ethnic African rebels and the Arab-dominated Sudanese government, there have been over half a dozen cease-fires or peace deals of various formats—all quickly breached by both sides" (p. 1).

In fact, beginning in 2004 and continuing through today, peace talks between the GOS and various rebel groups have been on and off affairs, with agreements often being broken by various and/or both sides within days, if not hours, of signing the agreements. In various cases and at various points in time, the intransigence of the GOS and/or rebel groups has placed one barrier after another in the way of finding a workable solution to the crisis in Darfur. The GOS has broken agreements both blatantly (attacking black African villages with Antonov bombers, helicopter gun ships and GOS troops and *Janjaweed*) and surreptitiously (whitewashing planes, attaching UN insignias to the wings and sides of the planes, and using the planes to transport weapons and personnel into Darfur). Various black African rebel groups have not only reneged on agreements, but purposely prevented other rebel factions from taking part in the peace talks. Throughout parts of 2007, some of the many rebel groups even began to treat their counterparts as enemies and engaged in battles with them. Not only that, but the various factions—currently, the UN estimates that there are up to 28 declared rebel factions (Gettleman, 2007, p. A6)—have even shot and killed civilians, raped black African women and girls, attacked and killed AU troops, and harmed and killed humanitarian aid workers.

Each rebel faction is eager to be involved in the peace talks and each no doubt has its own motives for doing so. Undoubtedly, many, if not most, are anxious to have their say regarding the fate of Darfur. And, as previously mentioned, all are undoubtedly cognizant of the new-found wealth and power that those residing in the south garnered upon the signing of the Comprehensive Peace Agreement, which finally brought to an end the twenty year war between north and southern Sudan.[9]

A peace agreement in Darfur was finalized in May 2006 (see details below), but it was signed by only one of three negotiating rebel groups— the SLA faction led by Minni Arkoy Minawi. Over time, and particularly from mid-2007 onwards, the lay of the land has gotten even more dangerous in Darfur. This is true for numerous reasons: the *Janjaweed* not only continue to attack black Africans but have began fighting amongst and between themselves; the various rebel groups continue to battle GOS troops and *Janjaweed* but have also begun fighting between and amongst themselves and attacking black African people in their villages and IDP camps; and roaming the region are bandits who continue to attack anyone and everyone, including IDPs and humanitarian workers. Disturbingly, and tellingly, a report entitled *Chaos by Design: Peacekeeping Challenges for AMIS and UNAMID*, Human Rights Watch (2007a) asserted that "the [GOS] continues to stoke the chaos, and, in some areas, exploit intercommunal tensions that escalate into open hostilities, apparently in an effort to 'divide and rule' and maintain military and political dominance over the [Darfur] region" (p. 1).

The Darfur Peace Agreement (DPA)

Following seven rounds of contentious negotiations, a peace accord, the Darfur Peace Agreement (DPA), was signed in May 2006. However, as Fadul and Tanner (2007) aptly put it, the peace agreement was "still-born" (p. 284). While the DPA was signed by GOS and the Minni Arkoy Minawi faction of the SLA, it was not signed by the SLA faction led by Abdel Wahid Mohamed al Nur nor by the Justice and Equality Movement led by Khail Ibrahim. Within a short time following the signing of the DPA, battles broke out between the non-signatories and the "government coalition," which included the SLA faction headed by Minni Arkoy Minawi.[10] Even greater violence was perpetrated by GOS troops and the *Janjaweed* against both black African rebel groups and black African civilians. As the attacks by the latter increased in number, there was a surge in the rape of girls and women, the murder of black African civilians, and thousands fled their villages seeking sanctuary in internally displaced persons camps or refugee camps in Chad. The most current attacks (those in mid- to late 2006 and all of 2007) have centered on both the relatively few remaining black African villages in Darfur as well as the IDP camps. Out of fear of being murdered should they venture outside the IDP camps, black African men insist that girls and women scavenge for wood needed to build fires to cook food even if it means (as it often does) that the females will be raped by GOS soldiers and *Janjaweed*.

Due to the ongoing violence which contributed to their ongoing insecurity, black African Darfurian civilians understandably looked askance at the DPA. As Fadul and Tanner (2007) note, there were other issues in regard to why the black Africans found the DPA a dubious proposition, and they included the lack of attention to: ". . . compensation [for the destruction of their villages and homes and the theft of their worldly goods], the rehabilitation of infrastructure, basic services, and reconciliation" (p. 286). The caveat, though, in regard to the latter statement was that "people always stressed these [compensation, rehabilitation of the infrastructure, reconciliation, et al] were secondary to security" (p. 286).

As the violence continued unabated month after month in the aftermath of the signing of the DPA, many black African Darfurians began asserting that "there could be no peace unless it was forced on the government militarily. In other words, peace depended on one of two things, a non-consensual deployment of Western troops or a rebel military victory—or both" (Fadul and Tanner, 2007, pp. 287, 288). Continuing, Fadul and Tanner (2007) observed that

> [a]s late as 2004, many Darfurian intellectuals criticized the decision to take up arms against the government. The brutality of Khartoum's reaction was predictable, they argued, and the violence had cast the region back many decades. By late 2006, it was striking to hear many of those same individuals say they believed armed rebellion was the only solution to Darfur's problems, despite disenchantment with the shortcomings and human rights abuses by rebel groups on the ground (p. 288).

In early December 2007, the UN Under Secretary General for Humanitarian Affairs, John Holmes, informed the UN Security Council that "280,000 people had been forced to flee the violence in Darfur this year [2007], that attacks on aid workers and their convoys had reached 'unprecedented levels' and that national authorities were closing off access to areas 'where there are tens of thousands of civilians in severe need' " (quoted in Hoge, 2007b, p. A10). The Human Rights Council in Geneva reported that "from June 20 to mid-November [2007], at least 15 land and air attacks were carried out against civilian centers in Darfur by government troops and their affiliated militias and one faction of the rebel Sudanese Liberation Army" (Hoge, 2007b, p. A10).

During the summer of 2006, the rebel groups who had not signed the DPA won a series of battles against the GOS, the *Janjaweed*, and Minni's SLA faction. This not only caused great consternation amongst GOS officials, but emboldened the rebel non-signatory groups.

As a result of the ongoing fighting and massive displacement of civilians, a vast number of black African Darfurians began to look askance at the efforts and credibility of the African Union mission (AMIS) in Darfur. More specifically,

Not only was AMIS weak but it was increasingly seen as partisan. The AU's role in imposing the DPA on the non-signatories compromised its neutrality in the eyes of those groups. In August, when the AU expelled the non-signatories from the AU-chaired Ceasefire Commission and AMIS was seen providing logistics to the forces of SLA-Minni amid escalating violence, many Darfurians concluded that the AU had taken sides (Fadul and Tanner, 2007, p. 308).

Such concern and doubts underscored for many the perceived need for the deployment of an international force in Darfur. The GOS, however, was not so sanguine about the idea. Although it repeatedly agreed to the deployment of an international force, it also repeatedly withdrew such agreements. Only incessant pressure from the international community finally forced the GOS' hand.

Late 2007 and Early 2008

The deployment of the AU/UN hybrid force has met one barrier after another. Well into December 2007, the GOS resisted the inclusion of non-African military personnel into the new force, the latter of whom were considered critical to the mission. The GOS also refused to provide land to the hybrid force, which was needed for supplying and housing troops. Likewise, the GOS refused to ease visa and travel restrictions, and was "blocking support staff and materials from the area through bureaucratic maneuvers" (Hoge, 2007a, p. A5). Additionally, the GOS asserted its right to "close down the [hybrid] force's communications when its own army was operating in the areas and was refusing to give United Nations planes clearances to fly at night" (Hoge, 2007a, p. A5). In effect, the GOS was making a mockery of its so-called promises to allow the deployment of the hybrid force and it was drastically impeding the international community's intention to provide African Darfurians with protection around the clock.

If the above was not enough of a hindrance to the deployment of the AU/UN hybrid force, in November 2007, UN Secretary General Ban Ki-moon complained vehemently that not a single country had donated helicopters for the hybrid force, which was restricting the mobility and transportation of the force.

Is There Agreement of Disagreement Among Legitimate Scholars as to the Interpretation of this Particular Genocide?

Various scholars, activists, politicians, individual governments, and others hold a wide-range of views in regard to whether the GOS and

Janjaweed attacks on the black Africans constitute genocide or not. In mid-2004, various U.S.-based activists and some U.S. politicians declared that genocide had been perpetrated in Sudan. For example, in July 2004, the United States Holocaust Memorial Museum's Committee on Conscience, which uses "graduated categories of urgency" (e.g., "watch," "warning," and "emergency") to warn of potential genocidal situations, signaled an "emergency" (e.g., "acts of genocide or related crimes against humanity are occurring or immediately threatened"). On July 22, 2004, both chambers of the U.S. Congress adopted concurrent resolutions (House Concurrent Resolution 467 and Senate Concurrent Resolution 133) in which they condemned the atrocities in Darfur as "genocide." Then, as previously mentioned, following a U.S. State Department-sponsored investigation, on September 9, 2004, U.S. Secretary of State Colin Powell declared that genocide had been perpetrated and was possibly still being perpetrated in Darfur.

Also, as previously mentioned, a subsequent investigation (December 2004/January 2005), conducted by the UN Commission of Inquiry into Darfur concluded that "crimes against humanity," not genocide, had been perpetrated in Darfur. The UN left the door open that upon subsequent study of the crisis and/or additional investigations by other bodies (presumably the International Criminal Court), it was possible that genocide might be found to have been perpetrated. (For a discussion of the ADT and COI findings, see Samuel Totten, 2006.)

In a May 7, 2004 report ("Sudan: Government Commits Ethnic Cleansing in Darfur") and later, in October 2007, in a paper ("Q & A: Crisis in Darfur"), Human Rights Watch declared that the GOS had committed both ethnic cleansings and crimes against humanity in Darfur. Amnesty International, another major human rights organization, has deemed the killings cases of crimes against humanity and war crimes, but has not taken a stand in regard to whether the atrocities amount to genocide or not. Following two on-the-ground investigations in Darfur (2004 and 2005) and an in-depth analysis of the data collected in such investigations (see, respectively, *Assault on Survival: A Call for Security, Justice and Restitution*, and *Destroyed Livelihoods: A Case Study of Furawiya Village, Darfur*), Physicians for Human Rights declared that the GOS had carried out a genocide in Darfur.

Among those scholars who assert that the atrocities perpetrated in Darfur do not constitute genocide are, for example: Mahmood Mamdami (2007), who argues in an article entitled "The Politics of Naming Genocide: Genocide, Civil War, Insurgency" that the situation in Darfur appears to be more a case of insurgency and counter-insurgency versus genocide; Alex De Waal (see *Newsweek*, 2007), who sees the crisis in Darfur as basically a war and not genocide; and Gerard Prunier

(2005 and 2007), who wavers between calling the crisis in Darfur "an ambiguous genocide" (2004), and in a later article, both a genocide and a case of ethnic cleansing (2007).

On the other hand, such scholars as Kelly Dawn Askin (2006), Gerald Caplan (2006), Stephen Kostas (2006), Eric Markusen (2006), and Samuel Totten (2004 and 2006) assert that the crisis in Darfur constitutes genocide. Furthermore, such noted anti-genocide activists as Jerry Fowler (2006) and Gregory Stanton (2006), both of whom are lawyers (Stanford Law School and Yale Law Schools, respectively), have also concluded that the atrocities committed in Darfur constitute genocide.

To establish whether a crisis/event is genocide or not, it is imperative to use the language of the UNCG as the means for examining the facts. Among the most critical words, phrases and conditions set out in the UNCG there are located in Article II:

> In the present Convention, genocide means any of the following acts committed with intent to destroy, in whole or in part, a national, ethnical, racial or religious group, as such:
>
> (a) Killing members of the group;
> (b) Causing serious bodily or mental harm to members of the group;
> (c) Deliberately inflicting on the group conditions of life calculated to bring about its physical destruction in whole or in part;
> (d) Imposing measures intended to prevent births within the group;
> (e) Forcibly transferring children of the group to another group.

In asserting that the crisis in Darfur constitutes a genocide, many scholars argue that there is ample evidence that the attacks by the GOS and *Janjaweed* have clearly resulted in a through c of Article II of the UNCG. The group that is under attack, they have argued, constitutes a racial group, and the issue of intent can be inferred from the events on the ground (e.g., what has taken place during the course of the attacks on the black African villages). More specifically, the aforementioned individuals provide analysis/rationales vis-à-vis their assertions that genocide has been perpetrated in Darfur by the GOS and the *Janjaweed.*

Stephen Kostas (2006), an International Bar Association Fellow at the Appeals Chamber of the International Criminal Tribunal for the former Yugoslavia, discussing Colin Powell's finding of genocide based on the analysis of the data collected by the U.S. State Department's Atrocities Documentation Project (ADP), writes as follows:

> First, they [Powell and Pierre Prosper, former U.S. Ambassador-at-Large for War Crimes, among others in the U.S. Government] noted that villages of Africans were being destroyed and neighboring Arab villages were not. Large numbers of men were killed and women raped. Livestock was killed and water polluted. In IDP camps, the GOS was preventing medicines and humanitarian assistance from going in despite persistent international calls for access. Examining these factors, they concluded there was a deliberate targeting of the group with the intent to destroy it.
>
> Prosper recalls the group examining the concepts of unlawful killing, causing of serious bodily and mental harm, and "the real one that got us, . . . was the deliberate infliction of conditions of life calculated to destroy the group in whole, or in part." Looking at the IDP camps, Prosper and Powell could not find any "logical explanation for why the Sudan government was preventing humanitarian assistance and medicine" into the camps "other than to destroy the group." The GOS was seen as offering unbelievable excuses, leading Powell to conclude that there was a clearly intentional effort to destroy the people in the camps who were known to be almost exclusively black African (pp. 121–122).

Gregory Stanton (2006), a Yale Law School graduate and a genocide scholar, asks and then asserts, "Was the killing [in Darfur by the GOS and *Janjaweed*] 'intentional'? Yes. According to the elements of crimes defined by the Statute of the International Criminal Court, genocide must be the result of a policy, which may be proved by direct orders or evidenced by systematic organization. Was the killing in Darfur systematically organized by the al-Bashir regime using government-armed *Janjaweed* militias, bombers, and helicopter gunships? Yes. Were the victims chosen because of their ethnic and racial identity? Yes. Fur, Massalit, and Zaghawa black African villages were destroyed, while Arab villages nearby were left untouched. . . . Does this conclusion constitute the intentional destruction, in part, of ethnic and racial groups? Yes. In short, the violence in Darfur is genocide, and it continues" (pp. 182–183).

Jerry Fowler (2006), a Stanford Law School graduate and Director of the United States Holocaust Memorial Museum's Committee of Conscience, argues the following regarding the issue of intent as it relates to the GOS and *Janjaweed*'s actions in Darfur: "U.S. Secretary of State Colin Powell concluded that intent could be inferred from the Sudanese Government's deliberate conduct. Inferring intent from conduct in the absence of direct evidence is widely accepted. The International Criminal Tribunal for Rwanda (ICTR) has delineated numerous circumstances that are relevant to determining 'intent' to destroy, many of which are present in the case of Darfur:

- "The general context of the perpetration of other culpable acts systematically directed against the same groups"
- "The scale of atrocities committed"
- "The 'general nature' of the atrocity"
- "Deliberately and systematically targeting members of some groups [black Africans] but not others [Arabs]"
- "Attacks on (or perceived by the perpetrators to be attacks on) the foundations of the group" [especially, the rape of the girls and woman, thus creating "Arab babies" and resulting in girls and women being considered "damaged goods" by their families and thus ostracized, which, in turn, generally, and automatically, precludes them from having children with their husbands or, if single, from even getting married and having children]
- "The use of derogatory language toward members of the targeted groups"
- "The systematic manner of killing"
- "The relative proportionate scale of the actual or attempted destruction of a group" (International Criminal Tribunal for Rwanda, 1998, paras. 523–524; International Criminal Tribunal for Rwanda, 2000, para. 166) (Fowler, 2006, p. 131).

Kelly Dawn Askin (2006) notes the following: "Rape as an instrument of genocide most often invokes subarticle (b) [of the UNCG] intending to 'destroy a protected group by causing serious bodily or mental harm to members of that group,' and (d) 'imposing measures intended to prevent births within a group'. . . . The Akayesu Judgment of the ICTR [International Criminal Tribunal for Rwanda] is the seminal decision recognizing rape as an instrument of genocide" (p. 150). Continuing, she argues that "There is every indication that the official policy of the GOS and *Janjaweed* forces is to wage, jointly or separate, concentrated and strategic attacks against black Darfurians by a variety of means, including through killing, raping, pillaging, burning and displacement. Various forms of sexual violence regularly formed part of these attacks. . . . Rape crimes have been documented in dozens of villages [now, in 2008, it is more like scores, and probably hundreds] throughout Darfur and committed in similar patterns, indicating that rape itself is both wide-spread and systematic" (p. 150).

Askin (2006) also comments on the epithets made by the attackers during the course of the rapes, which indicates, in various ways, a desire to "deliberately inflict on the group conditions of life calculated to bring about its physical destruction in whole or in part"; and "impose measures intended to prevent births within the group": "We want to change the color. Every woman will deliver red. Arabs are the husbands of those women" (quoted on p. 147); and "We will take your women and make them ours. We will change the race" (quoted on p. 147).

That which is delineated above is only a fraction of each individual's argument vis-à-vis why the Darfur crisis constitutes genocide.

Do People Care About This Genocide Today? If So, How Is That Concern Manifested?

Since 2003, the issue of Darfur has generated astonishing attention and concern among journalists, scholars, activists, university and high school students, church people, movie stars, film makers and others. Numerous journalists have written about the crisis in Darfur, and some have con-sistently done so. Most notably, Nicholas D. Kristof of *The New York Times* has made at least half a dozen trips to Darfur and the refugee camps in Chad, and has written extremely powerful and thought-provoking articles about what he witnessed, heard, and experienced. For his efforts, Kristof was awarded a Pulitzer Prize in 2006 for his series of articles on Darfur. Equally deserving of a Pulitzer Prize for her reporting on Darfur is Emily Wax, a journalist with the *Washington Post.* Her columns, too, over the years, have been extremely powerful and thought provoking. A less well-known but equally committed journalist to the Darfur cause is George Arnold, editorial writer for the *Arkansas Democrat Gazette.* Arnold has written at least half a dozen articles (and at least four or five editorials) on Darfur, all in an effort to educate and cajole his readership to begin to care about the ongoing genocide in Darfur.

A whole host of organizations and sub-organizations have arisen over the years that address the Darfur genocide. Among the most active are Save Darfur and STAND: A Student Anti-Genocide Coalition. The Save Darfur Coalition comprises "over 180 faith-based, advocacy and humanitarian organizations." The former claims that "the Save Darfur Coalition's member organizations represent 130 million people of all ages, races, religions and political affiliations united together to help the people of Darfur." The express purpose of The Save Darfur Coalition "is to raise public awareness about the ongoing genocide in Darfur and to mobilize a unified response to the atrocities that threaten the lives of two million people in the Darfur region."

Students Taking Action Now: Darfur (which has changed its name to STAND: A Student Anti-Genocide Coalition, and thus enlarged its focus) is comprised of student chapters in universities and high schools across the United States. The first U.S.-based STAND chapter was established at Georgetown University in Washington D.C. in 2004, shortly after President George W. Bush called Darfur "genocide." The students had attended a conference on Darfur at the United States Holocaust Memorial Museum and walked away thinking they had to do something to bring the issue of the Darfur genocide to the attention of the nation's students and beyond. That initial effort has expanded into an international network of student activism and now comprises more than 700 STAND chapters around the globe.

STAND has been active on numerous fronts, including the following: In January 2006, STAND initiated its Power to Protect campaign, which collected over one million postcards calling on President Bush to undertake more effective action vis-à-vis Darfur. In April 2006, STAND and the Genocide Intervention Network collaborated to bring more than 800 students from around the country to Washington, DC to lobby their elected officials. During the 2006–2007 school year, STAND students held six regional conferences at schools around the country, raised hundreds of thousands of dollars for civilian protection in Darfur, and was instrumental in getting more than 20 states and over 50 universities to divest funds connected in any way to Sudan. Additionally, STAND groups have held hundreds of awareness-raising events in cities around the world.

Among the most noted movie stars involved in bringing attention to the Darfur crisis are George Clooney, Mia Farrow, Don Cheadle, Matt Damon and, to a lesser degree, Brad Pitt. They have loaned their names to various efforts, have spoken at major rallies, helped to fund-raise, and, in the case of Cheadle, helped to produce a documentary and co-author a book on Darfur. Essentially, their "star power" has drawn immense attention to the crisis and in doing so have brought the issue to the consciousness of untold numbers of people.

Finally, over the past three years, numerous documentary films have been produced about the Darfur crisis, including but not limited to the following: "All About Darfur" (2005)"; Darfur Diaries" (2006); "Darfur Now" (2007); and "The Devil Came on Horseback" (2007).

At a minimum, all of the aforementioned efforts have helped to educate people about Darfur, keep the Darfur crisis front and center in people's (including politicians') minds, and not allowed the international community to totally ignore the plight of the victim population. It hasn't though, at least thus far, resulted in pushing the international community to provide real protection for the black Africans of Darfur. That said, one has to pause and ponder whether many more black Africans would have been killed had there not been such a clamour made over the atrocities carried out by the GOS and *Janjaweed*. There is no doubt that the killing by the GOS and *Janjaweed* has waxed and waned, and the latter is likely, at least in part, due to the fact that the international community has focused fairly sustained attention on the ongoing crisis in Darfur.

What Does This Genocide Teach Us If We Wish to Protect Others from Such Horrors?

The genocide in Darfur has taught humanity, once again, as if it really needed another lesson along this line, the following: that the inter-national community is more wedded to *realpolitik* than it is saving the lives of innocents; the UN Security Council is a group of disparate members whose primary focus is their own particular wants and needs and, as a body, it has no conscience to speak of; the UN Security Council's Permanent Five wield the power of life and death with their vetoes, but that doesn't constrain individual members from using their veto even when it will mean certain death to groups facing horrific atrocities, be they crimes against humanity or genocide; that individual nations and leaders talk a good game but at one and the same time, and more often than not, lack the political will to act when it counts (be it due to *realpolitik*, politics at home, or simply a lack of concern or a dearth of real care); that the time to act to save people from genocide is before genocide is found to have been committed (that is, early on when threats of and/or actual human rights violations far short of genocide are being carried out against a particular group); that all of the good intentions and efforts of activists can move many to action on the behalf of beleaguered others facing genocide but far too often, at least in today's world, they are overpowered by the *realpolitik* and the power of veto practiced by one or more of the Permanent Five members of the UN Security Council.

Conclusion

As the international community dithers, innocent people in Darfur continue to either be murdered, perish as a result of malnutrition, dehydration and lack of medication attention, and/or suffer rape at the hands of the GOS troops and *Janjaweed* (and increasingly, members of some of the rebel groups). Four long years have gone by since the start of the crisis in Darfur, and the international community continues to engage in talk over real action in an "effort" to ameliorate the problems that beset Darfur. Unfortunately, Darfur is a stark reminder that the world is no closer to solving, halting, let alone, preventing genocide than it was during the Ottoman Turk genocide of the Armenians (1915–1923), the man-made famine in Ukraine (1933), and the Holocaust perpetrated by the Nazis (1933–1945). The same is true, unfortunately, in regard to sexual assaults against girls and women during periods of violent conflict.

FIRST-PERSON ACCOUNTS BY SURVIVORS

The respondent [name has been deleted for sake of confidentialty] was born in 1972 in Andukeria, near Genenia in West Darfur. He is a Massaleit and had seven years of schooling. He first worked as a tailor and then a trader in produce.

This interview/oral history was conducted by Samuel Totten on 6/10/2007. It was conducted in the Gaga Refugee Camp in Eastern Chad. It was conducted under a lean-to within a larger compound with the respondent, interviewer and interpreter sitting on multicolored rugs.

I lived in Goker during the attacks. Goker is between Habilia and Geneina. Its population was about 2,600. I left Goker about one month ago.

The trouble in Darfur started long ago, in Darfur in 1994 and in Goker in 1995. Before, there were not a lot of camels in our area and then in 1995 more than 20,000 camels arrived. These camels, when they come along, they destroy everything. These camels were looked after by Arab people and the camels eat the plants that are growing and the Arabs say you can't do anything about it. When this happens, the people go and report it to the police and the police go and see the Arabs and the police come back and say, "These people are our people and we won't do anything to them." Because the head of the police are Arabs, and they have a program [an agreement] with the Arabs to destroy us. All of the farms were destroyed, including mine. They [the camels] ate all of the grain and plants.

After the rainy season, the farms was destroyed and the war between the Arabs and us began. In my own family, two of my cousins, both were farmers, were killed. They went to the market and they were returning and Arabs killed them, Arabs who had camels. The Arabs would stay in between villages and when our people visited friends or family members, the Arabs would rob and kill our people. They were criminals. This was the beginning of the *Janjaweed* [Arab militia who have conducted attacks, largely in conjunction with the troops of the Government of Sudan, on the villages of black Africans].

Because my cousins and others were killed at this time, all of our tribe members came together and fought the Arabs for six days and chased them way. Many of our people died and a lot of Arabs were killed. From our people, 190 were killed. All were fighters.

I, too, fought with those. We had no real weapons but we got weapons when we fought them. They had horses and camels and Kalashnikovs and Gems [shorter rifles than Kalashnikovs]. We fought in villages of a Massaleit and ate there and did not return home.

I was injured in the hand by a bullet. At the time I just salted the wound and bandaged it. I still do not have feeling in my thumb.

When we fought, the Arabs told us this country [Sudan] was not to be inhabited by slaves. When the Arabs were being beat, some started to run and others called out, "Don't run away from the slaves" and "This is a jihad against the slaves!"

After the battle, the government tried to help the Arabs and gave them horses, camels and money and weapons. And soon after, about one month, more Arabs came and attacked again. They came from different areas in Darfur, and Chad, and even Abeche [a major town in Eastern Chad, and which the Gaga Refugee camp is located near]. And the fighting continued through 2000. There was no solution unless you fought. There was no security.

We would set up ambushes because we knew the Arabs would attack us again. So, we were ready. Mothers of fighters would often come out to where we were fighting and beg their children to return. Most of us, though, would tell our mothers we were going to a meeting and not tell them we were actually going to fight. We knew the Arabs would attack us in the village if we didn't ambush them and we didn't want that. The Arabs come from as far away as Libya, Mauritania, and Egypt and some are even Palestinians.

As for my mother, she told me "You must fight even if you die because you are defending your people." Everyone knew if something wasn't done the Arabs would sneak up and attack and kill everyone. Of course, my mother feared that I would die.

In 2000, General Mohammed Ahmed Mustafa Deby came to meet with representatives of Massalit and Arabs and said he was a representative of the President of Sudan, al Bashir. In the meeting the representatives of the Massalit told the general that we were here before the Arabs came to Africa and all the tribes came to our areas and they lived peacefully but the Arabs came and started killing our people and so we fought them. The general said he was there to make a peace between us and the Arabs but he was deceiving us. Two months after this agreement, the Arabs started killing the leaders of the Massalit, and even some of the politicians inside Genenia.

After this, the Arabs started eliminating the educated people. There was a man named Ahmed Abdouffrag—an engineer and he went to Khartoum to ask the government to build roads in the Massalit area and he was killed in his home upon his return. This was in 2000. Some Arab people drove up to his home, called him out and shot and killed him.

Others who were killed were Ibrahim Darfouri, who was head of the legislative body in Genenia. His was wife was head of the Women's Union in Genenia. They were both killed the same day. They shot and killed them both. This, too, was in 2000.

People outside Genenia, leaders of other villages, were also killed. Saleh Dakoro, *umda* of Morley, was killed in 2001. He went to Genenia and on his way back some *Janjaweed* shot and killed him.

Yacoub Congor, another *umda*, was also eliminated in 2001. He was in the *suq* in Habilia and about 35 *Janjaweed* came into the suq, searched for him and one shot and killed him.

In 2002, the Arabs established their own villages in our areas. When our people were killed by the Arabs and went to the police, they said, "That's a tribal problem and we have nothing to do with it." But if a Massaleit killed even one Arab, the police would collect other police from other areas and even call the army and then come and attack the village [of the Massalit] where the Arab was killed.

The police would also go to other villages and arrest Massaleit [in retaliation for the one killing]. The police have a weapon called Fang, which is a rocket propelled grenade [RPG] and they would take the powder out of the shell and put it on the head of people and set it on fire and it would explode like diesel [gasoline]. I saw this with my own eyes.

You should know, all those people who were in Darfur and worked for the police, the army and security were all taken out of Darfur and moved away to other parts of Sudan and they were all replaced by *Janjaweed*.

They had another weapon where they would tie you to two vehicles—your arms to one and your legs to another—and they would drive off in separate directions, pulling our body apart.

And many people were arrested and taken to the security office, and many of those people have never been heard from again. And it's the *Janjaweed* who run the security office. All were red people.

Possibly around May 2002, Arabs from different nationalities were brought into Idelganim to train them [the local Arabs] to help them establish a state comprised of Darfur, Chad and the Republic of Central

Africa. al Bashir visited the camp and changed the name from Idelganim to Idelfoursan. He changed the meaning of the location, the camp, from "where goats live" to "where brave men with horses live."

Massalit from our tribe who are red like Arabs went into the training camps and posed as Arabs. Seven days after Omar Bashir visited the camp, Osama Bin Laden gave them [the Arabs] camels as presents. This place is east of Nyala in a village called Idelganim, near Korodfan. When these groups began moving about in Darfur, they were referred to as *gowat alsalam* (Peace Force). When they attacked, they would come in with 400 to 500 men on horses, surround the village and destroy it. And this was how our village was destroyed.

This day, about seven in the morning, in some villages near us, we saw horses, I cannot say the number, and three vehicles and helicopters. When the people were fighting at this time, the helicopters would land and take off but I don't know what they were doing. And we saw planes, all gray, Antonovs, come and go and we heard the dropping of bombs.

I left our village before it was attacked. We all fled right away, and I went to the police station and military in Goker [the regional head-quarters of Goker]. The village was burned down and I could see that as I was fleeing. We, many, many villagers, people from over 40 villages, about 6,000 people, stayed there [the aforementioned regional headquarters in Goker]. I stayed there from that time until one month ago, when I came here [Gaga camp in Eastern Chad]. Some organizations came there and helped us—such organizations as Red Cross and Oxfam.

I never returned to my village. There was nothing I could do there. The huts were built of grass and thus nothing remained after the fire.

In the village, there were about 700 cows, nine camels, and more than 2,000 goats, and 19 horses. I personally lost 28 cows and 61 goats.

So, from November 2003 to last month [June 2007] I was in an internally displaced camp. While our IDP [internally displaced persons] camp was not attacked, it was not peaceful. For example, women could not go out to collect firewood. If a woman went outside the camp, the *Janjaweed* would rape them. If they stayed inside, the government did not help provide wood for cooking. A man can't go out because if you go out yourself you'll receive one bullet [meaning, a man will be shot and killed]. The government also interferes with the distribution of food. There are many different types of food handed out by relief groups and the *Janjaweed* tells them not to give us certain food just to make us angry.

The African Union troops had an office in the IDP camp but there were very few men—only about thirteen. But when there was, for example, a crime, such as the rape of a woman, we'd tell them and they would say they would look for the criminals but always came back and said they couldn't find them.

I think some of the African Union (AU) troops are on the side of the *Janjaweed* and the government of Sudan. I say this because the *Janjaweed* bring the troops sheep and milk. We can see with our own eyes they bring such things. What else they may bring we do not know.

It is also true, some of the African Union troops truly help us. For example, the Rwandese soldiers are very good and helped us. So did troops from Eritrea. But troops from Nigeria, Chad, Cameroon, Egypt, and Libya are working for their own benefit, not the benefit of Darfur.

So, again, for example, if a person like you comes to speak to me [in Darfur] during the day, the *Janjaweed*, GOS troops and members of the AU will come at night and take me and kill me. And if something happens to you [meaning, black Africans], the Egyptian troops will even laugh.

Another time, in Mistere, where there are a lot of AU soldiers, the *suq* was attacked and two people, two traders, were killed and the market was looted, all by the *Janjaweed*, and all the AU soldiers did was take photographs during the attacks and nothing else.

One time, a journalist spoke to a person in our camp and that night some people—I'm not sure if it was *Janjaweed* or security people in the camp—went to his house. The man, though, thought there might be trouble so he had left his hut, but only after placing materials in his bed to make it appear he was sleeping there. Men burst into his room and fired four shots into the bed. The next morning we went to the African Union to report this, and the African Union soldiers went and got more soldiers, from all different countries, plus a man from a rebel group, JEM, to go to the man's house. When the soldier, who was from Egypt, saw the bullets he smiled. We told the one Rwandese soldier who was there that the killers would be back that night and asked him to take the man who was in danger to Genenia. The Rwandese soldier agreed but the Egyptian said no. We took the Rwandese soldier to the man who was hiding and when the soldier was about to take him to Genenia, the Egyptian said, "No, he is not to be taken there." The Rwandese soldier said, "Yes, he will be. It's our job to protect people." So, the Rwandese soldier took him to Genenia and the Egyptian just stood there and allowed him to do so.

The problem is truly worse than before—that is, worse with the African Union troops. Before they came, everyone knew there was ethnic cleansing (*tathir irgi*) and mass killing (*ibada jamia*) but after the AU came, because they insisted on coming in order to show they were doing something to help, [but,] all they do is take photographs and talk. And the violence continues. So, it's worse now, because there was hope there'd be real help but there's not. The situation is the same but the hope is gone.

We stayed in the camp for a long time, and we hoped that with the African Union the situation would be better but it never was so we decided to leave and come to Chad.

Several small villages between Genenia and Mornei were attacked at 6:00 in the morning and I saw a lot of horses and dust and vehicles, Toyota Landcruisers. The people who were being attacked flew toward our village. Many rode horses and many came on foot. And the enemy, the *Janjaweed* and the GOS, was chasing them, and we, too, fled—with all of us were donkeys and they were running.

As we were fleeing the *Janjaweed* would halt women with babies and force the women to show whether their children were boys or girls. And when the enemy caught a man, the man was killed. And if they caught a woman and she had a child, if the baby was a boy, they would kill him. They would take the baby boy and throw him on the ground and step on his throat and kill him. In other cases, they would throw the baby boys into the fire to burn alive. If the baby was a girl, they would leave them. The same for little girls. But if the girls were 13, 14, 15 or older, they often took them away for three or four days, and they [the girls] would often come back. But some never came back and we still don't know what happened to them.

Not from our village but others, people I know were taken and made slaves. The attackers would say in front of the people, "You, I am taking as a slave!" They would force such people to watch their animals as herders. They don't take big people [adults] but young boys about eight or nine years old.

The last days before I came to Gaga, there was interference by the government [of Sudan] in the work of the international organizations. What I mean is that one organization was formed by the Sudanese government and when they distributed food to us they told us we wouldn't get any food unless we went back to where we came from. This began two months before we came here [Gaga camp in Chad]. Then, when you went to your village, they would come and take pictures and pass them around and say, "Everything is alright." They would bring food once or twice, but then the *Janjaweed* would come and kill you. I refused to go back, as did my friends.

When we refused to return to our villages, for 50 days we did not receive any food. And there were no other organizations providing food for any of us. The only way we were able to eat is that we knew the future could be worse so while we received three meals a day, we only ate two meals; and when we started receiving no food, we began to eat only once a day.

And during this time, just by accident, some journalists passed (three men and one woman) by our camp, and we told these journalists we had no food for 50 days and the journalists reported this to a human rights organization. A human rights organization came to see us after seven days and when we told them our problem, they reported it to the Red

Cross, brought us food, and three days later, the other organization [the Sudanese organization] packed up all their food and left and never came back.

This is my daughter [indicating a little girl sitting in his lap], and I named her Condoleezza Rice. Her complete name is Condoleezza Mahjoub Oumar. I want to give Condoleezza Rice [the U.S. Secretary of State] this girl, my daughter, who is two years [old]. Because Condoleezza Rice came to visit us in Darfur when we were in a very bad situation. I have no means to contact Condoleezza Rice to tell her that I want to give her my child, and I wish I did.

Many people work for Darfur—the African Union, the United Nations, Kofi Annan (at one point, however, he gave the *Janjaweed* three months to turn in their weapons; can you imagine how many people could be killed in that time?)—Condoleezza Rice and Colin Powell [the former U.S. Secretary of state] worked more than all these others to help us. So, we do not forget people who help us, who help Africa. I wish I had a boy and a girl, because then I would give the boy to Colin Powell and the girl to Condoleezza Rice. I also know that Condoleezza Rice has no child and thus I would like her to have my child.

The respondent [name has been deleted for sake of confidentialty] is about 30 years old (not sure of her date of birth, it is a guess). She was born in the village of Tolos in West Darfur, which is near the larger town of Mornei. She is a Massaleit.

This interview/oral history was conducted by Samuel Totten on 6/10/2007. It was conducted in the Gaga Refugee Camp in Eastern Chad. It was conducted under a lean-to on which the interviewee, interviewer and interpreter sat. Approximately ten to fifteen family members (e.g., her children, mother, sister, nieces and nephews and others) sat and stood on the periphery listening in on the interview session.

When our village, Tolos, was attacked I was living with eight people in my home, my six children, me and my husband. Our village was attacked four years ago. I can't remember the month but it was about two months after Ramadan.

In the morning, early, we were taking breakfast, and we heard the planes. They are too loud, from far you can hear them.

The planes came first, then the trucks, and then the horses and camels. Some [*Janjaweed*] were on foot. The planes, Antonovs, flew over the village. They [the planes] were all white and the sides were red. They [three or four of them] dropped big things like *binil* [barrels], and they made fire. Everything caught fire, buildings, animals, people.

The planes dropped the big things and about 20 minutes after the Landcruisers came. Some were green color, some were black and green [camouflaged]. There were many, I don't know how many because at the time I was scared, but it might have been about 100. They came from all directions.

When we heard the big things falling and hitting, we ran out of the house but we didn't know where to go. The big things caused big holes, like wells.

Driving the cars were Sudaense soldiers. Most *Janjaweed* rode horses, camels and were on foot. On the trucks, they have a big gun [she is most likely referring to what are called *doskas*], and the soldiers held big guns, some red and some black [Bilgic, possibly of Italian make]. There were also *modra* [tanks] with men inside but you can't see them. Outside there is a big gun and everything was colored black and green. There were about ten modra. The camels and horses and Landcruisers were more than 400. They were crying louding as they came in, calling out "Nuba! Nuba!"

At that time, we were ten persons and we began running. I was with three of my sisters, my sister-in-law, my father's two sisters, and three were my neighbors. All of my children had run in fear and I didn't know where they were. My husband, too [was gone and she still does not know his whereabouts].

We ran outside the village to the West. There was a lot of shooting but none of us were hit.

I was so frightened, I left the village without my two babies and little four year old daughter who were inside our hut. I later found them because some one had grabbed them and run out with them.

As we were running I saw men from our village shot. They killed 27 men. They [the soldiers and *Janjaweed*] aimed at the men. I saw two of my fathers [her father's two brothers; in other words, her uncles, who are generally referred to as "fathers" by the black Africans] killed. We didn't have any guns in our village and they [the Government of Sudan troops and the *Janjaweed*] did all of the shooting.

I was looking and crying and running but what can I do? I was so fearful, didn't stop running and I was hysterical, crying and running. After the attack, we came back to our village and we found the dead bodies.

We ran for three days, to Habila. No food and no water.

Not for 23 days did I find my one son [name withheld for the sake of confidentiality], in Mornei on the way out in the bush. On the way out, we came across my husband who had two of our other sons in the bush. Then we went to Habila. We had nothing. Sometimes we went to the bush for firewood but we were attacked by the *Janjaweed*.

We returned to our village after ten days. We returned because it was safe. When we made it back, we did not find anything but bodies. There were about seven dead bodies.

Our animals, our cows, our sorghum, our millet, our clothes, nothing was left. Nothing. It was all burnt, destroyed. The whole village was destroyed.

We found three who were injured in a small valley, in different places. All three had been shot—one man in both arms and both legs and the other man in one leg and the other one in his hand.

We took the injured to Mornei on donkey and then they [the injured] were taken in automobile to Zallingi, east of Genenia. The people with the cars were black but I don't know if they were an organization or not. They were Sudanese, but I don't know where they were from. There was no hospital in Mornei and so they took them to Zallingi. The three are still living and one is here [in Gaga camp] in Block 7 and two are in Mornei.

When we left the village to return to Habilia, we came across the *Janjaweed* again, out in the bush. The *Janjaweed* were shooting guns and we began running. Because we are far away we could not hear what they were yelling at us. They followed us, but not too closely and then left.

In Habilia, we stayed without any work; sometimes we went into the bush to get firewood that we sold to buy food. We stayed there for two years, in an internally displaced persons camp.

Life was not good in the camp. There was not enough food and if you left the camp, the *Janjaweed* would sometimes beat us. There was not freedom.

I was attacked by the *Janjaweed*. We, men and women, were cutting firewood and they stopped us and beat us. They beat us with sticks for two hours. One person was injured very badly from the beating and he had head injures that left him feeling unwell.

Another time I was also out with five women and three girls (13 years old, 14 years old, and 15 years old) gathering firewood and the *Janjaweed* raped the three girls and a woman. We were about two hours from the camp, and we were on foot. When we first arrived at the area with the wood the *Janjaweed*, about twenty of them, were on camels and horses and came up on us very quickly. Some of them said, "We already took your land, why are you around here? We use your land and now we are going to use you."

We all started running away and four of us got captured, three girls and one woman. One girl who was captured was my sister's daughter, who was thirteen years old. From the morning until the evening the *Janjaweed* kept the girls and the woman.

When we reached the camp we told the mothers of the daughters about the capture of their daughters and the mothers went out and brought their daughters back on donkeys and took them to the hospital in Habilia. The four were badly injured because of the rape and the woman spent five days in the hospital and the girls were in for ten days. The girls were raped by many men, some by five, some by ten.

From the four girls, one got pregnant and had the baby. She was the one who was fifteen years. She is still in Habilia with the baby from the *Janjaweed*. When the girl's father heard about the baby from the *Janjaweed*, he got very angry and sick from his anger and died [possibly from a heart attack]. He was 50. He was not sick before that, but when he heard what happened he died.

We came to Gaga camp about one year ago. When we were in Habilia, there was no way you could go out without trouble from the *Janjaweed*. When we were in the Habilia camp, the *Janjaweed* came three times at night and attacked the camp. One time, they killed four guards, all [of whom] were Massaleit. So, it was not safe to stay there.

From Habilia, we, sixteen of us (me, my mother, my mother's sister, my own sister, my husband, my father, my six children, my husband's sisters, my husband's brothers) went to Genenia and from Genenia to Adre, and from Adre [in Chad, along the Chad/Sudan border] to Gaga. In the *suq* in Habilia we found a car to take us to Genenia. We stayed for two days in Genenia, in the station of cars. Already we were forced out of Sudan [Habilia] and Genenia is in Sudan so we did not want to stay. From Genenia we found a direct car to Adre in Chad. In Adre we stayed for two days. In Adre there is no camp or organization to help so we did not want to stay there. We reached Gaga by car we hired.

In Gaga, it took one month and ten days to get a tent. At that time, we lived outside the camp. Because there are many Massaleit in this camp, they would come out to see us and give us food.

The life in camp [the UNCHR camp in Gaga] is very difficult, but what can we do? There is no other way. When we first arrived, everything was fine, but now there is not enough food, not enough water, and not enough medicine.

With my husband and I live our four children and my mother. Before we got food every two weeks then it went to one month and now we have not had food for two months. So, now we have to go outside of the camp and work for Chadian people and they give us money and with it we buy millet. Sometimes, we buy sugar and sometimes okra and sometimes meat for our soup. We have had meat one time in months. We buy sugar more often because we like tea, so if we have money we can buy it every day, if not, then we don't. If we have money we also buy okra every day, if not we don't.

One day we get water and the next we don't. It's not regular. We don't know why this is so.

If we don't get water in the camp, we have to walk one hour on foot to get water out of the well. We get one *baka* [jerry can] of water from the well. I am the one who goes for the water and the *baka* with the water is very heavy so I can only carry one.

My baby [a little girl with a huge extended stomach], one and a half years, has had diarhoea for one year and we have seen a doctor here in Gaga ten times and he gave us medicine but it didn't do any good. We told the doctor and he gives more medicine and it doesn't do anything.

And when I make water [urinates] I feel very hot inside. This has gone on for three months. In Habilia I went to the doctor and got medicine for it and I felt better but here I go to the doctor and the medicine he gave me makes me feel no better

I don't have a lot of hope. If the Americans bring peace to Darfur and bring security then maybe life will get better, but here, I don't think so. If the UN [peace force] goes to Darfur, we'd like to go back to our country.

The respondent [name has been deleted for sake of confidentialty] is 17 years old and resides in the Gaga Refugee Camp in Eastern Chad. She is a Massalit.

This interview/oral history was conducted by Samuel Totten on 6/10/2007 It was conducted on a rug sitting in front of a UNCHR-issued tent with the sun beating down. A small makeshift fence made of tree branches surrounded the small, mostly dusty area which this woman and her family called home.

I was born during Ramadan but I don't know the day, month or year. I studied only one year in school. It was last year, here in Gaga.

I came to Gaga with my mother and my two sisters. One sister is 32 years and one is 20 years. In Masteri I lived with my mother and father and two sisters until three years ago. I met my husband, who is now 23, here in Gaga. I live with my husband and a baby girl, who is three months [old].

The government [of Sudan] used planes and trucks to attack us and the *Janjaweed* came on horse and camels and on foot. They came in the early morning just before sunrise and I was asleep. I first knew there was an attack because I heard the sound of weapons from the planes and the trucks. As soon as I heard the sounds I got up and ran from the hut. As we ran I heard some *Janjaweed* scream "Nuba *afnine*" [Nuba shit"]. I don't know how many *Janjaweed* and soldiers there were but maybe it was around 200. So many I can't count. Maybe 20 green and black [camouflaged] Landcruisers and hundreds of horses and camels.

The soldiers and *Janjaweed* chased us and they kept shooting men and boys. Many were killed. They also caught men and slashed them with long knives on the legs and arms, cutting off their arms and legs, and sometimes both on men—and sometimes both arms. Some who had their legs cut off were able to move, some could not. Those who survived were later given a new leg and a stick [crutch]. But those who had different sides of their bodies cut off [such as a right arm and a left leg] could not continue on. They could not walk. All of the attackers were wearing black and green and white [camouflaged].

At such times you do not look around for other persons, you take care of yourself. We (my mother and my two sisters) made it to Goagor in one day. But for three months we did not see my father. He went another way and we did not know it. He went to Tabrie in Chad, and then he came to find us in Goagor.

In my village, the *Janjaweed* and soldiers killed my second "father" [uncle] and his two sons. The two were older than me, but I don't know how old they were. They were all shot and killed. My second father was shot and as we, my two sisters and I, were running we saw him. He had just been shot in the side of his body and his insides came out the other side. We picked him up and placed him under a tree. We were very young then and very frightened and so we left him and rushed off.

Later, some people went back to the village and they saw my second father under the tree, dead. And at this time they also found the two sons of my second father, dead.

We stayed in Goagor for two years. We stayed with the people in the village there. There were about 200 people from Darfur, from different villages. When we were there we asked to farm but they said "How could you farm, you are refugees and have no land." And then when we went to go to the well, the Chadians caused us problems and told us we could not get water before them because we are refugees. So, we had to wait until every Chadian got water before trying to get some ourselves. We stayed there because we had no other place to go.

We finally decided to leave Goagor because many other refugees were going to Hajar Hadid and Gaga and since we were refugees we decided to go, too.

From Goagor we went to Gaga. We wanted to go to Hajar Hadid but we were told that there was no room for new refugees at Hajar Hadid and so we came to Gaga.

Gaga is [a] bad life because there is not enough food or water. I hope life will get better, but I don't know. The food [though] is not the important thing; the important thing is that we get our country back.

Mohammed Abdullah Arbab

The respondent was born on June 15, 1977 in Baouda, West of Congo Haraza-Beida in West Darfur. He completed school through the eleventh year. He is Massaleit. He is the umda of the UNCHR refugee camp, Farchana.

This interview was conducted by Samuel Totten on July 12, 2007 inside the tent of the respondent in the UNCHR camp of Farchana. Sitting in the crowded tent, which contained all of the interviewee's earthly possessions, were the interviewee, the interviewer and the interpreter. The initial interview lasted for just over two hours. At 4:50pm the interview had to be terminated for the day since there was a regulation that all non-residents had to be out of the camp by no later than 5:00pm. It was agreed that the interviewer and interpreter would meet the interviewee back at the same place, the interviewee's tent, the next morning at 8:00 to resume the interview. Unfortunately, an emergency arose in which the interviewee needed to assist someone who had become sick in the middle of the night and had to be taken to the camp hospital. Since the interviewer and interpreter had arranged to be taken to a different camp the next day this remarkable interview was never completed. As it stands, though, it contains insightful and important information on a broad array of issues.

Before the first attacks on our area in May 2002, the relationship with Arabs and black Africans was very good. There was even intermarriage.

We had no rebel groups in our village. The rebels at that time were in the north.

We heard about attacks on other Massalit prior to the attack on our village—about two months before we were attacked. Many villages in our areas were attacked before ours was attacked. We had nothing to help with—nothing. The Government of Sudan had Antonovs and the *Janjaweed* had weapons and horses, and all we could do to assist was go and help bury the dead bodies.

Beginning with the first attacks on our area, the Sudanese government gave Hamid Dawai weapons, vehicles, and equipment for communication. Brought in to work with Hamid Dawai was Jamal (with *Shurta*, the the Sudanese National Police) and Yasir (with the Sudanese Army), both with the rank of lieutenant. Then after this they attacked the first village, Kassia, on July 27, 2002. Thirteen huts were burned down and two villagers (Shiekha Dardama and Arbab Abou Koik) were killed. The attack was carried out in the early evening by both the *Jesh* (Sudanese Army) and the *Janjaweed*.

That night the dark came and the attackers returned to Beida. The villagers stayed in their homes for two days and then on Thursday the *Jesh* and *Janjaweed* attacked Kassia again. This time they killed seventeen people, destroyed the entire village by burning it down, stole all of the animals, and took the zinc roof of the school. Hamid Dawai's brother, Hasballa Dawai, was stabbed in the neck with a spear by a villager and killed. That was on Thursday, and then on Friday, three villages (Toucou/Toucoul, Migmesi, and Conga) were burned, totally burned down. In Toucou/Toucoul seven villagers were killed and in Migmesi one person was killed. The iman's brother was shot in the upper arm.

After the three villages were attacked and burned down, all of the villagers crossed the border into Chad, into such places as Amliona, Abassana, Matabano, Aboy, Sesi, and Berkangi. Then, on Monday, the *Janjaweed* and *Jesh* burned down villages called Andrig, Ajabani, Mermta, Temblei, Haraza, Bouta, Gobe, and Dim. The villagers from these villages could not go directly to Chad because right between their villages and Chad is a place, Aun Rado, where the *Janjaweed* are trained by the *Jesh*. So, the people, thousands, went to Kango Haraza in Darfur. They settled there for some days and the *Janjaweed* and the government returned and the area was burned down, and all the animals were stolen. And on the same day, several other villages, Awikar, Boukerei, Ararah, Megalo, and Kassedo were burned down. Out of this entire area, which is very big, only two villages remained—including Baouda, my village.

During many of these attacks, people were kidnapped and forced to work as guides to lead the *Jesh* and *Janjaweed* to important people.

In December 2002, they came and attacked Baouda and 25 people were killed. In Baouda, the attack was at 4:30 in the morning. The *Janjaweed* surrounded the village and before they started shooting they put fire on the houses, in the east part of the village. We didn't realize the *Janjaweed* had attacked the village, we just thought the village had caught fire. The houses were built of grass and we went to support and help the people with the fire. We heard about the fire because the owners were screaming. And when a man appeared to help with the fire the *Janjaweed* would shoot him. And when others heard the shooting they knew it was the *Janjaweed*. They were shooting with Kalashnikovs and Gem 4s. All the people rushed to their house to get their wives and children.

Everyone began to run towards Chad and as people ran, the *Janjaweed* shot them. The *Janjaweed* and *Jesh* wanted to kill them all, but Chad was only one kilometer away. The government also brought more soldiers in government vehicles, Landcruisers, gray military

Landcruisers, and all had *doskas* [large mounted automatic weapons] and they also had *animoks* [a big truck] that carries soldiers—up to 100 men. They chased people until they reached the *wadi*, which is at the border between Sudan and Chad. Then they [the soldiers and *Janjaweed*] returned and looted the village.

There were a lot of people who had sought refuge in our village from the other villages that had been destroyed, and many, many people were killed, so we don't know the number and since that day we have not returned to Sudan or our village.

I was on my way to help with the fire when I heard the sound of the shooting. The sound was very loud, and the *doskas* were firing, and the camels and horses were running into the village.

I returned to my house, got my wife and children (two girls, one two years and one four years), packed up my cart with a bag of clothes and some rugs to sleep on, hitched up my donkey, and when we were leaving the village, a leader of the *Janjaweed* called out to me. It was Algali Haron and he shot at me several times but the bullets didn't hit me. While on his horse, he grabbed me by the collar of my *gelabiah* and pulled me down from my cart and another *Janjaweed* called Salih Dardamo caught me from the back and held me as the other one stabbed me twice with a knife in the middle of the chest, just below the lungs. When he's stabbing me, my wife came up behind Algali Haron and hit him with an axe handle in the neck and knocked him down and my mother and my grandmother ran towards me and may father-in-law came to help me but he was shot by Salih Dardamo in the upper chest. (My father-in-law is now OK and is in Breidjing camp He has two wives so you can find him in Breidjing and Triendi camps.)

Salih Dardamo, who was all alone and surrounded by my family members, ran to his vehicle and raced off. I then put my father-in-law on the cart. We then crossed the wadi into Chad. Many of the people didn't make it as they were shot and killed.

Another one of my uncles was slashed by a bayonet and he was so bloody we thought he was dead so we didn't pick him up. But somehow he managed to get on his knees and made it to Chad.

Across the wadi was a Chadian garrison and some of the soldiers helped to fight off the *Janjaweed* and *Jesh* and were killed. This was inside Chad. The commander of the soldiers, Battalion Commander Tadjedin, was shot and killed inside Chad.

The dress of *Jesh* and *Janjaweed* were exactly the same—camouflague shirts and pants. The only difference is the *Jesh* had insignias showing rank and the *Janjaweed* had none. The *Jesh* and police also had something over their pockets, but I could not see what it was as I was not close enough.

The *Janjaweed* and *Jesh* were screaming at the villagers, *Abid* [Arabic for "slave"] and *amby* [Arabic meaning, "You have no religion"].

We settled across the *wadi* in Naclouta for one month. While there, the Chadian government tried by all means to protect us. But when people went to the *wadi* to get water or went to get their animals, the *Janjaweed* killed them. Sometimes the *Janjaweed* also stole our animals.

As we were escaping, I saw my cousin's husband, Alamin Idris, killed. He was shot in the *wadi*. There were many, many people who were killed. And nobody buried them, nobody returned there and thus they remained unburied. Some of them may have been carried away by the *wadi*, some may be buried by the sand, but many others have never been buried.

Other people in Kassia had tried to return and bury their dead and they were attacked by *Jesh* and *Janjaweed*. There, my father's brother, Khamiss Roy, was killed trying to do so.

After one month, the UNCHR came and picked us up in vehicles and took us to Farchana camp. When we arrived there were four blocks only and now there are 26. The first people arrived here on January 17, 2003, and we arrived in April 2003. Then in the beginning of 2004 I was selected to be *umda* of Farchana by the sheiks. The sheiks themselves nominated and elected me.

Before I was *umda* I was working with *Médécin Sans Frontières* in community service. I told the sheiks I didn't want to be *umda* but they insisted. At that time, we needed a person who could speak English and serve as a translator and they selected me as I know how to write and read. The most difficult aspect of the job is to make the people behave honestly.

The food we receive is not enough here [in the UNCHR refugee camp, Farchana], and there is a problem with water in April, May, and June; that is, there is a shortage. They give us a ration of twelve kilos of sorghum a month per person, but that is not enough. And we've never received meat. We have asked them to bring sardines [meaning fish in a can, not actual sardines] if they cannot provide us with meat, but they have not given us that either. They bring us sorghum only, every month. It's not ready to eat and and so we have to bring it to the flour mill and when you take it there they take half of it because you have no money to have it milled. So, you end up with six kilos.

Nothing special is provided for the babies, the infants. And those at one year and above only get sorghum as well.

We all wonder if there is no solution. The United Nations, the Security Council, and the Secretary General, they all make resolutions but fail to force the Sudanese government to obey. Some people are shocked by this, when the decisions are continually reversed. It makes people lose hope.

Notes

1 Colloquially, according to the black Africans of Darfur, *Janjaweed* means, variously, "hordes," "ruffians," and "men or devils on horseback."

2 The phrase "the first acknowledged genocide" is used here for it is possible that other genocides were and are being perpetrated in the early part of the twenty-first century but not detected yet by the international community. In fact, various scholars and political pundits have suggested that genocide could be underway in such places as the Democratic Republic of the Congo, and in far-flung areas across the globe where indigenous groups reside.

3 Civil war broke out in southern Sudan in 1983 and ended in 2005 as a result of a complex and prolonged international effort to bring the civil war to a close. It is estimated that some two million were killed during that twenty year period and another four million people were displaced. In fact, over the course of the war, at one time or another, about 80 percent of southern Sudan's people experienced displacement. The war began when the GOS implemented Islamic Sharia law throughout the country. Both Christian and animist peoples residing in the south were adamantly against such a law, and made their disenchantment known. Ultimately, the GOS and rebel groups from the south (comprised of individuals from the Christian and animist groups) engaged in the lengthy and deadly fight—the rebels to wrest the south from the GOS in the north and the GOS to regain control of the south and to banish the Christian and animists from their homes and land. As one journalist put it, "When government plane are not bombing [the] homes, churches, and schools [of the people in the south in the areas controlled by the Sudan Peoples Liberation Army or SPLA], armed Arab militias on horseback spread terror throughout the villages, killing men, raping women and taking way their domestic animals. The conflict in Sudan is one in which all known rules of war have constantly been violated" (Achieng, 2000, p. 1). A December 1998 report issued by the United States Committee for Refugees asserted that "Sudan's civil war has been characterized by an incremental ferocity that has left untouched practically no one in southern Sudan. . . . The government has systematically blocked food supplies to the south, attacked villages and driven large groups of people to areas where they could not survive. . . . It's a very deliberate strategy on the part of the government of Sudan to depopulate large parts of southern Sudan" (quoted in BBC News, 1998, pp. 1, 2)

4 Arab nomadic groups were, and are not, of course, of a single mind and thus should not be painted as a monolithic group or movement.

5 In regard to the establishment of the self-defense groups by non-Arabs in Darfur, Fadul and Tanner (2007) comment as follows:

> From the 1980s onwards, in Darfur and elsewhere, successive governments in Khartoum mobilized and armed Arab groups to do their bidding, mostly to attack and subdue populations considered hostile. The NIF [National Islamic Front] government furthered the tribal militia policy with the passage of the Popular Defense Act of 1989, making the PDF official. The government entrenched the policy in local government by elevating Arab traditional administrators above non-Arabs in the native Administration. . . . The Arab groups of western Sudan, Darfur, and Kordofan have been militarized for over two decades. By contrast, non-Arab communities mobilized along far more local lines, resorting to community-level strategies to try to ensure their protection. One such response was the establishment of self-defense committees. In the late 1980s and early 1990s, as Arab violence against non-Arab communities mounted, especially in western Darfur, and the state did not intervene, some of these communities started arming themselves. . . . These groups were poorly equipped and ill-coordinated, despite isolated attempts in the late 1980s and early 1990s to organize them. . . . They sold government sugar rations and livestock, and bought light weapons and ammunition from the Chadian military on the border.
>
> . . . The important point here is that the locus of these groups was the village and its outlying homesteads. There was little if any tactical cooperation among the self defense groups; if Arab militias attacked one village, the self defense force in the next village would most often just stay put until it in turn was attacked (p. 302).

6 In October 2006, the London-based Minority Rights Group International issued a report that asserted that United Nations' authorities were warned of ethnic tensions in Darfur as early as 2001 but chose to ignore the facts: "As early as 2001, the UN Commission on Human Rights' Special Rapporteur for Human Rights in Sudan began paying particular attention to Darfur, visiting the region in early 2002. His August 2002 report highlighted the violence in Darfur and noted Masalit claims that 'the depopulation of villages, displacement and changes in land ownership are allegedly part of government strategy to alter the demography of the region.' Despite his concerns, the 2003 Commission on Human Rights removed Sudan from its watch-list and ended the mandate of the Special Rapporteur" (Srinivasan, 2006, p. 6). Many argue that the international community was so intent on bringing the 20-year Sudanese civil war in the south to a close that it believed attention directed at Darfur might result in "a peace spoiler."

7 Tellingly, in interviews with black African Darfurian refugees in Gaga and Forchana refugee camps in eastern Chad during the summer of 2007, this author was told that Arab nomads had been provided with weapons and trained by the GOS as early as the mid-1990s. Furthermore, the so-called *Janjaweed* had been used by the Sudanese leadership since the late 1980s to supplement government troops in the fight against southern rebels (Prunier, 2005, p. 97), and it is certainly possible, if not highly probable, that many of them had roamed throughout Darfur and even joined nomadic groups as the latter herded livestock.

8 Each member of the Permanent Five of the UN Security Council can, alone, with a vote of "no" on any resolution defeat any motion or vote on an issue. The Permanent Five are the only members of the UN Security Council with such power.

9 Following a series of complex talks during 2002 and 2003, a Comprehensive Peace Agreement (CPA) was signed in Nairobi on January 9, 2005. The CPA provided for the sharing of power between the Government of Sudan (GOS) and leaders of the SPLM and determined that the main rebel leader, John Garang, would become the First Vice-President of Sudan. (Shortly after Garang became first vice-president, he died when his helicopter crashed during a storm.) An important provision of the CPA called for the sharing of revenues from oil, which had begun to be pumped in 1999, between the north and the south of the nation. Six years after the signing of the CPA, the south will be permitted to hold a referendum for self-determination and essential independence.

10 The signing of the DPA by Minni Arkoy Minawi did not bode well for him or his faction. Not only did his faction lose battle after battle with the rebel groups that refused to sign the DPA, but his men began to defect to the other side. By September 2006, it was estimated that up to 75 percent of his men had joined the non-signatory rebel groups. Furthermore, and understandably, many Darfurians began to look askance at Minni's collaboration with GOS troops and the *Janjaweed*.

References

Achieng, Judith (2000). "Sudan's Protracted War." *ICG News Desk.* August 25. Accessed at www.hartford-hwp.com/archives/33/137.html.

Amnesty International (2004). *Darfur: Rape as a Weapon of War: Sexual Violence and its Consequences.* London: Author. Accessed at: http://web.amnesty.org/library

Anonymous (2000). *The Black Book: The Imbalance of Power and Wealth in Sudan.* Khartoum: Author(s).

Apiku, Simon (2007). "African Darfur Troops Must Meet UN Standards—Adada." *Reuters,* August 16. Accessed at: www.reuters.com/resources/archive/us/20070816.html

Askin, Kelly Dawn (2006). "Prosecuting Gender Crimes Committed in Darfur: Holding Leaders Accountable for Sexual Violence." In Samuel Totten and Eric Markusen (Eds.) *Genocide in Darfur: Investigating Atrocities in the Sudan,* pp. 141–160. New York: Routledge.

Baldauf, Scott (2007). "Sudan: Climate Change Escalates Darfur Crisis." *The Christian Science Monitor.* July 27. Accessed at: www.cscomonitor.com/2007/0727/p01s04-woaf.html

BBC (2005). "UN Accuses Sudan Over Darfur Rape." July 29, n.p. Accessed at: http://news.bbc.co.uk/2/hi/Africa/4728231.stm

BBC News (UK Edition) (2004). "Sudanese Refugees Welcome Powell." June 30, 4 pp. Accessed http://news/bbc.co.uk

BBC Online Network (1998). "Millions Dead in Sudan Civil War." December 11. Accessed at: http://news/bbc.co.uk/1/hi/world/Africa/232803.stm

Cobham, Alex (2005). "Causes of Conflict in Sudan: Testing the *Black Book*." *Queen Elizabeth House, University of Oxford, Working Paper Series*. Oxford: University of Oxford. Accessed at: ideas.repec.org/p/qeh/qehw/ps/qehw.ps

De Waal, Alex (2004a). "Darfur's Deep Grievances Defy All Hopes for an Easy Solution." *The Observer* (London). July 25, p. 1. Accessed at: www.guardian.co.uk/sudan/story/0,14658,1268773.00.html

De Waal, Alex (2004b). *Famine That Kills: Darfur, Sudan*. New York: Oxford University Press.

De Waal, Alex (2004c). "Tragedy in Darfur: On Understanding and Ending the Horror." *Boston Review: A Poltical and Literary Forum*. October/November, n.p. Accessed at boston review.net/BR29.5/dewaal.html

Fadul, Abdul-Jabbar, and Tanner, Victor (2007). "Darfur After Abuja: A View from the Ground." In Alex de Waal (Ed.) *War in Darfur and the Search for Peace*, pp. 284–313. London and Cambridge, MA: Global Equity Initiative, Harvard University, and Justice Africa respectively.

Flint, Julie (2004). "A Year On, Darfur's Desapir Deepens." *The Daily Star* (Regional, Lebanon). December 30, p. 1. Accessed at: www.dailystar.com.lb/article.asp?edition_id=10&categ_id=5&article_id=11388

Flint, Julie, and De Waal, Alex (2005). *Darfur: A Short History of a Long War*. New York: Zed Books.

Fowler, Jerry (2006). "A New Chapter of Irony: The Legal Defintion of Genocide and the Implication of Powell's Determination." In Samuel Totten and Eric Markusen (Eds.) *Genocide in Darfur: Documenting Atrocities in the Sudan*, pp. 127–139. New York: Routledge.

Gettleman, Jeffrey (2007). "At the Darfur Talks in Libya, Rebel Unity Is as Scarce as the Rebels Themselves." *The New Times*, October 31, p. A6.

Global News Monitor (2004). "Genocide Emergency in the Darfur Region of Sudan." July 28, p. 2. http://www.preventgenocide.org

The Guardian (2006). "The Rape of Darfur. Special Reports." *Guardian Unlimited*, January 18, n.p. Accessible at: www.guardian.co.uk/sudan

Hoge, Warren (2007a). "U.N. Official Criticizes Sudan for Resisting Peace Force in Darfur." *The New York Times*, November 28, p. A5.

Hoge, Warren (2007b). "Lack of Donated Copters Harms Darfur Effort, U.N. Leader Says." *The New York Times*, December 7, p. A10.

Human Rights Watch (2002). "Biography of Hassan al Turabi." New York: Author. Accessed at: www.hrw.org/press/2002/03/turabi-bio.htm

Human Rights Watch (2004a). *Darfur Destroyed: Ethnic Cleansing by Government and Militia Forces in Western Sudan*. New York: Author. Accessed at: hrw.org/reports/2004/sudan0504/

Human Rights Watch (2004b). "Darfur Documents Confirm Government Policy of Militia Support: A Human Rights Watch Briefing Paper." New York: Author. July 20. Accessed at: hrw.org/English/docs/2004/07/19/darfur9096

Human Rights Watch (2004c). *Sudan: Government Commits "Ethnic Cleansing" in Darfur*. New York: Author.

Human Rights Watch (2007a). *Chaos by Design: Peacekeeping Challenges for AMIS and UNAMID*. New York: Author.

Human Rights Watch (2007b). "Q & A: Crisis in Darfur." New York: Author. Accessed at: www.hrw.org/english/docs/2004/05/05/darfur8536.htm

International Herald Tribune (2007). "Success Uncertain for New, U.N.-Sponsored Darfur Peace Talks." September 12. Accessed at www.iht.com/articles/ap/2007/09/12/africa/AF-GEN-Darfur-Peace-Talks.php

Kevane, Michael (2005). "Was the *Black Book* Correct? Regional Equality in Sudan." Santa Clara, CA: Santa Clara University, Department of Economics. Unpublished paper. Accessed at: understandingsudan.org/darfur/Was%20the%black%book%correct.doc

Kinnock, Glenys (2006). "The Rape of Darfur." *Guardian Unlimited*, January 18. Accessed at: www.guardian.co.uk/sudan

Kostas, Stephen A. (2006). "Making the Determination of Genocide in Darfur." In Samuel Totten and Eric Markusen (Eds.) *Genocide in Darfur: Investigating Atrocities in the Sudan*, pp. 111–126. New York: Routledge.

Lumeya, Fidele (2004). *Rape, Islam, and Darfur's Women Refugees and War-Displaced*. Washington, D.C.: Refugees International. Accessed at: www.refugeesinternational.org/content/article

Mamdani, Mahmood (2004). "How Can We Name the Darfur Crisis? Some Preliminary Thoughts." *Black Commentary*, p. 2. Accessed at: www.neravt.com/left/pointers.html

Mamdani, Mahmood (2007). "The Politics of Naming: Genocide, Civil War, Insurgency." *London Review of Books*, March 8. Accessed at: www.wespac.org/WESPACCommunity/DiscussionMessages/tabid/124/forumid/7/postid/408

Malan, Mark (2007). "Africom: A Wolf in Sheep's Clothing?" Testimony Before the Subcommittee on African Affairs, Committee on Foreign Relations, U.S. Senate, August 1. Accessed at: www.senate.gov-foreign/testimoy/2007/MalanTestimony070801/pdf

Mariner, Joanne (2004). *Rape in Darfur*. FindLaw's Writ—Mariner: October 27. Accessed at: writ.news.findlaw.com/mariner/20041027.html

Médecins Sans Frontières (2005). *The Crushing Burden of Rape and Sexual Violence in Darfur*. March 8. Paris: Author.

Médecins Sans Frontières (2005). "Persecution, Intimidation and Failure of Assistance in Darfur." *MSF Reports*. November 1. Paris: Author. Accessed at: www.msf.org/msfinternationa/invoke.cfm?objectid

Nathan, Laurie (2007). "The Making and Unmaking of the Darfur Peace Agreement." In Alex De Waal (Ed.) *War in Darfur: And the Search for Peace*, pp. 245–266. Cambridge, MA and London: Global Equity Initiative, Harvard University, and Justice Africa, respectively.

Newsweek (2007). "Dueling Over Darfur: A Human Rights Activist and an African Scholar Disagree—Vehemently—on the Best Way to Help Sudan." *Newsweek Web Exclusive*, November 8. Accessed at: www.newsweek.com/id/69004/output

Nieuwoudt, Stephanie (2006). "No Justice for Darfur Rape Victims." *Darfur Daily News*. October, n.p. Accessed at: iwpr.net/?p=acr&s=f&o=324842&apc_state=henpacr

Payne, Donald M. (2004). "Rep. Payne Urges Action at Congressional Black Caucus Press Conference on the Crisis in Darfur, Sudan"—Press Release, June 23, p. 1. Washington, D.C: U.S. Representative Donald M. Payne's Office.

Physicians for Human Rights (2006). *Assault on Survival: A Call for Security, Justice and Restitution*. Cambridge, MA: Author. Accessed at: physiciansforhumanrights.org/library/report-sudan-2006.html

Physicians for Human Rights (2005). *Destroyed Livelihoods: A Case Study of Furawiya Village, Darfur*. Cambridge, MA: Author. Accessed at: physiciansforhumanrights.org/sudan/news

Powell, Colin (2004). "Darfur." *Wall Street Journal*, August 5, p. 1.

Reeves, Eric (2007). "Darfur Betrayed Again: The UN/AU 'Hybrid' Force Steadily Weakens." August 24. Accessed at: www/sudanreeves/org/Article182.html

Reeves, Eric (2003). " 'Ethnic Cleansing' in Darfur: Systematic, Ethnically Based Denial of Humanitarian Aid Is No Context for a Sustainable Agreement in Sudan." SPLMToday.com, the official website of the SPLM/A, December 30, p. 1.

Refugees International (2007). *Laws Without Justice: An Assessment of Sudanese Laws Affecting Survivors of Rape*. Washington, D.C.

Stanton, Gregory H. (2006). "Proving Genocide in Darfur: The Atrocities Documentation Project and Resistance to Its Findings." In Samuel Totten and Eric Markusen (Eds.) *Genocide in Darfur: Investigating Atrocities in the Sudan*, pp. 181–188. New York: Routledge.

U.S. State Department (September 9, 2004). *Documenting Atrocities in Darfur*. State Publication 11182. Washington, D.C.: Author. 4 pp.

Sengupta, Somini (2004). "In Sudan, No Clear Difference Between Arab and African." *The New York Times, Week in Review*, October 3, p. 1. Accessed at: www.nytimes.com/2004/10/03/weekinreview/03seng

Srinivasan, Sharath (2006). *Minority Rights, Early Warning and Conflict Prevention: Lessons from Darfur*. London: Minority Rights Group International.

The Sudan Liberation Movement and Sudan Liberation Army (SLM/SLA) (2003). "Political Declaration." March 14. 4 pages. Accessed at: http://www.sudan.net/news/press/postedr/214.shtml

Sudan Tribune (2006). " 'Darfur Will be Foreign Troops' Graveyard'—Bashir." *Sudan Tribune*, February 27, p. 1. Accessed at: www.sudantribune.com/spip.ph?

Totten, Samuel (2006). "The U.S. Investigation into the Darfur Crisis and Its Determination of Genocide: An Analysis." In Samuel Totten and Eric Markusen (Eds.) *Genocide in Darfur: Investigating Atrocities in the Sudan*, pp. 199–222. New York: Routledge.

United Nations (2004). "Sudan: World's Worst Humanitarian Crisis"—Press Release, March 22. New York: Author, p. 2

United Nations Commission of Inquiry (2005). *UN Commission of Inquiry: Darfur Conflict.* New York: Author.

UN News Centre (2003). "As Refugees Pour into Chad from Sudan, UN Announces Plans for Safer Camps." *UN News Centre.* December 23. New York: United Nations. 2 pp.

Wax, Emily (2004). " 'We Want to Make a Light Baby': Arab Militiamen in Sudan Said to Use Rape as Weapon of Ethnic Cleansing." *The Washington Post*, June 20, pp. A01–02. Accessed at www.washingtonpost.com/wp-dyn/articles/A16001-2004Jun29.html

CHAPTER 18

Easier Said Than Done: The Challenges of Preventing and Responding to Genocide

BRIDGET CONLEY-ZILKIC and SAMUEL TOTTEN

Genocide is the intent to destroy a racial, ethnical, religious or national group as such. Beyond this concise definition it has also been described as "an odious scourge" (The 1948 United Nations Convention on the Prevention and Punishment of the Crime of Genocide), "the crime of crimes" (ICTR, 1998, para.16), and "a moral test" (Kristof, March 31, 2004). Failures to respond to the crime in the 1990s have elicited apologies from the United Nations, Organization of African States, France, Belgium, and the United States. Reparations have been paid. International legal proceedings have addressed states' obligations to respond and prevent. Various national legislative bodies have issued statements and laws regarding past cases of genocide. Civil proceedings have been brought against accused perpetrators of genocide in U.S. courts. And popular movements against genocide have made their voices most recently and loudly heard in response to genocide in Darfur, Sudan.

Clearly "genocide" means much more than its legal definition. Although the precise parameters of this excess meaning shift with time and perspective, at heart is an increased ethical imperative to focus on, respond to and memorialize cases of genocide be they imminent, on-going or historical. While that excess meaning should not be ignored, too often it overshadows empirical analyses of viable prevention and response for the sake of aspirational and idealized mechanisms.

The need to prevent and respond to genocide is easier to affirm in principle than to bring about in reality. This chapter introduces some of the reasons why prevention and response are difficult, reviews some of the work that has been done to organize preventative systems and some of the "tools" available for response, and suggests key changes that are necessary in order to improve current regimes of prevention and response.

One of the first difficulties of organizing effective prevention and response to genocide is "genocide" itself. In the cases of the Holocaust and Rwanda, the applicability of the term is almost entirely uncontested; in both cases there was an attempt by the perpetrator regime to completely destroy the targeted group. However, the United Nations Convention on the Prevention and Punishment of the Crime of Genocide (1948) does not limit the term to cases where perpetrators attempt to kill every member of the targeted group (see "Introduction" for a review of the definition). The vast majority of cases fall into this latter category, and in those instances, the border between massive atrocities targeted against civilians of certain groups and genocide is not clear. While the actual violence being perpetrated doesn't change if one calls it "genocide" or something else, the terminology matters because of the increased ethical imperative ascribed to "genocide." Too often once the specter of "genocide" looms, debates and discussion about prevention and response to the phenomenon are sidetracked by the single issue of whether or not "genocide" is indeed threatened or occurring and what extraordinary measure this particular crime warrants.

Several scholars and activists have suggested moving towards other terminology that does not include the overdetermined value of "genocide." Scott Straus argues that genocide "should then be conceptualized as belonging to a universe of cases of state-directed organized violence against civilians" (Straus, 2007, p. 499). To this end, various alternative terms have been proposed: atrocity crimes (Scheffer, 2007), ethnic cleaning, or simply "large-scale loss of life" (ICISS, 2001). Others have suggested that "crimes against humanity" is a more relevant and helpful term than genocide (Schabas, 2006). First codified in the charter of the International Military Tribunal (1945), "crimes against humanity" were limited to the context of international war. These crimes have subsequently been interpreted to cover situations of war and peace, including a range of acts committed along "widespread and systematic" patterns, that implies the acts are carried out intentionally (although not necessarily with "genocidal" intent).

The exceptional ethical imperatives that underwrite "genocide" do not exist to the same degree in the terms suggested above. This lack is both a potential disadvantage and an advantage. If exceptional prevention and response measures are deemed necessary to prevent the specific crime of genocide—versus the full range of other types of widespread violence against civilians—then something is lost in shifting away from this term. But this perception of loss begs the question: how prepared the international community is to take "exceptional" actions, and how such actions draw from more common approaches to conflict prevention and response. The potential advantages of imagining continuities between genocidal violence and other forms of violence that target civilians is that the threshold for action lowers. More diverse and nuanced mechanisms for prevention and response become necessary, as we will explore in depth below.

Preventing Genocide

What Counts as Genocide Prevention?

Genocide prevention constitutes any action undertaken to avoid the outbreak of genocidal violence, be they genocidal massacres or outright genocide. The paradox of genocide prevention is that in the end no one really knows if a specific series of actions has actually staved off genocide or not, for an event cannot be deemed genocide until it has actually been perpetrated. Therefore, efforts at genocide prevention need to seriously consider and address a broad spectrum of conflicts and potential conflicts that may or may not ever be considered genocidal. Such efforts must take a wide view of the context of the crisis;[1] address systemic issues (e.g., disenfranchisement of a group of people, deprivation of human rights, long-term effects of drought and/or famine); and work to ameliorate the immediate sources of social conflict. These concerns are the same as those of general conflict prevention activities, which are undertaken by a diverse field of governmental, international, and non-governmental organizations around the world. It cannot be emphasized too strongly that overlooking systemic issues can increase the chances of periodic, potentially genocidal, violence, even in post-genocidal societies.

However, one major difference between the prevention of genocide and the prevention of the full range of other atrocities is the legal obligation to prevent genocide. On February 26, 2007, the International Court of Justice (ICJ) issued a judgment in the case Bosnia-Herzegovina brought against the Federal Republic of Yugoslavia, which stated that the obligation to prevent genocide incurs "if the State manifestly failed to take all measures to prevent genocide which were within its power, and which might have contributed to preventing the genocide" (International Court of Justice, 2007). How this decision will impact the responsibility of other states to prevent genocide in the future is unclear.[2]

This extra obligation vis-à-vis preventing genocide raises several fundamental questions: What causes genocidal violence? and, why do some situations that exhibit many of the characteristics common to pre-genocidal situations never become genocides? Another way of asking this question is: are there specific elements necessary in order for genocidal violence to become manifest?

Research has shown that genocidal violence can be caused by a number of different factors: ideology (authoritarianism, nationalism, ethnocentrism); unequal distribution of power and/or wealth in "plural societies" or other forms of "social fragmentation" (Smith, 1998) such as ethnic hierarchies, discrimination, and disenfranchisement; and scarcity of and competition over resources. Research on the prevention of genocide is still at a relatively incipient stage, in terms of: identification of long-term causes of a wide range of inter-group violence and more immediate causes or "triggers" of *specifically genocidal violence*; developing and implementing fully operational and highly effective early warning systems; developing the most effective means of carrying out "preventive diplomacy"; and, ultimately, finding the most efficacious means for pre-venting genocide from becoming a reality.[3] Regardless of this missing information, quite a bit is known about signs that have commonly appeared before genocides, conditions common to many pre-genocidal situations, and factors that often produce large-scale violence. But knowledge is, of course, altogether different from the capacity and will to act on such knowledge.

Why the International Community Has Too Often Proven Ineffective in Preventing Genocide

The "international community" is a phrase that stands in for an often missing cohesion in the actions of the United Nations, key individual nations, multi-national organizations, and non-governmental organiza-tions. There are several key reasons why the international community has been ineffective at preventing genocide. The first, as alluded to earlier, is lack of consensus about whether or not a certain case "counts" as genocide. The second is a gap in early warning that is closely tied to crises-driven nature of international response. The third is a lack of political engagement among the nations and international organizations capable of responding to undertake meaningful action.

The gap in early warning about genocide exists despite solid evidence of patterns that have preceded genocides. Researching past cases of geno-cide, scholars have delineated discursive, legal and violent early warning signs that, while not definitive proof that a situation is heading towards genocide, indicates that a situation needs to be addressed in order to avoid mass violence, if not genocide. Among the discursive signs are the use of propaganda in government sponsored or condoned media (newspapers, radio, television); stereotyping; and use of disparaging comments that malign, dehumanize and/or single out for attack specific groups by government leaders. The latter include referring to members of a group as animals or insects (e.g., baboons, snakes, cockroaches) or illnesses (e.g., virus, tumor, cancer), and scapegoating members of a specific group. Legal changes that target specific groups can warn of impending large-scale violence, for instance: passing legislation that ostracizes specific groups of people or denies them fundamental rights; the appropriation of economic resources of members of a specific group; forcing people to wear certain symbols that single them out as "different"; or preventing individuals of a specific group from engaging in certain types of employment. And, there are often violent measures taken against groups, such as the perpetration of major human rights infractions against a particular group of people; forced deportations; the concentration of people in designated areas; extrajudicial killings; and the establishment of paramilitary groups that threaten the safety, well-being, and/or existence of members of a specific group of people. One of the most difficult warning signs to monitor—and perhaps the most important—is to understand when leaders have both the will to use violence and the means to do so. Evaluating the strength of extremists in evolving and complex political situations demands strong case-specific knowledge.

But whose job is it to watch for such signs? This work is done to varying degrees in the media, and by non-governmental organizations, the United Nations, and national governments.

Many have argued that, in the information age, it should be fairly easy to detect a potentially explosive or genocidal situation in the making. While the international print media is better than television media at covering simmering social conflicts, in general media based in the major industrialized countries rarely provide extensive coverage of emerging conflicts or social tensions, particularly in developing countries where such violence often occurs. Media turn to areas only (and sometimes not at all) when crises have already exploded and then usually depart soon after when the stories are no longer "newsworthy" or a crisis hits another part of the world.

Individual human rights, policy-oriented non-governmental organizations (NGOs), and coalitions of intergovernmental organizations, like the Forum for Early Warning and Emergency Response (FEWER), International Alert (London), and the Minorities at Risk Project (at the University of Maryland at College Park) monitor evolving situations around the world and recommend ways to improve social tensions and conflict. Local NGOs are often in the best positions for monitoring subtle changes within a society, but their influence is often limited inside their countries as well as internationally due their capacity to distribute information, uncertainty about their political agendas, or language differences. The influence of international NGOs and coalitions is also limited; their reports are often not conscientiously followed up or fully investigated by the UN or independent governments. In some situations, when warnings of pending genocide are reported over a period of months (or even years), policymakers on the receiving end tend to dismiss them. Referring to reports of impending atrocities in Rwanda before April 1994, Colonel Tony Marley, the U.S. State Department's political-military advisor in the region, asserted that " 'We had heard them cry wolf so many times' that the new warnings fell on deaf ears" (quoted in Kuperman, 2001, p. 105).

The United Nations has a range of agencies and special positions dedicated to gathering information about potential crisis situations. In addition to various Special Rapporteurs assigned to address key problems or areas, in 2004, the UN created the position of Special Advisor for the Prevention of Genocide and Mass Atrocities. Like the NGOs, though, often the reports of these various UN organs are treated with insufficient seriousness.

National governments, including the United States, collect information about threats of violence through various embassies and intelligence gathering agencies. However, intelligence gathering and analysis is not as strong as it could or should be when racial, religious, national, political, and ethnic strife is taking place. In some cases, early warning signals are either missed entirely or not pieced together in order to demonstrate that there is a pattern indicating the likelihood of genocide. Intelligence bodies can also fail to share their intelligence with other parties (including the United Nations). In 2000, the U.S. government created the Office of War Crimes and an Ambassador-at-Large-for-War-Crimes as a way to centralize information and policy on such matters inside the State Department, and while this office has helped support the tribunals for Yugoslavia and Rwanda, for example, it quickly became consumed with war crimes issues related to the "war on terror."

In short, there is no highly effective, centralized, global genocide early warning system. Undoubtedly, that is due to a host of reasons: the complexity inherent in moving from the theoretical to the practical; agreement over the operation of such a system and what it must, at a minimum, include in order to be effective; the costliness of such a project; where such a system would be housed and who would have operational oversight; the handling of such warnings by whom, to whom, and how they would be issued. What would be done once the warnings were issued? The international community seems to grasp intellectually, but has largely failed to act on, the fact that to prevent genocide prophylactic action must begin *as soon as* a specific group is, in some way, targeted for systematic ostracism, discrimination, or exclusion. Ameliorative action must be taken before the conflict or crisis breaks out in violence, for by the time violence breaks out and help is on the way, many hundreds, if not thousands or tens of thousands and more, may already be dead as a result of massacres or genocide. To wait until the "targeted" group is attacked violently or threatened with expulsion, if not death, constitutes a dangerous "waiting game." Despite many "lessons learned" due to catastrophic errors (by the United Nations, intergovernmental organizations, individual nations, NGOs (including many human rights organizations)) genocide scholars and activists are more reactive than pro-active in their efforts to halt genocide. Unfortunately, as Bruce Jentleson (1998) has argued, "Although the essence of the strategic logic of preventive diplomacy is to act early, before the problem becomes a crisis, it is often the same lack of a sense of crisis that makes it more difficult to build the political support necessary for taking early action" (p. 306).

When a strong enough consensus is reached among the various international and regional players that action is necessary, there is a range of measures that can be undertaken, such as: conducting fact-finding missions; focusing diplomatic efforts to help solve seemingly intractable problems; inserting confidence-building measures to reduce fear and distrust among parties;[4] working with governments and groups to address and ameliorate systemic problems (e.g., weak civil society, corrupt and/ or unjust state governance; systematic human rights violations; reducing equalities), mediating between actors;[5] negotiating peace-keeping agreements; deploying "preventive" peacekeeping forces (contingent on the agreement of the parties in conflict); employing various peace-building[6] measures; collecting weapons; and imposing sanctions (which work best when applied early on, employ a carrot/stick approach, and are tightly targeted).[7] Preventing genocide is politically complex and contingent on the situation on the ground, and none of these measures can guarantee ultimate success. But the costs of doing nothing, however, are infinitely higher. So why are warning signs not heeded?

Effective preventative measures are *not* most often derailed by lack of information or potential tools for affecting a situation. Rather, as Michael Barnett (who served with the United Nations Africa Desk prior to and during the 1994 Rwandan genocide) has argued, political will is the most commonly-missing ingredient:

> There is an unwritten belief that with knowledge the international community will act. Yet it was not the lack of knowledge that halted action in either Bosnia or Rwanda—it was politics. In both

cases, states and UN officials knew of but chose to ignore the war crimes that were being committed. In both cases UN Forces were on the ground and were eyewitnesses to acts of ethnic cleansing and genocide, and in both cases the rules of engagement prevented UN forces from coming to the active aid of civilians. More technologies and capabilities are no elixir and no substitute for a politics of engagement (Barnett, 1996, p. 156).

There are several factors that contribute to states' and organizations' lack of political engagement. Among them are an international system geared towards protecting national sovereignty, *realpolitik*, and lack of concern about abuses. The Treaty of Westphalia in 1648 established state sovereignty as the "defining principle of interstate relations and a foundation of world order" (Weiss and Hubert, 2001, p. 5) and its centrality to international relations was reaffirmed in the United Nations Charter (1945). In reality, though, sovereignty has always been more a right of the strong than the weak: colonial and imperial expansion, war, occupation, economic and other interventions throughout the centuries bear witness to this fact. But breaches of sovereignty were historically rationalized for reasons of *realpolitik*, action based on pragmatism and national self-interest, not for civilian protection. Many leaders thus interpreted sovereignty as a license to treat their citizens as they pleased and as insulation against attempts by any other nation or intergovernmental body to interfere in their internal affairs.

Increasingly sovereignty is being challenged by some nongovernmental activists and even within the United Nations General Assembly as a principle that should be limited in cases when large-scale atrocities against civilians are being carried out or tolerated by a state. This interpretation draws from various conventions outlining international human rights standards (e.g., the UN Declaration of Human Rights and the UN Convention on the Prevention and Punishment of the Crime of Genocide, among others), an emerging international legal regime with the capacity to prosecute individual criminal acts perpetrated by leaders, and the onset of the information age. Additionally, the United Nations Security Council (UNSC) has shown willingness to view internal problems of massive human rights abuses as a threat to the international order. This shift began during the Cold War when the UNSC issued sanctions and embargoes against Southern Rhodesia and South Africa for apartheid practices and expanded there considerably during the 1990s in response to a series of internal crises, including genocidal situations.[8]

Despite the fact that the international community and individual nations have increasingly responded to internal human rights abuses, *realpolitik* still plays a key role regarding who decides what actions to take, when, where, why, and how such actions are implemented. Samantha Power documents several examples of this in her 2002 study of U.S. response to genocide. In response to the unfolding human rights disaster in Bosnia, Secretary of State James Baker (a member of the 1988–1992 Bush administration), asserted that the United States did not "have a dog in this fight" (inferring that the United States had no interests there and thus was not about to get involved) (p. 267). Six days into the 1994 Rwandan genocide, Republican Senate minority leader Robert Dole commented that "The Americans are out, and as far as I'm concerned, in Rwanda, that ought to be the end of it" (p. 352). Power also notes that when "James Woods of the U.S. Defense Department's African Affairs Bureau suggested that the Pentagon add Rwanda-Burundi to its list of potential trouble spots, his bosses told him, in his words, 'Look if something happens in Rwanda-Burundi, we don't care. Take it off the list. U.S. national interest is not involved and we can't put all these silly humanitarian issues on lists. . . .'" (p. 342). And at the United Nations, effective response to human rights situations has too often been hampered by the permanent members of the Security Council (the United States, Great Britain, France, Russia and China) each of whom has at times used their veto power to halt strong actions and protect their national interests.

There is another reason why strong action sometimes fails to materialize, and that is the simple but profound fact that many governmental and intergovernmental officials have simply not cared about certain crisis situations. And, as Power argues regarding U.S. response, those policy-makers *who did care* and tried to change U.S. policy were rarely rewarded for their efforts and often their careers suffered considerably.

How can pressure be applied on the international community to act expediently in potentially genocidal situations? In addition to institutional and inter-institutional changes, there needs to be an informed and concerned public constituency who makes their voices heard. This is only now beginning to happen and there is much room for growth.

The Cost of Prevention Versus the Lack of Prevention

Not only is the prevention of genocide complex and difficult, it is costly in terms of "political capital" spent on such efforts: the hours consumed in diplomatic efforts; the varied effects of the imposition of sanctions (if and when they are used); and the costs incurred in developing and implementing, for example, conflict resolution, mediation and other types of programs whose express purpose is to ameliorate conflict and prevent violence.

Lack of prevention, though, is much more costly. First, and foremost, are the innocent lives engulfed in genocide. Among other costs are: the dangers posed to international stability by such violence; the tremendous difficulties and expense of responding during a genocide; and the danger of residue hatred (if not, the desire for retribution) felt by the remnant of survivors (which has, in the past, ignited new conflicts and genocidal actions years after the initial genocide).

Paying attention to complex systemic issues and social problems (which may contain potential seeds of genocide) is not only wise but far less costly than attempting to address them once violence has broken out and a crisis is underway.

When the Crises is at Hand: The Question of Response

Response to threats of genocide is often imagined as a single monolith of anonymous blue helmeted or camouflaged soldiers rescuing erstwhile victims while they push the perpetrators' backs to the wall. For those convinced that a genocide is occurring and demands extraordinary response, military intervention is conceived as a pure ethical good in response to the worst crime imaginable. For those who believe that responding to genocide is not a national or international priority, the demands of this idealized version too often provide an alibi for not exploring other response options that fall short of full armed intervention. In reality, response is neither as heroic nor as simple nor, thankfully, as limited as the ideal response would have it. Nations, the international community, and organizations have a range of response mechanisms they can use to protect lives during genocidal situations, including: influencing how violence is understood; delivering humanitarian aid; implementing legal tools; intervening with military forces; and deploying a range of diplomatic or political tools.

Often the range of response mechanisms is understood as operating along a single continuum—when one mechanism fails to do enough, advocates, policy-makers, and others should move on to the next more robust option. This grossly oversimplifies how situations unravel. Multiple actors undertake a range of response mechanisms simultaneously, with varying degrees of coordination and priority at any given moment. Calibrating and coordinating response always involves trade-offs between the improvements that different modes of response can offer and how each response might aid or hinder other available options at any given moment.

Influencing Knowledge and Understanding of Violence

The *New York Times* op-ed columnist Nicholas Kristof wrote in March 2004 that "nothing is so effective in curbing ethnic cleansing as calling attention to it" (Kristof, March 27, 2004). His optimism is a little overstated, as genocide in Darfur, Sudan would prove and as earlier media attention to Bosnia should have illustrated. But he has a point. The first step in sparking response to widespread violence against civilians is increasing knowledge and understanding of the situation. This work is undertaken by people from governmental organizations, international organizations, non-governmental organizations, popular grassroots movements, and the media, each with their own interests and varying degrees of influence.

Widespread targeting of civilians almost always occurs in the context of armed conflict (Shaw, 2007). Therefore, separating out, paying attention to and documenting attacks focused on civilian populations are key steps to understanding when and how genocide is threatened. The basic facts about a situation can be understood within multiple and contested frameworks: narratives of imperial or anti-imperial violence, "tribal" or "ancient" hatreds, acts of terrorism or anti-terrorism measures, collateral damage or anti-insurgency efforts, among other ways of making sense of a situation. To frame events within the narrative of human rights abuses is to attempt to extract individual acts of violence from their justifying framework and examine them against the backdrop of international legal standards. In the case of genocidal violence, a further step is necessary: human rights abuses need to be transplanted into a new narrative that addresses the perpetrator's overall "intent to destroy" a specific group.

However, debates about accurately identifying and responding to cases of genocide or potential genocide have too often stumbled over the single issue of whether or not the term "genocide" was used. The word, at least before Darfur, operated as a tripwire for policy-makers, as if its mere utterance would change all responsibility to respond. An example of this can be found in on June 10, 1994, while genocide was unfolding with brutal speed across Rwanda and the United States government tried its best to avoid labeling the killing as "genocide": State Department spokesperson Christine Shelly cautiously avoided calling events in Rwanda "genocide," referring to them instead as "acts of genocide" (Power, 2002, p. 363).

Ten years later, the U.S. government response to Darfur, Sudan was remarkably different. On September 9, 2004, U.S. Secretary of State Colin Powell testified before the Senate Foreign Relations Committee, stating that: "genocide has occurred and may still be occurring in Darfur" (Powell, 2004). Colin Powell had been careful to analyze the evidence[9] from Darfur under the light of the legal definition and he noted that the legal designation did not force any particular response: "Mr. Chairman, some seem to have been waiting for this determination of genocide to take action. In fact, however, *no new action is dictated by this determination*" (emphasis added). Powell then stated that the U.S. would "request a United Nations investigation."[10] In other words, the U.S. would follow the letter of the law. The ethical lightning bolt of "genocide" that in 1994 had been so carefully avoided was suddenly reduced to its legal definition—stripped bare.

But among college students, conservative Christians who had been involved in the conflict in Southern Sudan, Jewish groups, some members of the Congressional Black Caucus and others, the term ignited a fire. As Chad Hazlett and Rebecca Hamilton, two activists involved in the movement, wrote:

> Calling it genocide [reference to Colin Powell's testimony] elevated Darfur above other atrocities with high death tolls, seemingly highlighting it as the crisis most deserving of attention. The legitimacy the term gave to Darfur advocacy emboldened a fresh and growing pool of activists, convinced that the "worst crime imaginable" demanded an uncompromising response. (Hamilton and Hazlett, 2007, p. 343.)

Grassroots responses to the genocide in Darfur, Sudan, have proven that civilian groups can play a powerful role in determining how conflicts are understood. While they often lack the professionals' standards of fact-checking and research, activists have shown great creativity in seeking alternative modes of influence—divestment is an interesting point in case—as a means to influence policy. But popular activists and human rights professionals share some of the same limitations. Drawing attention to atrocities or naming them "genocide"—while necessary work to alter the landscape in which abuses are understood—does not stop the violence.

There are other limitations as well. "Genocide," with its extraordinary ethical imperatives, can dominate all other narratives for understanding a conflict. As a result, the simultaneous validity of different narratives explaining a conflict can be overlooked, producing divisions amongst people who might otherwise be allies in seeking ways to end violence. The focus can easily shift to rhetoric rather than response to on-going abuses. Additionally, the narrative of genocide tends to oversimplify a society by repeating and reinforcing the perpetrators' terms; by central-izing group identity as the single most important social issue; by defining groups solely as victim or perpetrator; and by overlooking social and historical complexities that could offer insight into the core problems.

The principles underlying promotion of human rights and advocating for military intervention are often in conflict. Finally, shifting the narrative framework to legal categories ("genocide" or "crimes against humanity") also has the effect (if not the intention) of prioritizing a legal response to a conflict, perhaps to the detriment of seeking other ways to respond.

Humanitarian Response

When genocides occur, large civilian populations are affected—by direct violence, massive displacement due to fleeing violence, or intentional forced displacement. Even segments of a society not directly targeted by perpetrators can face severe circumstances as a result of generalized violence. Bereft of shelter, food, and medical supplies, these populations find themselves in acute need of the most basic means of survival. This is where humanitarian aid steps in.

The oldest international humanitarian aid organization is the International Committee of the Red Cross, which describes itself as "an impartial, neutral and independent organization whose exclusively humanitarian mission is to protect the lives and dignity of victims of war and internal violence and to provide them with assistance" (ICRC, 2007).[11] While there are great variations in the operating principles of humanitarian organizations (in terms of affiliation with a particular religion or government, expertise and priority projects), the idea of neutral and impartial care of vulnerable populations underwrites the entire field of work.

Humanitarian aid workers have risked their lives to bring life-saving sustenance to people in genocidal situations across the world—undertaking major operations in Nigeria (1967–1970), Cambodia (along the Thai border beginning in late 1978), Kosovo (1999), Darfur, Sudan (2004–currently), and so on. In Bosnia (1992–1995), for example, within only 3 months of the start of the conflict, 2.6 million people were displaced. By its end, over half the Bosnian population of 4.4 million were displaced and at least 100,000 were dead. The United Nations High Commissioner for Refugees (UNHCR) took the lead in providing aid and their airlift into Sarajevo was the largest and longest such effort in modern history. Alongside UNHCR were over 250 non-governmental organizations responding to the crisis. Larry Hollingworth, field director for UNHCR, estimated in an interview in April 1995 that aid efforts had saved the lives of 100,000 people (ABC News, 1995).

The problem in Bosnia—and it is instructive for humanitarian action in general—is that while aid is urgent and necessary to tend to the basic biological needs of populations under immediate grave risk, it is not a response to genocide *per se*, but rather to the *effects* of genocidal policies on large civilian populations. In Bosnia, the problem of responding to genocide with humanitarian aid went one step further. The European Community, UN, and U.S. could not agree on a common political or military policy, and so used the aid effort as a show of their concern, and the imperative to continue that aid effort as a reason not to engage in more robust response.

The aid that kept civilians alive was not matched by a political will to protect them. Kofi Annan, UN Secretary General, and head of peace-keeping during both Bosnia and Rwanda, stated in the UN's 1999 report on Srebrenica:

> The problem, which cried out for a political/military solution, was that a Member State of the United Nations, left largely defenseless as a result of an arms embargo imposed upon it by the United Nations, was being dismembered by forces committed to its destruction. This was not a problem with a humanitarian solution. (United Nations, 1999, para. 491.)

In many cases, people cannot survive without aid and its significance as a response to crises that affect large populations should not be underestimated. Humanitarian aid is often the least controversial of responses because it does *save lives* without—in theory, anyway—taking political sides. It is also arguably the most operationally sophisticated of all response mechanisms, but it has distinct limitations.

As in Bosnia, concerns from aid workers, or those who favor a humanitarian response, that robust military or political interventions could disrupt the delivery of aid can produce disagreements about the highest priority: delivering aid, protecting civilians, or confronting perpetrators. Aid can also play a role in prolonging a conflict[12] by sustaining a conflict economy or enabling a government or armed rebel movement to ignore its responsibilities to the civilian population affected by violence. The most significant problem with the conception of aid as a response to genocide is that food, water, shelter, and medicine tend to only the most basic biological needs of a population; they cannot be a political solution to a crisis and certainly not to genocide.

Legal Response

A legal response to genocide can be a significant tool for identifying key individual's roles in perpetrating crimes, but has not yet proved to be capable of fundamentally altering an unraveling situation. Punishing perpetrators of genocide and crimes against humanity through judicial proceedings that expose their individual criminal responsibility is a worthy goal in and of itself, without any relation to promises of halting or mitigating on-going violence or preventing future violence. There is no question that legal proceedings have punished criminals with widely varying degrees of fairness: very limited and then aborted trials were held by Turkish leaders for their Ottoman predecessors for the Armenian genocide; Nazi leaders were brought to trial by the Allied forces and by governments of occupied nations; Khmer Rouge cadres are being tried in Cambodia beginning in 2008; Rwandan *genocidaires* continue to face trials in the International Criminal Tribunal for Rwanda (ICTR), national proceedings, and local forums called "gacaca"; war criminals from the former Yugoslavia are being tried at the International Criminal Tribunal for the Former Yugoslavia (ICTY) and in national proceedings; those accused of crimes in East Timor have faced uneven justice in Indonesian courts; Iraqi leaders were tried in national courts overseen by occupying US forces; Guatemala has undertaken a handful of cases relating to human rights abuses during its civil war; Ethiopia convicted its former dictator, Mengistu Haile Mariam, for genocide; and in Kosovo and Sierra Leone mixed national-international trials have brought perpetrators to justice. In 1998, the International Criminal Court (ICC) was established through treaty as a permanent international criminal court. And this is far from an exhaustive list of efforts to deal with massive human rights abuses through criminal proceedings. Of the proceedings mentioned, only those related to Srebrenica (Bosnia), Rwanda, Iraq and Ethiopia have found the accused guilty of genocide. It is a difficult crime to prove in advance of violence, while violence is on-going, and even after it has ended.

But beyond punishment of select individuals, what else can legal tools offer? The ICTY is mandated: "to deter further crimes; [and] to contribute to the restoration of peace by holding accountable persons responsible for serious violations of international humanitarian law" (ICTY, 2007). The ICTR asserts that its purpose is "to contribute to the process of national reconciliation in Rwanda and to the maintenance of peace in the region" (ICTR, 2007). The Rome Statute that established the ICC asserts that part of the court's role is to "put an end to impunity for the perpetrators of these crimes and thus to contribute to the prevention of such crimes" (ICC, 1998). However, evidence rests more heavily on tribunals not being able to accomplish all of these goals, but this is an open question as the legal response is still a relatively new tool and deterrence will take a good deal more time and research to prove or disprove.[13]

What is more ambiguous at best is the role a legal response plays in mitigating or halting on-going violence. It certainly was not the case with the creation of the ICTY in 1993, during one of the most violent periods of the Bosnian conflict and a full two years before the worst massacre to take place in Europe since World War II, at Srebrenica. The case for ICC indictments lessening violence in Darfur or the Congo is also not strong. However, it remains a question whether indictments could potentially offer moderates within a perpetrator regime the chance to rid themselves of radicals. On the other hand, legal proceedings could potentially foreclose opportunities for negotiating ends to conflicts and therefore genocides. If perpetrators feel they will end up in a court they may be less willing to make conciliatory moves. Mozambique and Uganda offer examples where amnesties have been used or considered to draw former perpetrators into a peace process. But one clear contribution international legal proceedings have made is increasing knowledge about how legal categories can inform understanding of on-going violence[14] and what types of violence are explicitly prohibited under international agreements.

Military Response

Armed intervention to halt atrocities and vanquish perpetrators is often portrayed as the only way to truly confront genocidal violence. This obscures not only variations in the forms that armed intervention can take, but also in the real accomplishments possible. Armed interventions in response to genocidal situations fall roughly into three general categories: biased or interested action; traditional peacekeeping; and coercive armed intervention with the goal of civilian protection.

Biased interventions are undertaken with the self-interest of the intervening force for their own security needs. This was the case when Allied forces defeated Nazi Germany and ended the Holocaust; the Vietnamese military toppled the Khmer Rouge regime in Cambodia; India intervened against Pakistan to aid Bangladesh; and the Rwandan Patriotic Front ended the 1994 genocide by pushing the perpetrator regime into neighboring Zaire.

These examples share four strong similarities. While violence against civilians factored into the rationale for all of these interventions, halting genocide was not a primary goal as much as defeating the perpetrator regime was. All of these interventions came after the victim group had already suffered enormous losses. All ended with the perpetrators removed from power (or removed from power over the victims). Finally, all these examples of victory were brought about with or were followed by a great deal of civilian suffering and death caused by or under the watch of the intervening forces. This final point is made not to equate the suffering brought about by war—although in some of these cases there was also intentional widespread violence against civilians—with that of intentional targeting of civilians that is genocide, but rather to point out that wars, even "just wars," are extremely violent and destructive.

There is another ending to biased armed intervention: the perpetrator regime wins or remains in power. Examples of this include: the Ottoman genocide of the Armenians (1915), Soviet assaults against ethnic minorities (in waves of violence increasing in the 1930s through the late 1940s), the Nigerian Civil War (1967–1970), Indonesia (1965–1966), Burundi (1972), Sudan's South (1985–2005) and Nuba Mountains (1991–1993), and the *Anfal* campaign against the Iraqi Kurds (1988). In each of these cases, the targeted victim group suffered terribly and many died. However, in not all cases did this mean their total destruction. In many cases, the perpetrators did not have sufficient coherency to carry out measures that the more extremist elements among them would have preferred, or while their attacks might have had limited genocidal intent (to destroy a group in a specific place, for example) once those interim goals were met, they backed down.[15] We are not arguing that any of these cases should be understood as successful or desirable ends to genocide, but rather that understanding the dynamics of such cases provides insight into how other such cases might be brought to an end.

The example of the Nigerian civil war in 1967–1970 offers one of the more complex scenarios of genocidal violence ending with the perpetrator regime in power. A wave of massacres of Ibo was carried out across Nigeria in 1966, killing 8,000 to 10,000, and injuring more. By the end of October 1966, 2 million Ibos had fled from throughout Nigeria to their eastern homeland (Ekwe-Ekwe, 1991, p. 63). An Ibo military leader, Colonel Ojukwu, took advantage of the situation to announce the independence of eastern Nigeria on May 30, 1967, naming the new state Biafra.

The Nigerian government, with General Odumegwu Gowon as president, responded by sending federal troops to challenge Biafran claims to independence. Some members of the Nigerian military made statements that indicated genocidal intent. For example, Benjamin Adekunle, a.k.a. "Black Scorpion," stated: "I want to see no Red Cross, no Caritas, no World Council of Churches, no Pope, no missionary and no UN delegation. I want to prevent even one Ibo from having even one piece to eat before their capitulation. We shoot at everything that moves and when our troops march into the center of Ibo territory, we shoot at everything, even at things that do not move . . ." (Amadi, 2007). But when the Nigerian military defeated the Biafran movement on January 14, 1970, General Gowon promoted an end narrative of "no victor, no vanquished." No large-scale killings of Ibo occurred.

This example raises some difficult questions: how does one know (and who could know, if anyone could?) whether statements by extremists are representative of the authorities who have decision-making power over a situation? Can aiding victims—or aiding rebel groups associated with targeted groups—prolong a conflict, which might otherwise end by drawing to a close the situation that made them vulnerable? The risks of being wrong in such an assessment are enormous. Who has the right to make such decisions when the outcome is not clear?

The second general category of armed intervention is traditional peacekeeping or monitoring, where the goals are limited to neutral, impartial, and consensual actions. Some actions are: monitoring agreements between armed combatants, delivering humanitarian supplies, monitoring of ceasefire violations and reporting of responsibility for armed attacks, patrolling national (often disputed) borders, etc. Some examples are: Bosnia (UNPROFOR 1992–1995), Rwanda (1993–1994), East Timor (1999), and Darfur (2005–currently). Beginning with the UN mission in Sierra Leone (1999), and in the shadow of enormous failures of peacekeeping forces to protect civilians in Bosnia and Rwanda, some peacekeeping missions were given stronger "civilian protection" mandates. Even with this language inserted into their mandates, such missions have had only limited success in actually accomplishing civilian protection. The "Report of the Panel on United Nations Peacekeeping Operations" (United Nations, 2000) led by Lakhdar Brahimi noted that too often mandates, staffing, and supplies were inadequate to the evolving situation into which peacekeepers were deployed. For instance, peacekeepers were often not given enough leeway in their rules of engagement to protect themselves or civilians; they were mandated to remain neutral, but when they did so in the face of massive abuses against civilians often a policy of appeasement resulted; best-case scenarios were often assumed when "worst-case" behavior was more the norm; forces were not deployed in sufficient numbers to pose a credible threat; and contributing countries were often unwilling to suffer casualties. The results of these shortcomings were several high-profile cases of peacekeeping failures—Bosnia and Rwanda among them (United Nations, 2000).

While improvements have been made not only at the United Nations but in other organizations capable of enacting peacekeeping missions, according to a 2006 report by Victoria Holt and Tobias Berkman, significant shortcomings continue to exist, particularly in regard to military doctrine, mandates, rules of engagement, training and resources to support missions with civilian protection as a core goal.

One step further along the continuum of traditional peacekeeping and more robust peacekeeping is coercive armed intervention with the goal of civilian protection—otherwise known as "humanitarian intervention" or "just war." Often vaunted as a necessary means to end genocide, this is the least tried of all such response measures. Examples—all of which provoked controversy about the level of force and right to authorization—can be found in Bosnia (with the 1995 NATO bombing campaign against Bosnian Serb communications networks), Kosovo (extended NATO bombing campaign in 1999), and to a limited extent in the Congo (EU intervention in summer 2003 and thereafter by MONUC). Although there are great variations in the mandates of the above mentioned interventions, each of them was conducted in the name of protecting civilian populations, not with the goal of defeating the perpetrator regime.

The report "The Responsibility to Protect" (R2P), by the International Commission on Intervention and State Sovereignty (2001), has had some success in re-orienting discussions of civilian protection by elaborating a general principle of an international responsibility to protect civilians when national government fails to do so. The report also presents specific criteria for when such interventions could be undertaken. This doctrine has gained supporters in the United Nations (Secretariat, General Assembly and Security Council), national governments (U.S., U.K., and Canada, among others), and non-governmental organizations (Human Rights Watch, Amnesty International, International Crisis Group, Refugees International), all of whom have begun to reference the basic principle of a responsibility to protect civilians.

However, there is no consensus on the very difficult issue of what this means in practice. The military capacity to enforce such a responsibility does yet fully exist, as Holt and Berkman report: "Multinational organizations and nations offer little evidence of preparing their forces to intervene in genocide or to stop mass violence as part of a stability or peace operation" (Holt and Berkman, 2006, p. 193). The problems of peacekeeping, notably reviewed in the Brahimi Report, did not disappear when the action was promoted under the heading of a new name. Difficult issues remain: balancing the use of force and the promotion of human rights, supplying troops and supporting them, and training and preparing for actions with the specific goal of civilian protection.

There are also conceptual controversies. Foremost among them is the matter of who decides when a situation warrants armed intervention? In the first instance, the authors of R2P posit the UN Security Council. But the report, recalling NATO's intervention in Kosovo, also envisions situations where a UNSC decision would not be forthcoming. Authorization of military force at this point is even trickier and has been cause for resistance to R2P from third world and developing countries, many of whom have suffered interventions under other rationales and would likely be the only places targeted for such interventions in the near future. There is also the fact that war produces unforeseen consequences.

It escalates violence, no matter how noble its original rationale is. War can also make other responses much more difficult, particularly negotiations and the delivery of humanitarian aid. It can arguably also make these measures easier, when a perpetrator regime is intentionally obstructing, but a positive outcome cannot be assumed.

Political Response

This category includes the full range of diplomatic responses, including: private discussions, public denunciations, sanctions (targeted or general), and negotiations. These measures can be tried separately, simultaneously, along a continuum, or in concert with other response tools. Unfortunately, coordinating the implementation of any of these measures by various nations and multi-national organizations to achieve the greatest effect is a separate problem in and of itself.

Genocide and massive targeting of civilians most often occur during war and end with the end of war. Therefore, negotiations designed to bring a conflict to an end can also serve to bring atrocities to an end. Some recent examples include: the two-decade-long conflict between Sudan's north and south ended in 2005 with the Comprehensive Peace Agreement; war in Bosnia-Herzegovina drew to a close with the 1995 Dayton Peace Accords; in Burundi, while it took several years for peace accords negotiated in 2000 to fully incorporate all the rebel groups and consolidate peace, the conflict ended through discussions with all major armed groups. All of these agreements have their faults and remain shaky, but they halted massive violence against civilians.

One difficulty of negotiations is that they necessarily entail entering into discussions with, and making concessions to, perpetrator regimes. When people have suffered intentional and direct onslaughts against their way of life, it is extraordinarily difficult and painful for them (or their advocates) to suggest compromises with the regime that inflicted such suffering. On the other hand, refusing to negotiate implies that the perpetrator regime can indeed be *defeated* or *severely handicapped* by other means. This cannot be assumed in many circumstances and may contribute to continued loss of life in the meantime. A second major difficulty is that those serving as mediators must be perceived as fair and neutral (enough), and capable of helping guarantee the terms of the agreement.

The example of even a failed peace process, like the one undertaken for Darfur from 2004 to 2006 illustrates the difficulties. While anti-genocide activists in the United States were advocating for a United Nations peacekeeping force to replace the African Union force in Darfur in Spring 2006, a major international push was made to end the conflict through negotiations. Previous rounds of the peace talks from 2004 to 2005 had produced very little: improvements in humanitarian access and ceasefires that were declared only to be simultaneously broken. Throughout this period, the government of Sudan was committing genocide against the civilian groups associated with the armed movements in Darfur. The dramatic discrepancy between the rhetoric and the actions rendered the talks largely meaningless.

In Spring of 2006, a seventh round of talks began in Abuja, Nigeria to try to achieve a comprehensive peace plan for Darfur that would end the conflict and the genocide. While the Sudanese government bore responsibility for the genocide, it benefited at the negotiations from the fact that it could present a coherent if inflexible position. The rebel movements that ostensibly represented the targeted victims, however, were divided and inexperienced. The process itself was rushed to meet deadlines that some negotiators felt were unreasonable (De Waal, 2006), but which the key international players—the United States and Great Britain—imposed and the African Union accepted. One stunning example of this rushed process is that the rebels and Sudanese government received copies of the proposed final agreement with only 5 days to review the plan's 515 paragraphs that addressed a wide-range of issues that would determine the future of the region—and only 2 days for those who were dependent on the Arabic translation of the text. Key rebel groups refused to sign: the JEM and the SLM faction led by Abdel Wahid. Alex de Waal, an adviser to the African Union for the negotiations, described how the AU and international mediators then closed in on Wahid:

> "You let me down!" he [Nigerian President and negotiator Olusegun Obasanjo] said, his fist in Abdel Wahid's face. Abdel Wahid began to explain, "You are our Baba, not just the Baba of Nigeria, but the Baba of Darfur, but I am demanding the rights for our people . . ." Before he could continue, Obasanjo seized him by the collar and pulled him into a side room, "I need to talk to you, boy." For more than two hours, a shuttle followed with Obasanjo, Zoellick and Benn pressing Abdel Wahid to sign (De Waal, 2006, pp. 278–9).

Wahid didn't sign, but De Waal stayed on in Abuja working to see if some of Wahid's concrete concerns could be answered. De Waal has noted that the distance between Wahid's concerns and the final agreement was not great in terms of substance; but the process had alienated Wahid completely. Meanwhile, the international negotiators stated that any groups who didn't sign would be considered "outlaws" (De Waal,

2006, p. 277), a designation that De Waal argues changed how Darfurians viewed the AU, seeing it as taking sides in the conflict and favoring the Government.

Was the Darfur Peace Agreement (DPA), as De Waal argued, Darfur's best chance for peace? Many had their doubts: could the Sudanese government be trusted to keep any agreement? Were the views of wider Darfurian society included in the discussions? Did any peace have a chance to survive without explicit reference to a new UN-led peace-keeping force? However, De Waal argued that despite its flaws, the DPA represented a chance for peace and an end to the genocide that would not come again any time soon:

> Axiomatic to a negotiated end to a war is that each side comes to terms with its former enemy. Many Darfurians still choke on this. After what they have suffered, it is understandable. [. . .]
>
> But the stark reality is that if Khartoum refuses to give ground to the rebels' final demands on how many of their troops are integrated in the national army, and the Movement leaders fail to grasp their best chance for peace, then Darfur faces a cataclysm. All those who believe in peace for Darfur will ask themselves whether we did enough to bring it about, and the needless deaths occur will scar our consciences (De Waal, 2007).

When the Darfur Peace Agreement failed to bring in all of the relevant players, the Sudanese government launched new attacks in Fall 2006[16] and the rebels also searched for military solutions to the conflict, causing yet more destruction, death and displacement in Darfur. By Fall 2007, when another round of talks was scheduled, the rebels had splintered further into 16 different factions, each with their own agendas and rendering a negotiating process infinitely more complex.

If the conflict and genocide had ended in Spring of 2006, countless lives would have been saved and the region could have begun recovery efforts and preparations for the 2009 national elections that could change Sudanese politics. Instead, the violence continues and has spread within Darfur and over the border with Chad. Negotiations cannot work, however, unless the parties are willing to participate in good faith and make compromises. Further, if the international community is to mediate any agreement, they must also be willing to commit to the process even if it takes longer than anticipated and to provide meaningful guarantees for its implementation.

There is no perfect response to genocide or massive crimes against humanity and certainly none that works the same way in every situation. Nonetheless, the tools mentioned above can be implemented to save lives. For those interested in improving the response to genocide, knowledge about the advantages *and* limitations of these tools is necessary.

Post-Genocidal Societies

In the aftermath of massive crimes against humanity and genocide, international aid and support for post-conflict reconstruction can mean the difference between helping a wounded nation and groups of people build a new society based on justice and peace, or watching it once again degenerate back into violent conflict. Any genocide prevention or response program should deal with post-genocide situations, and can include efforts such as: repatriation of internally displaced persons and refugees; demilitarization; establishing a fair and workable system of governance (including a fair and transparent electoral system); support for the development of fair and professional judiciary, police and military systems; re-building social infrastructure (e.g., roads, water, electric systems); bringing about economic reform; revising and implementing new and unbiased curricular programs in schools; implementing programs for reconciliation among the various actors; bringing alleged perpetrators to justice (thus avoiding impunity for crimes committed); and, possibly most significant of all, promoting and transitioning to a healthy democracy.

In Conclusion

Can genocide be prevented? Once it begins, can it be halted? How? With the ethical stakes of genocide so high, one would like the answers to be easy. They just are not. However, there are many things that could be done to improve prevention of violence directed against civilians and early warning for situations that threaten to explode. There are a series of response mechanisms—and the ones detailed here are not exhaustive—that can be implemented to save lives.

Without the willingness of an international body, a group of nations, or at the very least a single nation to act to prevent a genocide or respond early on, not even the most sophisticated and most efficiently operated genocide early warning system will be of much use, nor is the elaboration of any number of response mechanisms. The 1994 genocide in Rwanda provides ample evidence of this. Reports warning of impending genocide had been published well before it began. Linda Melvern documents some of these warnings in *A People Betrayed: The Role of the West in Rwanda's Genocide* (2000):

> In March 1993, a report was published revealing that in the previous two years those who held power in Rwanda had organized the killing of a total of 2,000 of its people, all Tutsi.

> [. . .] *There was little international concern when the human rights
> report came out* [italics added]. Only the Belgian government
> recalled its ambassador from Kigali for consultations, and the
> Rwandese ambassador in Brussels was told that Belgium would
> reconsider its economic and military aid unless steps were taken
> to rectify the situation. The French ambassador dismissed the
> massacres as rumors (p. 56).

After the genocide began, response was no better. The Organization of
African Unity's (OAU's) "International Panel of Eminent Personalities
(IDEP): Report on the 1994 Genocide in Rwanda and Surrounding
Events," formed to investigate the Rwandan genocide and to contribute
to the prevention of further conflicts in the region, stated that "the
UN's Rwandan failure was systemic and *due to a lack of political
will*" (italics added). The Panel found clear evidence that "a small
number of major actors," including Belgium, France, and the United
States, could have directly "prevented, halted, or reduced the slaughter"
(p. 140).

Changing how nations and international organizations prevent and
respond when genocide or massive human rights abuses are threatened
will require a better informed cadre of professional policy-makers who
recognize what genocide is and are expected to prioritize its prevention
and effective response; better systems of warning and response; and
finally, a better informed public who can help make these issues
mainstream political concerns.

"Political will" is often described as the most important missing
ingredient for better prevention of and response to genocidal situations.
But political will is generally the will to do something that is already
determined. Perhaps the most serious gap is in political *engagement*—
that is, long-term commitment to policies that promote democratic
access to, and equitable distribution of, power as well as crisis response
that is founded in the willingness to be responsive to the unique exigencies of a conflict so that the approach to resolving the problem is the one
best suited to solving it. Political engagement is something we should
demand of our governments, international organizations, and foremost,
ourselves.

Returning to the question with which we began—what does the
exceptional ethical imperative of genocide mean for the prevention of
and the response to the phenomenon? It has meant an urgency to "do
something," anything, to make the problem go away. What it should and
could mean is an extra obligation to search for the most effective,
informed, and sustainable means to prevent and respond to genocide.
This is not as easy or self-satisfying as measures solely foregrounded by

ethical imperative, but the problem of genocide demands that this search continue.

Notes

1   Stephen Steadman (1998) argues the following: "The single largest error in the conflict prevention literature is the tendency of scholars to analyze conflict as something divorced from its antagonists [. . .] few works that provide accurate diagnoses of different kinds of conflict situations and actors, specify alternative strategies of prevention and link the two in ways that could inform policy-making. We have myriad works on early warning, but little understanding of the organizational blinders that lead to missed information, incorrect diagnosis, and failed prevention" (pp. 67–68).

2   For more on this, see: Simons (2007), Schabas (2007), and Orentlicher (2007).

3   Genocide scholars have focused on eight major concerns vis-à-vis prevention of and response to genocide: the definition of genocide; processes of genocide; specific genocidal events; early warning signals; risk data bases; early warning systems; the adverse impact of the denial of past genocides; legal responses to genocide; and educational efforts at different levels of schooling (secondary, college, and university) and/or within governmental agencies (including legislative, judicial, and executive bodies, as well as the military). Complementary areas of inquiry include: conflict prevention; international law; intelligence gathering and sharing; preventive diplomacy; conflict management; conflict resolution; and peacekeeping. If there is to even be a hope of developing effective means to prevent and respond to genocide, genocide scholars and others must undertake a joint effort to a create greater synergism amongst the various aforementioned strands (Totten, 2004).

4   For example, "exchanges of information and verification, typically with respect to the use of military force and armaments; making military capabilities more transparent; establishing rules regarding the movement of military forces, and mechanisms for verifying compliance with such rules" (Malese, 2003a, p. 1);

5   In regard to the value of mediation in preventing violent conflicts, Bercovitch (1998) argues the following: "Because it offers a low-key, away-from-the-spotlight approach, because it is voluntary and non-coercive in nature (in which there is no blaming or labeling), mediation can be a particularly useful tool in a multifaceted regime of conflict prevention" (p. 248).

6   Malese (2003b) notes that "According to the United Nations document *An Agenda for Peace*, peacebuilding consists of a wide range of activities associated with capacity building, reconciliation, and societal transformation. Peacebuilding is a long-term process that occurs after violent conflict has slowed down or come to a halt. [. . .] Non-government organizations, on the other hand, understand peacebuilding as an umbrella concept that encompasses not only long-term transformative efforts, but also peacemaking and peacekeeping. In this view, peacebuilding includes early warning and response efforts, violence prevention, advocacy work, civilian and military peacekeeping, military intervention, humanitarian assistance, ceasefire agreements, and the establishment of peace zones" (p. 1).

7   See an Aspen Institute (1997) report (*Conflict Prevention: Strategies to Sustain Peace in the Post-Cold War World*) for a list of recommendations to strengthen and sustain conflict prevention programs: (1) Strengthened system of collecting and assessing information for conflict prevention at the United Nations, as well as publication of a UN early warning "watch list" of countries where deadly conflict may develop or escalate. (2) The United Nations needs to place higher priority on mobilizing political and material resources for conflict prevention. (3) More responsibility should be taken by regional states and organizations for preventing and pre-empting conflict in troubled states. Emerging regional arrangements and organizations should be strengthened by efforts of the United Nations and individual states so they can assure greater responsibility for undertaking the initial external preventive effort in potential conflict situations, such as advice, mediation, or "peer pressure." (4) In addition to region-specific prevention capabilities, the international community needs a dependable overall rapid response capability for situations careening out of control. (5) The economic tools wielded by states and by the international community need

to be fine-tuned for conflict prevention. (6) The role of development assistance in support-ing societies in managing diversity and harmful economic inequalities should receive more attention by the World Bank and other international and state aid agencies. (7) Post-conflict peacebuilding must be treated as a necessary element of conflict prevention, receiving priority and resources. (From the Executive Summary of the Report, n.p.)

8   See Weiss and Hubert, 2001, p. 9.
9   The State Department had commissioned a study, *Documenting Atrocities in Darfur* [http://www.state.gov/g/drl/rls/36028.htm] from a non-governmental organization, Coalition for International Justice. The Bush administration was also influenced by the long-time involvement of Christian conservatives in Sudan, where they had sided with Southern rebels against the government in Khartoum and the fact that Darfur hit the headlines in Spring 2004, just as the 10th anniversary of Rwanda was occurring.
10   The UN did indeed investigate the claims of genocide, but found that while crimes against humanity had occurred, it was not clear that the central government of Sudan had the necessary "intent" for the acts to qualify as genocide. The UN, EU, and African Union refrained from calling Darfur genocide. Only a small handful of non-governmental organizations did call it genocide, Physicians for Human Rights, and the U.S. Holocaust Memorial Museum among them.
11   The most profound challenge to the principles of the ICRC came during the Holocaust, when they maintained their silence about the fate of European Jews in order to maintain the regular functioning of their humanitarian responsibilities. See Jean-Claude Favez (1999).
12   See Alex De Waal (1997).
13   See Bloxham (2001) and Stover and Weinstein (2004).
14   See the *Crimes of War* project for one way that legal language has been harnessed to educate journalists about how to accurately report on unfolding events.
15   See De Waal and Conley (2006).
16   See Nathan (2007), p. 246.

References

ABC News (April 24, 1995). "The Peacekeepers: How the UN failed in Bosnia" an ABC news special with Peter Jennings.

Amadi, Sam (2007) in "Colonial Legacy, Elite Dissension and the Making of Genocide: The Story of Biafra," at http://howgenocidesend.ssrc.org/Amadi/index.html [accessed October 30, 2007].

Annan, Kofi A. (1999). "Development is the Best Form of Conflict Prevention," pp. 47–56. In Kofi A. Annan's *The Question of Intervention: Statements by the Secretary General*. New York: United Nations.

The Aspen Institute (1997). *Conflict Prevention: Strategies to Sustain Peace in the Post-Cold War World*. Queenstown, MD: Aspen Institute.

Barnett, Michael N. (1996). "The Politics of Indifference at the United Nations and Genocide in Rwanda and Burundi." In Thomas Cushman and Stejepan G. Mestrovic (Eds.) *This Time We Knew: Western Responses to Genocide in Bosnia*, pp. 128–162. New York: New York University Press.

Bercovitch, Jacob (1998). "Preventing Deadly Conflicts: The Contribution of International Mediation." In Peter Wallensteen (Ed.) *Preventing Violent Conflicts: Past Record and Future Challenges*, pp. 231–248. Uppsala, Sweden: Department of Peace and Conflict Research, Uppsala University.

Bloxham, Donald (2001) *Genocide on Trial: War Crimes Trials and the Formation of Holocaust History and Memory*. Oxford: Oxford University Press.

De Waal, Alex (1997). *Famine Crimes: Politics and the Disaster Relief Industry in Africa*. Bloomington: Indiana University Press.

De Waal, Alex (2006). "I will not Sign," London Review of Books, 30 November. Available at http://www.lrb.co.uk/v28/n23/print/waal01_.html access 10/31/2007 [Accessed November 3, 2007].

— (2007) "Personal View on Darfur Peace Talks," available online at http://www.ushmm.org/

conscience/analysis/details.php?content=2006–05–04–02&menupage=Sudan   [accessed November 2, 2007].

De Waal, Alex and Bridget Conley (2006). "Reflections on How Genocidal Killings are Brought to an End." New York: Social Science Research Council. Available at: http://how genocidesend.ssrc.org/de_Waal/

Ekwe-Ekwe, Herbert (1991). *The Biafra War: Nigeria and the Aftermath*. New York and Lampeter Ceredigion, Wales: Edwin Mellen Press.

Favez, Jean-Claude (1999) *The Red Cross and the Holocaust*, trans. by John and Beryl Fletcher. Cambridge: Cambridge University Press.

Hamilton, Rebecca and Chad Hazlett (2007). "Not on Our Watch: The Emergence of the American Movement for Darfur." In *War in Darfur and the Search for Peace*, ed. Alex De Waal. Cambridge: Harvard University Press.

Holt, Victoria and Tobias Berkman (2006). *The Impossible Mandate: Military Preparedness, The Responsibility to Protect, and Modern Peace Operations*. Washington, DC: Stimson Center. Available online at http://www.stimson.org/fopo/pdf/Complete_Document-TheImpossible_Mandate-Holt_Berkman.pdf [accessed November 19, 2007].

International Commission on Intervention and State Sovereignty (2001). "The Responsibility to Protect." Ottowa, Canada: The International Deveopment Research Centre. Available at: http://www.responsibilitytoprotect.org/ [Accessed October 2, 2007].

International Committee of the Red Cross (2007) "ICRC's Mission Statement." Available at: http://www.icrc.org/web/eng/siteeng0.nsf/html/68EE39. [Accessed October 16, 2007].

International Court of Justice (26 February 2007), "Press Releases: Application of the Convention on the Prevention and Punishment of the Crime of Genocide (Bosnia and Herzegovina v. Serbia and Montenegro)." Available at: http://www.icj-cij.org/presscom/index.php?pr=1897&pt=1&p1=6&p2=1 [accessed December 2, 2007].

International Criminal Court (17 July 1998), "Preamble to the Rome Statute of the International Court. Available at: http://www.icc-cpi.int/library/about/officialjournal/Rome_Statute_English.pdf [accessed November 6, 2007].

International Criminal Tribunal for Rwanda (ICTR) (4 September 1998). "Prosecutor vs Jean Kambanda: Judgment and Sentencing." Available at: http://69.94.11.53/default.htm [accessed November 3, 2007].

— (2007). "General Information: Introduction." Available at: http://69.94.11.53/default.htm [accessed October 19, 2007].

International Criminal Tribunal for the Former Yugoslavia (ICTY) (2007). "Bringing Justice to the Former Yugoslavia: The Tribunal's Core Achievements." Available at: http://www.un.org/icty/glance-e/index.htm [accessed October 19, 2007].

Jentleson, Bruce W. (2000). *Coercive Prevention: Normative, Political, and Policy Dilemmas*. Washington, D.C.: United States Institute of Peace.

Kristof, Nicholas (2004). "Starved for Safety," *New York Times*, March 31, 2004.

— "Will We Say 'Never Again' Yet Again?" *New York Times*, March 27, 2004.

Malese, Michelle (2003a). "Confidence Building Measures." Accessed at: Beyond Intractability: A Free Knowledge Base on More Constructive Approaches to Destructive Conflict, University of Colorado, Boulder. September, www.beyondintractability.org/essay/confidence_building_measures

Malese, Michelle (2003b). "Peacebuilding: What It Means to Build a Lasting Peace." Accessed at: Beyond Intractability: A Free Knowledge Base on More Constructive Approaches to Destructive Conflict, University of Colorado, Boulder. September, www.beyondintractability.org/essay/confidence_building_measures

Nathan, Laurie (2007). "The Making and Unmaking of the Darfur Peace Agreement." In *War in Darfur and the Search for Peace*, ed. Alex De Waal, p. 246. Cambridge: Global Equity Initiative, Harvard University and London.

Orentlicher, Diane (2007). "Justice in the Courts: An Interview with Diane Orentlicher." In *Voices on Genocide Prevention*, Washington, DC: U.S. Holocaust Memorial Museum March 29. Available at http://www.ushmm.org/conscience/analysis/details.php?content=2007–03–29.

Organization of African Unity's (OAU's) *International Panel of Eminent Personalities (IDEP): Report on the 1994 Genocide in Rwanda and Surrounding Events.*

Power, Samantha (2002). *"A Problem from Hell:" America and the Age of Genocide*. New York: Basic Books.

Powell, Colin (September 9, 2004). "The Crisis in Darfur: Testimony Before the Senate Foreign Relations Committee." (Washington, DC). Available at http://www.state.gov/secretary/former/powell/remarks/36042.htm

Schabas, William A. (2006). *The UN International Criminal Tribunals: The Former Yugoslavia, Rwanda and Sierra Leone*. Cambridge: Cambridge University Press.

Schabas, William (2007). "Whither Genocide? The International Court of Justice Finally Pronounces," *Journal of Genocide Research*, 9(2).

Scheffer, David (2007). "The Merits of Unifying Terms: 'Atrocity Crimes' and 'Atrocity Law,'" *Genocide Studies and Prevention* (2):1, 91–96.

Shaw, Martin (2007). *What is Genocide?* Cambridge: Polity.

Simons, Marlise "Genocide Court Ruled for Serbia Without Seeing Full War Archive," *New York Times*, April 9, 2007.

Stover, Eric and Harvey Weinstein (Eds.) (2004). *My Neighbor, My Enemy: Justice And Community In The Aftermath Of Mass Atrocity*. Cambridge: Cambridge University Press.

Straus, Scott (2007). "Second Generation Comparative Research on Genocide," *World Politics* 59, 476–501.

Totten, Samuel (2007). "The U.S. Investigation into the Darfur Crisis and Its Determination of Genocide: A Critical Analysis," pp. 199–222. In Samuel Totten and Eric Markusen (Eds.) *Genocide in Darfur: Investigating Atrocities in the Sudan*. New York: Routledge.

United Nations (19 November, 1999). "Report of the Secretary General Pursuant to General Assembly Resolution 53/35, The Fall of Srebrenica." Available at http://daccessdds.un.org/doc/UNDOC/GEN/N99/348/76/IMG/N9934876.pdf?OpenElement [accessed November 12, 2007].

United Nations (2000). "Report of the Panel on United Nations Peacekeeping Operations." Available at: http://www.un.org/peace/reports/peace_operations/ [accessed November 19, 2007].

Index